New Dictionary of Scientific Biography

VOLUME 5

MAC LANE–OWEN

Noretta Koertge
EDITOR IN CHIEF

CHARLES SCRIBNER'S SONS
An imprint of Thomson Gale, a part of The Thomson Corporation

Detroit • New York • San Francisco • New Haven, Conn. • Waterville, Maine • London

New Dictionary of Scientific Biography

Noretta Koertge

For more information, contact:
Gale Group
27500 Drake Rd.
Farmington Hills, MI 48331-3535
Or you can visit our Internet site at
http://www.gale.com

LIBRARY OF CONGRESS CATALOGING-IN-PUBLICATION DATA

New dictionary of scientific biography / Noretta Koertge, editor in chief.
p. cm.
Includes bibliographical references and index.
ISBN 978-0-684-31320-7 (set : alk. paper)—ISBN 978-0-684-31321-4 (vol. 1 : alk. paper)—ISBN 978-0-684-31322-1 (vol. 2 : alk. paper)—ISBN 978-0-684-31323-8 (vol. 3 : alk. paper)—ISBN 978-0-684-31324-5 (vol. 4 : alk. paper)—ISBN 978-0-684-31325-2 (vol. 5 : alk. paper)—ISBN 978-0-684-31326-9 (vol. 6 : alk. paper)—ISBN 978-0-684-31327-6 (vol. 7 : alk. paper)—ISBN 978-0-684-31328-3 (vol. 8 : alk. paper)
1. Scientists—Biography—Dictionaries. I. Koertge, Noretta.

Q141.N45 2008
509.2'2—dc22
[B]

2007031384

Editorial Board

M

MAC LANE, SAUNDERS (*b.* Taftville, Connecticut, 14 August 1909; *d.* San Francisco, California, 13 April 2005), *mathematics, category theory, mathematics education.*

Mac Lane in his long life made powerful and lasting contributions to world mathematics, notably by crystallizing with Samuel Eilenberg the concepts of category, functor, and natural transformation, and then extensively developing and applying them. Those concepts have become indispensable to twentieth- and twenty-first-century thinking about geometry, algebra, and logic and have a growing simplifying influence on analysis, statistics, and physics. One of the few universal mathematicians, Mac Lane was a towering figure because of his enormous work in research and teaching, but his career was also marked by a persistent struggle to bring about change and the acceptance of new ideas through participating in organizations whose tendency was rather to uphold the status quo. Mac Lane's doctoral students, including Irving Kaplansky, John Thompson, Michael Morley, and Robert Solovay, played important roles in twentieth century mathematical research. He was very active in the Mathematical Association of America, the American Mathematical Society, the National Academy of Sciences (NAS), and in the International Mathematical Union. He received numerous prestigious prizes for scientific achievement, including the National Medal of Science in 1989; in 1972 he was named an Honorary Fellow of the Royal Society of Edinburgh.

Early Life and Career. Mac Lane was 15 years old when his father died and he went to live with his grandfather. His father and grandfather were both pastors in the Congregationalist Church, and Mac Lane admired both of them for their courage in preaching nonconformist views such as Darwinism and pacifism, but he could never accept their religious ideas. An uncle financed his study at Yale University, where he graduated in 1930 with the highest academic standing in the history of the university, but he was not elected to the notorious Skull and Bones. He earned his master's degree in 1931 at the University of Chicago, where Eliakim H. Moore counseled him to go to Germany; he became the last American to earn a mathematics doctorate at the University of Göttingen of David Hilbert, Emmy Noether, Hermann Weyl, and Paul Bernays. He hid his copy of *Das Kapital* to prevent its being burned when he witnessed the Nazis taking control in January 1933. After his return to the United States, he taught mathematics at Cornell, the University of Chicago, and for ten years at Harvard University. In 1947 he became a professor at the University of Chicago, where his vigorous and inspired teaching continued well after his retirement in 1982.

Activities in Professional Organizations. From 1943 to 1981 Mac Lane was very active in various professional organizations. He served as director of Applied Mathematics at Columbia University from 1943–1945, on leave from Harvard, as part of the war effort. He was president of the Mathematical Association of America in 1951–1952, and began efforts at the national level to reform the teaching of mathematics. On 1 February 1952 he issued the directive to all sections of the MAA that minorities must have equal access to the academic and social functions of the association, contrary to the previous practice of some of the sections. From 1952–1958 he was chairman of the mathematics department at the University of Chicago, succeeding his friend Marshall Stone. In 1973–1974 he was president of the American Mathematical Society and was vice president of the National Academy of Sciences until 1981. During the eight years at the NAS he devoted much of his energy to chairing the Reports Review Committee, and was from time to time compelled to issue forceful calls for greater scientific seriousness—for example, in connection with a report on the effects of the military use of poisons in Vietnam. He did the same in other contexts, which, as one would expect, led to a mixed popularity.

Mac Lane strove valiantly to promote that closer unity between teaching and research that was so much the essence of his own mathematical life. To advance that purpose, he urged a merger of the professional societies, but succeeded only in creating one umbrella committee, the Joint Policy Board for Mathematics.

Through his organizational initiatives at the national level in the mid-1950s, he had applied his international mathematics experience to courses for high school teachers, which he and other active mathematicians taught. In the early 1960s, however, hopes for a progressive new math were frustrated when university presidents and government agencies cut the funding for these courses. Channelling energies into a retrogressive "new math," various authorities made organizational decisions that, in Mac Lane's view, tended to steer high school teachers towards outmoded pedagogical theories, instead of scientific thinking and mathematical content. Mac Lane's efforts to promote improved conditions for scientific research and education achieved only modest results, in spite of the great amount of time he spent in Washington. That experience contributed to his later analysis of what he saw as grave flaws in the methods for arriving at science policy in the federal government and the American university system.

Influential Textbooks. Fortunately, Mac Lane's energies were not entirely devoted to organizational efforts, but also to his own fruitful research and teaching and especially to the relation between them. His textbooks *A Survey of Modern Algebra* (1941, with Garrett Birkhoff), *Homology* (1963), *Categories for the Working Mathematician* (1971), and *Sheaves in Geometry and Logic* (1991, with Ieke Moerdijk) are still widely used in the early twenty-first century. Mac Lane's book with Birkhoff made Bartel van der Waerden's *Moderne Algebra* (1930) accessible to English-speaking undergraduates. The *Survey* was fundamental to the education of several generations, and Mac Lane rewrote the 1967 edition in order to respond explicitly to the growing need for the learning of category theory. All four of these textbooks fundamentally contributed to bringing new abstract research to students at the time when they needed to learn it.

Homological Functors and Abelian Categories. Forceful personality and energetic perseverance were not the only attributes that made Mac Lane so prominent; rather, the primary reason is that his central ideas were, and have remained, correct. He accurately summed up the achievements of the previous generation and passed them on, forever transformed in clarity and applicability. This process can be clearly discerned in the cases of homological functors and Abelian categories.

By 1940 Mac Lane and his friend Sammy Eilenberg had each made significant contributions to their respective fields of algebra and topology, and thus, through their collaboration on the challenging problems of Heinz Hopf and Norman Steenrod in algebraic topology, could gain access to the rich social patrimony of several centuries of mathematical development. Reflected through that access was sufficient knowledge of the forms of results, and especially of some main modes of the development of ideas, so that they were able to concentrate and isolate the explicit concepts that they called category, functor, and natural transformation. These explicit concepts were so correct as a reflection of the essence of various aspects of mathematical content and motion that they immediately provided a source of structures whose properties could be studied with fruitful results for mathematics in general. The concept of functor, almost immediately after its discovery by Eilenberg and Mac Lane in 1942 (and expounded by them in 1945) provided a structure to which axioms and deduced theorems could be applied; specifically, the axioms announced by Eilenberg and Steenrod in 1945 (and expounded by them in 1952) clarified the previous proliferation of geometrical constructions known as homology theories, and in turn made possible still richer such theories. Functorial homology theory became a cornerstone of the still ongoing research in algebraic topology. The axiomatic method could similarly be applied to categories themselves, as was then exploited by Mac Lane (in 1948, expounded in 1950). He captured the essence of linear algebra via the axiom that products and coproducts (which themselves can only sensibly be defined by categorical means) coincide in certain categories. Often such categories enjoy the internal representability of the solutions of any equation they contain; if they satisfy certain "exactness" conditions, such categories are called "Abelian" after the great Norwegian mathematician Niels Abel (1802–1829).

These Abelian categories quickly served their purpose as another cornerstone of algebraic topology and were host to a new branch of linear algebra that became known as homological algebra. Homological algebra had

Mac Lane

undergone extensive development in the collaboration of Eilenberg and Mac Lane in the late 1940s and early 1950s on the homology of groups. Over the next decades, Abelian categories underwent deep development by David Buchsbaum, Alexander Grothendieck, and Jean-Pierre Serre, and further by Maurice Auslander, Michael Barr, Peter Freyd, Peter Gabriel, Alex Heller, Barry Mitchell, Stephen Schanuel, Jean-Louis Verdier, Nobuo Yoneda, and others. Philosophically, those developments meant in particular that methods previously conceived as applying only to constant quantities could be extended to apply also to variable quantities, with powerful results.

Adjoint Functors. Axiomatic algebraic topology and homological algebra can both be described as having been new category theory, arising in a sense entirely within category theory, but in response to the needs of application. The most important instance of this phenomenon, it is generally agreed, is Daniel Kan's 1958 discovery of adjoint functors (which, in retrospect, were implicit in the Eilenberg-Mac Lane 1945 paper). This concept united a wealth of old and new examples, again exploiting the susceptibility of the appropriate structures to restricting properties that, as axioms, have powerful consequences and serve as a guide to further constructions, conjectures, and theorems. The particular problems occupying Kan concern the relation between the qualities of combinatorial homotopy theory and the qualities of quantities arising in differential vector calculus (a relation that lies at the basis of the finite element method in applied electro-magnetism, for example). Kan discovered that a functor from one category to another might be so special as to have another uniquely determined functor in the opposite direction that, while not actually inverting it, is the "best" approximation to an inverse (in either a left- or a right-handed sense). Typically, one of the two functors is so obvious that one might not have mentioned it, whereas its resulting adjoint functor is a construction bristling with content that moves mathematics forward.

One of many examples, whereby the use of adjoint functors helps old constructions become much more explicit and clear, is a construction which had played a key role in Mac Lane's research in Galois theory and explains the realization of conjugation on the complex numbers (the process of negating the generator i) as an inner automorphism (by j) of the larger enveloping algebra of Hamilton's quaternions. There is a similar realization of the mechanical flow on a phase space via an inner derivation by a Hamiltonian element in an algebra of operators. The conjugation example involves a two-element group in two different roles, and the mechanical example similarly involves an infinitesimal group of time translations. The "inner realization" construction is the left adjoint of the functor, determined by a given group G, which to every algebra A with a given representation of G by multiplication *in* A, assigns the action of G *on* A defined by

$$ag = g^{-1}ag.$$

The left adjoint to this process applies to any algebra with a given action of G on it, enlarging it in an optimal way to make the action inner; the resulting algebra, which contains this inner action of G in it, is usually non-commutative, even if the given one was commutative.

Adjointness and Logic. Naturally, Kan's discovery spurred a succession of new leaps forward within category theory in response to its relation with applications. Some of these were intimately related with Mac Lane's longstanding interest in logic and set theory. Already during the 1931 interval between his Yale degree and his studies at Göttingen, he had studied at the University of Chicago with Eliakim H. Moore. Moore too was a very strong personality who, coming from algebra, had, like Mac Lane, a burning desire and specific proposals to unify mathematical research and to reform mathematical teaching to that end. Mac Lane had taken up from Moore the quest to axiomatize set theory. Mac Lane's thesis at Göttingen had resulted from intense discussions with the set theorist Paul Bernays concerning the possibility of a formalized logic that could actually be used to guide mathematical proofs. During the next 30 years, however, Mac Lane did not concentrate his research on set theory or logic, although he did make valiant organizational efforts, promoting the formation of logic clubs among undergraduates and reviewing for the *Journal of Symbolic Logic.* He was pleased in the early 1960s when it became apparent that logic and set theory, insofar as they are mathematically relevant, can be characterized axiomatically as specific interlocking systems of adjoint functors: specifically

1. propositional logic symbolically presents parts of a universe of discourse in terms of pairs of operations like G & ( ) and G implies ( ), related by rules of modus ponens and deduction which say no more than that those operations are adjoint;
2. predicate logic treats, moreover, parts of several universes related by maps (for example projection maps), where the fundamental categorical process of composition is exemplified by substitution along the map (representing inverse image) that has a left adjoint, namely existential quantification along the map (representing direct image); and
3. higher-order logic treats, moreover, a system of several universes wherein, for any universe G, there are adjoint functors creating as new universes the G-cylinder and G-figure universes (also known as

function types; part of the adjunction property had been called lambda-conversion by Alonzo Church).

Set theory itself was quickly seen in a new light via adjointness; after all, the adjointness of function types expressed a fundamental transformation that had been used in functional analysis (and in its embryo, calculus of variations) for 250 years, and the belief that Georg Cantor's set theory would have an important role in analysis (as expressed at the first International Congress of Mathematicians in 1897 by Jacques Hadamard) had sprung from the intense work at that time which was bringing functional analysis to the light of day. Quickly overcoming his initial skepticism, Mac Lane recognized the decisive importance, for set theory and logic and their relationship to mathematics, of the explicitly adjoint character of these operations. He sprang into action: He made sure that the basics were published by making F. William Lawvere's *Elementary Theory of the Category of Sets* available through the University of Chicago library, and ensuring that an announcement of that work appeared in the *Proceedings of the National Academy of Sciences* (1964); he wrote expositions himself for all kinds of audiences; and he engaged in published polemics with recalcitrant set-theorists, right up to the new millennium (2000).

The Geometrical Use of Category Theory Gives Rise to New Category Theory. During the same period, Alexander Grothendieck was creating the new foundation for algebraic geometry, which was also based on categories and adjoint functors. He realized that the variable linear algebra that he (following Mac Lane) had developed in the late 1950s, is best viewed as an additional structure on a nonlinear kind of category, such as set-valued sheaves or analytic spaces. This led to the crystallization of a new kind of categories, which he called toposes because they were the brave new manifestation of the science of situation. (The Greek term was apparently chosen to signify a qualitative deepening of the analysis situs of Henri Poincaré.) These situations serve as the domains of variation for variable sets. In the 1970s students in Paris, at Harvard, and at other centers had to struggle to learn the topos theory through the 2000 pages (written with the help of Michael Artin, Jean-Louis Verdier, and others) that only the brain of a Grothendieck could really encompass.

Grothendieck retired suddenly in 1970, but the new algebraic geometry continued to develop. Meanwhile a simplified form of the topos theory had already sprung up, with motivations from continuum mechanics, but with new applications to set theory and logic. (That work, achieved in collaboration with Myles Tierney, was presented in 1970 by Lawvere at the International Congress of Mathematicians in Nice, France.) For a time those two trends, algebraic geometry and the new topos theory, were very slow in learning from one another, in contrast with the situation in the 1950s when category theory had been revolutionizing not only the framework of mathematics, but also its practice. There were logicians who, like Galileo's colleague, refused to look into "the telescope" that was provided by books on the topos-theoretic simplification of logic; there were also algebraic geometers who dismissed the modern topos geometry as "mere logic." Mac Lane did not despair in the face of these difficulties of communication and lack of mutual understanding.

That was precisely the sort of wrong that Mac Lane knew how to begin to set right: girding himself anew in the middle of his seventh decade, he set off for Cambridge where his lectures inspired Peter Johnstone to write the first book on the new topos theory (1977). In the middle of Mac Lane's ninth decade, yet another book appeared, the result of his collaboration with Ieke Moerdijk of the University of Utrecht in the Netherlands; this latter book, *Sheaves in Geometry and Logic* (1992), was necessary because the books that had appeared in the intervening twenty years on this emerging subject had still not covered all the varied developments. The book with Moerdijk shows clear traces of the hand of the master expositor: the systematic use of presheaf toposes and Kan adjoints and the careful exposition of the relation between the combinatorial topology of 1950 and the internal role of the adjointness formulation of logic.

Continuing Influence. Algebraic geometry, complex analysis, universal algebra, logic, and in fact any given field in mathematics has as neighbors other growing fields wherein the categorical method is already indispensable. Homotopy theory, for example, uses the Eilenberg-Mac Lane spaces (introduced in the mid-1940s) and is often based on Daniel Quillen's axioms, built on the categorical work of Peter Gabriel and Michel Zisman. As another example, the closed and enriched categories of Samuel Eilenberg and Gregory M. Kelly have led to a rejuvenated study of metric spaces and of generalized logic, unexpected when they were introduced in 1965 as the definitive solution to the problem of signs in algebraic topology. The force of the streams of these neighboring developments will eat away any resistance of remaining "islands" to the unification that the progress of mathematics requires.

When his formulation of the homology of rings was taken up and developed in 1961 by Umeshachandra Shukla, Mac Lane remarked that "as always, it is a pleasure to see how new ideas spread" (2005, p. 222). When visiting Soviet Georgia in 1987, he found to his delight a group of a dozen devoted and enthusiastic researchers in category theory and concluded, "it is remarkable to see how abstract mathematical ideas have international resonance" (2005, p. 331).

The enormous power of a correct idea cannot always be foreseen. Mac Lane found it hard to believe that already by the late 1950s, the fundamentals of category theory had penetrated into the midwestern farmlands, enabling fledgling students there to discuss and dream about its intimations of powerful unifying developments. The correctness of these explicit ideas was an electrifying inspiration to us then, and remains an enduring inspiration to scientific progress.

BIBLIOGRAPHY

WORKS BY MAC LANE

With Garrett Birkhoff. *A Survey of Modern Algebra.* New York: Macmillan, 1941.

With Samuel Eilenberg. "General Theory of Natural Equivalences." *Transactions of the American Mathematical Society* 58 (1945): 231–294.

"Groups, Categories, and Duality." *Proceedings of the National Academy of Sciences, U.S.A.* 34 (1948): 263–267.

Homology. Berlin: Springer-Verlag, 1963.

With Garrett Birkhoff. *Algebra.* New York: Macmillan, 1967.

Categories for the Working Mathematician. New York: Springer-Verlag, 1971.

"Origins of the Cohomology of Groups." *Enseignement Mathématique* 24 (1978): 1–29.

Selected Papers. Edited by I. Kaplansky. New York: Springer-Verlag, 1979.

With Samuel Eilenberg. *Collected Works.* Orlando, FL: Academic Press, 1986a.

Mathematics: Form and Function. New York: Springer-Verlag, 1986b.

"Concepts and Categories in Perspective." In *A Century of Mathematics in America,* Part 1, edited by Peter Duren. Providence, RI: American Mathematical Society, 1988.

With Ieke Moerdijk. *Sheaves in Geometry and Logic: A First Introduction to Topos Theory.* New York: Springer-Verlag, 1992.

"Contrary Statements about Mathematics." *Bulletin of the London Mathematical Society* 32 (2000): 527.

Saunders Mac Lane: A Mathematical Autobiography. Wellesley, MA: A. K. Peters, 2005.

OTHER SOURCES

Cartan, Henri, and Samuel Eilenberg. *Homological Algebra.* Princeton, NJ: Princeton University Press, 1956.

Eilenberg, Samuel, and Norman Steenrod. *Foundations of Algebraic Topology.* Princeton, NJ: Princeton University Press, 1952.

Johnstone, P. T. "An Elementary Theory of the Category of Sets." *Proceedings of the National Academy of Sciences, U.S.A.* 52 (1964): 1506–1511.

———. *Topos Theory.* London; New York: Academic Press, 1977.

Lawvere, F. William, and Robert Rosebrugh. *Sets for Mathematics.* Cambridge, U.K.: Cambridge University Press, 2003.

McLarty, Colin. "Saunders Mac Lane (1909–2005): His Mathematical Life and Philosophical Works." *Philosophia Mathematica* 13 (2005): 237–251.

F. W. Lawvere
Colin McLarty

MAIMONIDES, RABBI MOSES BEN MAIMON,

MAIMONIDES, RABBI MOSES BEN MAIMON, also known by the acronym RaMBaM (*b.* Córdoba, Spain, 1135 or 1138; *d.* Cairo, Egypt, 1204), *medicine, codification of the Jewish law, philosophy.* For the original article on Maimonides see *DSB,* vol. 9.

Maimonides is widely held to be the most important Jewish philosopher of the premodern period, perhaps of all times. His accomplishments in diverse branches of science, most especially medicine and astronomy, have contributed very much to the development of this attitude. The authority of Maimonides' thoughts on the relationship between science and religion are hugely enhanced by his eminence as a scientist. Maimonidean studies have burgeoned in the decades since the appearance of the first edition of *DSB,* and, along with this, his activity and literary legacy in the sciences have been closely scrutinized.

Interpolation of Maimonides's Epistemology. No aspect of Maimonides's involvement in the sciences has generated as much interest as the precise determination of the limits he placed on human knowledge, particularly with regard to the physical configuration of the heavens. A fundamental principle of cosmology, allegedly tracing back to Plato, stated that the motions of heavenly bodies are circular and centered upon Earth. In order to account for the apparent anomalies from uniform circular motion, astronomers employed devices such as eccenters and epicycles, which violate this principle. Maimonides was one of several prominent medieval thinkers who possessed a firm grounding in mathematical astronomy and who were deeply troubled that the models they used were not in keeping with the rules. Maimonides concluded his review of the difficulties besetting the astronomy of his day (*Guide of the Perplexed* 2.24), for which he could find no acceptable solution, with two contradictory remarks. First, he suggested that one cease speculations concerning things that are beyond the intellectual capacity of regular human beings. Immediately afterward, however, he

Maimonides. *Portrait of Maimonides.* © CORBIS.

admitted that he was confessing only his own inability to work out a solution. Someone else may indeed be able to provide a demonstration that will pave the way to a resolution, he suggested.

So what did Maimonides really think? In the introductory essay to his English translation of the *Guide,* Shlomo Pines argued that Maimonides would by no means place the solution to an astronomical puzzle beyond the reach of human intellects. Instead, he exaggerated the severity of the quandary for tactical reasons: Because Aristotle's claim that the universe is uncreated rests primarily on astronomical arguments, Maimonides found it useful to undermine as best he could the certainty of astronomy. In his *DSB* article Pines highlighted Maimonides' views on the limitations of human knowledge, and he weakened the connection between the astronomical quandary and the question of temporal creation.

A much more dramatic shift is evident in Pines's article, "The Limitations of Human Knowledge" (see bibliography). Pines exploited an unusual blend of texts in order to cast light upon Maimonides's position. These include, most importantly, a passage from a lost treatise by al-Fārābī, summarized—and rejected—by Ibn Bājja, in which al-Fārābī denies the possibility of knowledge of immaterial things (read literally, al-Fārābī is said there to deny the very existence of immaterial things), thus no metaphysics is possible. However, Pines also brought into the discussion two different theories of Ibn Bājja himself; another theory, which al-Fārābī is said to have preferred later on; and some key ideas propounded by Ibn Sīnān. Another, no less weighty conclusion to be drawn concerns the very purpose of human existence. Because metaphysical knowledge is impossible, the ultimate goal of life must lie in the political, that is, this-worldly, civic happiness.

It is not easy to reconcile all of these sources with each other. Their utility in ferreting out the true meaning of Maimonides's diverse statements is even more problematic. There is no direct evidence that Maimonides accepted any of the ideas said to derive from Ibn Bājja and the others: indeed, it is not certain that he was aware of all of them. Nonetheless, Pines stated quite clearly the conclusions that he wished to draw from his interpretation of Maimonides's final position (in the light of these sources), especially with regard to astronomy. Human intellection depends ultimately on the percepts of material objects. In fact, it is even more restricted than this: one can grasp only sublunar material objects. (Presumably, this is because the matter or the heavens, according to Aristotle, is essentially different from the stuff of sublunar objects). Clearly, the deity and the separate intellects are beyond human cognition; but even the heavens are intrinsically and irrevocably unknowable. This is true not only for ordinary people, but for philosophers as well, and even for most prophets. Taking Maimonides's citation of Numbers 12:8 at the end of *Guide* 2.24 quite literally, Pines averred that, according to Maimonides, only the biblical Moses was privy to the true configuration of the heavens.

Herbert Davidson vigorously pressed the difficulties in Pines's argument. According to him, Maimonides consistently maintained that the goal of life lies in intellectual attainment, rather than in the political life. Man can and must obtain demonstrative knowledge of the existence of God, the celestial spheres, and the active intellect, though knowledge of their essences is beyond the capacity of the human mind.

Josef Stern ("Maimonides on the Growth of Knowledge and the Limitations of the Intellect," in the 2004 volume edited by Roshdi Rashed and Tony Lévy) chose a different tack, drawing careful and precise distinctions between the impossibility of knowledge on the one hand, and limitations upon knowledge that is, in principle if not in fact, attainable, on the other hand. Knowledge of the deity is humanly impossible, for two complementary reasons. First, human intellection is in one way or another always intermeshed with the imagination, whose representations are necessarily sense-derived, hence material. Because God is not material in any way, He cannot be known by means of representations of this sort. Moreover,

Maimonides

there is ultimately no clear criterion by means of which one can perfectly distinguish between the intellect and the imagination. Therefore, there is no way of factoring out the distorting role of the imagination. Second, the syntax with which the human mind operates, that is to say, the subject-predicate structure of propositions, is necessarily composite. Hence, the mind cannot represent something perfectly simple, that is, utterly incomposite. Hence it cannot truly represent, and, thereby, know the deity. This is an insurmountable obstacle, intrinsic to the human mind.

As far as the heavens are concerned, Stern contended, Maimonides would claim that human knowledge of the heavens is only by way of their effects (the *quia* of the Latins), rather than by way of their causes (*propter quid*). This is a serious defect in the scientific character of astronomy, whose goal is always to furnish (final) causes for the subjects of their investigation. Be that as it may, why, even if the *telos* of the heavens is beyond human ken, can one not arrive at a satisfactory account of their three-dimensional structure, which is the issue at hand in *Guide* 2.24? In any event, Stern would agree that, strictly speaking, a correct solution is not humanly impossible.

Pines's final position, which interprets *Guide* 2.24 not as a tactical move, but rather as a straightforward, dogmatic claim that the true configuration of the heavens cannot be attained intellectually, made a deep impression upon research into Maimonides's astronomy. Two scholars in particular, Menachem Kellner and Gad Freudenthal, labored to situate Maimonides's purported agnosticism concerning the heavens within conventional (but problematic when applied to medieval science) categories in the history of science. Thus, for example, Maimonides emerges as an instrumentalist. On the other side of the fence, the present writer consistently defended Pines's first intuition. It is particularly important to note that Maimonides concludes the immediately preceding chapter (*Guide* 2.23) by observing that, when facing questions that indeed cannot be resolved by human logic, such as temporal creation, one resorts to rhetorical arguments. This supports the view that Maimonides's exclamations about his perplexity concerning unsolved astronomical issues serve a tactical end in his campaign to convince his readers of the temporal creation of the universe.

Works on the Exact Science. Neither Aristotle's account for the configuration of the heavens, nor that of Ptolemy, is free of doubt. By contrast, Maimonides voiced his belief in the perfection of Aristotelian physics. He introduced the second part of his *Guide* with a set of twenty-five premises—the first such catalog known to have been prepared. They are said to derive from the *Physics, Metaphysics,* and their commentaries, and to have been provided with a demonstration, either by Aristotle himself or by one the Peripatetics. Maimonides's motivation for preparing this list is clearly theological. These premises are required for establishing the existence of the deity as well for proving that He is neither a body nor a force within a body.

These premises enjoyed a life of their own as a concise summary of Aristotelian physics. Several commentaries were devoted exclusively to this portion of the *Guide.* A Muslim scholar, Muḥammad bin Abī Bakr al-Tabrīzī, wrote very extensive glosses, taking note of some of the novel and occasionally non-Aristotelian ideas then current in the eastern reaches of Islam. Al-Tabrīzī in turn was the most important source for Hasdai Crescas, whose thorough and penetrating critique of Maimonides's premises, and the Aristotelian system for which they form the scaffolding, has long been regarded as a turning point in the history of science.

Historical sources report an impressive amount of writing by Maimonides on the exact sciences. He is said to have authored several mathematical treatises, and to have corrected the mathematical encyclopedia of Ibn Hūd as well as Jābir ibn Aflaḥ's own correction to Ptolemy's *Almagest.* All that survives, however, are extensive notes to Apollonius's *Conics,* including notes to Ibn al-Haytham's reconstruction of book eight, and Maimonides's algorithm for computing the possibility of sighting the lunar crescent. The latter was written in Hebrew, and it was incorporated into *Mishneh Torah,* his great legal code. All the rest, including his extensive medical writings, were written in Arabic.

Otto Neugebauer provided the basic mathematical analysis of Maimonides's procedure with regard to the visibility of the lunar crescent. One computes a quantity, *b,* called the arc of vision (*qeshet ha-re'iyah*), which is, to simplify matters, the sum of the elongation subjected to a number of corrections (coordinate transformations, parallax, seasonal variations in rising time, latitude of Jerusalem) and two-thirds of the lunar latitude (uncorrected for parallax). Then, if *b* alone is greater than 14°, or if the sum of *b* and the elongation between the true Moon and Sun along the ecliptic is greater or equal to 22°, the crescent will be visible in the Jerusalem area, and if *b* is less or equal to 9°, the crescent will not be visible.

Identifying the sources of this method has proved to be quite difficult. Maimonides rounded off his computations, asserting, apparently correctly, that the round-off errors would cancel out; and he integrated into his computation certain values for the coordinates of Jerusalem. Neugebauer asserted that Maimonides depended upon the tables of al-Battānī for the mean motion of the sun and, toward the end of his analysis, intimated that Maimonides's entire procedure is found in al-Battānī. Though these claims are not without their difficulties, no other sources have been identified. However, some elements of

Maimonides's procedure do not appear to derive from al-Battānī, for example, his third longitude (the elongation after undergoing its second correction). This step, which is employed in some Indian visibility computation schemes, converts the elongation to the mixed coordinate system employing the pole of the equator and the ecliptic. Given the well-established connection between Indian and Andalusian astronomies, it seems likely that Maimonides learned of this step from the Andalusian scientific corpus, upon which he relied in all fields. However, one cannot rule out completely the possibility that this step was part of some ancient Jewish system which, as in India, made use of early, even pre-Ptolemaic, Hellenistic astronomy.

Maimonides was a firm and consistent opponent of astrology. According to the standard that he accepted, causal connections cannot be established by empirical methods alone (*tajriba*). There must be a demonstrable theoretical link (*qiyās*) between cause and effect. All the more so with regard to astrology, where the evidence for repeated linkages between stellar configurations and terrestrial events is at best questionable. Maimonides also detected a strong historical connection between paganism and astrology. However, it is not correct to claim that his opposition to astrology stemmed solely from this connection. Maimonides argued that the chief purpose of the Torah is to abolish falsity—not simply bad or unaccepted behavior, but false teachings about the world. It is, to use modern language, both a scientific and religious obligation (Maimonides would probably prefer to call this a fundamental human obligation) to reject the false and to uphold the true. Even if there never were any astral cults, astrology would still be false and *eo ipso* forbidden.

Views on Medicine. Medieval medicine, even of the most scientific variety, was forced to rely on experience in the case of remedies whose empirically proven therapeutic properties defied rational explanation by the standards of the day—that is, the purported ability of physicians to determine the heat, dryness, and so forth, of the substances that they employed. This situation required of Maimonides some flexibility with regard to the occult with regard to remedies. Nonetheless, here too Maimonides placed strict limits. In his commentary to the Mishnah (*Yoma* 8:4) he distinguished between medications whose efficacy is shown "by reason (*qiyās*) and credible (*qarība*) experience" and those that have no rationale, and whose empirical evidence is weak. According to Jewish law, remedies containing forbidden food substances can be taken only if they fall into the first category.

Given his firm commitment to scientific explanation, it is not surprising that Maimonides found miracles to be a major worry. In his early writings, he tended to look at miracles as natural phenomena—not everyday occurrences, to be sure, but then again not beyond the bounds of the possible. However, as his religious thought matured and, concomitantly, his doubts about the full explanatory power of science increased, he allocated to miracles a more significant role. Temporal creation, in particular, must be viewed as a miracle. It does not contradict Aristotelian science, which does not do more than explain, and correctly at that, the worldly phenomena (the world beneath the orb of the Moon, to be precise) encountered now. Nonetheless, there is no way that Aristotle can refute the claims that the world did not always operate in this manner, but rather came into being at a certain point (the beginning of time, to be precise), and, moreover, underwent a process of stabilization until the laws now in force became fixed. As noted above, the choice between creation and eternity is the choice between the more or less likely alternative, neither of which can be established with certainty. It is only in one of his very last writings, the *Letter on Resurrection* (dubbed by Pines *popular,* but viewed by many, including the present author, to present Maimonides's *true* position no less than any other writing), that Maimonides attempted to formulate a set of rules for determining whether or not a given event is miraculous.

His great renown as a physician notwithstanding, Maimonides's considerable legacy of medical texts is only in the early twenty-first century receiving serious attention. Gerrit Bos has undertaken the editing and translation of the entire corpus of Maimonidean medical writings, including the Hebrew and Latin translations as well as the original Arabic texts. A short essay on the synochous fever has been found appended to one of Maimonides's abridgments of Galen's writings, and some scraps of autograph medical jottings, as well as portions of Maimonides's medical library, have been identified in the Cairo *genizah.*

Maimonides's medical philosophy can be summarized as follows. The connection between mind and body is so strong, that the physician should as a rule first ask whether some emotional or psychic disturbance is the cause of the patient's complaint. As evidence for this, Maimonides cited his own experience: when his beloved brother was lost at sea, he was bedridden for an entire year, and even years later, the mere thought of this tragedy made Maimonides ill. The wise person follows a sound regimen to preserve health: the fool waits until he is ill before seeking medical advice. In keeping with his views on the mind-body connection, this means that the wise person should also seek spiritual counsel from doctors of the soul in order to inculcate apathy toward the vanities of this world, thus avoiding needless malaise. Maimonides's medical writings were written for a Muslim clientele, but the spiritual advice is clearly universal and nondenominational.

The physician should always choose the mildest form of intervention. If the malady can be treated by diet, then drugs should not be administered. If drugs are necessary, then the physician should employ simples before resorting to compounds. The patient should be weaned off drugs gradually. In medicine, as in the religious quest, Maimonides preferred the step-by-step approach, rather than dramatic leaps. Caution must be exercised to prevent the patient from becoming dependent upon medications. One's body is one's beast, and like a mule, it will become lazy if others do the work it ought to perform.

Maimonides recorded a few experiences of his early study of medicine in northern Africa. In medicine, as in astronomy, in biblical exegesis, and indeed in just about all fields of intellectual endeavor, Maimonides preferred the fruits of Andalusian and Maghrebi learning. As a rule, he endorsed the strictest economy of expression. However, he justified the bulk of medical books, given the great amount of information that they must contain. In particular, he observed, there is a major distinction to be drawn between medicine and the exact sciences. With regard to the latter it suffices to remember a few basic rules. The skilled practitioner can then derive at will whatever specific formula he may need. There is no need to burden the memory. However, medicine is not mathematics. It is a huge body of discrete data, which cannot be derived logically from some basic rules. Therefore, there is no escaping bulky books and a good memory.

This does not mean, however, that there is no logic to medicine. To the contrary: medical theory is founded upon reason and logical argumentation. The good physician should always be able to give a good reason for the course that he advocates. Indeed, in a letter to Samuel Ibn Tibbon (who translated the *Guide of the Perplexed* into Hebrew), Maimonides wrote that every evening he would review his medical books, so as to be able to provide a rationale for his medical advice.

SUPPLEMENTARY BIBLIOGRAPHY

WORKS BY MAIMONIDES

"Maimonides on the Synochous Fever." Translated by Y. Tzvi Langermann. *Israel Oriental Studies* 13 (1993): 175–198. This is a translation of a newly discovered medical treatise.

Maimonides on Asthma. Edited by Gerrit Bos. Provo, UT: Brigham Young University Press, 2002.

Moreh nevukhim. Translated by Michael Schwarz. 2 vols. Tel Aviv, Israel: University of Tel-Aviv, 2002. This is a new Hebrew translation and provides very full references to the secondary literature, passage by passage.

Medical Aphorisms, Treatises 1–5. Edited by Gerrit Bos. Provo, UT: Brigham Young University Press, 2004.

Maimonides

OTHER SOURCES

Davidson, Herbert A. "Maimonides on Metaphysical Knowledge." *Maimonidean Studies* 3 (1992–1993): 49–103.

———. *Moses Maimonides: The Man and His Works.* Oxford: Oxford University Press, 2005. Authoritative, provocative, up-to-date.

Freudenthal, Gad. "The Biological Limitations of Man's Intellectual Perfection according to Maimonides." In *The Trias of Maimonides: Jewish, Arabic, and Ancient Cultures of Knowledge,* edited by Georges Tamer. Berlin: de Gruyter, 2005.

Kellner, Menachem. "On the Status of Astronomy and Physics in Maimonides's Mishneh Torah and Guide of the Perplexed." *British Journal for the History of Science* 24 (1991): 453–463.

Kraemer, Joel L., ed. *Perspectives on Maimonides: Philosophical and Historical Studies.* Oxford: Oxford University Press, 1991.

Langermann, Y. Tzvi. "Maimonides on Astronomy: Some Further Reflections." In *Idem: The Jews and the Sciences in the Middle Ages.* Aldershot, U.K.: Ashgate, 1999.

———. "Maimonides and the Sciences." In *The Cambridge Companion to Medieval Jewish Philosophy,* edited by Daniel H. Frank and Oliver Leaman. Cambridge, U.K.: Cambridge University Press, 2003.

———. "Maimonides and Miracles: The Growth of a (Dis)belief." *Jewish History* 18 (2004): 147–172.

Levine, Hillel, and Robert S. Cohen, eds. *Maimonides and the Sciences.* Dordrecht, Netherlands: Kluwer, 2000. Some new essays, some reprints, on diverse aspects of Maimonides's involvement with the sciences.

Manekin, Charles H. *On Maimonides.* Belmont, CA: Thomson-Wadsworth, 2005. Short, excellent overview.

Neugebauer, Otto. "Astronomical Commentary." Appended to *Sanctification of the New Moon (Moses Maimonides, Code of Law, Book Three, Treatise Eight).* Translated by Solomon Gandz. New Haven, CT: Yale University Press, 1956.

Pines, Shlomo. "The Limitations of Human Knowledge according to al-Farabi, Ibn Bajja, and Maimonides." In *Studies in Medieval Jewish History and Literature,* edited by Isadore Twersky. Cambridge, MA: Harvard University Press, 1979.

Rashed, Roshdi, and Tony Lévy, eds. *Maïmonide Philosophe et Savant (1138–1204).* Leuven, Belgium: Peeters, 2004. Includes the study of Stern discussed in the entry, the two most important studies on Maimonides's involvement with mathematics (each written by one of the two editors), and a survey of Maimonides's medical opinions by the present author.

Seeskin, Kenneth, ed. *The Cambridge Companion to Maimonides.* Cambridge, U.K.: Cambridge University Press, 2005. Includes a comprehensive review of Maimonides's philosophy of science by Gad Freudenthal and further discussion of Maimonides's epistemology by Josef Stern.

Stern, Josef. "Logical Syntax as a Key to a Secret of the *Guide of the Perplexed.*" *Iyyun* 38 (1989): 137–166.

Twersky, Isadore. "Aspects of Maimonides's Epistemology: Halakah and Science." *From Ancient Israel to Modern Judaism* 3 (1989): 3–23.

Y. Tzvi Langermann

MAIRAN, JEAN-JACQUES DORTOUS DE

(*b.* Béziers, France, 26 November 1678; *d.* Paris, France, 20 February 1771), *physics.* For the original article on Mairan see *DSB,* vol. 9.

Mairan was a mathematician and an enthusiastic experimenter whose major works were on the formation of ice and on the aurora borealis. However, he was also interested in all the important topics addressed by the scientific community in the eighteenth century, among them, the shape of Earth, light, colors, sound, the composition of matter, and *vis viva* (the debate around the force of moving bodies and the conservation of matter). Despite his admiration for Isaac Newton and the high regard in which he was held by many of his contemporaries, his reputation as a dyed-in-the-wool Cartesian and being compared unfavorably to Bernard Fontenelle, his predecessor as secretary of the Paris Academy of Sciences, served to tarnish his image. Since the early 1970s, scholars have begun to remedy this and to reassess his contributions to the scientific culture of the eighteenth century by underlining in particular the significant role that he played in the propagation of the Newtonian "system."

Reputation. Mairan was a founding member of the Academy of Béziers; a member of the Imperial Academy of Sciences of St. Petersburg, the Royal Societies of London, Edinburgh, and Uppsala, the Institute of Bologna; and the Academy of Rouen. In 1741 he succeeded Fontenelle as secretary of the Academy of Sciences in Paris, a post held by only four men during the whole century.

Mairan enjoyed an excellent international reputation and exerted considerable influence on scientific progress in the eighteenth century. For example, Voltaire included him in the preface to *Alzire* (1736) with Pierre-Louis Moreau de Maupertuis, Rene-Antoine Réaumur, Charles-François Du Fay, and Alexis-Claude Clairaut as five of the most outstanding scientists and mathematicians of the century. Likewise, Jean Jallabert, professor of experimental philosophy and mathematics in Geneva, praised the observations and experimental methods of older scientists such as Newton, the Bernoullis (Jakob, Johann I and II, Daniel), Mairan, and Maupertuis in his inaugural address, titled *De philosophiae experimentalis utilitate, illusque et matheseos concordia* (Geneva, 1740).

Along with a voluminous correspondence, with innumerable contributions to the *Mémoires* of the academy, and with responsibility for the *Eloges* and for the *Histoire* of the academy for the years 1741, 1742, and 1743, Mairan wrote three prize-winning dissertations: one on barometric variations (1715), one on ice (1716), and one on light (1717) while still in Béziers. When the second edition of the *Dissertation sur la glace* was published in 1717, he became an associate of the Royal Academy of Sciences. After his move to Paris, he continued to publish dissertations on force, ice, and the aurora borealis. Mairan was interested in all the major scientific topics of the century—the shape of Earth, the nature of aurorae and their connection to sunspots and zodiacal light, motion, force, gravity, heat, light, colors, sound, barometric variations, universal attraction, the *vis viva* controversy, the nature and medicinal properties of electricity, the composition of matter, and scientific method; in short, a panoply of the scientific culture of the period.

Shape of Earth. Just as the academy prided itself on taking a neutral position on any topic until there was incontrovertible proof, Mairan prided himself on having an open mind. For example, he veered between opting for an oblate and a prolate shaped Earth, endeavoring to reconcile Gian Domenico and Jacques Cassini's measurements with the theory of centrifugal forces and the shortening of the pendulum. In his 1720 memoir he tried to prove that Earth was a prolate spheroid, and, in an attempt to accommodate troublesome and apparently incompatible facts, resorted to what Maupertuis in his 1738 critique of Mairan's argument considered the ingenious hypothesis of suggesting that if Earth had been prolate instead of spherical originally, it would now be, not oblate, but less prolate. In the end he agreed to abide by the results of the observations obtained by the academicians on the expeditions to Peru and to Lapland.

Light, Colors, and Sound. On the topic of light and colors, Mairan successfully repeated Newton's optical experiments at Béziers in 1716 and 1717, and in 1719 he reported on the second Latin edition of the *Opticks* at the request of the academy. Reluctant as he was to abandon a mechanistic explanation of the effects of light and to accept attraction as an innate property of matter, Mairan stressed what was for him the most important part of the *Opticks,* namely, the experiments and the physico-mathematical inductions that could be drawn from them. He was also interested in the analogy of the colors of the spectrum and the divisions of the monochord. He was at pains to explain through his theory of the propagation of sounds and the different elasticity of the particles of air why the various notes reach our ears without being confused.

***Vis Viva* and Other Controversies.** Few disputes in the eighteenth century generated as much fervor as the *vis viva* controversy in which Mairan played a major role. When Johann Bernoulli contested Colin Maclaurin's 1724 prize-winning paper on the laws of motion for perfectly hard bodies, his subsequent correspondence with Mairan resulted in the latter's 1728 memoir on the subject, which was then challenged by Émilie du Châtelet. The whole debate centered on the distinction made by Gottfried Wilhelm Leibniz between *forces mortes* and *forces vives,* with Mairan believing that all force was *force morte.*

Similar to Mairan's dispute with du Châtelet over *vis viva* was his dispute with Leonhard Euler over zodiacal light. Euler contended that the solar atmosphere was only a ring separated from the sun, like Saturn's rings, an argument which Mairan rejected, and which Euler himself eventually renounced.

Some twenty years later Mairan and Euler were still in disagreement—this time concerning Mairan's theory on the propagation of sound. As early as 1719, at the time of his report on the second Latin edition of the *Opticks,* Mairan proposed to the academy his thesis that air as the vehicle of sound consisted of an infinity of vibrating particles of differing elasticity. This theory was later elaborated in his 1737 memoir, *Discours sur la propagation du son dans les différents tons qui le modifient,* and rejected by Euler, who argued that all sounds are transmitted by the same particles of air, because each particle is capable of different vibrations that produce different sounds.

Scientific Method. Mairan, all his life, was preoccupied with methodological questions, and it was his spirited defense of systems in the preface to the fourth edition of the *Dissertation sur la glace* in 1749 that incensed Jean Le Rond d'Alembert. The latter wrote in the *Discours préliminaire* of the *Encyclopédie* that the time had passed for anyone to argue in favor of systems. In a letter to Gabriel Cramer in September 1749, he accused Mairan of confusing the real advantages of the systematic spirit with the doubtful advantages of metaphysical systems and hypotheses. However, Mairan was always careful to praise the usefulness of the true philosophical or geometric spirit as exemplified by René Descartes, while also recognizing the dangers that certain systems represented in the form of a plethora of sterile and illusory philosophical extravagances. In his *Eloge* of François Pourfour de Petit in 1741, for example, he had praise for Descartes's "immortal method" and for the care with which he conducted experiments. Mairan himself was a theoretician always in search of a mechanical model, but also a committed experimentalist and the instigator of a number of crucial experiments. In his *Mémoire sur la cause générale du froid en hiver et de la chaleur en été* (1719) he concluded that the method most likely to induce Nature to reveal her secrets is the constant interplay of experiment and reasoning.

Having condemned the abuse of certain systems and stressed the usefulness of others, such as Jean Jallabert's conjectures on the causes of electricity, for scientific progress, Mairan devoted the third part of his *Preface* to his hypothesis of subtle matter on which he based his discussion of ice. Mairan condemned subtle matter in the Cartesian sense of hard and inflexible particles filling the universe, a thesis which he said is untenable. However, he posited the existence of some kind of subtle matter that could account for a number of physical phenomena. How else, he asked, is one to understand action at a distance or electrical impulses? Subtle matter for Mairan was an active and invisible principle that provided a mechanical model of the universe and one which Newton had made use of in the *Opticks.*

Mairan's position on scientific method, in fact, was not so different from that of Étienne Bonnot de Condillac, whom d'Alembert so admired, and whose *Traité des systèmes* appeared in the same year as Mairan's *Preface* (1749). However, because many of his contemporaries perceived him to be a die-hard Cartesian, any favorable comment on systems that he might have made would have aroused suspicion.

Preoccupation with Newton. Mairan had a reputation as the last Cartesian in a predominantly Newtonian world and he was reluctant to jettison the vortex theory recognizing the problems that it had difficulty resolving. Despite this, it is not hard to show Mairan's fascination with Newton from virtually the beginning of his career. As early as 1717 in a letter to Firmin Abauzit in Geneva he admitted that Newton's explanation of the tides was free of the difficulties raised by the vortex theory, but that gravity as an inherent property of matter was hard to accept. In another letter to the same correspondent, written on 30 October 1717, he conceded that attraction regarded simply as a fact seemed to him to be highly likely. However, he drew his correspondent's attention to the end of the *Opticks,* where attraction was considered as essential a property of matter as extension. Although he admitted that there were places where Newton appeared to qualify this, on balance it seemed that this was indeed Newton's opinion.

In a letter to Gabriel Cramer dated 16 November 1732, Mairan showed himself to be thoroughly conversant with Newton's works, extolling Newton's "admirable theory" which, he said, seemed to be entirely consistent with the world as it is. He claimed to have accepted Newton's laws of motion of celestial bodies as a fact in his work on the aurora borealis. Indeed, in the *Éclaircissements* added to the 1754 edition of his work on the aurora modeled on Newton's *Queries* at the end of the *Opticks,* he maintained that the inviolable laws of universal gravitation were the basis of his whole system. However, he continued to reject attraction as an innate property of matter and to state that he could not provide the mechanistic explanation that no doubt lay behind the principle of attraction. In the meantime he was prepared to consider Newton's theory of universal attraction mathematically as Newton himself had done.

It is evident that Newton's writings were a model of scientific method for Mairan even in his early works. In his 1717 dissertation, for example, he praised the ingenious experiments on light that Newton had performed to establish the different refrangibility of colors, saying that these would be enough to immortalize his name. Also, according to Pierre Coste, who translated the *Opticks* into French, Mairan was the first in France to repeat Newton's optical experiments.

Conclusion. Jean-Jacques Dortous de Mairan should be remembered principally for three things: his work on ice and on the aurora borealis; his lifelong obsession with Newton, despite his not undeserved reputation as a Cartesian; and lastly, his enormous influence on the development and spread of scientific culture in the eighteenth century because of his voluminous correspondence and his prominent position as secretary of the Academy of Sciences, the power center of the scientific establishment.

Despite his reluctance to abandon completely Cartesian vortices and the plenum, he recognized the difficulties that these represented for an adequate understanding of the universe. Though anxious to explain physical phenomena by a mechanical model and uncomfortable with the concept of action at a distance, he accepted universal gravitation as a fact if not an inherent property of matter.

Lastly, his vast correspondence was a prime example of scientific networking, mirroring the intricate patterns of interdependence and mutual advantage crossing national frontiers. Through his network of correspondents, he was a conduit and facilitator of ideas.

SUPPLEMENTARY BIBLIOGRAPHY

WORKS BY MAIRAN

Dissertation sur les variations du baromètre. Bordeaux, 1715.

Dissertation sur la glace. Bordeaux, 1716; Béziers, 1717; Paris, 1730, 1749.

Dissertation sur la cause de la lumière des phosphores et des noctiluques. Bordeaux, 1717.

"Mémoire sur la cause générale du froid en hiver, et de la chaleur en été." In *Mémoires de l'Académie royale des sciences 1719.* Paris: Academy of Sciences, 1721.

"Recherches géométriques sur la diminution des degrés terrestres, en allant de l'Equateur vers les Poles." In *Mémoires de l'Académie royale des sciences 1720.* Paris, 1722.

"Discours sur l'estimation et la mesure des forces motrices des corps." In *Mémoires de l'Académie royale des sciences 1728.* Paris, 1730.

Traité physique et historique de l'aurore boréale. Paris, 1733, 1754. Published under the auspices of the Academy of Sciences.

"Discours sur la propagation du son dans les différents tons qui le modifient." In *Mémoires de l'Académie royale des sciences 1737.* Paris, 1740.

Histoire de l'Académie royale des sciences 1741. Paris, 1744.

Histoire de l'Académie royale des sciences 1742. Paris, 1745.

Histoire de l'Académie royale des sciences 1743. Paris, 1746.

MANUSCRIPT SOURCES

See the *Bibliothèque publique et universitaire de Genève* for Mairan's correspondence with Firmin Abauzit, Gabriel Cramer, and Jean Jallabert, principally Ms. Fr. 612 (Abauzit); Ms. Supp. 384 (Cramer); Ms. Supp. 140 (Jallabert).

See the Bernoulli-Edition, Universitätsbibliothek Basel, L1 a 661 for the Mairan-Bernoulli letters.

OTHER SOURCES

Beeson, David. *Maupertuis: An Intellectual Biography.* Oxford: Voltaire Foundation, 1992. On the shape of Earth debate.

Bone, Neil. *The Aurora: Sun-Earth Interactions.* New York: E. Horwood, 1991. A general discussion of the nature of aurorae.

Briggs, J. Morton, Jr. "Aurora and Enlightenment: Eighteenth-Century Explanations of the Aurora Borealis." *Isis* 58 (1967): 491–503. A useful discussion of the problems arising from the nature of aurorae encountered by eighteenth-century scientists.

Guerlac, Henry. "The Newtonianism of Dortous de Mairan." In *Essays on the Age of Enlightenment in Honor of Ira O. Wade,* edited by Jean Macary, 131–141. Geneva: Droz, 1977.

———. "Some Areas for Further Newtonian Studies." *History of Science* 17 (1979): 75–101.

Hall, A. Rupert. "Newton in France: A New View." *History of Science* 13 (1975): 233–250.The above essays by Guerlac and this one by Hall represent attempts to reassess Mairan's reaction to Newton.

Heilbron, J. L. "Experimental Natural Philosophy." In *The Ferment of Knowledge: Studies in the Historiography of Eighteenth-Century Science,* edited by George S. Rousseau and Roy Porter. New York: Cambridge University Press, 1980. A study of the eighteenth-century preoccupation with the nature of electricity.

Hine, Ellen McNiven. "Dortous de Mairan, the 'Cartonian.'" In *Studies on Voltaire and the Eighteenth Century* 266 (1989): 163–179. A discussion of the attraction that Newton had for Mairan, the Cartesian.

———. "Dortous de Mairan and Eighteenth-Century 'Systems Theory.' " *Gesnerus* 52 (1995): 54–65. On Mairan's disagreement with d'Alembert on the usefulness of systems.

———. *Jean-Jacques Dortous de Mairan and the Geneva Connection: Scientific Networking in the Eighteenth Century.* Oxford: Voltaire Foundation, 1996. Discusses the role of Mairan's correspondence network in the spread of Enlightenment thought.

Kleinbaum, Abby R. *Jean-Jacques Dortous de Mairan (1678–1771): A Study of an Enlightenment Scientist.* PhD diss., Columbia University, 1970. An excellent detailed analysis of Mairan's scientific work.

Taton, René. "The Beginnings of Modern Science: From 1450–1800." In *A General History of the Sciences*, edited by Rene Taton and translated by Arnold J. Pomerans. New York: Basic Books, 1964. A useful overview of science in the eighteenth century.

Ellen McNiven Hine

MALTHUS, THOMAS ROBERT

(*b.* near Dorking, Surrey, England, 13 February 1766; *d.* Bath, England, 23 December 1834), *political economy*. For the original article on Malthus see *DSB*, vol. 9.

An explosion of secondary literature on Malthus since the original *DSB*, publication of the catalogue of the Malthus family library in 1983, an important discovery of Malthus family documents in 1986 later sold to Kanto Gakuen University, publication of Malthus's collected *Works* (1986), definitive editions of the *Essay* and *Political Economy* in 1989, and the development since the 1970s of mathematical modeling in ecology have substantially modified the view of Malthus and his relevance for the history of science presented in the original article:

1. More accurate details of Malthus's biography have become known.
2. Studies of the confrontation of Malthusian population theory with Christian theology, and of the relation of each of these to ethics and political theory, have enriched the intellectual history of nineteenth-century science and religion.
3. A fuller understanding of Malthus's importance in the development of economic thought has transformed scholars' view of "Malthus the economist."
4. The mathematical core of the science of ecology can be viewed as a generalization of Malthus's original model of the equilibrium of a single human population.

Biography and the First *Essay*. The biography by Patricia James, subsequent biographical studies by John Pullen, and the later publication by Kanto Gakuen University of the Malthus family documents have shown that Malthus remained a faithful clergyman of the Church of England from his diaconal ordering in June 1789 to the end of his life. He was ordained a priest in March 1791 and served his curacy at Okewood punctiliously until preferment to the family living of Walesbury in 1803, the income from which allowed him to marry his "pretty cousin" Harriet Eckersall in 1804 and resign his college fellowship. That preferment was not a sinecure: As a non-residentiary, Malthus appointed and paid a curate and visited the parish regularly. Meanwhile he officiated and preached in the chapel at Haileybury, and like many clergymen of his generation had become "serious" (i.e. evangelical) by 1812 at the latest.

Scholars also know that Malthus made his first acquaintance with *Wealth of Nations* while still a pupil at Warrington Academy, was reading it six years later during his final term at Cambridge while preparing for ordination, and was undoubtedly the leading authority in England, both on that work and on political economy in general, when he accepted his professorial appointment at the East India College in 1805.

Studies in the early 2000s have shown that Malthus's first *Essay on Population* (1798), written while he was still assistant curate of Okewood, was a point-by-point rebuttal of William Godwin's attack on private property in *Political Justice*, which had nothing to do with any "Industrial Revolution" but much to do with the French Revolution. At its heart (chapter 10) is a mental experiment in the manner of David Hume. Human society is a system in stable equilibrium. If exogenously shocked, the system will return to equilibrium in the absence of further shocks. Population dynamics of the *Essay* are used to show that private property in land, combined with competition among landless workers, produces a stable economic equilibrium that is optimal in that it maximizes the surplus of food production over labor and capital costs. Upon that surplus depends everything "that distinguishes the civilized, from the savage state" (p. 287).

Theological Difficulties. In the first *Essay* the principle of population condemned the human race to "misery and vice" (p. 141). This would appear to deny the coexistence of the Divine attributes—especially those of benevolence and omnipotence—affirmed by orthodox monotheistic theology. Malthus attempted a naturalistic theodicy in the last two chapters (18 and 19) of the first *Essay*, according to which God is engaged in the creation of "mind" out of matter. But the attempt was confused and unsuccessful, and he was persuaded to omit it from subsequent editions. In the second *Essay* (1803) Malthus introduced the concept of "moral restraint" (not "natural restraint," cf. original article in *DSB*) to evade the inevitability of misery or vice, and made other smaller changes in his argument to render it more consistent with Anglican orthodoxy.

Meanwhile, William Paley and John Bird Sumner provided more satisfactory theodicies of the putative evil produced by population pressures. Their work was the basis of "Christian Political Economy" in the 1820s and 1830s, to which important contributions were also made

Thomas Malthus. **HULTON ARCHIVE/GETTY IMAGES.**

by Edward Copleston, Richard Whately and Thomas Chalmers. Whately's epistemological demarcation between religious and scientific knowledge became important later in the philosophy of science.

Because it adopted and incorporated Malthusian population theory, the nascent science of political economy had been reviled by many critics as "hostile to religion." "Christian Political Economy" defended the new science against what at that time was a very damaging charge. But its ideological thrust was to legitimatize *laissez-faire* in social policy, for which reason political economy continued to be viewed with alarm by Romantics, Christian socialists, Marxists and others.

Political Economy. Though his contribution to demography continued to be acknowledged—perhaps exaggerated—throughout the nineteenth century, Malthus's political economy was generally passed over in silence. This is because of his heterodox theory of "general gluts" which attempted to show that untrammeled market forces might be insufficient to correct mass unemployment. Lord Keynes had always been an admirer of Malthus however, and in 1936 produced his own, immensely influential version of the Malthusian doctrine, which together with his biographical essay on Malthus began a long process of reappraisal. This was stimulated by the international *Congrès Malthus* in Paris (1980) and fostered by the new literature referred to above. It culminated during the 1990s in major studies by Donald Winch (1996) and Samuel Hollander (1997). The effect of these has been to recognize the conceptual unity of Malthus's "demography" and his "economics," and to locate him at the center of the English School of political economy in the first third of the nineteenth century.

The Natural Sciences. It has long been known that Darwin and Wallace came to appreciate the scientific significance of the "struggle for existence" from reading Malthus. It has more recently been recognized that Malthusian population dynamics are the conceptual starting point of modern ecology. Standard textbooks of mathematical ecology in the early twenty-first century acknowledge Malthus as a pioneer (e.g. Kot, 2001, p. 11). An unconstrained, exponential population growth-rate, *r*, is sometimes labeled the "Malthusian parameter." More significantly, the related concepts of "density-dependence" and "carrying capacity" are seen to have their origin in Malthus's analysis of human population growth in a finite world (Vandermeer and Goldberg, 2003, pp. 10–11). For though by supplying more labor a growing population increases food production, the latter is subject to diminishing returns when food-producing resources are inelastic, hence the per-capita food supply will eventually fall to that level at which population is stationary. Malthus himself seems to have glimpsed the general, ecological implications of his argument: "The germs of existence contained in this spot of earth, with ample food, and ample room to expand in, would fill millions of worlds in the course of a few thousand years, Necessity, that imperious all pervading law of nature, restrains them within the prescribed bounds. The race of plants, and the race of animals shrink under this great restriction" (1798, p. 15).

SUPPLEMENTARY BIBLIOGRAPHY

WORKS BY MALTHUS

An Essay on the Principle of Population. London: Macmillan, 1966. Reprint of the first (1798) *Essay* for the Royal Economic Society. Facsimile reprint, essential for Malthus scholarship.

The Works of Thomas Robert Malthus. 8 vols. Edited by E. A. Wrigley and David Souden. London: William Pickering, 1986. The first collected works, especially valuable for Malthus's scattered and inaccessible pamphlet literature.

An Essay on the Principle of Population. 2 vols. Edited by Patricia James. Cambridge, U.K.: Cambridge University Press, 1989. The version published in 1803, with the variora of 1806, 1807, 1817 and 1826. Essential for Malthus scholarship.

Principles of Political Economy. 2 vols. Variorum Edition. Edited by John Pullen. Cambridge, U.K.: Cambridge University Press, 1989.

The Unpublished Papers in the Collection of Kanto Gakuen University. 2 vols. Edited by John Pullen and Trevor Hughes Parry. Cambridge, U.K.: Cambridge University Press, vol. I, 1997; vol. II, 2004. Contains many letters and papers by other members of the Malthus family and circle. Especially valuable as including four of Robert Malthus's previously unknown sermons.

OTHER SOURCES

Dupâquier, Jacques, A. Fauve-Chamoux, and E. Grebenik, eds. *Malthus Past and Present.* London and New York: Academic Press, 1983. English translations of a small selection of papers from the Paris *Congrès*, 1980.

Fauve-Chamoux, Antoinette, ed. *Malthus Hier et Aujourd'hui.* Paris: Éditions du Centre National de la Recherche Scientifique, 1984. French translations of a different but slightly overlapping selection of papers from the Paris *Congrès*, 1980.

Hollander, Samuel. *The Economics of Thomas Robert Malthus.* Studies in Classical Political Economy IV. Toronto: University of Toronto Press, 1997. Massive, exhaustive, authoritative.

James, Patricia. *Population Malthus: His Life and Times.* London and Boston: Routledge & Kegan Paul, 1979. Best available biography, but must now be supplemented by Pullen (1987), Waterman (1991) and the Kanto Gakuen papers.

Jesus College (University of Cambridge). *The Malthus Library Catalogue: The Personal Collection of Thomas Robert Malthus at Jesus College, Cambridge.* New York: Pergamon Press, 1983. See "Introductory Essay" by John Harrison.

Keynes, John Maynard. *Essays in Biography.* The Collected Writings of John Maynard Keynes, Vol. 10. London: Macmillan, for the Royal Economic Society, 1972. Essay 12, "Thomas Robert Malthus" (1933), is characteristically brilliant and still the best place to start.

Kot, Mark. *Elements of Mathematical Ecology.* Cambridge U.K.: Cambridge University Press, 2001.

Malthus Hier et Aujourd'hui. Congrès International de Démographie Historique, Paris-UNESCO 27, 28, 29 May 1980: Programme, Agenda. Paris: Société de Démographie Historique, 1980. Program includes papers on the relevance of Malthus for demography, ethnology, sociology, socialism, feminism, geography, theology, economic history, economics, evolutionary biology and ecology.

Pullen, John M. "Some New Information on the Rev. T. R. Malthus." *History of Political Economy* 19 (1987): 127–140.

Spengler, Joseph J. "Malthus's Total Population Theory: A Restatement and Reappraisal." *Canadian Journal of Economics and Political Science* 11 (1945): 83–110; 234–264. The earliest comprehensive analysis of Malthus's economic thought (still one of the best), by the leading Malthus scholar of his generation.

Tunzelmann, G. Nick von. "Malthus's 'Total Population System': a Dynamic Reinterpretation." In *The State of Population Theory: Forward from* Malthus, edited by David Coleman and Roger Schofield. Oxford: Blackwell, 1986. The most ambitious attempt since Spengler (1945) to capture the whole of Malthus's population theory.

Vandermeer, John H. and Deborah E. Goldberg. *Population Ecology: First Principles.* Princeton, NJ: Princeton University Press, 2003.

Waterman, A. M. C. *Revolution, Economics and Religion: Christian Political Economy 1798–1833.* Cambridge, U.K.: Cambridge University Press, 1991. Contains the only complete account of the nature and purpose of Malthus's argument in the first *Essay.*

———. "Analysis and Ideology in Malthus's 'Essay on Population'." *Australian Economic Papers* 31 (1992): 203–217. Mathematical reconstruction of the analysis of the first *Essay.*

———. "Reappraisal of 'Malthus the Economist,' 1933–97." *History of Political Economy* 30 (1998): 293–334. Survey of Malthus scholarship: Bibliography includes all important secondary literature up to 1997.

———. "New Light on Malthus: The Kanto Gakuen Collection." *Research in the History of Economic Thought and Methodology* 24A (2006): 141–152.

Winch, Donald. *Malthus.* Past Masters series. Oxford: Oxford University Press, 1987. Combines biography with a lucid and authoritative sketch of the whole range of Malthus's ideas in just over 100 pages.

———. *Riches and Poverty. An Intellectual History of Political Economy in Britain, 1750–1834.* Cambridge, U.K.: Cambridge University Press, 1996. State of the art in its field. Malthus gets center stage.

Wood, John Cunningham, ed. *Thomas Robert Malthus, Critical Assessments.* 4 vols. London and Dover, NH: Croom Helm, 1986.

A. M. C. Waterman

MANGOLD (NÉE PRÖSCHOLDT), HILDE

(*b.* Gotha, Germany, 20 September 1898; *d.* Auenstein near Stuttgart, Germany, 5 September 1924), *developmental biology, experimental embryology, pattern formation.*

Embryogenesis transforms the seemingly simple egg cell into an organized body of amazing complexity. A fundamental component of this process, called the organizer effect, was first documented in the doctoral dissertation of Hilde Mangold, published at the time of her death. This work, crucial for the 1935 Nobel Prize in Physiology or Medicine, ranks as the first breakthrough toward a mechanistic understanding of vertebrate development.

Life of Hilde Mangold. Hilde was born to Gertrud and Ernst Pröscholdt as the second of three daughters. Her father came from a family of artists who specialized in chinaware decoration but managed to acquire a soap factory

Hilde Mangold. *Hilde Pröscholdt Mangold with her son.* K. SANDER/UNIVERSITY OF FREIBURG/SCIENCE SOURCE/PHOTO RESEARCHERS, INC.

in Gotha, a provincial center of intellectual life. Hilde received the best education possible. She was one of the few girls to be admitted to the local high school and passed her final exam with best marks. Dissatisfied by a brief interlude at a "Pensionat" that trained prospective housewives, Hilde studied chemistry, philosophy, and fine arts at Jena University. After one term (winter 1918–1919) she shifted to Frankfurt and to zoology as her main subject.

There she was deeply impressed by a guest lecture by Hans Spemann, doubtless the leading experimental embryologist of that period. Spemann had just resigned from the Kaiser Wilhelm Institut für Biologie and moved to the idyllic setting of Freiburg (Baden, Germany). In the spring of 1920 Hilde moved there too. Impressed by her intellect and drive, Spemann accepted her for doctoral research after just one year of advanced training in biology. This training she shared with about a dozen fellow students, of whom two—Viktor Hamburger and Johannes Holtfreter—like Hilde herself were to leave indelible marks on developmental biology. The main teachers of this gifted and vividly interacting group were Fritz Baltzer and Otto Mangold.

In 1921, Hilde decided to marry Otto and adopted his family name. Despite considerable differences in years and in temper—Hilde vivacious, Otto steady and very systematic—the couple apparently developed a successful partnership in research as well as family life during the three years left to them. In December 1923 their son Christian was born and Hilde had to abandon work on her experiments—seemingly just for the time being. But she died on 5 September 1924, the victim of terrible burns suffered the previous day while trying to heat her baby's meal on an alcohol stove. She was buried in the family grave at Gotha; the tombstone carrying her portrait in bronze is still extant.

The Organizer Effect. This effect, named by Hans Spemann, is illustrated in Figure 1. It was first observed in experiments using salamander (newt) embryos at the

Mangold

onset of gastrulation, the process whereby cells destined to yield internal organs get shifted inside the previously hollow embryo (called the blastula). The aim was to understand the mechanisms causing the increase in ordered complexity (later called pattern formation) during embryogenesis. The organizer effect was documented by transplanting material from a certain region—called the dorsal lip—of a donor blastula into the belly region of another embryo of the same stage, the host (see Figure 1). Often, such transplants would locally initiate gastrulation and thereby move inward, accompanied by huge numbers of surrounding host cells. After further development, this cell complex could develop into a more or less complete additional body, made up of transplant cells intermingled with host cells that otherwise should have formed nothing but belly surface. Apparently, the transplanted material was capable of triggering (inducing) and guiding the formation of a well-organized body—it acted as an "organizer."

Under Spemann's guidance, Hilde Mangold in 1921 and 1922 performed 259 of these technically demanding "lip transplantations" for her doctoral thesis. Of the seventy-three surviving cases, twenty-eight developed in their belly regions recognizable components of an additional body. The individual degree of organization ranged from a feeble rudiment of the spinal cord (the as-yet-superficial neural plate, see Figure 1b) to a well-defined additional body (see Figure 1c). All but two of these additional embryos were of a chimeric (composite) constitution (see Figure 1d). With the ascent of genetic, biochemical, and molecular methods, Mangold's "mechanical" experiments seemed to fall into oblivion. However, once advanced molecular methods had passed their teething troubles, their practitioners came to appreciate her pioneering work—as documented by a dramatic rise in its citation frequency (Fässler and Sander, 1996).

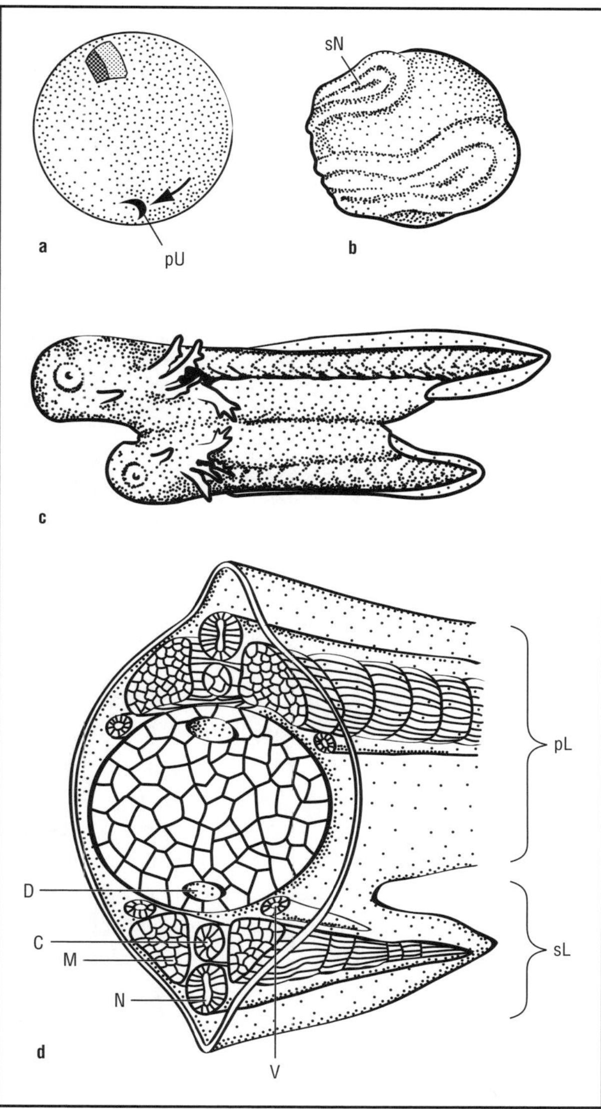

Figure 1. Demonstration of the organizer effect. (a) Dorsal lip material from a dark donor gastrula was transplanted onto a less pigmented host blastula about to gastrulate at pU. (b) The dark transplant has moved below the host's surface and caused this to form an additional neural plate of minor size (sN). (c) Coordinated cell movements in this neural plate and by internalized cells have shaped a small larval body attached to the host's belly region. (d) Cross section (at the left) of an adjacent part cut from the twin bodies shown in (c). The organ rudiments in the additional body (bottom) consist partly of cells derived from the transplant (marked in black). Bars indicate individual organs that primarily owe their character and positions to the organizer effect: C notochord; D intestine; M muscle segment; N spinal cord; V kidney precursor.

The Nobel Prize—Fables and Facts. In 1935, the Nobel Prize for Physiology or Medicine was awarded to Hans Spemann, expressly "for his discovery of the organizer effect in embryonic development." Some competitors, such as Sven Hörstadius, argued that this effect had been discovered already during a few exploratory experiments by Warren Harmon Lewis (1907) but—owing to a mistaken hypothesis of Wilhelm Roux (see Sander 1990, 1991)—Lewis had failed to recognize the effect, and never laid claim to it! The restriction of the prize to Spemann was considered unfair by some because it was Hilde Mangold who had delivered the experimental evidence. However, the prize can be awarded only to living persons.

Spemann himself no doubt deserved the honor because between 1914 and 1918 he had paved the way for Mangold's success. He developed all the techniques required, among them the delicate transplantation of small cell groups and the marking of transplant cells by taking the transplants from a different species—but as

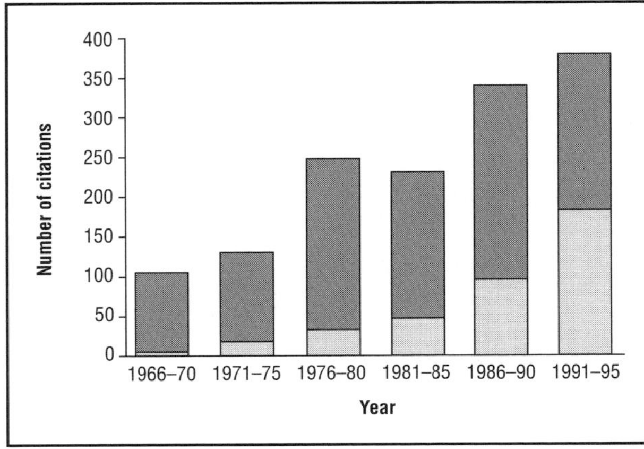

Figure 2. *Citation frequencies of Hans Spemann's publications. Number of references (citations) quoted during successive five-year periods in indexed publications. White parts of columns refer to Hilde Mangold's doctoral dissertation (Spemann and Hilde Mangold 1924). Black parts: Other publications of Hans Spemann.*

a newly installed professor (1919) he lacked the time to apply them in combination himself. He had, however, made predictions as to the outcome, of which one alternative—neural induction by the submerged transplant—was to prove correct. Spemann failed, however, to foresee the induction of a complete body and the chimeric constitution of individual organ rudiments (see Figure 1d)—clearly the most striking and overarching components of the organizer effect. They were revealed de novo by Hilde Mangold's experiments, and certainly should have earned her a share in the Nobel Prize. This, alas, was not to come true, but her name lives forth in the term *Spemann-Mangold organizer,* which became universally accepted.

BIBLIOGRAPHY

WORKS BY MANGOLD

"Ueber die Induktion von Achsenorgananlagen durch Transplantation eines Organisators." PhD diss., Albert-Ludwigs-Universität Freiburg, Germany, 1922. Typescript (no figures); stored at the Universitätsarchiv Freiburg.

With Hans Spemann. "Über Induktion von Embryonalanlagen durch Implantation artfremder Organisatoren." *Archiv für mikroskopische Anatomie und Entwicklungsmechanik* 100 (1924): 599–638. First and fundamental description of the organizer effect.

OTHER SOURCES

Fässler, Peter E. "Hans Spemann and the Freiburg School of Embryology." *International Journal of Developmental Biology* 40 (1996): 49–59.

———. *Hans Spemann (1869–1941)—Experimentelle Forschung im Spannungsfeld von Theorie und Empirie.* Berlin: Springer Verlag, 1997. Fully documented biography of Spemann.

———, and Klaus Sander. "Hilde Mangold (1898–1924) and Spemann's Organizer: Achievement and Tragedy." *Roux's Archives of Developmental Biology* 205 (1996): 323–332. Reprinted in Sander, 1997.

Hamburger, Viktor. "Hilde Mangold, Co-discoverer of the Organizer." *Journal of the History of Biology* 17 (1984): 1–11. Report by a famous labmate of Hilde Mangold.

———. *The Heritage of Experimental Embryology: Hans Spemann and the Organizer.* New York: Oxford University Press, 1988.

———. "Memories of Professor Hans Spemann's Department of Zoology at the University of Freiburg." *International Journal of Developmental Biology* 40 (1996): 59–63.

Hörstadius, Sven. *Über die Determination des Keimes bei Echinodermen.* Stockholm: Albert Bonnier, 1928. Claims that the organizer effect was discovered by W. H. Lewis in 1907.

Lewis, Warren Harmon. "Transplantation of the Lips of the Blastopore in *Rana palustris.*" *American Journal of Anatomy* 7 (1907): 137–143.

Sander, Klaus. "Von der Keimplasmatheorie zur synergetischen Musterbildung—Einhundert Jahre entwicklungsbiologischer Ideengeschichte." *Verhandlungen der Deutschen Zoologischen Gesellschaft* 83 (1990): 133–177. Illustrated history of developmental concepts.

———. "When Seeing Is Believing: Wilhelm Roux's Misconceived Fate Map." *Roux's Archives of Developmental Biology* 200 (1991): 177–179. Reprinted in Sander, 1997. Describes an error that may have prevented earlier discovery of the organizer effect.

———, ed. *Landmarks in Developmental Biology, 1883–1924: Historical Essays from Roux's Archives.* Berlin: Springer-Verlag, 1997.

———, and Peter E. Fässler. "Introducing the Spemann-Mangold Organizer: Experiments and Insights That Generated a Key Concept in Developmental Biology." *International Journal of Developmental Biology* 45 (2001): 1–11. A richly illustrated report.

Spemann, Hans. *Experimentelle Beiträge zu einer Theorie der Entwicklung.* Berlin: Verlag Julius Springer, 1936. Spemann's exposition of his lifelong research on amphibian embryogenesis. Reworked translation: *Embryonic Development and Induction.* New Haven, CT: Yale University Press, 1938.

Klaus Sander

MANSFIELD, CHARLES BLACHFORD

(*b.* Rowner, near Gosport, Hampshire, England, 8 May 1819; *d.* London, 26 February 1855), *aromatic organic reactions, chemistry, exploration, social reform.*

Mansfield

Charles Blachford Mansfield. SPL/PHOTO RESEARCHERS, INC.

The chemical and energy industries rely on processes for the separation of hydrocarbons. These were originally derived from coal tar, the by-product of the gas lighting and coke industries, and since the 1950s mainly from petroleum. In the late 1840s, Mansfield pioneered the separation of aromatic hydrocarbons such as benzene from coal tar, and from benzene he produced nitrobenzene, thus contributing to the later development of the synthetic dye industry. He was a social reformer, and also recorded the geography and resources of South America.

Charles Blachford Mansfield was born to the rector of Rowner when the latter was sixty years of age. His mother's family were descendants of Edward IV, and owned Osborne House, on the Isle of Wight, though it was sold to Queen Victoria after a brother-in-law lost a fortune on gambling. The proceeds enabled Mansfield to lead an independent life, and to follow his interests in science, industry, and social issues. His strong Christian values led him to take up the cause of education and improved conditions for the working classes.

Mansfield was educated at private schools, first at Twyford, then at Winchester, where he was so badly treated by one master that he suffered a breakdown at the age of sixteen. On recovery, he had a private tutor in Northamptonshire, and came to the notice of the Marquess of Northampton, president of the Royal Society, who encouraged a strong interest in science and ornithology. In October 1839 Mansfield entered Clare Hall, Cambridge, but did not graduate with a BA until 1846. In 1847 he joined the Royal College of Chemistry, since 1845 directed by August Wilhelm Hofmann, who undertook research into coal-tar products. Mansfield, as assistant to Hofmann, isolated abundant supplies of the hydrocarbons benzene (then called benzole) and toluene (toluol) by distillation of coal-tar naphtha. Realizing the commercial potential, he drew up a 50,000-word patent, filed on 11 November 1847. Specified uses included conversion of benzene, through the action of nitric acid, into nitrobenzene, a compound that came into use as a synthetic perfume. Mansfield's nitration allowed benzene and concentrated nitric acid to drop continuously from separate glass funnels into an upright coil of glass tubing, thereby preventing a great rise in the temperature. Other uses for benzene included illuminating gas, as described by Mansfield on 17 April 1849 before the Institute of Civil Engineers. He also proposed before the Royal Institution the use of benzene as a solvent. Benzene was later used extensively in dry cleaning. Mansfield had a good knowledge of metals and their salts, and in 1851–1852 lectured on metals before the Royal Institution. In his *Theory of Salts,* completed in 1855 he proposed a threefold system for classification of the elements that was not helped by an obscure system of nomenclature.

In January 1849 Mansfield went into business as a manufacturer in Hanover Square, not far from the Royal College of Chemistry. He assisted Read Holliday, a large tar distiller based in Huddersfield, to distill hydrocarbons, and promoted his "Gas or Air Light" illuminating machine. Mansfield resigned from the college in 1850. Hofmann was one of his customers, ordering nitrobenzene and its reduction product, aniline, for researches into aromatic bases. Mansfield also investigated a portable gas-producing unit, the enrichment of coal gas, and the manufacture of water gas. Following the discovery of the first synthetic, or aniline, dye by William Henry Perkin in 1856, the production of aromatic hydrocarbons and their nitro and amino compounds became essential to the synthesis of dyes, pharmaceuticals, explosives, and so on.

Mansfield's colleagues included Thomas Hughes, the Reverend Frederick Denison Maurice, Francis Cranmer Penrose, and Nevil Story Maskelyne. His close friendship at Cambridge with the writer Charles Kingsley involved religion, magic, mesmerism, science, nature, and female company. Mansfield, a shy individual, was a vegetarian, teetotaler, and nonsmoker, and, according to Kingsley, extremely handsome, which led him into a series of complex romances. In 1842 he married Catherine Shafto, but they separated soon after; when she refused a divorce, he engaged in further affairs and studied at the medical school of St. George's Hospital, London. Mansfield appears to have suffered from periods of mental instability and despair. This and his lifestyle no doubt explain why his graduation from Cambridge was delayed. In 1848, the year of revolutions, he cofounded, with John M. Ludlow and others, the Christian Socialist movement, visited Paris, and cared for the unwell Kingsley, another supporter of the Christian Socialists. Mansfield attempted to use a form of hypnosis called magnetizing to aid Kingsley.

Also in 1848, Mansfield participated in the establishment of what later became the South Paddington Working Men's College. During the 1849 cholera epidemic in London he helped with the provision of clean water. His strong social concerns, and the description of a balloon machine made in Paris, no doubt inspired his 1850 article "Hints for Hygea," published in the Tory *Fraser's Magazine.* There, perhaps stimulated by Michael Faraday's work on electricity, he took readers on a voyage by battery-powered hydrogen balloon to the utopian planet Hygea. Mansfield also prepared a description of steam-powered aerial navigation that was published posthumously.

In 1851 Mansfield proposed in the *Christian Socialist* that the Island of Sark be acquired for use as an experiment in socialism. In the same year he argued for a more equitable patent law. However, his Christian Scientist colleagues were unhappy with the revelation that he was keeping a mistress, though Mansfield countered that he was educating the lady and intended to marry her. That helped little, and the couple separated. In May 1852 Mansfield departed for South America, where in Brazil and Paraguay he wrote about the peoples, flora, fauna, and potential for British trade, and engaged in further romantic escapades. After his return to England in April 1853, Mansfield, at his home in Weybridge, Surrey, studied the fermentation of sugar, and carried on an affair with the wife of the writer George Meredith.

The success of Mansfield's distillation process attracted imitators, and in 1854 even a claim of priority from the Manchester chemist Frederick Crace Calvert. For hazardous distillations Mansfield rented a small room beside the Regent's Canal, close to St. John's Wood, where in 1855 he prepared specimens of aromatic hydrocarbons for display at the Paris Exhibition. On 17 February his still, tended by an assistant, burst into flames. Mansfield and the assistant were severely burned while attempting to remove the still from the building. They were rushed to the hospital, where several days later both died. Hofmann visited Mansfield in the hospital just before his death, and was greeted with the refrain: "Here lie the ashes of Charles B. Mansfield."

BIBLIOGRAPHY

WORKS BY MANSFIELD

Benzole: Its Nature and Utility. London, 1849.

"Researches on Coal Tar." *Journal of the Chemical Society* 1 (1849): 244–268.

"Hints for Hygea." *Fraser's Magazine* (1850).

Paraguay, Brazil and the Plate. Letters Written in 1852, 53.... With a Sketch of the Author's Life by C. Kingsley. Cambridge, U.K.: Macmillan, 1856.

A Theory of Salts: A Treatise on the Constitution of Bipolar (Two-Membered) Chemical Compounds. Edited by Nevil Story Maskelyne. London, 1865.

Aerial Navigation. Edited by R. B. Mansfield, with a preface by J. M. Ludlow. London: Macmillan, 1877.

OTHER SOURCES

Travis, Anthony S. *The Rainbow Makers: The Origins of the Synthetic Dyestuffs Industry in Western Europe.* Bethlehem, PA: Lehigh University Press, 1993.

Ward, Edward R. "C. B. Mansfield v. F. Grace[*sic*] Calvert: A Forgotten Controversy in the Coal Tar Industry." *Chemistry and Industry* (9 February 1957): 159–160.

———. "Charles Blachford Mansfield 1819–1855: Coal Tar Chemist and Social Reformer." *Chemistry and Industry* (25 October 1969): 1530–1537.

———. "Industrial Mixed Acid Nitration." *Ambix* 23 (1976): 199–200.

———. "Eminent Victorian: Charles Mansfield." *Chemistry in Britain* 15 (1979): 297–304.

———. "The Death of Charles Blachford Mansfield (1819–1855)." *Ambix* 31 (1984): 68–69.

Anthony S. Travis

MARCET, JANE HALDIMAND (*b.* London, England, 1769; *d.* London, 28 June 1858), *science education, popularization.*

Marcet was an influential writer of scientific books for general readers. She pioneered the use of conversation as a didactic genre, writing imaginary dialogues to introduce the elements of the sciences, including chemistry, natural philosophy, botany, and political economy. Her books were designed to make scientific knowledge available to readers who lacked access to formal education, but they also came to be used as textbooks, especially in women's colleges in the United States.

Born Jane Haldimand, she was the daughter of a Swiss merchant and the husband of a Swiss physician. Although she was born and brought up in London, and lived there for most of her life, she retained strong connections with the intellectual elite of Geneva, many of whom shared a commitment to public education that was a legacy of the Swiss Protestant Enlightenment. As a young woman, she served as hostess at her father's gatherings of intellectual acquaintances and supervised the education of

Marcet

Jane Haldimand Marcet. SCIENCE PHOTO LIBRARY.

her younger siblings after their mother's death in 1785. She cultivated a similar atmosphere of learning and enlightened conversation in her own household after her marriage to Alexander Marcet in 1799. During the early years of her marriage, she began to write scientific works in the style of dialogues. She completed *Conversations on Natural Philosophy* during this period, though it was not published until several years later.

The science of chemistry was attracting considerable public attention at this time. Her husband was lecturing on the subject at Guy's Hospital, while Marcet herself attended the lectures of Humphry Davy at the Royal Institution. Davy was drawing large audiences of men and women from London's fashionable elite to his spectacular and rhetorically crafted lectures. Marcet found that her grasp of chemical ideas was helped by discussing them with others. She and her husband invited Davy to dine with them, and the understanding of chemistry that she gained inspired her to write an introduction to the science in conversational form.

Conversations on Chemistry was published anonymously in 1806. The text presented the science in a domestic context, in which an instructor, Mrs. B. (perhaps modeled on Margaret Bryan, author of a popular astronomy text), taught her two female pupils, Emily and Caroline. Marcet disclosed her gender though not her identity in the preface, declaring that the book was intended particularly for female readers. She admitted some apprehension that chemistry might be thought an unsuitable subject for a woman to write about, but drew encouragement from the fact that various scientific institutions were then admitting women to lectures. She declared that the conversational style was particularly suited to their instruction, because women were not brought up to engage with abstract ideas or scientific language. The book nonetheless conveyed ample details about the latest scientific discoveries, including the new knowledge of gases, the powers of heat and electricity, and the isolation of new elements.

Marcet's *Conversations on Chemistry* was enormously successful. It was famously said by Michael Faraday to have inspired his interest in chemistry when he read it while working as a bookbinder's apprentice. Faraday later declared that Marcet had been "a good friend to … many of the human race" (Polkinghorn, 1993, p. 29). Seventeen further editions appeared in Britain, updated by the author as new discoveries were announced. A French translation went through four editions, and there were twenty-three in the United States, none of them authorized by Marcet. Some American editors added their own footnotes to her text and placed their own names on the title page. Their interventions helped the book attain its widespread popularity in the curriculum of women's colleges, where it was seen as having broadened the scientific education accessible to women.

At the same time, however, Marcet's work consolidated a demarcation between polite general knowledge and the specific practical knowledge of the technical arts. Mrs. B. insisted to her pupils that chemistry was not restricted to the arts, and she refrained from teaching pharmacy on the grounds that it "properly belongs to professional men" (vol. 1, p. 3). Women were to be allowed a general view of the basic principles of chemistry, but it was not expected that they would engage in its various fields of practical application.

Marcet's publishers encouraged her to repeat the success of her chemistry text with other works written in the same style. Her own interest was increasingly engaged by political economy, which she discussed with friends who included Henry Brougham, Thomas Malthus, and David Ricardo. Although, once again, doubts were expressed as to the suitability of the subject for women, Marcet's *Conversations on Political Economy* was widely praised when it appeared in 1816. Three years later, *Conversations on Natural Philosophy* was published, building upon what was by then the author's well-established reputation for clear and accessible introductory texts. Taking the same form of a dialogue, and with the same characters as the chemistry text, the book covered the topics of mechanics, astronomy, pneumatics, optics, and electricity.

Marcet moved from London to Geneva in 1820, after inheriting a substantial legacy from her father that allowed her husband to relinquish his medical practice. Two years later, she found herself widowed when he died suddenly on a visit to England. She divided her later years between Switzerland and London. Her last scientific work in the genre she had made so successful was *Conversations on Vegetable Physiology* (1829), based on discussions with the Swiss botanist Augustin-Pyrame de Candolle. Subsequent works included a primer on political economy for working people and a number of stories and pedagogical books for young children. Toward the end of her life, she finally allowed her name to appear on the title pages of new editions of her books, claiming the credit to which she was entitled for a remarkable career in scientific education that particularly benefited women.

BIBLIOGRAPHY

WORKS BY MARCET

Conversations on Chemistry: In Which the Elements of That Science Are Familiarly Explained and Illustrated by Experiments. 2 vols. London: Longman, Hurst, Rees, Orme, and Brown, 1806.

Conversations on Political Economy: In Which the Elements of That Science Are Familiarly Explained. By the Author of Conversations on Chemistry. London: Longman, Hurst, Rees, Orme, and Brown, 1816.

Conversations on Natural Philosophy: In Which the Elements of That Science Are Familiarly Explained and Adapted to the Comprehension of Young Pupils. By the Author of Conversations on Chemistry. London: Longman, Hurst, Rees, Orme, and Brown, 1819.

Conversations on Vegetable Physiology: Comprehending the Elements of Botany with Their Application to Agriculture. By the Author of Conversations on Chemistry. London: Longman, Rees, Orme, Brown, and Green, 1829.

OTHER SOURCES

Bahar, Saba. "Jane Marcet and the Limits to Public Science." *British Journal for the History of Science* 34 (2001): 29–49.

Coley, Noel G. "Alexander Marcet (1770–1822), Physician and Animal Chemist." *Medical History* 12 (1968): 394–402.

Knight, David. "Accomplishment or Dogma: Chemistry in the Introductory Works of Jane Marcet and Samuel Parkes." *Ambix* 33 (1986): 94–98.

Lindee, M. Susan. "The American Career of Jane Marcet's *Conversations on Chemistry*, 1806–1853." *Isis* 82 (1991): 8–23.

Morse, Elizabeth J. "Marcet, Jane Haldimand (1769–1858)." *Oxford Dictionary of National Biography*. Oxford: Oxford University Press, 2004. Available at: http://www.oxforddnb.com/view/article/18029.

Myers, Greg. "Fictionality, Demonstration, and a Forum for Popular Science: Jane Marcet's *Conversations on Chemistry*." In *Natural Eloquence: Women Reinscribe Science*, edited by Barbara T. Gates and Ann B. Shteir. Madison: University of Wisconsin Press, 1997.

Polkinghorn, Bette. *Jane Marcet: An Uncommon Woman.* Aldermaston, Berkshire: Forestwood Publications, 1993.

Rive, Augustus de la. "Madame Marcet." *Bibliothèque revue suisse et étrangère,* n.s. 4 (1859): 445–468.

Jan Golinski

MARGALEF, RAMON

MARGALEF, RAMON (*b.* Barcelona, Spain, 16 May 1919; d. Barcelona, 23 May 2004), *limnology, marine biology, ecology.*

Margalef was the most important Catalan and Spanish limnologist, marine biologist, and ecologist of the twentieth century. He was a pioneer and outstanding researcher in these fields, and he contributed greatly to several natural science branches, from limnology and biological oceanography to theoretical ecology. Margalef left an enormous body of scientific literature, consisting of more than 400 published scientific papers and a score of scientific books. Although not all of his papers were published in journals included in the Science Citation Index, for many years he was the most frequently cited Spanish scientist. In a list of ninety-five scientific pioneers from around the world, Margalef was considered to be one of the three most outstanding Spanish life scientists, the other two being Nobel Prize winners Santiago Ramón y Cajal (1852–1934) and Severo Ochoa (1905–1993). Margalef made outstanding contributions to aquatic ecology and general ecology, having postulated several unifying ecological concepts that address the functional and structural properties of ecosystems. These concepts, often controversial, have obtained since their initial formulations wide acceptance. Some of Margalef's most renowned achievements focused on topics that include the application of thermodynamics to the study of the ecosystem; the use of information theory to quantify the organization represented by the taxonomic diversity of the ecosystem, and using the species' diversity and connectivity as measures of ecosystem organization and complexity; the temporal development of ecosystems, that is, the ecological succession and the changes in ecological descriptors (such as production and structural organization of the ecosystem) occurring through this process; the ecological succession as an evolutionary framework of ecosystem development; the study of the small-scale spatial distribution of marine and freshwater phytoplankton, and the quantification of plankton diversity; the response of ecosystems to stress, and especially to the scarcity of nutrients (mainly phosphorus); the role of auxiliary energy and nutrient availability in the selection of phytoplankton life forms (the phytoplankton "mandala") and, more generally, in the production of organic matter both in the ocean and in the biosphere as a whole. The study of marine phytoplankton and of upwelling ecosystems allowed him to pave the way for the unification of physical and biological oceanography we take for granted today.

Margalef's book *Perspectives in Ecological Theory* (1968) and his articles "On Certain Unifying Principles in Ecology" (1963), "Life-forms of Phytoplankton as Survival Alternatives in an Unstable Environment" (1978), and "From Hydrodynamic Processes to Structure (Information) and from Information to Process" (1985) are classics regarding their citations by other authors. In particular, "On Certain Unifying Principles…" is considered to be among the top ten articles of twentieth-century biology.

The Making of a Naturalist. Margalef was an autodidact. Ramon was born in Barcelona, where his family emigrated from the once wine-rich Camp de Tarragona county, which was devastated by the phylloxera during the last decade of the nineteenth century. His father was a bank employee, but also very dedicated to a tiny orchard he owned. This familiar background may explain the interest of Ramon Margalef by nature from his first years. As a young man, he supplemented his education in Trade School with French, German, and mathematics, and he became interested in natural history and biology, especially that of aquatic environments. The Spanish Civil War interrupted his education; in 1938, while still a teenager, he was recruited into the Republican army. At the end of the war, and after serving an extended three-year period in the military, he worked as a clerk at an insurance company while continuing his research on Iberian aquatic ecosystems as a student at the Botanical Institute of Barcelona. Margalef read everything he could find on biology, physics, and other fields of science, which equipped him with an encyclopedic amount of knowledge. His earliest scientific publications, dating back to 1943, quickly established his talent and won him a scholarship, which allowed him to obtain a degree in biology. He studied in the University of Barcelona, completing in four years a five-year Natural Sciences career. In 1951, he defended (in the Complutense University of Madrid, where all theses must be presented in those years) his doctoral thesis on the "Temperature and Morphology of Living Beings," which addressed many questions that continued to be asked into the twenty-first century, and which interested Margalef all his life, including the changing responses of plant and animal growth, metabolism and production in relation to the environment temperature, as laboratory extensions of the well-known thermal rules (Allen's, Bergmann's, and so on).

In the 1940s, Margalef built his own microscope with an assortment of parts bought at flea markets. Over the years, he also built several other instruments in order to automatically obtain water and plankton samples, mimic natural conditions in the laboratory, or automatically process data from his experiments. Proof of the high quality of his inventions (actual prototypes that were later modified and improved) was that, for many years, the U.S. government gave him the money he requested to construct any kind of mechanical or electronic oceanographic or other instruments he devised.

Ecologist of World Fame. During that early period, Margalef was an indefatigable researcher. Not only was he an outstanding naturalist, he was also capable of making connections between very diverse aspects of biology, geology, physics, and chemistry. It was obvious that he had a rare kind of intelligence and that his knowledge exceeded by far that of his colleagues. Other scientists in higher positions (the botanist Pius Font I Quer, the zoologist Francisco García del Cid and the amateur naturalist Karl Faust) were aware of the excellence of Margalef's work and helped him to pursue his career with scholarships or by promoting his early research efforts. After World War II, Margalef visited numerous research centers and participated in many scientific meetings in the United States, thanks to an unlimited travel offer from the U.S. government. Subsequently, several American universities encouraged him to move to the United States with his family, an invitation he would have accepted gladly in order to leave science-barren postwar Spain, but the adverse opinion of his wife Maria Mir, also a biologist, whom he had married in 1952 and with whom he had four children, prevailed.

In 1950 Margalef began working at the Institute for Fisheries Research (Instituto de Investigaciones Pesqueras, IIP, later called the Institute for Marine Sciences), a division of the Spanish Research Council (CSIC), of which he was appointed director in 1966. Margalef promoted oceanographic research and the institute soon became a center of excellence in oceanography. He also converted the journal *Investigación Pesquera* (later renamed *Scientia Marina*) into a prestigious journal of Spanish marine science. Similarly, his works on limnology, which appeared mainly in *Publicaciones del Instituto de Biología Aplicada*, built an international reputation for that journal. When, in 1967, he was appointed to Spain's first chair in ecology at the University of Barcelona, he resigned his post at the IIP.

At the University of Barcelona, Margalef established the Department of Ecology and trained several generations of ecologists, limnologists, and oceanographers. After two decades of a fruitful academic career, he retired in 1987 and was appointed emeritus professor in 1996. Without the time-consuming commitments of teaching

Margalef

and active research, he continued to work, wrote on ecology and generously shared his knowledge with colleagues and friends until shortly before his death. Margalef trained hundreds of scientists in the classroom, in the laboratory, in the field, and at sea, lecturing to them and carrying out joint research not only at the University of Barcelona and the Institute for Fisheries Research but also at other centers around the world. From 1971 to 2001, he supervised around forty doctoral theses.

A prolific author with good command of half a dozen languages, Margalef read thousands of scientific books throughout his life, but he had a notable literary knowledge, too, especially of the classics. He also used his own books, which conveyed his ideas about the biosphere's organization and functioning, to teach university students and society in general.

Two remarkable and thorough university textbooks written in Spanish by Margalef deserve special mention: *Ecología* (1974) and *Limnología* (1983). For many years, *Ecología* was considered to be the best book on this field of science (as explicitly and separately expressed by the noted ecologists Eugene P. Odum and G. Evelyn Hutchinson) ever written in any language, both for its thorough analysis of this science and for supporting its encyclopedic data with a synthetic, coherent ecological theory. Margalef updated the ideas contained in it in later books: *La Biosfera: Entre la termodinámica y el juego* (1980), *Teoría de los sistemas ecológicos* (1991), *Oblik Biosfer* (in Russian, 1992) and *Our Biosphere* (1997). Margalef was also author and editor of many monographs, including *Introducción al estudio del plancton marino* (1950), "Los crustáceos de las aguas continentales ibéricas" (1953), "Los organismos indicadores en la limnología" (1955), *Comunidades naturales* (1962), *Ecología marina* (1967), and *The Western Mediterranean* (1985).

Margalef was a great popularizer of ecology. Among his books aimed at general audiences a few must be mentioned: *Ecología* (1981), which continues to be a bestseller; *L'ecologia* (1985, published on the occasion of a related exhibit); and *Planeta azul, planeta verde* (1992). He was a frequent contributor to several encyclopedias of natural history, especially *Història natural dels Països Catalans* (1992) and *Biosfera* (first published in Catalan, later translated into Japanese and English, *Biosphere*, 1993–1998). Margalef also participated in creating exhibitions aimed at the general public. In one of his articles advocating changes in the teaching of natural science, he stressed the importance of conveying the "simple facts about life and the environment not to forget in preparing schoolbooks for our grandchildren" (Margalef, 1984).

Contributor to Ecological Theory. Margalef's article "La teoría de la información en Ecología" (The theory of information in ecology, 1957) was his introductory lecture as a new member of the Barcelona Royal Academy of Sciences and Arts; later translated into English and published in *General Systems* (1958), it eventually reached a worldwide audience. In this article, Margalef suggested that the theory of information should also be applied to the study of species diversity in ecosystems (there are several "Margalef diversity indices," relating species numbers and their abundances, commonly used by ecologists). The interplay of matter and energy cycles at the ecosystem level translates as an information accumulation in the form of structure: the number of species, their interaction and their mutual interdependence. Thus, the species diversity of an ecosystem (or better, of one of its taxocoenosis, that is, one of its taxonomic components: their insects, plants, phytoplankton, whatever) can be considered as an information content. This information content increases with the number of species (the system being more heterogeneous) and decreases with the number of individuals of each species (the system being more homogeneous or monotone); this information is the inverse of the entropy of the system. Thus, any expression giving the information content of a system (not necessarily a biological one), such as the Shannon & Weaver (1963) index—$H = -\Sigma\, p_i \log_2 p_i$, where p_i is the proportion of the i-species in the total count—is suitable to explain the biological diversity of an ecosystem, and an easy method to ascertain its maturity, degree of organization, place in the ecological succession, degree of exploitation and so on.

At the time, ecology was still a young science, lacking both a theoretical reference framework and a corpus of stable paradigms comparable to those in other scientific fields. Margalef's 1958 paper, along with the article "On Certain Unifying Principles…" and the small book *Perspectives in Ecological Theory* (1968), which was translated into several languages, offered new and appealing ways of understanding ecology.

Margalef based his theoretical approach, which was holistic and integrative, on his extensive knowledge of aquatic ecosystems, which he had studied first as a naturalist, applying a botanical, zoological, and phytosociological perspective. He often acknowledged the influence other naturalists and ecologists had on his work, and explicitly cited, among others, F. E. Clements, H. W. Harvey, August Thienemann, Josias Braun-Blanquet, G. Evelyn Hutchinson and Eugene P. Odum; but having read so extensively, and having known personally so many ecologists, limnologists and oceanographers himself, it is hard to pinpoint only a few of them. Later he took a more general approach and gathered information about the structure and workings of the whole biosphere. He understood the ecosystem as a level of organization, made of complex elements connected in a non-permanent form by means of a network of flexible and adaptable interactions.

Superimposed on the network of matter and energy exchange (the classical trophic web), there is a network of information exchange, not totally coincident with the previous one. This ecosystem concept obeys macroscopic phenomenological laws, mainly physical and thermodynamical ones, and follows historical trends (the ecological succession) along which some function is optimized, namely the conversion of dissipated energy (or entropy production) in information (or structure). In plain terms, the Production/Biomass ratio (energy flux per unit biomass through the ecosystem) decreases along the ecological succession, as the amount of structure increases. This accretion of information, structure, complexity, and maturity is a self-organizing process; it was later called the Margalef principle on ecosystems.

Limnologist, Marine Biologist, and Biospheric Ecologist. Margalef excelled in the fields of limnology, marine ecology, and theoretical ecology. Working on his own, he set up the basis for studying the regional limnology of the Iberian Peninsula and the Balearic Islands, and later initiated the ecological research on one hundred Spanish reservoirs, which as of 2007 remained the only thorough analysis of this type worldwide. The International Society of Limnology awarded Margalef the Naumann-Thienemann Medal for "having shared his creative talents of discoveries, intuition, and synthesis of the ecological foundations of the limnological phenomena, and for his influence in the Hispanic world."

The study of marine plankton and primary production of the sea soon led Margalef to new quantitative approaches and to apply several new methods of evaluating the populations of the microscopic organisms living in the water column, such as consideration of species diversity, or other models derived from terrestrial ecology such as the concept of ecological succession. Probably his most outstanding contributions to ecology were recognizing the spatial organization of phytoplankton and the crucial role of external, auxiliary, or exosomatic energy in that structure. Prior to those observations, phytoplankton was considered to be simply a structureless cell suspension. He proposed a model for the production of organic matter in the ocean that combines the turbulence (dissipation of external energy) and the covariance of reactants (light, nutrients, organisms). The simplest form of this model, P (for production) = A (for turbulence) x C (for reactants covariance), was further elaborated and has come to be fully accepted.

Taking into account both space and the role of exosomatic energy in the structuring of biological communities was an approach that Margalef applied not only to the study of plankton, but also to other communities of the biosphere. This mode of thinking had proven to be advantageous in estimating species diversity and the connectance between different nodes of trophic webs. It also enabled him to study the patterns that could be elucidated from an analysis of ecological succession, which he was the first to identify as an evolutionary framework in the development of the ecosystem. From these ideas, an ecological theory emerged that, like everything in science, has been subject to modification, refutation, and evolution. This theory was Margalef's major contribution to ecology as an established scientific discipline.

Throughout all his scientific life he was especially interested in the role of phosphorus as a limiting factor in primary production, both in the sea and on land, and in his later years he pondered the changes the "shifting topology of landscape" (the transformation of world landscapes from natural areas spattered with few human settlements to urban-crowded areas with few natural remaining patches) will have on information, energy, and matter fluxes through ecosystem borders.

From his first publications on ecological theory until his last book, Margalef's role in furthering the understanding of the functioning of the biosphere has been acknowledged internationally. In 1988, the National Science Foundation recognized Margalef's research on the dynamics of marine phytoplankton, which he carried out during the 1960s and 1970s, and declared that his work on these subjects had been several decades ahead of its time, and had provided the foundations for subsequent biological research in that field. Indeed, Margalef is one of the very few scientists who contributed to both the theoretical and the practical development of a science.

Margalef also made contributions to biogeography, geology, human evolution, and human ecology. Including the human species in his general theory of the biosphere was among his most valuable but least-known contributions to ecology. His basic postulate was that man is to be viewed as a part of the biosphere (accordingly, he criticized the title of the United Nations program MAB, Man and the Biosphere, saying it should be renamed MIB, or Man *in* the Biosphere), in which it is necessary to consider human activity within a general ecological context to address many socioeconomical problems. He assimilated interactions between more and less mature natural systems to those occurring between social and political systems, and applied to man's activities the same concepts explaining ecosystem functioning: exosomatic energy, increasing of non-productive biomass along the succession, the Matthew principle, and so on.

Margalef received numerous and significant awards for his research and teaching activities, among them the A. G. Huntsman Award (1980, considered as the Nobel Prize in Oceanography); the Santiago Ramón y Cajal Prize of the Spanish Ministry of Education and Science (1984);

the Naumann-Thienemann Medal of the International Association of Theoretical and Applied Limnology (Societas Internationalis Limnologiae, SIL; 1989); the International Ecology Institute Prize (Germany, 1997); the American Society of Limnology and Oceanography (ASLO) Lifetime Achievement Award (2000); the Gold Medal Award of the Spanish Council for Research (CSIC; 2002); and the Gold Medal Award of the Autonomous Government of Catalonia (2003), and many others. Margalef was a member of several scientific academies in Spain and abroad, the U.S. National Academy of Sciences among them. In addition, he was an honorary member of several scientific societies around the world and was awarded *honoris causa* doctorates from several European and American universities. In science, receiving so many international awards is somewhat unusual, and it is even more unusual that professional recognition continues over half a century.

Ramon Margalef contributed enormously to the task of solving many of life's mysteries, and he did it, as Ivan Valiela (1994) observed, because "his ideas made us think, something enviable for any scientist." Margalef was an exemplary teacher and man of science, honored by the University of Barcelona, the various academies of which he was a member, the numerous research centers and universities that awarded him distinctions, and his country. He contributed remarkably to ecology, limnology, and oceanography, but liked to think of himself as a naturalist; indeed, he was a Galilean type naturalist (according to Gould, 1991, a Galilean naturalist is someone who not only enjoys the beauty of nature, as do the Franciscan naturalists, but who also thrives on discovering its secrets), and also a consilient one (Wilson, 1998, calls consilience a commitment to the fact that all the complexity of our world, both the physical and the human aspects of it, can be explained by the same general principles; Ros, 1999). He was one of the great minds of the natural sciences and biology, with a total dedication to science, but he was not insensitive to worldly affairs; on the contrary, he applied his knowledge of nature to gain a better understanding of the world that surrounded him. And, in spite of all his scientific wisdom, he was surely a greater human being than he was a naturalist.

BIBLIOGRAPHY

WORKS BY MARGALEF

With Miguel Massutí. *Introducción al estudio del plancton marino.* Barcelona: Patronato Juan de la Cierva, 1950.

"Los crustáceos de las aguas continentales ibéricas." *Instituto Forestal de Investigaciones y Experincias.* Biología de las aguas continentales X (1953): 1–243.

"Los organismos indicadores en la limnología." *Instituto Forestal de Investigaciones y Experincias.* Biología de las aguas continentales XII (1955): 1–300.

"La teoría de la información en Ecología." *Memorias de la Real Academia de Ciencias y Artes de Barcelona* 32 (1957): 373–449.

Comunidades naturales. Mayagüez: Instituto de Biología Marina de la Universidad de Puerto Rico, 1962.

"On Certain Unifying Principles in Ecology." *American Naturalist* 97 (1963): 357–374.

Editor. *Ecología Marina.* Caracas: Fundación La Salle de Ciencias Naturales, 1967.

Perspectives in Ecological Theory. Chicago: University of Chicago Press, 1968.

Ecología. Barcelona: Omega, 1974.

"Life-forms of Phytoplankton as Survival Alternatives in an Unstable Environment." *Oceanologica Acta* 1 (1978): 493–509.

La Biosfera: Entre la termodinámica y el juego. Barcelona: Omega, 1980.

Ecología. Barcelona: Planeta, 1981. For a wider audience than the 1974 book of the same name.

Limnología. Barcelona: Omega, 1983.

"Simple Facts About Life and the Environment not to Forget in Preparing Schoolbooks for Our Grandchildren." In *Trends in Ecological Research for the 1980s,* edited by J. H. Cooley and F. B. Golley. New York: Plenum Press NATO Conference Series, 1984.

"From Hydrodynamic Processes to Structure (Information) and from Information to Process." *Canadian Bulletin of Fisheries and Aquatic Sciences* 213 (1985): 200–220.

Editor. *Western Mediterranean.* Oxford, U.K.: Pergamon Press and International Union for Conservation of Nature and Natural Resources, 1985.

L'Ecologia. Barcelona: Diputació de Barcelona, Servei del Medi Ambient, 1985.

"Introducció al coneixement de la biosfera. Els ecosistemes pelàgics." In *Història Natural dels Paisos Catalans,* Vol. 14, edited by J. Terradas, N. Prat, A. Escarré, and R. Margalef. Barcelona: Enciclopèdia Catalana, 1989.

Teoría de los sistemas ecológicos. Barcelona: Universitat de Barcelona, 1991.

Oblik Biosfer (A View of the Biosphere). Moscow: Russian Academy of Sciences, Institute of Oceanography, 1992.

Planeta azul, Planeta verde. Barcelona: Prensa Científica, 1992.

"El planeta blau. Matèria per a la vida. Energia per fer i desfer. Éssers vius i informació." In *Biosfera,* edited by Ramon Folch. Barcelona: Enciclopèdia Catalana, 1993.

Editor. *Limnology Now: A Paradigm of Planetary Problems.* Amsterdam: Elsevier, 1994.

Excellence in Ecology. Book 10: *Our Biosphere.* Oldendorf/Luhe: International Ecology Institute, 1997.

OTHER SOURCES

Gould, Stephen J. *Bully for Brontosaurus: Reflections in Natural History.* New York: Norton, 1991.

Ros, Joandomènec. "Ramon Margalef, Limnologist, Marine Biologist, Ecologist, Naturalist." In *Homage to Ramon Margalef, or Why There is Such Pleasure in Studying Nature,* edited by Joandomènec Ros and Narcís Prat. Barcelona: Universitat de Barcelona, 1992.

———. *Proposicions il·luminadores i insensates: Reflexions sobre ciència.* Barcelona: Empúries, 1999.

Valiela, Ivan. "Review of *Homage to Ramon Margalef.*" *Scientia Marina* 58 (1994): 277.

Wilson, Edward O. *Consilience. The Unity of Knowledge.* New York: Knopf, 1998.

Joandomènec Ros

MARINUS OF TYRE (Tyre, Syria, Roman Empire, *fl.* c. 100 CE), *geography.*

Marinus was the author of a number of works on cartography, which are known solely from what Ptolemy (second century CE) relates about them in Book I of his *Geography.* Ptolemy speaks of Marinus as the most recent author to have dealt with the problem of constructing a map of the *oikoumenê,* the "inhabited world" (in effect, the part of the world known to Greco-Roman civilization). Most of what Ptolemy writes about Marinus is a review of his errors and infelicities. But at the outset he praises the thoroughness of his research, his critical attitude to his sources, and his readiness to correct his own work, and he makes it clear that the broad geographical conception portrayed in the *Geography* as well as the bulk of the detailed data are taken from Marinus.

Marinus assumed a spherical Earth having a circumference of 180,000 stades. (The size of the ancient geographers' stade is disputed, but that is not terribly important, because ancient geodesy relied on very crude distance estimates.) His *oikoumenê* comprised the three continents of Europe, Libya (Africa), and Asia, and he believed that Asia was joined to Libya not only at the head of the Red Sea but also by land south and east of the "sea of India" (the Indian Ocean), which was thus wholly enclosed and not connected to the ocean lying east of Europe and Libya. The northernmost known locality was Thoulê (the Shetlands?), slightly south of the Arctic Circle, and the westernmost was the Isles of the Blest (the Canaries). Ptolemy took over these assumptions. But Marinus deduced from the reports of various travelers that the *oikoumenê* extended 24° south of the equator and 225° east of the Isles of the Blest, much further in either direction than Ptolemy was willing to accept. The remotest places to the east of which his sources knew appear to have corresponded to China and Southeast Asia, and the southernmost to parts of the east coast of Africa a few degrees south of the equator. So far as scholars know, Greco-Roman geographical knowledge never surpassed these limits.

Marinus's most detailed and accurate information, of course, pertained to the Roman Empire and its immediate neighbors. Roughly two-thirds of the eight thousand or so localities listed in Ptolemy's geographical catalog were within the empire, and it is striking that in these regions Ptolemy's data reflect geographical conditions around the first decade of the second century CE, about half a century before Ptolemy wrote the *Geography.* This is probably when Marinus was active. Elsewhere, and especially in describing India and lands further east, Ptolemy had more recent informants.

Marinus advocated using a rectangular grid of meridians and parallels (i.e., a cylindrical projection) for drawing a world map. According to Ptolemy's report, Marinus did not actually produce a map in accordance with the last of his cartographical treatises, and it is not clear whether Ptolemy had access to any map executed according to Marinus's data or had to rely entirely on his writings.

BIBLIOGRAPHY

Berggren, J. Lennart, and Alexander Jones. *Ptolemy's Geography: An Annotated Translation of the Theoretical Chapters.* Princeton, NJ: Princeton University Press, 2000.

Honigmann, Ernst. "Marinos von Tyros." In *Realencyclopädie der Klassischen Altertumswissenschaft,* vol. 28. Stuttgart, Germany, 1930. Reviews the evidence for Marinus's writings.

Alexander Jones

MARK, HERMAN F. (*b.* Vienna, Austria, 3 May 1895; *d.* Austin, Texas, 6 April 1992), *chemistry, polymer chemistry, molecular structure, education.*

Mark was cited in a memorial program after his death as one who had "earned a lasting place in the history of polymer science through his research contributions, the successes of his students, his organizational genius, and his timeless promotion of polymer science. It is entirely accurate to say that Mark found polymers a curiosity and made them a science." Linus Pauling, while admitting that most chemists thought of Mark as a polymer pioneer, stressed that he thought of Mark "with affection and admiration, as a pioneer in modern structural chemistry and an important early contributor to its development" (Pauling, 1984, p. 337).

Early Life. This dichotomy is further emphasized by the two distinct phases of Mark's life—the years he spent in Europe and the years he spent in Canada and the United States. Born in Vienna, Mark was the oldest of the three children of Hermann Carl and Lili Mueller Mark. (He

Mark

originally spelled his own name "Hermann," but dropped the final "n" when he emigrated.) His father was a surgeon, a graduate of the Viennese School of Medicine, who spoke four languages fluently. Mark recalled in his autobiography that his early years up to his graduation from high school were a mixture of the discipline exacted by his parents when it came to school work and the freedom that ensued after that work was completed.

Mark filled his spare time with sports of all kinds, especially soccer and tennis, with skiing and skating occupying the winter months. As amateur musicians his parents instilled in him a love of music that was further bolstered by exposure to the Viennese music scene of world-class orchestras, operas, and plays. His interest in science was first implanted by Franz Hlawaty, his teacher in mathematics and physics, who made these traditionally hard subjects clear with his lucid explanations of principles and applications. It was further nurtured by a close high school friend, Gerhardt Kirsch. Four years older than Mark, Kirsch enrolled at the University of Vienna after graduation and took Mark, still a high school student, to hear lectures by such luminaries as Emil Fischer, Albert Einstein, Ernest Rutherford, and Marie Curie. At home, some of his father's classmates at the university, including Sigmund Freud, came to dinner. Listening to discussions between his father and some Zionist friends about Theodor Herzl and Chaim Weizmann, Mark became aware of potential changes in politics and culture, not realizing that his own idyllic youthful existence was soon to change.

Military Service and Education. Graduating from high school in 1913, Mark opted to get his required military service out of the way immediately by volunteering for a one-year stint, intending to start at the university in 1914. As a member of a mountain infantry regiment in the Austrian-Hungarian army, Mark was close to completing his year of service when World War I broke out. Mark served on the Russian and Italian fronts, rising to rank of lieutenant. He was wounded three times and received fifteen medals, including one of Austria's highest awards for bravery. In September 1914, Mark was sent home to recuperate from a serious leg wound and managed to complete one semester of graduate study in chemistry before he returned to the Austrian-Italian front. The war dragged on for three more years, and in 1918 Mark's unit was captured by the Italians. He spent the next eleven months as a prisoner of war in Monopoli.

Finally returning to Vienna in 1919, Mark immediately resumed his studies in chemistry with Wilhelm Schlenk and received his PhD in organic chemistry in 1921. In an oral history interview Mark said Schlenk was an attractive teacher whose techniques Mark adopted in his own career—"be very simple, make experiments, address the people visually and personally, and then always tell a few interesting stories in between. Don't make it too dry" (1986, p.1)

Molecular Structure Research. When Schlenk moved to the University of Berlin in 1921, Mark went with him as one of his assistants. Here he continued his research on trivalent carbon, which had been the subject of his PhD thesis, but within a short time Schlenk introduced him to Nobel laureate Fritz Haber, who was organizing a research institute on fiber chemistry within Kaiser Wilhelm Gesellschaft, the so-called Kaiser Wilhelm Institut für Faserstoffchemie. Haber explained why he needed an organic chemist with an interest in physical chemistry, and Mark quickly accepted the offer because "it was a new horizon and a big new institute with a lot of money" (Mark, 1986, p. 4). In August 1922 Mark married another Viennese, Marie Schramek, and they started their life together in a one-room apartment in Dahlem, a Berlin suburb.

The fiber research group was charged with improving the synthetic rayon fiber that the Germans made from cellulose because this rayon could not compete with natural fibers such as cotton and wool being used in other European countries. Told by institute director Reginald Oliver Herzog to determine the structure of rayon and cotton and cellulose with x-ray diffraction, Mark's group, headed by Michael Polanyi, embarked on a remarkable series of experiments. Because x-ray diffraction was a new technique, they constructed their own instrument with the assistance of other institutes in physics and physical chemistry. According to Polanyi, "Mark's experimental skill bordered on genius" (Morawetz, 1985, p. 593).

Because "you don't start climbing Mount Everest before you have climbed a large number of other peaks" (Mark, 1986, p. 5), Mark's group started by using x-rays to determine the structure of tin and zinc, progressing through inorganic compounds to larger organic compounds, and finally cellulose and rubber. Over the next four years more than fifty papers detailing their results brought considerable recognition to Mark's group. Einstein visited Mark's laboratory on a number of occasions and asked him to use their equipment to verify the Compton effect, which was crucial to Einstein's work, then being questioned by William Duane at Harvard because he could not repeat Compton's work. Mark's work was the first independent confirmation of the Compton effect, which pleased Einstein greatly.

Mark's work placed him in the middle of the ongoing controversy about whether natural fibers were large molecules, as claimed by Hermann Staudinger, or whether their properties could be explained by colloid chemistry.

In the end, the conclusions from the work on fiber formers were simple enough. They all consisted of long-chain molecules with molecular weights above 100,000. Some had a regular structure and could crystallize, while others could not. They all behaved like organic substances with respect to stereochemistry, composition and reactivity of functional groups. Most of their properties could be understood with covalent bonding along the chains and the van der Waals interactions between them.

I. G. Farben. In the summer of 1926 Haber introduced Mark to Kurt H. Meyer, a member of the board of directors of the German chemical company I. G. Farben. It was a repeat of the meeting Mark had with Haber four years earlier, only this time Mark was told that I. G. Farben was actually making fibers such as cellulose acetate and rayon that Mark had been studying from the loftier academic viewpoint. But the problem was still the same—the synthetics had a beautiful luster and were easily dyed, but they could not compete with the natural fibers on wet strength and abrasion resistance. I. G. Farben was setting up a fundamental fiber research laboratory, and they wanted Mark to work there, applying what he had learned in Berlin to help the company. They essentially wrote Mark a blank check, and he accepted, on the condition that he could do some fundamental research as well.

For the next six years, first as group leader and then as assistant research director, Mark produced another series of highly important papers on the chemistry of large molecules, including fiber structure, fiber spinning, synthetic rubber, and plastics. Applying fundamental studies to a technologically important problem, Mark showed that his crystallographic data could be used to predict the strength of an ideal fiber where it is only the breaking of covalent bonds that leads to mechanical failure.

At the same time, Mark and his assistant Raimund Wierl had discovered that the structure of gas molecules could be determined by studying their diffraction of a beam of electrons. In 1930 Mark showed the results to the visiting Linus Pauling, who later admitted that he could not contain his enthusiasm as he realized the impact of the discovery. Mark told Pauling he was not going to continue this work and gave Pauling the plans of the apparatus. When Pauling returned to California he constructed an instrument and over the next twenty-five years used it to determine the structure of 225 different substances that were crucial to his work in structural chemistry. Pauling was forever grateful to Mark not only for discovering the technique, but especially for Mark's generosity in sharing it with him.

By 1932 Mark had established himself as a gifted experimentalist who had made significant contributions to the structure of molecules and whose results were placing the fledgling concept of polymers on a firmer footing, as evidenced in part by the publication in 1930 of a handbook on polymer chemistry coauthored by Mark and Meyer.

Mark once said there were three main turning points in his life, and none of them was planned. The first was his meeting with Haber in 1922, the second was his meeting with Meyer in 1926, and the third was a meeting with I. G. Farben board member Wilhelm Gaus in 1932. According to Mark, Gaus told him bluntly that the company expected Adolf Hitler to gain power in Germany in the near future and that if he did, employment conditions would probably change although they could not predict how at the moment. Gaus projected that because Mark was a foreigner with a Jewish father, he might face difficulties beyond the company's control in the future. Because Mark had an excellent reputation in academic circles and had published widely, Gaus suggested that Mark look for a university position (Stahl, 1981, p. 66; Mark, 1986, p. 28).

Academic Program in Polymers. Mark found a haven in his native Vienna, where in 1932 he accepted an appointment as a professor of physical chemistry and director of the first chemistry institute at the University of Vienna. Mark set as his goal the organization of an institute for polymer research and education. With the assistance of some capable people Mark completed the task by 1936, when a new curriculum was in place to produce a polymer chemist.

Because he knew that industry was heavily involved in polymer synthesis, Mark decided instead to focus his research on the kinetics and the mechanism of polymerization reactions. Mark's efforts to establish a new program in polymer chemistry soon became well-known and attracted many students, some even from Russia. The chemical industry also made it clear that they were interested in hiring the graduates from Mark's program.

Mark's research on polymers continued unabated in Vienna, although now viscosity measurements, osmotic measurements and diffusion measurements replaced x-ray diffraction, and his papers were more theoretical in nature. During this very productive time he published more than seventy research papers and six books. In addition to looking at the mechanism of polymer formation in solution, Mark and his coworkers also focused on solution viscosity and its application to polymer systems. One important result was the Mark-Houwink equation, conceived by Mark and Roelof Houwink independently about the same time. Although it was semiempirical and unsophisticated, it was used for more than four decades to determine the approximate viscosity-average molecular weights of linear polymers and it still finds important applications in polymer chemistry today. Mark also collaborated with Eugene Guth in formulating a statistical theory of the elasticity of a flexible chain molecule, another important contribution from his Vienna years.

Now that his reputation as a polymer chemist was firmly established, Mark also needed to ensure the success of his institute in Vienna by securing funding from the chemical industry, primarily in England, publicizing it through lectures given throughout Europe and Russia, and attending scientific meetings in many different countries. All of this helped solidify his institute and Mark himself as a leader in the new science of polymer chemistry.

Escape to Canada. In the midst of deteriorating political conditions in Austria, Mark received a letter from Carl B. Thorne, the managing director of the Canadian International Paper Company in Montreal in May 1937. Noting Mark's work with cellulose, Thorne explained that "our lifeblood is cellulose." Thorne was concerned that their research laboratory was becoming obsolete because both the customers and the competition were becoming more sophisticated. Thorne wondered if Mark would be interested in becoming the research director of his paper company.

When Thorne came to Europe that summer, he cabled Mark and asked to meet in Dresden. Thorne repeated his offer, but Mark explained that it would not be possible to just walk away from his research institute and his students and never come back. Seeking a compromise, Mark suggested that he might come for a short time to reorganize the laboratory and train the people there in the new polymer techniques. After that, he could make periodic visits as a consultant. But Thorne really wanted a full-time research director, and though interested in Mark's proposal, he left the meeting with a curt "Let me see what else I can do."

Mark never realized at the time that this meeting would be his lifesaver after the Germans invaded Austria on 12 March 1938. Mark was arrested the next day and put in a Gestapo prison where he was interrogated about his association with I. G. Farben and Engelbert Dollfuss, a close friend who had served in Mark's unit in World War I. Dollfuss became the chancellor of the Austrian Republic and vainly tried to keep the country independent of the Nazis until he was assassinated in 1934. After four days Mark was released, but not before his passport was taken and his correspondence with Einstein confiscated.

After his release Mark went to the Canadian embassy and wired Thorne that he was ready to come to Canada. Thorne agreed, and arranged for an official letter of employment. With employment in Canada secured, Mark was able to get a Canadian visa, and with that came visas to pass through Switzerland, France, and England. To get his passport back, Mark appealed to a former schoolmate who was also a Nazi lawyer. It cost Mark a year's salary in bribes, but eventually the passport was returned.

Unable to withdraw any funds, Mark discreetly purchased platinum and iridium wire, which he shaped into coat hangers. On 10 May 1938, Mark, his wife, two boys, and a Jewish niece who was a prominent harpsichordist mounted a Nazi flag on the hood of their car, strapped skis and other gear to the top of the car, put their clothes on the coat hangers, and drove into Switzerland. Their passage to Canada was almost leisurely, thanks to Thorne who arranged for them to spend the summer in Switzerland, France, and England. Mark used the time in England to do some research on fibers, and even during the transatlantic voyage he worked on finishing the English edition of his *Physical Chemistry of High Polymeric Systems.* He arrived at the company plant in Hawkesbury, Ontario, on 26 September 1938. Mark would later exclaim, "Canada was heaven. Not only because it was in America, but because it had such a good reputation as a country and as a beautiful country. From then on everything was easy" (1986, p. 36).

Advancing Polymer Science. Mark found the laboratory at Hawkesbury to be the "state of the art cellulose chemistry of the early 1920s." It took him well over a year to bring the laboratory up to current standards. Much of this was supported and encouraged by du Pont, who was one of Thorne's best customers. Du Pont was using the wood pulp from the paper company to make a rayon that was a soft and luxurious textile fiber. In 1939 du Pont found that they could also make a rayon that was stronger, harder, and more durable. It was not very good for textile applications, but it made an excellent tire cord. Du Pont called it Cordura. Canadian International's wood pulp was not suitable for making Cordura, and Mark attacked the problem with his usual enthusiasm. He found that there was a substantial amount of low molecular weight material in the textile rayon, which was good as a plasticizer for extensibility, but was bad for tire cord tensile strength. After removing the low molecular weight material Mark made a number of samples of the new rayon and made Cordura from it. Within a year Mark had worked out all of the details to go from raw pulp to the final pulp that was suitable for Cordura.

In Canada, Mark renewed his contact with Eric S. Proskauer, a publisher of one of his books on polymers in Germany. Proskauer had emigrated to the United States in 1937 and with another émigré, Maurits Dekker, established Interscience Publishing Company. At a meeting in Montreal in 1939 Mark told Proskauer he would probably be returning to academia in the near future, and that

Mark

it was time to think of resuming publications in polymer science. Proskauer agreed. Because they were both immigrants, it was decided to begin with a volume on someone already established in the United States, and that was Wallace H. Carothers, the du Pont polymer chemist who discovered nylon and neoprene. Because Carothers had committed suicide in 1937, they felt this would be a fitting tribute to his genius. This was the first monograph in "High polymers; a series of monographs on the chemistry, physics and technology of high polymeric substances" that spanned more than thirty years and twenty-five volumes.

Brooklyn Poly. After solving the Cordura problem, Mark did not see any exciting problems in the future. To Mark, scaling up the Cordura process was an engineering problem and held no interest for him. When Mark reminded Thorne of a previous discussion in which he had said that he did not want to stay at the paper company forever, Thorne was furious. Thorne recalled how he helped Mark escape the concentration camps, and Mark knew he was in a difficult situation because he did owe his freedom to Thorne. Mark talked to the plant manager, Sigmund Wang, who advised him that the magic word was du Pont. "All you need to appease the boss is the word Du Pont," Wang said. "If you can convince him that Du Pont would look favorably on your move to the United States to a university which is somehow in contact with Du Pont, he would be agreeable because the whole mill lives from Du Pont" (Mark, 1986, p. 42). Between the two of them they eased Thorne's anger and opened the way for Mark to leave the paper company.

Through the development of the Cordura process Mark had made several contacts with du Pont people, and eventually made several trips to Wilmington, Delaware. One of those contacts was William Zimmerli, who was on the board of directors of the Polytechnic Institute of Brooklyn (now Polytechnic University). Because of his success on the Cordura project, Mark was recommended by Zimmerli to Raymond E. Kirk, Polytechnic's chemistry department chair, and Harry S. Rogers, the president, because Zimmerli felt that Polytechnic should become involved with polymers. Mark was given an adjunct professorship that was paid for by du Pont.

Kirk assigned Mark to the Shellac Bureau, a group that tested shellac being imported from India and then bleached it and delivered it to customers. Because the war was interfering with the shellac shipments, and Mark had experience with synthetic resins that mimicked shellac, he was able to help the bureau's research. But Mark's vision went far beyond shellac. With Kirk's blessing, Mark slowly began to develop a polymer program at Polytechnic which in 1946 became the Polymer Research Institute, the first of its kind in the United States.

But the war years saw Mark involved in some unusual projects. Because he had made measurements on the shear strength of snow and published papers on the heavy water content of glaciers, Mark was asked by the U.S. Army to assist in the field tests of a vehicle called the Weasel that would be used for combat in snow conditions. Mark and Turner Alfrey went to the Canadian Rockies where they made measurements relating the snow shear strength to the composition, and the slope angle under which the Weasel could maneuver.

This was so successful for the use of the Weasel in northern Europe that the army enlisted Mark's aid on the Ducq, an amphibious landing craft. Mark and Alfrey were able to determine the conditions under which the Ducq could be safely released from transport ships. Another wartime project was the so-called floating landing strip where the addition of a small amount of wood pulp to ice reduced its brittleness. The results have been used ever since in the construction of roads, air strips, bridges, and habitats in Arctic areas.

Polymer Research Institute. Toward the end of the war Mark turned his attention back to Brooklyn, where he intended to make the Polymer Research Institute a group with an international reputation. He also planned to initiate and sponsor the founding of similar institutions that would constitute a network of polymer research centers cooperating closely with each other. To this end Mark headed the planning committee of the Chaim Weizmann Institute of Science in Israel and maintained a lifelong association with that organization.

Mark served as director of the Polymer Research Institute until 1964, when he became emeritus. With his exceptional organizational skills he developed a curriculum, hired faculty, and began a research program. When the research began paying dividends Mark found that submitting papers to traditional journals resulted in a cursory dismissal with the explanation that the journal did not publish polymer papers. Undaunted, Mark founded the *Journal of Polymer Science.* New courses meant that new textbooks and reference works were needed, and they were quickly produced and published by Interscience. There were seminars and symposia, drawing people to Brooklyn and showcasing the developing polymer program there. And the tireless Mark was everywhere he could be, giving papers at scientific society meetings, industrial venues, and academic departments. In essence, Mark became *the* spokesperson for polymer science. He organized a special issue of *Scientific American* on polymers in which he wrote the lead article. He was profiled in the *New Yorker* under the title "Polymers Everywhere," and the *New York Times* carried articles about him for more than forty years, including the announcement of his receiving the National Medal of Science from President Jimmy Carter in 1979.

Graduates of the Polymer Research Institute had no difficulty finding jobs, not in academia, necessarily, but in the chemical industry, which was exploiting this new science to make new products that would impact almost every facet of daily life. And those who did maintain academic careers often set up their own polymer centers that produced more research and more experts in the field.

Mark remained active long past his obtaining emeritus status, and was noted for always looking ahead to the future of his science. For example, in the 1980s he led a study of fire-resistant polymers used in public places. Mark received many tributes to his scientific prowess, including numerous honorary degrees and medals. Polymer chemist Raymond Boyer explained that Herman Mark's contributions to the American plastics industry "has been immeasurable because it had so many primary and secondary effects of a highly ramified nature on all phases of polymer activity in the United States" (Boyer, 1966, p. 111), and Sir Eric Rideal noted succinctly that "there are no workers in the world in polymer science who at some point in their investigations are not indebted to his pioneering work" (Stahl, 1981, p. 80). Mark died after a brief illness at the home of his son, Hans Mark, chancellor of the University of Texas, at the age of ninety-six.

BIBLIOGRAPHY

WORKS BY MARK

With Hartmut Kallmann. "Über einige Eigenschaften der Compton-Strahlung" [Some properties of Compton radiation]. *Naturwissenschaften* 13 (1925): 1012–1015.

With Kurt H. Meyer. *Der Aufbau der hochpolymeren organischen Naturstoffe* [The structure of high molecular organic natural substances]. Leipzig, Germany: Akademische Verlagsgesellschaft, 1930.

With Eugene Guth. "Zur Statistchen Theorie der Käutschukelastizitat" [On the statistical theory of the elasticity of rubber]. *Zeitschrift fur Elektrochemie* 43 (1937): 683–686.

The General Chemistry of High Polymeric Substances. New York: Elsevier, 1940.

Physical Chemistry of High Polymeric Systems. New York: Interscience Publishers, 1940.

With George S. Whitby. *Collected Papers of Wallace H. Carothers on Polymerization.* New York: Interscience Publishers, 1940.

With Arthur V. Tobolsky. *Physical Chemistry of High Polymeric Systems.* 2nd ed. New York: Interscience Publishers, 1950.

"Giant Molecules." *Scientific American* 197 (March 1957): 80–89.

Giant Molecules. New York: Time, 1966.

"Polymer Chemistry: The Past 100 Years." *Chemical & Engineering News* (6 April 1976): 176–189.

"The Planning of the Weizmann Institute." *Rehovot* 9, no. 1 (1980): 3–7.

"Polymer Chemistry in Europe and America—How It All Began." *Journal of Chemical Education* 58 (1981): 527–534.

Interview by James J. Bohning and Jeffrey L. Sturchio at Polytechnic University, Brooklyn, New York, 3 February, 17 March, and 20 June 1986. Philadelphia: Chemical Heritage Foundation, Oral History Transcript #0030.

From Small Molecules to Large: A Century of Progress. Washington, DC: American Chemical Society, 1993. This autobiographical work is part of the series, "Profiles, Pathways and Dreams," edited by Jeffrey I. Seeman.

OTHER SOURCES

Boyer, Raymond I. "Herman Mark and the Plastics Industry." *Journal of Polymer Science, Part C* 12 (1966): 111–118.

Ginsberg, Judah. "The *Geheimrat.*" American Chemical Society. Available from http://acswebcontent.acs.org/landmarks/landmarks/polymer/pol_5.html.

Hunt, Morton M. "Polymers Everywhere." *New Yorker* 34 (1958): 13 September, 48–50; 20 September, 46–79.

Morawetz, Herbert. "Herman Mark—A Legend in His Lifetime." Unpublished typescript, oral history transcript #0030, research file, Chemical Heritage Foundation, Philadelphia. This research file is rich in other resources on Mark, including photocopies of *New York Times* articles taken from Mark's 85th birthday scrapbook.

———. "Herman Mark, 'The Geheimrat' at 90." *Macromolecules* 18 (1985): 593–594.

Pauling, Linus. "Herman Mark and the Structure of Crystals." *Chemtech* (June 1984): 334–337.

Program for "Polymers to the Year 2000 and Beyond, a Memorial Symposium for Herman F. Mark." Polytechnic University, Brooklyn, New York, 9 October 1992.

Proskauer, Eric. "A Tribute to Dr. Mark." *Journal of Polymer Science, Part A: Polymer Chemistry* 26, no. 9 (1988): vii–ix.

Saxon, Wolfgang. "Herman F. Mark Dies at 96; A Pioneer in Polymer Chemistry." *New York Times,* 10 April 1992.

Stahl, G. Allen, ed. *Polymer Science Overview: A Tribute to Herman F. Mark.* Washington, DC: American Chemical Society, 1981.

James J. Bohning

MARR, DAVID COURTNAY (*b.* 19 January 1945, Essex, England, *d.* 17 November 1980, Cambridge, Massachusetts), *cognitive neuroscience, computational neuroscience, information processing, representation, theoretical neuroscience, vision.*

During his tragically brief career, Marr founded the discipline that has come to be known as computational neuroscience. He developed the codon theory of information processing in the brain, which claims that the brain's

Marr

central function is statistical pattern recognition. He also recognized the fundamental distinction between the computational, algorithmic, and implementational levels of theory in describing brain function. Above all, he was interested in answering the question: What is it that the brain does?

Early Years. David Courtnay Marr was born in Essex, England. He attended Rugby, a British public school (similar to a private high school in the United States), on scholarship. In 1963, he went to Trinity College of Cambridge University, where he obtained BS and MS degrees in mathematics in 1966. Then, instead of pursing mathematical study, he switched his focus to neuroscience and studied neuroanatomy, neurophysiology, and molecular biology, earning a doctorate in theoretical neuroscience under the supervision of Giles Bradley in 1969. After obtaining his PhD, Marr accepted an appointment to the scientific staff of the Medical Research Council Laboratory of the Molecular Biology Department in Cambridge in the division of Cell Biology, working under Sydney Brenner and Francis Crick.

The results of his dissertation, essentially a theory of cerebellar function, inspired his three articles published between 1969 and 1971. Marr's published theory was mathematical, but it also reflected the known anatomical and physiological data of the time. Despite the immense advances in neuroscience afterward, much of Marr's theoretical work from his dissertation remained viable and relevant in the early twenty-first century. In the three articles, Marr described a possible function for each of three major brain structures: the cerebellum, the archicortex (the older part of the cerebral cortex), and the neocortex. Each of the answers dovetails with the others around the basic idea that the brain is a sophisticated pattern recognition device, working in a very high-dimensional feature space. The basic feature in all of these functions is a "codon," or a subset of properties that perhaps individual cells fire in response to.

The cerebellum, Marr surmised, learns the motor skills associated with actions, movements, and posture. The cerebellar Purkinje cells learn to associate particular actions with the contexts in which they are performed. Marr suggested that they do this by modifying their synapses using some sort of codon representation. Later, after learning, the Purkinje cells initiate the appropriate actions when exposed to the correct context alone. Many researchers still agree with the broad outlines of Marr's theory regarding how the cerebellum works.

In his second article, Marr then extended this idea to more general types of statistical pattern recognition and conceptual learning, arguing that this principle is probably behind many aspects of basic brain function. Marr called this idea his Fundamental Hypothesis: "where instances of a particular collection of intrinsic properties (i.e. properties already diagnosed from sensory information) tend to be grouped such that if some are present, most are, then other useful properties are likely to exist which generalize over such instances. Furthermore, properties often are grouped in this way" (1970, pp. 150–151). These ideas foretold much of contemporary neural network modeling, which assumes that learning consists in optimizing underlying probabilistic representational space.

Take the problem of facial recognition as an example. Humans can recognize one another's faces, even though they are all very similar to one another and one never sees them in exactly the same position or with the same expression as one did formerly. One can recognize the frontal view of smiling face as the same face seen frowning in profile last week. How does one do this? How does one keep track of all the properties that make up a face, and how does one know which properties are important to keep track of?

Consider a multi-dimensional graph in which each dimension represents one property of some complex object, like a face. Each point in the multi-dimensional space of the graph would then represent one possible face in one possible configuration. These points can be grouped together in graphs that are close to one another into "sub-volumes." Even though these grouped points are close to one another, which properties have which value will not be the same across points. Indeed, looking at the values of individual properties one at a time may not reveal whether their respective multi-dimensional points would be close together in space.

It turns out that the points associated with one particular face, seen from a variety of angles and with a variety of expressions is usually concentrated in a single and obvious sub-volume. To learn to recognize faces most efficiently, instead of learning all the possible values for each individual property, it is best to learn the distribution of sub-volumes in the multi-dimensional space. And that, thought David Marr, is exactly how the brain does it. In the early twenty-first century, neural network modelers tried to figure out what these graphs look like and exactly how one should be sensitive to the sub-volumes in the space.

These sorts of models require extensive memory so that the organ or machine can track and tally the probabilities of various events. Moreover, this memory has to react to the shape of the sub-volumes instead of something lower-level and more detailed, such as location along the axis of the graph. In this sense, it can be said that the memory retrieves its information based on content, not on physical attributes. Marr's third essay argues that the hippocampus fulfills this function. To make this argument, Marr combined the abstract mathematical constraints on the combinatorial possibilities of his theoretical codons with the latest data on hippocampal anatomy and physiology. He borrowed Donald Hebb's idea that the brain learns by modifying its synaptic connections through experience and gave a rigorous mathematical proof that his model can recall things very efficiently, even when only given partial content. Finally, Marr outlined several specific and testable predictions of hippocampal structure and function—such as synapses in the hippocampus that can be modified by experience—many of which were later corroborated by others.

Around 1971, Marr's intellectual interests shifted from general theories of brain function to the study of more specific brain processes. He effectively abandoned the idea of creating abstract theories of brain function, which he came to believe were too vague to explain how anything actually works. By 1972, he had concluded that it would be necessary to understand the details of the specific brain mechanisms and the cognitive tasks they support in order to fully explain the brain. From this nascent idea, he went on to invent the field of computational neuroscience, the legacy for which he is best known. Marr first expressed these ideas publicly in 1972 at a workshop on brain theory organized by Benjamin Kaminer at Boston University. At this event, Marr opined that there was an "inverse square law" for theoretical research: the value of research varies inversely with the square of its generality. Eventually this idea was published in a two-page book review in *Science* (Marr, 1975, p. 875).

Massachusetts Institute of Technology. In 1973, Marr joined the Artificial Intelligence (AI) Laboratory at the Massachusetts Institute of Technology (MIT) as a visiting scientist. At first, he had planned to stay only a few months, but finding the intellectual climate quite stimulating, he ended up staying for the rest of his career. Cambridge, Massachusetts, was already at the intellectual center for advances in both computational modeling and neuroscience. Things happened quickly there, and Marr rapidly became one of the central figures in MIT's dominance in AI. He saw early on that a marriage between the disciplines would be enormously fruitful. He wrote to his mentor and friend, Sydney Brenner, in September of 1973: "I have been thinking about the future. Presumably, as a result of the Lighthill report, AI must change its name. I suggest BI (biological intelligence). I am more and more impressed by the need for a functional approach to the CNS [central nervous system] and view it as significant that the critical steps for the retina were taken by land, the only scientist in the field actually concerned with handling real pictures.… I see a bright future for vision in the next few years, and am anxious to stay in the subject, doing my own AI research as well as acting as interface with neurophysiology.

At the AI laboratory at MIT, Marr embarked on a research program that sought to outline the computations involved in visual processing. Testing his ideas on computer models, Marr embodied a new approach in his work, combining insights from the new field of AI and those from neuroscience. Influenced by Horn's algorithm for computing lightness and by Land's retinex theory, Marr focused first on the functions of the retina, with great excitement and promise of groundbreaking results. As he writes to Brenner in July 1973,

> Nick Horn, co-director of the vision mini-robot project, came up with a beautiful algorithm for computing Land's retinex function. It is not quite the one actually used, but was near enough to enable one to take the last steps. I am busy tying up all the detailed anatomy and physiology now, and am very hopeful that the whole thing will turn out to be very pretty. But the retinex is the real secret. … One of our wholly new findings is that the so called center-surround organization of the retinal ganglion cells is all a hoax! It is nothing but a by-product of showing silly little spot stimuli to a clever piece of machinery designed for looking at complete views. That will put the cat among the pigeons in a very satisfying manner!

During this time, Marr's thought was undergoing a transition from believing that computational descriptions are on a par with neurophysiological data to holding that the computational framework was the foundation supporting neurophysiology. Early during his stay at MIT, Marr became convinced that there simply was not enough empirical data to support any general theories of brain processing. Indeed, he suspected that it might turn out that the brain would not support any useful general theory of processing. As a result, he began to criticize the most popular theories of modeling brain function at the time. In a review of the conference proceedings for a summer school institute on the physics and mathematics of the nervous system (held in Trieste, Italy, in August of 1973), Marr takes broad swipes at catastrophe theory, automata theory, learning automata theory, and neural net theory. His basic complaint is that theoreticians do not connect their theories to actual data. It might very well turn out that there is no general theory of brain function; instead, there will only be local understandings of particular brain processes.

In this review, he complains that even neural net theory, the most "biological" of modeling approaches, falls short of its goals:

> [T]here are two problems. First, the brain is large but it is certainly not wired up randomly. The more we learn about it, the more specific the

> details of its construction appear to be. Hoping that random neural net studies will elucidate the operation of the brain is therefore like waiting for the monkey to type *Hamlet.* Second, given a specific function of inevitable importance like a hash-coded associated memory, it is not too difficult to design a neural network that implements it with tolerable efficiency. Again, the primary unresolved issue is *what* functions you want to implement and *why.* In the absence of this knowledge, neural net theory, unless it is closely tied to the known anatomy and physiology of some part of the brain and makes some unexpected predictions, is of no value. (1975, p. 876)

Modeler's reactions to his harsh criticisms were decidedly mixed.

At the same time, Marr espoused a positive program. His central positive idea was that in order to understand any system, one must first understand both the problems it faces and the form that possible solutions could take. One must focus there, instead of on the structural details of the mechanisms themselves. Marr called these two types of understanding "computational" and "algorithmic," respectively. He placed these two *desiderata* above the third sort of understanding, the "implementational" level. In the brain, the implementational level would refer to the anatomy and physiology of the relevant neural areas involved in perception, action, and cognition. Marr also switched from working on retinal functioning to working with Tomaso Poggio, then housed at the Max Planck Institute in Tubingen, to develop theories of binocular stereopsis.

In 1977, Marr accepted a faculty appointment in the Department of Psychology at MIT, where he was given a continuing appointment and promoted as tenured full professor in 1980. In addition to his collaboration with Poggio, Marr also worked with Michael Ullman, Eric Grimson, Ellen Hildreth, H. Keith Nishihara, Whitman A. Richards, and Charles F. Stevens, among others. During this period, Marr also developed theories on low-level image representation and on shape and action characterization. Marr's book, *Vision: A Computational Investigation into the Human Representation and Processing of Visual Information,* written during the last months of his life, summarized the results of these collaborations.

In his book, Marr described vision as proceeding from a two-dimensional visual array (on the retina) to a three-dimensional description of the world as output. His stages of vision include a "primal sketch" of the scene, based on feature extraction of fundamental components of the scene, including things such as edges, color, movement, and so forth. The primal sketch is translated into a "2.5 D" sketch of the scene, which is a subject-centered perception of visual information. Finally, this model is converted into a "3 D" model, in which the scene is visualized on a continuous, three-dimensional objected-centered coordinate map. In virtue of how it integrated neural data with principles from computing and other related fields, Marr's book redefined the study of human and machine vision and continues to influence artificial intelligence research and research in computational neuroscience. Sadly, Marr was diagnosed with acute leukemia during the winter of 1978 and died from complications of the disease on 17 November 1980, in Cambridge, Massachusetts. His book was published posthumously in 1982.

During his time at MIT, people were in awe of Marr, and some of his proposals were taken simply as dogma. Consequently, his influence upon the research trajectories of many was profound. For an example, consider Marr's influence on his colleague Steven Pinker's work in shape recognition. The simplest way to recognize a shape would be to use some sort of template, a stored representation that imitates the shape of the object. However, if the object is shifted, rotated, or distorted, any simple template-matching mechanism will make errors. At the same time, midsized objects are things that humans all can recognize easily. To solve this problem, Marr suggested that human brains define shapes on a coordinate system centered on the object itself. As a shape moves, the coordinate system moves with it, and so one's "template" for the shape remains unchanged.

Pinker tested Marr's theory in numerous different ways. In one experiment, people memorized complex shapes presented in a certain orientation. The shapes were then presented in another orientation as a test to see how long it took people to name them. If Marr were right that humans represented shape invariantly across all orientations, people should be equally fast at recognizing objects in any orientation. But if humans were good at shape recognition because they had memorized shapes in the various orientations they had seen before, then they should identify objects at orientations they had seen before faster than objects seen in entirely new orientations.

Pinker found that Marr's hypothesis that shape learning is independent of orientation was only partly right. In general, subjects took a longer time to recognize objects in orientations they had not seen before. However, when the object's shape was symmetrical, they recognized it equally quickly, regardless of orientation. Perhaps humans have an object-centered coordinate system that is in fact mapped directly onto an object, regardless of orientation, but only for one dimension at a time.

Many of the details of Marr's specific theory of computational vision were refuted by neurophysiological data and insights not available in the 1970s. Nonetheless, his basic insight that good theories in the brain and behavioral sciences can combine mathematical rigor with neurally-based data remains as a fundamental component of computational neuroscience. Moreover, his emphasis on asking why a brain process is occurring, instead of merely looking for a differential equation that describes it, was adopted by most neurophysiologists in the early 2000s.

BIBLIOGRAPHY

WORKS BY MARR

"A Theory of Cerebellar Cortex." *Journal of Physiology* (London) 202 (1969): 437–470.

"A Theory for Cerebral Neocortex." *Proceedings of the Royal Society of London* (Series B) 176 (1970): 161–234.

"Simple Memory: A Theory for Archicortex." *Philosophical Transactions of the Royal Society of London* (Series B) 262 (1971): 23–81.

"The Computation of Lightness by the Primate Retina." *Vision Research* 14 (1974): 1377–1388.

"Approaches to Biological Information Processing." *Science* 190 (1975): 875–876.

"Early Processing of Visual Information." *Philosophical Transactions of the Royal Society of London* Series B, 275 (1976): 483–524.

With Tomaso Poggio. "Cooperative Computation of Stereo Disparity." *Science* 194 (1976): 283–287.

With Tomaso Poggio. "From Understanding Computation to Understanding Neural Circuitry." *Neurosciences Research Program Bulletin* 15 (1977): 470–491.

With H. Keith Nishihara. "Representation and Recognition of the Spatial Organization of Three-dimensional Structure." *Proceedings of the Royal Society of London* Series B, 200 (1978): 269–294.

With Tomaso Poggio. "A Computational Theory of Human Stereo Vision." *Proceedings of the Royal Society of London* Series B, 204 (1979): 301–328.

With Ellen Hildreth. "Theory of Edge Detection." *Proceedings of the Royal Society of London* Series B, 207 (1980): 187–217.

"Artificial Intelligence: A Personal View." In *Mind Design*, edited by John Haugeland, 129–142. Cambridge, MA: MIT Press, 1981.

Vision: A Computational Investigation into the Human Representation and Processing of Visual Information. San Francisco: W. H. Freeman, 1982.

With L. M. Viana. "Representation and Recognition of the Movements of Shapes." *Proceedings of the Royal Society of London* Series B, 214 (1982): 501–524.

OTHER SOURCES

Edelman, Shimon, and Lucia M. Viana. "Marr, David (1945–1980)." In *International Encyclopedia of the Social and Behavioral Sciences*, edited by Neil J. Smelser and Paul B. Baltes, 9256–9258. Oxford: Elsevier Science, 2001.

Vaina, Lucia M., ed. *From the Retina to the Neocortex: Selected Papers of David Marr*, vol. 1. Cambridge, MA: Birkhauser Boston, 1991.

Valerie Gray Hardcastle

MARSILI (OR MARSIGLI), LUIGI FERDINANDO

(*b.* Bologna, Italy, 20 July 1658; *d.* Bologna, 1 November 1730), *natural history, geography, oceanography, mineralogy, politics of science.* For the original article on Marsili see *DSB*, vol. 9.

Between 1975 and 2005 the complex figure of Marsili was widely studied by scholars interested in various aspects of his life and work. Knowledge of him developed through a variety of perspectives: the distinctly European dimension of Marsili's thinking and his initiatives; the part he played in the founding of the Institute of Sciences of Bologna and his views on the relationships between the new experimental science and the modern state; the special role he attributed to geography, as the discipline in which everything known about a place can be unified and made useful for its rulers; his idea of the necessary synergy between science and the arts, and the ways in which he put this into practice in his own researches and in his projects for new scientific institutions. In addition to these, fresh insights were achieved into the value of his pioneering studies in geology and oceanography.

The very title of John Stoye's ample and well documented biography, *Marsigli's Europe*, indicates the broad scope of this Bolognese nobleman's experience as soldier and virtuoso. The two identities were not separate but deeply interwoven throughout his life. As is shown by Stoye, and before him from Raffaella Gherardi, Marsili also addressed his scientific and political concerns beyond Christian Europe, towards the Ottoman Empire, its institutions, language, antiquities, and natural history. Marsili spent most of his life abroad: in the Habsburg dominions, in Provence, Switzerland, the Low Countries, and England. Nevertheless he succeeded in persuading the Bolognese senate and Pope Clemente XI to reform the teaching of natural philosophy and mathematics in Bologna, with the resulting foundation of the Istituto delle Scienze e delle Arti (and not of the Accademia delle Scienze, as Francesco Rodolico states in the original article on Marsili). The new institution was inaugurated in 1714, and in the course of some twenty years acquired a library, an observatory, physics and chemistry laboratories, a natural history museum, and a museum of military arts, where experimental courses were taught using instruments and materials at the outset mostly donated by Marsili himself. The institute also included two academies, the Accademia delle Scienze and the Accademia di Belle Arti (the Clementina, named after the pope). The former had been in existence since 1691 as the Accademia degli Inquieti, and in 1705 Marsili offered to house it in his family home, to which he would dispatch the books, instruments, and natural specimens he collected all over Europe, and where an observatory was then built on the roof. This private institute, which was to develop through the researches of Eustachio Manfredi, Francesco Vittorio Stancari, and other young Inquieti, constituted the embryo of the future public institution.

Marsili's inspiration for the project of forming an institution which would teach the new subjects by experiment and observation ("through the eyes, and not through the ears," in his words), came from his teachers, Marcello Malpighi, Geminiano Montanari, and Giandomenico Cassini, all followers of Galileo who were linked to the Accademia del Cimento, as well as being in touch with the Royal Society in London and the Académie des Sciences in Paris. Marsili himself became a foreign member of both, in 1699 (not in 1722, as Rodolico says) and in 1715 respectively.

As Gherardi has shown, Marsili's political vision of science was also derived from a direct experience of the power apparatuses of the modern state, in the course of his career as a general in the Imperial Army and his acquaintance with the Viennese court. His researches on the Danube basin, from every standpoint, including cartography, astronomy (for calculating longitude), geology, mining, hydrology, natural history, later published in the six great volumes of his *Danubius Pannonico-mysicus* (1726), were made possible thanks to vast financial resources and the work of hundreds of individuals who included engineers and artists. In Marsili's mind, geography, as a multifaceted discipline able to unify all knowledge of a particular location, thereby enabling its political control, was a necessary tool for the formation of state rulers both in peace and war time (Farinelli, 1979 and 1992).

Marsili's first significant collaborator was the German Johan Christoph Müller, who coordinated his field surveys and drew the majority of related illustrations and maps. The originality of Marsili's method of inquiry is manifest in the sustained iconic representations of nature and its human transformations carried out in the course of his travels and military campaigns. Besides Müller, Marsili was served by artists such as Georg Christoph Einmart, an engraver and astronomer from Nuremberg, the latter's daughter Maria Clara, and the Bolognese Raimondo Manzini, "a specialist in the illustration of nature" (Olmi, 2000, p. 273). It was thanks to his cartographic skills and his deep knowledge of the disputed territories that Marsili was elected imperial plenipotentiary in the negotiations to define new boundaries after the peace of Karlowitz, which, in 1699, put an end to the war between the Habsburg Empire and the Turks.The original article in the *DSB* rightly gave considerable importance to Marsili's researches on geology and on oceanography. New studies of these have enriched scholars' knowledge of them. Anita McConnell ("The Flowers of Coral," 1990) shows how Marsili's opinion that coral was a plant was not immediately refuted by the community of natural philosophers "in deference to his social standing." The view of Jean-Andre Peysonnel that coral was animal in nature was eclipsed by Marsili's *Histoire physique de la mer* (1725) dedicated to the Paris Academy of Sciences and prefaced by Herman Boerhaave, and not published until 1752.

Marsili's background as a high-ranking officer trained in mining engineering during a long stay in eastern Europe enhanced his acute powers of observation on geological field trips.

In his study "Luigi Ferdinando Marsili, Geologist" (2003), Ezio Vaccari notes that the research Marsili undertook in the Swiss Alps (1705), observing and describing their various morphological and structural features, bore out essential elements of his theory on the structure of mountains, which he subdivided into three morphological units. Marsili planned to write a treatise on the organic structure of the earth, a work never completed. According to Marabini and Vai (2003), his studies of the gypsum formations in the Apennines can be seen as one part of this project and as an example of the innovative character of his geological method and of the wide-ranging perspective he maintains, even when his starting point lies in local and extremely detailed observation.

Even in this field Marsili never forgot his pedagogical concerns. In the rich collections of geological and paleontological material he donated to the Istituto he left an invaluable legacy to future scholarship that was later preserved in the science museums of the University of Bologna (Sarti, 2003).

SUPPLEMENTARY BIBLIOGRAPHY

Listed are editions or facsimiles of Marsili's works issued after 1981.

WORKS BY MARSILI

Relazioni dei confini della Croazia e della Transilvania a sua maestà cesarea. Edited by Raffaella Gherardi. 2 vols. Modena, Italy: Mucchi, 1986.

Ragguaglio della schiavitù. Edited by Bruno Basile. Rome: Salerno, 1996. (In appendix: *Memoriale a Giuseppe re de' romani figlio di Leopoldo imperadore scritto dal co(nte) Luigi Marsigli tornato dalla schiavitù a Bologna.*)

Bevanda asiatica: trattatello sul caffè. Edited by Clemente Mazzotta. Rome: Salerno, 1998.

Danubius Pannonico-Mysicus, tomus I. Edited by Antal András Deák. Budapest, Hungary: Vizugyi Muzeum, Leveltar es Konyvgyujtemeny, 2004. (Includes a facsimile of the 1726 Hague-Amsterdam edition, and texts in Hungarian, Latin, English.)

OTHER SOURCES

Angelini, Annarita, ed. *Anatomie accademiche III. L'Istituto delle Scienze e l'Accademia.* Bologna, Italy: Il Mulino, 1993. Contains *Introduzione* by A. Angelini, pp. 13–310, and a documentary appendix, pp. 311–571.

Cavazza, Marta. *Settecento inquieto. Alle origini dell'Istituto delle Scienze di Bologna.* Bologna, Italy: Il Mulino, 1990.

———. "I due generali: le vite parallele di Vincenzo Coronelli e Luigi Ferdinando Marsili." In *Un intellettuale europeo e il suo universo. Vincenzo Coronelli (1650–1718),* edited by Maria Gioia Tavoni. Bologna, Italy: Costa, 1999.

Farinelli, Franco. "Il filosofo e la città: Luigi Ferdinando Marsigli e l'Istituto delle Scienze." In *La città del sapere: i laboratori storici e i musei dell'Università di Bologna,* testi di Pier Luigi Cervellati et al. Milan, Italy: A. Pizzi, 1987.

———. "Multiplex Geographia Marsilii est difficillima." In *I segni del mondo. Immagine cartografica e discorso geografico in età moderna,* edited by Franco Farinelli. Scandicci, Italy: La Nuova Italia, 1992.

Gherardi, Raffaella. *Potere e costituzione a Vienna fra Sei e Settecento: il "buon ordine" di Luigi Ferdinando Marsili.* Bologna, Italy: Il Mulino, 1980.

Marabini, Stefano, and Gian Battista Vai. "Marsili's and Aldrovandi's Early Studies on the Gypsum Geology of the Appennines." In *Four Centuries of the Word Geology. Ulisse Aldrovandi 1603 in Bologna,* edited by Gian Battista Vai and William Cavazza. Bologna, Italy: Minerva Edizioni, 2003.

McConnell, Anita. "L. F. Marsigli's Voyage to London and Holland, 1721–1722." *Notes and Records of the Royal Society of London* 41 (1986): 39–76.

———. "A Profitable Visit: Luigi Ferdinando Marsigli's Studies, Commerce and Friendships in Holland, 1722–23." In *Italian Scientists in the Low Countries in the XVIIth and XVIIIth Centuries,* edited by C. S. Maffioli and L. C. Palm. Amsterdam and Atlanta, GA: Rodopi, 1989.

———. "The Flowers of Coral—Some Unpublished Conflicts from Montpellier and Paris During the Early Eighteenth Century." *History and Philosophy of Life Sciences* 12 (1990): 51–66.

———. "L. F. Marsigli's Visit to London in 1721, and His Report on the Royal Society." *Notes and Records of the Royal Society of London* 47 (1993): 179–204.

Olmi, Giuseppe. "L'illustrazione naturalistica nelle opere di Luigi Ferdinando Marsigli." In *Natura-Cultura. L'interpretazione del mondo fisico nei testi e nelle immagini,* edited by Giuseppe Olmi, Lucia Tongiorgi Tomasi, and Attilio Zanca. Florence, Italy: Olschki, 2000.

Sarti, Carlo. "The Istituto delle Scienze in Bologna and its geological and paleontological collections in the 18th Century." In *Four Centuries of the Word Geology. Ulisse Aldrovandi 1603 in Bologna,* edited by Gian Battista Vai and William Cavazza. Bologna, Italy: Minerva Edizioni, 2003.

Sartori, Renzo. "Luigi Ferdinando Marsili, Founding Father of Oceanography." In *Four Centuries of the Word Geology. Ulisse Aldrovandi 1603 in Bologna,* edited by Gian Battista Vai and William Cavazza. Bologna, Italy: Minerva Edizioni, 2003.

Spallanzani, Mariafranca. "Le 'Camere di storia naturale' dell'Istituto delle Scienze di Bologna nel Settecento." In *Scienza e letteratura nella cultura italiana del Settecento,* edited by Renzo Cremante and Walter Tega. Bologna, Italy: Il Mulino, 1984.

———. "Le Camere di Storia naturale." In *I luoghi del conoscere. I laboratori storici e i musei dell'Università di Bologna,* edited by Franca Arduini et al. Milan, Italy: A. Pizzi, 1988.

Stoye, John. *Marsigli's Europe: The Life and Times of Luigi Ferdinando Marsigli, Soldier and Virtuoso.* New Haven, CT and London: Yale University Press, 1994.

Vaccari, Ezio. "Mining and Knowledge of the Earth in Eighteenth-century Italy." *Annals of Science* 57 (2000): 163–180.

———. "Luigi Ferdinando Marsili, Geologist: From the Hungarian Mines to the Swiss Alp." In *Four Centuries of the Word Geology. Ulisse Aldrovandi 1603 in Bologna,* edited by Gian Battista Vai and William Cavazza. Bologna, Italy: Minerva Edizioni, 2003.

Marta Cavazza

MARTIN, ARCHER JOHN PORTER

(*b.* Upper Holloway, London, 1 March 1910; *d.* Llangarron, Herefordshire, 28 July 2002), *analytical chemistry, chromatography, biochemistry.*

Martin was effectively the founder of modern chromatography, a method of separating different compounds in a mixture. The Italian-born Russian chemist Mikhail Tswett is usually credited with invention of chromatography at the beginning of the twentieth century, but the form of chromatography he developed—absorption chromatography—was rarely used for more than two decades after his early death and is hardly ever used in the early twenty-first century. By contrast, Martin invented three forms of chromatography—partition chromatography, paper chromatography, and gas-liquid chromatography—which were rapidly adopted and are still used intensively as of 2007. Even the other two forms of chromatography in common use—thin-layer chromatography and high-performance liquid chromatography—owe much to Martin's work. But if Martin's development of chromatography was a remarkable achievement, rewarded by a Nobel Prize in chemistry in 1952, his career illustrates how a moment—or even several moments—of scientific genius is not the same as being a scientific genius. Martin's research work thus sheds new light on the nature of scientific discovery. Martin's life after winning the Nobel Prize at the relatively early age of forty-two illustrates the problem of not knowing what to do after achieving the ultimate accolade, a problem which has also afflicted other Nobel Laureates.

Childhood and Early Research. During his career, Martin combined an interest in biochemical problems with a love of practical mechanics. This may have been—at least partly—a result of his family background. His father,

William Archer Porter Martin, was a medical practitioner whose forefathers were landowners in the north of Ireland. His mother, Lilian Kate Martin (née Brown), was the daughter of John Brown, who ran a plumbing and gas-fitting business in Hove, Sussex. A more immediate influence, however, was his elder sister Nora, who showed him chemistry experiments in the family's garden shed; they had moved to Bedford in 1920. Martin was probably dyslexic, as he was barely able to read until he was nine; but he went to Bedford School, a middle-of-the-road private school, when he was eleven. There he showed his interest in making things and in methods of separation by studying fractional distillation—a technique that was already crucial to the development of the burgeoning oil-refining industry—and making his own distillation column from coffee tins and lumps of coke. It is not surprising that when he went up to Peterhouse, Cambridge, in 1929 he had a scholarship to study chemical engineering.

In his early days at Cambridge, Martin was drawn into the circle of the well-known biochemist J. B. S. (John Burdon Sanderson) Haldane. This friendship was crucial to Martin's career. If he had not been taken up by Haldane, he would not have switched to biochemistry and would not have been accepted to do postgraduate research. In the unlikely event that he had been accepted, he certainly would not have completed his PhD without Haldane's support. It is hard to say what would have happened otherwise, but it is likely Martin would have become an obscure—if rather eccentric—chemical engineer. As a result of his switch in mid-degree to biochemistry and because he was already suffering from the severe depression that plagued him for much of his life, Martin only got a lower second class degree.

His initial research, on the conversion of B-carotene to vitamin A with C. P. (Charles Percy) Snow and Philip Bowden, was a complete failure, mainly thanks to Snow, who gave up chemistry soon afterward. With Haldane's assistance, Martin then moved to the nutritional laboratory in the biochemistry department. He worked with Leslie Harris and Tommy Moore on the isolation of Vitamin E and then with Sir Charles Martin (no relation) on the isolation of the anti-pellagra factor, but in both cases the Cambridge researchers were pre-empted by other groups overseas. During this research, however, Martin had developed a cumbersome countercurrent solvent extraction apparatus to separate different biochemical compounds. Another crucial meeting in Martin's life took place in early 1938 when Sir Charles introduced Martin to a fellow graduate student Richard L. M. Synge, who was working on the separation of acetylated amino acids. Martin and Synge then worked together to develop a better countercurrent extraction apparatus.

Development of Partition and Paper Chromatography. At this point, Sir Charles Martin suggested to his namesake that he take a job as a biochemist at the Wool Industries Research Association (WIRA) in Headingly, Leeds, rather than pursue his earlier ambition to become a chemical engineer. Archer Martin carried on, building more and more elaborate countercurrent setups, but tired of trying to get the inefficient and temperamental apparatus to work properly. He then had a revolutionary idea that transformed separation science. He had already seen the need for the two solvents to reach equilibrium rapidly so that the extraction could be carried out in a reasonable time, and realized that the best way of achieving this was by using very fine droplets. But if he used fine droplets the solvent would not move quickly and the benefit of achieving a rapid equilibrium was cancelled out. It suddenly struck him that there was no need for both the solvents to move; one could be held in a fine state on a stationary medium and the other solvent would move through it.

By this time, Martin had been reunited with Synge, who had come to WIRA in 1939. They decided to use silica gel as the solid support, as it could hold almost its own weight in water and was chemically inert. They were able to separate acetylated amino acids from the hydrolysis of wool protein, using methyl orange as an indicator, much more efficiently than with the countercurrent apparatus they had hitherto used. Martin and Synge demonstrated partition chromatography at a meeting of the Biochemical Society held at the National Institute for Medical Research, Hampstead, on 7 June 1941. Their practical achievement was supported by their development of the theory of partition chromatography; within a short space of time Martin was able to model the behavior of peptides and other compounds with a fair degree of precision. In their paper on this new technique, published in *Biochemical Journal* in November 1941, Martin and Synge suggested that a carrier gas could be used instead of a liquid for the mobile phase: gas-liquid chromatography was developed by Martin a decade later. They also proposed the use of fine particles and high pressures to improve the separation: the main features of high-pressure liquid chromatography, which was introduced in the mid-1970s. It must not be forgotten that this breakthrough took place during World War II. At the same time as they were inventing solid-liquid partition chromatography, Martin and Synge were also developing cloth that provided protection against mustard gas.

Column-based partition chromatography was a great improvement over Tswett's adsorption chromatography and countercurrent extraction, but it still had limitations. In particular, Martin and Synge soon discovered it did not work well with certain amino acids. Just as Martin had taken the older adsorption chromatography and adapted it, they now turned to paper chromatography, which had been originally described by Friedlieb Ferdinand Runge in 1850. Filter paper adsorbed water, was cheap, and readily available (an important consideration in wartime). Martin and Synge found that paper-based partition chromatography was eminently suitable for amino acids and required only tiny amounts of material, a crucial concern in biochemical research. Their new collaborator, A. Hugh Gordon, suggested using ninhydrin as an indicator to detect the spots of purified amino acids formed in the process.

Synge moved to the Lister Institute for Preventive Medicine in Chelsea, London, in 1943, and his place was taken by Gordon and Raphael Consden. Martin and his colleagues went on to develop two-dimensional paper chromatography, which uses one solvent (or mixture of solvents) in one direction, after which the paper is turned through ninety degrees and a new solvent is employed. The first public demonstration of paper chromatography took place at a meeting of the Biochemical Society held at the Middlesex Hospital, London, on 25 March 1944.

Development of Gas Chromatography. After an unhappy spell as head of the biochemistry division of Boots Pure Drug Company in Nottingham in 1946–1948, Martin joined the staff of the Medical Research Council (MRC), initially at the Lister Institute in London. In 1950 he joined the National Institute for Medical Research (NIMR), the flagship institute of the MRC, when it moved from Hampstead to Mill Hill on the northern outskirts of London. Martin needed the right partner to work with and an understanding boss. At Mill Hill, he was fortunate on both counts. He formed a working partnership with Tony James and reported to the director, Sir Charles Harington, who considered originality and intelligence to be more important than keeping the rules and having management skills. Mill Hill in this period also produced another great scientific maverick, James Lovelock. This was fortunate, as Martin rarely wore a tie and turned up for work in the summer in shorts and sandals.

Having developed partition chromatography and paper chromatography, Martin had become interested in crystallization in a column (later known as zone refining) but could not achieve worthwhile results. He was rescued from this dead end by a request from his NIMR colleague George Popják for a simple method of separating small amounts of mixed fatty acids, which arose from his investigation of the biosynthesis of milk fatty acids in a lactating goat. To help Popják (and to give Lovelock something more worthwhile to do), Martin returned to a concept he had explored with Synge almost a decade earlier but not pursued, namely gas-liquid chromatography. In essence, as previously, this was the addition of a liquid interface to an existing technique—gas-solid absorption chromatography—which had been developed earlier. The mobile phase was now a gas (usually nitrogen) and the stationary phase was Celite, coated with a suitable liquid and placed in glass tubes. The column was heated by a jacket containing boiling ethylene glycol (this well-known antifreeze has a boiling point of 180° C).

The problem with gas chromatography was finding a suitable method of detecting the separated components as they left the so-called column (which soon became a coil). Acidic and basic compounds were popular in the early work as they could be measured by standard titration. Martin and James used their first gas-liquid chromatography set-up to separate a mixture of amines and then used this information to identify the odoriferous principle of stinking goose-foot (*Chenopodium vulvarium*). They demonstrated the new technique at the meeting of the Biochemical Society held at the NIMR on 20 October 1950. By the time they repeated their demonstration at the Dyson Perrins Laboratory in Oxford, during the meeting of the International Union of Pure and Applied Chemistry in September 1952, they had extended the scope of gas chromatography to mixtures of fatty acids (in the form of their methyl esters) and hydrocarbons.

Whereas the impact of partition chromatography had been relatively slow, partly because of the war and Martin's modest status at the WIRA—Martin did not become a Fellow of the Royal Society until 1950—gas-liquid chromatography attracted attention almost immediately. Despite its greater complexity, this new technique spread like wildfire in 1952 and 1953. This was partly a result of Martin's higher profile as a Nobel Laureate—he won the Nobel Prize for chemistry with Richard Synge in 1952 for partition chromatography—and partly the result of a pent-up demand in academia and industry for a technique that would separate tiny amounts of relatively volatile compounds quickly and cleanly. This was particularly true in the rapidly developing petrochemical industry and gas chromatography was taken up enthusiastically by companies such as Anglo-Iranian Oil Company (which became British Petroleum—later BP—in 1954), Shell, and Imperial Chemical Industries (ICI). Martin himself concentrated on the development of detection methods for gas chromatography and developed the gas density balance for this purpose in September 1953. The gas density balance was typical of Martin's innovations. It was an elegant masterpiece of intricate engineering, but it was far too complicated for most chemists to construct or use, and it was rapidly superseded by other detectors.

Later Career. Martin's career after 1954 was uneventful by any standard and could even be described as unsuccessful. It is worth asking why this was the case. Having spent nearly two decades developing new methods of separating compounds, Martin had achieved all his goals. His later

Archer John Porter Martin. AP IMAGES.

projects, mainly of a biochemical nature, were rather unfocused and soon petered out. Martin had succeeded when he was working with other gifted scientists with strong personalities who ensured that the research stayed on track and disabused Martin of his more eccentric ideas while at the same time developing the good ones. A good example of the eccentricity of some of his ideas was his proposal for a tornado-making machine at a cocktail party in Houston in the 1970s.

After he left the NIMR in 1956, Martin worked largely on his own and the practical mechanic side of his personality became dominant. He spent much of his time tinkering with machinery rather than concentrating on serious scientific research. In the late 1950s and 1960s, following the discovery of the double helix, biochemistry was rapidly becoming molecular biology. Lacking close contact with other leading biochemists, Martin failed to appreciate the major changes in his field. His biochemical research with its aim of isolating biologically active factors harked back to Cambridge in the 1930s. Martin did not have the managerial or organizational skills to become a senior manager in a major organization, a successful businessman, or a head of an Oxbridge college. He was neither a good team player nor an inspiring leader. Martin had shot both of his bolts and had nothing more to offer.

Leading scientists, even Nobel Laureates, often become marginalized in their later careers by working as freelance consultants, or they exist on the edge of academia by holding honorary or visiting research fellowships. Martin's later career encompassed both options and neither option turned out well. Martin left the NIMR in part because he was angry that the British government had sold his patent for the gas density balance to an American firm. But there was really nothing left for Martin to do at Mill Hill. He was not very successful as head of the physical chemistry division—a post to which he had been appointed in 1952—and he was clearly not suitable for consideration as a possible successor to Sir Charles Harington as director. With the aim of becoming a consultant for Griffith & George (he was even listed as director of research of Griffith & George in the Royal Society yearbook for 1960) and other companies interested in his work on gas chromatography, Martin used his Nobel Prize money in 1957 to buy Abbotsbury, a large house in Elstree near Mill Hill, riddled with dry rot and standing in a large overgrown plot. At Abbotsbury Laboratories, as it was rather grandiosely named, Martin acted as a consultant, made gas density balances, and carried out biochemical research. Between 1969 and 1974, he also held a visiting professorship as a *bijzonder hoogleraar leer der analogiën* (special professor in the science of analogies) at the Technical University of Eindhoven. This post also gave him the opportunity to act as a consultant to Phillips Electronics during his visits to the Netherlands.

Matters appeared to take a turn for the better when David Long arranged for Martin to become a consultant for the Wellcome Foundation at its research laboratories in Beckenham, Kent, with the expectation that he would tell the firm which research topics were likely to be useful and thus worth exploring further. This was probably not a good idea, as Martin was much better at generating ideas than at judging which were sound. When Long left Wellcome in 1973, he arranged for Martin to be given funding by the Medical Research Council to set up a research group at the University of Sussex, where John Cornforth—his former colleague at the NIMR—was now based with other leading chemists, including Joseph Chatt, Alan Johnson, and Harry Kroto.

Martin's later research can be divided into three areas: isolation of biologically active compounds, work in broader areas, and mechanical developments. At Abbotsbury, he concentrated on the isolation of anti-inflammatory factor from milk, liver, and eggs. At the Wellcome and the University of Sussex in the 1970s he attempted the isolation of insulin from pig gut. In the 1960s, Martin conceived the idea of "microengineering" and in particular the concept of a micromanipulator that could replace the hand in delicate scientific work. Subsequently, these ideas were validated by the introduction of nanotechnology, on one

Martin

hand, and the development of microsurgery, on the other. If Martin had been working closely with other scientists, this line of research might have been fruitful; working on his own, he was unsuccessful. While he was at Sussex, Martin was interested in the biological mechanism of smell. On the mechanical side, Martin worked with Frans Everaats of TU Eindhoven on improvement of electrophoresis, a separation technique Martin had wished he had taken up earlier in the 1940s when it was still being developed. At the Wellcome Foundation, Martin used his mechanical expertise to develop a vacuum pump for freeze-drying and a handheld high-pressure pump for the needle-free administration of vaccines.

At this point, Martin's career began to unravel completely. Annoyed about the miners' strike in 1973–1974 and the return of the Labour Party to power, in 1974 Martin suddenly took up a Robert A. Welch Professorship at the University of Houston, Texas, without formally giving up his position at Sussex. The faculty at Houston looked forward to working with Martin and they gave him unlimited funds to purchase equipment. As there was no statutory retirement age for the well-paid Welch Professors, he looked set to fulfill his wish to continue with research until he was in his eighties. However, when he arrived in Houston, his fellow faculty members found Martin profoundly unsettling. American chemists viewed a research professorship as an opportunity to pursue an energetic research program. Martin saw it as an opportunity to spend his time in a leisurely manner, wander around, tinker with the machinery in the basement, and think. He tried to extract a protein from potato skins and his laboratory was soon full of rotting potato skins.

If this was not bad enough from the faculty's point of view, Martin kept getting into trouble with the university authorities in various ways. For instance, he created a storm in the student body over his views about race and intelligence. He believed that less intelligent people should be paid not to have children whereas very intelligent people (such as himself) had a duty to procreate. He also had controversial views about the punishment of criminals, arguing that they should be given the option of radiation treatment that would artificially age them instead of a prison sentence. At a time when the Unification Church was actively seeking links with influential academics, it cut its ties with Martin because of his contentious views. The faculty's patience finally snapped and his professorship was terminated in 1979, a unique event in the annals of the Welch Professorships.

Around this time, Martin started to suffer from severe forgetfulness, which was eventually diagnosed as Alzheimer's disease in 1985. He would leave his car engine running, forget to turn off taps, and fail to turn up to give lectures. On the occasion of his seventy-fifth birthday he had the prepared text of a speech with him, but he was unable to read it. Nonetheless, the leading chromatographer Ervin Kováts was able to obtain a position for him at the University of Lausanne and hoped that Martin could collaborate with pharmaceutical firms on his anti-inflammatory factor, but nothing came of this, probably because of Martin's worsening mental condition. When Martin retired in 1984, he moved with his wife—Judith (née Bagenal) whom he had married in 1943—to Cambridge. His mental condition deteriorated, and although he took part in the trials of donepezil (Aricept), he was moved to a nursing home in 1996. At the time of his death, Martin was living in a nursing home in Llangarron, Herefordshire, near his daughter's home.

BIBLIOGRAPHY

WORKS BY MARTIN

With Richard L. M. Synge. "Separation of the Higher Monoamino-Acids by Counter-Current Liquid-Liquid Extraction: The Amino-Acid Composition of Wool." *Biochemical Journal* 35 (1941): 91–121.

With Raphael Consden and A. Hugh Gordon. "Qualitative Analysis of Proteins: A Partition Chromatographic Method Using Paper." *Biochemical Journal* 38 (1944): 224–232.

With Anthony T. James. "Gas-liquid Partition Chromatography: The Separation and Micro-Estimation of Volatile Fatty Acids from Formic Acid to Dodecanoic Acid." *Biochemical Journal* 50 (1952): 679–690.

"The Development of Partition Chromatography." Nobel Lecture, 12 December 1952. Available from nobelprize.org/nobel_prizes/chemistry/laureates/1952/martin-lecture.pdf.

On the Uses of Analogy. Eindhoven, Netherlands: Technische Hogeschool Eindhoven, 1964. Available from http://alexandria.tue.nl/extra2/redes/martin1964.pdf.

OTHER SOURCES

Lovelock, James. "Obituary: Archer John Porter Martin." *Memoirs of the Fellows of the Royal Society* 50 (2004): 157–170.

Morris, Peter J. T. "Martin, Archer John Porter, 1910–2002." *Oxford Dictionary of National Biography.* Online edition, January 2006. Available from http://www.oxforddnb.com/index/101077176.

Porter, Ruth, ed. *Gas Chromatography in Biology and Medicine.* London: Churchill, 1969. Martin's CIBA Foundation lecture. Although it appears to be autobiographical, it was written by someone else using notes made during the lecture.

Stahl, G. Allan. "Interview with Archer J. P. Martin." *Journal of Chemical Education* 54 (February 1977): 80–83.

Peter J. T. Morris

MASLOW, ABRAHAM (*b.* New York, New York, 1 April 1908; *d.* Menlo Park, California, 8 June 1970), *psychology, psychology of personality, humanistic psychology.*

Maslow was a prominent personality theorist and one of the best-known American psychologists of the twentieth century. Skeptical of behaviorism and psychoanalysis, Maslow worked to develop a more expansive theory of human motivation, one that could accommodate the powerful influence of biology and the environment while honoring the human capacity for free will. Entitled the "hierarchy of needs," Maslow's theory provided the foundation for a wide-ranging program to reform the discipline of psychology. Convinced that psychology was selling humanity short, Maslow hoped to change the discipline in its entirety, and to this end he played a leading role in establishing "humanistic psychology" in the late 1950s. In the 1960s Maslow's emphasis on self-expression and the human capacity to transcend limitations found a mass audience across a wide spectrum of people in search of a new vocabulary of selfhood, and he became a guru to both business executives and the counterculture. In 1968 his renown was acknowledged by his election as president of the American Psychological Association.

Origins and Education. Although Maslow lived to see his ideas enter the American mainstream, he always thought of himself as the "marginal man, the Outsider, the rejected person who has no home" (Maslow, 1960, p. 13). Born into a Russian Jewish immigrant family in Manhattan in 1908, Maslow felt little affinity for his body, his family, or his faith. His father, Samuel Maslow, was a cooper, but it was his mother, Rose Maslow (his father's first cousin), who played a larger and particularly menacing role in his upbringing. As an adult, Maslow described her as a kind of anti-mother: the very opposite of the stable, nurturing "Yiddishe Mameh" so revered in the Eastern European Jewish immigrant community. "My mother, a horrible woman, hated me utterly" he recalled bitterly (Maslow, 1932). Maslow felt particularly aggrieved by his mother's vicious attacks on his physical appearance. Rose would frequently complain about her son's ugly, skinny body; as much as he hated her, Maslow found it difficult not to internalize this message. He developed a near-paralyzing self-consciousness that at times prevented him from entering a subway car so as not to inflict his pathetic physicality on the rest of humanity.

Haunted by a desire for a powerful body, Maslow reacted angrily to his mother's unrelenting reminders of his physical limitations. Over time, hatred for Rose grew into a generalized antipathy for everything she represented—including Jewish religious practice. Maslow recalled feeling that Judaism "was a totally nonsensical religion" and that "all people who were religious were either hypocrites or feeble-minded" (Maslow, 1960, p. 23). Although he was disdainful of Jewish religious tradition, Maslow developed a deep appreciation for "Jewish heritage that sent me to school books and libraries as a matter of course" (Maslow, 1979, p. 950). As a youth he spent much of his spare time in the library, and by the time he reached adolescence, Maslow was well on his way to becoming part of what David Hollinger (1996) has described as a community of "free-thinking Jews." These were Jews who "took little interest in Judaism but did not become Christians, and who, even more portentously, brought a skeptical disposition into the American discussions of national and world issues" (p. 19).

Anti-Semitism was a crucial catalyst in Maslow's burgeoning skeptical sensibility. Although he felt little affinity for his faith or his culturally symbolic frail body, he quickly learned that being a Jew was as much a cultural identity as it was a form of religious expression. He heard teachers speaking contemptuously of him as "that smart Jew," and throughout his youth he was tormented by gangs of anti-Semitic thugs (Hoffman, 1988, p. 4). Deeply resentful, Maslow dreamed of "destroy[ing] the priests & the churches that had hurt me so much" (Maslow, 1979, p. 387). These dreams stayed with him long after he left the ethnically divided neighborhoods of New York City, and they helped condition the iconoclastic, "outsider" posture that characterized Maslow's approach to psychology.

Enamored with ideas from an early age, Maslow enrolled as an undergraduate philosophy major at the City College of New York in 1926. Intellectually restless and unsure of what to do with his future, Maslow transferred to Cornell in 1927 and then moved to the University of Wisconsin in 1928. At Wisconsin, Maslow found the direction he was looking for in the work of well-known behaviorist psychologist John B. Watson. Behaviorist psychology hit Maslow like a religious epiphany: "I suddenly saw unrolling before me into the future the possibility of a *science of psychology*, a program of work which promised real progress, real advance, real solutions to real problems. All that was necessary was devotion and hard work" (Maslow, 1979, p. 277). With Watsonian behaviorism as his inspiration, Maslow dedicated himself to psychology, completing a BA in 1930 and then enrolling in Wisconsin's graduate program.

In graduate school Maslow studied experimental psychology under the supervision of Harry Harlow at the University of Wisconsin, and he wrote his doctoral dissertation on the relation between sexual conduct and dominance hierarchies in monkeys. A hard-working and original student, Maslow was highly regarded by Harlow, who later described him as a "fine monkey man" (Harlow,

1972). Although Maslow undertook no further research on primates after graduate school, the experience of working with monkeys made an enduring impression on him. He remained convinced that primates represented an unadorned and truthful view of what was fundamentally human. "I always felt about the monkeys and apes," he later remarked, "as if I was seeing the roots of human nature laid bare" (Maslow, 1979, p. 331). For the rest of his career, Maslow viewed society as something that was influential but fundamentally artificial. As a humanistic psychologist, he argued that psychological development involved transcending the artifice and constraints of socialization and releasing an inborn biological potential.

Although Maslow spent more than five years studying primate behavior, he was never completely enamored with the structure and ethos of laboratory psychology. As a young graduate student he commented critically on the "publish or perish" mentality that pervaded the laboratory and the kind of atheoretical anti-intellectualism that this ethos breeds. Maslow was equally critical of the scholarly substance of psychology. As a graduate student, he was convinced that the discipline had become hostage to a scientistic sensibility that put loyalty to method ahead of intellectual creativity. Subsequent exposure to Adlerian psychology and cultural anthropology further entrenched this idea, and by the early 1950s the intellectual poverty of psychology had become a cornerstone of Maslovian thought.

Early Career. After graduating from the University of Wisconsin with a PhD in 1934, Maslow tried to obtain an academic appointment, but in the anti-Semitic context of the 1930s his applications met with little success. However, he did obtain a postdoctoral fellowship in New York City at Teachers College, Columbia University, working under the direction of the renowned psychologist Edward Thorndike. At Teachers College Maslow continued his research on sexuality and dominance, but instead of using primates as subjects he now employed female undergraduates, arguing that "girls [are] more tractable" ("Barnard Girls," 1936). In a series of papers based on this research, Maslow maintained that there was a fundamental continuity between human sexuality and primate sexuality: "In general," he remarked in a 1942 article, "it is fair to say that human sexuality is almost exactly like primate sexuality with the exception that cultural pressures added to the picture, drive a good deal of sexual behavior underground into fantasies, dreams, and unexpressed wishes" (Maslow, 1942, p. 291).

Maslow's productivity and intellect impressed Thorndike, but anti-Semitic hiring practices continued to thwart his progress. Effectively barred from more prestigious institutions, Maslow was hired in 1937 by Brooklyn College, a predominantly Jewish teaching-intensive institution. The job was poorly paid and left little time for research, but it did keep Maslow in New York City at a time of extraordinary intellectual ferment. The city was home to a remarkable collection of American intellectuals and German émigré scholars. In what little spare time he had, Maslow became acquainted with such distinguished figures such as Alfred Adler, Ruth Benedict, Karen Horney, and Erich Fromm, all of whom emphasized the social basis of behavior and, to varying degrees, individual agency. Under their influence, Maslow became increasingly sensitive to the impact of culture on personality, arguing in a 1937 paper that "we must treat the individual first as a member of a particular cultural group, and only after treat him as a member of the general human species" (p. 418).

With the encouragement of Benedict, Maslow sought to apply his newfound cultural awareness through anthropological fieldwork. He obtained a grant from the Social Science Research Council and spent the summer of 1938 on the reserve of the Northern Blackfoot Indians near Calgary, in Alberta, Canada, in order to study dominance and emotional security among native people. The trip was an eye-opening experience for Maslow, and it led him to question further the cultural limitations of psychological techniques and concepts. In New York City Maslow had developed a questionnaire to test personal dominance, but to his dismay he soon discovered that it had limited value. "The test was ridiculously useless when used to measure secure people" he later remarked. "Many of the questions in this test were completely incomprehensible to the Blackfoot; others were merely funny" (cited in Hoffman, 1988, p. 123). Ironically, the fieldwork also prompted Maslow to question the very idea that had prompted him to undertake the trip in the first place: the centrality of culture. Having spent the summer interacting with the Blackfoot people, Maslow was struck not by their cultural distinctiveness but by their common humanity. The Blackfoot seemed to have the same basic character types and psychological issues as members of the larger culture; some of the values and modes of expression were different, but the people were the same. "I found almost the same range of personalities as I find in our society," he reported. "I am not struggling with a notion of a 'fundamental' or 'natural' personality" (cited in Hoffman, 1988, p. 128).

Human Motivation. At Brooklyn College Maslow's heavy teaching load left little time for research, but the relative importance and relationship of biology and culture on personality remained active in his mind. Increasingly convinced that personality was biological, Maslow was nevertheless dissatisfied with existing biologically based formulations, most particularly psychoanalysis, that reduced motivation to a single impulse. Drawing again from the stimulating intellectual environment of New York City, he began to reflect on the implications of a lecture by the celebrated German psychologist Max Wertheimer on the significance of behavior that was not directly related to physiological needs (e.g., playfulness and aesthetic enjoyment).

Maslow also became fascinated by the motivational structure of many of the distinguished scholars with whom he had interacted. They were, as a group, warm, friendly, intellectually creative, and personally dynamic. How did they become this way? "They were puzzling" he later remarked. "They didn't fit. It was as if they came from another planet ... [What] I knew didn't explain them" (cited in Hoffman, 1988, p. 152). In reflecting on these "good human beings," Maslow (1945) was undertaking something relatively unusual in psychology. Psychoanalytically inspired theory was based largely on the study of people experiencing personal difficulties. This approach had clearly yielded a wealth of insight, but Maslow argued that it had resulted in a distorted and unduly narrow conception of human motivation. A new theory was needed, one that would integrate existing formulations from psychoanalysis and behavioral psychology with insights derived from the study of the "psychologically healthy."

The result of these theoretical deliberations was Maslow's most celebrated work: his theory of motivation, known as the "hierarchy of needs." First published in 1943, the theory maintained that human beings were motivated by five sets of hierarchically arranged goals: physiological needs, safety, love, esteem, and self-actualization. When satisfaction had been achieved at one stage, the motivational focus of the person would shift to the next goal. This new and "higher" need would then "dominate the conscious life" of the person and "serve as a center of organization of behavior" (Maslow, 1943, p. 395). In proposing this theory, Maslow stressed the limitations of each need. Once a need had been satisfied, it no longer served as a source of motivation. For example, once a hungry person had a reliable source of food "other (and 'higher') needs emerge and these, rather than physiological hungers, dominate the organism" (Maslow, 1943, p. 375).

In acknowledging the biological and environmental basis of behavior, the hierarchy drew on existing psychological theory. However, Maslow's theory also posited the existence of an additional innate human need that was located at the summit of the hierarchy. Known as "self-actualization," this need referred to a biologically based sense of inner destiny, a "desire for self fulfillment ... to become everything that one is capable of becoming" (Maslow, 1943, p. 382). Although self-actualization was a relatively small component of Maslow's original paper, it took up an increasingly large portion of his attention in his subsequent work, and he became closely identified with the term.

Humanistic Psychology. Maslow left Brooklyn College in 1951 and joined the faculty at the newly established Brandeis University. Hired as chair of the Psychology Department, Maslow played an important role in building the new department and attracting such distinguished faculty as Richard Held, Ulrich Neisser, Kurt Goldstein, and George Kelley. Amidst his numerous administrative duties, Maslow wrote *Motivation and Personality* (1954), a groundbreaking work that attracted considerable attention within psychology. At its center was an extended discussion of the hierarchy of needs and a consideration of how the science of psychology could contribute to a new, life-affirming set of human values. It was a hopeful message imbued with a distinctively American spirit of optimism. However, it went against the grain of an American psychology that was still wedded to behaviorism and animal experimentation.

Keenly aware of the unorthodox nature of his ideas, Maslow presented in this work both a critique of contemporary psychology and a commentary on human nature. He chastised mainstream psychology for elevating a devotion to scientific method over a commitment to real human experience, noting that "the science [of psychology] as a whole too often pursues limited or trivial goals with limited methods and techniques under the guidance of limited vocabulary and concepts" (Maslow, 1954, p. 354). The discipline was "means centered" insofar as it emphasized technique, when it should be more "problem centered"—concerned with the reality of human psychology (Maslow, 1970, p. 11). Inspired by psychology's potential but convinced that the field was misdirected, Maslow devoted himself to the task of moving the discipline's boundaries, thereby creating a "larger jurisdiction for psychology" (Maslow, 1968, p. xv). This was as much a metaphysical ambition as it was a bureaucratic project. Psychology's larger jurisdiction was to be a zone where conventional distinctions no longer applied: science, religion, psychology, and pseudo-science would all merge into one persuasive and empowering idiom that could take humanity to a higher plane of experience.

Maslow's critique resonated with a number of psychologists long frustrated with the limitations of mainstream psychology. Increasingly aware of a growing community of like-minded psychologists, in the late 1950s and early 1960s Maslow helped establish an institutional framework for an alternative psychology, known as "humanistic" or "third-force" psychology. In 1961 he helped found the *Journal of Humanistic Psychology* and in 1963 he helped establish the Association for Humanistic

Abraham Maslow. © UPI/BETTMANN/CORBIS.

Psychology, an organization that included prominent psychologists such as Charlotte Bühler, Rollo May, Henry Murray, and Carl Rogers. Building on the success of this humanistic project, Maslow published *Toward a Psychology of Being* (1962); he applied humanistic psychology to business in *Eupsychian Management* (1965) and to science in *The Psychology of Science* (1966).

After coming to Brandeis, Maslow largely abandoned empirical work in favor of theoretical innovation and analysis. Though he worked outside the laboratory, Maslow continued to view his work in scientific terms, and he was convinced that the hierarchy of needs was a statement of scientific fact and not an expression of social value. Promoting the theory as "science," contributed to its influence, but the hierarchy of needs was not without a political and cultural context. The placement of material needs as a precondition for higher needs is less a universal human truth than a reflection of American middle-class sensibilities. American values are also evident in the pronounced individualism of his psychology. Echoing liberals such as Adam Smith, Maslow placed the autonomous individual at the center of his psychology, and he argued that unobstructed self-interest was the best way to ensure the public good. Although Maslow strenuously denied the charge, his approach appeared to condone an individualistic, self-seeking approach to life and a culture of narcissism. Feminist theorists have also suggested that the vision of selfhood as a hierarchy is itself a reflection of a Western male bias that privileges autonomy and independence at the expense of relatedness and reciprocity.

Maslow was not indifferent to such criticism, and he commented pointedly on the Western male values that are contained in the ostensibly neutral discourse of science. He was in fact a pioneering figure in his explicit acknowledgment of the gendered character of science and in his attempt to transcend the rigid dichotomy of masculinity-femininity. Despite his awareness of these issues, Maslow found it difficult to completely abandon the scientism of his youth. He continued to view science "as a God" and looked to biology as a basis for psychology and ethics (1979, p. 426). His stinging criticisms of the shortcomings of scientific psychology were accompanied by an unwavering biological essentialism in which "truth, goodness, beauty, [and] justice" would ultimately be explained through "biochemical, neurological, endocrinological substrates or body machinery" (1971, p. 22).

Psychological Guru. The social ferment of the 1960s propelled Maslow onto the national stage. Many Americans had become dissatisfied with the gray-flannel conventionality of the 1950s, and in humanistic psychology they discovered a refreshing alternative and an important ideological resource. Influential feminists such as Betty Friedan (1963) drew on Maslow's concept of self-actualization to explain the alienation of American women. For counterculture activists such as Abby Hoffman, the language of self-actualization was a warrant to challenge convention and trust inner impulses (Hoffman, 1980). "Maslovian theory laid a solid foundation for launching the optimism of the sixties" Hoffman remarked. "Existential, altruistic and upbeat, his teachings became my personal code" (p. 26). Maslow himself was uneasy about the spiritual and political conclusions that others drew from his work, and in his private correspondence he characterized student activists as "perpetual adolescents" and complained bitterly about "dominant, castrating" women (1979, p. 603, p. 77).

Maslow held no such reservations about another group attracted to his ideas: American business. In 1962 Maslow spent part of the year as a paid consultant for Non Linear Systems, a California-based engineering firm. The firm's president, Andrew Kay, had a reputation for innovative management techniques, and he was eager to apply Maslow's humanistic ideas to his company. Although Maslow was a longtime academic, he found the experience of working in a business environment invigorating, and he spent hours discussing the relevance of humanistic psychology to the practical problems of American industry. In 1965 he published the results of his observations in a book titled *Eupsychian Management*. The book took its curious title from the term *eupsychia*—a word Maslow had invented to refer to a utopia of self-actualized people. In innovative management, Maslow saw the possibility of putting American society on a more psychologically healthy foundation. Although Maslow was overly ambitious in gauging the potential of his ideas to transform society, the hierarchy became a staple in discussions of organizational behavior; in business schools it continues to enjoy the status of a classic among classics. Maslovian thought remains an important touchstone for meaning-based jobs, human relations training, and worker participation in management.

Although Maslow promoted a psychology of hope and transcendence, he found little repose in his private life, and he often complained of feeling unappreciated by his family, colleagues, and students. Election to the presidency of the American Psychological Association in 1968 was a welcome surprise, but Maslow remained frequently stressed and dissatisfied. In 1970 he died of a heart attack at age sixty-two, survived by his wife Bertha Goodman and his two children, Ann and Ellen. His final major work, *The Farther Reaches of Human Nature,* was published posthumously in 1971.

Maslow remains a figure of considerable renown in psychology. A recent study polled 1,725 members of the American Psychological Society, asking them to list the top psychologists of the twentieth century (Haggbloom, 2002). Maslow ranked tenth, ahead of such distinguished figures as Carl Jung, John Watson, and Lewis Terman. The "hierarchy of needs" has evolved into a psychological classic familiar to every psychology undergraduate, and although humanistic psychology remains a marginal presence in academic psychology, Maslow's work has helped to diversify the field's questions and categories. For all of his influence on academic psychology, Maslow's most enduring legacy is cultural. Since his death his work has provided the foundation for countless popular psychologies, and his psychological language of "needs" and "self-actualization" has become part of the everyday idiom of American selfhood.

BIBLIOGRAPHY

Maslow's papers are on deposit at the Archives of the History of American Psychology, University of Akron. The collection contains correspondence, photographs, and unpublished journals and manuscripts.

WORKS BY MASLOW

Unpublished journal. Archives of the History of American Psychology, University of Akron, 1932.

"Personality and Patterns of Culture." In *Psychology of Personality,* edited by R. Stagner. New York: McGraw Hill, 1937.

"Self-esteem (Dominance-feeling) and Sexuality among Women." *Journal of Social Psychology* 16 (1942): 259–294.

"A Theory of Human Motivation." *Psychological Review* 50 (1943): 370–396.

"Journal of Good Human Beings." Unpublished manuscript, Maslow Papers, Archives of the History of American Psychology, University of Akron, 1945.

Motivation and Personality. New York: Harper and Row, 1954. 2nd ed., New York: Harper and Row, 1970.

"Interview with Dorothy Lee." Maslow Papers, Archives of the History of American Psychology, University of Akron, 1960.

The Psychology of Science: A Reconnaissance. New York: Harper and Row, 1966.

Toward a Psychology of Being. New York: Van Nostrand Reinhold, 1968 (original work published in 1962).

Eupsychian Management: A Journal. Homewood, IL: R. D. Irwin, 1965.

The Farther Reaches of Human Nature. New York: Viking Press, 1971.

The Journals of A. H. Maslow. Monterey, CA: Brooks/Cole Publishing, 1979.

OTHER SOURCES

"Barnard Girls Taking Place of Scientist's Apes." *New York Herald,* 15 May 1936. Maslow Papers, Archives of the History of American Psychology, University of Akron.

Cullen, Dallas. "Maslow, Monkeys and Motivation Theory." *Organization* 4 (1997): 355–373.

Daniels, Michael. "The Myth of Self-actualization." *Journal of Humanistic Psychology* 28, no. 1 (1988): 7–38.

Friedan, Betty. *The Feminine Mystique.* New York: Norton, 1963.

Matuyama

Haggbloom, Steven J. "The 100 Most Eminent Psychologists of the 20th Century." *Review of General Psychology* 6 (2002): 139–152.

Harlow, Harold. "Reflections on Abraham Maslow." Unpublished manuscript. Maslow Papers, Archives of the History of American Psychology, University of Akron, 1972.

Herman, E. *The Romance of American Psychology: Political Culture in an Age of Experts.* Berkeley: University of California Press, 1995.

Hoffman, Abbie. *Soon to Be a Major Motion Picture.* New York: Perigee Books, 1980.

Hoffman, Edward. *The Right to Be Human: A Biography of Abraham Maslow.* Los Angeles: Jeremy Tarcher, 1988.

Hollinger, David A. *Science, Jews, and Secular Culture: Studies in Mid-twentieth-century American Intellectual History.* Princeton, NJ: Princeton University Press, 1996.

Nicholson, Ian A. M. "'Giving Up Maleness': Abraham Maslow, Masculinity and the Boundaries of Psychology." *History of Psychology* 4 (2001): 79–91.

Shaw, Robert, and Karn Colimore. "Humanistic Psychology as Ideology: An Analysis of Maslow's Contradictions." *Journal of Humanistic Psychology* 28 (1988): 51–74.

Ian A. M. Nicholson

MATUYAMA MOTONORI

(*b.* Usa, Oita Prefecture, Japan, 25 October 1884; *d.* Yamaguchi, Japan, 27 January 1958), *physics, geophysics, theoretical geology.*

Some discoveries are made before their time in the sense that there is a long delay from the time of discovery to the time when it is generally accepted. A good example is the paleomagnetic research by Japanese geophysicist Matuyama Motonori. In 1929 he proposed that the most recent reversal of the geomagnetic field took place in the early Quaternary. The chronology of geomagnetic reversals over the last five million years was established during the 1960s, contributing to the success of the theory of ocean floor spreading. These investigations identified four intervals of geomagnetic polarity, named the Brunhes normal, Matuyama reversed, Gauss normal, and Gilbert reversed epochs. The name of the Matuyama reversed epoch commemorates Matuyama's discovery three decades earlier.

Early Life. Matuyama Motonori changed his family name two times in his life. He was born in small village near the Usa Shrine in Oita prefecture on 25 October 1884. His name was at first registered as Suehara Motonori after his mother's family name, Suehara Kou. His father, Sumie Tengai, was a Zen Buddhist priest. When Tengai became the chief priest at an eminent Zen Buddhist temple in Yamaguchi, Tengai with his family migrated from Oita to Yamaguchi. At this time, Motonori changed his family name to Sumie. Finally, when he married in 1910, he changed his family name to Matuyama by adopting the name of his father-in-law.

Gravimetric Studies. Matuyama's research activity incorporates a wide range of geophysical research, including early papers on seismology, glacial ice deformation, and volcanology. Although his most influential work was investigating the remanent magnetization of basaltic rocks in Japan and neighboring countries, his major work was related to a gravimetric study. He entered the Imperial University in Kyoto (now Kyoto University) in 1908 and graduated in 1911. Then he was accepted in postgraduate school. His mentors were Shida Toshi and Shinjyo Shinzo, with whom he began his investigation of gravitation. He published his first report "On the Elasticity of the Earth and Earth's Crust," in 1912, coauthored with Shida.

In 1913 Matuyama was appointed lecturer at the Physical Institute of Kyoto University. He began studying coral reefs in 1915, when he noticed uplift in the Mariana Islands and subsidence in the Marshall Islands in the West Pacific. He stressed the importance of measuring the seabed shift and its angle of these areas. By a recommendation of Terada Torahiko, member of the Imperial Academy of Japan, to the Japanese Association for the Advancement of Science, tide gauge stations in the Saipan and Jaluit islands were established for that purpose.

In 1916 Matuyama became an assistant professor at the Geophysical Institute. His doctoral dissertation was published as "Determination of the Second Derivative of the Gravitational Potential on the Jaluit Atoll," in 1918. It suggested that minute features in the gravity field could reveal subsurface structure.

In 1919 Matuyama was sent abroad for two years. At the University of Chicago he performed experimental geology. Matuyama made laboratory models of glaciers, and by subjecting them to pressure and other variables, he studied deformation in ice. The paper detailing his findings was "On Some Physical Properties of Ice," published in *Journal of Geology* in 1920. On the basis of this work, he was recommended for membership in the honorary scientific society, Sigma Xi. Also in honor of his work, the Matuyama Rocks (66°40' S, 66°35' W) in the British Antarctic Territory were named in his honor. On his return to Japan in 1921, he was appointed the first professor at the Institute of Theoretical Geology in the Geological Institute.

Research on Earth's Magnetic Field. Matuyama was the first paleomagnetist to investigate the important questions of the timing of the reversal of Earth's magnetic field. In surveying magnetic anomalies in Japan, he found that the

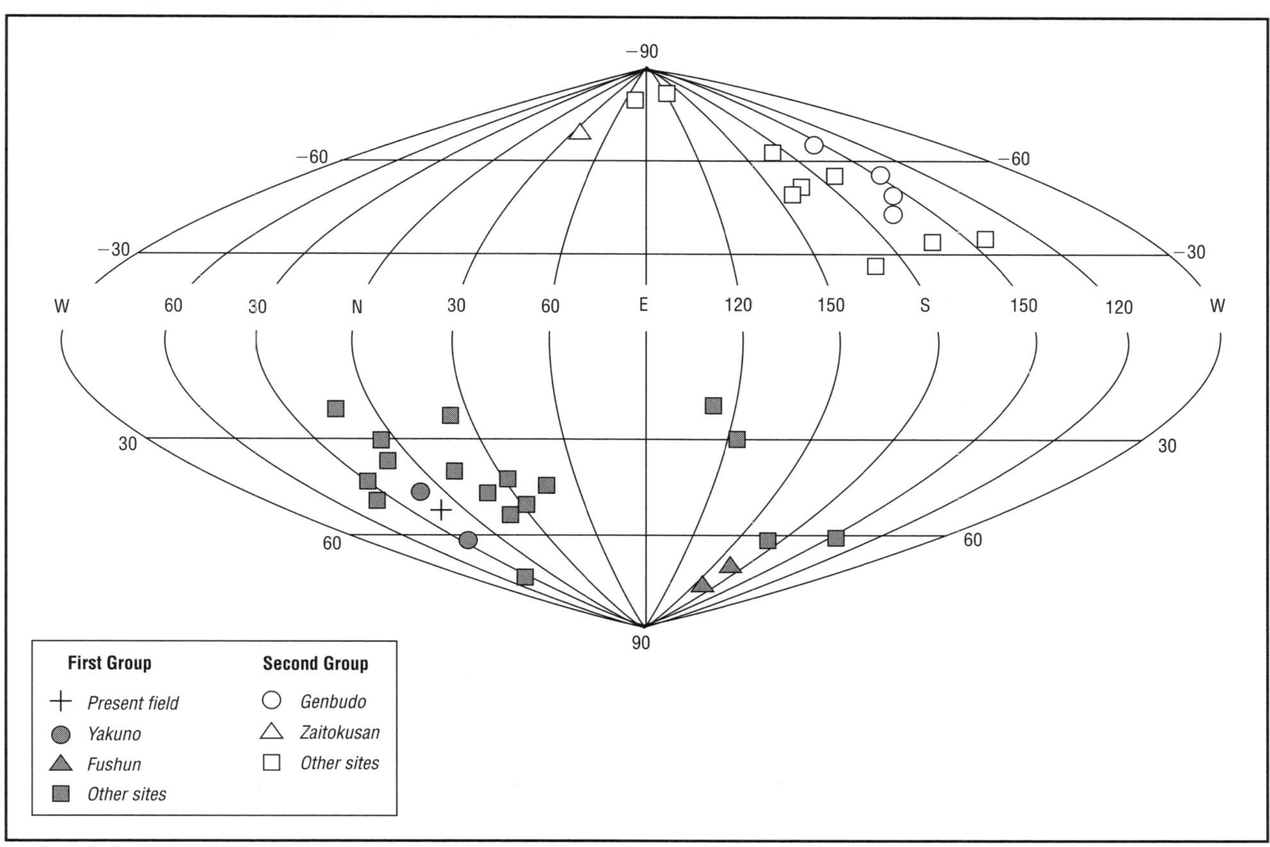

Figure 1. *The direction of magnetisation of basalt in Japan, Korea and northeastern district of China. Closed symbols represent normal polarity; open symbols represent reversed polarity.*

magnetic field was less intense over certain volcanic formations than it was elsewhere. This surprised him because volcanic formations contain magnetite, which might be expected to enhance the strength of the local magnetic field. The anomaly inspired him to investigate the matter. He collected samples from many parts of Japan and measured their magnetism. Early in April 1926, a specimen of basalt from Genbudo in the Hyōgo prefecture, a celebrated basalt cave, was collected for the purpose of examining its magnetic properties. When this block was tested by bringing it near a freely suspended magnetic needle, its magnetic north pole was found to be directed to the south and above the horizontal direction. This is nearly opposite to the present geomagnetic field at that locale. In May of the same year, four specimens of basalt were collected from Yakuno in Kyoto prefecture. When tested, their magnetic axes were found to nearly coincide with the present geomagnetic field. Genbudo and Yakuno are not very far from each other and have nearly the same magnetic field. Their basalts probably resulted from lavas of Quaternary eruptions. Subsequently, he collected more than one hundred specimens of basalt from thirty-six locations in other parts of Japan, in Tyosen (Korea), and in Manchuria (the northeastern region of China).

His most significant work based on these collections is "On the Direction of Magnetization of Basalt in Japan, Tyosen, and Manchuria" (1929). In this article he noted that the magnetism of the rocks fell into two distinct groups. One group, including the rocks from Yakuno, was directed toward the present geomagnetic field (normal magnetization). The other group, including rocks from Genbudo, was opposite the present field (reversed magnetization). His acute observation that the polarity of a rock correlated with its stratigraphic position or age led him to propose that long periods existed in Earth's history during which the polarity of the magnetic poles was the opposite of what it is now. However, for a long time his proposal was not accepted because geophysicists still did not have a sensible theory for the origin of the geomagnetic field. The response of his fellow scientists was neither disbelief nor outrage, but, rather, silence.

Gravity over the Japan Trench. From 1927 through 1932, Matuyama extended his determinations of gravity to new regions, notably Korea and Manchuria. He also explored the oceanic abyssal regions near the Caroline and Mariana island groups in the West Pacific and found free-air gravity anomalies in both of these tropical areas.

In 1934 and 1935 Matuyama led a gravity survey of the Japan Trench, a deep depression on the Pacific Ocean floor near Japan, in a submarine using instruments perfected by F. A. Vening Meinesz. This could be submerged to depths where the effects of waves on swinging pendulums became negligible. The Japan Trench is the site of frequent seismic activity, and the undersea earthquakes there trigger tsunamis. Later, one of his successors correlated the earthquakes with gravity anomalies.

Matuyama retired from Kyoto University in 1944. In his postretirement years he became the first president of Yamaguchi University. At both universities he actively engaged a large group of assistants and students in his research. He was well known as a devotee of Noh plays, the classic form of Japanese dance drama. He died of leukemia on 27 January 1958 at Yamaguchi.

Posthumous Vindication. The works of Matuyama played a dramatically important role in the progress of plate tectonics theory. A few years after Matuyama's death, Allan Cox began his research on geomagnetic reversals. The main result of his research was to corroborate Matuyama's conclusion of thirty years earlier, that the geomagnetic field had reversed its polarity at some time in the early Quaternary. Cox and others developed the remarkable geomagnetic polarity time scale. They named the most recent epochs Brunhes and Matuyama to honor two geophysicists who were among the first to perceive the significance of reversed magnetization in rock. Consisting of rock, the ocean floor produced—as it newly emerged from the midocean ridges—the pattern of the zebra stripes shown in oceanic magnetic anomaly profiles.

BIBLIOGRAPHY

WORKS BY MATUYAMA

With Shida Toshi. "On the Elasticity of the Earth and Earth's Crust—Part 3—Note on Hecker's Observation of Horizontal Pendulums." *Memoirs of the College of Science and Engineering, Kyoto Imperial University* 4, no. 1 (1912): 187–224.

With Shida Toshi. "On the Elasticity of the Earth and Earth's Crust—Part 6—Change of Plumb Line Referred to the Axis of the Earth as Found from the Result of the International Latitude Observations." *Memoirs of the College of Science and Engineering, Kyoto Imperial University* 4, no. 1 (1912): 277–284.

"Determination of the Second Derivative of the Gravitational Potential on the Jaluit Atoll." *Memoirs of the College of Science, Kyoto Imperial University* 3 (1918): 17–68.

"On Some Physical Properties of Ice." *Journal of Geology* 3 (1920): 607–631.

"On the Direction of Magnetization of Basalt in Japan, Tyosen, and Manchuria." *Proceedings of the Imperial Academy Japan* 5 (1929): 203–205.

今始庵だより [Letters from Konjian]. Yamaguchi, Japan: private publication, 1954.

OTHER SOURCES

Charton, Barbara. *A to Z of Marine Scientists.* New York: Facts on File, 2003.

Cox, Allan, ed. *Plate Tectonics and Geomagnetic Reversals.* San Francisco: W. H. Freeman, 1973.

Glen, William. *The Road to Jaramillo: Critical Years of the Revolution in Earth Sciences.* Stanford, CA: Stanford University Press, 1982.

Maenaka Kazuaki. 日も行く末ぞ久しき－地球科学者松山基範の物語 [The days pass away forever: The life story of earth scientist Matuyama Motonori]. Tokyo: Bungeisha, 2006.

Kazuaki Maenaka

MAUCHLY, JOHN WILLIAM

(*b.* Cincinnati, Ohio, 30 August 1907; *d.* Ambler, Pennsylvania, 9 January 1980), *computer science, physics, meteorology, statistics.*

Mauchly conceived of and co-invented, with John (J.) Presper Eckert, the Electronic Numerical Integrator and Computer (ENIAC), generally recognized as the world's first general-purpose, digital electronic computer. The ENIAC was designed and built between March 1943 and November 1945 at the University of Pennsylvania as a wartime project supported by the U.S. Army Ordnance Department. Comprising more than 17,000 vacuum tubes, the machine could perform 5,000 additions per second (and 350 multiplications and approximately 100 divisions or square-root operations per second), making it two to three orders of magnitude faster than the fastest numerical computing machinery then available.

Despite this technical achievement, the historical significance of the ENIAC and Mauchly's contributions to it lie primarily in establishing the general feasibility of electronic computers and their application to general data processing. Together with Eckert, Mauchly established the Eckert-Mauchly Computer Corporation in December 1947 (which was acquired by Remington Rand in 1950) and built the first commercially successful digital computer, the UNIVAC I (1951), to be sold in the United States.

Family Background and Early Life. John Mauchly was born in 1907 to Sebastian J. and Rachel Scheidemantal Mauchly in the town of Hartwell, Ohio, a suburb of Cincinnati. John's father, "S. J." Mauchly, was a high school science teacher who decided to pursue a PhD in physics (degree received in 1913) at the University of Cincinnati. S. J. Mauchly examined the relationship between atmospheric electricity and radio propagation, and he developed an instrument capable of measuring the vertical component of the Earth's magnetic field. This work and invention earned him a prestigious position at the Carnegie Institution of Washington (Washington, D.C.) and its newly established Department of Terrestrial Magnetism. John's father then secured his scientific reputation by discovering the diurnal (daily) variation in the Earth's magnetic field. John was influenced by his father's reputation and the meticulous attention to data that would guide both individuals' careers.

S. J. Mauchly's position at the Carnegie Institution brought the family to the Washington suburb of Chevy Chase, Maryland. Chevy Chase, at the time, was a brand-new streetcar suburb that offered quite a few members of the nation's emergent scientific elite an opportunity to assert a middle-class identity. Life in the suburbs reinforced John's aspirations for achievement. John entered McKinley Technical High School in 1921. McKinley was a strong college preparatory school affiliated with the U.S. Navy Yard in Washington. Mauchly excelled in a wide range of subjects. He also became the editor in chief of the school newspaper and earned the rank of commandant in the Washington area High School Cadet Corps.

The other significant influence in John's early life was the electrical and electromechanical culture of the 1920s. As a youth, John tinkered with his Meccano set, and with electrical devices such as a buzzer and battery. During grade school he devised a block signaling system for his model railroad set. By the time he was in high school, his interest in electrical apparatus afforded him a part-time job repairing electrical appliances for his neighbors and in helping to lay their household lines. In college he also spent a summer as part of an electrical work crew in North Carolina.

Mauchly entered Johns Hopkins University in 1925. Owing partly to his interest in electricity, as well as the requirements of his engineering scholarship, he first chose electrical engineering as his major. However, during his sophomore year he transferred into Hopkins's doctoral program in physics via a special program for high-achieving students. This decision may have reflected the continued influence of his father. The father also fell prey to a serious ailment—later diagnosed to be bacterial encephalitis—that took his life on Christmas Eve 1928. While still pursuing his doctoral degree, John Mauchly married Mary Augusta Walzl on 30 December 1930; the couple would have two children.

Early Research Involving Calculations. To properly understand Mauchly's contributions to the field of digital computing, it is important recognize that he began his career as a molecular physicist and not as someone dedicated to machine computation. He began his PhD under Gerhard Dieke, a Dutch émigré physicist known for his work in mass spectroscopy. This work introduced Mauchly to the rigors of calculation. Mass spectroscopy produced a series of photographic traces as intermediate data. It was necessary to then work backward through the physical models to computer molecular energy levels. This was a time when "computers" still referred to men and women who performed computations using calculating machinery. Such work required individuals, including Mauchly, to come up with a meticulous "plan of calculation" that carefully laid out a rigorous procedure for the work.

Mauchly completed his dissertation on "The Third Positive Group of Carbon Monoxide Bands" in 1932. The work was good enough to earn him his PhD; it did not immediately earn him a job. The year 1932 was simply a bad time to graduate. Aside from the Great Depression, U.S. research universities had begun to absorb the initial wave of scientific émigrés. Subatomic physics had also eclipsed molecular physics as the most promising area of study. Mauchly was able to secure a teaching position in 1933 at Ursinus College (Collegeville, Pennsylvania), a small liberal arts college located outside of Philadelphia. This provided him with an income, but neither the time nor resources with which to pursue research. Mauchly attempted for a while to continue his work in molecular physics using borrowed data, but eventually he began seeking other forms of data upon which he could perform analysis.

Mauchly spent the three summers between 1936 and 1938 as a "temporary assistant physicist and computer" at the Department of Terrestrial Magnetism—under his father's former supervisor, John Fleming. Being at DTM gave Mauchly access to their extensive repository of data on atmospheric electricity. Mauchly was also befriended by Julius Bartels, another scientific émigré, who brought with him a statistical approach to the study of geophysical morphology. Prior to Mauchly's arrival Bartels had extended Mauchly's father's observations by identifying a separate twenty-seven-day cycle in the Earth's magnetic field. Given that this corresponded to the Sun's period of rotation, this established an important connection between sunspots, cosmic rays, and the Earth's magnetic field. Excited by the prospect that his father's data could be massaged to generate new findings, Mauchly

Mauchly

proceeded to comb through the DTM data in search of other regularities.

Based on Bartels's insights, Mauchly developed a new approach to bivariate statistics. Using this technique, he felt he had identified a diurnal depression in midday ion densities that also exhibited a correlation between angle of incidence (as measured at observatories located at different latitudes) and the intensity of a solar effect. However, the article he submitted to the *Journal of Terrestrial Magnetism and Atmospheric Electricity* was turned down by Fleming, who served as the editor of the journal. Fleming rejected the article on the grounds that Mauchly lacked the theoretical understanding necessary to draw general conclusions about the cause of magnetic variation in the upper atmosphere. Mauchly also suspected that Fleming had apprehensions about allowing someone outside of DTM to publish an article using the institution's data.

The subsequent turns in Mauchly's career go a long way toward explaining the diverse forms of knowledge that he brought to the origins of the digital electronic computer. Fleming's initial rejection led Mauchly in several related directions. First, it caused Mauchly to shift his interests to meteorology. If the DTM's atmospheric data had to be regarded as private, the daily weather maps and precipitation data generated by the U.S. Weather Bureau were entirely in the public domain.

Fleming had also challenged Mauchly for relying on too short a period of analysis, and here Mauchly met his supervisor's challenge through two complementary strategies. The first was to delve further into statistics. A stronger statistical argument could legitimate inferences made from a limited pool of data. Corresponding with the Princeton statistician Samuel Wilks and the Columbia statistician Harold Hotelling enabled Mauchly to develop a more formal, if derivative technique for multivariate statistics called the "sphericity test." Fleming now accepted Mauchly's article, published in 1940 as "A Significance Test for Ellipticity in the Harmonic Dial," though it was clearly rewritten to emphasize the new statistical technique instead of theoretical inferences about the ionosphere. Separately, Mauchly produced a general account of his statistical technique, published in 1940 as "Significance Test for Sphericity of a Normal N-Variate Distribution" in the *Annals of Mathematical Statistics*, a leading statistical journal. These were the principal technical publications Mauchly issued prior to his work on the ENIAC.

Growing Interest in Computing. A complementary turn was his newfound interest in computing and computing machinery. At Ursinus Mauchly began employing students to work with the weather data, using funds provided by the National Youth Administration, a part of the Works Projects Administration. He also found several occasions to study the latest calculating machinery, including the IBM tabulators on display at the 1939 New York World's Fair and the Complex Number Calculator developed by George Stibitz at Bell Telephone Laboratories. Working from the published literature, Mauchly developed an analog computing instrument known as a harmonic analyzer (an analog computer uses continuous electrical signals or mechanical motion to directly model physical phenomena), which could identify regularities in statistical data.

As a physicist Mauchly was also exposed to the new "logic" tradition in physics. Electronic "scaling" circuits and "coincidence" circuits emerged as important components within the particle detectors used by atomic physicists. Upon coming across a 1939 article written by E. C. Stephenson and Ivan Getting in *Review of Scientific Instruments*, Mauchly began to consider how scaling circuits, which in effect could "count," could be used for high-speed calculating machinery.

Even as he began to explore this idea, his work in numerical meteorology began to bear some fruit. He presented his initial findings during the 1940 meeting of the American Association for the Advancement of Science in Philadelphia. It was during this presentation that Mauchly met John Atanasoff. Through considerable coincidence, Atanasoff was a molecular physicist at Iowa State College who had turned to computational machinery as a means of extending his scientific career. Atanasoff had designed, and, with the aid of his graduate assistant, Clifford Berry, built a specialized computer that used electronics to help solve large systems of linear equations as found in molecular physics and other disciplines.

A main point of historical dispute has to do with the knowledge Mauchly derived from a visit with Atanasoff in Iowa. Although the Atanasoff-Berry Computer was never fully operational, all of the electronic components were assembled and available for demonstration. Mauchly spent several days in Iowa conversing with Atanasoff and his assistant. Atanasoff was also speaking with members of the National Defense Research Committee (the civilian U.S. science mobilization effort) and became aware of the broader use of electronics for computing.

What can be said is that as a result of this visit Mauchly grew excited about the prospects of electronic computers. Given his interest in statistics, Mauchly could envision a very different machine more similar to the mechanical calculators he used for his statistical work. He redoubled his efforts in electronics. He also decided to enroll in a war training program in electronics at the University of Pennsylvania. Then, when the opportunity arose, Mauchly abandoned his tenured position at Ursinus to take up a teaching position in electrical engineering at Penn.

The ENIAC. Mauchly played a crucial role in the development of the the ENIAC (Project PX according to its wartime designation) along with Presper Eckert and other colleagues at the University of Pennsylvania's Moore School of Electrical Engineering. Physically, the ENIAC was made up of forty frames arranged in a U-shaped layout whose length totaled eighty feet. These frames housed thirty semi-autonomous units, of which twenty were called *accumulators,* which behaved basically like adding machines in that they could add, subtract, or store a ten-digit number and its sign (+/-). There were two other arithmetic units, namely a *high-speed multiplier* and a *divider/square-rooter.* The ENIAC also had three *function tables* with a large array of manual switches whose values could be read at electronic speeds. These function tables were necessary to represent the nonlinear, incalculable component of the mathematical equation for exterior ballistics (the flight of an artillery shell), which was considered the most important application by ENIAC's sponsor, the Army Ordnance Department.

Meanwhile, the easiest way to recognize the novel design of the ENIAC is by looking at its programming system. It is significant in this respect that the ENIAC's accumulators did not have all of the functions of an adding machine. While a mechanical adding machine stores two numbers, x and y, in computing the sum x + y, an accumulator was designed to store only one number so that every addition (and subtraction) had to occur by precisely coordinating the action of two different units. Similar coordination was required to perform both multiplication and division. Coordination was achieved through a system of wires and plug boards that routed a *program pulse.* The first program pulse was generated by the ENIAC's *initiating unit.* And whereas there was a *master programmer* used to execute a particular operation for a fixed number of iterations, programming the ENIAC required the careful coordination of events at the scale of the entire machine. (Though not part of its original design, the ENIAC could also execute a conditional branch instruction through a procedure known as *magnitude discrimination,* which tested for the sign of a given number. This was a later addition, not made by Mauchly.)

While this description is a way to visualize the ENIAC as it was designed, it remains an anachronistic description that obscures the design's historical origins. Historically the ENIAC and Mauchly's contributions to it emerged through the confluence of several related developments. The first was the development of an analog mechanical computing instrument known as the *differential analyzer,* and the presence of one of these units at the Moore School. The differential analyzer was developed by Harold Hazen and Vannevar Bush at MIT, an extension of which was made by Moore School instructor Irven Travis under contract with the Army Ordnance Department.

Upon completing this work, Travis gained recognition as a regional expert on computing instruments, and was hired by General Electric as a consultant. One of the reports Travis wrote for GE described the possibility of a numerical alternative to the differential analyzer, one that was based on ganging together a bank of adding machines; he also mentioned the possibility that electronics might be necessary to deliver the requisite speed. Mauchly insisted that he never saw a copy of Travis's report. However, Mauchly did speak with Travis at some length about computing machines prior to Travis's departure for a war assignment.

Finally, war mobilization brought the Army Ordnance Department, and its new Ballistic Research Laboratory (Aberdeen, Maryland), to renew its affiliation with the Moore School. In addition to commandeering the Moore School's differential analyzer, BRL asked the Moore School to assemble a human computing unit, and to use numerical methods to produce ballistics tables. That such work was taking place at the Moore School was well known; Mauchly's wife, Mary, also served as one of the human computers prior to the Army's evaluation of the ENIAC proposal.

For a while, Mauchly's interests remained with meteorology. However, as his interest in electronic computers grew, the Army's need for ballistics tables—and the considerable backlog that existed by late 1942—provided a suitable rationale for building one. Though the evidence here is scarce, it appears that Mauchly did consider the possibility of designing the numerical equivalent of a differential analyzer using the circuit design techniques employed by Atanasoff (Atanasoff basically used coincidence, or real "logic" circuits rather than counters, to perform arithmetic). Kindly rebuffed by Atanasoff based on the advice Atanasoff received from his patent attorney, Mauchly turned instead to the idea mentioned, if not sketched out by, Travis. Though the idea was not fully original, it at least "belonged" to the Moore School.

The ENIAC's design was clearly influenced by the attempt to implement a numerical alternative for the differential analyzer. What one sees as its "data-flow architecture" owes its origins to the differential analyzer (and to analog computers more generally), where "data" travel simultaneously throughout the system during computation. However, numerical methods were substantially different from those of analog computation. Computation had to take place through sequential operations that spread the computation out over time. This was something entirely familiar to the human computers who produced ballistics tables; it was also something familiar to Mauchly through his knowledge about creating a "plan of calculation." Moreover, so long as the ENIAC was designed to support numerical calculation, it was not limited to a specific class of mathematical problems, as was the differential analyzer. The ENIAC, in any event, was an amalgam of these two technical traditions.

The fact that wartime exigencies led to a rushed design effort is evident in both versions of the ENIAC "proposal." The first was an informal memo submitted by Mauchly to the Moore School's war projects supervisor in August 1942; the second was the formal proposal Mauchly and Eckert submitted to the army in April 1943 with the assistance of at least one other engineer. Though both documents spoke of a central programming device, neither had any substantial description of how such a unit would allow the ENIAC to execute a defined sequence of operations. There was still no design for the programming system when the army officially approved the project in June 1943.

The ENIAC's programming system emerged in a rather contingent manner. Following standard engineering practice, the project engineers set out to demonstrate a proof of concept by assembling two accumulators. It was necessary to interconnect the two units to provide a meaningful demonstration. And despite mention of a central program control unit, it was easier to implement the interconnection through a local system of controls placed on each accumulator. Hoping, nevertheless, not to have to substantially reengineer the accumulator as they moved beyond the two-accumulator test, those on the project, including Mauchly, made an educated guess about the number of local controls necessary for future use. Most likely, the decision to take such an approach was reinforced by the fact that the differential analyzer, in its normal mode of operation, was physically reconfigured for each equation. This was the historical origin of the distributed programming system that became the hallmark of the ENIAC.

The historical literature has been somewhat divided about Mauchly's contributions to the actual development of the ENIAC. The most important thing to note is that Mauchly served as a consultant, rather than as the project's director. Project PX was a major wartime project, one that the university did not entrust to an untenured faculty member with so little background in electronics. This is not to say that Mauchly had no role in the project. Mauchly kept an eye on the validity of the mathematical algorithms, was among those who reviewed the programming system, and was actively involved with filing patent disclosures. (Aside from his interests in doing so, this was made necessary by the university's contractual obligations to the military.) Mauchly also served as an important sounding board for Eckert on all aspects of the ENIAC's design. Yet, so long as Project PX was cast as an engineering endeavor, where the Moore School was expected to deliver the machine described in the proposal, the principal expertise required for doing so lay with the Moore School engineers. As the project wore on, Mauchly, at least in the eyes of the engineers, became more an adviser to the project than someone directly involved in the crucial task of building the machine.

However, existing accounts of Mauchly's contributions are based on a misconception of the process of invention. Moreover, the historical literature tends to lump together Mauchly and Eckert's contributions and describe them as sole inventors, which is itself an artifice of the system of assignments in the U.S. patent system. Mauchly's contributions, and those of his colleagues at the University of Pennsylvania, were incremental in nature, in a way that is consistent with what is known in general about the inventive process.

It should also still be clear that Mauchly played a crucial role in the invention of the ENIAC. Despite all of the resources that were devoted to war research, Mauchly alone possessed the different forms of knowledge and technical interests, and resided at an institutional location that produced a versatile, digital electronic computer during World War II. Other technical developments in electronics and the considerable advances in applied mathematics during the war would have ensured that a digital electronic computer was not far off on the horizon. Nevertheless, Mauchly stood at the crucial juncture necessary to "invent" the ENIAC.

Subsequent Career. Shortly after the war, and the successful completion of the ENIAC, Mauchly suffered a personal tragedy when his wife, Mary, drowned in an accident in 1946. In 1948, Mauchly married Kathleen "Kay" McNulty, a mathematician who had been one of the first ENIAC programmers. After the war, Mauchly also found an opportunity to try his hand at entrepreneurship. The cultural cachet of being an "inventor" was not something so easily cast aside. Mauchly, along with Eckert, established the Electronic Controls Company in 1946, and the firm was formally incorporated as the Eckert-Mauchly Computer Corporation in December 1947. Working first with a contract from the U.S. Census Bureau (the contract was also supervised by the National Bureau of Standards), Eckert and Mauchly began cultivating a market for their digital computer, the UNIVAC I. At EMCC, and then at Remington Rand, Mauchly focused his energies on the study of computer applications and on marketing. He was among those who helped develop a computer's early instruction sets (the operations that any given computer directly recognizes and supports), by working with the early programmers at the National Bureau of Standards.

Mauchly's self-taught marketing skills were eventually eclipsed by the professionally trained marketing staff of

John Mauchly. *Dr. John Mauchly with suitcase-sized computer.* **AP IMAGES.**

Remington Rand. In 1959 he left the firm to create his own independent consulting firm, Mauchly Associates, which he then followed with another venture, Dynatrend, in 1967. Here he found a more permanent niche as a consultant within the emerging computer services industry, where he helped to introduce quantitative project management techniques to U.S. construction firms and other businesses.

Mauchly and Eckert would have retained their reputation as the inventors of the digital electronic computer had it not been for an acrimonious patent dispute (*Honeywell v. Sperry Rand Corp*), filed with the federal district court in Minnesota, whose 1973 decision invalidated the 1964 ENIAC patent. Debates from this latter period have polarized historical memories, and have tended to occlude Mauchly's contributions. Mauchly retired to the quiet suburb of Ambler, Pennsylvania, outside of Philadelphia. He died in 1980, at age seventy-two following several bouts with illness. His wife, Kathleen Mauchly, survived him, marrying the photographer Severo Antonelli in 1985; Kathleen McNulty Mauchly Antonelli died in April 2006.

BIBLIOGRAPHY

John Mauchly's papers may be found in the Annenberg Rare Book and Manuscript Library, University of Pennsylvania, Philadelphia, Pennsylvania. See also UPD 8.10, ENIAC Papers (ENIAC Patent Trial Collection, 1864-1973), University Archives and Records Center, University of Pennsylvania.

WORKS BY MAUCHLY

"A Significance Test for Ellipticity in the Harmonic Dial." *Journal of Terrestrial Magnetism and Atmospheric Electricity* 45 (September 1940): 145–148.

"Significance Test for Sphericity of a Normal N-Variate Distribution." *Annals of Mathematical Statistics* 11 (1940): 204–209.

OTHER SOURCES

Akera, Atsushi. *Calculating a Natural World: Scientists, Engineers, and Computers during the Rise of U.S. Cold War Research.* Cambridge, MA: MIT Press, 2006.

Aspray, William. *John von Neumann and the Origins of Modern Computing.* Cambridge, MA: MIT Press, 1990.

Burks, Alice R., and Arthur W. Burks. "The ENIAC: First General Purpose Electronic Computer." *Annals of the History of Computing* 3 (1981): 310–389. Best article-length technical description of the ENIAC.

———, and Arthur W. Burks. *The First Electronic Computer: The Atanasoff Story.* Ann Arbor: University of Michigan Press, 1988.

Costello, John. "As the Twig Is Bent: The Early Life of John Mauchly." *IEEE Annals of the History of Computing* 18 (1996): 45–50.

Goldstine, Herman H. *The Computer: From Pascal to von Neumann.* Princeton, NJ: Princeton University Press, 1993. A historical account published by one of the participants. Originally issued in 1972.

McCartney, Scott. *ENIAC: The Triumphs and Tragedies of the World's First Computer.* New York: Walker, 1999. An accessible, nonacademic history of Mauchly and Eckert.

Stern, Nancy. *From ENIAC to UNIVAC: An Appraisal of the Eckert-Mauchly Computers.* Bedford, MA: Digital Press, 1981.

Atsushi Akera

MAUPERTUIS, PIERRE LOUIS MOREAU DE

MAUPERTUIS, PIERRE LOUIS MOREAU DE (*b.* St. Malo, France, 28 September 1698; *d.* Basel, Switzerland, 27 July, 1759), *mathematics, mechanics, natural philosophy, life sciences.* For the original article on Maupertuis see *DSB,* vol. 9.

Maupertuis was an original and eclectic thinker whose contributions to the science of the eighteenth century ranged widely across fields and genres. He was at the center of scientific activity from the 1730s through most of the 1750s, first in Paris and then in Berlin. His career was fraught with controversies and contradictions, bitterness and triumph. Expending considerable effort in forging a public reputation, initially as a mathematician, then more broadly as a man of letters and a philosopher, he ventured into the speculative areas of life science and metaphysics as well as mathematics and mechanics. He was a favorite of princes and duchesses, and a friend of some of the best mathematicians and philosophers of his day. His major scientific work falls into the following categories: geodesy (the shape of Earth), rational mechanics (principle of least action), and life science (reproduction and heredity). In addition, he wrote on mathematics, cosmology, metaphysics and the philosophy of language. When the original *DSB* article was written, very little research on Maupertuis had made use of unpublished sources (especially letters), or sources held in archives outside of Paris, and as a result, Maupertuis's published works had not been linked to their historical and cultural context. This update offers a revised perspective on the scientific work of this Enlightenment figure. For a full account of Maupertuis's career, institutional position, scientific correspondence, and works, see Terrall (2002), which has full references to unpublished archival material.

Maupertuis has been remembered, in the history of science and in physics and biology textbooks (Glass, 1959; Guéroult, 1934; and Brunet, 1938) for certain of his ideas that gained significance through some relation, genealogical or not, to more modern concepts such as evolution or the dynamical principle of least action. Though his reputation as a brilliant innovator was largely eclipsed by the end of the eighteenth century, in part because of Voltaire's witty attacks, in his day Maupertuis was a major player in the European scientific and literary worlds. The social location of science and philosophy in these worlds, where hierarchical power relations coexisted with the cosmopolitan and egalitarian ideals of the republic of letters, informed the articulation of Maupertuis's ideas, the self-conscious presentation of these ideas to his contemporaries, and the reactions they provoked.

Defense of Newtonian Theory. Although Newton's mathematics was well known in France around the turn of the eighteenth century, Maupertuis was one of the first French mathematicians to defend the Newtonian theory of gravitation. He traveled to London in 1728, where he made social contact with Newtonian mathematicians and physicists, and other members of the Royal Society. This trip, however, was not in any substantive way the source of his Newtonianism. His own work on attraction, especially the mathematical application of gravitation theory to the vexed problem of the shape of the Earth, dates from somewhat later, after his mathematical studies with Johann Bernoulli in Basel. Bernoulli was anything but a Newtonian. He objected strenuously to empty space and action-at-a-distance, and he considered Continental mathematics, in the Leibnizian tradition, far superior to that of the English. His importance for Maupertuis's mathematical career, documented in their extensive correspondence, cannot be overestimated.

Little did Bernoulli suspect, while he painstakingly reviewed Maupertuis's mathematical problem solutions, that his protégé would subsequently become famous as a pioneering French Newtonian. In fact, Maupertuis

Pierre Louis de Maupertuis. *Engraving of the expedition led by Maupertuis.* SPL/PHOTO RESEARCHERS, INC.

solidified his position in the Paris Academy of Sciences in the early 1730s with a series of papers applying Leibnizian analysis to problems from Newton's *Principia.* He made a conscious choice to work on controversial material, but he did not initially present it as a defense of Newton. His work in geodesy came directly out of this Leibnizian-Newtonian mathematics, because the shape of Earth was a problem Newton had discussed in some detail. Having established his credibility in the academy on the basis of mathematics, Maupertuis published a comparison of Cartesian and Newtonian cosmologies for a non-specialist audience. This book, *Discours sur les figures des astres* (1732), brought the theory of universal attraction to the attention of a literary audience in France well before Voltaire wrote his *Letters on the English* (1738). Indeed, Voltaire admired Maupertuis's book and turned to the mathematician for clarification of Newtonian physics.

Geodetic Expedition. In 1736 Maupertuis led a high-profile expedition mounted by the academy to make astronomical and geodetical measurements in the Arctic. This expedition, the product of a dispute about measuring and calculating techniques with implications for the Newtonian theory of gravitation, gave Maupertuis the opportunity to expand his reputation outward from the specialist environment of the academy and the mathematics community to the genteel literary public. On his return from Lapland, he was hailed as a hero by the social elite, who appreciated the exotic combination of Arctic travel and mathematical acumen. He was also lionized by Voltaire and his allies, because the Lapland results supported Newton's mathematical deduction that Earth must be slightly flattened at the poles. The Paris Observatory astronomers, headed by Jacques Cassini, were less enthusiastic about the new measurements, which called into question their own measurements of the Paris meridian. Cassini objected to Maupertuis's astronomical practices and to his use of mathematics; although the Paris meridian measurements seemed to imply an elongated Earth, this was strictly an empirical matter and had nothing to do with Cartesian mechanics. (There was no Cartesian explanation for an elongated Earth.) Although the conflict was complicated by Cassini's hostility toward universal gravitation, this was not essentially a dispute about cosmology. Nevertheless, because of the unmistakable Newtonian overtones of the flattened Earth, the Lapland expedition brought related cosmological and philosophical issues into the public eye.

Berlin Academy and Principle of Least Action. By 1740, Maupertuis's expedition account had made him famous throughout Europe. Frederick II, the new king of Prussia, attempted to woo him to Berlin to revitalize the Prussian Academy of Sciences. Disillusioned about the prospects for a viable academy in Berlin after an initial visit in 1740 to 1741, when Frederick was at war in Silesia, Maupertuis ultimately succumbed to the Prussian monarch's flattering attentions. He moved to Berlin in 1745 as president of the Academy of Sciences and as a key player in the lively intellectual life of the court at Potsdam, where several French philosophers and writers had taken refuge from censorship at home. Maupertuis governed the Berlin Academy autocratically, modeling his administrative style on that of the Prussian king. He was genuinely interested in enhancing the reputation of Berlin as a home for serious scientific and philosophical endeavors, and he worked hard to attract foreign scholars to Berlin—a project that met with only mixed success.

Shortly before moving to Berlin, Maupertuis introduced the principle of least action to the Paris Academy, in a paper about the refraction and reflection of light. He framed it as a mathematical version of the metaphysical economy principle that nature acts as simply as possible: "Whenever there is any change in nature, the quantity of action necessary for this change is the smallest possible" (1756, Vol. 4, p. 36). In Berlin, unlike Paris, the academy devoted official attention to speculative philosophy, or metaphysics (one of the academy's classes was devoted to this subject, explicitly excluded from the Paris Academy). Maupertuis's first paper in Berlin derived the principle of least action for mechanics (including static equilibrium) from a metaphysical economy principle. Because it was both a unifying principle and a mathematical expression of final causes, he not only brought together different problem areas in physics (optics, mechanics, and statics), but also made his principle the cornerstone of a proof for the existence of God. Maupertuis used the Berlin Academy to promote his rational mechanics, based on this *extremum* principle. He found an exceptionally able and willing ally in Leonhard Euler, who applied the variational calculus to problems outlined by Maupertuis in less rigorous form. Maupertuis revisited his metaphysical-mechanical principle in several publications, most extensively in *Essai de cosmologie* (1750), where he made mathematical physics the cornerstone of a rationalist theology that found evidence for God in the most universal principles and offered an alternative to natural theology based on admiration of the details of divine design.

Theory of Generation. Maupertuis was also well known for his theory of generation. In *Vénus physique* (1745, an expanded version of a short anonymous work published the previous year), he gathered evidence from microscopy, anatomy, animal breeding, and everyday experience to argue for an epigenetic theory of fetal development. In this model, male and female seminal fluids, made up of heterogeneous corpuscles derived from the different parts of the parents' bodies, combine to form germs, the particles are driven by their own teleological *instincts* or *affinities* for each other. These active properties allow for many possible outcomes within certain parameters, and they locate the capability to produce order in organic matter itself. Maupertuis used chemical affinities, forces of a different order than mechanical forces of impact, to describe organic forces. Strong affinities between those elements "appropriate for forming traits similar to those of the individual parent" account for resemblances between parents and offspring (1980, p. 139).

Maupertuis refined his notion of the forces responsible for organization in *Système de la nature* (1751). The focus here shifted from arguments about preexistence and epigenesis to a fuller justification of a dynamic conception of matter. Chemistry retained its analogical role as the counterpoint to mechanical reductionism, but in spite of their selectivity and flexibility, affinities could not fully explain organic form and function. "We must have recourse to some principle of intelligence, to something similar to what we call desire, aversion, memory" (Maupertuis, 1756, Vol. 2, p. 147). Desire and aversion operate as forces analogous to the affinities that propel, unite, and separate chemical substances; memory links each organic element to its corresponding part in the parent organism. Every element "retains a kind of memory (*souvenir*) of its previous situation and will resume it whenever it can, in order to form the same part in the fetus" (Vol. 2, p. 158).

Though his position in Berlin did give him a high profile, Maupertuis was frustrated in his efforts to transform the Prussian academy to his own specifications. He became increasingly combative and embittered about the situation in Berlin. In the 1750s his health deteriorated as he suffered recurrent bouts of debilitating fever and lung disease. He engaged in a bitter and rather pointless controversy with a former friend, Samuel König, about the authorship of the principle of least action. (For a full account of the institutional and intellectual ramifications of this dispute, see Terrall, 2002, Chap. 9.) Voltaire also turned against him in this period, due not so much to philosophical differences as to personal resentment and competition for favor with the Prussian king. It was often said, in the 1750s and subsequently, that Maupertuis's poor health was due to his contretemps with Voltaire. This was certainly not the case. He continued in this period to produce new work, especially on generation and inheritance, and to re-edit older texts for new editions. His final contribution to the Berlin Academy journal in 1756 reprised his metaphysical mechanics in the context of a discussion of epistemology and the necessity of the laws of motion. He left Berlin for France for the final time in 1756, on the eve of the Seven Years' War, and spent the last three years of his life (1756–1759) caught between allegiance to France, his native land, and to Frederick, his most illustrious patron. He died at the home of Johann Bernoulli in Basel on his way back to Berlin in 1759.

SUPPLEMENTARY BIBLIOGRAPHY

WORKS BY MAUPERTUIS

Vénus physique: suivi de La lettre sur le progres des sciences. Edited by Patrick Tort. Paris: Aubier-Montagne, 1980.

Oeuvres de Mr. de Maupertuis. 4 Vols. Lyon, France : J.M. Bruyset, 1756.

OTHER SOURCES

Beeson, David. *Maupertuis: An Intellectual Biography.* Oxford: Voltaire Foundation, 1992.

Brunet, Pierre. *Étude historique sur la principe de la moindre action.* Paris: Hermann, 1938.

Glass, Bentley, William Straus, and Owsei Temkin, eds. *Forerunners of Darwin, 1745–1859.* Baltimore, MD: Johns Hopkins University Press, 1959.

Greenberg, John. *The Problem of the Earth's Shape from Newton to Clairaut.* Cambridge, U.K.: Cambridge University Press, 1995.

Guéroult, Michel. *Dynamique et métaphysique leibniziennes.* Paris: Les belles lettres, 1934.

Hoffheimer, Michael. "Maupertuis and the Eighteenth-Century Critique of Preexistence." *Journal of the History of Biology* 15 (1982): 119–144.

Terrall, Mary. *The Man Who Flattened the Earth: Maupertuis and the Sciences in the Enlightenment.* Chicago: University of Chicago Press, 2002.

Mary Terrall

MAYOR (FORMERLY MAYER), ALFRED GOLDSBOROUGH

(*b.* Frederick, Maryland, 16 April 1868; *d.* Loggerhead Key, Dry Tortugas, Florida, 24 June 1922), *marine biology, taxonomy, ecology.*

A pioneer in jellyfish and comb jelly taxonomy, Mayor was the author respectively of the monumental three-volume *Medusae of the World* and the classic *Ctenophores of the Atlantic Coast of North America.* Also the founder and director of the Tortugas Laboratory of the Carnegie Institution of Washington, the first tropical marine laboratory in the Western Hemisphere, he later conducted seminal work on the ecology of coral reefs.

Education and Formative Career. The son of the noted American physicist Alfred Marshall Mayer and Katherine Duckett Goldsborough, Mayor evidenced an interest in natural history and scientific illustration at an early stage of his life, but, following the wishes of his father, enrolled in a program in engineering and physics in the Stevens Institute of Technology, in Hoboken, New Jersey. After graduating from that institution in 1889, he pursued advanced study in physics, first at Clark University and later at the University of Kansas, but decided in 1892 to enroll in the zoology program at Harvard University.

As a student in the marine biological laboratory of Alexander Agassiz, in Newport, Rhode Island, during the summer of 1892, Mayor displayed a special affinity for the study of jellyfishes and extraordinary skill in illustrating them in color. His ability soon came to the attention of Agassiz, a renowned marine zoologist and director of Harvard's Museum of Comparative Zoology. Agassiz invited Mayor to coauthor a book with him on the medusae, or jellyfishes, of the western Atlantic Ocean. Mayor gladly assented, but, because of his early interest in butterflies and moths, his mathematical ability, and the influence of the Harvard zoology instructor Charles Benedict Davenport, Mayor elected to conduct a study of lepidopteran wing scales as the topic of his dissertation. He completed this statistical study under the direction of the morphologist Edward L. Mark, and received the doctor of science degree from Harvard in 1896.

In the meantime, he accompanied Agassiz on collecting excursions to the Caribbean in 1893 and to Oceania on three occasions between 1896 and 1900. During this time, Agassiz also sent Mayor to several locations on the eastern coast of North America and to the Dry Tortugas to collect specimens of medusae and ctenophores. In addition, Agassiz appointed Mayor as an assistant in the Museum of Comparative Zoology. Despite chafing under the authoritarian style of Agassiz, Mayor held that position until 1900, when he was appointed as the curator of zoology for the Brooklyn Museum.

Director of Tortugas Laboratory. By then, Mayor was the author or coauthor of numerous articles and monographs and had gained international notice for his work, which included (either alone or with Agassiz) fifty-three new taxa, or scientific names and descriptions, of jellyfishes and comb jellies. During his four-year tenure at the Brooklyn Museum, Mayor succeeded in building the collections of that institution, launching two scientific journals, and continuing his research. He yearned for a higher position, however, and, in 1902, shortly after learning of the interest of the newly formed Carnegie Institution of Washington in establishing a marine biological laboratory, he began a vigorous campaign to persuade its trustees to develop such a station in the Gulf of Mexico, on Loggerhead Key, in the Dry Tortugas, with the hope that he would be appointed as its director. His efforts came to fruition late in 1903, when the Carnegie Institution established the Tortugas Laboratory, and appointed Mayor as the director of the first tropical marine biological laboratory in the Western Hemisphere.

The initial group of researchers arrived at the Tortugas Laboratory during the late spring and early summer of 1905. Open only from late March to early August of each year, the laboratory proved to be ideal for the study of tropical marine life, but it faced formidable problems because of its isolation and the frequency of hurricanes in the area. Nevertheless, Mayor attracted scores of able scientists to the laboratory, and conducted research on his own as well, including many studies of jellyfish pulsation. He also continued his taxonomic research and his work on the medusae book, a project from which Agassiz withdrew in 1904.

Mayor decided to expand the scope of the work, and titled it *Medusae of the World.* Published in 1910, the three-volume study gained immediate recognition. Comprising 735 pages of text, 428 text figures, and 76 colored plates, all prepared by Mayor, this work was still being cited frequently almost a century after its publication. In 1912 Mayor published a book on the ctenophores, or comb jellies, of the western Atlantic, and it has endured as well. Eighty-seven taxa of jellyfish and comb jellies described by Mayor and Mayor and Agassiz remain valid today.

In 1913 Mayor extended the mission of the laboratory to encompass the South Pacific, and began to focus his research on the ecology of coral reefs. He continued his seasonal studies there through 1921, investigating the effects of temperature, depth, and silt on coral growth and conducting research on the nature of reef-formation. He employed a diving helmet in an effort to develop a fuller understanding of the origin and development of reefs. One of the several grids he laid out was located many years later, making a long-term comparison possible. In recognition of his contributions, the National Academy of Sciences elected Mayor to membership in 1916. An ardent patriot who blamed Germany for launching war in 1914, he came to loathe his Teutonic-based name, and had it legally changed from Mayer to Mayor in August 1918.

Personal Information. In 1900 Mayor married Harriet Randolph Hyatt, daughter of the able naturalist Alpheus Hyatt and a gifted sculptor. They had four children: Alpheus Hyatt, Katherine, Brantz, and Barbara. Harriet contracted tuberculosis around 1910, and later spent many months in a sanatorium and in Europe in an effort to recover. Her condition improved, and she lived to the age of ninety-two. Mayor later caught the disease, and, debilitated by its effects, died at Loggerhead Key on 24 June 1922, after fainting and falling into shallow water there. A year later, friends and fellow researchers at the Tortugas Laboratory erected a monument to him on Loggerhead Key. After the death of Mayor, the Tortugas Laboratory received less support from the Carnegie Institution, though it continued to operate through the 1939 season. Mayor's legacy continues, however, through his classic books, one hundred publications, eighty-seven valid taxa, nineteen patronyms, and a host of significant papers published by the scientists who conducted research at the Tortugas Laboratory during his administration.

BIBLIOGRAPHY

A complete bibliography of Mayor's publications appears in Lester D. Stephens and Dale R. Calder, Seafaring Scientist. *Major collections of Mayor's papers are in the following repositories: American Philosophical Society Library, Philadelphia, Pennsylvania; Brantz and Ana Mayor Private Collection, Hanover, New Hampshire; Brooklyn Museum Archives, Brooklyn, New York; New York Public Library, Manuscripts and Special Collections, New York, New York; Princeton University Library, Department of Rare Books and Special Collections, Princeton, New Jersey; Syracuse University, E. S. Bird Library, Special Collections Department, Syracuse, New York.*

WORKS BY MAYOR

Medusae of the World. 3 vols. Carnegie Institution of Washington Publication 109. Washington, DC: Carnegie Institution of Washington, 1910. Reprint edition, Amsterdam: Asher, 1977.

Ctenophores of the Atlantic Coast of North America. Carnegie Institution of Washington Publication 162. Washington, DC: Carnegie Institution of Washington, 1912.

OTHER SOURCES

Betz, Joseph J. "Pioneer Biologist." *Sea Frontiers: Bulletin of the International Oceanographic Foundation* 11, no. 5 (1965): 286–295.

Colin, Patrick L. "A Brief History of the Tortugas Laboratory and the Department of Marine Biology, Carnegie Institution of Washington." In *Oceanography: The Past,* edited by Mary Sears and Daniel Merriman. New York: Springer-Verlag, 1980.

Davenport, Charles Benedict. *Biographical Memoir of Alfred Goldsborough Mayor, 1868–1922.* Washington, DC: National Academy of Sciences, 1926. Although informative, this account is flawed by its eugenics bias.

Ebert, James D. "Carnegie Institution of Washington and Marine Biology: Naples, Woods Hole, and Tortugas." *Biological Bulletin* 168 (1985): 172–182.

Stephens, Lester D., and Dale R. Calder. *Seafaring Scientist: Alfred Goldsborough Mayor, Pioneer in Marine Biology.* Columbia: University of South Carolina Press, 2006.

Lester D. Stephens

MAYR, ERNST WALTER (*b.* Kempten, Bavaria, Germany, 5 July 1904; *d.* Bedford, Massachusetts, 3 February 2005), *ornithology, zoogeography, systematics, evolutionary biology, history and philosophy of biology.*

As an architect of the synthetic theory of evolution of the 1940s, Mayr analyzed the origin of biodiversity and the concept of biological species, making the species problem a central concern of evolutionary biology. Later he became an influential historian and philosopher of biology.

Early Ornithological Career. Mayr was the middle of three brothers. Their father Otto Mayr was a successful jurist and an enthusiastic naturalist. On weekends, he and his wife Helene Pusinelli showed their children birds, flowers, mushrooms, and fossils. Mayr thus became a young naturalist and soon spent nearly every free minute of his life watching birds around Dresden, where Mrs. Mayr had moved with her boys after the death of her husband in 1917. Immediately after Ernst had passed his high school examination in February 1923, he discovered a pair of rare migrating ducks, an observation that brought him in contact with Dr. Erwin Stresemann in Berlin, Germany's leading ornithologist.

Following a family tradition Mayr intended to become a medical doctor and entered medical school in Greifswald on the coast of the Baltic Sea in 1923. He had selected this university because of the excellent birding areas nearby. Between semesters he worked as a volunteer for short periods at the Museum of Natural History in Berlin with Erwin Stresemann, who wrote of him in a letter: "I have discovered … a rising star, a young studiosus med[icinae] by the rare name of Mayr, of fabulous systematic instinct. Unfortunately, he will probably have to wither away as a medical doctor. If only one could always place the right man in the right position!" (12 July 1924; see Haffer, 1997, p. 215). In February 1925 Stresemann persuaded Mayr to switch to zoology and to major in ornithology, partly by promising to place him on an expedition to the tropics later on. This was a temptation Mayr could not resist. He transferred to the University of Berlin, passed his doctoral examination summa cum laude in June 1926, and was immediately employed as an assistant curator at the Museum of Natural History in Berlin.

Mindful of his earlier promise, Stresemann arranged, in late 1927, a one-man expedition for Mayr to New Guinea, jointly financed by the Berlin museum, the American Museum of Natural History in New York, and Lord Walter Rothschild in Tring, United Kingdom. Mayr collected birds on five poorly known mountain ranges in New Guinea between early 1928 and June 1929. When he was ready to return home, he received an invitation to join the American Museum's Whitney South Sea Expedition in the Solomon Islands. He did so and returned to Germany only in April 1930 and then worked on his collections from eastern New Guinea. In January 1931 he accepted the American Museum's invitation to be a visiting research associate for one year to study the bird collections from the islands of the southwest Pacific. When, in 1932, the American Museum purchased Rothschild's large bird collection, Mayr became the curator of the Whitney-Rothschild collections in New York. His motivation for leaving Germany was not political but rather the simple reason that his position in the United States was better, scientifically, than any he could expect in Germany.

Ornithology and Zoogeography. During the 1930s Mayr studied primarily bird collections from Oceania. A continuous stream of research articles appeared, followed by book-length contributions on the birds of New Guinea (1941), the southwest Pacific (1945), the Philippines (1946, with J. Delacour), and northern Melanesia (2001a, with J. Diamond). These studies formed the basis for Mayr's analysis of variation and speciation in birds. He described twenty-six new species and 445 new subspecies of birds, many cases of simple and complex geographic variation of species, and discussed numerous borderline cases between subspecies and species.

Based on these studies Mayr established the basic principles of an equilibrium theory of island biogeography. The size of an island fauna is determined by an equilibrium between immigration and extinction, size and elevation of the island, and distance from other land masses. His interpretation of the origin of several forms of Australian tree runners (*Neositta*) in humid refuges during dry climatic periods of the geological past was the first detailed presentation of Pleistocene speciation for birds of the Southern Hemisphere. His studies of the birds of the Indonesian Archipelago convinced him that most species had reached the various islands by dispersal across ocean barriers rather than over land bridges for which he found no evidence. Mayr also influenced ornithology by encouraging amateurs in the New York region to undertake serious biological studies of birds, by publishing Margaret M. Nice's pioneering population study of the song sparrow, by establishing bird family relations when cataloging and arranging the Rothschild collection, and as well as by editing, in later years, the continuation of James L. Peters's *Check-List of Birds of the World.*

The Evolutionary Synthesis. In the 1930s, based on Darwinian evolutionary theory, Mayr also collected data for a comprehensive evolutionary analysis of geographical variation and speciation in birds (and other animals), especially after establishing contact with Theodosius Dobzhansky in 1935. At a symposium organized by

Mayr

Dobzhansky in December 1939, Mayr spoke on "Speciation Phenomena in Birds." This was a decisive step into his evolutionary career and led to his giving (jointly with Edgar Anderson) the Jesup Lectures at Columbia University (New York) in March 1941. Mayr expanded the manuscript of his lectures, which was published as *Systematics and the Origin of Species* (1942). This volume became a cornerstone of the evolutionary synthesis of the late 1930s and 1940s, when a largely unified evolutionary theory emerged.

Biological evolution comprises two major components: adaptive development of populations through time, and multiplication of species or the origin of organic diversity. The mathematical population geneticists Ronald Aylmer Fisher, Sewall Wright, and J. B. S. Haldane had solved, with their publications in 1930 through 1932, the first of these problems (the Fisherian synthesis, Mayr, 1999a, p. xiv): They had convincingly shown that small mutations and natural selection play the main roles in the gradual process of adaptive evolution of populations over time (phyletic evolution, anagenesis, or evolution as such). The other main problem, the origin of diversity (multiplication of species, speciation, or cladogenesis), was solved during the evolutionary synthesis between 1937 and 1950 (Mayr, 1993).

In general, this period saw a synthesis: (1) between the thinking in three major biological disciplines—genetics, systematics, and paleontology; (2) between an experimental-reductionist approach (geneticists) and an observational-holistic approach (naturalists-systematists); and (3) between an anglophone tradition with an emphasis on mathematics and adaptation and a continental European tradition with emphasis on populations, species, and higher taxa. The three genetical aspects (then not new insights) that were firmly and universally adopted during the evolutionary synthesis were: (1) that inheritance is "hard," there is no "soft" inheritance of acquired characters; (2) that inheritance is particulate, that is, the genetic contributions of the parents do not blend but remain separate, to be differently recombined in future generations; and (3) that most mutations are very small and evolution therefore is gradual. This latter aspect in particular permitted a synthesis between genetics and systematics, because the naturalists had always insisted that evolution and speciation are gradual (continuous) and occur without sudden steps. The naturalists had to give up any belief in soft inheritance and to learn that a selective advantage of even small changes of the genotype could account for gradual evolution. In addition, the evolutionary synthesis led to a refutation of the three anti-Darwinian paradigms—(a) the typological-saltational, (b) the teleological-orthogenetic, and (c) the transformationist-Lamarckian theories.

Based on his background as a naturalist-systematist in Russia during the 1920s, Dobzhansky (1937) produced a first synthesis between the views of the naturalists-systematists and the geneticists. The other architects of the evolutionary synthesis widened the path that Dobzhansky had blazed—Ernst Mayr (1942, species and speciation), Julian Huxley (1942, general evolution), George Gaylord Simpson (1944, paleontology), Bernhard Rensch (1947, macroevolution), and G. Ledyard Stebbins (1950, botany). At an international conference in Princeton, New Jersey, in January 1947 there was general agreement among the participating geneticists and naturalists-systematists on the nature of species, the gradualness of evolution, the importance of natural selection, and the populational aspect of the gradual origin of species. A synthesis indeed had taken place. Some differences that remained at that time included the problem of the target of selective demands, which, for the population geneticists, continued to be the gene, whereas the naturalists-systematists insisted it was the individual as a whole. In general, a unification of biology

> was not an objective in the minds of any of the architects of the synthesis during the 1930–1940 period. They were busy enough straightening out their own differences and refuting the antidarwinians to have time for such a far-reaching objective. It wasn't until the 1950s when most of the previous difficulties had been resolved that one could begin to think seriously about the role of evolutionary biology in the whole of biology and about the capacity of evolutionary biology to achieve a unification of the previously badly splintered biology. (Mayr, 1993, p. 33; see also Smocovitis, 1996, p. 202)

Recent research has indicated that the evolutionary synthesis was an international program to which also several other workers in Germany contributed (Mayr, 1999b; Reif et al., 2000).

During the 1940s, Mayr was also active as a community architect founding specialty groups beyond ornithology, first within the Committee of Common Problems of Genetics, Paleontology, and Systematics (1942–1949) and later within the Society for the Study of Evolution (1946 ff.). He also served as founding editor of the society's journal *Evolution* (1947–1949). Each year, between 1943 and 1952, Mayr and his family spent several summer weeks at Cold Spring Harbor Biological Laboratory, Long Island, where, in discussions with colleagues, he acquired his extensive knowledge of advanced genetics and molecular biology.

Biological Species. Many researchers thought of species as morphologically defined groups of individuals, whereas others, including Mayr, considered species as breeding groups. His concise definition reads "Species are groups of interbreeding natural populations that are reproductively [i.e., genetically] isolated from other such groups" (Mayr, 1969, p. 26; see also 1942, p. 120). Isolating mechanisms maintain the integrity of species by protecting their gene pools from hybridization with other species and, as Mayr showed, arise as a by-product of divergence during the process of speciation (see below). Criteria to infer subspecies or species status of geographically separated populations are derived from the study of related forms that are in contact and do or do not hybridize. The rather frequent occurrence of closely similar ("sibling") species and of conspicuous variants within species convinced many biologists of the validity of the biological species concept.

The history of this concept goes back to the early nineteenth century. Building on the work of Stresemann, Rensch, and Dobzhansky, Mayr combined systematic, genetic, and ecological aspects and thus established the biological species concept in all its ramifications. Although he was not the originator of the biological species concept, he demonstrated its validity more convincingly than anyone else before and proposed a superior definition.

The Problem of Speciation. Evolutionists understood since the Fisherian synthesis (see above) how and why populations of species change over time, yet species are distinct—they do not hybridize with or blend into one another. How can one separate species arise from another (parental) species? Some geneticists (saltationists like William Bateson, Hugo de Vries, and Richard Goldschmidt) believed that new species arise instantaneously by large mutations, sudden steps in which either a single character or a whole set of characters together become changed. By contrast, the naturalists-systematists were gradualists and believed that speciation is a populational process, a gradual accumulation of small changes often by natural selection. The rate of such gradual change varies from slow to relatively fast depending on the strength of selective demands and on the size of the populations in which the changes are taking place (faster in small populations).

Mayr's theory of allopatric speciation from geographically separated populations had been proposed earlier by some evolutionists, but it was his clear synthesis that convinced geneticists and zoologists generally of the common occurrence of such processes: Either a previously continuous species range is split into two or more parts (through sea-level changes or climatic-vegetational changes) or a small isolated founder population is established by dispersal of a few individuals of a parental species across a barrier. Each isolated population then evolves independently, gradually diverging from one another. When sufficient genetic differences have accumulated, the parental and daughter populations may come in contact without hybridizing—a new (daughter) species has originated. Mayr emphasized that, despite the striking gaps between the species of a local flora and fauna, the gradual evolution of new species is no longer a puzzle, and can indeed be illustrated by numerous examples in extant faunas. He never ruled out that sympatric speciation (without geographic isolation) occurs in certain groups of animals, but felt for a long time that convincing evidence was lacking. When the simultaneous acquisition of mate preference and niche preference in a population was demonstrated for cichlid fishes and parasitic insects during the 1980s and 1990s, he accepted this mode of speciation. These preferences isolate two populations in a similar manner as geographic separation.

Mayr's specific contributions to the evolutionary synthesis were his analyses of the nature of biological species and of the origin of organic diversity. Speciation and other processes in evolution are not simply a matter of genes but of populations and of species. His 1942 volume explained a large part of evolutionary theory well known to naturalists-systematists but not to geneticists, particularly species and speciation and the role of geography in the evolution of populations and species. The volume demonstrated the importance of taxonomic research for evolution.

In more general terms and including later contributions, Mayr dealt with variation and population thinking, species concepts, the dual nature of evolution (phyletic evolution and speciation), the unity of the genotype, and accident versus adaptation in evolution. His most important papers have been reprinted in two volumes of essays (1976, 1988). He did not publish a textbook on evolution, although his books *Animal Species and Evolution* (1963) and *Populations, Species, and Evolution* (1970) come close. In the book *What Evolution Is* (2001b), published when he was ninety-seven years old, he gave a clear and concise exposition of modern evolutionary biology.

Mayr opposed the early view of population geneticists that evolutionary change is an input and output of genes, like adding certain beans to a beanbag and withdrawing others. Instead he called attention to the frequency of interaction among genes, to their changing selective values, and to the general cohesion of the genotype. Other topics he studied and discussed were behavior and evolution, the emergence of evolutionary novelties, sexual selection, and Haeckel's biogenetic law. Mayr proposed or introduced from foreign languages many terms in systematics and evolutionary biology like allopatric (geographically separated), founder principle, population thinking, semispecies, and superspecies. He also showed that, if the individual is the target of selective demands, neither the theory of neutral evolution nor the adaptationist program are in conflict with Darwinism. The same applies to the theory of punctuated equilibrium proposed by Niles Eldredge and Stephen J. Gould; Charles Darwin was already aware of highly unequal rates of evolution. On the other hand, Mayr emphasized that biologists are still quite ignorant about evolution in most groups of invertebrate animals, of fungi, protists, and the prokaryotes.

Career after the Evolutionary Synthesis. In 1953 Mayr accepted the position of Alexander Agassiz Professor of Zoology at the Museum of Comparative Zoology (MCZ), Harvard University, in Cambridge, Massachusetts, and entered the second phase of his life work. He lectured on evolutionary biology and taught seminars on specific topics, because such courses had not been offered at Harvard for a long time and leading textbooks of biology treated evolution quite superficially. Sixteen graduate students obtained PhD degrees under his guidance between 1955 and 1973. Mayr was director of the MCZ during the period from 1961 to 1970.

As advisor to the U.S. National Academy of Sciences, he served as a member of the Biology Council during the 1950s and of the Committee on Research in the Life Sciences during the 1960s, for which services he received the National Medal of Science in 1969. Later he was awarded the Balzan Prize of Italy and Switzerland (1983) as "the greatest living evolutionary biologist," Japan's International Prize for Biology (1994) as "the outstanding systematist in the world," and Sweden's Crafoord Prize (1999) for his "fundamental contributions to the conceptual development of evolutionary biology"—these awards constitute the "Triple Crown of Biology."

History and Philosophy of Biology. The third phase of Mayr's career, devoted to developmental historiography and a modern philosophy of biology, began during the late 1950s when, at the same time, he continued as an active worker in the fields of systematics, species, and evolution. His contributions to the history and philosophy of biology were based on several decades of empirical research in biology (1976, 1988, 2004). He was particularly interested in the history of scientific problems and their solutions, in tracing an idea, concept, or controversy back to its sources, devoting sufficient attention to the general context of different time levels. Mayr began his work on the history of biology from the perspective of someone who had been very active in shaping that history. Some historians have faulted his approach to history, even labeling it Whiggish, a criticism that Mayr (1990) rejected from his personal point of view. Because the evolutionary synthesis is so central to contemporary biology, historians continue to revise our understanding of how it happened (Smocovitis, 1996).

Mayr's historical magnum opus is *The Growth of Biological Thought: Diversity, Evolution, and Inheritance* (1982), where he traced the complete life history of each problem of evolutionary biology and exposed the historical and philosophical relations between systematics, evolution, and genetics. In general, Mayr saw the development of science as an increasing emancipation of scientific knowledge from religious, philosophical, and other ideological beliefs. He advocated that, in scientific progress, various competing paradigms may exist side by side and more or less pronounced "revolutions" may occur in times of normal science. Changes of concepts have a much stronger effect on the development of the sciences than new factual discoveries.

He wrote extensively on Charles Darwin and his times (1991), emphasizing that in 1859 Darwin had proposed not one theory of evolution but five independent theses with respect to evolution: (1) Evolution as such, that is, change of populations through time; (2) common descent of all living organisms; (3) multiplication of species; (4) gradual evolutionary change instead of sudden (saltational) changes within populations; and (5) natural selection as a mechanism of evolutionary change. Analysis of these five theses constitute Mayr's most significant contribution to the history of evolutionary biology. The differing fate of these theses after 1859 indicate their independence. Most authors, who had accepted the first thesis, rejected one or several of Darwin's other four theses. The core thesis of natural selection was not generally accepted until the 1940s during the modern synthesis. Likewise, the term *Darwinism* has several different meanings: Darwinism as the creed of the Darwinians refers to their rejection of special creation: he who believed in the origin of the diversity of life through natural causes was a Darwinian. Darwinism as selectionism has been a primary meaning since the evolutionary synthesis of the 1940s as well as for a few early naturalists. Neo-Darwinism is Darwinism without soft inheritance, the inheritance of acquired characteristics.

Mayr argued that Darwin was the first to apply "population thinking" when he proposed the concept of natural selection (based on the uniqueness of individuals in a population). Mayr considered most or all of Darwin's contemporaries to be typologists, to whom the underlying type or essence of a species had reality and variation was irrelevant. "The replacement of typological thinking by population thinking is perhaps the greatest conceptual revolution that has taken place in biology" (1963, p. 5). Mayr's conceptualization of population thinking is a major contribution to the philosophy of biology.

Mayr with the Leidy medal. *Ernst Walter Mayr (left) receiving Leidy medal from Dr. Phillip Calvert (right) as Charles MB Cadwalader (center) watches.* AP IMAGES.

He also emphasized that no biological phenomenon is explained fully until both its functional/environmental (proximate) causes and its evolutionary (ultimate) causes are determined. For example, a northern warbler starts its fall migration on a particular night because of certain physiological/environmental (proximate) causes and because of the general genetic disposition of the bird (evolutionary causes). According to Mayr, the genetic program of an individual is the result of selection that acted upon untold generations and that program is a causal factor which differs fundamentally from physicochemical causes. The many peculiarities of life such as uniqueness and variability, historical contingency, genetic program, diversity, and natural selection necessitate a specific philosophy of biology that excludes both essentialism (typology) and reductionism (explanation purely by molecular structure). In the face of the growth of molecular biology, Mayr vigorously defended organismic and evolutionary biology, but he welcomed molecular biology as such. Experiment is not the only valid method of science, Mayr stated; observation, comparison, and the construction of historical-narrative explanations are also legitimate and important methods in the physical and biological sciences.

Mayr drew ethical implications from three of the five Darwinian theses (1984): The theory of common descent deprived humans of their unique position in the world and of their right to exterminate any other species of animals or plants. The theory of natural selection showed Mayr that altruistic behavior is of selective advantage in closely related individuals of small populations of early humans. Evolution as such countered the idea that humans have no obligation for the future, either with respect to the world's environment or its fauna and flora. His world view of evolutionary humanism is conscious of the evolutionary past of humans and is aware of their responsibility for the community as a whole and for posterity. Humans are challenged to develop an ethic that can cope with the new situation. Mayr believed overpopulation is the core problem that faces humankind and a change in attitude toward family size is needed: voluntary birth control appears to be not enough and he recommended a set of incentives to be built into the tax system, pension system, and welfare system in the hope that this will lead to zero population growth throughout the world.

Mayr was very skeptical about the existence of extraterrestrial intelligence. Living molecular assemblages might have originated on other planets at some stage of their history. However, it is highly improbable that intelligence followed and humans are most probably alone in this vast universe.

Mayr received the George Sarton Medal of the History of Science Society (1986) and was nominated a Fellow of the Center for the Philosophy of Science in Pittsburgh (1993). The Rockefeller University in New York awarded him the Lewis Thomas Prize: Honoring the Scientist as Poet (1998) and an annual Ernst Mayr Lecture was established in Berlin, Germany (1997). He received a total of seventeen honorary doctoral degrees from universities around the world. Mayr served as president of the Society for the Study of Evolution (1950), of the American Ornithologists' Union (1956–1959), of the Thirteenth International Ornithological Congress (1962), of the American Society of Naturalists (1962–1963), and of the Society of Systematic Zoology (1966). He published twenty-one books and over 750 scientific articles, about 200 after his retirement in 1975.

Summarizing, Mayr was a cataloger in much of his ornithological work, which formed the empirical basis for his later theoretical studies. He was a major synthesizer of biology, an effective disseminator of biological principles, and a master analyst who dissected such complex concepts as population thinking and Darwin's five theses of evolution. New theories that Mayr proposed as an innovator include his theories of island biogeography and of the founder principle of speciation. He was convinced of the uniqueness of each individual organism (population thinking) and of the necessity of the historical approach for an understanding of organic beings.

Personality. Exceptional energy, resolution, ambition, and self-confidence were personal traits that guided Mayr when he went on his one-man expedition to New Guinea in 1928 and during many other periods in his life, in his leadership role in evolutionary studies in the United States during the 1940s, and in his spokesmanship for systematics and evolutionary biology when molecular biology threatened to dry up all the research funds during the 1960s. He was driven by an unlimited curiosity, had strong opinions, hated beating around the bush, and made sweeping statements. To take an unequivocal stand and to fight for his views appeared to him of greater heuristic value than to evade the issue. Therefore some of his colleagues considered him to be dogmatic.

However, he was friendly and easygoing. He had no fixed visiting hours as director of the MCZ and anybody could meet with him any time. He promptly reviewed manuscripts in detail for friends, students, and journal editors, and supported students and young colleagues in many other ways. Mayr helped found the Society for the Study of Evolution and served as secretary and first editor of its journal *Evolution,* and he helped the *Journal of the History of Biology* to get started in the 1960s. He was generous with his time and with the money he received for academic prizes, all of which he gave to purposes of education and conservation. He was tolerant regarding racial, religious, and ethnic differences and he appreciated the unknown in science and religion. His driving enthusiasm for scientific work until the last month of his life was remarkable.

Mayr influenced the history and philosophy of biology by all the help he gave to neophyte historians and philosophers. His views were strongly held, but he also thought that others had the right to disagree with him, even if they were lowly graduate students.

Mayr had married Margarete ("Gretel") Simon of Freiburg, Germany, in 1935; they had two daughters, Christa (1936) and Susanne (1937), and became U.S. citizens in December 1950. He enjoyed generally good health throughout most of his long adult life. In 1934 his left kidney had to be removed but he lived to be over one hundred years old. After his wife had passed away in 1990, he managed his household alone until he moved to a comfortable retirement home in Bedford near Cambridge, Massachusetts, in 1997. On 5 July 2004 he celebrated his hundredth birthday in excellent physical and mental health.

During his last year he gave numerous interviews and published his last book, *What Makes Biology Unique?* Four symposia were held in his honor, two of which he attended. After a short illness he died quietly and peacefully on 3 February 2005. His ashes were scattered by his family and a few close friends along a path overlooking a lake at his beloved country place in New Hampshire, which he had acquired in 1954 and where he had spent many months of his long life.

BIBLIOGRAPHY

A complete bibliography is provided by J. Haffer in the volume edited by W. J. Bock and M. R. Lein (2005), and in Haffer's biography of Mayr, Ornithology, Evolution, and Philosophy—The Life and Science of Ernst Mayr (1904–2005) *(2007). Mayr papers containing his correspondence are kept in the following archives: (1) Pusey Library, Harvard University Archives, Cambridge, MA, and (2) Staatsbibliothek Preussischer Kulturbesitz Berlin, Potsdamer Str., Manuscript Division.*

WORKS BY MAYR

List of New Guinea Birds. New York: American Museum of Natural History, 1941.

Systematics and the Origin of Species from the Viewpoint of a Zoologist. New York: Columbia University Press, 1942.

Birds of the Southwest Pacific. New York: Macmillan, 1945.

With J. Delacour. *Birds of the Philippines.* New York: Macmillan, 1946.

Animal Species and Evolution. Cambridge, MA: Belknap Press of Harvard University Press, 1963.

Principles of Systematic Zoology. New York: McGraw-Hill, 1969.

Populations, Species, and Evolution. Cambridge, MA: Belknap Press of Harvard University Press, 1970. An abridgment of *Animal Species and Evolution.*

Evolution and the Diversity of Life: Selected Essays. Cambridge, MA: Belknap Press of Harvard University Press, 1976.

With William B. Provine, eds. *The Evolutionary Synthesis: Perspectives on the Unification of Biology.* Cambridge, MA: Harvard University Press, 1980.

The Growth of Biological Thought: Diversity, Evolution, and Inheritance. Cambridge, MA: Belknap Press of Harvard University Press, 1982.

"Evolution and Ethics." In *Darwin, Marx, and Freud: Their Influence on Moral Theory,* edited by A. L. Caplan and B. Jennings. New York: Plenum Press, 1984.

Toward a New Philosophy of Biology: Observations of an Evolutionist. Cambridge, MA: Harvard University Press, 1988.

"When Is Historiography Whiggish?" *Journal of the History of Ideas* 51 (1990): 301–309.

One Long Argument: Charles Darwin and the Genesis of Modern Evolutionary Thought. Cambridge, MA: Harvard University Press, 1991.

"What Was the Evolutionary Synthesis?" *Trends in Ecology and Evolution* 8 (1993): 31–34.

"Introduction, 1999." *Systematics and the Origin of Species from the Viewpoint of a Zoologist.* Paperback ed. Cambridge, MA: Harvard University Press, 1999a.

"Thoughts on the Evolutionary Synthesis in Germany." In *Die Entstehung der Synthetischen Theorie: Beiträge zur Geschichte der Evolutionsbiologie in Deutschland 1930–1950,* edited by T. Junker and E.-M. Engels. Verhandlungen zur Geschichte und Theorie der Biologie 2. Berlin: Verlag für Wissenschaft und Bildung, 1999b.

With J. Diamond. *The Birds of Northern Melanesia: Speciation, Ecology, and Biogeography.* New York: Oxford University Press, 2001a.

What Evolution Is. New York: Basic Books, 2001b.

What Makes Biology Unique: Considerations on the Autonomy of a Scientific Discipline. New York: Cambridge University Press, 2004.

OTHER SOURCES

Bock, W. J., and M. R. Lein, eds. *Ernst Mayr at 100: Ornithologist and Naturalist.* Ornithological Monographs, no. 58. Washington, DC: American Ornithologists' Union, 2005.

Dobzhansky, Theodosius. *Genetics and the Origin of Species.* New York: Columbia University Press, 1937.

Greene, John, and Michael Ruse, eds. "Special Issue on Ernst Mayr at Ninety." *Biology and Philosophy* 9, no. 3 (July 1994).

Haffer, Jürgen. *Ornithologen-Briefe des 20. Jahrhunderts.* Ökologie der Vögel, vol. 19. Ludwigsburg, Germany: Holzinger, 1997.

———. *Ornithology, Evolution, and Philosophy—The Life and Science of Ernst Mayr (1904–2005).* New York: Springer, 2007.

Huxley, Julian. *Evolution, the Modern Synthesis.* London: Allen & Unwin, 1942.

Reif, W.-E., T. Junker, and U. Hossfeld. "The Synthetic Theory of Evolution: General Problems and the German Contribution to the Synthesis." *Theory in Biosciences* 119 (2000): 41–91.

Rensch, Bernard. *Neuere Probleme der Abstammungslehre.* Stuttgart, Germany: Enke, 1947.

Ruse, M. "Ernst Mayr 1904–2005." *Biology and Philosophy* 20 (2005): 623–631.

Simpson, George Gaylord. *Tempo and Mode in Evolution.* New York: Columbia University Press, 1944.

Smocovitis, Vassiliki Betty. *Unifying Biology: The Evolutionary Synthesis and Evolutionary Biology.* Princeton, NJ: Princeton University Press, 1996.

———, et al. "Collection of Articles on Ernst Mayr at Ninety." *Evolution* 48 (1994): 1–43.

Stebbins, G. Ledyard. *Variation and Evolution in Plants.* New York: Columbia University Press, 1950.

Jürgen Haffer

MCCLINTOCK, BARBARA

MCCLINTOCK, BARBARA (*b.* Hartford, Connecticut, 16 June 1902; *d.* Huntington, New York, 2 September 1992), *genetics, maize, cytology, developmental regulation.*

In her six-decade career, McClintock had three achievements of the sort that transform a field. First, in the late 1920s and early 1930s, she worked out the cytology of the maize plant, a problem that had stymied geneticists for years. This work made her reputation among geneticists. Second, twenty years later, she discovered transposable elements, genes that change position among the chromosomes. She won a Nobel Prize in the category of Physiology or Medicine for this discovery in 1983. Transposable elements made her world famous, but the way they were interpreted has obscured her third achievement: the development, in the 1960s and 1970s, of a vision, unique in its time, of the genome as dynamic and highly responsive to external stimuli. The reasons that this last achievement might have transformed developmental biology and genomics, but has not, revealed some of the social processes at play in the making of a scientific reputation.

Born in 1902 in Hartford, Connecticut, McClintock soon moved to Flatbush, Brooklyn, where she grew up. Although she was named Eleanor, very early she began to be called Barbara; as a young adult she changed her name legally. Her father, Thomas Henry McClintock, was a physician, respectable and middle class. Her mother, Sara Handy McClintock, descended from a long line of Boston bluebloods who traced their ancestry to the Mayflower. McClintock was a middle child, with two older sisters and one younger brother. Late in life, she recalled that her parents had allowed her the freedom to pursue her interests and did not pressure her to perform in school or to conform socially—she located this as a source of the fierce independence she showed throughout her adult life. She attended Erasmus Hall High School, graduating at age sixteen. Her father supported her intention to attend college and she was accepted to Cornell University in Ithaca, New York, which for its day had an impressive record of admitting women. McClintock entered the agriculture college, which is part of New York's state university system, in the fall of 1919. All of McClintock's degrees were from Cornell: a bachelor of science (1923), master of arts (1925), and PhD (1927).

Making Maize Cytogenetics. When McClintock arrived at Cornell, it was becoming a world center for the study of maize genetics. Harvard's Edward Murray East and Cornell's Rollins Emerson were the top two maize geneticists in the country. Through the late 1910s and the 1920s, Emerson built Cornell into a center of maize genetics research and a clearinghouse for data, methodological tips, and professional gossip. By the late 1920s, Cornell's maize program boasted several professors and many brilliant graduate students and postdoctoral fellows, seminars and conferences, ample funding from the U.S. Department of Agriculture (USDA), and a world-class reputation. Maize was clearly the most vigorous, exciting specialty of genetics at Cornell in those years.

One of Emerson's important early discoveries was a so-called mutable allele, which spontaneously mutated back and forth from the wild type form during the development of the plant. Its effects are evident in the colorful mottled and striped kernels on almost any ear of holiday "Indian corn." For Emerson, this mutable allele suggested a key to the physiology of the gene. Yet maize geneticists felt hampered by their inability to map genes to specific sites on chromosomes, as the fruit fly geneticists had been doing since the midteens. Maize workers had identified genetic linkage groups—clusters of genes that tend to be inherited together—but had not been able to correlate them to individual chromosomes. At the end of the 1920s, maize genetics stood about where *Drosophila* genetics had been in the 1910s.

McClintock brought maize into its "classical" phase. While still a graduate student, she became the research assistant to the cytologist Lowell Fitz Randolph. Randolph drew her into his research on maize chromosomes. She quickly developed into a virtuoso of the microscope; she had that sense of the instrument scientists call "feel." With this virtuosity added to a startling intelligence, candid personal style, and hot temper, McClintock was universally admired but not always liked. Her friends were intensely loyal, but she made enemies easily—particularly with those in positions of authority. A bitter skirmish with Randolph ended their collaboration and she began to work under Lester W. Sharp.

Near the end of her work with Randolph, McClintock had discovered a triploid, a maize plant with a complete third set of chromosomes. In its offspring, she found a plant with a single extra chromosome, a phenomenon known as trisomy. McClintock used it to crack the greatest problem in maize genetics at the time. An extra chromosome alters the normal Mendelian inheritance pattern, giving instead a "trisomic ratio." By technical innovation and careful observation, McClintock learned to distinguish among the ten maize chromosomes. She could therefore tell which chromosome was tripled in a given plant. If that plant showed a trisomic ratio for a gene in a known linkage group, then she could confidently locate that linkage group to that chromosome. In *Science* magazine in 1929, she published the first chromosome diagram for maize. By 1932, she had mapped eight of the ten linkage groups to their respective chromosomes, and colleagues had mapped the others.

Assigning linkage groups to chromosomes is based, of course, on the assumption that the genes lie on the chromosomes. An implication of the chromosome theory of heredity is that cytological crossing over, in which two chromosome arms physically cross one another and exchange segments, corresponds to genetic crossing over, in which an allele changes linkage groups. Still, no one had yet confirmed this correlation unequivocally. In 1931, McClintock and graduate student Harriet Creighton did so in "A Correlation of Cytological and Genetical Crossing-Over in *Zea mays,*" a paper considered a classic of cytogenetic technique and reasoning.

McClintock's work helped usher in the golden age of maize genetics in the first half of the 1930s. In 1932, Cornell hosted the Sixth International Congress of Genetics. The Emerson and East schools were turning out superb

Barbara McClintock. *Barbara McClintock holding an ear of corn, circa 1975.* HULTON ARCHIVE/GETTY IMAGES.

students who were colonizing other programs, predominantly at big land-grant universities in the midwestern Corn Belt. Knowledge of maize cytogenetics exploded, with large numbers of new genes discovered, characterized, and mapped to the chromosomes. For the international congress, the Cornell maize geneticists planted a living chromosome map: ten rows of corn, one for each chromosome, with a plant for each genetic locus in the correct order down the row. With her brilliant microscopic technique and cleverly designed, meticulously executed experiments, McClintock was one of the brightest lights of this era.

Golden age or no, it was the Great Depression. Jobs were few, jobs for women were fewer still, and jobs for "difficult" women fewest of all. Yet Emerson supported McClintock on his USDA grant after her PhD, and she then received two distinguished fellowships, from the National Research Council (1931–1933) and from the Guggenheim Foundation (1933–1934). The Guggenheim fellowship took her to Berlin, where she intended to work with the fruit fly geneticist Curt Stern. Stern, however, had been working in Thomas Hunt Morgan's laboratory at the California Institute of Technology. When Adolf Hitler came to power in 1933, Stern, a Jew, wisely decided not to return to Germany. McClintock, however, was urged to go anyway.

In Berlin, she befriended Richard Goldschmidt, another notoriously prickly personality. Goldschmidt introduced her to the group of German geneticists who were exploring the physiology of the gene, cytoplasmic inheritance, and the relation of genes to embryological development. When Berlin, the capital of the Nazi state, grew too depressing for McClintock, he arranged for her to escape to Freiburg, where she worked in the laboratory of Friedrich Oehlkers, another member of the group. As Jan Sapp showed in his *Beyond the Gene* (1987), a central concern of this school was the "paradox of nuclear equivalence": if, as everyone assumed, a gene is "on" all the time, and if each cell contains all the genes, how do different cell types arise? How do development and differentiation occur? The Germans' answer was that some regulatory machinery must lie outside the nucleus, in the cytoplasm. McClintock returned early from Germany, but only after absorbing an interest in gene regulation that remained for the rest of her life.

In 1936, McClintock took her first and only regular university faculty appointment, at the University of Missouri. The head of the botany department was Lewis J. Stadler, a distinguished maize geneticist and longtime McClintock admirer and collaborator. At Missouri, from descendants of Stadler's x-rayed strains, McClintock developed a strain of corn in which chromosomes would rip themselves apart. The chromosomes break at cell division, the broken ends find one another, and they fuse again. But if broken ends from different chromosomes fuse, they will be pulled apart again at the next division, breaking the chromosomes anew and repeating the cycle. She called this the breakage-fusion-bridge (BFB) cycle and published it in 1938. She quickly turned BFB into a research tool. When the chromosomes break, mutations are often produced. McClintock began to use BFB the way others used x-rays, as a tool for generating mutations. With x-rays, one generated random mutations over all the chromosomes and screened perhaps thousands of plants. But BFB occurs at a predictable site on a given chromosome, thus providing a means of producing directed mutations. This was a boon—especially for McClintock, who preferred to grow small numbers of plants and tend them all herself.

McClintock hated the restrictions and tedium of academic life. She found the students dull, the faculty meetings stultifying, and the bureaucracy and arbitrary rules intolerable. A widespread anecdote has it that she shocked

McClintock

the faculty by climbing in the window of her locked laboratory after hours. True or not, it captures how she bridled at authority. As always, she concentrated her antipathy on the man in charge, in this case Stadler. She became almost paranoid about Stadler's "machinations"; she became convinced that he was undermining her and was about to fire her. She told the story this way for years, and many accounts relate her version of the story. But in fact, she was offered a promotion with tenure and turned it down. When it became clear to Stadler that McClintock would leave Missouri, he strove to find her a place where she would be happier. He succeeded with Milislav Demerec, a former Emerson student who was in 1940 the interim (soon to be permanent) director of the Carnegie Institution of Washington's Department of Genetics, at Cold Spring Harbor on New York's Long Island.

Controlling Elements. McClintock joined the Carnegie staff at Cold Spring Harbor in 1941. The small research laboratory, tucked among the grand estates of Long Island's Gold Coast, was not well suited to maize genetics. It could not provide the dozens of acres most corn geneticists required. Its annual rhythms—busy summers chocked with meetings and courses and quiet winters with only the small permanent staff to talk to—clashed with the routines of maize genetics. McClintock complained that summer visitors continually tramped through her cornfield, looking to chat, during the busiest time of her year. Yet the resources would suffice. McClintock could grow the one hundred to two hundred plants she needed each season on a sandy acre by the water's edge. And Cold Spring Harbor, almost uniquely, offered what she needed more than land or privacy: freedom from teaching, administration, and grant writing. She had nothing to do but science. Though clashes with various directors prompted occasional thoughts of leaving, she remained at Cold Spring Harbor for fifty-one years, until her death.

In 1944, she crossed two strains of maize that underwent the BFB cycle. The experiment was designed as a straightforward exercise in gene mapping: she hoped to generate new mutations on chromosome 9 and locate them relative to known genes. But the plants fairly exploded with new mutations, including several new mutable alleles. McClintock saw immediately that she had disrupted something fundamental among the chromosomes. The entire set of chromosomes—what came to be called the genome—had become unstable and was throwing off mutations right and left. One mutable gene in particular caught her attention. At first it appeared to cause chromosome breakage. She called it *Ds,* for *Dissociator.* She later regretted the name, because she soon found that *Ds* did many things besides break chromosomes. A second locus, *Activator* (*Ac*), needed to be present in order for *Ds* to operate. Mapping the new loci proved unusually difficult. Whenever she thought she had one of them isolated to a particular location, it would appear somewhere else in the next generation. In the spring of 1948, she realized that both *Ds* and *Ac* were changing positions, physically moving from one site to another. When *Ds* inserted next to a gene, that gene would be silenced or altered. When *Ds* jumped away again, the gene would be restored to normal function. *Dissociator* seemed to create mutable alleles.

The term *transposition* had existed in the genetics literature for decades. Well-known events such as translocations and shifts resulted in the transposition of a gene from one location to another. McClintock used the word *transposition* to describe the action of *Ds* and *Ac.* Her transposition was novel in that only one gene seemed to be moving at a time; it was physically excising itself from the chromosome and reinserting at another location.

Transposition per se was never what interested McClintock most. It provided her with a mechanism for the genomewide disruption she had witnessed in the 1944 experiment. In a normal plant, she reasoned, the mobile elements must be under some sort of control, which enables them to regulate when genes turn on and off during the development of the plant. This was her answer to the paradox of nuclear equivalence. She imagined a massively coordinated system of thousands of mobile elements, turning genes on and off as the organism developed. Each cell type in the organism would be produced by a characteristic pattern of transpositions. McClintock imagined that in the 1944 experiment, she must have disrupted that control system, liberating masses of rogue mobile elements that transposed out of control and produced the welter of new mutations. By 1950 she was calling her mobile elements "controlling elements."

The fact of transposition was immediately confirmed and rapidly accepted by the maize community. By the fall of 1950, transposition was confirmed by Robert Nilan and Royal Alexander Brink at the University of Wisconsin. In June 1951, McClintock gave what would become a famous talk on controlling elements at the Cold Spring Harbor Symposium, which Brink attended. In 1953 Peter Peterson, at the University of Iowa, independently isolated another mobile element. Through the 1950s, other researchers requested seeds from McClintock's controlling-element strains. No one doubted that transposition occurred in maize.

Few, however, accepted McClintock's interpretation of these findings, their putative role as controllers of development. Brink, for example, preferred to call them transposable elements rather than controlling elements, believing his term less interpretive than hers. The question hinged on whether or not the transpositions were random. McClintock hurt her own case by refusing to publish more than a tiny fraction of her mountains of data;

she relied instead on enigmatic talks and elliptical reviews. When, in 1961, François Jacob and Jacques Monod published their operon theory of gene control in bacteria, she followed immediately with review in the *American Naturalist* of the parallels between bacterial operons and maize-controlling elements. The bacterial operon, she argued, was merely a simpler, cruder mechanism in a simpler, cruder organism.

With the discovery of transposition in bacteria in 1967 and 1968, the accretion of accepted knowledge began to bury McClintock's theory of genetic control. Meanwhile, the operon model was firmly established as the model of gene regulation. Transposition began to be seen as universal—and as not being a challenge to the operon. With a bacterial model for transposition, molecular studies of the phenomenon took off. Transposition is widespread and complex and has had a large impact on genome structure. Later, molecular studies of transposition led to a new interpretation of mobile elements as genomic parasites, very important in evolution, but not the driving force of development McClintock had believed them to be.

McClintock was recognized as the founder of a new and important field. She began to win science's big prizes, and in 1983 was awarded an unshared Nobel Prize in Physiology or Medicine. But that prize was bittersweet, because it codified transposition as her major discovery and buried the concept that was most important to her: the genetic control of development.

The Dynamic Genome. McClintock worked little with transposition after 1953. In her controlling element work, she labored to keep the elements stationary, so she could better study their effects. Through the late 1950s and the 1960s, she probed ever-stranger phenomena but resolutely retained a language and methodology of classical genetics that was increasingly unable to cope with her findings. She invented new terminology—such as *presetting* and *erasure*—that had no correlates in the rest of the genetics literature. She explored the evolution of domestic corn, devising a novel method of mapping the evolutionary distribution of strains or "races" of maize throughout the Americas.

The last phase of her career was devoted to integrating genetics, development, and evolution into a sweeping vision of organic change on different time scales. That vision was at odds with the prevailing view of the nucleus as a hereditary vault, in which genetic information is stored and protected from the random insults of daily life. In the 1970s, McClintock made a series of brief "natural history" studies of the reprogramming of the developmental-genetic program by tadpoles metamorphosing into frogs, gall wasps on trees, and local plants. How could one set of genes make two such different organisms or tissues? The genes do not change—only the pattern of their activity changes. She understood that both internal and external forces could shape that pattern. In her Nobel Prize speech, she referred to the genome as a "sensitive organ of the cell," responsive to the environment. In the years since, the vision of the genome as dynamic, not static, has become mainstream. In experimental biology, the field of evolutionary developmental biology (evo-devo) uses molecular tools to answer questions McClintock posed about patterns and timing of gene expression—and looks back to the German physiological geneticists as forerunners. In biomedicine, multigene and gene-environment interactions have become an intense field of study. Each of these fields might have acknowledged McClintock as a pioneer, but to date neither one has.

McClintock thus became a victim of her own reputation. In interviews, she told her story as one of scientific neglect and ideas ahead of their time. Because she was famous for transposition, it seemed it must have been transposition that was neglected. As a canonical narrative emerged, her reputation was cemented: she would be remembered as the discoverer of transposition, not of genetic control.

BIBLIOGRAPHY

McClintock's papers are collected at the American Philosophical Society Library, in Philadelphia. This collection includes several boxes of correspondence, her reprint collection, and a large, challenging, and rewarding set of her laboratory and field notes. The archives at Cold Spring Harbor Laboratory, Cornell University, the Carnegie Institution of Washington, and the Guggenheim Foundation also contain small McClintock collections. In addition, several collections at the Lilly Library of Indiana University, in Bloomington, and the George Beadle collection at the California Institute of Technology Archives in Pasadena contain McClintock-related material.

WORKS BY MCCLINTOCK

"Chromosome Morphology in *Zea mays*." *Science* 69 (1929): 629. The first published ideogram, or chromosome diagram, of maize.

With Harriet Creighton. "A Correlation of Cytological and Genetical Crossing-Over in *Zea mays*." *Proceedings of the National Academy of Sciences of the United States of America* 17 (1931): 492–497. A classic paper correlating genetic and cytological crossing-over.

With Marcus M. Rhoades. "The Cytogenetics of Maize." *Botanical Review* 1 (1935): 292–325. An excellent review of maize cytogenetics at the end of the "golden age."

"Chromosome Organization and Gene Expression." *Cold Spring Harbor Symposia on Quantitative Biology* 16 (1951): 13–47. Her most-cited article; the published version of her famous Cold Spring Harbor talk, reportedly but implausibly received with disbelief and jeering.

"Some Parallels between Gene Control Systems in Maize and in Bacteria." *American Naturalist* 95 (1961): 265–277.

With T. Angel Kato Y. and Almiro Blumenschein. *Chromosome Constitution of Races of Maize: Its Significance in the Interpretation of Relationships between Races and Varieties in the Americas.* Chapingo, Mexico: Colegio de Postgraduados, Escuela National de Agricultura, Mexico, 1981. The result of a twenty-five-year effort to understand the evolution of cultivated maize.

"The Significance of Responses of the Genome to Challenge." *Science* 226 (1984): 792–801. Her Nobel lecture.

The Discovery and Characterization of Transposable Elements: The Collected Papers of Barbara McClintock. Edited by John A. Moore. New York: Garland, 1987. Collects many, but not all, of McClintock's papers from the late 1930s to the mid-1960s.

OTHER SOURCES

Barahona, A. "Barbara McClintock and the Transposition Concept." *Archives Internationales d'Histoire des Sciences* (Paris) 46, no. 137 (1997): 309–329.

Coe, Edgar, and Lee B. Kass. "Proof of Physical Exchange of Genes on the Chromosomes." *Proceedings of the National Academy of Sciences of the United States of America* 102, no. 19 (2005): 6641–6646. An analysis of Creighton and McClintock's famous article of 1931.

Comfort, Nathaniel C. "Two Genes, No Enzyme: A Second Look at Barbara McClintock and the 1951 Cold Spring Harbor Symposium." *Genetics* 140, no. 4 (1995): 1161–1166.

———. "'The Real Point Is Control': The Reception of Barbara McClintock's Controlling Elements." *Journal of the History of Biology* 32 (1999): 133–162.

———. "From Controlling Elements to Transposons: Barbara McClintock and the Nobel Prize." *Trends in Biochemical Sciences* 26, no. 7 (2001): 454–457. How McClintock came to be known for transposition.

———. *The Tangled Field: Barbara McClintock's Search for the Patterns of Genetic Control.* Cambridge, MA: Harvard University Press, 2001.

Kass, Lee B. "Current List of Barbara McClintock's Publications." *Maize News Letter* 73 (1999): 42–48. Also available from http://www.agron.missouri.edu/mnl/73/.

———. "Records and Recollections: A New Look at Barbara McClintock, Nobel Prize–Winning Geneticist." *Genetics* 164, no. 4 (2003): 1251–1260.

———, and Christophe Bonneuil. "Mapping and Seeing: Barbara McClintock and the Linking of Genetics and Cytology in Maize Genetics, 1928–1935." In *Classical Genetic Research and Its Legacy: The Mapping Cultures of Twentieth-Century Genetics,* edited by Hans-Jörg Rheinberger and Jean-Paul Gaudillière. London and New York: Routledge, 2004. Covers McClintock's career prior to controlling elements.

Keller, Evelyn Fox. *Reflections on Gender and Science.* New Haven, CT: Yale University Press, 1985. Chapter 9, "A World of Difference," is a philosophical look at McClintock's role in science.

———. *A Feeling for the Organism: The Life and Work of Barbara McClintock.* Tenth Anniversary Edition. New York: W. H. Freeman, 1993.

Nathaniel C. Comfort

MCCREA, WILLIAM HUNTER (*b.* Dublin, Ireland, 13 December 1904; *d.* Lewes, Sussex, United Kingdom, 25 April 1999), *astronomy, astrophysics, cosmology, physics, mathematics.*

Sir William McCrea was a tall, gentle man who talked very slowly. But his impish wit clearly showed he was a quick thinker. From the time he began his PhD studies in 1926 under Ralph H. Fowler until nearly the time of his death, McCrea made contributions to mathematics, physics, and almost every area of astronomy, including planetary physics, astrophysics, comets, interstellar hydrogen chemistry, Newtonian cosmology, relativistic cosmology, and steady state cosmology. McCrea's achievements began early: In a series of papers culminating in 1929–1930, McCrea, following up on work originally begun by Cecilia Payne, demonstrated that hydrogen dominated the solar atmosphere, laying down the basis for what became the accepted view that the ratio of hydrogen to helium is about 3:1.

Although he moved to Derbyshire when he was two, McCrea was always proud of his Irish heritage, and maintained close ties to his homeland throughout his life and work. His later connection to Armagh Observatory, and especially its director Eric Lindsay, did much to sustain that venerable institution during some of its darkest days, just preceding Lindsay's appointment in 1937. Then, beginning with a mysterious 1940 phone call from the Irish mathematician (and Taoiseach, or prime minister of Ireland) Éamon de Valera, McCrea was intimately involved in the establishment and initial running of Ireland's justifiably well regarded School for Theoretical Physics. Later, when Ireland's pulling out of the British Commonwealth led Irish scientists to fear isolation, McCrea was responsible for siting the Royal Astronomical Society's third summer meeting in Dublin (1950)—its first convening outside the United Kingdom. Similarly, in 1957 he helped to persuade the British Association for the Advancement of Science to hold its annual meeting in Dublin. Throughout all this, and nearly to the end of his life, McCrea also had special interest, not to mention success, in encouraging young Irish scientists and students to work in United Kingdom labs, his own included.

Born in Dublin on 13 December 1904, he died after several years of declining health in Lewes, Sussex, on 25 April 1999, leaving behind his three children Isabel,

Sheila, and Roderick. Marian, his wife of many years, had died four years earlier. McCrea's death marked the end of an era in British astronomy. Indeed, that era's very existence owed much to McCrea's own contributions. McCrea attended Chesterfield Grammar School, and went up to Cambridge in 1923 with an entrance scholarship to Trinity. While at Cambridge, he was awarded a Rayleigh Prize in Mathematics, and became a Rouse Ball Senior Student at Trinity. As if this were not enough, McCrea concurrently earned a first-class BSc honors degree in mathematics from the University of London.

In 1928–1929 McCrea was a visiting research student in Göttingen. At that time Göttingen functioned as a finishing school for mathematical physicists drawn from all over the world—McCrea just missed America's Howard P. Robertson, and studied alongside the Canadian and future Nobel Prize–winner Gerhard Herzberg. At Göttingen he found himself in a hotbed of mathematical physics, both pure and applied: Harald Bohr lectured on periodic functions, and Lev Landau on number theory, while David Hilbert and John von Neuman were the stars of the new mathematics of relativity and quantum mechanics. McCrea was to apply his Göttingen studies immediately in his work on solar atmospheric composition, and shortly thereafter in general relativity and cosmology.

Career Path. After returning from Göttingen, McCrea took an appointment as lecturer in mathematics in Edinburgh; two years later he moved to Imperial College as reader in mathematics, where he stayed until 1936. At that time he moved back to Ireland, to the chair in mathematics at Queen's University, Belfast. Taking war leave from Queen's in 1943, he went to work for Patrick M. S. Blackett in the Admiralty in London. He did not leave London for the next twenty-three years: from 1944 until 1966 he served as professor of mathematics and head of department at the University of London's Royal Holloway College. McCrea's final move was to the Astronomy Center in Sussex, an institution whose fraught history and birth he had been intimately involved in. Interestingly, it was his first and only official appointment in an astronomy institution!

During his career McCrea accumulated many honors. He became a Fellow of the Royal Society in 1952; served as president of the Royal Astronomical Society (RAS) from 1961 to 1963; was an RAS Gold Medallist in 1976; and was knighted in 1985. He was also a member or fellow of the London Mathematical Society, Royal Irish Academy, and the Royal Society of Edinburgh. In addition to visiting at many universities, McCrea received honorary degrees from five of them. In 1988 he was made a Freeman of the City of London.

Cosmological Research. McCrea is perhaps best known for his work in modern relativistic cosmology. He was in on it from the start. In late September 1931, the British Association for the Advancement of Science held a special session devoted to the evolution of the universe, a topic of considerable interest following Edwin Powell Hubble's measurements of what appeared to be galactic velocity red-shifts, which soon came to be associated with the expanding cosmological models that Alexander Friedmann and Georges Lemaître had developed from general relativity theory. Participants in this session, which by its nature constituted the quasi-official origin of modern relativistic cosmology, included all the leading senior workers in the field, for example, Arthur S. Eddington, Willem de Sitter, Edward Arthur Milne, and Herbert Dingle among others. McCrea arrived at the session in a rush, accompanied by the equally young and new astronomer George Cunliffe McVittie, whom he had befriended in Edinburgh. "We got there late," McCrea was to say later, "and there was a huge overflow crowd. They opened up another room, and set up a loudspeaker, and that's how we attended the meeting" (Smith interview, 1978). From that point on, McCrea and McVittie were each going to be a lot closer to the action.

The two collaborated on a problem Eddington had set, namely seeing whether a Friedmann-Lemaître expansion, leading to a de Sitter end-state, could be generated from an Einstein beginning state. They did not make much progress; the mathematics, they noted, were formidable. But this introduction to expanding universe models marked the beginning of a lifetime of work in the field for both men.

McCrea's next project achieved very real success in reducing cosmology's mathematical formidability. A 1933 paper coauthored with Oxford's Milne demonstrated the possibility of a Newtonian cosmology, something that no one before, including Isaac Newton himself, had believed could be done. Their results provided a generally available, much simpler model of the universe than relativistic cosmology's model. Using their model, one could very easily show many results relevantly similar to relativistic results without resorting to the intricate complexities of the general theory of relativity. Of all McCrea's accomplishments, this one earned him the greatest measure of gratitude from the world's astronomy students!

His relationship with Milne demonstrates what a deep and loyal friend McCrea could be. Milne was a brilliant, moody person, original yet sometimes arcane in his thinking, and his evident role was to play philosophical gadfly, confronting more conservative sorts such as McVittie and, especially, Dingle. Milne was a controversial figure, and it cost him emotionally. It is hard to imagine Milne soldiering on without the quiet support of

McCrea. In one letter, written shortly after the tragic death of his first wife, a horribly depressed Milne thanks McCrea for his "generous encouragement." The two men stayed close until Milne's untimely death in 1950; McCrea kept their correspondence throughout most of his life.

During the 1930s and up until the war, McCrea worked on a multitude of problems in astronomy and astrophysics. One area that interested him considerably was the problem of confronting relativistic cosmology with observations; his 1935 paper on the subject laid the foundations for decades of subsequent work.

Once the war started, McCrea withdrew—on his own choosing—from the cosmological fray, and, under Blackett, focused on operational research. After the war, it was back to astrophysics, astronomy, and cosmology. In this last field his influence was once again, and soon, of monumental significance.

Steady State Controversy. In addition to having been one of only two persons to hold the four RAS offices of president, secretary, treasurer, and foreign correspondent, McCrea also served as editor of both leading RAS publications, *Observatory* and *Monthly Notices.* It was during service on the latter that he single-handedly initiated one of the more exciting phases of modern cosmology, the controversy over the steady state theory of the universe.

In this theory, Hermann Bondi and his co-author Thomas Gold proposed that, contrary to the then-orthodox relativistic expanding universe theory, the universe did not have an origin in time, but rather had always been as it is now, expanding due to a continuous creation of matter, thereby achieving, as its name indicated, a steady-state. How the original article introducing the theory got accepted for publication is classic McCrea.

During summer 1948, McCrea was serving the RAS as secretary, whose job it was to delegate referees for submitted manuscripts. "I was alone at the time, I think it must have been at the Long Vac. When manuscripts came in, I was supposed to appoint a reviewer, so when Bondi's manuscript came in, as I was alone, I appointed myself to be reviewer, reviewed the manuscript, and then, as Secretary, accepted it for publication" (Smith interview, 1978, p. 24).

McCrea told this story with a twinkle in his eye. As nearly everyone interested or active in the fields of astronomy, physics, and cosmology knows steady state theory was enormously controversial throughout its lifetime, with passionate devotees and equally passionate haters always set against one another, frequently in print, and sometimes even in public. RAS meetings during the controversy were often fraught with tension among the members. Without McCrea's intervention it is doubtful that the theory would have seen light of day, let alone such an illustrious venue as *Monthly Notices* for its introduction.

McCrea was attracted to the steady-state theory from the beginning, for several reasons. First, of course, was the simple fact of his role in its initial publication. Secondly, although the theory's invoking of a continuous creation of matter—rather than having all matter created in one instant at t_o —offended many physicists, McCrea was not one of them. Indeed, over the next several years he worked to discover a method to integrate continuous creation into the relativistic field equations. His success was announced in a May 1951 paper "Relativity Theory and the Creation of Matter," which once and for all settled the question whether the steady-state theory was compatible with general relativity.

Yet, although these reasons were strong ones, there was a third set of reasons that strongly inclined McCrea to pursue the steady-state theory rather than orthodox relativistic expanding theories. It would not be unfair to characterize these reasons as "philosophical." From the very beginning of his work in the field, McCrea had sought to confront cosmological theory with observation, in part simply to restrain excursions of theorists' imaginations, and in part to provide evidence for choosing between competing models. As the 1930s became 1940s, it became evident to him and other workers that observational tests for cosmological theory were not thick on the ground. While McCrea put aside his research during the war, he did not stop thinking about this central problem. When the Bondi-Gold theory came along, it offered distinct advantages over relativistic expanding universe theory in this regard. As McCrea would later note, "The simple steady-state model was unique. On conceptual grounds this was … a high recommendation. On observational grounds, it rendered the model as vulnerable as possible to observational test" (McCrea 1968, p. 1296). Bondi and Gold had argued that their theory predicted several specific observations—H-He ratios, galactic density counts, etc.—which, if they failed, would contradict the theory. McCrea liked both the specificity of the predictions, and their logic. As he argued, correctly, predictions that are verified can only provide support for a theory, they cannot verify the theory itself. Contradictions, by contrast, rule out a theory *tout court.* Bondi, following Karl Popper, emphasized that steady-state was more scientific than relativistic expanding universe theory because it was specifically and directly *falsifiable.* McCrea appreciated this point about steady-state theory.

Yet, even though he was instrumental in the presentation and development of the steady state theory, when evidence accumulated against it, McCrea gave it up. In review articles in 1968, 1970, and 1984 he specifically addressed the basic cosmological models and evaluated their performance against the available physical evidence, indicating specifically where the steady-state theory had been falsified by observational evidence.

By his later years at Sussex's Astronomy Center, McCrea had become somewhat skeptical of the cosmological enterprise in general, and Big Bang cosmology in particular. In the end, it seemed that he was disappointed in all cosmological models, perhaps because they failed the high standards he held for both the nature of evidential support and our physical understanding of astronomical processes.

One of McCrea's more satisfying affairs was the RAS 160th Anniversary Dinner in early 1980. Having been asked to address the gathering, he responded, "Oh, surely Professor X of such and such other Society would be a better choice," only to be told that "he would be good but he would go on too long." McCrea: "So I said 'What about Professor Y of yet another Society?' 'Yes, but he would be serious' was the answer to that one. So I began to get the message—short and silly is what's wanted" (McCrea, 1980). In the end, what the listeners got was wit, surely, but coupled with wisdom, a typical McCrea performance.

Later Years. A few years later McCrea reflected on his travels and professional experiences in an attempt to explain some of the dynamics of the preceding fifty years of astronomy. His work revealed an amazing genealogy, a fully developed family tree of astronomy's researchers, teachers, and students at several of the great world centers of the discipline. This work, along with his masterful chapter in R. J. Tayler's *History of the Royal Astronomical Society*, remains excellent testimony to both McCrea's care for his profession, and his care to get the facts right.

McCrea's ninetieth birthday in December 1994 was a festive occasion at the RAS, with speeches given, toasts made, and many wishes for long life. Some of the material was published, most happily a tribute in the *Irish Astronomical Journal* to "Sir William McCrea at 90: A Great Irish Astronomer."

McCrea believed that astronomy, and especially cosmology, could never be separated from deeper meaning. "Cosmology requires, I venture to assert, the concept of Creator and of personality, and together these mean God" (Yourgrau and Breck, p. 72). Supporting this view was McCrea's religious faith. As he later told an interviewer: "I'm a practicing Christian, and Anglican, and I can claim a real faith. I know there are many problems and puzzles, but one is conscious, at the very least, that there must be a purpose in one's existence" (Smith Interview, 1978, p. 36).

A similar sentiment appears at the end of his RAS 160th anniversary talk. It is worth quoting at length:

> After 160 years, the Universe around us that we contemplate as astronomers and geophysicists, is as mysterious as when the Society was founded. We know a great deal more than our founders did about the structure of the Universe. Who would say that we have learned any more about its meaning and purpose? In raising our glasses to the health of our sciences let us hope that in the coming years they will bring us not only still further knowledge of the structure and operation of the Universe, but also some spark of light upon these profounder mysteries.

BIBLIOGRAPHY

WORKS BY MCCREA

With Edward A. Milne. "Newtonian Universes and the Curvature of Space." *Quarterly Journal of Mathematics* 5 (1934): 73–80.

"Observable Relations in Relativistic Cosmology." *Zeitschrift für Astrophysik* 9 (1935): 290–314.

"E. A. Milne." *Monthly Notices of the Royal Astronomical Society* 111 (1951): 160–170.

"Relativity Theory and the Creation of Matter." *Proceedings of the Royal Society of London,* ser. A, 206 (1951): 562–575.

"Cosmology." *Reports on Progress in Physics* 16 (1953): 321–363.

"Cosmology—A Brief Review." *Quarterly Journal of the Royal Astronomical Society* 4 (1963): 185–202.

"Cosmology after Half a Century." *Science* NS 160 (21 June 1968): 12951–11299.

"A Philosophy for Big-Bang Cosmology." *Nature* 228 (1970): 21–24.

"Models, Laws, and the Universe." In *Cosmology, History, and Theology,* edited by Wolfgang Yourgrau and Allen D. Breck. New York: Plenum, 1977.

Interview with Robert W. Smith, 22 September 1978. College Park, MD: Niels Bohr Library, American Institute of Physics,

"Address by Professor W. H. McCrea, FRS, at the RAS 160th Anniversary Dinner." *Quarterly Journal of the Royal Astronomical Society* 21 (1980): 220–223.

"Physics and Cosmology: Some Interactions." In *The Big Bang and Georges Lemaître: Proceedings of a Symposium in Honour of G. Lemaître Fifty Years after his Initiation of Big-Bang Cosmology, Louvain-la-Neuve, Belgium, 10–13 October 1983,* edited by A. Berger. Dordrecht, The Netherlands: Reidel, 1984.

"Cambridge Physics 1925–1929: Diamond Jubilee of Golden Years." *Interdisciplinary Science Reviews* 11 (1986): 269–284.

"Clustering of Astronomers." *Annual Review of Astronomy and Astrophysics* 25 (1987): 1–22.

"The Decade 1931–1940." In *History of the Royal Astronomical Society,* vol. 2, edited by Roger J. Tayler. Palo Alto, CA: Blackwell Scientific, 1987.

Interview with George Gale, 12 October 1988.

OTHER SOURCES

Kragh, Helge. *Cosmology and Controversy: The Historical Development of Two Theories of the Universe.* Princeton, NJ: Princeton University Press, 1996.

McNally, D. "Sir William McCrea at 90: A Great Irish Astronomer." *Irish Astronomical Journal* 24 (1997): 49–54.

North, John David. *The Norton History of Astronomy and Cosmology.* New York: Norton, 1994.

George Gale

MCCULLOCH, WARREN STURGIS

(*b.* Orange, New Jersey, 16 November 1898; *d.* Old Lyme, Connecticut, 24 September 1969), *neurophysiology, cybernetics, cognitive science.*

McCulloch was a central figure in the early cybernetics movement. Cybernetics emerged from the interaction of anthropologists, mathematicians, neurophysiologists, physicists, psychiatrists, and psychologists with the financial backing of the Josiah Macy Jr. Foundation. Cybernetics analyzed biological, psychological, and social phenomena in terms of positive and negative feedback, communication, information, and computation. Cybernetic ideas have since diffused widely, but most notably into the fields of artificial intelligence, cognitive science, communication, and computer science.

McCulloch's education ranged widely. At Carteret Academy in Orange, New Jersey, a private high school for boys, he devoted extra study to mathematics and Latin and also had a keen personal interest in poetry and secret codes. In the fall of 1917, he enrolled at Haverford College in Haverford, Pennsylvania, but with the outbreak of World War I, he transferred to Yale to be a part of the Yale Naval Training Unit. After a few months of active duty spanning the end of the war, McCulloch decided to remain at Yale. He graduated in 1921 with a major in philosophy. In 1923 he graduated from Columbia University with a master's degree in psychology, then turned his sights to psychiatry at Columbia's College of Physicians and Surgeons, graduating with an MD in 1927. McCulloch completed his internship and residency at Bellevue Hospital in New York City; he then returned to Columbia for a year to work in the Neurosurgical Laboratory in the Department of Neurology before returning to Bellevue for a year. He spent a year in graduate work in mathematical physics at New York University in 1931–1932 before serving a stint on the admission service at Rockland State Hospital in New York. What followed was a thirty-five-year career of scientific and philosophical investigation of the mind and brain.

The majority of McCulloch's subsequent scientific career falls into three periods corresponding to the institutions where he drew his salary: the Laboratory of Neurophysiology at Yale University's Medical School; the Illinois Neuropsychiatric Institute at the University of Illinois Medical School; and the Research Laboratory for Electronics at the Massachusetts Institute of Technology (MIT).

At Yale. Johann Gregorius Dusser de Barenne was Sterling Professor of Physiology and head of Yale's Laboratory of Neurophysiology from 1930 until his death in 1940. McCulloch joined Dusser de Barenne on a fellowship in 1934, but eventually worked himself up to the rank of assistant professor in 1940. During his years at Yale, McCulloch established himself as a neurophysiologist and authority on the sensory and motor cortex, working primarily with macaques and chimpanzees. An important component of his research concerned the functional organization of the brain. On the hypothesis that a particular region of the brain is dedicated to one specific function, say, motor control of the arm, the question of functional organization asks how that region is connected to other regions dedicated to other functions, such as motor control of the leg. Dusser de Barenne and McCulloch's principal tool was strychnine neuronography. This technique involved applying a dilute colored solution of strychnine to the exposed surface of an animal's cortex. The strychnine would induce distinctive, easily measured electrical activity in the brain region to which the poisoned neurons projected. This method was a great advance over degenerative techniques that involved performing one surgery to destroy a portion of the brain, then waiting several weeks to perform a second surgery to ascertain what pathways in the brain may have deteriorated as a result of the destruction. Clearly, much more data could be collected in one day with strychnine neuronography than could be collected in months with degenerative methods. Further, by measuring the effects of the strychnine with electronic apparatus, the method allowed for more precise measurements than mere gross sensory or motor responses to stimuli.

A second significant research project for Dusser de Barenne and McCulloch concerned the ways in which an electrical stimulus applied to one point of the cortex facilitates or extinguishes motor responses to a second test stimulus. For many decades, it had been known that a given stimulus could facilitate the motor effects of a second stimulus. Dusser de Barenne and McCulloch, however, discovered that there are conditions under which a given stimulus could extinguish the motor effects of a second test stimulus. What made this interesting to them was that the extinguishing effect could not be explained in terms of fatigue of the stimulated neurons. Large initial stimuli did not induce the extinction as well as did just supraliminal stimuli. Were the effect a matter of fatigue, they reasoned, the effect would be proportional to the

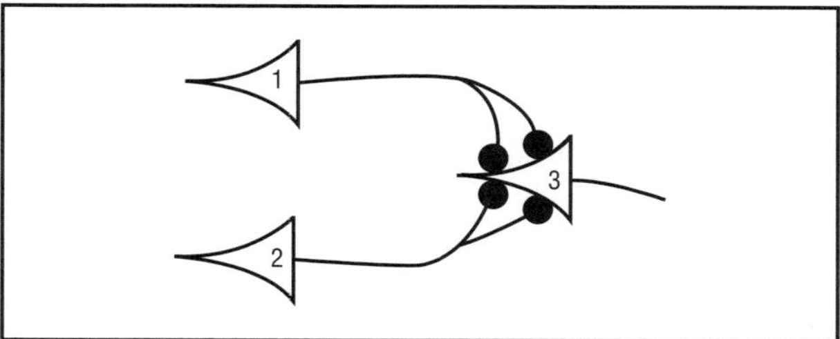

Figure 1. *McCulloch-Pitts network for disjunction.*

intensity of the initial stimulus. In other words, the extinguishing effect seemed to reveal something about the mechanisms of normal brain function. Five years' worth of investigation on these facilitating and extinguishing phenomena led them to the conclusion that multiple factors were involved, one of them being reverberating electrical activity in closed loops of neurons. This was especially rewarding to them, since just a few years before this Rafael Lorente de Nó had used anatomical evidence to argue for the existence of closed loops of neurons.

In June 1940, Dusser de Barenne died suddenly of heart disease. Rather than continue its support of neurophysiology, the faculty of Yale's Medical School decided to reallocate Dusser de Barenne's endowed chair to another discipline, leading to the incorporation of the Laboratory of Neurophysiology into John Fulton's Laboratory of Physiology. With considerable disappointment and frustration, McCulloch felt compelled to search for another academic appointment. With the help of friends, he was appointed director of research at the newly created Illinois Neuropsychiatric Institute starting 1 September 1941.

At the University of Illinois. While McCulloch's stature was growing during his time at Yale, the move to Chicago enabled him to flourish as his own intellectual, working on research projects of his own conception. It also dramatically expanded McCulloch's range of scientific connections. At the Neuropsychiatric Institute, he continued to work on purely physiological and neurophysiological projects, such as tests of glucose tolerance, carbohydrate metabolism, and the anatomical mapping of neuronal pathways in the brain. His best-known contributions from his time in Chicago, however, were the product of interdisciplinary collaborative projects beyond the confines of the institute. He also indulged his literary side through his involvement with the Chicago Literary Club and in later years was proud of the fact that a collection of his poetry, *The Natural Fit* (1959), was the first poetry ever published by the society.

Among his earliest new friends in Chicago was a medical school student, Jerome Lettvin, who introduced McCulloch in turn to his younger friend, Walter Pitts. For many years, McCulloch had thought that it should be possible to describe the activity of networks of neurons using some form of Boolean logic of sentences. This was to be a formalization of some of the early-twentieth-century qualitative theories of the role of networks of neurons underlying psychological processes. From his work at Yale, McCulloch had also come to believe that closed loops of neurons played an important role in brain activity. Pitts was just the partner McCulloch needed in order to formalize his logical conception of nervous nets. Though still a very young man of eighteen, Pitts had for some years been studying logic and mathematics on his own. Moreover, he had allied himself with Nicolas Rashevsky's group in mathematical biophysics at the University of Chicago and for about a year had been working on a project to use differential equations to describe the electrical activity in closed loops of neurons. Realizing their confluence of interests, McCulloch and Pitts set about forging what came to be their most significant paper, "A Logical Calculus of the Ideas Immanent in Nervous Activity." This work, published in 1943 in Rashevsky's journal, *Bulletin of Mathematical Biophysics*, gave logico-mathematical form to the idea that networks of neurons compute logical functions.

"A Logical Calculus": Two Ideas. There are two principal ideas in "A Logical Calculus." The first, and most influential, is that it is possible to establish formal equivalences between formulas in an extension of Boolean logic and networks of on-off neurons that contain no closed loops. As a simple example, consider the network of three neurons shown in Figure 1. The formula McCulloch and Pitts would use to describe this network would be $N_3(t) \equiv N_1(t-1) \vee N_2(t-1)$, which asserts that the neuron N_3 will fire at time t if, and only if, either neuron N_1 fires at time $t-1$ (an earlier instant of time) or neuron N_2 fires at time $t-1$. McCulloch and Pitts assumed that it required two excitatory inputs to cause a neuron to fire; they inserted two such inputs from both neuron N_1 and neuron N_2. As a second example, there is the network shown in Figure 2. McCulloch and Pitts would describe this network using

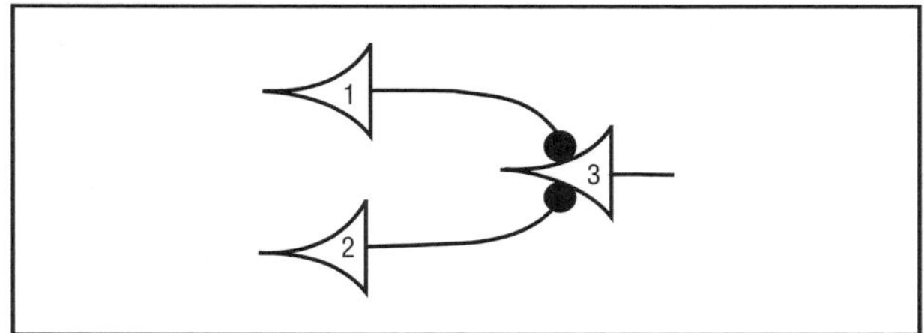

Figure 2. *McCulloch-Pitts network for conjunction.*

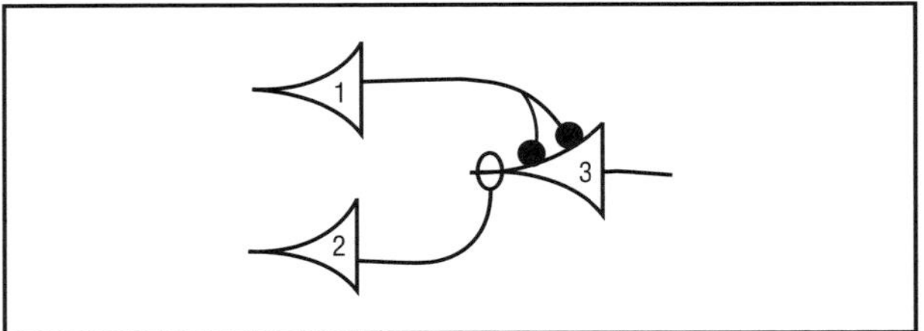

Figure 3. *McCulloch-Pitts networks for A and not-B.*

the formula $N_3(t) \equiv N_1(t-1) \,.\, N_2(t-1)$, which asserts that N_3 will fire at time t if, and only if, both N_1 fires at time $t-1$ and N_2 fires at time $t-1$. A third example is the network shown in Figure 3, with positive excitatory synapses shown as black dots and negative inhibitory synapses show as open circles. McCulloch and Pitts would describe this network using the formula $N_3(t) \equiv N_1(t-1) \,.\, {\sim}N_2(t-1)$, which asserts that N_3 will fire at time t if, and only if, both N_1 fires at $t-1$ and N_2 does not fire at $t-1$. The technical challenge of this idea lay in showing how any network not containing closed loops could be described using a formula in the system McCulloch and Pitts had developed and in showing how any formula in the system could be used to generate an equivalent network.

The second major idea in "A Logical Calculus" was the suggestion that closed loops of neurons could be used to explain memory, purposive behavior, homeostasis, and various psychiatric disorders. So, McCulloch and Pitts's work provided formal descriptions of what was then the intuitively appealing hypothesis that short-term memory consists of electrical activity in closed loops of excitatory neurons. This kind of short-term memory could complement a kind of long-term memory constituted by modifications to the connections among neurons. The links to purposive behavior and homeostasis came about through McCulloch's extramural interactions. While working on "A Logical Calculus," McCulloch learned of Arturo Rosenblueth's, Norbert Wiener's, and Julian Bigelow's ideas of positive and negative feedback loops and their relation to purposive behavior. According to their analysis, purposive behavior is simply behavior guided by negative feedback. Aiming for a goal is a matter of having some mechanism that detects deviation from that goal and uses negative feedback to correct for the deviation. Closed loops of neurons might provide such a mechanism.

"A Logical Calculus": The Upshots. "A Logical Calculus" thus helped establish common ground between McCulloch and Pitts, as well as others who were interested in the emerging theory of computation, computer engineering, information, and communication and their application to a broad spectrum of biological, psychological, and sociological phenomena. The practical upshot of this common interest was the initiation of a series of interdisciplinary conferences on "circular causality" to be sponsored by the Josiah Macy Jr. Foundation, with McCulloch as conference chairman. Each conference, initially held at six-month intervals, then later at one-year intervals, featured some five or perhaps ten papers separated by ample time for extensive discussion. In fact, the discussion was widely heralded as the high point of the conferences. In time, the ten conferences of the series attracted an impressive array of mid-twentieth-century luminaries, including the anthropologists Gregory Bateson and Margaret Mead, the engineer Claude Shannon, the mathematicians John von Neumann and Norbert Wiener, the philosopher F. S. C. Northrop, the physiologists Ralph Gerard and Rafael Lorente de Nó, the psychiatrist Lawrence Kubie, and the psychologists Heinrich Klüver and Donald Marquis.

Aside from its influence on the cybernetics movement, "A Logical Calculus" for many years inspired additional research in Nicolas Rashevsky's mathematical biophysics. Attempts to clarify, simplify, and extend the results in "A Logical Calculus" also led more mathematically inclined investigators to develop what came to be known as automata theory. In later years, the paper served as an important reference point for other mathematical treatments of neural networks, such as Frank Rosenblatt's work on perceptrons.

The other noteworthy collaboration between McCulloch and Pitts at about this time was "How We Know Universals: The Perception of Auditory and Visual Forms" (1947). This paper showed how one might account for Gestalt invariants in the visual perception of sizes and shapes and in the auditory perception of musical chords in terms of structures that could be mapped onto specific brain structures.

At MIT. During the course of the Macy conferences, McCulloch finished his eleventh year at the Neuropsychiatric Institute. By then, he had had his fill of the responsibilities of directing a research operation involving some forty faculty, students, and staff. He and his wife, Rook, also wished to return to the East Coast to be closer to their summer home, a farm in Old Lyme, Connecticut. Topping it off, there was the prospect of working in a neurophysiology group with Lettvin and Pitts, who had already moved to Cambridge, with the further hope of attracting Patrick Wall to their group. Adding a neurophysiology group to MIT's Research Laboratory for Electronics was intended to more fully implement Wiener's vision of a center for cybernetic ideas. MIT would, thus, become the institutional home to the fruits of the Macy conferences. All of which made a move to MIT in October 1952 seem eminently attractive.

Unfortunately for all involved, the move did not bear the fruit that was expected. Just as the negotiations for McCulloch's move were reaching their conclusion, a personal rift arose between Wiener and McCulloch, Pitts, and Lettvin. Much to McCulloch's, Pitts's, and Lettvin's disappointment, Wiener refused to have anything to do with them. This was the most dramatic development of the MIT years, but diverse interests also led the members of the group in different directions.

The break with Wiener was especially difficult for Pitts. Although always a troubled individual, the following years saw Pitts simply refuse to complete the work he needed to do for his PhD. Despite heroic efforts by Lettvin, McCulloch, and others, Pitts progressively lost interest in research and turned to long periods of self-destructive behavior. Lettvin and Wall perhaps remained most true to the original conception of an experimental group in neurophysiology. They took the lead in experimental work on the spinal cord and the use of strychnine during the early 1950s. In the late 1950s, Lettvin and Humberto Maturana produced some of the classic results in vision science. Using sophisticated microelectrodes, they found that cells in the frog's retina respond selectively to moving black dots. In other words, the frog's eye responded to things that looked like the frog's prey, namely, moving flies. Their subsequent publication, "What the Frog's Eye Tells the Frog's Brain" (1959), with McCulloch and Pitts as coauthors, became one of the most frequently cited papers in vision science.

McCulloch, for his part, contributed to the experimental work the group was doing on the spinal cord, the use of strychnine, frog vision, and neuron physiology, but his heart had moved away from experimental work in the direction of more purely logical and mathematical investigations. One of his later projects at MIT concerned how the brain could compute reliably given the unreliable, probabilistic activity of individual neuronal action potentials. He became interested in probabilistic, multivalued logics in contrast to the deterministic, two-valued logic of McCulloch-Pitts networks. Another project, pursued most extensively with William Kilmer, was the development of a theory of the reticular formation of the brain as a command and control center.

While at MIT, McCulloch indulged many more of his personal proclivities, some to good effect and some to not so good. A naturally gregarious extrovert with a talent for public speaking, during the 1950s and 1960s, McCulloch was frequently on the road giving lectures. He spoke on computers, cybernetics, and bionics at universities and conferences in the United States and in Europe. He also served as an advisor to the National Aeronautics and Space Administration and was the first elected president of the American Society for Cybernetics. Over the course of his travels, McCulloch met many bright and aspiring scientists whose careers he did his best to promote. Perhaps in part because of his experiences with the young Pitts and his fondness for young people in general, McCulloch also frequently gave lectures at high schools in Connecticut, Massachusetts, New Jersey, and New York. Less good for McCulloch was his love of scotch and filterless cigarettes. They apparently cut his life short while he was reading a research paper at his farm in Old Lyme.

BIBLIOGRAPHY

McCulloch's professional papers are available for scholarly use at the American Philosophical Society Library in Philadelphia.

WORKS BY MCCULLOCH

With W. Pitts. "A Logical Calculus of the Ideas Immanent in Nervous Activity." *Bulletin of Mathematical Biophysics* 5 (1943): 115–133.

With W. Pitts. "How We Know Universals: The Perception of Auditory and Visual Forms." *Bulletin of Mathematical Biophysics* 9 (1947): 127–147.

The Natural Fit. Chicago: Chicago Literary Club, 1959. A pamphlet of poetry, reprinted in *The Embodiments of Mind.*

With J. Y. Lettvin, H. R. Maturana, and W. H. Pitts. "What the Frog's Eye Tells the Frog's Brain." *Proceedings of the IRE* 47 (1959): 1940–1951.

The Collected Works of Warren S. McCulloch. Edited by Rook McCulloch. Salinas, CA: Intersystems Publications, 1989. An extensive, but still incomplete, collection of McCulloch's publications and lectures. The primary omissions are published abstracts from conference proceedings.

The Embodiments of Mind. Cambridge, MA: MIT Press, 1989. A sampler of McCulloch's publications and lectures from 1943 to 1964. This collection obviously does not at all represent the work McCulloch carried out at Yale.

OTHER SOURCES

Abraham, T. "(Physio)logical Circuits: The Intellectual Origins of the McCulloch-Pitts Neural Networks." *Journal of the History of the Behavioral Sciences* 38 (2002): 3–25.

———. "Integrating Mind and Brain: Warren S. McCulloch, Cerebral Localization, and Experimental Epistemology." *Endeavour* 27 (2003): 32–36.

Arbib, M. "Warren McCulloch's Search for the Logic of the Nervous System." *Perspectives in Biology and Medicine* 43 (2000): 193–216.

Kenneth Aizawa

MCVITTIE, GEORGE CUNLIFFE

(*b.* İzmir, Turkey, 5 June 1904; *d.* Canterbury, United Kingdom, 8 March 1988), *astronomy, applied mathematics.*

McVittie mathematically explored cosmological models, drawing out consequences to match against observations. His 1956 book *General Relativity and Cosmology* was for years the major mathematical presentation of relativistic cosmology. He built the astronomy department at the University of Illinois into a significant research and teaching program, and as secretary of the American Astronomical Society shaped its programs.

Early Life. McVittie's birth was followed by that of a brother in 1906 and a sister in 1908. His maternal grandfather, Georg Weber, a native of Alsace, taught French at the Evangelical School in İzmir and wrote archaeological books on Ephesus and Smyrna (as İzmir was named when it was an ancient Greek city). George's father, Francis, born in Blackpool, went out from England around 1890 as secretary to a licorice importer, married in 1903, lost his job in 1905, obtained an agency to import American rolltop desks in 1907, developed his own primitive department store by 1914, and after World War I prospered buying up British Navy stores in the Aegean Islands and reselling them in Smyrna (as İzmir again was named, after the Greeks took it from the Turks in 1919). George later remembered his father as a hardheaded Victorian businessman whose only idea was that life was about making money.

Francis could not afford to send his sons to public school in England, from which they were cut off anyway by World War I. Nor did he want his sons mixing with the natives, so they were tutored at home. George first encountered relativity theory in an engineering journal, after which his father imported a book on the theory, which George found unintelligible. Francis also bought a 3-inch naval telescope in 1919. Late in life, George would claim that he had never made an astronomical observation, other than detecting with a radio antenna from the top of a tall building the passage of *Sputnik.* Nor would he ever take more than a single astronomy course, a graduate one on stellar structure.

Home tutoring was successful; George passed the Cambridge University entrance examinations with distinction in 1921. School fees and the cost of living were lower in Edinburgh, however, and George arrived there in August 1922 to find lodging and enter the university, in civil engineering, a practical subject his father approved of.

The rest of the family was on vacation in London in September when the Turks retook İzmir, and in the process destroyed much of the city and the McVittie business. Francis found employment in London as secretary of a relief committee for British who had fled Smyrna, and George joined him there, typing and copying letters. Francis soon built a small business in London importing and repairing oriental carpets.

In their relief work the McVitties impressed an Edinburgh businessman, who raised a subscription of six hundred pounds as a loan to Francis, repayable, if he ever recovered his business in İzmir, and if not, a gift, to see George through university. George also won a small scholarship, and entered Edinburgh University in 1923, a year after his earlier, aborted attempt.

His heart was set on a master of arts in mathematics and natural philosophy, which he received in 1927, with first-class honors. His now impoverished father had less influence over George and his choice of studies. University regulations required taking two subjects in the humanities, and years later George would attribute the origin of his uncompromising empiricist attitude perhaps to a series of lectures on Plato, Aristotle, Immanuel Kant, John Locke, George Berkeley, and David Hume.

Cosmological Studies. Most physicists and astronomers then were perplexed by Einstein's relativity theory, while mathematicians could more readily participate, through theory if not observation, in the exciting new quest to know the structure of the universe. Edmund Whittaker, professor of mathematics at Edinburgh, contributed perhaps more to the development of relativity theory than any other British mathematician. He was an outstanding teacher who explained his subject clearly. Although it was unusual then even for junior staff, let alone students, to be invited to professors' homes, Whittaker hosted tea parties for students at his house on Sundays and sometimes informal dances in his drawing room.

In 1927 McVittie won a scholarship of 200 pounds for three years of graduate study. Other than in Oxford, it was expected that anyone showing promise in mathematics would finish off at Cambridge. McVittie stayed in less-expensive Edinburgh for another year, collecting a second fellowship involving some teaching and learning more from Whittaker, before he moved to Cambridge to study with Arthur Eddington, the professor of astronomy there. Eddington, when praised as one of only three persons who understood Einstein's relativity theory, is said to have thought a moment before asking who was the third.

Twice a term McVittie cycled out to the Cambridge observatory, where he was shown by a maid into Eddington's study. Eddington would look up from his desk, giving the impression that he was wondering who this young man was and why had he come. Eddington seemed distant, unapproachable, and unintelligible. Compared with Edinburgh, McVittie found the atmosphere at Cambridge suffocating.

Also there were philosophical incompatibilities. Eddington pursued mathematically elegant theories, and he was trying to reconcile quantum mechanics and relativity theory. McVittie preferred to pin down things with observations. He hoped to develop mathematically possible cosmological models of the universe and then use observations to choose among them.

In 1929 the American astronomer Edwin Hubble announced his discovery of an empirical relation between red shifts of spectral lines in light from spiral nebulae and the apparent brightness of the nebulae. The red shifts could be interpreted as Doppler shifts, implying motions of the nebulae, and apparent brightness was taken as an indicator of distance. Greater velocities for more distant nebulae suggested an expanding universe. In Edinburgh, Whittaker suggested to a student that he should look into the possibility of interpreting Hubble's red shifts in the context of general relativity. In Cambridge, however, it seemed, at least to McVittie, that no one other than himself had much interest in Hubble's new velocity-distance relationship. A large gulf existed between mathematical physics and observational cosmology.

At the beginning of 1930 Eddington did put McVittie to work on the problem of whether Albert Einstein's static model of the universe is stable. The problem, however, had already been studied by Georges Lemaître, a Belgian astrophysicist, a Catholic priest, and a student with Eddington in 1923–1924. Indeed, Lemaître had sent Eddington a reprint of his 1927 paper on a homogeneous universe of constant mass and increasing radius accounting for the radial velocity of the extragalactic nebulae. But by 1930 Eddington had forgotten about Lemaître's work. Published in a relatively minor journal, *Annales de la Société Scientifique de Bruxelles,* Lemaître's paper was easily overlooked by astronomers (although it was listed in the 1927 *Astronomischer Jahresbericht,* the annual survey of scientific papers on astronomical topics). A talk by Eddington in London at the end of January 1930 caused Lemaître to realize that Eddington did not remember his earlier work on an expanding universe. Lemaître wrote to Eddington, reminding him of the 1927 paper. Somewhat shamefacedly, Eddington showed Lemaître's letter to McVittie. Seeing that the problem of the stability of the static model had already been solved, McVittie became very discouraged, and temporarily abandoned research in cosmology.

Dropping the question of the stability of Einstein's mathematical model of the universe after only a few weeks' diversion allowed McVittie to complete in 1930 his PhD thesis on unified field theories. Einstein had proposed unifying electromagnetism and gravitation, and McVittie worked out several possible solutions. None, however, survived comparison with observations. This failure produced in McVittie a skeptical attitude toward unified field theories and a belief that the meaning of any set of field equations was best obtained by working out particular exact solutions. McVittie published his first three scientific papers on this topic, one in 1929 and two in 1930.

Early Career. McVittie obtained a position in 1930 as assistant lecturer in mathematics at Leeds, where he gave nine hours of lectures a week to undergraduates. The salary of 350 pounds per year sufficed during the Great Depression. In 1934 he married Mildred Bond Strong. They would have no children. Her father, John, was a professor of education in Leeds, and her brother, Kenneth, would become in 1964 the first director general of intelligence, Ministry of Defense.

Promotions normally were obtained by moving to another university, and McVittie moved up to lecturer in applied mathematics at Liverpool, with a salary of 450 pounds, in 1934, and to reader (equivalent to associate professor in the United States) in mathematics at King's College, University of London, in 1936. He could now attend meetings of the Royal Astronomical Society at Burlington House in London more regularly, and he became more interested in astronomy.

McVittie published nine more papers between 1930 and 1934, two jointly with William McCrea, who at the beginning of 1930 was a lecturer with Whittaker at Edinburgh. McVittie and McCrea examined what would happen to an Einstein universe were it given a prod: would condensations cause it to begin expanding or collapsing? On his own, McVittie showed mathematically that the Lemaître universe, departing from the equilibrium Einstein state, can expand or contract, and an initial contraction can be started by the formation of condensations. He went on to develop the mathematics necessary to tackle the problem of whether the universe would expand or contract when a condensation formed, but he did not answer the question.

McVittie grew skeptical of Hubble's observations and their interpretations, and by the mid-1930s he felt muddled. Nonetheless, in his *Cosmological Theory* of 1937 he calculated astronomical observables, hoping to select a particular universe in agreement with observation. But the mathematical methods he developed would prove more important than any cosmological conclusion. McVittie's dissatisfaction with Hubble's interpretation of his observations became the central theme of what had been intended as a review of the observational situation in cosmology that McVittie prepared for a joint meeting in 1939 between the Royal Astronomical Society and the Physical Society of London. Hubble had assumed corrections to his observed magnitudes of spiral nebulae for the dimming effect of the red shifts of the nebulae. McVittie argued in considerable mathematical detail that Hubble's assumptions were not valid in an expanding universe of general relativity, and concluded that it was impossible to advance beyond a few very tentative conclusions without introducing arbitrary and unjustified hypotheses.

Also during the 1930s McVittie debated Edward Arthur Milne, an astronomer at Oxford. At this time, philosophy professors at Oxford knew a priori that space was Euclidean, and they were equally convinced that the theory of relativity was false. Particularly bothersome to Milne was the contention that we probably would never know why space is expanding rather than contracting, both being equally probable in relativity theory. In his commonsense explanation, Milne rejected the notions of curved space and expansion of space, and proposed instead a group of nebulae moving in Euclidean space in random directions with different velocities. Such a model would soon acquire the appearance of an expanding group, the nebulae with highest velocities naturally having receded farthest from the starting point. McVittie found Milne's mathematics very interesting, differing as it did from that of relativistic cosmology, but he thought Milne's philosophy was silly. A strict empiricist, McVittie was quite content to let observations determine whether the universe was expanding or contracting; he felt no need, as had Milne, for theory to explain either expansion or contraction.

War Intervenes. As threat of war grew, McVittie registered with the Royal Society in 1938 for mathematical meteorological work, since obviously no astronomy would be involved in the war. While reading up on meteorology, he realized that relativity theory provided a mathematical apparatus applicable to the study of fluids, and into the 1950s he published several papers on gas dynamics.

In November 1939 McVittie was sent to the Government Communications Headquarters at Bletchley Park to decipher German weather messages and help prepare weather forecasts for air operations over German-held territory. Also, deciphered weather reports from locations in the Atlantic Ocean revealed positions of German submarines and helped reduce shipping losses. McVittie began the work single-handedly, but by 1943 headed a staff of sixty. He received the Officer of the Order of the British Empire for wartime contributions.

McVittie later recalled that World War II was a discontinuity in his scientific interests, but that is an exaggeration. He had continued to pursue his interest in cosmology during the early 1940s, in debates with Milne and with Arthur Geoffrey Walker, Milne's student. Indeed, there had been periods when McVittie had thought he would go crazy if he kept on dealing with ciphers, and his cosmological quarrels with Milne were welcome relief.

McVittie returned to King's College in 1945, and in 1948 he became professor of mathematics and head of the department at Queen Mary College, University of London. At King's, McVittie tutored Arthur C. Clarke in applied mathematics. Clarke later collaborated with Stanley Kubrick on the script for the movie *2001: A Space Odyssey,* in which the computer reported: "I am a HAL nine thousand computer Production Number 3. I became operational at the HAL Plant in Urbana, Illinois, on January 12, 1997." Clarke's choice of Urbana, home of the University of Illinois, for HAL's birthplace is explained by McVittie's presence there as chair of the astronomy department. How an English mathematician ended up in another field of study on another continent also calls for explanation.

McVittie in America. The 1950 meeting of the International Union of Mathematicians was to be held at Harvard University. British currency regulations allowed McVittie to take very little money out of the country, and he cast about for lecture engagements in America to pay his way. He obtained invitations to the Michigan Summer School for astronomers and to Harvard's astronomy department for the entire fall semester. McVittie and the head of Queen Mary College were "temperamentally unsuited to produce a fruitful collaboration," so McVittie later recalled in an oral interview for the American Institute of Physics—they were not "simpatico"—and both welcomed a temporary separation.

There were few American astronomers then; the large group of post–World War II students was just beginning to graduate. And even fewer were equipped to deal with cosmology. McVittie made a very favorable impression at Harvard, where his lectures were the beginning of his important role in introducing the study of relativity into the astronomy and physics graduate school curricula in the United States. Furthermore, Mrs. McVittie, a meticulous and conscientious housekeeper, found America a welcome change from Britain, where rationing and shortages after the war made it hard for women to run households.

In the fall of 1950 the dean of liberal arts and sciences at the University of Illinois asked Harlow Shapley, director of the Harvard College Observatory, if Illinois should revive its astronomy department—its only professor had recently retired—and with whom. (The correspondence is preserved at the university, under Staff Appointments Papers.) Initially Shapley recommended several American astronomers, but on 27 October 1950 wrote that he had just learned that McVittie, "a man of considerable ability and accomplishments, one of the best remaining in England, which is going into an astronomical slump," wanted to stay in America. Shapley added that Mrs. McVittie was a very attractive personality, had appreciable social interests, as did her husband, and both would be bright additions to the social life of any university.

Further praise for McVittie came from Leo Goldberg at the University of Michigan Observatory. He had tried to find a way to keep McVittie at Michigan, but his budget would not allow for the addition of another senior staff member. The mathematics department at Michigan was also interested in McVittie, but suffered the same budget limitation. Goldberg wrote on 3 May 1951, "As I understand it, you have no very extensive observational facilities at Illinois, and a theorist like McVittie would be ideally suited to your situation.… One reason for Dr. McVittie's success as a lecturer is his great personal charm and warm personality.… If you get McVittie, you will be adding a really distinguished man to your faculty."

More guarded was Martin Schwarzschild at the Princeton University Observatory. He had been struck by McVittie's "lack of astronomical background," but also

> by his eagerness to get more thoroughly acquainted with a larger body of astronomical facts. I rather think that this limitation in his acquaintance with astronomical data and observations has rather seriously hampered his effectiveness in theoretical astronomy and astrophysics. I could, however, well imagine that a position in this country with the many possibilities here to get in contact with astronomical observations and with its probable necessity of undergraduate teaching in astronomy might soon fill up Dr. McVittie's astronomical knowledge and then give him the possibility to apply his mathematical ability to astronomical problems with full effectiveness.

McVittie was offered and accepted the position at Illinois, beginning in the fall of 1952. Meanwhile, Queen Mary College obtained a new head and with him a new spirit. By the summer of 1952 McVittie was regretting leaving. Politicians in Illinois had opposed hiring yet another foreigner at the university, and the university president was fired a year later partly for his hiring policies. McVittie, however, never encountered any animosity. With his acerbic wit and pithy comments on the foibles of institutions and their constituents, Mac, as McVittie was called, enlivened faculty and professional society meetings. He was always critical, always usefully, always wittily, never hurtfully.

At Illinois, McVittie set up courses in astronomy, a master's degree program, and eventually a PhD program. He taught mathematical topics: relativity, cosmology, celestial mechanics, and dynamics. By 1956 the department had expanded to four astronomers, including Stanley P. Wyatt Jr., who wrote an outstanding astronomy textbook, at the expense of research McVittie wished he might otherwise have done. By 1969 the department had nine senior faculty members, three research associates, two dozen PhD students, and many undergraduate students taking elementary astronomy courses.

McVittie's work in mathematical aspects of cosmology led, in 1952, to his demonstration that a continuous creation process could exist in a suitably chosen general relativity model of the universe. This model might have bridged the gulf between relativistic cosmologists and proponents of the new steady state theory, who insisted that the universe will always appear the same to any observer. (First proposed in 1948 in England, steady state theory featured an expanding universe with constant density because new mass was being created out of nothing.) Most opponents of steady state cosmology, however, ignored McVittie's mathematical demonstration and continued to view relativistic cosmology and the continuous creation of matter as irreconcilable. It was not hard to set aside McVittie's conclusion, inasmuch as he, himself, had noted that the method employed in his paper was that of a priori cosmology, in which a model universe is developed not from observational data but from certain principles to which the universe purportedly conforms. These principles, believed reasonable because they were in agreement with the investigator's epistemological or philosophical views, really were restrictions imposed by the investigator on possible universes.

McVittie was opposed to steady state theory and its rationalistic fancies, as he termed them. Given a lack of reliable data, it was especially tempting in cosmology to substitute logic for observation. McVittie, however, strongly resisted. He rejected the hypothesis of continuous creation of matter as an unnecessary hypothesis. It was also a violation of energy conservation and basic rules of scientific reasoning. McVittie limited himself to what little could be determined about the universe from observation alone. He later remembered that he had been glad to get away from England and the hullabaloo, as he characterized it, about the new revelation of steady state theory.

At Illinois, Edward C. Jordan, in the Electrical Engineering Department and soon to be its chairman, encouraged McVittie to take up radio astronomy. In 1956 they jointly appointed George W. Swenson Jr., an electronics expert specializing in antenna design, to build a radio telescope, with funding from the Office of Naval Research.

Radio telescopes could detect objects farther away than could optical telescopes, and counts of radio sources at successive limits of brightness were more accurate than for optical sources, because the flux density of radio sources was comparatively more easily measured. McVittie worked out mathematically a formula for the predicted number of radio sources to successive limits of brightness (i.e., distance) for several model universes. Then he examined observations from radio telescopes in Australia and in England, only to infer from the data that changes occurred in the strengths of radio sources over time. Furthermore, the reported observations from Australia and England were not in harmony with each other. So, characteristically, McVittie called for further observations before a meaningful choice could be made between different cosmological models.

The required observational work would not be done at Illinois. Swenson, more interested in making instruments than in making use of data they produced, was often on leave at the National Radio Astronomy Observatory between 1964 and 1968. Furthermore, funding was reduced during the shift of federal support for science from the military to the National Science Foundation.

More successful than his radio astronomy research program at Illinois was McVittie's effort to have set aside from human-made interference a frequency band for radio astronomy. In 1963 the Federal Communications Commission declared television channel 37 a silent zone for ten years—to facilitate listening for little green men on Mars, so rumor said. Protection was extended to the whole world by resolution of an Extraordinary Administrative Radio Conference held in Geneva that same year; Swenson was scientific advisor to the U.S. delegation.

McVittie published *General Relativity and Cosmology* in 1956, and a second edition in 1965. For years it was the major mathematical presentation of relativistic cosmology. McVittie understood science as a method of correlating as much apparently disconnected sense data as possible into a rational scheme of thought: a theory. Newtonian mechanics was one such scheme, quantum mechanics a second, and general relativity a third means of interpreting data supplied by observation. McVittie mathematically developed consequences of the theory to match against observations. For McVittie in the 1950s, cosmology was an exercise in detection with a few elusive clues and some cautious preliminary conclusions, but no finality was then possible.

McVittie also wrote *Fact and Theory in Cosmology*, a popular account for readers without mathematical knowledge, published in 1961. Again he welded together astronomical observations with cosmological theories, but without the detailed mathematical proofs in *General Relativity and Cosmology*. In addition to general relativity, McVittie also included steady state theory and Milne's model in his study. Again, theories provided interpretations of data. And again, McVittie doubted that observational proof of any highly specific model of the universe would be forthcoming in the foreseeable future.

McVittie served as secretary of the American Astronomical Society from 1961 to 1969 and was influential in shaping its programs at a time of rapid growth in astronomy. He served as secretary (1958–1964), vice president (1964–1967), and president (1967–1970) of Commission 28 (Galaxies) of the International Astronomical Union (IAU). He chaired a 1961 IAU symposium and edited the resulting book: *Problems of Extra-Galactic Research* (1962).

Return to England. McVittie retired from the University of Illinois in 1972 and returned to England, where he became honorary professor of theoretical astronomy at the University of Kent. He was active there teaching colorfully and enthusiastically, supervising research students, and doing research until a year before his death. Under his influence a research group on relativity grew up in the mathematics department.

McVittie also was active in the Canterbury Archaeology Trust and the excavation in the city center of a Roman theater and temple precinct. Only then did he learn the history of his maternal grandfather and his work in archaeology.

McVittie was a Fellow of the Royal Society of Edinburgh, the Royal Astronomical Society, and the Royal Meteorological Society; Morrison Lecturer at the Lick Observatory in 1956, John Simon Guggenheim Memorial Foundation Fellow in 1962 and 1970, and Chaire Georges Lemaître at the University of Louvain in 1974. Asteroid 2417 McVittie is named in his honor.

BIBLIOGRAPHY

McVittie prepared a thirty-page autobiographical sketch around 1976 at the request of the Royal Society of Edinburgh, of which he was a fellow. A copy is in the George C. McVittie Papers, 1928, 1935, 1938–1975, 0.3 cubic feet, University of Illinois at Urbana-Champaign Archives. The sketch includes descriptions of his researches and a list of scientific publications to 1975. Copies of the autobiographical sketch are also at the Royal Society of Edinburgh and the American Institute of Physics. At Illinois see also Staff Appointments Papers (2/5/15) box 660, folder George C. McVittie, for correspondence from astronomers appraising McVittie's qualifications for the position he took up at the University of Illinois. Amplifying the autobiographical sketch is: George McVittie. Oral history interview by David DeVorkin. 1978. Niels Bohr Library, American Institute of Physics, College Park, MD.

WORKS BY MCVITTIE

With W. H. McCrea. "The Contraction of the Universe." *Monthly Notices of the Royal Astronomical Society* 91 (1930): 128–133. Derives mathematically that an Einstein universe containing a single condensation would start contracting.

"The Problem of n Bodies and the Expansion of the Universe." *Monthly Notices of the Royal Astronomical Society* 91 (1931): 274–283. Shows mathematically that the Lemaître universe, departing from the equilibrium Einstein state, can expand or contract, and an initial contraction can be started by the formation of condensations (particles of greater density than the surrounding matter).

"The Mass-Particle in an Expanding Universe." *Monthly Notices of the Royal Astronomical Society* 93 (1933): 325–339. Develops the mathematics necessary to tackle the problem of whether the universe will expand or contract when a condensation forms, but does not answer the question.

"Milne's Theory of the Expansion of the Universe." *Nature* 131 (1933): 533–534. Both Milne's theory and relativistic cosmology were in accordance with observation, and it seemed impossible to decide definitely for or against either theory solely on the basis of the recession of spiral nebulae.

"The Spiral Nebulae and the Expansion of the Universe." *Physical Society of London Reports* 1 (1934): 24–29. McVittie concluded that observations could not, at that time, discriminate between relativistic cosmology and E. A. Milne's cosmological model, and that the choice was thus almost entirely a matter of personal taste.

Cosmological Theory. London: Methuen, 1937. 2nd ed. New York: John Wiley, 1949.

"Observation and Theory in Cosmology." *Proceedings of the Physical Society of London* 51 (1939): 529–537. Ostensibly a review of the observational situation in cosmology prepared for a joint meeting in 1939 between the Royal Astronomical Society and the Physical Society of London, but primarily a critique of assumptions made by Edwin Hubble in correcting his observed magnitudes for the dimming effect of red shifts.

"A Model Universe Admitting the Interchangeability of Stress and Mass." *Proceedings of the Royal Society of London, Series A, Mathematical and Physical Sciences* 211 (1952): 295–301. A relativistic cosmological model with continuous creation of matter.

General Relativity and Cosmology. London: Chapman & Hall, 1956. 2nd ed. London: Chapman & Hall, 1965, and Urbana: University of Illinois Press, 1965. For years the major mathematical presentation of relativistic cosmology.

"Model Universes Derived from Counts of Very Distant Radio Sources." *Publications of the Astronomical Society of the Pacific* 70 (1958): 152–159. Based on counts from Sydney and Cambridge.

Fact and Theory in Cosmology. London: Eyre & Spottiswoode; New York: Macmillan, 1961. A popular account for readers without mathematical knowledge.

"Rationalism versus Empiricism in Cosmology." Book review of *The Universe at Large,* by H. Bondi; *Rival Theories of Cosmology,* by H. Bondi, W. B. Bonnor, R. A. Lyttleton, and G. J. Whitrow; *The Nature of the Universe,* by F. Hoyle; and *Towards a Unified Cosmology,* by R. O. Kapp. *Science* 133 (1961): 1231–1236.

Editor. *Problems of Extra-Galactic Research.* New York: Macmillan, 1962.

"An Anglo-Scottish University Education." In *The Making of Physicists,* edited by Rajkumari Williamson. Bristol, U.K.: Adam Hilger, 1987.

OTHER SOURCES

Chisholm, Roy. "George McVittie: Honorary Professor, University of Kent." *Vistas in Astronomy* 33 (1990): 79–81.

Davidson, D. "George McVittie's Work in Relativity." *Vistas in Astronomy* 33 (1990): 65–69.

Gale, George. "Cosmology: Methodological Debates in the 1930s and 1940s." Available in the *Stanford Encyclopedia of Philosophy* from http://plato.stanford.edu/entries/cosmology-30s/. On the cosmological debate during the 1930s and 1940s and McVittie's role in it, especially in England from 1935 to 1937.

Hide, Raymond. "Brief Comments on George McVittie's Meteorological Papers." *Vistas in Astronomy* 33 (1990): 63–64.

Knighting, E. "War Work, 1940–1945." *Vistas in Astronomy* 33 (1990): 59–62.

Lemaître, G. "Un univers homogéne de masse constante et de rayon croissant, rendant compte de la vitesse radiale des nebuleuses éxtra-galactiques." *Annales de la Société Scientifique de Bruxelles* 47 (1927): 49–56. Translated and reprinted as "A Homogeneous Universe of Constant Mass and Increasing Radius Accounting for the Radial Velocity of Extra-Galactic Nebulae." *Monthly Notices of the Royal Astronomical Society* 91 (1931): 483–490.

MacCallum, M. A. H. "George Cunliffe McVittie (1904–1988)." *Quarterly Journal of the Royal Astronomical Society* 39 (1989): 119–124.

McCrea, William. "George Cunliffe McVittie (1904–88) OBE, FRSE. Pupil of Whittaker and Eddington: Pioneer of Modern Cosmology." *Vistas in Astronomy* 33 (1990): 43–58. An appreciation by McVittie's early collaborator.

Osterbrock, Donald E., Laurence W. Fredrick, Frank K. Edmondson, et al. "McVittie and the American Astronomical Society." *Vistas in Astronomy* 33 (1990): 75–77.

Runcorn, S. K. "George McVittie: His Breadth of Scientific Interest." *Vistas in Astronomy* 33 (1990): 39–42.

Sánchez-Ron, José M. "The Reception of General Relativity among British Physicists and Mathematicians (1915–1930)." In *Studies in the History of General Relativity,* edited by Jean Eisenstaedt and A. J. Kox. Boston, Basel, and Berlin: Birkhäuser, 1992.

———. "George McVittie: The Uncompromising Empiricist." In *The Universe of General Relativity,* edited by Jean Eisenstaedt and A. J. Kox. Boston, Basel, and Berlin: Birkhäuser, 2006.

Swenson, George W., Jr. "George McVittie." *Physics Today* 42, no. 3 (March 1989): 128–132. Obituary notice by McVittie's radio telescope colleague at the University of Illinois.

———. "Building a Department of Astronomy." *Vistas in Astronomy* 33 (1990): 71–73.

Norriss Hetherington

MEDAWAR, PETER BRIAN (*b.* Rio de Janeiro, 28 February 1915, *d.* London, 2 October 1987), *immunology, transplant biology, medicine.*

Sir Peter Medawar is best remembered for developing the theory of acquired immunological tolerance, thus laying the foundation for successful organ and tissue transplantation. For this work he received, along with Sir Frank Macfarlane Burnet, the Nobel Prize for Physiology or Medicine in 1960. A central figure in twentieth-century British science, as a gifted writer he also explored the beauty and power of scientific thinking for a wider public.

Early Years. Medawar was born the son of Nicholas Agnatius Medawar (a salesman of Lebanese extraction) and Edith Muriel Dowling, who was British. He spent his early years in Brazil, where he learned Portuguese and developed a love of opera. The family returned to England for a brief period, and Medawar and his brother remained in England when his parents returned to Brazil. From 1928 to 1932 he attended Marlborough College, where he endured harassment due to his lack of athletic ability and his Middle Eastern features, which led others to assume he was Jewish. It was, however, at Marlborough that he developed a love of biology, a passion that he took to Oxford, where he studied zoology at Magdalen under the tutelage of the eminent anatomist John Z. Young. He received a first in zoology in 1935, and in the same year was appointed Christopher Welch Scholar and Senior Demonstrator at Magdalen. At this time, he began working at the Sir William Dunn School of Pathology under the future Nobel laureate Sir Howard Florey; he would remain in Oxford until after World War II. During this period of his life, he would be Rolleston Prizeman (1942), Senior Research Fellow of St. John's College (1944), and university demonstrator in zoology and comparative anatomy (also 1944). In 1946 he was elected a Fellow of Magdalen; he was awarded a DSc in 1947, and soon afterward was appointed Mason Professor of Zoology at the University of Birmingham (at the suggestion of Sir Solly Zuckerman).

On Growth and Form. Medawar's first scientific work involved studying extracts from malt that inhibited the growth of chick fibroblasts (connective tissue cells), studies that versed him in the emerging field of tissue culture. The factor identified was a carbohydrate rather than a protein and has not as of 2007 been fully characterized. When he showed Florey the first draft of his manuscript, Florey was not impressed, saying the paper was more philosophical than scientific; yet the paper, "A Factor Inhibiting the Growth of Mesenchyme," was published in 1937 following Florey's recommendation that Medawar consult with some chemists. As Mitchison comments, this paper already had many of the distinctive features of Medawar's later work: "powerful ideas, able to place a simple fact in the widest possible context; a highly distinctive style, able to manipulate with total confidence a vocabulary far wider that that usually employed within science; and the authority … to assign previous work to its place within a novel conceptual framework" (1990, p. 286).

This work spurred Medawar on to examine the growth of cells in culture. Building on the works of Charles Sedgwick Minot, Ludwig von Bertalanffy, and Julian Huxley, and using mathematical modeling of growth, Medawar assimilated and clarified the earlier works while investigating aspects of it in depth. While Medawar would shift his research during World War II into the field that would bring him eventual fame, he often returned to the problems of growth in all its manifestations and, for example, extensively discussed human demographics in his 1959 Reith Lectures for the British Broadcasting Corporation (BBC). In addition, he examined D'Arcy Wentworth Thompson's analyses of relative growth and applied them to human problems, and he was one of the few who attempted to utilize—albeit unsuccessfully—Thompson's method of transformed coordinates, a method that would only be mathematically formalized in the 1980s with the development of geometric morphometrics.

The Immunology of Transplantation. Medawar's work during World War II would eventually create a new branch of science, the immunology of transplantation. With the war raging—and bombings increasing the number of burn victims—the problem of skin graft rejection became particularly serious. Conventional wisdom held that preventing rejection was a matter of surgical skill; Medawar's work would demonstrate that this was instead a biological problem.

The War Wounds Committee of the British Medical Council assigned Medawar to work with Thomas Gibson at the Burn Unit at Glasgow Infirmary. In 1943 they produced a paper ("The Fate of Skin Homografts in Man") that would for the first time use experimentation and observation to systematically study the rejection process. To do so, Gibson transplanted a set of grafts (termed *autografts*) taken from a burn victim and a second individual (termed *homografts,* or later *allografts*) onto the patient's back. At intervals, some of these small "pinch" grafts were removed and studied histologically by Medawar, who observed that the autografts succeeded, but allografts failed after initial acceptance. Importantly, a second set of allografts were rejected more rapidly than the first. Thus, to Gibson and Medawar, the rejection process appeared to have characteristics of an immunological response.

Medawar returned to Oxford and continued his study of allograft rejection using rabbits as his model organism. In a series of papers for the War Wounds Committee, he confirmed the existence of the time delay before rejection commenced, used demographic techniques to study survival times for grafts, and described invasion of the grafts by lymphocytes, thus strengthening the case for rejection being due to an immune reaction.

Peter Brian Medawar. AP IMAGES.

Subsequent work suggested that the lymphocytes—rather than the antibodies they produced—were responsible for destroying the allograft.

Medawar examined methods that could prevent or slow the allograft reaction. One such means was the use of steroids, which had been noticed to reduce lymphocytes and to inhibit the immune response. Medawar, Rupert Billingham (1921–2002), Elizabeth Sparrow, and Peter L. Krohn began an examination of the effect of subcutaneously administered cortisone on graft survival, and found that the treatment lengthened survival times by a factor of three or four. This discovery provided the basis for subsequent successful attempts to enhance kidney graft survival using corticosteroids.

In 1947 Medawar moved to Birmingham, where he built a research group around Billingham and Leslie Brent, both of whom would follow him to University College, London (UCL), in 1951 when Medawar was appointed Jordell Professor of Zoology and Comparative Anatomy. Brent described the six years following the move to London as being the most creative and momentous of their lives (2005, p. 39), and in a series of papers the trio would lay the groundwork for modern transplantation immunology.

Medawar

Central to their work was the examination of skin transplantation in twin cattle. The Edinburgh geneticist Hugh P. Donald had challenged Medawar to find a method to distinguish between dizygotic and monozygotic twins in cattle. Medawar suggested that skin grafting would provide such a test, reasoning that if grafts were mutually accepted, the twins would have to be monozygotic (genetically identical). Much to the surprise of Medawar and Billingham—who were working with two technicians on an Agricultural Research Council farm in Staffordshire—virtually all the grafts were accepted, including those from twins that were definitely dizygotic. What could have caused such tolerance? As it happens, in 1945 an American, Raymond D. Owen, had shown that dizygotic twin cattle have two populations of red blood cells: their own and cells derived from their twin while in the womb (in this, cattle are different from humans due to their synchorial placenta). Medawar and Billingham realized that the acceptance of foreign grafts was due to this exchange, thus supporting a hypothesis put forward in 1949 by Burnet and Frank J. Fenner. Billingham, Medawar, and Brent then set out to experimentally examine this acquired tolerance using inbred strains of mice.

Within two years, the team had successfully induced tolerance to skin allografts by introducing donor cells into fetal mice. Cells were prepared from the spleen, testes, and kidney of a donor and placed in the abdominal cavity of a fetal recipient. This resulted in tolerance of the recipient for allografts from individuals who were genetically identical to the donor. The results were described in a paper published in *Nature*—a paper that, fifty years later, the British Transplantation Society described as the most important paper in the history of transplantation. Its importance lay in demonstrating that graft rejection could be overcome by purely biological means that did not require immunosuppressive drugs. A series of papers ("Quantitative Studies on Tissue Transplantation Immunity") followed in rapid succession, and the third paper was seen by Brent as their magnum opus (and by Mitchison as the group's "crowning glory"). Appearing in *Philosophical Transactions of the Royal Society* in 1956, the paper described a series of experiments which established that tolerant individuals were usually chimeric (i.e., possessing a combination of donor and recipient cells), examined possible mechanisms of tolerance, and concluded that tolerance was brought about by a deletional mechanism. (It was Burnet who would famously propose elimination of self-reactive lymphocyte clones in 1960.) While the mechanism was unknown in 1956, what was clear was that tolerance-of-self (the immune system's ability to tolerate the organism's own cells) must itself be acquired by exposure of the system to self-molecules during the process of development.

The Nobel Prize. In 1960 Medawar and Burnet were awarded the Nobel Prize for their work on immunological tolerance. Introducing the laureates, Sven Gard of the Royal Caroline Institute noted that "[i]mmunity is our perhaps most important defense against a hostile surrounding world. By penetrating analysis of existing data and brilliant deduction, and by painstaking experimental research you have unveiled a fundamental law governing the development and maintenance of this vital mechanism." While Burnet and Fenner had speculated about the existence of tolerance in 1949, it took the experimental work of Medawar, Billingham, and Brent to demonstrate the phenomenon. It may be wondered why Billingham and Brent were not included in the award. As Brent himself notes, that would have meant that Fenner and, indeed, Owen would probably have had to be included as well. Medawar himself publicly acknowledged the contributions of Billingham and Brent on British television the day the award was announced and in his memoirs stated that "I was terribly sorry that the distinction could not be so far divided as to have included my friends Bill [Billington] and Leslie. I could—and did—share my portion of the prize money with them, but that's not the same thing."

Later Work. Moving from UCL in 1962, Medawar was appointed director of the National Institute for Medical Research and, in 1971, head of the transplantation section of the Medical Research Council's Clinical Research Center, a post he held until the year before his death. The Nobel Prize brought fame to Medawar and, while he became a public intellectual, he continued to investigate aspects of immunology. He studied immunological privileged sites (places such as the brain where lymphocytes do not occur and thus where allografts can survive indefinitely). In particular, he examined why the mammalian fetus is not rejected, deciding that neither privilege nor the action of hormones can explain acceptance of the foreign tissue. With Sparrow, he continued his examination of the use of corticosteroids to prolong skin grafts. He examined the use of antilymphocyte serum as an agent to prevent graft rejection. He continued this scientific research even after his stroke of 1969, while spending a significant amount of time communicating his views on scientific method to fellow scientists and the public. (A representative sample of these writings is collected in *Pluto's Republic* and *The Threat and the Glory.*)

Influenced by T. D. "Harry" Weldon, A. J. Ayer, and Karl Popper, Medawar was particularly interested in seeing science as a hypothetico-deductive enterprise that was not restricted to the examination of scientific problems. While experiment and testing were important, Medawar saw the true mark of science, which he famously described as the "art of the soluble," to be the creative act in which a new idea was generated. Following from Popper, he held that these ideas could never be formally proven true.

Medawar's view on biology is best exemplified by a portion of his Nobel banquet speech given on 10 December 1960:

> It is [...] a sign of the times—though our brothers of physics and chemistry may smile to hear me say so—that biology is now a science in which theories can be devised: theories which lead to predictions and predictions which sometimes turn out to be correct. These facts confirm me in a belief I hold most passionately—that biology is the heir of all the sciences.

Medawar's interest in the theory of biology and the nature of scientific inquiry is nicely illustrated in his 1974 paper presenting "A Geometric Model of Reduction and Emergence." In this short piece, he noted that biology contains "contextually distinctive notions" at the level of the organism that are "peculiar to and distinctive of" that level and are thus "not obviously reducible to the notions of the level immediately above [ecology] or higher still [chemistry and physics]" (p. 57). These notions include "heredity," "infection," "immunity," "sexuality," and "fear." He goes on to provide a thought-provoking discussion of "the sense of diminishment" that results from "analytical reduction" (p. 62). Yet this antireductionism did not lead to "fuzzy" thinking—one has only to read his justly famous review of Pierre Teilhard de Chardin's *The Phenomenon of Man* to see that was not the case.

In addition to his Nobel Prize, Medawar received much recognition for his work. He was elected Fellow of the Royal Society of London (1949), was the Society's Croonian Lecturer in 1958, and received its Royal Medal in 1959. He was awarded a C.B.E. (Commander of the British Empire) in 1958, a knighthood in 1965, a C.H. (Companion of Honour) in 1972, and an O.M. (Order of Merit) in 1981.

In February 1937 Medawar married Jean Shinglewood Taylor (1913–2005), whom he met as an undergraduate in Oxford, and with whom he had four children. In 1969 Medawar suffered a stroke while giving an address at the British Association for the Advancement of Science's annual meeting in Exeter. This left him partially paralyzed and under the care of Jean, who collaborated with him on some of his later writings. He suffered several more strokes and eventually died from one in 1987. Further details of his life can be found in his autobiographical *Memoir of a Thinking Radish* (1986) and Jean's memoir, *A Very Decided Preference* (1990).

BIBLIOGRAPHY

A complete bibliography of Medawar's work is contained in the microfiche version of the article by Avrion Mitchison (cited below). Medawar's correspondence and papers are at the Wellcome Library for the History and Understanding of Medicine, London.

WORKS BY MEDAWAR

"A Factor Inhibiting the Growth of Mesenchyme." *Quarterly Journal of Experimental Physiology* 27 (1937): 147–162.

"The 'Laws' of Biological Growth." *Nature* 148 (1940): 772–772.

With Thomas Gibson. "The Fate of Skin Homografts in Man." *Journal of Anatomy* 77 (1943): 299–310.

"The Behaviour and Fate of Skin Autografts and Skin Homografts in Rabbits." *Journal of Anatomy* 78 (1944): 176–199.

"A Second Study of the Behaviour and Fate of Skin Homografts in Rabbits." *Journal of Anatomy* 79 (1945): 157–176.

With Wilfrid E. le Gros Clark. "Size, Shape, and Age." In *Essays on Growth and Form*, edited by Wilfrid E. le Gros Clark and P. B. Medawar. Oxford: Clarendon Press, 1945.

With Rupert E. Billingham and Leslie Brent. "'Actively Acquired Tolerance' of Foreign Cells." *Nature* 172 (1953): 603–606.

With Rupert E. Billingham, Leslie Brent, and Elizabeth M. Sparrow. "Quantitative Studies on Tissue Transplantation Immunity. I. The Survival Times of Skin Homografts Exchanged between Members of Different Inbred Strains of Mice." *Proceedings of the Royal Society of London, Series B* 143 (1954): 43–57.

With Rupert E. Billingham and Leslie Brent. "Quantitative Studies on Tissue Transplantation Immunity. II. The Origin, Strength, and Duration of Actively and Adoptively Acquired Immunity." *Proceedings of the Royal Society of London, Series B* 143 (1954): 58–80.

With Rupert E. Billingham and Leslie Brent. "Quantitative Studies on Tissue Transplantation Immunity. III. Actively Acquired Tolerance." *Philosophical Transactions of the Royal Society of London, Series B* 239 (1956): 357–414.

"The Homograft Reaction (Croonian Lecture 1958)." *Proceedings of the Royal Society of London, Series B* 148 (1958): 145–166.

"D'Arcy Thompson and *Growth and Form*." In *D'Arcy Thompson: The Scholar-Naturalist*, edited by Ruth D'Arcy Thompson. Oxford: Oxford University Press, 1958.

"The Phenomenon of Man." *Mind* 70 (1961): 99–106.

"A Geometric Model of Reduction and Emergence." In *Studies in the Philosophy of Biology: Reduction and Related Problems*, edited by Francisco J. Ayala and Theodosius Dobzhansky. Berkeley: University of California Press, 1974.

Advice to a Young Scientist. London: Harper & Row, 1980.

Pluto's Republic. Oxford: Oxford University Press, 1982.

The Limits of Science. New York: Harper & Row, 1984.

Memoir of a Thinking Radish. Oxford: Oxford University Press, 1986.

The Threat and the Glory. Oxford: Oxford University Press, 1990.

OTHER SOURCES

Brent, Leslie. *A History of Transplantation Immunology.* London: Academic Press, 1997.

———. "Billingham, Rupert Everett" *Biographical Memoirs of Fellows of the Royal Society of London* 51 (2005): 33–50. Provides further details on the collaboration between Billingham, Brent, and Medawar.

Medawar, Jean S. *A Very Decided Preference: Life with Peter Medawar.* Oxford: Oxford University Press, 1990.

Mitchison, Avrion. "Peter Brian Medawar." *Biographical Memoirs of Fellows of the Royal Society of London* 35 (1990): 283–301.

"The Nobel Prize in Physiology or Medicine 1960." Available from http://www.nobelprize.org.

John M. Lynch

MEEHL, PAUL EVERETT (*b.* Minneapolis, Minnesota, 3 January 1920; *d.* Minneapolis, 14 February 2003), *psychology, philosophy, psychiatry.*

Meehl was a theoretical psychologist and philosopher of science who contributed several important conceptual formulations to psychology, most notably a demonstration of the superiority of actuarial against intuitive prediction. A practicing psychotherapist, he played an important role in the medicalizing of American psychology.

Polyvalent Beginnings. Meehl came to psychology out of deep personal motives: His father's suicide during the Great Depression and his mother's death five years later from a misdiagnosed brain tumor led him to question fatal human motives and fallible judgment. Intellectually precocious and voracious, his first encounter with his future work was his reading, at age twelve, Karl Menninger's *The Human Mind.* In his autobiography, Meehl said he found this blend of contemporary psychiatric nosology and therapeutic optimism a "healing Damascus experience" (1989, p. 339). Before Meehl was fifteen he had read extensively in psychology—popular behaviorisms as well as Sigmund Freud—and revealed a taste and talent for epistemology, reading Bertrand Russell. He was especially influenced by Alburey Castell's lucid 1935 textbook *A College Logic,* and honed his formal logical skills debating with adolescent peers. Castell, a University of Minnesota faculty member, was limned as Frazier's critical interlocutor in B. F. Skinner's *Walden Two;* similarly, Meehl became a gadfly critic of psychology's scientific enterprise.

Meehl entered the University of Minnesota in 1938, intending to follow the premedical course, but he migrated to psychology, graduating with an undergraduate degree (with a minor in biometry) in 1941. His main undergraduate influence in psychology was Donald G. Paterson, a practical psychometric specialist and an early proponent of vocational guidance, from whom he gained expertise in the measurement of human abilities and a predisposition to consider psychology as inseparable from its applications. It was fortunate that, in 1940, Herbert Feigl moved from Iowa to Minnesota, where he finished the rest of his career. Feigl, a highly cultured colleague of the Viennese logical positivists, found in Meehl a kindred spirit and a lifelong friend. Through Feigl, Meehl had access to a rich, well-articulated theoretical approach to the unity of science and liberalized versions of neopositivism. Meehl remained at Minnesota for graduate work—indeed, he remained at Minnesota for the remainder of his career, retiring as Regents' Professor of Psychology in 1990—and was mentored by another exponent of the style of Minnesota psychology known as "Dustbowl Empiricism," Starke Rosecrans Hathaway. Hathaway was one of the earliest medical clinical psychologists in the United States and had just finished assembling, in conjunction with the neuropsychiatrist J. Charnley McKinley of the medical faculty, a psychometric instrument designed specifically for identifying and classifying psychiatric disorders, the Minnesota Multiphasic Personality Inventory, or MMPI.

Meehl, rated unfit for service during World War II because of a heart defect, remained at Minnesota during the war years. While continuing to work with Feigl and Hathaway, Meehl became one of the group of graduate students who associated closely with Skinner in the midst of a most fertile conceptual period, when he was working simultaneously on shaping, language, and the social implications of behaviorism, leading to the writing of *Walden Two.* Skinner, after moving to Indiana from Minnesota at the end of the war, thought highly enough of Meehl that he offered him his first academic position. Meehl, however, declined it, having established himself as not only a psychometric specialist but also as a clinician, seeing his first clients in 1942. Meehl received a PhD in clinical psychology in 1945, entering that profession just as it came of age in economic and social terms. His thesis focused on people with psychopathology who are able to compensate for it and appear normal. The search for latency, psychopathic and otherwise, determined the direction of his career.

The Search for Latent Entities. From the outset, Meehl strove to create a theoretical framework that could contain both clinical and experimental psychology and that would allow the existence of latent mental entities. Meehl was impressed early on by an experience in which Hathaway gave him several psychiatric case studies and asked him, blind to the diagnosis and to the MMPI profile, to find similarities between them. Meehl identified a behavioral regularity (sexual nonaggressiveness) the group of cases, and was surprised when Hathaway revealed that they had been sorted not by psychiatric diagnosis but only by the similar simple pattern of their scores on the MMPI. Meehl likened this procedure of "looking at the person through the test" to pulling oneself up by one's own bootstraps, and "bootstrapsing" became a familiar Meehl theme and technique.

While continuing to work on the development of the MMPI, Meehl, by now a faculty member in psychology at Minnesota, entered into a long-term collaborative relationship with his behaviorist colleague Kenneth MacCorquodale, researching aspects of Edward C. Tolman's theory of latent learning. Tolman and his coworkers had contended that, in rats, learning could take place implicitly without direct reinforcement. By the mid-1940s Tolman had evolved several versions of a theory incorporating not only empirical behavioral data but also theoretical terms that he eventually came to call cognitive structures. In 1948 MacCorquodale and Meehl published "On a Distinction between Hypothetical Constructs and Intervening Variables" in *Psychological Review,* streamlining the vocabulary used to define the relations between theory and data across several contemporary learning theories. They conceived a distinction between terms that functioned to summarize or abstract empirical data and that could, if necessary, be reduced to the data level (intervening variables) and terms at a high level carrying "surplus meaning," which could not be completely reduced to data (hypothetical constructs). This was a move away from a narrow operationalism and toward a modern neurocognitive view of learning, the brain, and the mind. Meehl and MacCorquodale made an explicit connection between hypothetical constructs and underlying neurology, and D. O. Hebb utilized this distinction as a basic element of his seminal 1955 paper "Drives and the Conceptual Nervous System." The hypothetical construct-intervening variable conception has proved durable and useful not only in psychology but in fields as diverse as computer science and molecular biology.

Meehl's next significant contribution to theoretical psychology was again collaborative, the product of a working group investigating test validity for the American Psychological Association in 1954. This paper, "Construct Validity in Psychological Tests," coauthored with Lee Cronbach and published in *Psychological Bulletin* in 1955, introduced the idea of the nomological net, an idea drawn from several sources in empirical-realist philosophy. The net provides coherence and explanation through individual theories that exist at a conceptual level as constructs, ligated to each other through logical coherence and to physical reality (through a level of intervening variables) by connections to empirical data. Between 1955 and the end of his career, Meehl, in several papers, evolved the following formal logical schematization of the network of relations between theory and data (simplified here to its basic elements):

$$(\mathbf{T} \cdot \mathbf{A} \cdot \mathbf{C}) \rightarrow \mathrm{O}$$

with T and A representing primary and auxiliary theories respectively, C representing conditions of observation, experimentation, or individuals, conjunctively leading to O, empirical observations. Strongly influenced by Hans Reichenbach's 1938 text *Experience and Prediction*—he referred to it in both his first and last (posthumously) published papers—as well as by his own psychometric background, he conceived this conceptual network as essentially probabilistic. Theories, maintained Meehl, borrowing from his philosophical contemporary Arthur Pap, are "open concepts," provisional and corrigible. Meaning emerges in reciprocal relations between all elements of the system, "seeping upward" from data, and spreading downward and laterally from theories and auxiliaries. The nomological net, in Meehl's view, is continually being mended by the addition of new postulates, new observations, and new interconnections at all levels.

During the 1950s Meehl's search for latent entities took a more explicit clinical turn, as he shifted focus to psychiatric syndromes, in particular schizophrenia. Meehl, now established in clinical practice, had already garnered extensive experience with the phenomenology of schizophrenia, contributing a case study on catatonia to Arthur Burton and Robert E. Harris's *Case Histories in Clinical and Abnormal Psychology* in 1947 and editing, along with Hathaway, an extensive collection of case studies aligned with MMPI profiles. Sometime during this period Meehl encountered the description of "pseudoneurotic schizophrenia" published in 1949 by Paul Hoch and Philip Polatin. This syndrome, in which underlying schizophrenic pathology is overlaid and masked by virtually all other psychiatric syndromes including depression, anxiety, and hypochondria, was at once a supreme diagnostic challenge and an apt exemplar of latency. Meehl became more explicitly psychoanalytic in orientation, undergoing training analysis with Bernard Glueck, a student of Sandor Rado, an independent-minded Freudian. Rado theorized that a collection of personality traits lay behind schizophrenia, terming this the schizotype.

In 1962 Meehl presented, as his presidential address to the American Psychological Association, a theory of schizophrenia that postulated an underlying, genetically determined neural deficit (schizotaxia) leading to, through learning, the formation of a set of personality characteristics (the schizotype, or schizotypy, in Meehl's terms), which could, under certain environmental and social conditions, lead to the expression of phenotypic schizophrenia. This theory was one of the earliest modern postulates of a behavioral-genetic theory in psychology and has proved a durable source of research conjecture in psychiatry. Meehl's work on schizophrenia and diagnosis led to two significant related contributions: the revival of the concept of anhedonia and a statistical taxonomic approach to mental entities.

The concept of a lack of pleasure had fallen into disuse as interest in psychological hedonism waned during the 1920s. Meehl's approach to pleasure is a good example of his approach, his eclecticism, and his range. In 1950 Meehl established the noncircularity of the law of effect by showing that reinforcers were transitive across situations. Then, proceeding to clinical observations, he focused specifically on the lack of pleasure observed in schizophrenics. To describe this lack of pleasurable feeling he borrowed Rado's term *anhedonia,* which had come into psychoanalysis from older psychologies such as those of William James and Théodule Ribot, to name an internal entity, a measurable individual-difference variable for which he proposed measurement scales. Finally, late in his career, he considered this latent hedonic dimension in the context of economics and proposed a theory of measurable relative pleasure utilities in contrast to Pareto optimality.

Meehl became interested in problems of classification while developing methods to test competing genetic hypotheses of schizophrenia. Eventually he came to the conclusion that many psychological types and traits—pathological and nonpathololgical—form taxonic classes. "There are gophers," said Meehl, "there are chipmunks, but there are no gophmunks" (1995, p. 268). Meehl came to see "carving nature at its joints" as a prime focus of scientific interest, and he invented several novel statistical techniques to reveal patterns indicating taxonic class membership from empirical data, which he grouped under the heading "bootstrapsing taxometry." Development of these techniques with several colleagues, notably David Faust, Robert Golden, and Niels Waller, occupied much of Meehl's attention after 1980.

The search for mental entities forms the contextual background for Meehl's philosophy of mind. Though Meehl thought of himself as an avocational philosopher in contrast to the "card-carrying" members of that discipline, he had substantial credentials in the field and was one of the founding members of the Minnesota Center for the Philosophy of Science in 1953. During the next forty years he produced, singly and in collaboration with others, including Wilfrid Sellars and Herbert Feigl, substantial contributions on emergence, the mind-body problem, and freedom and determinism. In conjunction with a defense of Feigl's mind-brain identity thesis, Meehl utilized thought experiments involving the autocerebroscope, by which one's brain activity could be read off the cortex and projected onto a screen, allowing comparison between reports of perceptions and brain activity. This conceptual device anticipated, as Meehl noted late in his career, current progress in neuroimaging and its correlation with cognitive states.

While Meehl maintained that, from a physical perspective, identity held its own even when conflicts were introduced between cerebroscope readings and cognized self-reports of states—a foreshadowing of current modular theories of mind—he also demonstrated considerable weakness in this monistic view at the semantic level of qualia. Likewise, regarding freedom and determinism, Meehl opted for a middle-ground view, locating decisions in a probabilistic space within a deterministic system, a "tertium quid." Meehl adopted a "cafeteria" approach to philosophy, assembling what he felt was needed for the tasks at hand. He also kept an open mind about the subjects that could be admissible in a scientific, realist psychology, writing extensively on religion and parapsychology (he contributed the article on the subject to the *Encyclopaedia Britannica* in 1962) as well as on Freudian theory—dream analysis in particular.

Critique of Practice. Complementary to Meehl's focus on entities is his extensive critique of how theory guides practice both in science and in psychotherapy and the ways in which this might miscarry. Meehl's first and most well-known contribution in this area was the result of ten years' effort at the beginning of his career. Published in 1954 after it had been turned down by several publishers, *Clinical vs. Statistical Prediction: A Theoretical Analysis and a Review of the Evidence* became an immediate classic that was reprinted forty-two years later after more than thirteen thousand copies had sold. This work is the Rosetta Stone of Meehl's critical approach, containing the essence of his critiques of method and clinical practice. His starting point was Theodore Sarbin's contention that clinicians' predictions of outcomes are always inferior to actuarial predictions in principle.

In contrast to this view, Meehl invoked Hans Reichenbach's distinction between the "context of discovery" and the "context of justification." Clinicians, maintained Meehl, function both as theory constructors and theory verifiers. As constructors, they often make predictive statements emerging from novel combinations of unique clinical data—Meehl used a dream interpretation from Theodor Reik as an example—for which no actuarial track record exists. The unique functions of clinicians, Meehl stressed, were in pattern finding and theory building, rational but at a level different from that at which precise actuarial verification could obtain. However, when actuarial data existed that could be combined to make predictions via regression equations, the situation was different. Meehl conducted a pioneering meta-analysis, tabulating the results of twenty studies in which clinicians and actuarial clerks worked with the same data. The results showed that, with one exception that Meehl admitted with many qualifications, clinicians were not superior to, and frequently inferior to, the actuarial calculation, a result verified several times over in subsequent studies by Meehl and many collaborators and independent researchers. *Clinical vs. Statistical Prediction* was a stimulus both for development of automated systems for test interpretation and diagnosis, as well as an important step in the development of a psychology of cognitive biases. Meehl maintained that it was unethical and socially irresponsible to fail to use actuarial prediction systems when they were available, and he campaigned vigorously for their use through the rest of his career.

The next element in Meehl's critique concerns the actual practice of clinical psychology. Meehl drew on both his statistical expertise and his penchant for formal logical dissection to reveal, in a chapter in his 1973 compilation *Psychodiagnosis* titled "Why I Do Not Attend Case Conferences," a bestiary of diagnostic gaffes and fallacies, ranging from statistical mistakes such as ignoring population base rates to logical ones such as the volunteering of entirely irrelevant information or overgeneralization from personal experience, for example the Uncle George's Pancakes Fallacy (a client storing uneaten pancakes in the attic is not exhibiting pathology because "good ole Uncle George used to do that"). Both Meehl's conception of the clinician as theorist as well as his logical analysis of practice are at the forefront here. Clinicians would produce more interesting insights were they to function at a higher logical level, and they would be more accurate if they would aspire to the logic embodied in neurology grand rounds. Beginning in the mid-1960s and continuing through the rest of his career, Meehl expanded his critique to the collective scientific progress of psychology, which he saw as fitful at best, especially in its "softer" areas (for example, personality and social psychology). Adopting much of Karl Popper's approach, Meehl criticized both the statistical basis and the logic of psychology's scientific practices. Psychology errs, he claimed, in trying to validate theories of dubious verisimilitude with weak statistical methods.

Adding to the contemporary critique of null hypothesis significance testing (NHST), Meehl claimed that tests of directional hypotheses showing statistical significance corroborated substantive theories weakly, failing not only to conclusively reject false theories but also producing ambiguous records of confirmatory evidence for true ones. Meehl also compared the specificity of prediction from theory in physics and psychology and found psychology wanting. Borrowing a meteorological metaphor, he said that psychology appears content to predict that it will rain in April rather than to predict precise amounts of rainfall on specific April days. From the viewpoint of formal logic, taking a positive significance test result as evidence for the truth of the theory under test was an elementary logical mistake—affirming the consequent. Until this faulty logic could be replaced with a valid *modus tollens* procedure, and theories were proposed that would generate point predictions that could be conclusively rejected, psychological theories would tend to generate high rates of spurious confirmation under NHST and would linger until they, like Douglas MacArthur's old soldiers, "faded away."

Later, reacting to criticisms by Imre Lakatos, Paul Feyerabend, and others, Meehl would adopt a more nuanced view of how theory might be amended even after failing strong falsification tests, and still later Meehl devised a taxonomic method, cliometrics, which utilized criteria of successful science to classify research programs, historical and current, as either productive or "degenerating." As an immediate methodological corrective, Meehl advocated reporting confidence intervals rather than statistical significance in summaries of research results. But ultimately psychology will progress faster when its theories are sounder, and Meehl urged psychologists to look to less statistical but equally rational and empirical disciplines for models for theory building, especially history, law, and psychoanalysis. Interestingly, Meehl saw psychoanalysis, one of his essential sources of theory as a clinician (though he could not devise formal tests for its theoretical claims), as drifting into degeneration, describing himself as a "60% Freudian" in 1973 but a "33% Freudian" in 1992.

Principled Practical Eclecticism. Along with his principled eclecticism in theory and philosophy, Meehl had a plainspoken practical attitude toward applied psychology. He was, by his own account, temperamentally suited to the practice of law and eventually taught in Minnesota's Law School. From that vantage point he addressed practical problems such as the conceptual foundations of the insanity defense and defended lawyers' use of the "fireside inductions"—commonsense generalizations about human behavior—against psychologists' insistence on experimental results. Sometimes, Meehl argued, it is practitioners outside psychology who are ahead in terms of knowledge. A practical behaviorist, he was not averse to quoting, in many situations, what he called "Meehl's Malignant Maxim": The best predictor of future behavior is past behavior. As a therapist, he practiced both classical psychoanalysis (he had a couch in his office) and, concurrently, Albert Ellis's rational-emotive therapy, in which clients are encouraged to confront the reality of failures and rejection directly, admit mistakes, and dispute their bad logical choices.

A social meliorist and libertarian, Meehl was, however, under no illusions about either human goodwill or the political process: correspondence from him bore the legend "Caligula for Proconsul" on the envelope, and he made a very good case for the idea that one might as likely be killed driving to the polls as that one's vote would decide a national election. Yet Meehl saw participation in a democracy as an ethical imperative, and he considered the taxpaying citizen who underwrote his salary his primary social responsibility. Meehl reserved his strongest opprobrium, however, for intrusions of political views into science, and wrote, toward the end of his life, a lengthy defense of the necessity for the independence of science in the face of political objections to its content.

Meehl was extensively honored for his work, winning many of the main achievement awards offered within organized psychology, including the American Psychological Association's Distinguished Scientific Contributor Award in 1958 and its Award for Outstanding Lifetime Contribution to Psychology in 1996. He was elected a member of the National Academy of Sciences in 1987. His ultimate goal for psychology was unity via what he called the "five noble traditions": psychometrics, behavior theory, behavior genetics, descriptive psychiatry, and psychoanalysis. Meehl once said, referring to *Clinical vs. Statistical Prediction,* that he had been "socially reinforced for writing something which hardly anyone believes" (1996, p. v), but his formulations of psychology's scientific vocabulary are ubiquitous and ineluctable. His challenge to psychologists to improve theory and practice remains open.

BIBLIOGRAPHY

Meehl's papers are cataloged on his Web site, "Paul E. Meehl, 1920–2003," available from http://www.tc.umn.edu/~pemeehl/. Regularly updated by his wife, Leslie J. Yonce, this site contains a complete bibliography and links to more than half of Meehl's papers.

WORKS BY MEEHL

Psychodiagnosis: Selected Papers. Minneapolis: University of Minnesota Press, 1973. Includes Meehl's American Psychological Association address on schizophrenia, Cronbach and Meehl, Meehl and MacCorquodale, and the "Case Conferences" chapter.

"Hedonic Capacity: Some Conjectures." *Bulletin of the Menninger Clinic* 39 (1975): 295–307.

"The Selfish Voter Paradox and the Thrown-Away Vote Argument." *American Political Science Review* 71 (1977): 11–30. Meehl at the peak of his logical game.

"Autobiography." In *A History of Psychology in Autobiography,* vol. 8, edited by Gardner Lindzey. Stanford, CA: Stanford University Press, 1989.

Selected Philosophical and Methodological Papers. Minneapolis: University of Minnesota Press, 1991. Collection of essential papers through 1989; contains Meehl's main contributions to the philosophy of mind, to the critique of scientific method, and to law.

"Bootstraps Taxometrics: Solving the Classification Problem in Psychopathology." *American Psychologist* 50 (1995): 266–275. Good entry point for taxometrics.

Clinical vs. Statistical Prediction: A Theoretical Analysis and a Review of the Evidence. Northvale, NJ: Jason Aronson, 1996. Reprint of the 1954 edition with a new introduction.

"Relevance of a Scientist's Ideology in Communal Recognition of Scientific Merit." *Psychological Reports* 83 (1998): 1124–1144. Discussion of the relation of politics and science.

"Cliometric Metatheory III: Piercian Consensus, Verisimilitude, and Asymptotic Method." *British Journal for the Philosophy of Science* 55 (2004): 615–643. Complete discussion of cliometrics.

OTHER SOURCES

Cichetti, Dante, and William M. Grove, eds. *Thinking Clearly about Psychology.* Vol. 1: *Matters of Public Interest*; Vol. 2: *Personality and Psychopathology.* Minneapolis: University of Minnesota Press, 1991. These two volumes, Meehl's Festschrift, survey the range of applications of his thought.

Peterson, Donald R. *Tough Notes from a Gentle Genius: Twelve Years of Correspondence with Paul Meehl.* Hillsdale, NJ: Erlbaum, 2005. Revealing exchange of letters between Meehl and one of his students, covering the last twelve years of Meehl's life.

Peterson, Gail. "A Man of Many Gardens." *Behavior and Philosophy* 33 (2005): 85–89. A sympathetic and personal life sketch.

Rozeboom, William W. "Meehl on Metatheory." *Journal of Clinical Psychology* 61 (2005): 1317–1354. Thorough survey of Meehl's methodological contributions.

Waller, Niels G., and Scott O. Lilienfeld. "Paul Everett Meehl: The Cumulative Record." *Journal of Clinical Psychology* 61 (2005): 1209–1229. Part of a Meehl memorial issue of this journal, this biographical account also contains an analysis of the rate and content of Meehl's reading.

David C. Devonis

MELITENIOTES, THEODORE (*b.* Constantinople, c. 1320; *d.* Constantinople, 8 March 1393), *astronomy.*

A product of the Senatorial class, Meliteniotes was born around 1320 in Constantinople. A high ecclesiastical official, he was Great Sacellarius (Treasurer), and

Meliteniotes

around 1360, he became *Didascalos tōn didascalōn;* that is, director of the Patriarchal School. His religious bent was Palamite and anti-Latin. He died 8 March 1393. His output was voluminous. He composed an exegetical work on the Gospels in three sections, and an *Astronomical Tribiblos* in three books. He may be the author of an allegorical poem on *Sôphrosynè* (Temperance), attributed to a certain Meliteniotes. In this pedantic and heterogeneous poem are found many descriptions and digressions, including a catalog of precious stones, a veritable dictionary of mineralogy.

The *Astronomical Tribiblos* is a treatise on astronomy in three books, according to a tripartite division dear to the author, probably in homage to the Holy Trinity. The autograph manuscript is preserved, *Vaticanus gr.* 792. According to its examples it was evidently composed around 1352.

Book 1 contains an introduction, a small treatise of arithmetic, and a treatise on the construction and use of the plane astrolabe with detailed drawings. The introduction develops a history of astronomical science, seen by the author as having biblical origins, and drawing inspiration from Flavius Josephus and Strabo. He strenuously condemned astrology, but affirmed that astronomy may be of service to the faith, citing the miraculous eclipse at the Passion of Christ. The arithmetical part explains the arithmetical operations in the sexagesimal system: multiplication, division, square root, fractions, addition and subtraction, and proportional interpolation. Meliteniotes drew on the ancient authors whose names he cited (Theon, Pappus, Syrianus, and John Philoponus), but especially his Byzantine predecessors, whom he did not name, George Pachymeres and Theodore Metochites, as well as making his own personal contribution. The treatise on the astrolabe explained, to begin with, the construction of the instrument and then its use. He mentioned seventeen stars to be placed on the spider, but without giving their coordinates. In order to ensure that the instrument would not become useless after a period, because of the precession of the equinoxes, Meliteniotes explained how to draw a spider without stars. This is the only Greek treatise to develop this possibility.

Book 2 is devoted to the astronomy of Ptolemy, whose calculations he explained in the manner of Theon of Alexandria, both according to the *Almagest* and the *Handy Tables.* The calculations were illustrated by detailed examples for 25 December 1352 (except for a lunar eclipse, 23 October 1352, and a solar eclipse, 7 August 1347). No theoretical explanation is provided. At the end of Book 2 the author mentioned the need to correct Ptolemy's tables, both because of copyists' errors which entered the tables, and because of the defects in the instruments of observation. These produced errors imperceptible at the time of Ptolemy, but accrued over the centuries. The author promised to correct the tables when he might find the time, away from the ecclesiastical business that absorbed him and the headaches that left him prostrate.

Book 3 was devoted to Persian astronomy, that is the tables used by George Chrysococces in his *Persian Syntaxis,* the *Zīj ī-Īlkhānī* of Naṣīr al-Dīn al-Ṭūsī. Meliteniotes certainly used the work of Chrysococces, but he differed at a number of points: the transcriptions of Persian words were different, and several errors of Chrysococces were corrected. For example, the longitude of Constantinople is correctly put at 49°50' (in place of the Ptolemaic value of 56° used by Chrysococces). Meliteniotes, who copied in his own hand the *Laurentianus* 28/17, containing the teaching of Shams Bukhārī, also had access to sources earlier than Chrysococces. In this book Meliteniotes uses the same examples as in Book 2, but he made no explicit comparison between the results obtained from Ptolemy's tables and those from the Persian tables. Book 3 was a great success and was widely copied with many variations under the title *Paradosis tōn Persikōn kanonōn.*

It is not known whether Meliteniotes actually taught astronomy, but the pedagogical character of his work is evident. The *Tribiblos* introduced no scientific innovation, yet it played apparently an important role. By his personality and by the important offices that he held in the church, Theodore Meliteniotes seems to have prescribed the study of astronomy as part of the training of the senior Byzantine clergy. By his strenuous condemnation of astrology he dissociated the Persian tables from any astrological application, contrarily to the *Persian Syntaxis* of Chrysococces, whose avowed aim was the practice of astrology. Finally, he led the way to an improved understanding of the Persian methods, even if he did not eliminate all the errors that disturbed the work of Chrysococces.

BIBLIOGRAPHY

Astruc, Charles. "Le livre III retrouvé du commentaire de Théodore Méliténiotès sur les Evangiles (Paris. gr. 180)." *Travaux et mémoires* 4 (1970): 411–429. Commentary of the Gospels.

Dölger, Franz. "Die Abfassungzeit des Gedichtes des Meliteniotes auf die Enthaltsamkeit." *Annuaire de l'Institut de philologie et d'histoire orientales* 2 (1934): 315–330. On the poem *Sôphrosynè.*

Leurquin, Régine. "La Tribiblos astronomique de Théodore Méliténiote (Vat. gr. 792)." *Janus* 72, no. 4 (1985): 257–282.

———. *Théodore Méliténiote. Tribiblos Astronomique.* livre 1, *Corpus des Astronomes Byzantins* 4. Amsterdam, Gieben, 1990. livre 2, *Corpus des Astronomes Byzantins* 5–6, Amsterdam, Hakkert, 1993. Greek text with French translation and commentary.

Miller, E. "Poëme allégorique de Méliténiote." *Notices et Extraits des manuscrits de la bibliothèque impériale* 19, no. 2 (1858): 1–138. Greek text.

Tihon, Anne. "L'astronomie byzantine à l'aube de la Renaissance (de 1352 à la fin du XVe siècle)." *Byzantion* 66 (1996): 244–280.

Anne Tihon

MENARD, HENRY WILLIAM (*b.* Fresno, California, 10 December 1920; *d.* La Jolla, California, 9 February 1986), *marine geology.*

H. William Menard, informally known as Bill, was one of several scientists who led the systematic mapping of the deep oceans after World War II. This was the first detailed study of most of the Earth's surface, and one that, by leading to plate tectonics, revolutionized geology.

Early Years. Menard grew up in Los Angeles with his adoptive parents Henry William and Blanche, attending the California Institute of Technology (Caltech) as a geology undergraduate. He joined the Naval Reserve in 1941, going on active service in photo interpretation and intelligence after graduation in 1942. After the war he returned to Caltech for an MS, and then moved to Harvard for a PhD for a study of sedimentation, in which he applied the kind of simple quantitative methods he would use throughout his career.

In 1949, Menard returned to California to join the Sea-Floor Studies section of the Naval Electronics Lab in San Diego, where he studied bathymetry and marine sediments, combining navy soundings and data collected on oceanographic expeditions, many done jointly with the Scripps Institution of Oceanography (SIO), where he became a part-time lecturer in 1951 and full-time (and lifelong) faculty member in 1955. This exploration of the oceans by a few institutions was the first attempt to map the geology and topography of some very large regions, in Menard's case, much of the Pacific.

An example of what could be found was Menard's discovery, on his first deep-sea expedition in 1950, of an undersea mountain range (the Mid-Pacific Mountains) and of the Mendocino fracture zone, a large straight feature of rough topography offsetting seafloor of different depths. With data from subsequent surveys Menard located more of these features, all approximately parallel, in the northeast Pacific.

Deep-Sea Sedimentation. Menard's initial work in marine geology was a rethinking of deep-sea sedimentation, pointing out that the notion of an undisturbed sea floor was invalid, and invoking turbidity currents as a major source of sediments. The discovery of the fracture zones, which were unlike anything known on land, turned his attention to describing and explaining the source of these and other large-scale ocean features. Between 1950 and 1965, Menard, with other SIO scientists, led deep-sea expeditions to all parts of the Pacific, gradually refining what was known about this part of the ocean. After an initial focus on the fracture zones, in the late 1950s he became as interested in the oceanic rises, both the existing East Pacific Rise and possible previous rises shown by the existence of drowned islands. Always ready to try a new hypothesis, Menard attempted several syntheses of the known ocean data using temporal changes within a fixed pattern of continents and oceans. These summary accounts made many of the findings of oceanography available to a wider audience of geologists, and culminated in the book *Marine Geology of the Pacific* (1964), which unfortunately became largely obsolete soon after publication, when the new concepts of seafloor spreading and plate tectonics—very largely based on marine geology—completely changed the paradigm for understanding the ocean floor.

Though Menard had played no role in developing these new concepts, he was quick to adopt them and to realize how important they were. Having (by his own account) accepted the basic ideas by late 1966, over the next few years he and his students used magnetic, geological, and bathymetric data to determine the history and origin of many features of the northeast Pacific, an activity that had major implications for the understanding of the geology of western North America. The northeast Pacific, with faster spreading and more obvious complexities than the Atlantic, could not be explained through constant spreading. With his students, Menard extended concepts of seafloor spreading to include variations in spreading direction and changes in the nature of plate boundaries.

Though plate tectonics explained much, there were still topics it did not address, and much of Menard's research from the 1970s until his death was devoted to these areas, in particular the record of uplift and subsidence preserved in islands and submarine mountains. By combining his wide knowledge of particular instances with new concepts such as uplift by flexure from nearby loads and reheating of the lithosphere, he continued to address long-standing questions about the origins of high atolls and guyots, a topic described for the general reader in his last book, *Islands* (1986).

Menard's interests extended well beyond his professional specialty, notably to areas such as resource availability, shown in his work on manganese nodules, and later on a novel evaluation of the efficiency of exploration for oil. In 1974 he published a textbook discussing geology and resources. These wider interests also led him to an episode of public service, as director of the U.S. Geological Survey from 1978 through 1981.

Menard also had a strong interest in the history of geology, about which he wrote several articles and two books. The first book, *Science: Growth and Change* (1971) grew out of his year (1965–1966) at the White House Office of Science and Technology, and examined patterns of scientific growth and how these affected different branches of science and those who pursued them, and showed how subfields of geology had grown at very different rates. The other book, *The Ocean of Truth* (1986), was a combined memoir and history of marine geology and continental drift, describing how the explorations that Menard and others had led had provided convincing evidence for continental drift and plate tectonics. Menard's interest in making his science known to the public was expressed through popular articles and a book (*Anatomy of an Expedition,* 1969) describing what it was like to explore at sea. These works show his considerable wit, also present (though more muted) in his professional writings.

Menard's achievements brought him wide recognition, including election to the National Academy of Sciences in 1968, and the William Bowie Medal of the American Geophysical Union in 1985.

Menard brought to all of the areas he studied a zest and enthusiasm for research, and a desire to share his findings, that was a pleasure to those who worked with him at sea and ashore. He married Gifford Merrill in 1946; they had three children.

BIBLIOGRAPHY

WORKS BY MENARD

With Robert S. Dietz. "Mendocino Submarine Escarpment." *Journal of Geology* 60 (1952): 266–278.

"Deformation of the Northeastern Pacific Basin and the West Coast of North America." *Bulletin of the Geological Society of America* 66 (1955): 1149–1198.

"The East Pacific Rise." *Science* 132, no. 3441 (1960): 1737–1746.

With Tanya Atwater. "Changes in Direction of Sea Floor Spreading." *Nature* 219 (1968): 463–467.

With Marcia K. McNutt. "Evidence for and Consequences of Thermal Rejuvenation." *Journal of Geophysical Research* 87 (1982): 8570–8580.

The Ocean of Truth: a Personal History of Global Tectonics. Princeton, NJ: Princeton University Press, 1986.

OTHER SOURCES

Fisher, Robert L., and Edward D. Goldberg. "Henry William Menard." *Biographical Memoirs of the National Academy of Sciences* 64 (1988): 267–276.

Duncan Carr Agnew

MENDEL, JOHANN GREGOR (*b.* Heinzendorf, Austria [later Hynčice, Czech Republic], 22 July 1822; *d.* Brünn [later Brno, Czech Republic], 6 January 1884), *botany, genetics, meteorology.* For the original article on Mendel see *DSB,* vol. 9.

Mendel scholarship has traditionally been guided by the questions posed by Ronald Fisher in 1936: what did Mendel discover? How did he discover it? And what did he think he had discovered? Answers to these seemingly naïve, but politically and epistemologically charged questions have varied considerably over time. For Mendel's "rediscoverers" in 1900, the law of segregation was the centerpiece of Mendel's discovery. Commemorating the fiftieth anniversary of the rediscovery of Mendel's paper, Cyril Dean Darlington pointed out that it was only now, fifty years later, that geneticists were about to rediscover what Mendel had truly discovered, namely the material nature of the determinants of heredity, which Mendel had called "elements."

Geneticists paid attention to Mendel's historical achievements in order to strengthen and defend their discipline, which by 1950 had become stigmatized as a reactionary science in countries under Communist control. In 1962, the American human geneticist Curt Stern visited Brno to speak with Jaroslav Kříženecký, who had been dismissed as professor of animal breeding and genetics in 1950 and had been imprisoned for two years in 1956. Stern and Kříženecký wanted to organize an international conference at Brno on the occasion of the hundredth anniversary of the publication of Mendel's *Pisum* paper. The Mendel museum in Brno, which had been closed down in 1950, was renovated in 1963, and the conference took place in 1966, despite Kříženecký's untimely death in 1964. Both events marked the "rehabilitation" of Mendel and genetics as a scientific discipline in the Communist block.

Since then, historians have moved on from Fisher's questions to emphasize questions about the intellectual and social context in which Mendel worked: what were biologists' prevailing ideas about variation and heredity? What practical problems concerning hybridization faced breeders in Moravia? Biographical studies have revealed other important details about Mendel's life, such as his work in meteorology. Sociologists of science have analyzed the Mendel story as a reflection of changing interests in the scientific community. This article is divided into two sections, the first on Mendel's life and nineteenth-century background, the second on his hybridization studies and their relationship to evolution and the development of genetics.

Overview of Mendel's Career. Mendel's father was a diligent and industrious peasant and his mother was a

Mendel

Johann Gregor Mendel. © BETTMANN/CORBIS.

gardener's daughter, a fact biographers have seen as instrumental in stimulating their son Johann's interest in growing plants. Mendel's education included six years at the gymnasium (secondary school) in Troppau (Opava) and two years at the Lyceum attached to the university of Olmütz (Olomouc), where he studied philosophy, mathematics, and physics as preconditions for university study.

In 1843 Mendel entered the Augustinian monastery in Brno with the name Gregor, finding there the best possible conditions for pursuing his studies. During his theological studies in Brno, Mendel attended courses in agriculture at the Philosophical Institute, where he became acquainted with the role of hybridization in creating new plant varieties. In 1849 the abbot at Brno, Cyrill Napp, sent him as a substitute teacher to the gymnasium at Znojmo.

From 1851 to 1853, in his studies at the University of Vienna, Mendel paid much attention to physics, mathematics, chemistry, and plant physiology, and acquired the theoretical background and the skill required to perform experiments and undertake independent research. The teaching of the physicist Christian Doppler had a formative impact on Mendel's experimental methodology. He also took courses at the university from Franz Unger, who was an early proponent of cell theory and interested in paleobotany, biogeography, and hybridization.

In 1854 Mendel was appointed teacher of physics and natural history at the newly established Realgymnasium in Brno. He devoted all his free time to his long-term research program on plant hybridization (principally peas), drawing on the experience of breeders and plant hybridization experiments conducted by botanists. Mendel became a member of a number of regional associations of breeders, agriculturalists, and naturalists.

In 1864 Mendel was elected abbot of the monastery and entrusted with new duties. The previous extent of experimentation ended, but he did not lose his interest in the problem. A recently discovered fragmentary note (Orel, 1996, p. 187) shows that in the mid-1870s he returned to the enigma of *Hieracium* hybrids (see below) and found that cross-fertilization of these polymorphic species yielded segregating multifactorial traits in accordance with his theory of variable hybrids.

In 1857 Mendel began his meteorological observations in the monastery and was soon recognized as the authority on this subject in Moravia. He published the results of meteorological observations made throughout the province, and promoted weather forecasting. He wrote some magazine articles about promising new ways to transmit weather data to Vienna and to disseminate weather forecasts to farmers. His remarkable theoretical knowledge and talent for observation is shown in his ten-page report on the whirlwind in Brno in October 1870. He used physics to explain its origin through the meeting of two air streams of different dimensions and properties, arising shortly after the occurrence of the storm.

Having been elected abbot, Mendel was soon appreciated for his support for applying hybridization techniques to create new plant varieties. His newly built apiary became a pioneering research site for the improvement of beekeeping. He paid special attention to investigating controlled crossing to create a new race of bees. After his death in 1884 Mendel's achievements were recognized by plant breeders and beekeepers. His naturalist colleagues commemorated his activities in meteorology and his hybridizing experiments (Matalová, 1984).

Background: Concepts and Questions. Mendel's study can be viewed narrowly as a sequence of hypotheses tested through experiments, which led to the explanation of the essence of heredity. But to fully appreciate the questions that inspired Mendel and the methods that he used, he must be placed within a rich, multilayered context that historians have begun to evaluate. Scholars now know that Mendel was influenced by a wide variety of problems and ideas stemming both from major botanists and local Moravian agriculturalists.

His main innovation was his transition from questions about inheritance and transformation of species to answers involving transmission and distribution of individual traits. He selected the genus *Pisum* (garden peas) as the best experimental model plant. He reduced the problem to be investigated to discrete trait pairs (of seeds and plants) that existed in alternative forms and were reliably distinguishable. His aim was to explain the "generally applicable law of formation and development of hybrids" as one way of "finally reaching the solution to a question about the developmental history [*Entwicklungs-Geschichte*] of organic forms." (1865, pp 3–4; Kříženecký, pp. 57–58; see Stern and Sherwood, p. 2). Here, as for most German scientists of his day, the term *Entwicklung* embraced development at both individual and species levels.

Sander Gliboff (1999) has argued that Unger's combination of plant morphology and biogeography provided the overarching intellectual framework for Mendel's hybridization studies. Unger's goal was to discover patterns and quantified laws of distribution and Entwicklung, including historical *Entwicklung* (i.e., species transformation). His method counted plant species and followed their changing proportions in the flora over geographic space or over geological time. What Unger wanted to provide was a "physics" of the plant organism. Gliboff finds the parallels to Mendel's famous pea studies to be striking. The monk looked at a short-term *Entwicklung*, but employed a similar methodology: he quantified the changing proportions of the different traits, from generation to generation, and formulated laws of change.

Roger Wood and Vítězslav Orel have brought to light the existence of a unique regional network of sheep breeders and professors of agriculture and science in Moravia, which provided the immediate social and intellectual context for Mendel's work. In 1814, this group formed a Sheep Breeders' Society in Brno; they were trying to find ways to control the characteristics of the animals they bred. Producers of fruit trees and vines were also interested in problems of heredity. In 1818, this society was engaged in a search for a law of hybridization. They realized that traits might be hidden, yet somehow transmitted to future generations.

The abundant communication of animal and plant breeders with naturalists in Moravia in the 1830s (before Mendel came to Brno) led them to ask about the definition of species, the force of hybridization, and the creation of heritable new kinds of plants. Professor Johann Karl Nestler indicated how nature produces, "through forces beyond the hand of man," constant natural species and how, in contrast, humans modify the variations in organisms "with increasing or disappearing inheritance" (Wood and Orel, 2005, p. 262). The discussion of sheep breeding culminated at the annual meetings in Brno in 1836 and 1837, with the formulation of the physiological research question: what is inherited and how? One of the active participants in these discussions was Napp, who would admit Mendel to his monastery in 1843.

Staffan Müller-Wille and Orel (2007) offer a detailed analysis of Mendel's relationship to botanical hybridizers and his innovative concern with transmission of single traits. Those earlier hybridizers (unlike twentieth-century geneticists) were concerned with species evolution, not inheritance of single traits. Mendel built on hybridizers' concepts and questions, yet developed creative new methods and answers that would later be powerful tools for the Mendelians. His main innovation was his transition from questions about inheritance and transformation of species to answers involving transmission and distribution of individual traits.

Müller-Wille and Orel start with Carl Linnaeus, who in 1751 defined species as lineages that (in the same environment) always produced identical progeny down the generations. Varieties, in contrast, manifested differences caused by external differences in temperature, wind, soil, and so on. Soon, however, Linnaeus encountered what he called *constant varieties*—plants that did not seem to fit with the strict distinction of species and varieties, and which he interpreted as resulting from hybridizations. Over the next century botanists investigated hybrids, seeking laws of inheritance and classifying types of progeny in terms of species as whole bundles of traits. Could new species be formed by hybrid crosses between existing species? Were species so stable and distinct that hybrids would either be sterile or inevitably revert to one parental type? Or were species so fluid that they were immensely malleable, with chaotically varying progeny?

In 1849 Carl Friedrich Gärtner attributed the variability resulting from hybridization to the interaction of the "inner natures" of the parent species. Gärtner believed a formative force (*Bildungskraft*) caused the form of a species, and in hybridization the forces of the different species interacted; often over time one force would predominate, and over generations the progeny would gradually return to that force's type. If two specimens appeared similar, the way to discern whether they belonged to the same species was to cross them with yet another species. If both specimens gave rise to similar progeny when outcrossed, that proved the specimens belonged to the same species, i.e., had the same inner nature. If the specimens produced different progeny when outcrossed, they belonged to different species. Upon further crossing of hybrids, he found bewilderingly many combinations of traits, for which he vainly sought a law.

Taking up the search for that law, Mendel, like Linnaeus, defined a species (*Art*) as a lineage that, under equal

Mendel

environmental conditions, produced identical offspring. For instance, his tall pea plants were one species, his short ones another. (English translations of Mendel's paper obscure this point, as they variously render *Art* as "species," "variety," "stock," or "strain.") Here we see his crucial innovation: crossing species that differed only in one easily distinguishable trait simplified the problem and enabled him to discern basic patterns, such as the 3 : 1 ratio from the self-pollination of hybrids.

Crossing two parental species produced pea plants that resembled one parent, but these were variable hybrids because their descendants varied. In the next generation, one quarter of the plants resembled one grandparent (e.g., tall) and bred true when self-pollinated (all progeny were tall): they belonged to the same species as that grandparent. Another quarter resembled the other grandparent (e.g., short) and bred true, which showed they belonged to the same species as that grandparent. The remaining 50 percent were variable hybrids.

In further generations, ever more of the progeny belonged to one or the other ancestral species, because the constant species members bred true, plus some of the offspring of hybrids belonged to constant species. This explained the "reversion" to ancestral types. But unlike his predecessors, Mendel saw no gradual process: each pea plant was either a member of a constant species or a variable hybrid. Mendel also worked out the more complex mathematical patterns when crossing species that differed in two or more traits.

In experiments with other plant species Mendel wished to determine whether the laws of development discovered for *Pisum* were also valid for other plants. He mentioned that one experiment with *Phaseolus,* regarding the shape of the plant, was in agreement with the same law. The second experiment, about change of coloration, he explained in terms of a *composite series* made up of independent colors $A = A1 + A2 + \ldots$

Thus, like Gärtner, Mendel used hybridization to determine the inner nature that revealed if a plant was an exemplar of a species or a hybrid. But, to explain those phenomena, Mendel wrote neither of species forms (like earlier hybridizers) nor of pairs of genes (like later geneticists); rather he referred to discrete types of reproductive cells that were associated with the regular development of certain characteristics, and thus with different types or species of plants.

Each egg or pollen cell had a certain constitution (Mendel used the somewhat general term *Beschaffenheit*). Members of pure species produced germ cells with all the same constitution, for instance the potential to make short plants. When they combined to make a new plant, all the cells shared that constitution, hence the same species continued (all the progeny were short). Hybrid plants produced two types of germ cells. When different germ cells met in hybridization, one trait would dominate (e.g., tall), but the hybrid plants produced equal numbers of each kind of pollen and eggs (e.g., tall and short). The constitution of the germ cell was the cause underlying the mathematical laws describing the patterns of variable hybrids, and the constancy of pure species (see second part for more).

After 1865 Mendel paid greatest attention to experiments with *Hieracium,* for which he found different results from peas. When he crossed two species, the appearance of members of the first generation varied greatly, yet the next generation appeared uniform and so did further descendants. Mendel called these *constant hybrids,* that is, new, true-breeding species. He believed that in such hybridizations the constitutions of the pollen and egg were "entirely and permanently accommodated together" and the resulting plant would produce germ cells that all shared the same constitution. Thus it *was* possible for hybridization to produce new species, but not in the lawless indefinite variety some earlier hybridizers had thought possible.

When Mendel delivered his lectures on his pea plant experiments to the newly founded Brno Natural Science Society in 1865, his audience did not grasp his answers to the research questions formulated in Brno thirty years before (Orel and Wood, 2005). Nor was his work taken up widely. The figure of Mendel as an ignored scientific genius has become so conventional that in 2000 the sociologist of science Steve Fuller used him as the standard case of the unrecognized discoverer who proposes a scientific novelty and suffers neglect. However, rather than suffering, Mendel's feeling (recorded by Abbot F. Bařina, who was the last novice Mendel accepted into the monastery) was as follows:

> Though I have had to live through many bitter moments in my life, I must admit with gratitude that the beautiful and good prevailed. My scientific work brought me much satisfaction, and I am sure it will soon be recognized by the whole world. (Křížený, 1965, p. 6)

Augustine Brannigan has argued that Mendel was not completely forgotten, but that his contemporaries understood him to be talking about species hybridization, and claiming that the descendants of hybrids tend to revert to ancestral types. Around 1900 the "rediscoverers" of Mendel instead picked up on his mathematical laws of transmission of particular traits. Jan Sapp has analyzed how various Mendelians interpreted Mendel in light of controversies in twentieth-century genetics and evolution. There are also ongoing controversies over the level at which Mendel understood the implications of his experiments (Monaghan and Corcos, 1990; Falk and Sarkar, 1991; Orel and Hartl, 1999).

SUPPLEMENTARY BIBLIOGRAPHY

See also Olby's bibliography, below. The translations of Mendel's paper into other languages are summarized in Folia Mendeliana *8 (1973) and 9 (1979). English and German texts can be found at http://www.mendelweb.org/.*

WORKS BY MENDEL

"Versuche über Pflanzenhybriden." *Verhandlungen des naturforschenden Vereines in Brünn* 4, Abhandlungen (1866): 3–47. Reprinted with corrections from a copy of the manuscript in: *Fundamenta Genetica,* edited by Jaroslav Kříženecký. Prague: Czechoslovak Academy of Sciences,1965a. Translated in *The Origins of Genetics: A Mendel Source Book,* edited by Curt Stern and Eva R. Sherwood. San Francisco: Freeman, 1966.

"Ueber einige aus künstlicher Befruchtung gewonnenen Hieracium-Bastarde." *Verhandlungen des naturforschenden Vereines in Brünn* 8, Abhandlungen (1869): 26–31. Translated as: "On Hieracium-Hybrids Obtained by Artificial Fertilisation" in Stern and Sherwood.

OTHER SOURCES

Brannigan, Augustine. *The Social Basis of Scientific Discoveries.* Cambridge, U.K.: Cambridge University Press, 1981.

Corcos, Alain F., and Floyd V. Monaghan. *Gregor Mendel's Experiments on Plant Hybrids: A Guided Study.* New Brunswick, NJ: Rutgers University Press, 1993.

Dunn, L. C. "Mendel, His Work and His Place in History." *Commemoration of the Publication of Gregor Mendel's Pioneer Experiments in Genetics,* special issue of *Proceedings of the American Philosophical Society* 109 (1965): 189–198.

Fairbanks, Daniel J., and Bryce Rytting. "Mendelian Controversies: A Botanical and Historical Review." *American Journal of Botany* 88 (2001): 737–752.

Falk, Raphael, and Sahotra Sarkar. "The Real Objective of Mendel's Paper: A Response to Monaghan and Corcos." *Biology and Philosophy* 6 (1991): 447–451.

Frolov, Ivan Timofeevich, and S. A. Pastusnyi. *Mendel', mendelizm I dialektika.* Moscow: Mysl', 1972.

Fuller, Steve. *Thomas Kuhn: A Philosophical History for Our Times.* Chicago: University of Chicago Press, 2000.

Gliboff, Sander. "Gregor Mendel and the Laws of Evolution." *History of Science* 37 (1999): 217–235.

Kříženecký, Jaroslav. *Gregor Johann Mendel: 1822–1884. Texte und Quellen zu seinem Wirken und Leben. Festgabe der Deutschen Akademie Naturforscher Leopoldina zum Mendel Memorial Symposium 1865–1965, August 1965 in Brünn.* Leipzig, Germany: J. A. Barth, 1965.

Matalová, Anna. "Response to Mendel's Death in 1884." *Folia Mendeliana* 19 (1984): 217–221.

Monaghan, Floyd V., and Alain F. Corcos. "The Real Objective of Mendel's Paper." *Biology and Philosophy* 5 (1990): 267–292.

Müller-Wille, Staffan, and Vítězslav Orel. "From Linnaean Species to Mendelian Factors: Elements of Hybridism, 1751–1870." *Annals of Science* 64, no. 2 (April 2007): 171–215.

Orel, Vítězslav. *Gregor Mendel: The First Geneticist.* Oxford: Oxford University Press, 1996.

———. "Contested Memory: Debates over the Nature of Mendel's Paradigm." *Hereditas* 142 (2005): 98–102.

———, and I. Cetl. *The Secret of Mendel's Discovery.* In Japanese. Tokyo, 1973.

———, and Daniel L. Hartl. "Controversies in the Interpretation of Mendel's Discovery." *History and Philosophy of the Life Sciences* 16 (1994): 423–464.

———, Françoise Robert, and Jean Robert Armogathe. *Mendel, 1822–1884: Un inconnu célèbre. Un savant, une époque.* Paris: Belin, 1986.

Sapp, Jan. "The Nine Lives of Gregor Mendel." In *Experimental Inquiries,* edited by H. E. Le Grand. Dordrecht, Netherlands: Kluwer Academic Publishers, 1990. Available from http://www.mendelweb.org/MWsapp.html.

Stubbe, Hans. *Kurze Geschichte der Genetik bis zur Wiederentdeckung der Vererbungsregeln Gregor Mendels.* Jena, German Democratic Republic: Fischer, 1963. Translated as *History of Genetics, from Prehistoric Times to the Rediscovery of Mendel's Laws.* Cambridge, MA: MIT Press, 1972.

Wood, Roger J., and Vítězslav Orel. *Genetic Prehistory in Selective Breeding: A Prelude to Mendel.* Oxford: Oxford University Press, 2001.

———, and Vítězslav Orel. "Scientific Breeding in Central Europe during the Early Nineteenth Century: Background to Mendel's Later Work." *Journal of the History of Biology* 38 (2005): 239–272.

Vítězslav Orel
Staffan Müller-Wille

Relationship of Mendel to Mendelian Genetics. The name Gregor Mendel has long been closely associated with the study of heredity and variation, a field of studies to which the name "genetics" was given in 1906. Four decades earlier Mendel's research on hybridization was published, and by 1906 he had long been dead. How strong, then, is the claim for Mendel as founder of this great science? The British evolutionist, Sir Gavin de Beer, had no doubt on the matter. In 1965 he declared, "There is not known another example of a science which sprang fully formed from the brain of one man." To an audience at the Royal Society that year he explained: "It is not often possible to pinpoint the origin of a whole new branch of science accurately in time and place … But genetics is an exception, for it owes its origin to one man, Gregor Mendel, who expounded its basic principles at Brno on 8 February and 8 March 1865" (De Beer, p. 154).

Clearly Mendel had nothing to do with the establishment of the institutions associated with genetics. Rather, sixteen years after his death, it was William Bateson, aided by the Royal Horticultural Society, who, in the English-speaking world, began to map out the discipline that in 1906 he christened "genetics," and in 1909 published the first full scale English text, *Mendel's Principles of Heredity.* The same year appeared Wilhelm Johannsen's German text, *Elemente der exakten Erblichkeitslehre.* Was it then an exaggeration on De Beer's part to claim that the science "sprang fully formed" from Mendel's brain? To address this question let us summarize briefly the core features of the Mendelian genetics established in the early years of the twentieth century, then anatomize Mendel's paper of 1865, in order to assess the extent of the dependence of the former on the latter.

Early Mendelian Genetics. The central concept of Mendelian genetics was that of the "factor" or "gene." In the simplest case, it was claimed, an hereditary trait is determined by two such factors, one from each parent. For a given hereditary trait, every cell in the organism has one paternal and one maternal copy of each. Bateson called them "allelomorphs," later abbreviated to alleles. In the germ cells, however, only one of the two alleles would be present, because in forming these cells the two factors or alleles would have been "segregated" into different daughter germ cells. Subsequent fusion of germ cells in fertilization would restore the two-fold constitution from which arise the cells of the new organism. Neither Bateson nor Johannsen wished to identify their proposed hereditary units with specific particles in the cell.

By 1915, however, Thomas Hunt Morgan and his group in New York had created maps showing the relative locations of these hereditary determinants on the chromosomes of the fruit fly. The concept of the gene as a material particle was thus introduced. Meanwhile Johannsen, wishing to put an end to confusions between the observed characteristics of an organism and its genetic constitution, had introduced the terms *gene*, *genotype*, and *phenotype.* Mendelian factors were henceforth and increasingly referred to as genes, and hereditary transmission was used to refer to genes rather than to characteristics.

Although it was soon recognized that Mendelian heredity governs characteristics that blend and have small variations, as well as those that are nonblending and have large variations, the early Mendelians concentrated their research on the latter. These, they claimed, give little if any opportunity for natural selection to play its creative, adaptive role. That role requires the variations to be small so that they can be accumulated in a gradual stepwise manner. Acting on large nonblending variations, natural selection would be no more than a sieve, weeding out the nonadaptive. Supporters of Darwinian evolution therefore considered Mendelian research a diversion, irrelevant to the problems of evolution. As a result it took some three decades to achieve a synthesis between Darwinism and Mendelian genetics. What, then, were Mendel's views on hereditary particles and Darwinian evolution, and how close was his research to that of the early Mendelians?

Mendel's Theoretical and Experimental Contributions. Mendel's research was carried out before chromosomes had been described, but not before it was established that every cell comes from the division of a preexisting cell, and that fertilization is the union of two germ cells. He accepted these conclusions as some did not, Charles Darwin for one. Furthermore, Mendel believed that the development of the organism proceeds "in accord with a constant law based on the material composition [*Beschaffenheit*] and arrangement of the elements that attained a viable union in the cell" (Stern and Sherwood, p. 42; Kříženecký, p. 88). His was a materialist account. But nowhere did he speak of just two elements or factors for an hereditary trait. Most often he used phenotypic language. Thus he described "traits that pass into hybrid association ... unchanged" (Stern and Sherwood, p. 9; Kříženecký, p. 63) rather than elements or factors. Germ cells he described as "endowed with the potential [*Anlage*] for creating identical individuals" (Stern and Sherwood, p. 24; Kříženecký, p. 74). Here *Anlage* translated as "potential," "disposition," or "rudiment" bespeaks Mendel's appreciation of the nineteenth century distinction between "hereditary constitution" and the observed characters or traits. The other location for such language is in a letter to Carl Nägeli in 1870. In discussing the determination of sex he referred to the Anlage for the functional development of the sex organs, and suggested that the germ cells are "different as regards the sex anlage" (Stern and Sherwood, p. 97). *Anlage,* admittedly, has multiple meanings, from blueprint to potential and predisposition, but these two occasions in which Mendel used the word make clear that when attending to the level of cells, he could stop the characteristic talk and turn to the language of hereditary constitution. The early Mendelians, for the most part, were no more consistent than Mendel in this respect.

Mendel was one among several who in the nineteenth century used letter notation to represent hybridizations, among them Nägeli and Max Wichura. Mendel knew their work, but had rightly rejected the fractional law of inheritance upon which they relied. The referents of Mendel's letters, however, were, like theirs, the "forms" of the plants. When he turned to the reproductive cells of the hybrids, though, Mendel used such notation to refer to the germ cells. Thus his representation of the pairs of germ cells that come together when the hybrid *Aa* reproduces and of the resulting offspring is:

$$\frac{A}{A}+\frac{A}{a}+\frac{a}{A}+\frac{a}{a}=A+2Aa+a$$

Mendel

The letters on the right side of the equation clearly refer to the foundation cells (zygotes) produced, their kinds, and the proportions between them, in terms of the kinds of plants they yield. Had he been referring to factors, the expression on the right side of the equation would be: $AA + 2Aa + aa$.

Mendel, it seems, did not picture cells, whether of hybrids or of pure species, as possessing two elements per trait that go their separate ways when the germ cells are formed. Such a conception would have meant that a separation between pairs of elements occurs whether the elements are like or unlike. But in forming the germ cells he suggested: "all elements present participate in completely free and uniform fashion, and only those that differ separate from each other" (Stern and Sherwood, p. 43; Křížencký, p. 88). His language conjures up the separation of pepper grains from a mixture with mustard seeds rather than paired elements in the cell. And why not? Bateson rightly called the segregating cell division "out of which each gamete comes sensibly pure in respect of the allelomorph it carries," Mendel's "essential discovery" (Bateson, 1928, p. 245).

Mendel's interpretation of his results in terms of the cell theory was just one of the many brilliant features of his 1865 paper. Although the idea of *pairs* of elements in the cells is missing, the notion of pairs is contained in one central and indispensable feature of his experimental design, namely his "constant differing traits" (*konstant differierende Merkmale*). These were his chosen seven traits, each of which differed in its expression in different strains, not in a "more or less" manner, but "decisively." Thus for the trait height, strains were either tall or short, for seed color, either green or yellow etc. These were the "differing characters" or character-pairs (*je zwei differierende Merkmale*). His success in establishing their independence from one another in hereditary transmission gave him the confidence to deny that species are unified entities that only act as wholes. Thus prepared, he could unravel the confused accounts of the behavior of hybrid descendants in the literature, and explain the alleged greater variability of cultivated plants over their wild relatives in terms of the frequency of spontaneous hybridization and the ensuing recombination of independently transmitted characters.

Mendel's experimental procedure was unique in its day. Here he drew inspiration from physics and, Gliboff believes, from botany, possibly from the work of Unger (Gliboff, 1999). Mendel tested the true-breeding quality of thirty-four varieties of pea for two seasons (1854–1856) before he started the hybridizations. He grew twenty-two of these varieties as controls throughout the experiment (1856–1862) to check that they continued true when no crossbreeding occurred. Some plants in the experiment were grown under glass to see if protection from insects gave results differing from those obtained from plants grown outside where insects might have interfered. He harvested peas in their thousands in order to achieve statistically significant results.

His interpretation of the results was also unprecedented. Having been trained in combinatorial mathematics he was well aware of the numerical relations between the terms in the expansion of a binomial. Thus $(A + a)^2 = A^2 + 2Aa + a^2$—the three terms related as 1 : 2 : 1 (when *Aa* cannot be distinguished from *A*, the ratio becomes 3 : 1). This meant that he did not just report data showing a three-fold predominance of one class of offspring over the other, but he saw the significance of the approximation of his data to 3 : 1. Such a ratio would be produced if the germ cells of the hybrid *Aa* are "pure," i.e., are of the type *A* or *a* but not *Aa*, and if both are produced in equal numbers, and all combinations in fertilization are realized equally.

Historical research has revealed that two of the three "rediscoverers" of Mendelian heredity, Hugo de Vries and Carl Correns, had read Mendel in the 1890s, Correns before he carried out his hybridization experiments (Rheinberger, 1995), De Vries only after he had arrived at the 3 : 1 ratio independently (Stamhuis et al., 1999; Meijer, 1995). But it was reading Mendel's paper possibly for the second time that alerted him to the great significance of these ratios. The third rediscoverer, Erich Tschermak, had completed his experiments before reading Mendel, but he did not arrive at the full Mendelian explanation of his results (Olby, 1985, pp. 120–123).

However, all the rediscoverers' papers were eclipsed by Mendel's stunning achievement. It was clearly Mendel who first set out the design of the hybridization experiments subsequently carried out by his rediscoverers. His remarkable experimental methodology, as Müller-Wille and Orel have shown, belongs in the long tradition of plant hybridization going back to Linnaeus (Müller-Wille and Orel, 2007). Yet Mendel's introduction of the "character-pair" as an independent unit in hybridization, his statistical sophistication, and his creative application of cytology were major innovations. They constituted major tools of the Mendelism that followed. Moreover, even in 1900 Mendel's results were more impressive than those of his rediscoverers, and this they acknowledged.

On these grounds Mendel stands out as the preeminent figure in the prehistory of Mendelism. However, if the attribution of founder status to Mendel is accepted in De Beer's terms, it should not imply the presence in Mendel's work of features only introduced in the following century.

Mendel and Evolution. Some historians have argued that Mendel's experiments and their theoretical explanation were directed against Darwin's theory of evolution by natural selection (Callender 1988; Bishop 1996). Mendel encountered species transformism first in the rather speculative tradition of *Naturphilosophie* when he became friendly with a fellow Augustinian, Franz Matthaeus Klacel. According to the *Naturphilosophen* a "world spirit" has worked within organisms, transforming them into higher and more complex forms over long periods of time. Mendel again met with transformism in the teaching of Unger at the University of Vienna. There he learned of the work of the German plant hybridists, Joseph Kölreuter and Gärtner, and of the debate as to whether new species might have arisen by hybridization. Already in the winter of 1853 he must have been considering a project with *Pisum* on the lines of the experiments for which he is now famous. And as the introductory and the concluding sections show, he was, like Gärtner, concerned to address the question of whether there are hybrids that remain as constant as do their originating species.

Although Mendel visited London in 1862 as a member of Brno's delegation to the International Exhibition there, he never met or corresponded with Darwin. We know that Mendel read and wrote marginalia in his own copy of the 1863 German translation of *The Origin of Species*. These, like the concluding section of his 1865 paper, show clearly that he did not accept Darwin's views on the source of variation (Stern and Sherwood, pp. 37–38; Křiženecký, pp. 84–85). This negative response was not on account of religious concerns, for Mendel, though a devout Christian, took a very liberal view of Christianity and was certainly not a supporter of the biblical creation story. When he referred publicly to "the spirit of the Darwinian teaching" (Stern and Sherwood, p. 51), he did not criticize or denigrate it.

But Darwin's claim that all variation is directly or indirectly traceable to changes in the conditions of life Mendel rejected, as he surely did Darwin's claim that the role of hybridization in generating variation has been "greatly exaggerated" (Darwin, 1861, p. 20). Both Mendel and, earlier, his teacher Unger, had conducted transplant experiments to test the alleged lasting effects of changed conditions and had not found them. Because Darwin believed crossbreeding dilutes new variations, he saw it as a deterrent to their establishment. But Mendel knew from his experiments that the disappearance of some characters following crossbreeding does not necessarily lead to their loss. For Mendel, therefore, Darwin's theory needed fundamental revision. (But Darwin could have responded to Mendel that the genetic recombination generated by hybridization would not alone supply sufficient novel variations. Hence arose the suggestion of abrupt, hereditary variations independent of hybridization, as in the work of Bateson [1894] and the mutation theory of De Vries [1901].)

To describe Mendel as a convinced Darwinian would thus be misleading. Rather, what little evidence we have would suggest that he was a transformist who, unlike Darwin, perceived in the genetic recombination following hybridization a rich source of variation upon which selection could act. To read more into his work seems unjustified.

SUPPLEMENTARY BIBLIOGRAPHY

See also Müller-Wille and Orel's bibliography above.

Bateson, William. *Materials for the Study of Variation Treated with Especial Regard to Discontinuity in the Origin of Species.* London: Macmillan, 1894.

———. "Presidential Address to Section D." *Report of the British Association* 1904. Reprinted in Bateson, Beatrice. *William Bateson, F.R.S. Naturalist. His Essays and Addresses Together with a Short Account of His Life.* Cambridge, U.K.: Cambridge University Press, 1928.

———. *Mendel's Principles of Heredity.* Cambridge, U.K.: Cambridge University Press, 1909.

Bishop, B. E. "Mendel's Opposition to Evolution and to Darwin." *Journal of Heredity* 87 (1996): 205–213.

Callender, L. A. "Gregor Mendel—An Opponent of Descent with Modification." *History of Science* 26 (1988): 41–75.

Correns, C. "G. Mendel's Regel über das Verhalten der Nachkommenschaft der Rassenbastarde." *Berichte der deutschen botanischen Gesellschaft* 18 (1900): 158–168.

Darwin, Charles R. *On the Origin of Species by Means of Natural Selection, or the Preservation of Favoured Races in the Struggle for Life.* 3rd. ed. London, 1861. Translated by Victor Carus, *Über die Entstehung der Arten im Tier und Pflanzenreiche durch natürliche Züchtung.* Stuttgart, 1863. Mendel's copy.

De Beer, Gavin. "Genetics: The Centre of Science." *Proceedings of the Royal Society of London, Series B, Biological Sciences* 164 (1966): 154–166.

De Vries, Hugo. "Sur la loi de disjonction des hybrides." *Comptes rendus hebdomadaire des séances de l'Académie des sciences* 130 (1900): 845–847.

———. *Die Mutationstheorie: Versuche und Beobachtungen über die Entstehung von Arten im Pflanzenreich.* Leipzig, Germany: Veit, 1901. Translated by J. B. Farmer and A. D. Darbishire as *The Mutation Theory: Experiments and Observations on the Origin of Species in the Vegetable Kingdom.* 2 vols. Chicago: Open Court, 1909–1910.

Heimans, J. "Mendel's Ideas on the Nature of Hereditary Characters: The Explanation of Fragmentary Records of Mendel's Hybridizing Experiments." *Folia Mendeliana* 6 (1971): 91–98.

Henig, Robin Marantz. *The Monk in the Garden: The Lost and Found Genius of Gregor Mendel, the Father of Genetics.* New York: Houghton Mifflin, 2000.

Iltis, Hugo. *Gregor Johann Mendel: Leben, Werk und Wirkung.* Berlin: Julius Springer, 1924. Translated by Eden and Cedar Paul. *Life of Mendel.* London: George Allen & Unwin, 1932.

Reprinted 1966. Note that pp. 207–408 of the German edition were excluded from the English translation.

Johannsen, Wilhelm. *Elemente der exakten Erblichkeitslehre.* Jena, Germany: Fischer, 1909.

———. "The Genotype Conception of Heredity." *American Naturalist* 45 (1911): 129–159.

Kimmelman, Barbara A. "Organisms and Interests in Scientific Research: R. A. Emerson's Claims for the Unique Contributions of Agricultural Genetics." In *The Right Tools for the Job: At Work in Twentieth-Century Life Sciences,* edited by Adele E. Clarke and Joan H. Fujimura. Princeton, NJ: Princeton University Press, 1992.

Mawer, Simon. *Gregor Mendel: Planting the Seeds of Genetics.* New York: Abrams/Field Museum, Chicago, 2006.

Meijer, Onno. "Hugo de Vries No Mendelian?" *Annals of Science* 42 (1985): 189–232.

Olby, Robert. "Mendel No Mendelian?" *History of Science* 17 (1979): 53–72. Reprinted with minor changes in Olby, *The Origins of Mendelism.* 2nd ed. Chicago: Chicago University Press, 1985.

———. "Horticulture: The Font for the Baptism of Genetics." *Nature Reviews: Genetics* 1 (2000): 65–70.

Paul, Diane, and Barbara Kimmelman. "Mendel in America: Theory and Practice, 1900–1919." In *The American Development of Biology,* edited by Ronald Rainger, Keith R. Benson, and Jane Maienschein. Philadelphia: University of Pennsylvania Press, 1988.

Rheinberger, Hans-Jörg. "When Did Carl Correns Read Gregor Mendel's Paper?" *Isis* 86 (1995): 612–618.

Roberts, H. F. *Plant Hybridization before Mendel.* Princeton, NJ: Princeton University Press, 1929. Reprinted New York: Hafner Publishing Co., 1965.

Stamhuis, Ida, Onno Meijer, and E. J. Zevenhuizen. "Hugo de Vries on Heredity: Statistics, Mendelian Laws, Pangenesis, Mutation." *Isis* 90 (1999): 238–267.

Weiling, Franz. "Descent of the Prelate Cyrill Napp, the Spiritual Mentor of J. G. Mendel." *Sudhoffs Archiv* 55, no. 1 (1971): 80–85.

———. "Historical Study: Johann Gregor Mendel, 1822–1884." *American Journal of Medical Genetics* 40, no. 1 (1991): 1–25; discussion 26.

Tschermak, Erich. "Über künstliche Kreuzung bei Pisum sativum." *Zeitschrift für das landwirtschaftliche Versuchswesen in Oesterreich* 3, no. 5 (1900): 465–555.

Robert Olby

MENDELEEV, DMITRII IVANOVICH

(*b.* Tobolsk, Siberia, Russia, 8 February 1834; *d.* St. Petersburg, Russia, 2 February 1907), *chemistry, periodic table.* For the original article on Mendeleev see *DSB,* vol. 9.

Recognition of Mendeleev as the most important, although not the only, developer of the periodic law has strengthened in recent years, and his contributions to other areas of science and learning have begun to be explored in greater detail by scholars. Interest in Mendeleev's work has continued in the early twenty-first century, and a small but steady stream of studies continues to flow from scholars both inside and outside of Russia.

Although a considerable part of the work on Mendeleev's output considers the various aspects of the periodic law and its discovery—his most important contribution to science—there is a growing interest in Mendeleev's scientific work for the Russian government, his involvement with practical issues of agriculture and industry, his critique of spiritualism, and his scientific research on the theory of solutions and on gas laws, among other aspects of his life and work. All of these provide a fuller context in which to better understand his central scientific contributions.

The Periodic Law and its Reception. B. M. Kedrov's article in the original *Dictionary of Scientific Biography* (1981; *DSB*) brought his conception of the discovery of the periodic law to a broader audience and this view has since become widely accepted by many scholars. In brief, Kedrov argued that Mendeleev formulated the main contours of the periodic law during the course of one day, 17 February 1869 on the Russian calendar (1 March by the Gregorian calendar in use in the West). Mendeleev had recently been appointed to the chair of chemistry at St. Petersburg University and was writing his own general chemistry textbook for use in his classes. By early in 1869, Mendeleev had finished the first part of the textbook, ending with a chapter on the halogens, and moved on to the alkali metals. He was then faced with what group to consider next. The logical choice was the alkaline earth metals, but some other metals had similar properties, so Mendeleev would have to choose which way to proceed. On 17 February, he began to compare the atomic weights of these various groups of elements, which Kedrov identified as the key step in the discovery of the periodic law. Over the course of this day, Mendeleev increased the numbers of elements he was able to arrange in groups in several rough drafts of a table. To help in this process, he made a series of cards on which he wrote the symbols and main properties of the sixty-three then-known elements and began to play what Kedrov called chemical solitaire. At the end of the day, he drafted a clean copy of his table of elements and sent it to be printed.

There are serious deficiencies with Kedrov's account that are beginning to be recognized and discussed by a larger group of scholars, even though a few historians of chemistry (mainly residing in St. Petersburg) had long

Mendeleev

Dmitrii Ivanovich Mendeleev. *Dmitry Ivanovich Mendeleev, circa 1894.* HULTON ARCHIVE/GETTY IMAGES.

provided alternate views of Mendeleev's discovery. Kedrov provided an extremely detailed, almost hour-by-hour recreation of the so-called day of one great discovery. However, the evidentiary basis of this reconstruction is shaky, because the few archival documents Kedrov used cannot definitively be dated to that one day and may not even refer to the incidents claimed by Kedrov. In addition, Kedrov tended to overlook the evidence provided in Mendeleev's textbook as a guide to his thoughts during the months surrounding 17 February. Kedrov's belief that the key step in the discovery involved the alkali metals and what elements to discuss after this group is implausible, because no hesitation can be noted in Mendeleev's prior plans for his textbook and the chemical properties of the alkali earths make them the natural successors, despite some other elements having a few similar properties. Also, Kedrov's emphasis on Mendeleev's comparison of various natural families of elements by the atomic weights of their members is likewise implausible because many of these groups did not have clearly established weights and other properties in 1869.

In contrast to Kedrov's view of the discovery taking place on one day, a credible case can be made for a longer process of discovery that lasted well over a year. When Mendeleev first began writing his textbook from 1867–1869, he formulated a framework for thinking about the elements, which included, among other ideas, an abstract conception of a chemical element using its atomic weight as the fundamental feature that determined its chemical energy and consequently also its chemical properties. By early 1869 Mendeleev had arrived at the concept that trends in properties of elements corresponded to increases in their atomic weights. However, a system based only on this criterion did not satisfy him, because the different periods exhibited varying characters, such as the number of elements in them and the rate of change of some of the elements' properties. In constructing this early fragmentary table, he employed analogies between atoms and organic compounds, including the idea that elements could be viewed as similar to isomers in organic chemistry. Using this idea from organic chemistry, he identified two classes of elements, where some chemical elements with similar atomic weights have different chemical properties, whereas other elements with similar atomic weights have similar chemical properties. He continued to struggle with his desire for a unified table that would have a symmetrical structure.

The version of the table he completed on 17 February 1869 was a compromise between Mendeleev's two main taxonomical criteria: physico-chemical relationships and chemical relationships. This table clearly showed the physico-chemical criteria of the periodic change in the properties of the elements based on their atomic weights (his first taxonomic requirement), but much less well the chemical relationships between the different elements in one column (group; his second desideratum). This compromise table was similar to those of some of his predecessors, but it did not satisfy Mendeleev's thirst for what he termed a natural system of elements. To construct this type of a system, he needed to find chemical criteria that could unite elements of the different classes. By the end of 1869 or early in 1870, Mendeleev had settled on the use of the highest forms of oxygen compounds (higher salt-forming oxides and their corresponding hydrates and salts) as the essential chemical criterion. Using this idea, Mendeleev recognized that the characteristic properties of the elements determine the highest oxidation state of these elements and the properties of these compounds: "[T]he natural arrangement of elements in groups according to the size of the atomic weight corresponds to the amount of oxygen that these elements can hold in the highest salt-forming oxides" (1958, p. 57). He used this principle to solve his main classificatory problem of uniting elements of different classes and by November 1870 was able to create a natural system of elements. Although this did not resolve all of his problems, such as placement of the rare earths, it did allow him to formulate the

— 70 —

но въ ней, мнѣ кажется, уже ясно выражается примѣнимость выставляемаго мною начала ко всей совокупности элементовъ, пай которыхъ извѣстенъ съ достовѣрностію. На этотъ разъ я и желалъ преимущественно найдти общую систему элементовъ. Вотъ этотъ опытъ:

			Ti=50	Zr=90	?=180.
			V=51	Nb=94	Ta=182.
			Cr=52	Mo=96	W=186.
			Mn=55	Rh=104,4	Pt=197,4
			Fe=56	Ru=104,4	Ir=198.
			Ni=Co=59	Pl=106,6,	Os=199.
H=1			Cu=63,4	Ag=108	Hg=200.
	Be=9,4	Mg=24	Zn=65,2	Cd=112	
	B=11	Al=27,4	?=68	Ur=116	Au=197?
	C=12	Si=28	?=70	Sn=118	
	N=14	P=31	As=75	Sb=122	Bi=210
	O=16	S=32	Se=79,4	Te=128?	
	F=19	Cl=35,5	Br=80	I=127	
Li=7	Na=23	K=39	Rb=85,4	Cs=133	Tl=204
		Ca=40	Sr=87,6	Ba=137	Pb=207.
		?=45	Ce=92		
		?Er=56	La=94		
		?Yt=60	Di=95		
		?In=75,6	Th=118?		

а потому приходится въ разныхъ рядахъ имѣть различное измѣненіе разностей, чего нѣтъ въ главныхъ числахъ предлагаемой таблицы. Или же придется предполагать при составленіи системы очень много недостающихъ членовъ. То и другое мало выгодно. Мнѣ кажется притомъ, наиболѣе естественнымъ составить кубическую систему (предлагаемая есть плоскостная), но и попытки для ея образованія не повели къ надлежащимъ результатамъ. Слѣдующія двѣ попытки могутъ показать то разнообразіе сопоставленій, какое возможно при допущеніи основнаго начала, высказаннаго въ этой статьѣ.

Li	Na	K	Cu	Rb	Ag	Cs	—	Tl
7	23	39	63,4	85,4	108	133		204
Be	Mg	Ca	Zn	Sr	Cd	Ba	—	Pb
B	Al	—	—	—	Ur	—	—	Bi?
C	Si	Ti	—	Zr	Sn	—	—	—
N	P	V	As	Nb	Sb	—	Ta	—
O	S	—	Se	—	Te	—	W	—
F	Cl	—	Br	—	J	—	—	—
19	35,5	58	80	190	127	160	190	220.

Periodic Table. *Mendeleev's first periodic table, 1869.* THE LIBRARY OF CONGRESS.

periodic law in its entirety: "the essence, the nature of elements, is expressed in their weight, i.e., in the mass of the substance entering into the reaction… The physical and chemical properties of elements, appearing in the properties of the simple and complex bodies they form, stand in a periodic dependence…on their atomic weight" (1949, p. 907). He summarized his findings in a long paper published in 1871 in Justus Liebig's *Annalen der Chemie*, later calling it "the best summary of my views and ideas on the periodicity of the elements." Although he did some further work on developing the periodic law after this time, his main attention shifted to other interests.

It took many years for Mendeleev's periodic law to become accepted by a majority of scientists. Kedrov, in his *DSB* article, claims that the discovery of gallium, scandium, and germanium—earlier predicted by Mendeleev—was "of decisive importance in the acceptance of the law." However, Mendeleev made many other predictions that turned out to be incorrect. This has led to a debate among scholars over whether prediction or

Mendeleev

accommodation (the ability of the theory to incorporate known facts) was the primary factor in the acceptance of Mendeleev's periodic law. For example, Brush has shown that scientific journals and textbooks began to discuss the periodic law only after the confirmation of Mendeleev's predictions. He suggests that chemists gave more weight to these novel predictions, which then can help explain why Mendeleev's work is remembered whereas the others who claimed to discover the periodic law have been forgotten. Alternatively, Scerri believes that the successful predictions served mainly to draw attention to Mendeleev's periodic law itself and that once scientists became aware of it, they valued the way it successfully incorporated known facts. In addition, other aspects of the periodic law—such as its ability to correctly place beryllium and other difficult elements in the table—helped it gain gradual acceptance from scientists by about 1890.

Long before the discovery of isotopes, chemists realized there was something deeply puzzling about Mendeleev's Periodic Law. It was not based on atomic weights per se, but on periodicities in the order of atomic weights. In the first edition of his textbook, Mendeleev speculated that "internal differences of the matter that comprises the atoms of similar elements" could be the reasons for their differences in properties (1949, p. 191). In the fifth edition (1889), Mendeleev singled out mass as the key determinant of periodicity. He later (sixth edition, 1895) used an analogy with Newton's law of gravitation to argue that mass is the source of periodicity. Even though we do not have an explanation for this relationship of periodicity on mass, he asserted, it can be accepted, just as we accept the law of gravitation—also without explanation—because it works.

Mendeleev's Work in Other Fields. Russian scholars have long examined the totality of Mendeleev's varied activities both inside and outside of science, although they have devoted most of their attention to examining the periodic law and its consequences. In his *DSB* entry, Kedrov provided a brief summary of many of these activities. Scholars outside of Russia, however, have not paid much attention to Mendeleev's activities other than the periodic law until relatively recently (Gordin, 1998, 2001, 2003, 2004; Rice, 1998; Brooks, 1998, 2003; Almgren, 1968, 1998; Stackenwalt, 1976, 1998). This recent work has opened important new perspectives on Mendeleev.

It is difficult to make sense of Mendeleev's intentions in pursuing many of his varied activities—such as his sudden abandonment of work on the periodic law in 1871 in order to take up research on gas laws funded by the Imperial Russian Technical Society, his widely scattered activities as an economic consultant, his writings on theoretical economics, his research on smokeless gunpowder, among others—but some possible clues are emerging. Gordin has viewed Mendeleev as a conservative reformer who wished to bring order to the world around him—both the scientific as well as political worlds. At first Mendeleev hoped to use scientific societies and expert opinions as a way to organize the necessary development of the Russian Empire after the changes wrought by the Great Reforms Era. For example, Mendeleev used the Russian Physical Society as the organizer of a commission to investigate spiritualist claims during the 1870s. What mainly concerned Mendeleev, it seems, was the spiritualists' desire to encroach upon what Mendeleev saw as scientific territory by interpreting natural phenomena. Although Mendeleev gained some measure of renown for his participation in this commission and his activities against spiritualism, he did not succeed in vanquishing spiritualist beliefs from Russian society. Kedrov quotes Mendeleev's statement that "spiritism was rejected," but this was not the case; Russian spiritualism continued to flourish long after this time.

Gordin has argued that Mendeleev's rejection for full membership by the St. Petersburg Academy of Sciences in 1880 initiated an imperial turn in Mendeleev's thinking. From that time on, Mendeleev devoted more of his attention to concerns that would require empire-wide organization and changes. Thus, he began to become involved with the economic development of Russia, as in his efforts to reform the tariff and in his actions as director of the Chief Bureau of Weights and Measures. In these activities Mendeleev at first functioned closely with high-ranking government bureaucrats and then he became one himself. Soviet historians of science often implied that Mendeleev held anti-tsarist views, but in fact he firmly supported the government, although he had disputes with some officials while working well with others.

Mendeleev had a long interest in issues dealing with metrology when he was appointed the scientific curator of the Depot of Weights and Measures in 1892. Especially in the decade prior to this appointment, he had become deeply involved in various economic matters, including his leading work on the revision of the tariff structure from 1889 to 1892 under the auspices of the Ministry of Finance. Mendeleev drew up an expansive plan for his new institution, which was soon transformed into the Central Bureau of Weights and Measures in 1893 with himself as director. He envisioned an institution that would carry out both practical activities and purely scientific research, and he greatly enlarged both its staff and purview. The main goals of the new institution were to unify the many different weights and measures used in the diverse Russian Empire, achieve their regulation in trade and industry, and orchestrate the eventual conversion to the metric system. The first task tackled by the bureau was the renovation of the prototypes of the official standards of weights and measures employed in Russia. At the same

Mendeleev

time, Mendeleev and his colleagues conducted research on various metrological questions, most of them related in some way to the renewal of the prototypes. For example, the researchers made extremely precise determinations of the weight of one liter of air and one liter of water, and conducted studies on how to increase the precision of balances as well as on techniques of weighing, among others. Also, Mendeleev founded a new scientific journal in which the results of this research could be published and made available to scholars both in Russia and abroad. When the prototypes had been prepared and tested, Mendeleev drafted a new law (enacted in 1899) on standardization that codified the prototypes and created the framework for their use in the unification of standards throughout Russia. One of the major provisions of the law was for the gradual adoption of the metric system in Russia. This law also gave the bureau responsibility for a network of local stations and inspectors to verify the accuracy of weights and measures used in trade and commerce throughout the empire. Meanwhile, Mendeleev began to develop plans for establishing standards of measurement for liquids, gas and water flows, electricity, light, and others. Mendeleev and the bureau received strong support for all of these (sometimes very costly) activities from the minister of finance, especially under Count Sergei Iu. Witte (1892-1903). However, Mendeleev had to temper his plans for expansion in the years before his death, likely due to Witte's resignation as well as to the financial pressures related to the Russo-Japanese War (1904-05) and the military buildup after the war.

SUPPLEMENTARY BIBLIOGRAPHY

WORKS BY MENDELEEV

Sochineniia. 14. Moscow-Leningrad: Izdatel'stvo Akademiia Nauk SSSR, 1949.

Periodicheskii zakon. Osnovnye stat'i. Moscow: Izdatel'stvo Akademii Nauk SSSR, 1958.

Zavetnye myski. Polnoe izdanie [Cherished thoughts]. Moscow: Mysl', 1995. The version of this work in the Soviet-era Collected Works contains many deletions. This version is the same as the original 1905 edition.

S dumooiu o blage rossiiskom: Izbrannye ekonomicheskie proizvedeniia. Novosibirsk, Russia: Nauka, 1991.

Mendeleev on the Periodic Law. Selected Writings, 1869–1905. Edited by William B. Jensen. Mineola, NY: Dover, 2002.

OTHER SOURCES

Almgren, Beverly. "Mendeleev: The Third Service, 1834–1882." PhD diss., Brown University, 1968.

———. "D. I. Mendeleev and Siberia." *Ambix* 45 (1998): 50–66.

Bensaude-Vincent, Bernadette. "L'éther, élément chimique: un essai malheureux de Mendéléev (1902)?" *British Journal for the History of Science* 15 (1982): 183–188.

———. "La genése du tableau de Mendeleev." *La recherche* 15, no. 159 (1984): 1207–1215.

———. "Mendeleev's Periodic System of Chemical Elements." *British Journal for the History of Science* 19 (1986): 3–17.

Brooks, Nathan M. "Mendeleev and Metrology." *Ambix* 45 (1998): 116–128.

———. "Dmitrii Mendeleev's *Principles of Chemistry* and the Periodic Law of the Elements." In *Communicating Chemistry: Textbooks and Their Audiences*, edited by A. Lundgren and B. Bensaude-Vincent. Canton, Massachusetts: Science History Publications, 2000.

———. "Developing the Periodic Law: Mendeleev's Work during 1869–1871." *Foundations of Chemistry* 4 (2002): 127–147.

———. "D. I. Mendeleev kak ekonomicheskii sovetnik Rossiiskogo pravitel'stva." In *Vlast' i nauka, uchenye i vlast': 1880-e—nachalo 1920-kh godov*, edited by N. N. Smirnov. St. Petersburg: Dmitrii Bulanin, 2003.

Brush, Stephen G. "Prediction and Theory Evaluation in Physics and Astronomy." In *No Truth Except in the Details: Essays in Honor of Martin J. Klein*, edited by A. J. Kox and Daniel M. Siegel. Dordrecht, Netherlands: Kluwer Academic, 1995.

———. "The Reception of Mendeleev's Periodic Law in America and Britain." *Isis* 87 (1996): 595–628.

Dmitriev, Igor S., ed. *Mendeleevskii sbornik.* St. Petersburg: St. Petersburg University Press, 1999.

———. "Nauchnoe otkrytie *in statu nascendi:* periodicheskii zakon D. I. Mendeleeva." *Voprosy istorii estestvoznaniia i tekhniki* 1 (2001): 31-82.

———. *Chelovek epokhi peremen. Ocherki o D. I. Mendeleeve i ego vremeni.* St. Petersburg: Khimizdat, 2004a. A collection of Dmitriev's important studies on Mendeleev.

———. "Scientific Discovery *in statu nascendi*: The Case of Dmitrii Mendeleev's Periodic Law." *Historical Studies in the Physical and Biological Sciences* 34 (2004b): 233–275. A summary of Dmitriev's important re-interpretation of the contexts of Mendeleev's discovery which includes a detailed critique of Kedrov's account of the discovery of the periodic law. For the more extensive Russian version of this article, see Dmitriev (2001).

Dobrotin, R. B., N. G. Karpilo, L. S. Kerova, and D. N. Trifonov. *Letopis' zhizni i deiatel'nosti D. I. Mendeleeva.* Leningrad: Nauka, 1984.

Gordin, Michael D. "Making Newtons: Mendeleev, Metrology, and the Chemical Ether." *Ambix* 45 (1998): 96–115.

———. "Loose and Baggy Spirits: Reading Dostoevskii and Mendeleev." *Slavic Review* 60 (2001): 756–780.

———. "The Organic Roots of Mendeleev's Periodic Law." *Historical Studies in the Physical and Biological Sciences* 32 (2002): 263–290.

———. "Measure of All the Russias: Metrology and Governance in the Russian Empire." *Kritika* 4 (2003a): 783–815.

———. "A Modernization of 'Peerless Homogeneity': The Creation of Russian Smokeless Gunpowder." *Technology and Culture* 44 (2003b): 677–702.

———. *A Well-Ordered Thing. Dmitrii Mendeleev and the Shadow of the Periodic Table.* New York: Basic Books, 2004.

An important study that focuses on Mendeleev's work other than the periodic system.

Kaji, Masanori. "On Mendeleev's Path to the Discovery of the Periodic Law: Analysis of His Work of 1854–1869." In Japanese. *Kagakusi Kenkyu: Journal of the History of Science (Japan)* 26 (1987): 129–139.

———. *Mendeleev's Discovery of the Periodic Law of the Chemical Elements. The Scientific and Social Context of His Discovery.* In Japanese. Sapporo, Japan: Hokkaido University Press, 1997.

———. "D. I. Mendeleev's Concept of Chemical Elements and *The Principles of Chemistry*" *Bulletin of the History of Chemistry* 27 (2002): 4–16.

Makarenia, A. A. *D. I. Mendeleev i fiziko-khimicheskie nauki: Opyt nauchnoi biografii D. I. Mendeleeva*, 2nd ed. Moscow: Energoizdat, 1982.

———, and A. I. Nutrikhin. *Mendeleev v Peterburge.* Leningrad, Russia: Lenizdat, 1982.

Nekoval-Chikhaoui, Ludmilla. "Diffusion de la classification périodique de Mendeleev en France entre 1869 et 1934." Ph.D. diss., Univ. Paris-Sud U.F. R. Scientifique d'Orsay, 1994.

Rawson, Don C. "The Process of Discovery: Mendeleev and the Periodic Law." *Annals of Science* 31 (1974): 181–204.

———. "Mendeleev and the Scientific Claims of Spiritualism." *Proceedings of the American Philosophical Society* 122 (1978): 1–8.

Rice, Richard E. "Mendeleev's Public Opposition to Spiritualism." *Ambix* 45 (1998): 85–95.

Scerri, Eric R. *The Periodic Table. Its Story and Its Significance.* Oxford: Oxford University Press, 2007.

Smith, J. R. "Persistence and Periodicity: A Study of Mendeleev's Contribution to the Foundation of Chemistry." Ph.D. diss., University of London, 1976.

Stackenwalt, Francis Michael. "The Economic Thought and Work of Dmitrii Ivanovich Mendeleev." Ph.D. diss., University of Illinois at Urbana-Champaign, 1976.

———. "Dmitrii Ivanovich Mendeleev and the Emergence of the Modern Russian Petroleum Industry, 1863–1877." *Ambix* (1998): 67–84.

Tishchenko, V. E., and M. N. Mladentsev. *Dmitrii Ivanovich Mendeleev, ego zhizn' I deiatel'nost: Universitetskii period, 1861–1890 gg.* Moscow: Nauka, 1993. Published as *Nauchnoe Nasledstvo*, vol. 21.

Trifonov, D. N. "Versiia-2. (K istorii otkrytiia periodicheskogo zakona D. I. Mendeleevym)." *Voprosy istorii estestvoznaniia i tekhniki* no. 2 (1990): 24–36; no. 3 (1990): 20–32. A critique of Kedrov's version of the discovery of the periodic law.

Zamecki, Stefan. "Mendeleev's First Periodic Table in Its Methodological Aspect." *Organon* 25 (1995): 107–126.

Nathan M. Brooks

MENZEL, DONALD HOWARD (*b.* Florence, Colorado, 11 April 1901; *d.* Cambridge, Massachusetts, 14 December 1976), *astronomy, theoretical astrophysics, solar physics, gaseous nebulae.*

Menzel was one of the first American astronomers to place modern physics at the core of astrophysical practice. He used quantum physics to study the nature of gaseous nebulae; the solar atmosphere, chromosphere, and corona; and also to explore the structure of the atom itself. He founded two solar observatories and was a major broker in international astronomy at midcentury. He achieved popular notice as an author of astronomical themes, nature studies, and science fiction, but most widely as a critic and skeptic of efforts directed to the study of unidentified flying objects and the nature of their occupants.

Early Life and Training. Menzel was a grandson of a Civil War veteran who settled in Denver, Colorado. Menzel's father, Charles Theodor Menzel Jr., worked as a railroad clerk and ticket agent in Florence, Colorado, where Menzel was born, and then moved his family to the remote town of Leadville, where he became a station manager. Menzel spent his early childhood under rather difficult conditions. By 1910, however, his father had saved enough money to purchase a mercantile company and store in Leadville and the family prospered.

His mother, Ina Grace Zint, managed the growing family, and maternal grandmother, Hattie Prince Zint, looked after the children's training, encouraging in particular the water coloring and woodburning arts. They were a serious Lutheran family, devoted to learning. His parents tried unsuccessfully to enter Menzel in public school before he was old enough, and when their application was rejected, his father got him a library card and encouraged reading. Menzel relished the science fiction of the day, including in particular Jonathan Swift's *Gulliver's Travels*, Jules Verne's books, and Johann David Wyss's *Swiss Family Robinson.* He was fascinated by the scientific questions raised in this literature.

Menzel identified with a small group of boys who engaged in general roughhousing, which prompted his father to teach him how to box, and Menzel was eventually accepted as a boy who could defend himself. He continued to pursue reading, and even wrote a prize-winning poem, "The Little Stars," which convinced him he had a future as a writer. He played chess, learned Morse code, and built radios, and was an avid rock and mineral collector, eventually using his accumulated treasures as a means of income through selling iron pyrite, galena, and blue-lead sulfide to tourists. Drawn by his father to the railroad, Menzel was able to ride local trains of various sorts; he remembered in particular his rides through Fremont

Menzel

Pass, where his first large solar observatory was built many years later.

Menzel was a fast learner and precocious student. He graduated high school at age sixteen after the family had moved to Denver in 1915 and entered Denver University in 1917, graduating from there in only three years. He majored in chemistry but also pursued astronomy, especially after viewing a solar eclipse in 1918, and then a bright nova outburst. Herbert Howe, professor of mathematics and astronomy and also dean of the College of Liberal Arts, befriended Menzel, eventually granting him access to the 20-inch (59-centimeter) refractor at Chamberlain Observatory. Although he declared for chemistry, Menzel loved astronomy and observing variable stars. Through another member of the Denver faculty, Menzel came into contact with Raymond Smith Dugan of Princeton University, a leading variable star observer, and Dugan helped him join the American Association of Variable Star Observers.

Upon graduation Menzel stayed local, entering the graduate school and obtaining a master's degree in one year in mathematics and astronomy, in the spring of 1921 at the age of twenty. By then he and Dugan had corresponded to the point where Menzel was offered a studentship at Princeton, working for Dugan and required to observe and analyze eclipsing binary star systems. Menzel would be a special student at first, because the director of the Princeton University Observatory, Henry Norris Russell, was concerned that his training thus far had been very narrowly constrained; in spite of his contact with Howe, he was largely self-educated in astronomy.

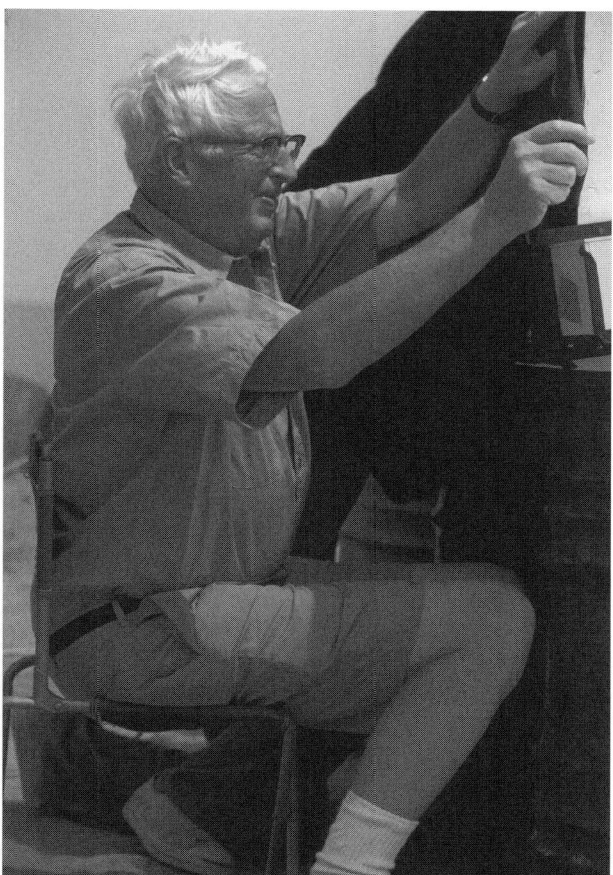

Donald Howard Menzel. *Menzel waiting to view a solar eclipse.* © JONATHAN BLAIR/CORBIS.

Graduate Years at Princeton and Harvard. Entering Princeton in the fall of 1921, Menzel quickly mastered Dugan's visual photometer on the Halsted Observatory's 23-inch (58-centimeter) refractor, and distinguished himself in his studies. He roomed with the only other astronomy graduate student, Bancroft W. Sitterly, but came into contact with highly competitive students in mathematics and physics.

Coursework under Russell exposed Menzel to the forefront of astrophysics, namely the application of the principles and practices of the modern physicist to the study of astronomy. Russell concentrated on the analysis of physical processes and mathematical shortcuts to their elucidation, which fascinated Menzel. He started studying related fields in physics and mathematics, taking courses and attending lectures by Oswald Veblen, Luther Eisenhart, and Henry Fine. Encouraged by John Q. Stewart, the third member of the Princeton astronomy faculty who held a dual appointment in physics, Menzel studied physical optics and the quantum theory of radiation under Augustus Trowbridge, and eventually Stewart directed him to explore laboratory experiments on the absorptive properties of sodium as one means of gaining insight that would be useful for studying the chemical compositions of the atmospheres of the Sun and stars.

Through his variable star work and through Russell, Menzel spent a summer at the Harvard College Observatory, working for Harlow Shapley on his surveys of the distribution of nebulae and the distances to the Magellanic Clouds. But his continued exposure to physics, taking courses from Karl Taylor Compton in atomic theory in particular, again directed by Stewart, wedded him to astrophysics. He was therefore poised to take advantage of an extraordinary set of circumstances: the emergence of Meghnad Saha's ionization equilibrium theory and its mathematical elucidation by Ralph Howard Fowler and Edward Arthur Milne, as well as by Russell and Stewart, and the presence of an enormous cache of spectroscopic data at Harvard that was ripe for further analysis in light of this new theory. Russell accordingly sent Menzel to Harvard for his third graduate year 1923–1924, to exploit

Menzel

this material, specifically to measure line intensities to calibrate the Harvard classification sequence of stellar spectra to a physical temperature scale.

Menzel soon found that he was not alone in the Harvard plate stacks. The British scholar Cecilia Payne was ardently pursing the same questions. After a period of adjustment, they both exploited the collection effectively. Menzel wrote up his findings, analyzing arc line spectra for metals for which Russell had series relations.

During his graduate school years at Princeton, Menzel came into contact with Hugo Gernsback and eventually began writing popularly, his work appearing in Gernsback's pulp *Amazing Stories.* Menzel suspected, correctly, that such activities were frowned on. He managed to hide the extent of his writing by using pseudonyms. His writing for *Amazing Stories* apparently did not begin until he had his PhD and was bound for his first position.

Lick Observatory. It is not clear why Menzel took a teaching position at the University of Iowa; certainly this was not the sort of position Russell would have recommended if he had high hopes for his graduate student. Menzel recalled offers from Gernsback to become an associate editor of *Amazing Stories*, a standing offer from Denver and from various high schools, and said only that he chose Iowa because it offered a decent salary and the promise of time and opportunity for research. But after a year teaching at the university, and a short appointment at Ohio State University, he became dissatisfied and contacted Russell for advice. Now Russell acted promptly, supporting Menzel's candidacy for a junior position at the Lick Observatory, operated by the University of California, a position Menzel obtained without difficulty.

Russell was anxious to have his student at Lick so that he would have access to its marvelous observational resources, including photographic records from many solar eclipse expeditions such as flash spectra that held the key to the structure of the solar reversing layer, the region where its absorption spectrum originated. Menzel accordingly arrived at Lick, and Russell directed his attention to this cache of material. By 1930 Menzel had revolutionized knowledge of the solar atmosphere and its chromosphere.

Although Lick was a great mountain observatory, it was a classic astronomical institution, where careers were narrowly defined by instrumentation and the will of the director. Menzel, trained under Russell, believed in broader professional vistas and chafed at the many chores he was expected to handle. He even felt his monumental work on the solar atmosphere was poorly received by Lick astronomers, especially when they advised him not to publish the theory portion in his observatory monograph, an extensive discourse on his application of wave mechanics, but to reserve it for some appropriate journal that entertained such fuzzy stuff. As Robert Grant Aitken wryly advised him, Lick was an "Observatory!" where data were collected and recorded. "Leave the theory to the poor, underprivileged British astronomers," Aitken quipped, "such as Milne and Eddington, who don't have an observatory" (Menzel unpublished autobiography, pp. 210, 222–223). Menzel often recalled this quip many years later, but at the time, it was demoralizing. Menzel found the faculty on the Berkeley campus far more collegial, and spent as much time there as he could, teaching fine students, and attracting some of them, including Fred Whipple, to do their thesis work at Lick. He also sought escape in his continued clandestine writing for Gernsback.

Move to Harvard. Menzel had managed to secure a junior position for Whipple at Harvard in 1931, and remained in contact with Shapley. When Harry Plaskett left Harvard for Oxford in 1932, Russell, knowing of Menzel's unhappiness at Lick, suggested Menzel as Plaskett's replacement. Arriving at Harvard on 1 September 1932, one day after he had helped observe a solar eclipse from Fryeburg, Maine, as his last duty for Lick, Menzel brought to Harvard a considerable cache of data on planetary nebulae spectra that he now hoped to exploit. He had already written on physical processes in gaseous nebulae in his last months at Lick Observatory, but it needed further physical analysis and discussion. He collaborated with Joseph Boyce, whom he had come to know at Berkeley but who was now at the Massachusetts Institute of Technology (MIT), as well as with Payne, and through the 1930s continued research along two related lines: gaseous nebulae and the outer regions of the solar atmosphere.

Menzel had been fascinated by the source of the illumination in nebulae since 1926 when he suggested, but then rejected, the possibility that the emission lines of the hydrogen Balmer series seen in nebulae were the result of photoionization and recombination caused by ultraviolet radiation from the central stars. Nevertheless, Menzel continued his interest in the causes of nebular illumination and formed a series of collaborations and group studies at Harvard on physical processes in gaseous nebulae, engaging bright students such as Lawrence Aller, James Baker, Leo Goldberg, and others. Starting in 1937 and lasting through 1945, he led studies that were the first to systematically blend observational data and wave theory to calculate temperatures, electron densities, and compositions in planetary nebulae, in terms of derived temperatures of the stars responsible for illuminating the gas. This work, expressed in a series of eighteen papers, helped to establish the careers of his finest students.

Throughout the decade, Menzel became a member of Shapley's senior staff, along with Bart Bok, Payne, and Whipple. In the mid-1930s Shapley promoted Menzel to

Menzel

associate professor and tenure. Menzel also engaged in high-profile eclipse expeditions. Most significant was an international effort to observe the Siberian eclipse of 1936, for which he developed, in conjunction with MIT physicists, a set of large high-dispersion spectrographic devices made of a lightweight magnesium alloy. He also secured technical assistance and support from the Dow Chemical Corporation, the Folmer-Graflex Company, and Bausch & Lomb, and invited a team of radio physicists from the Cruft Physics Laboratory to examine the effect of the eclipse on the Heaviside layer, using radio transmitters and receivers placed in proximity to the station within the path of totality. Menzel was thus the first astrophysicist to collect optical and radio phenomena to explore how solar activity controlled the Earth's ionosphere. This goal led to his western expeditions and the establishment of two major solar observatories.

Menzel shared the astronomers' dream of observing the solar corona at will, not having to wait for the occasional solar eclipse. The need to record continuous variations in solar activity and to correlate these to earthy atmospheric phenomena was becoming the most obvious practical application of astronomy since the rise of celestial navigation. In 1935 he approached the U.S. Department of Agriculture with a proposal to apply coronal studies to search for links between solar activity and weather, beyond what he thought mere sunspot numbers or even the controversial solar constant correlations produced at the Smithsonian Astrophysical Observatory (SAO) could show.

In 1930 Bernard Lyot's new invention, a coronagraph, showed that one could photograph the solar corona outside an eclipse, under the pristine conditions of the Pic Du Midi Observatory in the Pyrenees. Menzel's proposal, however, was to create an electronic version he called a Coronavisor that would subtract skylight and photospheric glare electronically. Following the ideas of A. Melvin Skellett of the Bell Telephone Laboratories, and not in any way reminiscent of Lyot's simple photo-optical design, Menzel did not think it was necessary to observe from a high, dry altitude where scattered light would be minimized. His proposal was funded, but progress was slower than hoped, and though he was clear in his intentions, to build a physical laboratory at Harvard's Oak Ridge observing station some 30 miles (48 kilometers) west of campus specifically for the study of solar terrestrial relations, by late 1937 the grant had been expended and there was nothing tangible to show for the effort. Only then did he apply Lyot's designs, and begin thinking of a western observatory.

Menzel asked his student Baker to design and build the lenses, and engaged the talents of Brian O'Brien's staff at the University of Rochester Institute of Optics as well as the expertise of the PerkinElmer Corporation and the collegiality of Lyot. He planned to take his instrument to Lick Observatory, but delays and his search for sites that at least matched Lyot's drew him eventually back to his mountain home and a site near Leadville, which he found in 1939 on hikes with his father.

When government support ceased in 1939, Menzel had to let his staff go, and turned to a young graduate student, Walter Orr Roberts, to continue the work. Roberts had worked at Kodak for C. E. Kenneth Mees and had interests that closely meshed with Menzel's. By the spring of 1940, a 4-inch (10-centimeter) instrument was being tested at Oak Ridge and was bound for installation at Climax, Colorado, at some 11,500 feet (3,505 meters) elevation, with much of the construction support provided by the Climax Molybdenum Company, after Menzel appealed to them for help. Over the summer, the station was built, and by the end of the summer, the first photographs of prominences by Roberts gave great hope that success was near. It would take another year, to October 1941, before the corona was captured. Roberts was the one who did it, while Menzel remained the enabler, faced with constant funding problems. But soon, Menzel went to war, and found an eager new funder.

War Work. In its first half-year of operation, the Climax station had secured evidence linking coronal activity to subsequent ionospheric storm activity on Earth. This and intelligence reports hinting that the Germans were building an ionospheric monitoring network using coronagraphs soon led the National Defense Research Committee to fund Climax. Throughout the war, Climax data were sent directly to the National Bureau of Standards for analysis. Menzel, at the center of making all this happen, remained at Harvard as he entered war work late in the year.

Menzel's first project, an Office of Scientific Research and Development (OSRD) contract, was to design and build optical gun sights devices for tracking aircraft that were using the Sun for cover, exploiting his experience with coronagraphs. But he also enrolled in a navy correspondence course in cryptanalysis, the result of a lingering childhood fascination with ciphers and codes and the knowledge that such skills were needed. Menzel had already studied cryptology when he was at Berkeley, fascinated through chance contacts with others taking these courses, and later came to know Howard Engstrom, who would join the Washington office of the Chief of Naval Communications. In 1941, Menzel's ability to rapidly and creatively complete coding assignments impressed the navy, which by September asked him to take part in training women at Radcliffe College and other seven-sister colleges. This program soon extended to Harvard graduating seniors and in all several hundred students received training and eventual commissions in the navy. He was in the midst of this activity when, in the fall of 1942, he was commissioned a lieutenant commander and assigned to the Office of the Chief of Naval Communications, after one month of intensive training and indoctrination in a secret program on the Harvard campus. In Washington, however, his responsibilities extended to the theory of radio wave propagation and exploited his knowledge of solar physics, cryptanalysis, and his experience and fascination for shortwave ham radio. He soon met the navy's expectations by finding ways to match radio frequencies to ionospheric conditions, primarily to facilitate the detection of enemy submarines.

Serendipitously aligned with the program he set in place at Climax and the National Bureau of Standards, Menzel was now on active duty using the solar observations to predict changes in radio communication conditions and thereby to create a system of managing operational radio frequencies. Eventually he commanded a section that kept records of all naval radio messages, both friendly and intercepted, and collaborated with the National Bureau of Standards and the Department of Terrestrial Magnetism of the Carnegie Institution of Washington to produce comprehensive data sets for the transmission characteristics of the atmosphere as a function of time. Menzel was also directed to join various Wave Propagation committees of the Joint and Combined Chiefs of Staff, and he ultimately chaired these national and allied efforts to maintain coordinated research in the subject and promote the systematization of radio fade-out predictions.

Menzel also contributed to extending the effectiveness of radar countermeasures, mainly to obtain a better understanding of anomalous propagation phenomena that could confuse radar intelligence and techniques for submarine direction finding and communications. After developing the theory and practical methods of identification, he tested them under operational conditions in Panama. Menzel later recalled that it was experience gained in these circumstances that led him to become one of the most vocal and visible debunkers of reported UFO phenomena, a duty he relished. At the end of the war Menzel prepared an "Elementary Manual of Radio Propagation" that in 1948 was published commercially.

In the closing months of the war Menzel turned back to issues relating to ship communications and code breaking, but he and others also began to sense that a shakedown was likely to come among the various services in the postwar world for control of wave propagation responsibilities. In concert with Edward Uhler Condon, then the director of the Bureau of Standards, as well as J. Howard Dellinger, director of the Interservice Radio Propagation Laboratory within the bureau, Menzel outlined the need for an agency that could provide systematic services after the war. His outline included a worldwide network for ionospheric and weather data gathering and a centralized facility for processing the information. The proposal—and a multimillion dollar annual budget—were approved up the line, and resulted in the establishment of the civilian Central Radio Propagation Laboratory (CRPL) of the National Bureau of Standards, as of 2007 located in Boulder, Colorado.

Menzel recalls being asked by Condon at war's end to take over the direction of the CRPL, as Dellinger was soon to retire. He was tempted, to be sure, but he was also aware of what his new expertise could mean to astronomy, especially radio astronomy. The fact that the Sun emitted a complex radio signature had been carefully guarded during the war, but the release of such information in peacetime would be explosive. Menzel was also keenly aware of the possibility of using shortwave radar to bounce signals off the Moon, and what this might mean not only for communications but for improving knowledge of the lunar orbit. Though he arranged for several conferences of navy astronomers and communications personnel, nothing came of these suggestions at the time. What was clear to Menzel, apparently, was that he might best exploit his newly found knowledge, expertise, and military and government contacts as a Harvard professor, and not an active duty officer. In any case, he returned to Harvard but remained a special consultant for the CRPL and remained active in both military and civilian Washington circles in other capacities for the rest of his career. In addition to the offer from Condon, Menzel had other offers from the Naval Electronics Laboratory and from associates planning to develop electronic computers. As a consultant, Menzel found his work on behalf of the CRPL especially engrossing, allowing him to suggest major changes, such as the removal of the CRPL from Washington in favor of Boulder, Colorado, near a university and in the comparative proximity of his High Altitude Observatory (HAO) at Climax. The University of Colorado was ready to provide assistance, facilities, and joint appointments to the CRPL, and also offered the advantage of graduate student manpower. Gaining the approval of locals as well as Washington, Menzel remained intimately involved in the design and construction of the CRPL over the years, becoming as well an honorary member of the Boulder Chamber of Commerce. He was also an active member of the National Bureau of Standards Visiting Committee.

Postwar Institution Building. Menzel and much of the Harvard College Observatory staff returned to their prewar positions under conditions that can only be described as highly polarized. Menzel and Whipple, especially, had experienced vastly wider horizons made possible through

The Moon. *Dr. Donald Howard Menzel indentifies features in Moon photo.* AP IMAGES.

the application of new technologies and government funding. Other members of the Harvard senior staff, mainly Shapley, Bok, and to some extent Payne (Payne-Gaposchkin after her 1934 marriage to the Harvard astronomer Sergei Gaposchkin), were wary of government intervention, and especially resisted military funding. But by the late 1940s, they all keenly knew that what they needed was a major infusion of new support, if only to maintain what they had built as a competitive facility for teaching and research.

There was also significant friction between Shapley and the Harvard administration, mainly with President James Bryant Conant. In an attempt to normalize the observatory and to reduce the director's autonomy, in 1945 Conant created the Harvard College Observatory Council (HCOC), consisting of senior staff and the director. Among the members of the HCOC, Menzel was much closer to the Harvard administration than Shapley, especially to Dean Paul Buck. He represented modern lines of activity and closer ties with campus departments than Shapley or the others. In a series of reorganizations in the late 1940s, prompted by the Harvard administration, Buck designated Menzel as chairman of the Department of Astronomy, responsible for coordinating the teaching load. Shapley countered by designating Bok as associate director and his implied successor, but soon Menzel was designated associate director for solar research. Menzel recalls that Shapley was infuriated by all this, but the actual series of events, and their intent, remained unclear. In any event, the HCOC approved this reorganization because it did distribute chores more equitably.

Immediately after the war, Shapley and the HCOC agreed that the observatory needed a major infusion of funds and planned a campaign. Conant, however, blocked Shapley's fundraising efforts in the mid-1940s, in preference for a combined Harvard campaign. These steps virtually ensured that the observatory would be in crisis at Shapley's retirement, which was due in September 1952, and was being enforced by Conant. Tensions rose again in 1950, when Conant and Buck asked the observatory to consider becoming a regular campus department, placing the directorship of the observatory and chairmanship of the department on a rotating cycle. Shapley and the HCOC firmly rejected this idea, but they all knew that deep changes were afoot.

In 1951 Shapley and the HCOC pleaded with the administration to choose a successor expeditiously. Instead, Conant asked J. Robert Oppenheimer, as a member of the Board of Overseers, to convene a blue-ribbon panel of physicists and astronomers to assess Harvard astronomy. With Shapley's retirement in September 1952, Buck asked Menzel to be acting director, prompting Bok to resign as associate director. The HCOC remained, but there was great tension throughout the observatory. While the committee deliberated, Shapley's people, including Bok and much of the junior staff, were clearly at odds with Menzel and Whipple, and it became Menzel's job not only to get the HCOC working again, but to satisfy the complaints of the committee.

Menzel immediately began a series of reforms in line with the desires of the Harvard administration, condemning buildings that had fallen into disrepair, giving notice to groups within Shapley's extended observatory family, such as the American Association of Variable Star Observers, that they had to move out of the observatory, culling and regularizing the observatory library book holdings, and, most sensitive of all, culling the famed Harvard photographic plate collection and divesting Harvard's interest in its southern station at Bloemfontein in South Africa. At the same time, less controversial to the rank and file, Menzel was also taking steps to divest Harvard of any financial responsibility for the HAO in Colorado, in favor of a new station at Sacramento Peak in New Mexico, in proximity to air force and army ordnance missile testing facilities near Alamogordo and White Sands, New Mexico.

Menzel's New Mexico project was originally an attempt to seek out a complementary observing site to HAO for fuller seasonal coverage. HAO had been officially incorporated in 1948 as an independent organization affiliated with Harvard and the University of

Colorado, managed by Menzel's former student Roberts. In the postwar world, with the relaxation of wartime pressures and reductions in wartime funding, and with Conant's restrictions on Harvard campaigns for financial support in favor of his central university effort, Menzel was frustrated, maintaining Climax with private donations. Thus in his retrenchment campaign, Menzel included Climax. Beyond funding problems, there had been another deeply fractious issue.

In the spring of 1950, responding to what later were revealed to be accusations by Colorado businessmen, two air force officers presented Menzel with charges of disloyalty that could result in the revoking of his security clearances, and all employment as consultant to the air force, which included Sacramento Peak. The air force was funding Sacramento Peak, facilitated by Menzel's close relationship with the air force Cambridge Research Laboratories, within the Air Materiel Command. This facility was just being built, with John W. Evans and Roberts tasked to provide scientific direction and improved instrumentation, when Menzel's loyalty hearings started in Boston. These hearings took place between late May and early June 1950, but deliberations dragged into 1951, when Menzel was finally exonerated after enlisting Harvard lawyers and an impressive list of staunch backers with Washington connections. But the whole affair tested Menzel's relations with Roberts and the Colorado businessmen. In fact, Roberts was also investigated for alleged subversive activities, mainly his public lectures and addresses.

By October 1952, freshly installed as acting director and faced with the challenge of bringing the observatory and its far-flung assets into line with Harvard policies, Menzel was writing critical letters to Roberts regarding his management of HAO. He accused Roberts of being more focused on production than good research and asserted there was a lack of good supervision overall. Evans was now at Sacramento Peak full time, and Roberts was encountering serious cost overruns building new instrumentation. In March 1953, Menzel alerted Buck to problems at Climax, and how these were drawing the critical attention of other solar astronomers such as Robert R. McMath and Leo Goldberg at Michigan. By October 1954, formal relations between the two observatories ceased, though Menzel expressed the hope that they would still be loosely linked through a wide consortium he called the Solar Associates.

Directorship of HCO. Even though Menzel was made acting director, he was not originally in line for the directorship. The Oppenheimer committee did not regard any of the remaining faculty to be capable of restoring Harvard astronomy to the front ranks, and even considered among other options closing all the observing stations and creating a wholly new department that would take the forefront in theoretical astrophysics. With the committee's initial report on the state of astronomy in hand by the end of 1952, Conant then asked Oppenheimer to search for a new director, and this took another full year, as he and Harvard administrators negotiated first with Bengt Strömgren, then with Jan Oort, and finally, equally unsuccessfully, with Otto Struve. During the year, Menzel's actions in revamping the observatory, making it more responsive to campus standards, improving the infrastructure through cutbacks and efficiencies, more than impressed the administration. In the spring Payne-Gaposchkin wholeheartedly supported Menzel, writing to Buck that under Menzel's leadership there was now more solidarity and cohesion than division, that Menzel was taking steps to broaden and strengthen astrophysics and, most importantly, that he was improving relations with Harvard campus departments such as physics and chemistry, and the applied sciences at MIT. Cross-field research was then an important buzzword for the Harvard administration, and Payne-Gaposchkin used it deftly in her promotion of Menzel. Endorsements such as these led to Menzel's appointment in January 1954, initially for a five-year period.

As director, Menzel set about consolidating relations with Sacramento Peak, improving the Oak Ridge Station, mainly through supporting Bok's development of a radio telescope there. Menzel also took the initiative to bring the Smithsonian Astrophysical Observatory (SAO) to Harvard in 1955. Menzel was among those the new Smithsonian Secretary Leonard Carmichael turned to for advice about the future of the SAO, which had been in Washington, DC, for more than a half-century but had fallen behind the front ranks in modern astrophysics, concentrating solely on monitoring the Sun's output of energy. After deliberating options, which included moving SAO to Colorado to be part of HAO, Carmichael decided that the best route to take would be to associate SAO with a major university, and Menzel stepped in to suggest Harvard, eventually with Whipple as the SAO director. At the time, the SAO had dwindled to an observatory virtually in name only. What both Menzel and Whipple realized was that by bringing the SAO association to Harvard, they were opening up a new route to government funding at a time when this type of support was rapidly increasing. The Smithsonian had considerable resources and also provided a mechanism to bring classified work to Harvard, or so thought McGeorge Bundy, who had replaced Buck as dean of the faculty when Conant departed and Nathan Pusey was installed as Harvard's new president. In the spring of 1955 SAO became part of the Harvard College Observatory, and Whipple built up a new staff with programs relating to upper atmosphere studies, meteoritics, and satellite tracking, preparing for the onset of the International Geophysical Year in 1957.

Menzel also enjoyed contact with Senator John F. Kennedy when Kennedy was asked, as a member of the Board of Overseers, to chair the HCO visiting committee in 1958. Through frequent meetings in both Cambridge and Washington over the next several years, Menzel secured Kennedy's endorsement for expanding HCO facilities, in concert with increased support from the Smithsonian, and also became an informal advisor on science policy.

Although the spectacular growth of the astronomical facilities overall during Menzel's tenure as director was mainly due to Whipple's efforts, Menzel managed to make significant improvements to staff and facilities as well, establishing a radio astronomy facility in Fort Davis, Texas, supporting radio studies with the spacecraft Mariner 2, strengthening both experimental and theoretical studies in spectroscopy and atomic physics, and greatly strengthening the teaching and PhD production of the department of astronomy. His most significant hire was to bring Goldberg back to Harvard in 1960 to take over and greatly expand solar physics, mainly through taking a strong role in the Orbiting Solar Observatory mission of the National Aeronautics and Space Administration's (NASA). Bringing Goldberg back to Harvard was a major accomplishment for Menzel. Goldberg was one of his most capable students and had worked closely with him in one of his most fruitful problem areas: the calculations of the intensities of absorption lines.

Goldberg also shared Menzel's goal of establishing a truly powerful astrophysical facility in the west, in Hawaii. This dream became one of Menzel's greatest preoccupations in the last years of his chairmanship. In the early 1960s, Menzel sought to establish a large observatory facility on 13,000-foot (3,962-meter) Mauna Kea. Although he garnered interest from NASA, Menzel was unable to secure the endorsement of the HCOC, which he later recalled as a serious upset at the time. His frustrations, he felt, led ultimately to a heart attack in 1965, at age sixty-four. Menzel endured open-heart surgery and many months of recuperation, and resigned his directorship in favor of Goldberg, who succeeded him in 1966. Menzel retired in 1970.

Menzel married Florence Kreager in 1926; they met during Menzel's brief tenure teaching at Ohio State, where she was a student. Florence proved to be an important asset at the Lick Observatory; her sociability and grace helped to make the serious Menzel more acceptable to the close-knit Lick staff and students alike. She continued to be even more open and accessible to students and junior faculty at Harvard and was remembered fondly by many of Menzel's associates. They had two daughters, Suzanne and Elizabeth.

Although his most cited works remain his contributions to physical processes in gaseous nebulae, and his devotion to both observational and theoretical astrophysics remain among his most lasting legacies, Menzel is most popularly remembered in the early twenty-first century as a tireless debunker of the UFO phenomenon, a subject he wrote on frequently and never ceased to disparage. He is also remembered by colleagues, students, and casual astronomy enthusiasts alike for his indefatigable efforts to observe solar eclipses worldwide and to enthuse about them and other sky-watching activities through his popular writing, which continued throughout his career. His interests always ranged far beyond the strict bounds of astronomy and included radio propagation, communications problems, radio electronics, and electronic intelligence, specifically navy efforts known collectively as electronic intelligence (ELINT). In retirement, he continued to offer his services to both the military and to industry interested in electronic communications systems and technologies. In 1973 he became scientific director of Electronic Space Systems Corporation (ESSCO), a defense electronics and communications company in Concord, Massachusetts, known for manufacturing radomes and radio telescopes.

BIBLIOGRAPHY

The bulk of Menzel's professional papers are contained in Donald Howard Menzel, 1931–1986 HUG 4567 at the Harvard University Archives, Pusey Library, Cambridge, Massachusetts. Also at Harvard are his records as HCO director, and related collections, including Records of the Harvard College Observatory (UAV 630.37.x), Records of the High Altitude Observatory (UAV 631.10.x), and Records of the Dept. of Astronomy (UAV 169.12.x). He deposited his records dealing with UFO phenomena at the American Philosophical Society, and his files covering his loyalty hearings and potential loss of security clearance are housed at the University of Denver.

WORKS BY MENZEL

With William W. Coblentz and Carl O. Lampland. "Planetary Temperatures Derived from Water-Cell Transmissions." *Astrophysical Journal* 63 (1926): 177–187.

"The Planetary Nebulae." *Publications of the Astronomical Society of the Pacific* 38, no. 225 (1926): 295–312.

"Pressures at the Base of the Chromosphere: A Critical Study of Milne's Theories." *Monthly Notices of the Royal Astronomical Society* 91 (1931): 628–652.

"Crocker Eclipse Expedition to Fryeburg, Maine: Report on the Jumping-Film Spectrographs." *Publications of the Astronomical Society of the Pacific* 44, no. 261 (1932): 356–358.

With Joseph C. Boyce and Cecilia H. Payne. "Forbidden Lines in Astrophysical Sources." *Proceedings of the National*

Academy of Sciences of the United States of America 19, no. 6 (1933): 581–591.

With Henry Norris Russell. "The Terrestrial Abundance of the Permanent Gases." *Proceedings of the National Academy of Sciences of the United States of America* 19, no. 12 (1933): 997–1001.

With Chaim L. Pekeris. "Absorption Coefficients and Hydrogen Line Intensities." *Monthly Notices of the Royal Astronomical Society* 96 (1935): 77–112.

With Henry Norris Russell and Cecilia H. Payne-Gaposchkin. "The Classification of Stellar Spectra." *Astrophysical Journal* 81 (1935): 107–118.

"The Theoretical Interpretation of Equivalent Breadths of Absorption Lines." *Astrophysical Journal* 84 (1936): 462–473.

With Leo Goldberg. "Multiplet Strengths for Transitions Involving Equivalent Electrons." *Astrophysical Journal* 84 (1936): 1–10.

"Physical Processes in Gaseous Nebulae. I." *Astrophysical Journal* 85 (1937): 330–339. With different coauthors, many of them his students, Menzel published eighteen papers in this series between 1937 and 1945.

With Leo Goldberg. "The Solar Corona and Ultraviolet Radiation." In *Centennial Symposia, December 1946: Contributions on Interstellar Matter, Electronic and Computational Devices, Eclipsing Binaries, [and] the Gaseous Envelope of the Earth*, 279. Harvard Observatory Monographs, no. 7. Cambridge, MA: Harvard Observatory, 1948.

With R. Grant Athay, Jean-Claude Pecker, and R. N. Thomas. "The Thermodynamic State of the Outer Solar Atmosphere V A Model of the Chromosphere from the Continuum Emission." *Astrophysical Journal Supplement* 1 (1955): 505.

With R. Grant Athay. "A Model of the Chromosphere from the Helium and Continuum Emissions." *Astrophysical Journal* 123 (1956): 285.

Our Sun. Rev. ed. The Harvard Books on Astronomy. Cambridge, MA: Harvard University Press, 1959.

Editor. *Fundamental Formulas of Physics*. 2 vols. New York: Dover, 1960.

Editor. *Selected Papers on Physical Processes in Ionized Plasmas*. New York: Dover, 1962.

With Bruce W. Shore. "Generalized Tables for the Calculation of Dipole Transition Probabilities." *Astrophysical Journal Supplement* 12 (1965): 187.

A Field Guide to the Stars and Planets, Including the Moon, Satellites, Comets, and Other Features of the Universe. London: Collins, 1964. Revised edition with Jay M. Pasachoff. Boston: Houghton Mifflin, 1983.

Editor. *Selected Papers on the Transfer of Radiation*. New York, Dover, 1966.

With Bruce W. Shore. *Principles of Atomic Spectra*. Wiley Series in Pure and Applied Spectroscopy. New York: Wiley, 1968.

"Oscillator Strengths, f, for High-Level Transitions in Hydrogen." *Astrophysical Journal Supplement* 18 (1969): 221.

With Fred L. Whipple and Gerard de Vaucouleurs. *Survey of the Universe*. Englewood Cliffs, NJ: Prentice-Hall, 1970.

OTHER SOURCES

Aller, Lawrence H. "Menzel's Physical Processes in Gaseous Nebulae." *Astrophysical Journal* 525 (1999): 265–266.

Bauer, Craig, and John Ulrich. "The Cryptologic Contributions of Dr. Donald Menzel." *Cryptologia* 30 (2006): 306–339.

Doel, Ronald E. *Solar System Astronomy in America: Communities, Patronage, and Interdisciplinary Science, 1920–1960*. Cambridge, U.K.: Cambridge University Press, 1996.

Goldberg, Leo, and Lawrence H. Aller. "Donald H. Menzel." *Biographical Memoirs of the National Academy of Sciences* 60 (1991): 149–167.

Hoskin, M. A., and Owen Gingerich, eds. "Donald H. Menzel Centenary Symposium." *Journal for the History of Astronomy* 33, part 2, no. 111 (2002). Includes essays by Bogdan, DeVorkin, Layzer, Osterbrock, Liebowitz, and Pasachoff.

David DeVorkin

MERIAN, MARIA SIBYLLA

(*b.* Frankfurt am Main, Germany, 4 April 1647; *d.* Amsterdam, Netherlands, 13 January 1717), *entomology, botany, natural history, ethnography.*

Merian, a leading naturalist, was bold to travel to Surinam, then a Dutch colony, in 1699 at the age of fifty-two in search of exotic plants and insects. Merian was one of the few—and perhaps the only European woman—who voyaged exclusively in pursuit of her science in the seventeenth or eighteenth centuries. Accompanied only by her twenty-one-year-old daughter Dorothea Maria, whom she trained from childhood as a painter and assistant, Merian collected, studied, and drew insects and plants of the region for two years. Returning to Amsterdam, Merian published her major work, *Metamorphosis insectorum Surinamensium,* which included sixty illustrations detailing the reproduction and development of various insects. In addition to broadening significantly the empirical base of European entomology, Merian's text and glorious illustrations also captured for Europeans "plants never before described or drawn" (commentary to plate 35). Her work was much celebrated in her time for its empirical accuracy and artistic brilliance.

The daughter of the well-known artist and engraver, Matthäus Merian the elder, Merian learned the techniques of illustrating—drawing, mixing paints, and etching copperplates—in her father's workshop. It was this training in art that gave Merian her entrée to science; the primary value of her studies of insects derived from her ability to capture in fine detail what she observed. In early modern science, women commonly served as observers and illustrators. The recognized need for exact observation

Maria Sibylla Merian. *Illustration of a pair of Common Morpho butterflies by Merian.*

in astronomy, botany, zoology, and anatomy in this period made that work particularly valuable.

Although Merian married Johann Graff, an apprentice to her stepfather Jacob Marrel, in 1665, she functioned throughout her life as an independent woman directing her own business interests, training young women in her trade, experimenting with technique, and following her own scientific interests. In Nürnberg, Frankfurt, and later Amsterdam she established thriving businesses—selling fine silks, satins, and linens painted with flowers of her own design. In Nürnberg, Merian also began her scientific career with the publication of her *Der Raupen wunderbare Verwandlung und sonderbare* (Wonderful transformation and special nourishment of caterpillars) in 1679. In fifty copperplates, she drew the life cycle of each caterpillar—from egg to caterpillar to cocoon to butterfly—attempting to capture each change of skin and hair and the whole of their life cycle. From a financial point of view, Merian undertook her study of caterpillars in an attempt to find other varieties that, like the silkworm, could be used to produce fine thread. Though she claimed to have found such a caterpillar in Surinam, she never brought it into production.

Merian's second book, *Neues Blümenbuch* (1680), featured flowers drawn from life designed to provide guild artists with designs for painting and embroidery. Merian was renowned for both the new techniques she developed to enhance the durability of her colors and her new printing techniques developed to capture the living beauty of flowers.

In the mid-1680s, Merian (or "Graffin," as she called herself) divorced her husband, reclaimed her father's famous name, and moved with her two daughters to the utopian Labadist community. Merian was no doubt active in the community's self-sufficient economy: baking bread, weaving cloth, and printing books. During her ten-year stay, she also sharpened her scientific skills, learning Latin and studying the flora and fauna sent from the Labadist colony in Surinam (she later used these connections for her journey to South America).

Voyage to Surinam. Having studied insects since the age of thirteen, Merian moved in 1691 to Amsterdam, the hub of Dutch global commerce, to study the city's rich natural history collections. Here Merian prepared 127 illustrations for a French translation of Johann Goedart's *Metamorphosis et historia naturalis insectorum.* She also met Caspar Commelin, director of the botanical garden, who would later assist her in adding Latin plant names and bibliography to the text of her *Metamorphosis.* Disappointed that Dutch natural history collections displayed only dead specimens, Merian set out to do her own research: "This all resolved me to undertake a great and expensive trip to Surinam (a hot and humid land) where these gentlemen had obtained these insects, so that I could continue my observations" (Merian, 1705, An Den Leser).

Like other naturalists of the period, Merian relied on Amerindians and African slaves for assistance in bioprospecting: in finding, identifying, and procuring choice specimens. In her *Metamorphosis* she emphasized—as was common in this period—information given directly to her by the Indians. These included uses of plants in medicine (cotton and senna leaves cured wounds; seeds of the peacock flower induced abortions), foods (a recipe for Cassava bread), buildings, clothing, and jewelry. Ship lists indicate that Merian brought her "Indian woman" with her to Amsterdam, but nothing more is known about this woman.

Overcome with malaria, Merian was forced to leave Surinam in 1701 sooner than she had intended. Her trip was a great success for both her science and business. In addition to publishing her *Metamorphosis,* she enlarged her trade in exotic specimens. Before leaving Surinam, she arranged with a local man to continue to supply her with all manner of butterflies, insects, fireflies, iguanas, snakes, and turtles for sale in Amsterdam. A number of Merian's brandy-preserved own specimens were displayed in the town hall.

Merian financed her own research and scientific projects. She spared no expense in preparing her Surinam volume, which she sold by subscriptions. Well received by the learned world, Merian's three books appeared in a total of twenty editions between 1680 and 1771.

Merian left her mark on entomology. Six plants, nine butterflies, and two beetles are named for her. Her training and skills did not die with her, but were carried on by her daughters who completed the third volume of her Surinam book. In 1717, her daughter Dorothea Maria moved to Saint Petersburg, where she and her husband, George Gsell, became court painters. Their daughter (Merian's granddaughter) eventually married Leonard Euler.

BIBLIOGRAPHY

WORKS BY MERIAN

Der Raupen wunderbare Verwandlung und sonderbare. Nürnberg, 1679.

Neues Blümenbuch. Nürnberg: J.A. Graffen, 1680.

Metamorphosis insectorum Surinamensium. Amsterdam, 1705.

OTHER SOURCES

Davis, Natalie Zemon. "Metamorphoses: Maria Sibylla Merian." In *Women on the Margins: Three Seventeenth-Century Lives.* Cambridge, MA: Harvard University Press, 1995.

Pfister-Burkhalter, Margarete. *Maria Sibylla Merian, Leben und Werk 1647–1717.* Basel, Switzerland: GS-Verlag, 1980.

Rücker, Elisabeth. *Maria Sibylla Merian (1647–1717): Ihr Wirken in Deutschland und Holland.* Bonn, Germany: Presse- und Kulturabteilung der Kgl. Niederländischen Botschaft, 1980.

Schiebinger, Londa. "Scientific Women in the Craft Tradition." In *The Mind Has No Sex?: Women in the Origins of Modern Science.* Cambridge, MA: Harvard University Press, 1989.

———. *Plants and Empire: Colonial Bioprospecting in the Atlantic World.* Cambridge, MA: Harvard University Press, 2004.

Ullmann, Ernst, ed. *Leningrader Aquarelle.* 2 vols. Leipzig, Germany: Edition Leipzig, 1974.

Wettengl, Kurt, ed. *Maria Sibylla Merian (1647–1717): Artist and Naturalist.* Ostfildern, Germany: G. Hatje, 1998.

Londa Schiebinger

Merton

MERTON, ROBERT KING (*b.* Philadelphia, Pennsylvania, 4 July 1910; *d.* New York, New York, 23 February 2003), *sociology of science and knowledge, social theory.*

Merton was the preeminent figure in the sociology of science in the generation following World War II. For Merton, this discipline concerns the social factors that make it possible for science to flourish. These factors range from values and conditions in the wider society that promote science to social norms internal to the scientific community that regulate the distribution of rewards. However, the actual content of scientific knowledge, that is, its theories, concepts, or methods, is outside the scope of Mertonian sociology of science. Merton's other sociological interests included the relations among social structure, deviance, and anomie; ethnic relations and urban sociology; mass communications; complex social organizations or bureaucracies; the sociology of the professions, especially the medical profession and medical education; and the methodology and sociology of social research. He brought the problem of unintended consequences to the attention of sociologists, developed the method of using focus groups, and coined many new terms and phrases that have come into common parlance, including "role model," "self-fulfilling prophecy," and "dysfunction." As a social theorist, Merton was rivaled only by Talcott Parsons among postwar American sociologists, and Merton easily surpassed Parsons as a literary stylist.

Merton was born Meyer R. Schkolnick on 4 July 1910 to working-class eastern European Jewish immigrants in Philadelphia. He adopted Robert K. Merton as his stage name during his adolescent career as a performing magician, after his mentor in the magic trade—and future brother-in-law—told him that the name he had initially chosen, Merlin, was rather hackneyed. He chose his first name from Jean-Eugène Robert-Houdin, the magician who inspired Harry Houdini (Ehrich Weiss). By the time he began undergraduate studies at Temple University in 1927 his friends knew him as Bob Merton, and he legally changed his name at nineteen. At Temple, Merton became the research assistant to the sociologist George E. Simpson. Simpson brought Merton to his first meeting of the American Sociological Association, where he met Pitirim Sorokin, who encouraged him to pursue graduate work in sociology at Harvard University. Merton received his doctorate in 1935 and stayed on for a few years as a tutor and an instructor. He then taught for two years at Tulane University, where he quickly rose to chairman of the Sociology Department.

Finally, in 1941 Merton joined the faculty at Columbia University, where he spent the rest of his teaching career, retiring in 1984 with the rank of university professor. Here he educated many students in the sociology of science and collaborated with Paul Lazarsfeld at his Bureau of Applied Social Research. Over the course of his career, he was awarded many fellowships, prizes, and honorary degrees. To list only some of the most notable, he was a Guggenheim Fellow in 1962–1963; a Fellow of the Center for Advanced Studies in Behavioral Sciences in Stanford, California, in 1974; and a MacArthur Fellow from 1983 to 1988; and he was awarded the National Medal of Science in 1994. He was married to the sociologist Harriet Zuckerman, who was also on the Columbia faculty. By a previous marriage to Suzanne M. Carhart, whom he had met at Temple, he was the father of Robert C. Merton, the Nobel Prize–winning economist, and Stephanie Tombrello and Vanessa Merton.

Puritan Values and Science. Merton presented most of his sociological work in the form of learned essays, rather than book-length studies. One notable exception is his PhD dissertation, originally titled "Sociological Aspects of Scientific Development in Seventeenth-Century England." He successfully defended this thesis in December 1935, with the sociologists Sorokin, Parsons, and Carle C. Zimmerman, and the historian of science George Sarton serving on his dissertation committee. Sarton especially took a keen interest in Merton's work, and offered to publish it in *Osiris,* a journal that published longer studies and other articles in the history of science that were not appropriate for publication in *Isis,* which Sarton also edited. A revised version of Merton's dissertation appeared with the new title, "Science, Technology, and Society in Seventeenth-Century England," in *Osiris* in 1938. It was finally published as a separate book in 1970 under this title.

In this work, Merton set out to investigate how science as a social institution was interdependent with religion and the economy in the seventeenth century. He thought that seventeenth-century science was still too young to have been valued for its own sake, and had to be justified in terms of other values. This idea led him to two investigations. The first is a quantitative study of the degree to which the direction taken by scientific research was influenced by socioeconomic and military needs, such as solving the problems presented by pumping water out of mines, determining longitude at sea, and aiming cannons. The second is an inquiry into the ways in which Puritan values may have facilitated the development of modern science. In his preface to the 1970 edition, Merton explains that as he was studying the writings of seventeenth-century scientists in preparation for his thesis, he was struck by their Puritan religious commitments. This brought to his mind Max Weber's work, *The Protestant Ethic and the Spirit of Capitalism* (1904–1905), in which the author had tried to establish a link between ascetic Protestantism and capitalism. Turning once again to Weber's book, Merton found that Weber had suggested that sociologists investigate the connection between ascetic Protestantism and science. Merton took up the challenge, in spite of some resistance from Sorokin, who was skeptical of Weber's claims.

Sarton tried but without success to get Merton to cut back on the parts dealing with religion for the published version. Merton himself says that the part dealing with economic and military needs is clearer. Nevertheless, it is the link between Puritanism and science that captured scholars' attention at that time, providing an ironic example of those unintended consequences that so fascinated Merton. Merton suggests that the attention given to this link may have been due to its having seemed highly improbable to scholars in the 1930s, who were more accustomed to thinking of science as being at loggerheads with religion. The notion that Puritan values helped make the growth of science possible has since become known as the "Merton Thesis," thus exemplifying the phenomenon of eponymy in science, or naming a contribution to knowledge after its contributor, a topic to which Merton also devoted much of his attention later.

The Merton Thesis is not a claim about the intentions or motivations of individual scientists. Nor is it a claim about certain religious or theological doctrines, or even a specific church, promoting scientific research. Instead, the thesis is about how affectively charged values or ideals associated with one social institution made possible the rise of a very different social institution. According to Merton, the Puritan values or "ethos" on which early science drew include the glorification of the Author of Nature through the discovery of order in the universe. A second Puritan value is that one should work toward achieving what the seventeenth-century chemist Robert Boyle called the "comfort of mankind" here on Earth. Science was thought to promote the general good through its technological applications. A third value is the Puritan exaltation of reason, which was believed to distinguish humans from the animals and keep the passions in check. However, the Puritans did not value the idle use of reason in mere speculation, but held that reason must be subservient to experimentation, which they associated with the kind of practical, industrious, physical work that they also valued.

Merton explains that Puritanism was not a necessary condition for the rise of science; other ideologies or value systems could have played the same role. Indeed he generalized his thesis to include other forms of ascetic Protestantism, including eighteenth- and nineteenth-century German Pietism as well as seventeenth-century English Puritans. Even in the historical circumstances in which the Puritan ethos did play a role, the economic, technological, and military needs of England also played key parts. Thus, the Puritan ethos was not a sufficient condition for the rise of modern science, either. The fact that science subsequently evolved into a secular institution that often stood in opposition to the ascetic Protestantism from which it arose exemplifies for Merton the irony of history and the problem of unintended consequences.

Unfortunately, only five hundred copies of the *Osiris* volume containing Merton's dissertation were printed, and because the journal was printed in Belgium in 1938, even these soon became unavailable to scholars because of wartime conditions. Because the dissertation remained out of print until 1970, the Merton Thesis was probably better known to a generation of sociologists through a much shorter paper, titled "Puritanism, Pietism, and Science," published in *Sociological Review* in 1936. This paper was republished in Merton's widely read anthology, *Social Theory and Social Structure,* which went through three editions, in 1949, 1957, and 1968, and more than thirty printings.

The Merton Thesis generated much controversy. In response to George Becker's (1984) empirical, historical critique, Merton (1984) broke his thesis down into three different claims of increasing levels of abstraction, and argued that empirical criticisms applied only to the lowest level, the particular sociohistorical claim about ascetic Protestantism in seventeenth-century England or eighteenth- and nineteenth-century Germany having the unintended effect of encouraging and legitimizing the growth of science. The middle-range hypothesis was that the emergence of science required, among other things, a specific ethos or set of attitudes and values that could have derived from some other institution, such as religion. At the most abstract level, his claim was that social institutions in general, including science and religion, are dynamically interdependent. However, by insulating these last two claims from counterevidence, Merton only raises questions about their empirical support.

Science and Ideology. Merton's interest in the social conditions that make science possible also extended to his own time. In a paper called "Science and the Social Order," delivered at the American Sociological Association in 1937 and published the following year in the journal *Philosophy of Science*, Merton examines the ways in which Nazi politics and ideology were interfering with science in Germany. As Merton sees it, by the twentieth century the success of science had led to its being able to enjoy a high degree of independence and autonomy from other social institutions, relative to the seventeenth-century science he had studied for his dissertation. However, this degree of autonomy could occur only in liberal democratic societies, and was currently being challenged in the Third Reich, in which, notoriously, contributions by Jewish scientists were proscribed.

Robert K. Merton. HULTON ARCHIVE/ GETTY IMAGES.

The ethos of science, which this paper characterizes as including intellectual honesty, integrity, organized skepticism, disinterestedness, and impersonality, was in conflict with the Nazi political order. For these totalitarians, the ethos of science represented little more than liberal, bourgeois, cosmopolitan biases. Merton explains that the conflict between science and Nazism is *psychological* rather than logical. Although it may seem as though scientific skepticism can challenge the beliefs on which political authority rests, from a purely logical point of view, to show the empirical basis or causes of beliefs is not to deny their validity. However, political authorities, like religious authorities, demand an attitude of loyalty and unqualified acceptance. Drawing on the theories of the French sociologist Émile Durkheim, Merton argues that every social institution carves out a sacred sphere of beliefs that is not to be profaned by scientific analysis.

With this preliminary account of the ethos of science, Merton is beginning to shift the focus of his attention away from the relationship between science and the wider society and toward the norms internal to the scientific community. He further develops these ideas about the ethos of science in a paper titled "A Note on Science and Democracy," where he says that recent attacks on science have led scientists to reexamine the norms and values on which science depends. This essay was first published in the new *Journal of Legal and Political Sociology* in 1942, and was subsequently republished under various titles in several anthologies of Merton's works, including *Social Theory and Social Structure* (1949), *The Sociology of Science* (1973), and *On Social Structure and Science* (1996). In this widely read paper, Merton analyzes the ethos of science into four interdependent norms, described below. This analysis served as a theoretical framework for subsequent work in the sociology of science by Merton and the students he trained at Columbia.

The Norms of Science. Merton defines the ethos of science as "that affectively toned complex of values and norms which is held to be binding on the man of science" (1973, pp. 268–269). The values are the institutional goals of science, and these legitimate the social norms of science, which are the means to achieving these ends. The institutional goal of science is to extend what he calls "certified knowledge," which is defined by the methods of science as "empirically confirmed and logically consistent statements of regularities" (p. 270). Merton's conception of scientific knowledge, with its emphasis on empirical regularities—and apparent neglect of their underlying theoretical explanations—reflects the influence of the positivist philosophy of that time. But for Merton, because the goal of science is to *extend* such knowledge, the institution of science also places a value on originality.

The institutional norms of science derive from its goal and methods. They are binding on the scientist not only because they are productive of the ends of science, but because "they are believed right and good. They are moral as well as technical prescriptions" (p. 270). These norms are maintained in existence by rewarding scientists for behaving in ways that conform to them, and in varying degrees they make up at least part of the scientist's conscience. They have never been explicitly codified by scientists; rather, Merton inferred them from his reading of the history of science. They include:

Universalism. According to this norm, claims to truth are to be evaluated in terms of universal or impersonal criteria, and not on the basis of the race, class, gender, religion, or nationality of the scientists proposing them. Nazi proscriptions of "Jewish science" and Soviet dismissals of Mendelian genetics as "bourgeois metaphysics" are clearly in violation of this norm.

Communism. During the Cold War years, this came to be known as the norm of "communalism." It calls for the common ownership of scientific discoveries and for scientists to give up their intellectual property rights in exchange for recognition and esteem. Secrecy is the very antithesis of this norm: scientific knowledge belongs in the public domain. The capitalist notion of proprietary technical knowledge is also in opposition to this norm.

For Merton, the scientific norm of communism explains the phenomenon of eponymy. Having a contribution to this common store of knowledge named after oneself is one of the few rewards available to scientists. This norm also helps to explain priority disputes. It is precisely because scientists are rewarded for original contributions to the stock of knowledge that it matters who discovered something first.

Disinterestedness. According to this norm, scientists are rewarded for acting in ways that outwardly appear to be selfless. That is, scientists do not seem to be working for money or other external rewards, but instead for the good of science. However, disinterestedness is not a matter of individual motivation, but rather the way in which the institution of science distributes rewards. Scientists may be motivated by a selfish desire to achieve fame and recognition or by an altruistic desire to benefit humanity, but what they are rewarded for is their behavior, not their motives, and they are rewarded for acting in ways that appear disinterested.

Merton thought that this norm could explain what he believed to be "the virtual absence of fraud" in science (1973, p. 276). That is, it is because scientists know that others will check their work that they will act in ways that can be characterized as disinterested. How much research misconduct occurs is of course debatable. But Zuckerman (1977) argued that the fraud that does occur attests only to a breakdown in the norm of distinterestedness.

Organized Skepticism. For Merton, this is both an institutional and a methodological norm, according to which no claims to truth are held sacred. All are subject to empirical and logical criticism. As mentioned above, it is this norm that pits science against religious and political authorities.

Merton characterizes these four norms as mutually reinforcing. Indeed, they are not logically independent of one another. For instance, in his account of what he takes to be the low rate of research misconduct, disinterested behavior among scientists depends on the norm of organized skepticism.

The Mertonian Paradigm Comes of Age. After the 1942 paper on the norms of science, Merton appears to have retreated from the sociology of science for a while. In 1949 he resigned as the associate editor for sociology of science from the journal *Isis,* explaining that he was turning his attention instead to the study of social structure and mass communication. Ironically, in his foreword to Bernard Barber's *Science and the Social Order* in 1952, he complained that the sociology of science was being neglected, and suggested that this may be due at least in part to sociologists not perceiving science as presenting any pressing social problems. Although he was working with Elinor Barber on the role of serendipity or chance connections in science, the book that they wrote together, *The Travels and Adventures of Serendipity: A Study in Sociological Semantics and the Sociology of Science,* was not published (in English) until 2004.

Change came in the late 1950s. Beginning with his presidential address to the American Sociological Association in 1957, Merton wrote and published a series of papers over approximately the next ten years that addressed such things as priority disputes, the reward system of science, problem choice, and multiple discoveries. These papers drew on the theoretical framework he had established in the 1942 article, which also served to define the sociology of science in the United States for a generation of sociologists. During this period he directed dissertations in the sociology of science by Zuckerman, the brothers Stephen Cole and Jonathan Cole, and others. In addition, he wrote *On the Shoulders of Giants: A Shandean Postscript* (1965), a seriously lighthearted inquiry, written in the form of an extended letter to a friend, into the origins of Isaac Newton's famous aphorism, "If I have seen further it is by standing on the shoulders of giants."

Merton's essays in the sociology of science during this period developed his theoretical framework by taking up such problems as scientists deviating from the norms of science or being subject to conflicting norms. His account of deviance in science drew on his more general theories of social anomie. For Merton, an anomic situation arises when a culture gives rise to aspirations that not everyone can realize, which results in deviant behavior and a cynical rejection of the moral rules. In science, deviance is a response to the discrepancy between the huge emphasis on original research and the difficulty most scientists experience in trying to make original contributions. However, Merton continued to think that misconduct in science, such as plagiarism and fabrication of data, was relatively rare.

Merton also applied the notion of sociological ambivalence to science. Ambivalence arises when individuals are subject to opposing norms. This may happen not only in science but in any social institution. It can arise either through conflict between different social statuses occupied by the same individual or within a single status, in which there are incompatible normative expectations. For instance, Merton saw Charles Darwin's hesitancy in publishing his theory of evolution as exemplifying a norm of humility, which works against the drive to achieve recognition for original research. More generally, the norm of communalism dictates that scientists should

Merton

make new knowledge available to others as quickly as possible, but there is a counternorm that says that they ought not to rush into print. Organized skepticism cautions scientists against being the victims of the latest fads, but the value placed on originality entails a counternorm that prescribes openness to new ideas. However, Merton cautioned that these norms and counternorms are not necessarily contradictory to each other. Barry Barnes and Alex Dolby (1970) have suggested that perhaps the actual norm in science is to steer a middle path between two extremes.

Another departure from the ethos of science is discussed in a paper titled "The Matthew Effect in Science," presented to the American Sociological Association in 1967 and published in *Science* the following year. Merton gives this name to the phenomenon of credit tending to accrue more to scientists who are already well known, taking the term from the New Testament book of Matthew (25:29), where it says "For unto every one that hath shall be given, and he shall have abundance: but from him that hath not shall be taken away even that which he hath" (1973, p. 445). Although this effect may appear to conflict with the norms of universalism and communism, Merton argues that it is in fact functional for science, by bringing new work to the attention of the scientific community more rapidly.

Critiques of the Mertonian Program. The Mertonian paradigm began to lose its dominant position in the sociology of science after the publication of Thomas Kuhn's *The Structure of Scientific Revolutions* (1962). As this work shows scientists being guided in their work by the paradigms or exemplary achievements of specialized communities, sociologists came to realize that what scientists take to be the very content of their disciplines is relevant to a sociological understanding of science, after all. Sociologists also began to suspect that Merton's interpretation of priority disputes may have been misconceived. As Kuhn argues, to ask whether the English clergyman and chemist Joseph Priestley (1733–1804) or the French chemist Antoine-Laurent Lavoisier (1743–1794) discovered oxygen first is to overlook the differences between what these scientists thought their experiments showed, as well as between what they thought and how oxygen is conceived in the early twenty-first century.

Barnes and Dolby (1970) were among the first sociologists to raise these kinds of Kuhnian objections. Kuhn taught them that scientific education emphasizes dogmatism, not skepticism. They argue that the Mertonian norms are derived from a conception of the goals of science, not from an empirical study of actual science. At best, they express the norms that scientists profess, not the ones that guide them in their research. Furthermore, Barnes and Dolby find that the norms of science have changed as science evolved from a largely amateur endeavor in the seventeenth century, through a professional, academic phase, to its present state, in which it is no longer autonomous from national and military interests.

Michael Mulkay (1976) subsequently offered an even more radical critique. He maintains that the Mertonian norms belong to an ideology that scientists use to justify their demands for public support without public scrutiny, claiming that such scrutiny is unnecessary because quality is guaranteed by norms and values internal to science. To show that these norms actually govern science, one would have to show that they are linked to the distribution of rewards. However, when referees evaluate a scientific paper or research proposal, they have no way of telling whether the authors adhered to these norms, and base their decisions on the content of the paper or proposal. Furthermore, referees take into account such factors as institutional affiliation and not just universalistic criteria.

Toward the end of the 1970s, sociologists of scientific knowledge began to challenge the intellectual authority of science and to argue that its content was shaped by social interests, social networks, and the use of rhetoric and persuasion. Merton could never accept the relativism that these views implied, and remained a firm believer in scientific progress. However, more recent years have seen a turning away from relativism and a renewed interest—at least among philosophers of science—in the relationship between democracy and science.

BIBLIOGRAPHY

WORKS BY MERTON

Social Theory and Social Structure: Toward the Codification of Theory and Research. New York: Free Press, 1949. Perhaps the most widely read collection of Merton's most important papers on theoretical sociology, social structure, sociology of knowledge, and sociology of science. Additional papers were added in subsequent editions, with the 1968 edition (New York: Free Press) being the most complete.

On the Shoulders of Giants: A Shandean Postscript. New York: Free Press, 1965. An inquiry into the origins of Newton's famous aphorism, written in the form of a letter to a friend.

Science, Technology, and Society in Seventeenth-Century England. New York: Harper & Row, 1970. A reprint of the 1938 publication of his revised doctoral dissertation, with a new preface.

The Sociology of Science: Theoretical and Empirical Investigations. Edited by Norman W. Storer. Chicago: University of Chicago Press, 1973. Contains nearly all of Merton's important papers in the sociology of science and knowledge up until the time of publication.

Sociological Ambivalence and Other Essays. New York: Free Press, 1976. Contains essays concerning the problem of conflicting norms in science and other walks of life.

The Sociology of Science: An Episodic Memoir. Carbondale: Southern Illinois University Press, 1979. Reproduces Merton's introduction to *The Sociology of Science in Europe,* edited by Merton and Jerry Gaston, in which Merton gives an account of the relationship of his work to that of others in the history, philosophy, and sociology of science.

"The Fallacy of the Latest Word: The Case of 'Pietism and Science.'" *American Journal of Sociology* 89 (1984): 1091–1121. Replies to Becker (see below).

On Social Structure and Science. Edited by Piotr Sztompka. Chicago: University of Chicago Press, 1996. Anthology of Merton's work in a variety of sociological fields. Includes a select bibliography of works by and about him. Also contains his 1994 autobiographical address to the American Council of Learned Societies, "A Life of Learning," which is especially good for the early years. This address can also be found in the 1997 volume cited below.

"De-Gendering 'Man of Science': The Genesis and Epicene Character of the Word *Scientist.*" In *Sociological Visions,* edited by Kai Erikson. Lanham, MD: Rowman and Littlefield, 1997. Also contains "A Life of Learning."

With Elinor Barber. *The Travels and Adventures of Serendipity: A Study in Sociological Semantics and the Sociology of Science.* Princeton, NJ: Princeton University Press, 2004. Originally completed in 1958, investigates the history of the term *serendipity* and the role of serendipity or chance connections in science.

OTHER SOURCES

Barnes, S. Barry, and Robert G. A. Dolby. "The Scientific Ethos: A Deviant Viewpoint." *Archives Européennes de Sociologie* (*European Journal of Sociology*) 11 (1970): 3–25. A critique of Merton's views on the norms of science.

Becker, George. "Pietism and Science: A Critique of Robert K. Merton's Hypothesis." *American Journal of Sociology* 89 (1984): 1065–1090. Questions the connection between German Pietism and science.

Clark, Jon, Celia Modgil, and Sohan Modgil, eds. *Robert K. Merton: Consensus and Controversy.* New York: Falmer, 1990. Contains biographical essays as well as critical discussions of all aspects of his contributions to sociology.

Cohen, I. Bernard. "The Publication of *Science, Technology, and Society:* Circumstances and Consequences." *Isis* 79 (1988): 571–582. Contains useful biographical information about Merton as a young scholar.

———, ed., with the assistance of K. E. Duffin and Stuart Strickland. *Puritanism and the Rise of Modern Science: The Merton Thesis.* New Brunswick, NJ: Rutgers University Press, 1990. Contains a long essay by Cohen on the impact of the Merton Thesis, which is followed by several critiques of the Merton Thesis and replies by Merton.

Coser, Lewis A., ed. *The Idea of Social Structure: Papers in Honor of Robert K. Merton.* New York: Harcourt Brace Jovanovich, 1975. Contains essays about the man and his work, including one by Lazarsfeld about his years working with Merton at the Bureau of Applied Social Research. Also includes a nearly complete bibliography of his writings up until 1975.

Crothers, Charles. *Robert K. Merton.* Chichester, U.K.: Ellis Horwood; New York: Tavistock, 1987. A concise introduction to the man and his works, written for undergraduates.

Feldhay, Rivka, and Yehuda Elkana, eds. "'After Merton': Protestant and Catholic Science in Seventeenth-Century Europe." *Science in Context* 3 (1989): 3–302. Special issue of the journal containing eleven papers critiquing and extending the Merton Thesis, in addition to some historical material on Merton and Sorokin.

Feuer, Lewis S. *The Scientific Intellectual: The Psychological & Sociological Origins of Modern Science.* New York: Basic, 1963. Argues that, contrary to Merton and Weber, the inspiration for modern science was not Puritanism but a hedonistic, libertarian ethic.

———. "Science and the Ethic of Protestant Asceticism: A Reply to Professor Robert K. Merton." *Research in Sociology of Knowledge, Sciences, and Art* 2 (1979): 1–23. Presents additional historical evidence that favors his own hypothesis over Merton's.

Gieryn, Thomas F., ed. *Science and Social Structure: A Festschrift for Robert K. Merton.* Transactions of the New York Academy of Sciences, ser. 2, vol. 39. New York: New York Academy of Sciences, 1980. Several of the papers in this volume address Merton's ideas on the ethos or norms of science, sociological ambivalence in science, multiples, and eponymy. There is also a discussion of Merton's influence.

———. "Eloge: Robert K. Merton, 1910–2003." *Isis* 95 (2004): 91–94. An appreciative note by one of Merton's former students.

Hunt, Morton. "'How Does It Come to Be So?' Profile of Robert K. Merton." *New Yorker* 36 (1961): 39–63. Widely cited account of his early years.

Mongardini, Carlo, and Simonetta Tabboni, eds. *Robert K. Merton and Contemporary Sociology.* New Brunswick, NJ: Transaction, 1997. Contains critical analyses of Merton's work by mostly European sociologists, written for academics.

Mulkay, Michael. "Norms and Ideology in Science." *Social Science Information* 15 (1976): 637–656. Includes a critique of the Mertonian norms.

Schultz, Ruth. "The Improbable Adventures of an American Scholar: Robert K. Merton." *American Sociologist* 26 (1995): 68–77. Reveals something of the personal side of Merton.

Sztompka, Piotr. *Robert K. Merton: An Intellectual Profile.* New York: St. Martin's Press, 1986. A somewhat more detailed study than Crothers's book.

Wood, Paul, ed. *Science and Dissent in England, 1688–1945.* Burlington, VT: Ashgate, 2004. Several of the papers in this collection address the historical evidence for the Merton Thesis.

Zuckerman, Harriet. "Deviant Behavior and Social Control in Science." In *Deviance and Social Change,* edited by Edward Sagarin. Beverly Hills, CA: Sage, 1977. Application of Mertonian framework to research misconduct.

Warren Schmaus

Migdal

MIGDAL, ARKADY BENEDIKTOVICH (*b.* Lida, Russian Empire [later Belarus], 11 March 1911; *d.* Princeton, New Jersey, 9 February 1991), *physics, nuclear theory, condensed-matter theory.*

Migdal was among the increasingly rare theoretical physicists after World War II who felt equally at home in nuclear and particle physics as well as the physics of condensed matter, occasionally venturing into plasma theory as well. Beginning in nuclear theory, he predicted a giant dipole resonance in photoabsorbtion processes in 1944 (experimentally confirmed three years later). His work on phonons in the 1950s offered one of the first productive applications of quantum field theory to the solid state, and he also made major contributions to the theory of Fermi liquids. He then took the lessons from this work back to nuclear theory, where he derived an early rigorous treatment of strong interactions inside nuclei, and later also saw his original ideas on pion condensation extended in unexpected ways. Because he counted Lev Davidovitch Landau as a teacher, Migdal is often identified as a member of the Landau School, though Migdal was ambitious enough and close enough to Landau in age to pursue a friendly rivalry of sorts. (Only Migdal dared arrive late at Landau's famous theory seminar in Moscow.) The author of several textbooks that showed a generation of theorists how to carry calculational tools such as Green's functions and Feynman diagrams from one domain to another, Migdal taught at the "Soviet MIT" (the Moscow Engineering Physics Institute, MIFI) and ventured successfully into science popularization, warranting the designation of a "Migdal School" in the eyes of many contemporaries.

Early Career. Arkady Benediktovich Migdal was born in the Jewish Pale of Settlement, in what was then the Vilna province of the Russian Empire, slightly south of present-day Vilnius, Lithuania. His father Beinus Migdal made a meager living as a pharmacist, though little else is known about his early family life. The region suffered greatly from the ebb and flow of world war, revolution, and civil war in the 1914–1921 period. It was occupied repeatedly by Germans, Poles, and Russians before it was eventually incorporated into the newly constituted Polish state during the interwar period. (It had once belonged to the long-defunct Polish-Lithuanian Commonwealth). Like many peers at the time, Migdal's family moved to Leningrad (later St. Petersburg) in search of better fortunes in the 1920s. (Subsequently Arkady would usually change his patronymic from the Yiddish-inflected Beinusovich to the more Russian Benediktovich.) It was in Leningrad that Migdal received his secondary education, and even managed to publish a brief pedagogical note on the Atwood machine before his eighteenth birthday.

Migdal's career as a physicist got off to a rocky start after his initial enrollment in the physics faculty at Leningrad State University in 1929. Soviet universities had just introduced so-called "brigade" methods into the curriculum in a hasty attempt to encourage collective modes of learning, and in the spring of 1930 Migdal was among several students kicked out for rebelling against the new system. Formalism, apoliticism, and antisocial behavior were among the formulaic charges leveled at the students, and Migdal in particular was faulted for a "slapdash attitude toward shock work." (Borrowed rather incongruously from the industrial context of the First Five Year Plan, "shock work" designated production efforts above and beyond the agreed-upon norms.) He spent a couple of months in jail, but the brigade methods were soon abandoned and the students readmitted. His troubles did not cease, however, because his "bourgeois" family members faced difficulties finding an economic niche for themselves once the looser strictures of the Bolsheviks' New Economic Policy during the 1920s were abandoned. Beginning in 1929 more centralized planning, headlong industrialization, and stricter "red" criteria for the social credentials of Soviet white-collar workers were introduced. The following year Migdal's father was laid off, before eventually being exiled to Kazakhstan for three years in 1932 for engaging in gray-market activities. He took ill and died not long after, with Migdal forced to look after his mother in Leningrad in the meantime.

Like many children of socially suspect parents in his generation, Migdal also completed a lengthy practical stint at an electronic instrument factory to shore up his proletarian credentials, and then stayed on as a consultant. His many obligations tore him away from his studies, and he was expelled from the university again in March 1933. It was another two years before his factory supervisors managed to get him re-enrolled in evening courses at the university, where V. A. Fock was among his teachers. He finally graduated at the end of 1936 and immediately embarked on advanced study at the Leningrad Physico-Technical Institute. His first advisor, M. P. Bronshtein, was only five years older, but he quickly steered Migdal toward theoretical nuclear physics. (Bronshtein was arrested in August 1937 during the Great Purges, never to return.) For Migdal the importance of the new subject matter was highlighted at the Third All-Union Conference on Nuclear Physics held in Leningrad in October 1938, though its lively debates took place without the foreign physicists who had participated in two previous rounds. Migdal made his professional debut that same year with an article on neutron scattering in ferromagnets, and proceeded to develop an expertise in atomic ionization processes. In 1939 he developed an approximation method he labeled "tossing," in order to solve certain problems associated with the ionization of atoms by neutrons. (The technique found its way into numerous quantum mechanics textbooks, including his own some thirty years later.) By the time Migdal defended his first (*kandidatskaia*) dissertation in Leningrad in 1940, he had already won the esteem of Yakov Il'itch Frenkel, Igorvgen'evich Tamm, and Landau, the dominant Soviet theorists at the time.

After these labors Migdal was already judged mature enough to proceed directly to work on the advanced *doktorskaia* dissertation, and he moved to Moscow to work with Landau. With Landau as an advisor, he developed an interest in recent experimental results in superconductivity and superfluidity, some of which were issuing from his institutional home at P. L. Kapitza Institute for Physical Problems. Landau had already launched into the development of his famous theory of superfluidity (published in May 1941), but in 1940 Migdal independently derived an exact calculation of the heat capacity for the collective portion of the superfluid helium well below the λ-point (what Landau dubbed the "phonon part"). After showing the calculation to Landau—who duly acknowledged it in his paper—Migdal retreated, somewhat regretfully, from trying to develop a more complete theory in Landau's shadow. He turned instead to the study of photoabsorption by atomic nuclei.

Though this phenomenal domain was well removed from liquid helium, Migdal nonetheless employed a similar set of tools, adopting a collective model that selected dynamic variables associated with the collective motion of a large number of nucleons (e.g., the deformation parameters describing surface vibrations and rotations of a nucleus). The resulting work on nuclear decay mechanisms, and especially quadrupole and dipole γ emission, formed the basis for his dissertation in 1943, as well as a related paper in English in 1944. In this work Migdal offered theoretical grounds for the large dipole resonance centered around 17 megaelectron volts (lower for heavy nuclei, higher for lighter ones), a phenomenon first noted tentatively by Walter Bothe and Wolfgang Gentner in 1937, but described authoritatively only a decade later by George C. Baldwin and G. S. Klaiber. In Migdal's description, the energy maximum of giant dipole resonances (GDR) is governed by the symmetry energy in the Bethe-Weizsäcker formula for the binding energy of the nucleus and by the average kinetic energy of the nucleons. GDR has since become a cottage industry for collective dynamics that extends even to so-called metallic clusters.

Basic Research in the Soviet Nuclear Weapons Complex. Late in the war, Migdal was invited to join I. V. Kurchatov's Laboratory No. 2, later known as the Institute of Atomic Energy ("Kurchatov Institute"). Like many physicists of his generation, he found himself confronted with the novel demands of classified research, and for more than a quarter century he found it expedient to make the necessary accommodations, perhaps because this initially offered relative security in the late Stalin era, when state-sponsored anti-Semitism reached a peak. Though some of this work came at the cost of priority claims internationally, Migdal retained direct access to Kurchatov until the latter's death in 1960, and he proved adept at winning precious personnel and resources for fundamental research, eventually heading "Sector 10," the institute's general nuclear theory group. He did not lack for contact with the finest physicists of the postwar generation, collaborating with G. I. Budker on calculations for an early design of a homogeneous finite reactor and serving as an official opponent for Andrey D. Sakharov's dissertation defense in November 1947. The Soviet weapons complex underwrote several other results that were slow to reach the public eye. In the early 1950s Migdal led a group working on controlled thermonuclear synthesis, and performed important calculations with Viktor Mikhailovitch Galitskii on the distribution of cyclotron radiation in magnetized thermonuclear plasma. With S. I. Braginskii he also developed a qualitative theory of processes accompanying the inertial pinch effect. These works were only declassified in a 1958 collection on the physics of plasma edited by Mikhail Aleksandrovich Leontovich.

While little is known about Migdal's classified research, he did simultaneously manage to follow developments in the nascent field of pion physics after the war, publishing a survey with Yakov Abramovich Smorodinskii. The next major "public" problem he tackled at the Kurchatov Institute was the resonant interaction of slow nucleons in a nuclear reaction, which surely grew out of concerns from weapons work and reactor design. For a three-body system the challenge was to describe possible final-state interactions for *pp*, *np*, and *nn* scattering, where it was especially difficult to extract experimental information about the scattering length a_{nn}. At a Landau theory seminar in 1950, Migdal demonstrated that the posited interactions between the final products of a nuclear reaction leading to three particles could strongly influence the energy and angular distribution of those final products. For small relative momenta, the energy distribution for the *nn* reaction was shown to be essentially dependent on a_{nn}, a result first published by Kenneth Watson in 1952, and eventually released for international publication by Migdal in 1955. The accuracy of their distribution functions was not great, but some of the theory's working assumptions formed the starting point for the more exacting techniques developed—for example, those developed by Ludwig D. Faddeev a decade later.

In 1953 Landau and Isaak Yakovlevich Pomeranchuk performed a series of calculations in classical electrodynamics showing how multiple scattering could

Arkady Migdal. SHEILA TERRY/SCIENCE PHOTO LIBRARY.

interfere with bremsstrahlung. The suppression of the bremsstrahlung stemmed from the interference between photons generated along individual portions of the electron trajectory, but their suppression calculation failed at the same level that the classical bremsstrahlung calculation failed, when $k \sim E$. Migdal attempted a fully quantum mechanical calculation in 1956, which had the advantage of covering the entire energy range. Treating multiple scattering as a kind of Fokker-Planck diffusion process, he worked out the average radiation per collision while taking into account the interference between the radiation from different collisions. In the absence of suppression processes, Migdal's cross-section matched up well with the Bethe-Heitler cross-section, and the approach was robust enough that it remains in use in the twenty-first century, albeit with modern correction terms. He also found the cross-section for pair production, though these calculations only applied to an infinite-thickness target. Only in 1993 did the E-146 collaboration at the Stanford Linear Accelerator Center (SLAC) perform truly detailed experimental tests of Landau-Pomeranchuk-Migdal (LPM) suppression theory, whose subsequent modifications held up remarkably well.

Superconductivity and Superfluidity; Finite Fermi Systems. During the 1950s Migdal was one of many who set their sights on the theory of superconductivity, mastering many of the formal issues in this vast domain and even skirting close to the solution ultimately found by John Bardeen, Leon Neil Cooper, and John Robert Schrieffer in 1957. Working mostly with adiabatic perturbation theory and second quantization, he initially made only modest contributions, but eventually became the first to apply non-perturbative diagrammatic methods to electron-phonon interactions in metals in 1958. Gersim Matveevich Eliashberg extended the technique to superconductors two years later. Migdal truly hit his stride once he learned of Landau's theory of Fermi liquids in 1957, quickly offering a general result in corroboration of the Landau picture. For non-interacting collections of particles obeying Fermi statistics at low temperatures, the chance of finding any

Migdal

particle at a given energy drops sharply to zero above the Fermi energy E_F. For interacting particles it is natural to assume that this energy cut-off will be somewhat smoothed out, but Migdal found that the cut-off is much sharper than expected (the "Migdal jump"), and can be used to define E_F, thus shoring up the generality of the quasiparticle concepts in Fermi liquid theory.

Landau's theory covered weakly excited states in infinite systems of interacting fermions, and Migdal and his closest associates soon realized that its applicability extended from liquid He^3 to nuclear many-body theory. In various papers and an original textbook Migdal argued forcefully for the parallels in the descriptive frameworks, and made the major modifications necessary to apply his theory to finite systems such as nuclei. With his close colleague Galitskii, he developed the Green's function techniques in 1958 that began to bring analytical properties, spectral expansions, dispersion relations, and even the exact formula for the ground-state energy within reach of the nuclear physicist. Migdal's approach was semi-phenomenological in the classic style of the Landau School, with equations derived from first principles, but with parameters for quantities such as quasiparticle energies and wave functions and quasiparticle-quasihole interactions carefully calibrated with suitable experiments. Migdal expanded the interaction at the Fermi surface in terms of Legendre polynomials, and the art came in choosing the correct general experimental parameters (Landau-Migdal parameters) to use the theory to make connections to other, seemingly unrelated phenomena. (In the finite case, as Migdal showed, these parameters become density dependent.) At low energies the nucleus behaves like a gas of quasiparticles interacting via pair forces dependent on the nuclear density (Migdal forces). The theory of finite Fermi systems—extensively formalized by Migdal in a 1965 textbook by that name—provided a framework for virtually any nuclear structure calculation, whether self-consistent or non-self-consistent (in the sense of Hartree-Fock).

The richness of this general research program was manifested in the flood of papers produced by Migdal and his colleagues and students in the 1960s. Migdal made connections between superfluidity and nuclear moments of inertia, identified nuclear analogies to one-particle excitations in Fermi systems, and, with Anatoly Ivanovich Larkin, treated the case of zero temperature and *S*-wave pairing. Isotopic and isomeric shifts in atomic and mesoatomic spectral lines were treated, as were magnetic and quadrupole moments, while calculations of beta-decay and muon-capture probabilities also found their way into the FFS program.

Neutron Stars, Pion Condensation, and Quantum Chromodynamics. Migdal was elected a corresponding member of the Academy of Sciences in the autumn of 1953, along with many other contributors to the Soviet thermonuclear weapons program; full academician status came more than a decade later. The lure of working in the Soviet weapons complex dimmed over time, however, as Soviet civilian physicists were gradually permitted to attend more international conferences in the 1960s. Migdal was also drawn to "civilian" diversions such as boxing, mountain climbing (especially popular among Soviet physicists), scuba diving (he was one of the first practitioners in the Soviet Union), sculpting, and jewelry making. Following yet another argument with the authorities over censorship and delays in publication in 1971, Migdal finally transferred to the recently founded Landau Institute of Theoretical Physics.

Around the time of his move to the Landau Institute, Migdal developed an interest in the behavior of Bose and Fermi systems in strong external fields. As early as 1959 he had hinted that superfluidity of nuclear matter might have interesting cosmological consequences for neutron stars, predicting that such stars would have a superfluid state with a transition temperature corresponding to 1 mega-electron volt. In a series of papers culminating in a massive 1978 review essay that became his most cited article, Migdal explored the range of phenomena that nucleon media subject to extreme conditions might manifest. In 1971 he suggested that the boson vacuum in a sufficiently strong external field would be unstable, and that matter in a neutron star subject to these conditions could undergo a phase transition. Dubbing this "pion condensation" (by analogy with Bose condensation), Migdal postulated the existence of superdense nuclei for which the energy gained in the phase transition would be offset by the energy loss due to contraction of the nucleon medium. Unfortunately, the effective nuclear charge $Z > 1600$ required to achieve the effect was scarcely realistic, but the hypothesis nonetheless had other suggestive consequences, including the appearance of spin-isospin ordering of a nucleus subject to one-pion exchange forces. Numerous physicists sought more realistic physical analogues (e.g., the strengthening of *l*-forbidden M1 transitions) that might exhibit behaviors hinting at the possibility of pion condensates. More generally, Migdal and his associates were developing a new domain of nuclear physics dealing with non-nucleonic degrees of freedom, with consequences for understanding the equation of state of hadronic matter. Many of these developments were later summarized in a posthumous volume written in collaboration with E. E. Saperstein, M. A. Troitsky, and D. N. Voskresensky.

In his later years Migdal applied some of the techniques he had employed with pion condensates to study another set of hadronic phenomena: gluons, the gauge bosons in quantum chromodynamics. The ideas were much the same: intense external color fields applied to gluons might force them to undergo boson condensation. The classical Yang-Mills theory of quantum chromodynamics (QCD) is scale-invariant, however, so the condensate energy must be characterized by a dimensional parameter specifying the external source, and the problem of quark confinement is thus neglected. Though the introduction of broken scale invariance does permit one to circle back to the confinement problem, Migdal did not achieve everything he had hoped with his models, despite his readiness to learn some of the elements of string theory in his seventies. Coming from the (relatively) more pragmatic precincts of nuclear many-body theory to the more rarified realm of QCD, Migdal occasionally advocated (with tongue firmly in cheek) resorting to the TV method, meaning "trivial vulgarization," when parametrizing desired quantities in the theory. Not all particle theorists were amused. Yet as some of his colleagues remarked, it was not just that Migdal had come to elementary particle theory, but that the theory itself had come to him in the course of the 1970s, adopting some of the "Migdal-type" qualitative methods that the teacher had indeed been advocating in his 1975 textbook, *Qualitative Methods in Quantum Theory.*

Migdal remained at the Landau Institute of Theoretical Physics for the remainder of his career, although increased travel opportunities and lecture stints in the 1980s eventually led to an affiliation with Princeton University, where his son Alexander also taught physics, and where he spent his final months before succumbing to stomach cancer in early 1991. In addition to his son, he left a wife, Tatyana, and a daughter, Marina.

BIBLIOGRAPHY

WORKS BY MIGDAL

"Rasseianie neitronov v ferromagnetikakh." *Doklady Akademii Nauk* 20 (1938): 555.

"Ionizatsiia atomov pri iadernykh reaktsii." *Zhurnal eksperimental'noi i teoreticheskoi fiziki* 9 (1939): 1163.

"Quadrupole and dipole γ-radiation of nuclei." *Journal of Physics* 8 (1944): 331.

With Ia. A. Smorodinskii. "Iskusstvennye π-mezony." *Uspekhy fizicheskikh nauk* 41 (1950): 133–152. A review paper quickly dated due to its treatment of so-called "varitrons" (meson-like particles whose existence was never confirmed), it is still useful as a reflection of his research concerns during a lengthy period of classified work when he published little else.

"Bremsstrahlung and pair production in condensed media at high energies." *Physical Review* 103 (1956): 1811–1820.

"The Momentum Distribution of Interacting Fermi Particles." *Journal of Experimental and Theoretical Physics* 5, no. 2 (1957): 333–334.

With V. M. Galitskii. "Application of the Methods of Quantum Field Theory to the Many-Body Problem." *Journal of Experimental and Theoretical Physics* 34 (1958): 139.

"Superfluidity and the Moments of Inertia of Nuclei." *Nuclear Physics* 13 (1959): 655–674.

"Single-Particle Excitations and Superfluidity in Fermi Systems with Arbitrary Interaction: Application to the Nucleus." *Nuclear Physics* 30 (1962): 239–257.

"A New Approach to the Theory of Nuclear Structure." *Nuclear Physics* 57 (1964): 29–47.

With Anatoly I. Larkin. "Theory of Superfluid Fermi Liquids: Application to the Nucleus." *Journal of Experimental and Theoretical Physics* 19 (1964): 1478.

"Nuclear magnetic moments." *Nuclear Physics* 75 (1966): 441–469.

Theory of Finite Fermi Systems and Applications to Atomic Nuclei. Translated by S. Chomet. New York: Interscience, 1967. Second ed., 1983.

With Vladimir P. Krainov. *Approximation Methods in Quantum Mechanics.* Translated by Anthony J. Leggett. New York: W. A. Benjamin, 1969.

"Vacuum Stability and Maximum Fields." *Journal of Experimental and Theoretical Physics* 34 (1972): 1184.

"π condensation in nuclear matter." *Physical Review Letters* 31 (1973): 257–260.

"Phase Transition in Nuclear Matter and Multiparticle Nuclear Forces." *Nuclear Physics* A210 (1973): 421–428.

"O psikhologii nauchnogo tvorchestva." *Nauka i zhizn'* 2 (1976): 3.

With G. A. Sorokin, O. A. Markin, and I. N. Mishustin. "Pion Condensation and Stability of Abnormal Nuclei." *Physics Letters* 65B (1977): 423–426.

Qualitative Methods in Quantum Theory. Translated by Anthony J. Leggett. Reading, MA: W. A. Benjamin, 1977.

"Instability of Yang-Mills Equations and Gluon-Field Condensation." *Journal of Experimental and Theoretical Physics Letters* 28 (1978): 37.

"Pion Fields in Nuclear Matter." *Reviews of Modern Physics* 50 (1978): 107–172.

Poiski istiny. Moscow: Molodaia gvardiia, 1983.

"QCD and the Structure of Hadrons." *Nuclear Physics* A478 (1988): 95–102.

With E. E. Saperstein, M. A. Troitsky, and D. N. Voskresensky. "Pion Degrees of Freedom in Nuclear Matter." *Physics Reports* 192 (1990): 179–437.

OTHER SOURCES

Archive of the Russian Academy of Sciences in Moscow, fond 524, op. 1 (1936–1944), d. 281. Includes Migdal's personnel file at the time of his application to doctoral study in 1940.

Agasian, N. O., et al., eds. *Vospominaniia ob akademike A. B. Migdale.* Moscow: Fizmatlit, 2003. Reminiscences by colleagues; includes Migdal's complete bibliography.

Beliaev, S. T., V. G. Vaks, I. I. Gurevich, et al. "Arkady Benediktovich Migdal (on his Seventieth Birthday)." *Soviet Physics Uspekhi* 24 (1981): 336–339.

Danos, M., B. S. Ishkhanov, N. P. Yudin, et al. "Giant Dipole Resonance and Evolution of Concepts of Nuclear Dynamics (On the 50th Anniversary of A. B. Migdal's Paper 'Quadrupole and Dipole γ Emission from Nuclei')." *Physics Uspekhi* 37 (1995): 1297–1307.

Khodel, Victor, and Eduard Saperstein. "Arkady B. Migdal." *Nuclear Physics* 555 (1993): vii–xv.

Party-Komsomol Group. "Lzheudarnikov—von iz brigady." *Studencheskaia pravda* (9 April 1930): 3. Migdal's expulsion from Leningrad State University.

Karl Hall

MILANKOVIĆ (MILANKOVITCH), MILUTIN

(*b.* Dalj, Austria-Hungary [now Croatia], 28 May 1879; *d.* Belgrade, Yugoslavia, 12 December 1958), *celestial mechanics, mathematical physics, climatology, geophysics, civil engineering, history of science.*

Milanković revolutionized the understanding of climate dynamics. He put the astronomical theory of climate on a firm mathematical basis and founded cosmic climatology by calculating the temperature conditions on planets of the inner solar system, and the depth of the atmosphere of the outer planets. In particular he calculated the impact of Earth's secular orbital cycles on climate changes and explained the origin of the Pleistocene ice ages. The perennial periodic orbital variations (eccentricity, obliquity, precession) considered in his canon of insolation, along with their influence on planets' climates, today are called Milanković cycles.

Milanković was a Serbian mathematician, born in the Slavonia region, part of Austria-Hungary (now Croatia), where his ancestors settled at the end of the seventeenth century after the great migration of Serbs from Kosovo and Metohija province. His family was wealthy, and through the centuries esteemed as philosophers, inventors, professors, lawyers, and civil servants. Milanković's father Milan was a merchant who died early, leaving behind a wife and six children, Milutin being the oldest of them. Tutored by his mother Jelisaveta and uncle Vasa Muačević, Milanković was thoroughly educated at home and at high school in Osek (now Osijek). His teacher of mathematics, Vladimir Varićak, later a member of the Yugoslav Academy of Sciences, noticed his exceptional abilities and remained his lifelong friend and advisor.

In 1896 Milanković enrolled at the Technical School in Vienna, with a major in civil engineering. Eight years later he gained a PhD in technical sciences with a thesis titled *Theory of Pressure Curves,* published in 1907. In his successful career as a civil engineer he was particularly interested in the theory of reinforced concrete. His ability to solve civil engineering problems mathematically was evident in his early articles and in his six patents granted in Austria, Hungary, and Yugoslavia. Milanković never abandoned his first profession: even as a renowned scientist he constructed buildings, railroads, airports, bridges, dams, and aqueducts all over central Europe. In 1956 he designed an edifice of the maximal height that could be constructed on Earth: a rotationally symmetrical building made of reinforced concrete over 21 kilometers high, with base diameter of over 112 kilometers (though it is unrealistic, since it does not take into account wind effects). In 1909 Milanković came to Belgrade University and became a citizen of the Kingdom of Serbia. He taught a course in applied mathematics, uncommon for European universities, which included three seemingly diverse subjects: rational mechanics, celestial mechanics, and theoretical physics. It was this approach that, in his opinion, helped him establish climatology as an integral, holistic science.

His original contribution to celestial mechanics is called Milanković's system of vector elements of planetary orbits. He reduced six Lagrangean-Laplacian elliptical elements to two vectors determining mechanics of planetary movements. The first specifies the planet's orbital plane, the sense of revolution of the planet, and the orbital ellipse parameter; the second specifies the axis of the orbit in its plane and the orbital eccentricity. By applying those vectors he significantly simplified the calculation and directly obtained all the formulas of the classical theory of secular perturbations.

Milanković started working on the astronomical theory of climate in 1912. His work was interrupted constantly by turbulent events. In 1914, he married Christina Topuzović, a beautiful and well-educated daughter of a wealthy merchant. But at the same time World War I broke out and the Austro-Hungarian authorities arrested him while he was spending his honeymoon in Dalj. He was interned in Budapest, where he was allowed to work in the library of the Hungarian Academy of Sciences. His wife joined him, and their only child, son Vasko (named after his dear uncle), was born there at the end of 1915. His work was adversely affected by the Austrian plunder of Belgrade University during World War I and the German devastation of Belgrade during World War II, including the bombing of the national library, the mathematical institute he founded, and the press that had just published his book. He also was forced to leave his home for several months because of the severe Allied bombing of Belgrade. Through all this hardship he constantly elaborated his theory for nearly four decades. He published about forty important papers until 1941, when he combined them in his masterwork *Canon of Insolation and the Ice-Age Problem.*

Encouraged by German geophysicist Alfred Wegener, who promoted the theory of continental drift, Milanković also worked on a theory of secular wandering of Earth's rotational poles, calculating how over the centuries Earth's crust moves relative to the poles. This theory, which appeared in Beno Gutenberg's *Handbuch der Geophysik* (Manual of Geophysics; 1933), mathematically follows the poles' trajectories, explaining the drift of Earth's solid crust over its fluid substratum as a consequence of the steady influence of centrifugal forces on unevenly distributed masses of continents and oceans. At first the theory was readily accepted, but in decades after Milanković's death, when Wegener's theory was gradually transformed into plate tectonics, it was ignored. Even so, it seems that Milanković discovered one of the essential causes of pole movements, which cannot be entirely neglected.

Curve of Insolation. Astronomical theories of climate involve changes in Earth's orbital geometry that affect seasonal and latitudinal distribution of incoming solar radiation. They emerged in the nineteenth century, most prominently in the work of James Croll, who influenced Charles Lyell. By 1890, because of uncertainties in the timing of ice ages and deficiencies in the stratigraphic record, the astronomical theory was largely disregarded for at least three decades. Geologists and climatologists were trying to find the cause of the ice ages in Earth's autonomous system (atmosphere–ocean–ice) as well as in the "solar theory," which postulated variations in the output of the Sun. None of these theories could be adequately tested.

Milanković applied himself to reviving the astronomical theory when it was nearly entirely abandoned, having almost every geologist against it. He realized that the astronomical theory had fallen into disrepute not because of any intrinsic weakness, but because of insufficient knowledge of celestial mechanics and Earth history. Determined to refine it, he built a mathematical apparatus for an exact survey of the insolation (the word is derived from incident solar radiation) of a planet, as well as the distribution and effects of heat in its atmosphere, and created a method for calculating the consequent alterations of the climate.

He founded his theory of climatology as an exact science in six papers, published between 1912 and 1914, devoted to the mathematical relationship between a planet's insolation and its temperatures. In 1917, he finished a comprehensive manuscript "Mathematische Grundlagen der kosmischen Strahlungslehre," published three years later as *Théorie mathématique des phénomènes thermiques produits par la radiation solaire.* There he resolved the problem of thermodynamics of inner planets of the solar system and attained the first reliable predictions about the present climates of Mercury, Venus, Mars, and the Moon, generally still valid, with the exception of Venus.

After 1920, when cooperation with Wladimir Köppen and Alfred Wegener began, Milanković turned his attention exclusively to Earth's climate, specifically the problem of ice ages. His primary focus was the insolation of Earth in the last six hundred thousand years at middle latitudes. The best-known result of the work was the "Curve of Insolation," first published in 1924, in Köppen and Wegener's book *Die Klimate der geologischen Vorzeit.* Being coincident with contemporary dating of four Alpine glacial periods, determined fifteen years earlier by Albrecht Penck and Eduard Brückner, the curve soon became widely accepted as a geological calendar for calibrating the paleoclimatological timescale.

Canon of Insolation. The canon of insolation is a general astronomical theory of climate applicable to planets with a solid crust. It is a comprehensive mathematical picture of planets' solar climates (the theoretical climate of a planet determined only by insolation) in which Earth is a particular case. Since the explanation of insolation dynamics was obtained by astronomical calculation similar to the predictions of solar and lunar eclipses (usually called the canon of eclipses), Milanković gave the same name to his work. The canon has two parts, named by the author *astronomical* and *physical;* the first explains how orbit affects insolation and the second how insolation affects climate.

The "astronomical" part explains the influence of orbital changes on planets' insolation in various seasons and latitudes. It is based on the law of gravitation, which explains the secular (over many centuries) variations in a planet's motion and enables their calculation, and the law of radiation, which explains how the solar insolation reaches the planets. Slow, but steady secular variations of the three Milanković cycles determine seasonal and latitudinal distribution of insolation, and the heating pattern of a planet.

Variations in eccentricity of Earth's orbit from an almost exact circle to a slightly elongated shape (eccentricity 0.06) with periodicity of about one hundred thousand years alters the relative lengths of the astronomical seasons (the four periods between the two equinoxes and two solstices) and affects temperature differences between those seasons. Variation in obliquity (nutation) tilts Earth's axis away from a line perpendicular to the orbital plane from 22.1° to 24.5° with periodicity of about forty-one thousand years. When the axis is more strongly tilted, the difference of annual insolation between the equator and the poles is smaller, but this increases the thermal differences between summer and winter, especially at high latitudes. Precession is a revolution of Earth's axis, completed in

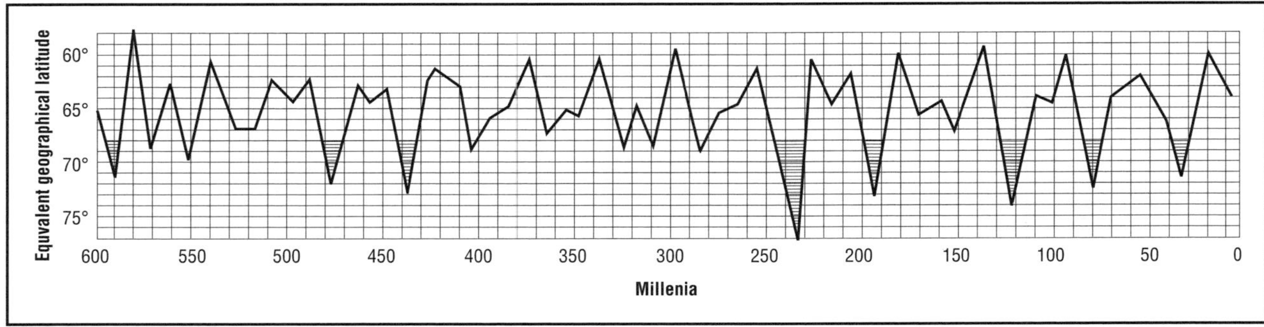

The first Milanković's Curve of Insolation, published in 1924.

about twenty-three thousand years, which, depending on eccentricity, cyclically varies the relative length of the seasons by slowly shifting the equinoctial points along the orbit. It is also visible as a secular circular moving of the celestial pole relative to the stars.

Milanković calculated how persistent changes of those parameters, taken together, modify insolation of the uppermost layer of the atmosphere in certain latitudes over the centuries. Considering ice ages, he concluded that the seasonal differences had a decisive role in the initiation of glaciations. To eliminate the everchanging differences of lengths and irradiation of astronomical seasons, Milanković introduced the concept of caloric half-years: caloric summer was the half-year when every day received more insolation than any day in the winter half. This solution not only enabled an exact mathematical description of the secular march of seasonal irradiation, but also of its most important effect—the secular displacement of the snow line.

The exact recalculations of the three orbital changes and the precise resolution of their climatic impact is the *punctum saliens* of Milanković's theory. First, he investigated and calculated how the seasonal insolation at 55°, 60°, and 65°—the belt most sensitive to changes in the temperature balance sheet—varied over the centuries. Later he redid those calculations with refined parameters. At Belgrade Observatory he initiated the redoing of Urbain-Jean-Joseph Leverrier's calculations of changes in Earth's eccentricity, obliquity, and precession for the last million years, using the most accurate data. Then he calculated the latitudinal insolations from –75° to +75° (for each 5°) and their change for each caloric season. Thereby he produced tabulations and charts of classical and permanent importance and published them in 1930.

Milanković deduced, by analyzing curves of insolation, that in the polar regions the effects of the variations in obliquity dominate over the other two cycles. In tropical regions the synergetic variations of eccentricity and precession, which change the length of seasons, are dominant. At middle latitudes, especially between 50° and 65°, all the three astronomical elements are equally influential.

While the astronomical part of the theory calculated the insolation reaching the upper layers of the atmosphere, the physical part is devoted to the relationship between the changing insolation and the temperatures of ground and atmosphere. It demonstrates mathematically how the Sun's rays pass through the atmosphere, reach the ground, and by warming it also heat the atmosphere, causing the diurnal and annual change of temperatures. Milanković was the very first who calculated temperatures of the upper atmospheric layers.

Milanković concluded that summer was more crucial for ice ages than winter. He formulated a mathematical relation between summer insolation and the altitude of the snowline, and determined how much increase in snow cover would be induced by a decrease in summer insolation (more precisely, insolation during the caloric half-year). Not only did ice cover more territory, it reflected heat, further cooling the summer. He also noted that insolation on the Northern Hemisphere might completely dominate Earth's climate, since two-thirds of the land area is located there. It is the ground that synchronizes the ice ages in both hemispheres, and the latitude 65° N is a region critical for the initiation of glaciers.

Challenges and Confirmations. After broad acceptance in the 1930s and 1940s, Milanković's theory was nearly abandoned in the next two decades. The objections came first from meteorologists who (again) claimed that insolation changes due to the variations of orbital elements were too small to perturb the climate system extensively. Then the paleontological samples collected on the land surface and dated by the new carbon-14 method showed a significant disagreement with the theory.

In 1955 Cesare Emiliani (1922–1995) noted in the *Journal of Geology* the general correspondence of Milanković's curves with historical fluctuations of $^{18}O/^{16}O$, confirming the main advantage of the canon of insolation: it provides predictions that can be tested. After Milanković's death, a crucial test was conducted by the international CLIMAP (Climate: Long-Range Investigation, Mapping, and Prediction) research program, which focused on the reconstruction of glacial climates by analyzing fossil evidence from ocean cores. Results published in 1976 by James Hays, John Imbrie, and Nicolas Shackleton showed that oxygen isotope data from deep-sea cores confirm the existence of the Milanković cycles. The CLIMAP evidence strongly supports his essential concept that orbital variations exert a significant influence on climate.

In 1988 the COHMAP (Cooperative Holocene Mapping Project) mapped out the patterns of global climate change over the past eighteen thousand years, demonstrating the central role of Milanković forcing, along with the response of the climate system. Further confirmation of the theory came from the SPECMAP (Spectral Mapping Project), which showed that the climate system appears to act in response to insolation forcing in each Milanković cycle. Whereas the reaction of the climate system seems mostly linear in the precession and nutation cycles, the climatic result of the eccentricity variations is nonlinear, with large Northern Hemisphere ice sheets providing a vital source of climatic inertia.

New insights raise a series of new questions that challenge Milanković's theory. There is geological evidence for the presence of nonorbital spectral peaks in the climate record. The detailed mechanisms involved in the transformation of orbit parameter variations into climate variations are so far unknown and consequently the response time between astronomical forcing and climate change cannot be accurately determined. Nevertheless, Milanković's theory can still be tested and it is frequently confirmed by making the "simplest possible" assumption, namely, that frequencies in the system input (orbital variations) appear linearly in the system output (climate variations). Many independent investigators appear to see clear evidence of such astronomical forcing, as well as evidence suggesting that the climate system responds nonlinearly to all Milanković frequencies.

All those problems confronting the canon of insolation do not impugn its validity as a method on which contemporary climatology is based. Milanković revived the moribund astronomical theory of climate and established a firm conjunction between it and the geosciences, linking the exact sciences (celestial mechanics, spherical astronomy, and mathematical physics) and descriptive sciences (geology, climatology, geography, oceanography, and glaciology). He set a reliable method for reconstruction and prediction of climate, which is basically still valid.

> The basis of all sciences involved in any theory of paleoclimates can be found in the Milanković Canon. Critically read, it will remain forever a milestone in climate science. It is owing to the careful work by Milanković that we may expect to start to understand how the earth system is responding to the astronomical forcing and how it might behave in the future. (Berger and Mesinger, 2000, p. 1617)

Varied Accomplishments. Milanković was also the author of the reformed Julian calendar, which was accepted in 1923 at the Panorthodox congress in Constantinople, but was never implemented. This calendar is more accurate than the Gregorian, and it is so attuned that the first deviation between the two would occur in 2800. It also suggests that the date of Easter should not be calculated from cycles of golden numbers and epacts (a system of numbers corresponding to the different length of the solar and the lunar year) any more, but determined by astronomical observations.

Milanković was intently interested in the historical evolution of the scientific fields he worked in, considering it fundamental for understanding of any current problem. He wrote textbooks on celestial mechanics, a history of astronomy, two histories of technics, and one novelized general history of science. His literary talent is mostly obvious in *Through Distant Worlds and Times,* a popular history of astronomy written in epistle form, which had several German and Serbian editions.

Milutin Milanković was a member of the Serbian Academy of Sciences, the Yugoslav Academy of Sciences and Arts in Zagreb, the German Academy of Natural Scientists Leopoldina, Halle, the Institute of Science, Literature and Arts, Venice, and other scientific associations. His name is given to a Moon crater (+170, +77), to a Mars crater (+147, +55), and to a small planet (1936GA). In 1993 the European Geophysical Society established a medal in his name.

BIBLIOGRAPHY

WORKS BY MILANKOVIĆ

"Theorie der Druckkurven." *Zeitschrift für Mathematik und Physik* 55, no. 1/2 (1907): 1–27.

"Prilog teoriji matematske klime" [On the mathematical theory of climate]. *Glas Srpske Kraljevske Akademije* (Belgrade) 87 (1912): 136–160.

"Über ein Problem der Wärmeleitung und dessen Anwendung auf die Theorie des solaren Klimas." *Zeitschrift für Mathematik und Physik* 62 (1913): 63–77.

Théorie mathématique des phénomènes thermiques produits par la radiation solaire. Paris: Gauthier-Villars et Cie, 1920.

With W. Köppen and A. Wegener. *Die Klimate der geologischen Vorzeit.* Berlin: Gebrüder Borntraeger, 1924. ("Curve of Insolation" published for the first time as Milanković's original contribution).

"Mathematische Klimalehre und Astronomische Theorie der Klimaschwankungen." In *Handbuch der Klimatologie*. Vol. 1, *Allgemeine Klimalehre*, edited by Wladimir Peter Köppen and Rudolf Geiger. Berlin: Gebrüder Borntraeger, 1930.

"Säkulare Polverlagerungen." In *Handbuch der Geophysik*, Bd 1, Lieferung 2, Abschnitt VII. Hrsg von Beno Gutenberg. Berlin: Gebrüder Borntraeger, 1933.

Durch ferne Welten und Zeiten: Briefe eines Weltallbummlers. Leipzig, Germany: Koehler und Amelang, 1936.

"Astronomische Mittel zur Erforschung der erdgeschichtlichen Klimate." In *Handbuch der Geophysik*. Vol. 9, edited by Beno Gutenberg. Berlin: Gebrüder Borntraeger, 1938.

"Kanon der Erdbestrahlung und seine Anwendung auf das Eiszeitenproblem" [Canon of insolation of Earth and its application to the problem of the ice ages]. Belgrade: Königlich serbischen Akademie, 1941. Translated as *Canon of Insolation and the Ice-Age Problem* by Israel Program for Scientific Translations. Published by the U.S. Department of Commerce and the National Science Foundation, 1969. Reprinted in 1998 by the Serbian Agency for Textbooks/ Alven Global. Japanese translation: *Kiko hendou no tenmongaku teki riron to hyouga jidai.* Translated by Kenji Kashiwaya et al. Tokyo: Koko Syoin, 1992. Serbian translation: "Kanon osunčavanja i njegova primena na problem ledenih doba." Translated by Milan Ćirić. Belgrade: Zavod za udžbenike, 1997.

Astronomska teorija klimatskih promena i njena primena u geofizici [Astronomical theory of climate change and its application in geophysics]. Belgrade: Naučna knjiga, 1948.

Uspomene, doživljaji, saznanja [Reminiscences, experiences, knowledge]. I–III. Belgrade: Srpska akademija nauka i umetnosti, Vol. I, 1979, Vol. II, 1952, Vol. III, 1957. Milanković's autobiography, with extensive explanations of his theory (over 900 pages).

OTHER SOURCES

Berger, André, and Fedor Mesinger. "Canon of Insolation." *Bulletin of the American Meteorological Society* 81 (2000): 1615–1618.

———, Fedor Mesinger, et al., eds. *Paleoclimate and the Earth Climate System. Proceedings of the Milutin Milanković Anniversary Symposium.* Belgrade: Serbian Academy of Science and Arts, 2005.

———, John Imbrie, James D. Hays, et al., eds. *Milankovitch and Climate: Understanding the Response to Astronomical Forcing.* 2 vols. Dordrecht, Netherlands: D. Reidel, 1984.

Emiliani, Cesare. "Pleistocene Temperatures." *Journal of Geology* 63 (1955): 538.

Hays, James D., John Imbrie, and Nicolas J. Shackleton. "Variations in the Earth's Orbit: Pacemaker of the Ice Ages." *Science* 194 (1976): 1121–1132.

Ibbeken, Hillert. *Orbit and Insolation: The Milankovitch Theory.* VHS videorecording by Institut für Geologie, Geophysik und Geoinformatik, Und Zentralinstitut für Audiovisuelle Medien, Freie Universität. Berlin, 1993.

Imbrie, John, and Katherine Palmer Imbrie. *Ice Ages: Solving the Mystery.* Short Hills, NJ: Enslow Publishers, 1979.

Indjic, Milica. "Bibliografija Milutina Milankovića" [Bibliography of Milutin Milanković]. Belgrade: Srpska akademija nauka i umetnosti, 1994. Basic text in Serbian, citations in respective languages.

Milanković, Vasko, ed. *Milutin Milanković: From His Autobiography.* Katlenburg-Lindau, Germany: European Geophysical Society, 1995. Excerpts from *Reminiscences, Experiences, Knowledge.*

Petrovic, Aleksandar. *Milutin Milanković and the Mathematical Theory of Climate Changes.* Belgrade: Serbian Society of History of Science, 2002. In English.

Aleksandar Petrovic

MILGRAM, STANLEY (*b.* New York, New York, 15 August 1933; *d.* New York, New York, 20 December 1984), *psychology, social psychology, social science.*

Milgram is generally regarded as one of the most important and controversial psychologists of the twentieth century largely because of his most famous work—a path-breaking series of experiments on obedience to authority. He also made pioneering contributions to cross-cultural research, the nature of social networks, and urban psychology. Historically, Milgram's obedience studies have overshadowed his other scientific contributions because of their troubling implications about human nature and because of the ethics of the experimental methods he used to obtain his findings.

Early Development and Education. Milgram was born in the Bronx, New York, on 15 August 1933, to Eastern European Jewish parents, Samuel and Adele, who had emigrated separately to the United States around the time of World War I. Samuel was a baker, and Adele assisted him in the store in addition to running their household.

Stanley attended the local elementary school, PS 77, and James Monroe High School. At Monroe he was placed in honors classes and graduated in only three years. He was a member of Arista, the honor society, and became editor of the school newspaper. He also worked on stagecraft for school productions, an experience he drew on later to help infuse his experiments with the dramatic elements that made them such credible and powerful experiences for his subjects.

He enrolled in Queens College and majored in political science with a minor in art. During the summer of 1953 he took a trip to Europe, taking a French language course at the Sorbonne, in Paris, and touring France,

Milgram

Spain, and Italy. The trip made him a lifelong Francophile and imbued him with an appreciation of the distinctive atmospheres of cities, a precursor of his later professional interest in urban psychology.

Graduate Education at Harvard. Although initially Milgram had planned to enter the foreign service corps, during his senior year he heard about the Department of Social Relations at Harvard University. Its unique interdisciplinary approach appealed to Milgram, who changed his plans and applied to the program with a goal of obtaining a PhD in social psychology. At first he was rejected because he had not taken any psychology courses at Queens. Undeterred by this setback, he took six different psychology courses at three different New York area colleges during the summer of 1954 to make up his deficit, enabling his acceptance as a special student in the fall.

At Harvard, Gordon Allport became his mentor; the two developed a lifelong friendship. Milgram also developed close relationships of mutual respect with Jerome Bruner and Roger Brown. However, the person who became his most important scientific influence—Solomon Asch—was not a regular member of the Harvard faculty. Asch had come to the department as a visiting lecturer during the 1955–1956 academic year, and Allport assigned Milgram to serve as his teaching and research assistant.

Asch had brought a Gestalt orientation to social psychology, and his research was characterized by a fusion of philosophic depth and an uncluttered style of research. Milgram's own accessible research style and his belief that "simplicity is the key to effective scientific inquiry" (1974, p. 13) had the imprint of Asch's influence.

Asch had become well known for his pioneering work on conformity using a laboratory paradigm that he invented. In his experiments, subjects were led to believe they were participating in a study of perceptual judgment. On each trial, the task of the subject, who was seated with six or seven other participants, was to indicate which one of a triad of vertical lines was equal in length to a fourth line. Each participant was to announce his match, in turn. All but one of the subjects were actually confederates who gave, unanimously, incorrect answers on specific "critical trials," and the lone naive subject was one of the last to give his answer. Would the subject yield to group pressure and also give an incorrect match, or would he maintain his independence and announce the correct answer?

Although there were wide variations among the subjects, on the average they yielded to the bogus majority on about one-third of the trials. Asch went on to conduct many different variations of his basic procedure, such as varying the size of the pressure group, increasing the difficulty of the task by reducing the differences among the three stimulus lines, and rupturing the unanimity of the bogus majority.

Hoping to emulate Asch in his professional career, Milgram would come up with a distinctive experimental paradigm and then "worry it to death," as Brown put it (unpublished interview with author, 23 June 1993) For his doctoral dissertation, he did a cross-national comparison of conforming tendencies in Norway and France, using a variation of the Asch procedure involving sound rather than visual stimuli. It was a highly ambitious study—even Allport, who invariably was supportive of Milgram's efforts, tried to dissuade him. First, in 1957–1958, he set up a lab and collected data in Oslo, and the following year duplicated the procedures near Paris. Overall, he found significantly more conformity in Norway than in France. Although rarely recognized as such, this was a pioneering piece of work—one of the first scientific studies of cross-national differences in behavior. It was also a personal milestone for Milgram. He now saw that he was capable of doing original research. His achievement also made him aim high in his future research career and not be willing to settle for the mundane.

In the fall of 1959, Milgram accepted an invitation from Asch—who was then a visiting member at the Institute of Advanced Study in Princeton—to help him edit a book on his conformity research, a book that was never published. Concurrently, Milgram was writing up his dissertation. Although the circumstances turned out to be less than ideal, he was able to deliver it to Allport by the required deadline and was awarded his PhD in June 1960.

Yale and the Obedience Experiments. While still with Asch in Princeton, on 3 May 1960, Milgram received a letter from Leonard Doob, a senior social psychologist in Yale's Department of Psychology, informing him of an opening and inviting him to visit if he was interested. The meeting with Doob resulted in an offer from Yale. Milgram accepted and he began at Yale in the fall of 1960 as an assistant professor. In December 1961 he married Alexandra (Sasha) Menkin. They had two children, Michele born in 1964 and Marc in 1967.

By the time he left Asch in June 1960, Milgram had already decided that he wanted to study obedience to authority. He conducted some pilot studies and applied for a grant from the National Science Foundation. As soon as the grant was approved, in May 1961, Milgram started working out the details of his planned experiments, which he conducted beginning in August of that year in Linsly-Chittenden Hall on Yale's Old Campus.

The basic laboratory procedure went as follows: The experimenter told the subject that the purpose of the experiment was to study the effects of punishment on learning, and that his job was to teach another subject (the

Shock Generator. *Stanley Milgram's shock generator.* FROM THE FILM *OBEDIENCE* © 1968 BY STANLEY MILGRAM, © RENEWED 1993 BY ALEXANDRA MILGRAM, AND DISTRIBUTED BY PENN STATE MEDIA SALES.

learner) to memorize a list of adjective-noun word pairs. The teacher sat in front of a shock machine with thirty lever switches arrayed horizontally on its front panel—each one corresponding to increasing shock voltages in 15-volt steps, beginning with 15 volts and ending with the 450-volt maximum. Whenever the learner—sitting in an adjacent room—made a mistake, the teacher had to give him a shock and, on each subsequent error, he had to increase the intensity of the shock, one step at a time. The learner reacted to the shocks with screams that became increasingly pitiful and desperate, until he finally fell silent and stopped giving answers. Actually, unbeknownst to the subject, the shock machine was a realistic-looking prop and no actual shocks were delivered to the learner, a confederate who only feigned his suffering. Milgram found that about two-thirds of the subjects were fully obedient to the experimental authority and continued to the maximum shock level.

During the course of the 1961–1962 academic year, Milgram conducted more than twenty different experimental variations to answer specific questions. Among the findings, the amount of "shock" given declined:

1. with decreasing distance between the subject and learner;
2. with increasing distance between experimenter and subject;
3. when the subject saw two other "subjects" defying the experimenter;
4. when the subject could choose the amount of shock to give in response to the learner's mistakes;
5. when the experimenter called a halt to the proceedings, even though the learner insisted that they continue.

Male and female subjects were equal in their degree of obedience—65 percent were fully obedient. Coincidentally, the obedience experiments partially overlapped the trial of Adolf Eichmann (which began 11 April 1961, in Jerusalem) for his role in the murder of six million Jews

Obedience experiment. *Subject in obedience experiment at shock generator.* FROM THE FILM *OBEDIENCE* © 1968 BY STANLEY MILGRAM, © RENEWED 1993 BY ALEXANDRA MILGRAM, AND DISTRIBUTED BY PENN STATE MEDIA SALES.

during the Holocaust. The Israeli government carried out his death sentence on 31 May 1962, four days after Milgram had run his last subject, presaging a more substantive connection that was to be made later between the obedience experiments and the behavior of the Nazis during World War II.

There are two important lessons to be drawn from the results of the obedience experiments. First is the extreme willingness of individuals to obey legitimate authority, even when the orders conflict with one's moral principles. Second is the causal power of the situation to override stable, personal beliefs and values. For example, obedience varied as a function of subject-learner distance even though the wrongfulness of hurting another person remained unchanged.

The enduring impact of the obedience experiments is manifested in two ways. First, it has altered some prevailing views of human nature. It has generally been assumed that there is a direct line between the kind of person an individual is and his or her actions. But the obedience experiments have shown that one need not be evil or aberrant to act inhumanely. While individuals would like to believe that, when confronted with a moral dilemma, they will act as their consciences dictate, Milgram's experiments have revealed that, under the weight of powerful social pressures, one's moral sense can readily be trumped.

The second enduring legacy of the obedience research is its impact on research ethics. Milgram had used deception and created an unusually stressful experience for his subjects, which they had not anticipated. The controversy stirred up by his research, together with a handful of other ethically questionable studies, such as the Tuskegee Syphilis Study, led to the formalization of principles for the protection of human research subjects by the U.S. government—their most visible manifestation being the requirement of screening and approval of research proposals by Institutional Review Boards (IRBs).

While still at Yale, after completion of the obedience experiments, Milgram devised the lost-letter technique as a way of measuring community attitudes. The technique involves "losing" letters addressed to different recipients in various locations, such as stores and sidewalks. The proportion of letters that end up being mailed serves as a behavioral indicator of attitudes. For example, in one study conducted in New Haven, Connecticut, Milgram found that only about a third as many letters addressed to Friends of the Nazi Party or Friends of the Communist Party were mailed than ones addressed to medical research associates or a private individual. Over the years, it has been the most frequently used unobtrusive measure of attitudes. It is a procedure that does not involve personal contact, and, as such, gave Milgram a much-needed respite from the intense, confrontational experience of the obedience experiments.

Return to Harvard. As he ended his first three years at Yale, Milgram was invited to join the Department of Social Relations at Harvard. While he could have continued at Yale, Milgram considered Harvard an "academic Eden," and he accepted a position there as an assistant professor in the fall of 1963.

At Harvard, Milgram focused on two areas of research. First was a continuation of his lost-letter technique. For example, in 1964, he used it to predict the outcome of the Johnson-Goldwater presidential contest. Second, he embarked on a totally new course of research—"the small world problem." Ithiel de Sola Pool, a political scientist at the Massachusetts Institute of Technology (MIT), and Manfred Kochen, a mathematician with International Business Machines (IBM), had developed a theoretical model that predicted that large social networks could be traversed by a relatively small chain of acquaintances, and Milgram decided to test it empirically with a procedure that he devised, "the small world method." In one study, he gave a folder to each of a group of randomly selected "starters" in Omaha, Nebraska, and told them to send it on to a particular stockbroker in Boston, by sending it on to close acquaintances who they thought would move it closer to the target. Only about 25 percent of the chains were completed. But, among those chains, the results were supportive of the small-world idea. On the average, it took about six intermediaries for a starter to reach the target.

According to Charles Kadushin, a social network researcher, by the late 1980s, the small-world method had become "one of the critical tools of network analysis" (1989, p. xxiv). Since the early 1990s, the broader public became aware of Milgram's discovery of the small-world phenomenon via a Broadway play titled "Six Degrees of Separation." More importantly, in 1998, two applied mathematicians at Cornell, Steven Strogatz and Duncan Watts, significantly expanded the domain of applicability of the small-world concept. They made the startling discovery that Milgram seems to have identified an underlying principle that is pervasive in the physical world, and not limited to social contacts. They found that the small-world effect—the remarkable ability of very large networks to be traversed in only a small number of steps—can be found in domains as wide-ranging as the electric power grid of the western United States and the neural pathways of nematode worms.

In the fall of 1966, Milgram came up for consideration for promotion and tenure by Harvard's Department of Social Relations. After a lengthy and contentious debate, the promotion and tenure committee reached a negative decision. Apparently, some members of the committee continued to be troubled by his obedience experiments and, according to his colleague, Roger Brown, ascribed to him "some of the properties of the experiment. That is, they thought he was sort of manipulative, or the mad doctor, or something of this sort. … They felt uneasy about him" (unpublished interview with author, 23 June, 1993).

Studying the Psychology of City Life. Being turned down by the place he considered "academic Eden" was a traumatic experience for Milgram. He was offered, and accepted, a position at the Graduate Center of the City University of New York (CUNY) to head their newly developing PhD program in social psychology in the fall of 1967. In the process, he went from a lecturer to a full professor—skipping the assistant and associate professor levels—at double his Harvard salary. Yet the fact that he did not get any offers from more prestigious universities gnawed at him, and he did not expect to stay at CUNY more than five years.

As it turned out, CUNY worked out much better than expected, and he remained there until his untimely death from a heart attack in 1984. Toward the end of his stay at Harvard, he had begun to develop an interest in the scientific study of cities. Now, city life became a central focus of his interests, and his belief that social psychology could be applied to urban issues became manifest both in the curriculum of the doctoral program he now headed and the kind of research that he and his students conducted. CUNY's doctoral program became the first social psychology program in the United States with an urban emphasis.

In 1970 Milgram published "The Experience of Living in Cities," in *Science*, which laid the foundation for the newly developing field of urban psychology. Besides presenting a number of innovative experiments, Milgram introduced the unifying concept of "overload" to help

Milgram

make sense of the various differences in behavior between city and small-town residents that he and his students and others had found. Borrowing from cybernetics, Milgram used the concept of overload to describe a system that is barraged by more input than it can process. Milgram argued that modifications in behavior engendered by urban living can be seen as representing the various ways that individuals tried to adapt to the sensory onslaught of city life.

At the suggestion of Harry From, a graduate student with a background as a filmmaker, in 1972 they collaborated on an award-winning film, "The City and the Self," based on Milgram's *Science* article. Milgram developed a passion for filmmaking and, between 1974 and 1976, he and From produced four other films on various topics in social psychology.

Among the studies generated by his interest in city psychology, three are especially noteworthy. First, he studied the mental maps of New Yorkers and Parisians, using methods that he invented—because, as he explained: "The image of the city is not just extra mental baggage; it is the necessary accompaniment to living in a complex and highly variegated environment. … People make many important decisions based on their conception of a city, rather than the reality of it" (1977, pp. 8, 89). and second, he conducted research on subway norms. Stimulated by his mother-in-law's complaint about riders not offering their seats to a gray-haired lady like her, he had his students approach seated subway passengers and ask them for their seats. They found, much to everyone's surprise, that 56 percent of the subjects gave up their seats, even without any justification for the request. Third, he identified a species of urban life, which he dubbed "familiar strangers"—persons one sees day after day and yet never interacts with. Milgram's students photographed clusters of commuters at a train station while waiting for their trains to Manhattan. When shown the photographs, on the average, commuters reported seeing four familiar strangers, while the average number of passengers they had spoken to was 1.5. Milgram believed that the tendency not to interact with familiar strangers was a form of adaptation to urban overload. These individuals are depersonalized and treated as part of the scenery, rather than as people with whom to engage.

Perhaps the most important experiment Milgram conducted while at CUNY investigated the antisocial effects of television. Its importance lies not so much in the findings, but in the methodology used. Over the course of a year during 1970 and 1971, funded by a quarter-million dollar grant from CBS's Office of Social Research, Milgram and a research associate, R. Lance Shotland, conducted a series of field experiments to study the negative effects of television viewing. Milgram was able to get CBS to produce a particular episode of their popular prime-time series "Medical Center," tailored to fit the needs of his experiment. Three different versions were produced, all with the identical story line, but differing in their endings: two of them depicted variations of an antisocial act, while the third ended in a prosocial act. Across a series of eight experiments, viewers saw one of the three versions of the episode and then a few days later were given the opportunity to carry out a destructive act similar to what was depicted in the antisocial versions. The results indicated that viewers of the antisocial versions were no more likely to act destructively than viewers of the prosocial version or those who watched another, thematically different episode from the series. What makes this study unique is that this was the first, and only, time a mass media researcher was able to get stimulus materials custom made for the specific needs of an experiment, and thereby achieve maximal control over the independent variable.

Defining Characteristics of Milgram's Approach. Although Milgram identified solidly with social psychology, he disagreed with its heavy emphasis on theory-driven research aimed at testing directional hypotheses. In contrast, Milgram's approach was phenomenon-centered and, as such, represents a continuation, through Asch, of the Gestalt tradition. At the same time, his boundless confidence in studying a wide range of social phenomena scientifically makes him supremely Lewinian. The main driving force behind most of Milgram's research was a relentless curiosity, rather than theory testing. Typically it was a quest to verify the existence of a phenomenon or regularity in behavior suggested by subjective experience, and, once established, to identify the factors that led to variations in the observed phenomenon. Hence his body of research encompassed a wide range of mostly unrelated topics.

Outcome. Yet, below surface appearances, one can find the following unifying commonalities that, in their totality, define Milgram's style of research: outcome measures that are observable, discrete, and dichotomous. Milgram was first and foremost an experimentalist who was able to study a wide variety of phenomena within the structural confines of the randomized experiment. He considered the use of the experimental method an essential feature of social psychology. But he was not dogmatic about this, because ultimately for Milgram the choice of method was dictated by the requirements of the behavior being studied, not vice versa. When the problem called for it, he readily used less powerful research methods. The unifying characteristic of Milgram's data-gathering techniques was in the nature of the target behaviors he studied. In most of his studies, the outcome measure was discrete and dichotomous: It was essentially a *yes* or *no* answer to the

Milgram

question of whether a given behavior occurred. Did New York City subway riders give up their seats when requested to? Were lost letters differing in the admirability of their targets mailed or not? This undoubtedly was what made much of Milgram's research so compelling. In contrast to the relativism and ambiguity inherent in many continuous measures (e.g., a point on a numerical scale), the discrete, observable acts comprising most of Milgram's findings lent them a quality of absoluteness, clarity, and conclusiveness that made their implications readily discernible to both lay and professional readers.

The Salience of Moral Issues. In descriptions of his studies, Milgram often saw the behavior under focus as representing the resolution of a conflict between two behavioral alternatives, one of which the person ought to have chosen according to moral, or at least normative, standards.

Clearly, of all of Milgram's work, the most heavily imbued with moral significance was his obedience research. In those studies Milgram confronted two moral issues, the first by design and the second largely (though not solely) in response to criticisms of the ethics of the experiments. The first moral issue was embedded in the conflict situation Milgram's subjects found themselves in—a conflict between obeying legitimate authority and following the dictates of one's conscience. The second moral issue raised by the obedience experiments had to do with Milgram's treatment of his subjects. Beginning with Diana Baumrind (1964), a number of writers have debated the ethics of placing subjects in the extremely stressful situation Milgram created and of deceiving them about the true purpose of the experiment. A moral perspective also pervaded many of Milgram's other writings. Thus, for example, he saw withdrawal from moral and social involvement with others as one of the consequences of the stimulus overload characteristic of urban life. Milgram even brought a moral viewpoint to phenomena one would not normally conceptualize in those terms. Thus, he saw the Asch group-pressure experiments as representing a "dilemma of truth versus conformity," one that the person had to resolve in a manner that was either "consistent with or in opposition to moral values" (1977, p. 92).

The Primacy of Situational Determinants. As already noted, Milgram was an experimentalist who was able to apply the experimental method to a wide variety of phenomena. Milgram was also an experimentalist in the sense that situational factors had primacy in his thinking as potential determinants of behavior. One of the strongest statements in this regard comes toward the end of Milgram's (1974) book:

> The disposition a person brings to the experiment is probably less important a cause of his behavior than most readers assume. For the social psychology of this century reveals a major lesson: often, it is not so much the kind of person a man is as the kind of situation in which he finds himself that determines how he will act. (p. 205)

Style, Not Just Substance. Milgram's writing was invariably lucid and readable, whether he was addressing fellow psychologists reading a journal report of one of his experiments or readers of a general-circulation magazine. A wry sense of humor peppered his work throughout his career. He was at his best when his humor turned to sarcasm, using it as a deadly weapon in scholarly combat. One critic of the obedience experiments argued that Milgram's subjects saw through the deception but pretended not to because they did not want to ruin the experiment. Milgram (1972) replied, "Orne's suggestion that the subjects only *feigned* sweating, trembling, and stuttering to please the experimenter is pathetically detached from reality, equivalent to the statement that hemophiliacs bleed to keep their physicians busy" (p. 140).

Milgram effectively communicated psychological knowledge to the broader public through his writings and interviews. As he did not shy away from appearing in mass-circulation magazines, he was able to reach a wide audience. For example, an excellent concise article about his obedience research appeared in *TV Guide* to coincide with the airing of *The Tenth Level*, a television drama based on the obedience experiments. Milgram had an appreciation for the journalist's craft, and he even edited a book consisting of newspaper and magazine articles on psychological topics meant for the introductory psychology course.

BIBLIOGRAPHY

WORKS BY MILGRAM

"Issues in the Study of Obedience: A Reply to Baumrind." *American Psychologist 19* (1964): 848–852.

"Some Conditions of Obedience and Disobedience to Authority." *Human Relations 18* (1965): 57–76. An early summary of many of the conditions in the obedience experiment, it won Milgram the annual Socio-Psychological Award for 1965 from the American Association for the Advancement of Science (AAAS).

"Interpreting Obedience: Error and Evidence (A Reply to Orne and Holland)." In *The Social Psychology of Psychological Research*, edited by Arthur G. Miller. New York: Free Press, 1972.

Obedience to Authority: An Experimental View. New York: Harper & Row, 1974. Milgram's most definitive and complete account of his obedience research, together with a less than satisfactory attempt at theorizing about his findings, it was a finalist in the National Book Awards and has been translated into eleven languages.

The Individual in a Social World: Essays and Experiments. Reading, MA: Addison-Wesley, 1977. The most complete collection of Milgram's writings, with connecting narrative added by him. A second edition, appearing posthumously in 1992, was edited by former students John Sabini and Maury Silver and contains articles written after the first edition.

OTHER SOURCES

Blass, Thomas. "Understanding Behavior in the Milgram Obedience Experiment: The Role of Personality, Situations, and Their Interactions." *Journal of Personality and Social Psychology* 60 (1991): 398–413. The most complete literature review of the obedience paradigm. Although most of it is accessible to a broad readership, some sections require a background in the social sciences.

———. *The Man Who Shocked the World: The Life and Legacy of Stanley Milgram.* New York: Basic, 2004. The first and to date only comprehensive biography of Milgram. Highly readable, it was named one of the best science books of the year by *Discover* magazine.

———. "Stanley Milgram.com." Informational Web site on Milgram. Available from http://www.stanleymilgram.com.

Kadushin, Charles. "The Small World Method and Other Innovations in Experimental Social Psychology." In *The Small World*, edited by Manfred Kochen. Norwood, NJ: Ablex, 1989.

Miller, Arthur G. *The Obedience Experiments: A Case Study of Controversy in Social Science.* New York: Praeger, 1986. A thoughtful and highly readable examination of the obedience experiments, emphasizing the controversies surrounding them.

Thomas Blass

MILL, JOHN STUART

(*b.* London, England, 20 May 1806; *d.* Avignon, France, 8 May 1873), *philosophy, economics.* For the original article on Mill see *DSB*, vol. 9.

Mill's most important contribution to science was to provide an inductive methodology for it. He did so in his *System of Logic*, particularly in books three to five, where he defines induction as "the process by which we conclude that what is true of certain individuals of a class is true of the whole class, or that what is true at certain times will be true in similar circumstances at all times" (1843, p. 188). Mill believed that such inferences provide a crucial step in scientific inquiry. In typical scientific cases involving several hypotheses and various computations, Mill advocated what he called the deductive method, consisting of three steps: first, a set of inductions to the laws involved; second, ratiocination or calculation, involving combining the laws together with specific initial conditions so as to generate predictions; and third, verification of these predictions by observation and experiment.

Mill's view of scientific method has had many severe critics, including William Whewell (1794–1866) and Charles Sanders Peirce (1839–1914) in the nineteenth century, and many philosophers of science in the twentieth century. Some claim that Mill was erroneously assuming a fallacious principle of induction by simple enumeration, according to which whenever all observed A's have been B it is legitimate to infer that all A's are B. Mill, however, was making no such assumption. He was simply offering a definition of induction or inductive generalization while allowing that some inductions are justified whereas others are not. Indeed, he devotes an entire section to when inductive generalizations are fallacious. His view is that the question is an empirical one, the answer to which varies depending on the kinds of instances and their properties. People may need only one observed instance of a chemical fact about a substance to validly generalize to all instances of that substance, whereas many observed instances of black crows are required to generalize about all crows. This is due to the empirical fact that instances of chemical properties of substances tend to be uniform, whereas bird coloration, even in the same species, tends not to be.

A related criticism is that Mill's inductive philosophy ignores the idea of severely testing a hypothesis; for example, it fails to consider how the sample from which the induction was made was generated. But again this is a vast oversimplication. Mill emphasizes that the generalizations of concern to science are causal laws, and, in one of the most famous sections of his work, he offers "four methods of experimental inquiry" for determining causes. Mill writes:

> When a fact has been observed a certain number of times to be true, and is not in any instance known to be false; if we at once affirm that fact as an universal truth or law of nature, without ever testing it by any of the four methods of induction, or deducing it from other known laws, we shall in general err grossly. (p. 373)

More generally, for Mill whether an inductive generalization from "these A's are B" to "all A's are B" is justified depends on a variety of empirical factors, including how the A's were selected.

Some critics claim that Mill trivializes the scientific enterprise by restricting inductions to generalizations from facts ascertainable simply by opening one's eyes and looking (for example, the fact that these crows are black); and that in so doing he did not allow inferences to more typical theoretical scientific conclusions. Again, this is an oversimplication. What Mill required is that inductions be made from known facts and that the latter be

Mill

John Stuart Mill. *John Stuart Mill, circa 1870.* HULTON ARCHIVE/GETTY IMAGES.

established by observation and experiment (or from previously established inductions). But his view of what counts as established by observation and experiment is quite broad. He cites examples of inductions in astronomy and physics from empirically established facts about the magnitudes of particular planets in the Solar System, their mutual distances, the shape of the Earth and its rotation, and gravitational forces between the Sun and the planets. Mill did reject the claim of many physicists of his day that the wave theory of light had been empirically established. He did so not because light waves cannot be seen, but on the ground that no legitimate induction had yet been made to the existence of the vibrating luminiferous ether, though he allows that such an inference might be possible in the future from the experimental establishment of other facts.

Another major criticism, offered particularly by advocates of a hypothetico-deductive (H-D) account of science, is that Mill's first step in his deductive method, the inductions to the laws, is not needed in science. Some, following Karl Popper (1902–1994), say that such a step is illegitimate, since, as David Hume (1711–1776) argued, inductive generalizations are never justified. For the hypothetico-deductivist, the scientist begins not by inductively inferring a hypothesis or law, but by making a guess or conjecture. Following this, H-D theorists say, agreeing with Mill, there is ratiocination and verification of predictions. If the predictions turn out to be true, then some H-D theorists will conclude that the hypothesis is probably true, while others (following Popper) will reject this conclusion and say that we can conclude only that the hypothesis has not been shown to be false.

Mill rejected both ideas. From the fact that our hypotheses yield predictions that turn out to be true, we cannot conclude that our hypotheses are probably true, because of the competing hypotheses objection: there may well be hypotheses incompatible with ours which yield the same successful predictions. This can be so, Mill argues against Whewell, even if the predictions are novel and even if the system of hypotheses is simple and coherent. By contrast, from our successful predictions, if we simply conclude (with Popper) that our hypotheses have not been shown to be false, we are not satisfying one of the fundamental aims of science, which Mill regards as "discovering and proving general propositions" (p. 186). Only by including the inductive step, Mill insists, can one avoid the competing hypothesis objection and infer the probable truth of the hypotheses.

Finally, most critics have a field day with Mill's principle of the uniformity of nature, which he claims warrants inductions, namely that "what happens once will, under a sufficient degree of similarity of circumstances, happen again … as often as the same circumstances recur." Critics regard this as an unnecessary, unjustified, and vague assumption. Mill's discussion of this principle is admittedly somewhat confusing. But perhaps a charitable if plausible interpretation is this: Instead of asserting boldly but vaguely that nature is uniform, Mill is claiming less boldly and less vaguely that there are uniformities in nature, that is, there are general laws governing various types of phenomena. This is an empirical claim. Some of these laws are initially arrived at inductively, without presupposing any particular laws or even that there are laws of nature. These can then be used to strengthen inductive inferences to the existence of other laws, which are inductively arrived at. For example, Newton used the inductively inferred fact that the motions of the moons of Jupiter are governed by a central inverse-square force exerted by Jupiter on those moons to strengthen the inductive inference that a central inverse-square force is exerted by Saturn on its moons to produce their similar motions.

SUPPLEMENTARY BIBLIOGRAPHY

WORKS BY MILL

A System of Logic: Ratiocinative and Inductive. London: Longmans, 1843 (1959).

OTHER SOURCES

Achinstein, Peter. *Particles and Waves: Historical Essays in the Philosophy of Science.* New York: Oxford University Press, 1991.

Peirce, Charles S. *Collected Papers of Charles Sanders Peirce.* Edited by Charles Hartshorne and Paul Weiss. Cambridge, MA: Belknap Press of Harvard University Press, 1960–1966.

Popper, Karl R. *The Logic of Scientific Discovery.* New York: Basic, 1959.

Skorupski, John. *John Stuart Mill.* London: Routledge, 1989.

Snyder, Laura J. *Reforming Philosophy: A Victorian Debate on Science and Society.* Chicago: University of Chicago Press, 2006.

Whewell, William. *The Philosophy of the Inductive Sciences, Founded upon Their History.* 2nd ed. 2 vols. London: Parker, 1847.

Peter Achinstein

MILLER, NEAL ELGAR

(*b.* Milwaukee, Wisconsin, 3 August 1909; *d.* Hamden, Connecticut, 23 March 2002); *learning, motivation, psychotherapy, hypothalamus, biofeedback, behavioral medicine.*

The newsletter of the American Psychology Association (APA) has ranked Miller among the ten most eminent psychologists of the twentieth century. Highly influential as a learning theorist, neuroscientist, science statesman, educator, and, above all, a consummate experimentalist, Miller authored eight books and more than 276 articles.

The great variety of areas in which Miller made important conceptual and research contributions mainly concerned reward and motivation mechanisms: 1) underlying thought processes and behaviors relevant to problem solving in psychotherapy, 2) as mediated by the nervous system, and 3) involved in learning control over *voluntary* (conscious) skeletal-muscle and *autonomic* (normally unconscious) internal-organ response systems for minimizing stress, treating disease, and promoting health. Furthermore, his career shows psychology's evolution from a largely theory-driven but relatively data-impoverished experimental discipline in the 1930s to one that in the early twenty-first century integrates a vast body of clinical, social, and physiological knowledge.

Promising Early Years. Miller was the only child of Irving E. and Lily Rose Miller. His father obtained his PhD at the University of Chicago, where he studied with John Dewey and James Rowland Angell (later president of Yale University), and after several teaching positions elsewhere became professor of educational psychology at what later became Western Washington State College in Bellingham. His son Neal was a gifted child and avid reader. He gave his father credit for surreptitiously guiding his education by bringing home books and articles and leaving them lying casually about. After Miller read them, he noticed they disappeared to be replaced by others.

He earned his bachelor's degree in 1931 at the University of Washington, where he had a major learning theorist, Edwin R. Guthrie, as a teacher. Only in his senior year did he decide on psychology as a career because one could be near its frontier and get into research without first having to go through so much specialized work and also because it combined his interests in writing, people, and science in general. He worked with the famed IQ researcher Louis M. Terman at Stanford University, and obtained his master's degree there in 1932. But beforehand, he took advanced experimental psychology with Walter R. Miles and, because of his proficiency in physics and chemistry, helped Miles to put all the apparatuses in the Stanford Laboratory in good working order. Therefore, when Miles was invited to join the psychology faculty at Yale, he took Miller with him for doctoral work.

Laws of Learning and Foresight: Seeking a Unified Theory. At Yale, Miller came under the influence of Clark L. Hull, the most prominent learning theorist of his time. Hull's program aimed at showing how the principles of classical conditioning, discovered in Pavlov's lab, could be applied to understanding Edward Thorndike's trial-and-error learning, human verbal learning, and higher mental processes such as purposeful, goal-oriented, and foresightful behavior, now described as cognitive. For example, in 1935, in his PhD dissertation Miller demonstrated that, by using the letter *T* as the critical cue (stimulus) predicting a shock and the number *4* as the neutral one predicting no shock, a learned change in the electrical conductivity of a person's skin—now elicited by the critical cue but not by the neutral one—could be transferred from the cues' overt presentations to the person's merely thinking about them. From this emerged the idea that the mental acts of thinking, remembering, and imagining are themselves responses that can then function as cues (*response-produced cues*) to which other responses can be made and are subject to the same laws of learning as are external responses and cues. These mental responses, unconstrained by the real-time sequencing of cues in the physical world, permit the playback of events in reverse of their actual happenings. Thereby, one can work backward in one's mind's eye from a hoped-for goal along a route that better illuminates how to reach it than groping blindly forward from the start. It is such use of response-produced cues that Miller identified as the basis for much foresightful behavior in problem solving.

Extending the Quest to Freudian and Social Phenomena. As a result of an insight Miller had about the similarity between Freud's conception of repression and Pavlov's conception of inhibition, he resolved to extend Hull's program to an examination of Freudian theory and practice in terms of the laws of learning. Accordingly, he obtained a postdoctoral fellowship to study in Vienna at Freud's Psychoanalytic Institute, where he underwent a didactic analysis with Heinz Hartmann. He long regretted he had turned down at least one analytic session with the great Freud himself because an hourly fee of $20 seemed more than he could afford.

In 1936 Miller returned to Yale as instructor in psychology and research assistant psychologist in the multidisciplinary Institute of Human Relations. Observing a dominant male monkey self-mutilate when prohibited from attacking a competitor given his harem, Miller thought of the Freudian concept of aggression-turned-inward. The result, in 1939, was his book, *Frustration and Aggression*, coauthored, among others, with the sociologist John Dollard. Its major hypothesis, as later reformulated in the journal *Psychological Review*, claimed that when a segment of society is frustrated from attaining its goals it tends—depending on what avenues are open or closed for expressing that frustration—to relieve it as angry persecutions against an innocent, less powerful segment. Examples included Miller's European encounters with anti-Semitism inflamed by the still-lingering economic privations from reparations required of Germany after World War I.

Hull originally hypothesized that a response is *reinforced* (strengthened) if immediately followed by a reduction in a need. However, the assumption was that all needs drive (motivate) responses to reduce them. But some needs cannot do so because they cannot be detected (for example, the need to escape carbon monoxide). Thus, in *Frustration and Aggression*, Hull's hypothesis was restated by Hobart Mowrer and Miller as the *drive-reduction hypothesis*, which now dealt only with detected needs, henceforth, defined as *drives*. In its strong form, the drive-reduction hypothesis asserts that the only events that can act as reinforcers of a response are those that immediately follow it and are themselves soon followed by a reduction in the drive motivating it or are highly associated with that drive's later reduction. Assessing this strong form's validity was the concern of much of Miller's later research.

While testing in rats the Freudian idea of reaction formation, Miller noted the following: Hungry rats trained to go down a short alley for food and then given an electric shock at the goal tended on subsequent trials to approach part way and then stop, stopping further away the stronger the shock had been. From such observations emerged Miller's theoretical-experimental analyses of *approach-avoidance conflict behavior*. Published as "Experimental Studies of Conflict Behavior," in 1944, these stated that if a goal is something an organism both wants and fears, there is an approach tendency to it, called an approach gradient, that grows stronger the nearer one gets to it but there is also an avoidance gradient that does the same. However, the avoidance gradient increases more rapidly with nearness than does the approach. The gradients often will cross each other—at that intersection the organism's approach will stop. But just how close to the goal that will be depends on the relative strengths of the approach gradient versus the avoidance one.

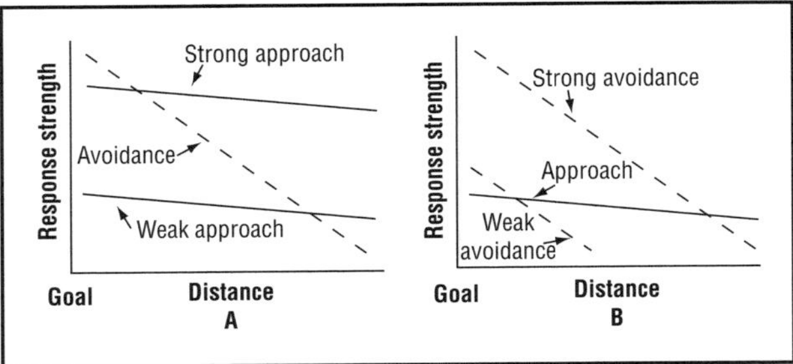

Figure 1. *Effects of Changes in Strength of Approach and Avoidance. Diagram A demonstrates that with an increase in the strength of approach tendencies, the intersection of approach with avoidance is not only moved nearer to the goal but also occurs at a higher point on the avoidance gradient. Diagram B demonstrates that decreasing the strength of avoidance increases the height of the point of intersection. Thus, in both cases, even though the goal in conflict is more closely approached, the amount of anxiety actually aroused at these intersections will be greater, a seeming paradox that accords with Freud.*

In 1939 Mowrer hypothesized that any fear—or anxiety, as it is called when its source is vague or unconscious—that is induced by a noxious situation is then acquired by the cues associated with that situation. Thus, the fear subsequently can be induced by those cues alone and motivate responding to them. Most importantly, a reduction of this acquired fear by escaping or avoiding those cues will reinforce any specific response doing so. Miller rigorously tested this hypothesis of fear as an acquirable—that is, learnable—drive by first shocking rats in the white side of a two-compartment box until they learned to run rapidly through a door into the black side to escape shock. Afterward, when put in the white side with the door closed but without shock administered, they defecated and showed other signs of having learned to fear the cues there to which shock had become associated. If, by trial and error, they then rotated a small wheel, which opened the door and allowed them to escape the white side's cues and, thus, the fear itself, they quickly learned to rotate the wheel for escape on subsequent nonshock trials. This confirmed Mowrer's hypothesis.

Miller

Principles of Learning in the Acquisition of Social Behavior. In 1941, the year Miller became an associate professor, he and Dollard wrote another book, *Social Learning and Imitation,* to show how a wide range of human behavior can be understood by knowing a few important principles of learning plus the social-condition contexts in which the learning takes place. In the book they listed four fundamentals necessary for instrumental learning, that is, for the remembering of which behaviors—guided by what signposts—have proven, for future reference, to be instruments of success in achieving one's goals:

1. DRIVE (or Motivation); a person must want something. A drive may be innate, as with hunger, or it may be learned, as with fear or the desire for money.
2. CUE (or Stimulus); a person must notice something. A cue may be response-produced, as with the thought of the letter *T* in the experiment already described.
3. RESPONSE; a person must do something. A response may be an overt act or a central nervous system event, such as a thought, a perception, or paying attention.
4. REWARD (or Reinforcement); a person must get something that is wanted. A reward following a response to a cue strengthens the tendency for the cue subsequently to elicit the response. A reward may be a learned one, such as getting money. Pain is a stimulus that elicits fear, and a reduction in pain or fear strengthens (rewards) any response immediately followed by that reduction.

An Interruption: Contributions in the War Years. In World War II, Miller served in the U.S. Army Air Corp (1942–1946). As a captain, he helped develop tests to select cadets likely to succeed in pilot training. He also initiated a study of factors contributing to fear and courage in combat. After being promoted to major, he helped identify behavioral and perceptual areas where improvements could be made in pilot training and in hitting targets via fixed gunnery. John C. Flanagan, one of his Army Air Corps colleagues, years later commented that Miller also instituted a pilot flight-check evaluation list "which provided the basis for today's procedures, making my flights on commercial airlines much more pleasant and giving me more confidence that the airline pilots will do the right things (Flanagan to Miller, 3 September 1980, unpublished letter).

Retrospectively, in 1987, Miller wrote that his program's success resulted from three factors: (1) finding something that the Air Force needed and that psychologists could deliver—initially, selection of personnel, (2) delivering it, and (3) then providing data proving it had been delivered. These wisdoms he adapted to achieving success in the many other missions for which he later served as a statesman in psychology and other behavioral sciences.

Learned Basis of Freudian Phenomena Revisited. When the war ended in 1946, Miller returned to Yale, where he attained tenure in 1947. He married Marion Edwards—a social worker there—in 1948. He was awarded full professorship in 1950 and appointed the first recipient of the James Rowland Angell Chair of Psychology in 1952. Again he collaborated with Dollard, taking psychoanalysis as a point of departure for analyzing psychotherapy as learning. As part of that effort Miller published an article, *Theory and Experiment Relating Psychoanalytic Displacement to Stimulus-Response Generalization,* in which, harkening back to his "Experimental Studies of Conflict Behavior," he posited the following: When the approach to a stimulus is inhibited by conflict with an avoidance of that same stimulus, responses tend to displace to other stimuli that are still similar enough to motivate the prospect of a successful approach but are dissimilar enough to minimize the interfering avoidance. For example, given the Freudian Oedipal conflicts between a young son's erotic love of his mother and retaliatory fear of his father, one can understand the displacement implied in the old vaudeville song, "I want a girl just like the girl [but not the same one, God forbid] that married dear old dad." This and other predictions were borne out by three other studies on displacement, all in 1952.

In 1950 appeared another Miller book with Dollard, *Personality and Psychotherapy: An Analysis in Terms of Learning, Thinking, and Culture.* It was immensely influential in training the first post–World War II generation of clinical psychologists in the treatment of the neuroses and was, for years, widely used as a text in learning theory. It paid special attention to how in therapy the appropriate use of response-produced cues, particularly verbal ones, can facilitate generalizations between likenesses that should be perceived in one's life but maladaptively are not and distinctions between differences that, likewise, should be perceived but, again, are not.

While writing *Personality and Psychotherapy,* Dollard and Miller submitted a proposal, encouraged by the Ford Foundation, to study coping behavior in normal people. But the foundation responded that, because of a policy change, it would take more than a year to decide whether to fund studies in that area. This unendurable delay forced the two researchers apart to formulate separate projects to support themselves. From the National Institute of Mental Health, Dollard found funding for the analysis of

Fat rat. *A rat whose ventromedial nucleus of its hypothalamus has been destroyed causing it to ravenously eat until it has gained many times its normal weight. Note, the pointer on the scale does not indicate that the rat weighs 80 grams but rather 1080 grams.* **PHOTOGRAPH BY J. A. F. STEVENSON; SUPPLIED BY THE INTELLECTUAL ESTATE OF NEAL E. MILLER; COURTESY OF EDGAR COONS.**

psychotherapeutic interviews. From the same source, Miller found funding for studies of the mechanisms of reinforcement.

Into the Gut and the Brain. Around 1950–1952, Miller started turning to physiological interventions because they offered unique opportunities to test the strong form of the drive-reduction hypothesis of reinforcement against competing possibilities. For example, instead of the reinforcing value of food for a hungry animal residing in the food's ability to reduce hunger, might it instead be either the pleasures of taste or of the swallowing of the food that is reinforcing? But, if one could reward behavior by reducing hunger while bypassing both taste and swallowing, that would clearly support the drive-reduction hypothesis. Indeed, delivery of food to a hungry rat via a tube directly into its stomach rewarded the learning of correct choices in a T-maze for that delivery. This supported the drive-reduction hypothesis of reward but did not discount that taste and swallowing could also be rewarding.

A preliminary step to yet another plan for testing the drive-reduction hypothesis was to lesion (destroy) the ventromedial nucleus in the hypothalamus of a rat's brain, which then causes overeating and obesity. If this overeating had all the aspects of normal hunger, Miller could then proceed to the test proper. However, contrary to hunger motivation, these lesioned rats, while eating a larger amount of highly palatable foods than normal rats, worked less hard for food and were less tolerant of less palatable foods. This result spoiled his plan but taught

Miller

him the importance of taking a variety of measures before inferring the nature of an underlying state—a lesson which he in 1961 strongly communicated in print as a cautionary tale for psychologists working in the brain.

The salience of the brain approach was heightened by two dramatic findings in the mid-1950s. One was the discovery by James Olds and Peter Milner of sites in the lateral hypothalamus that rats find rewarding to self-stimulate with volleys of brief electrical pulses by pressing a lever. The other was a reverse discovery by Jose Delgado, Warren Roberts, and Miller of sites where electrical stimulation would motivate cats to learn a response to escape or avoid the stimulation. But it was puzzling that at some sites cats would learn a response to terminate stimulation but not a response to avoid it—an observation leading to the discovery of the reward-escape effect in which Gordon Bower was involved. Implanted rats showing this effect cycled repeatedly between pressing a lever to turn on the stimulation and rotating a wheel to turn it off. In 1957 Miller seized this opportunity for an unusual test of some drugs. He showed that methamphetamine enhanced and chlorpromazine reduced the rewarding aspects of the cycle while leaving the punishing aspects unaffected. This was a first evidence of what later was recognized as the involvement of the neurotransmitter dopamine in promoting reward. Miller presented these data and others with Herbert Barry to drug companies to advertise the potential benefits of behaviorally evaluating pharmacological agents. With his encouragement, this approach was to become the field of behavioral psychopharmacology.

Another advantage of implanting electrodes in the lateral hypothalamus was to search there in rats for where W. R. Hess in cats had found that stimulation could induce them to eat. But as Miller much later reported in his autobiographical article, "Behavior to the Brain to Health," the search took two years before yielding success. Edgar Coons discovered the site where rats, even thoroughly satiated, would eat ravenously while the current was on but stop immediately when it was turned off. Behavioral tests confirmed that the electrically elicited eating had all the earmarks of normally motivated hunger. Then why, contrary to the drive-reduction hypothesis, would these animals not press a lever to turn the hunger off but would press to turn it on? Miller noted in a *Federation Proceedings* article that Coons had found that amphetamine raises the threshold required to elicit feeding and lowers that required to sustain self-stimulation, showing that a single system does not subserve both self-stimulation and feeding. Also Coons later found that, at the lowest current required to elicit eating, the rat would NOT press a lever for it unless food was available to eat while the current was on—just as the drive-reduction hypothesis would predict.

The phenomenon of stimulation-elicited hunger lent itself to yet another question. Was hunger a learnable drive like fear? If so, would not a satiated animal then eat in the presence of a cue to which the experience of being hungry had in the past been closely associated? Other attempts with Arlo K. Myers to demonstrate such learning had proved a failure, but that could be because the slowness of onsets and offsets of normal hunger attenuated its association with the cue too much. The rapidity, however, with which stimulation-elicited hunger could be turned on whenever a designated cue was presented made for a much better test. However, as Miller reported in 1964, unstimulated eating in satiated animals was never observed to occur in the presence of the cue, even after numerous trials of pairing stimulation-elicited eating with that cue.

Major Recognitions and High Public Service. By 1962 his growing reputation and impact as a scientist was such that Miller was asked to chair a panel that made a published report to the President's Science Advisory Committee on the needs of the behavioral sciences and how to meet them. It was a report over which he said he "sweated blood." In further recognition of this impact, Miller was extended in 1964 the country's highest scientific award, the National Medal of Science, handed to him in person by President Johnson. The citation accompanying it reads, "For sustained and imaginative research on principles of learning and motivation and illuminating behavioral analysis of the effects of direct electrical stimulation of the brain."

At the time Miller moved to Rockefeller University in 1966 a great urgency was being felt by the many disparate disciplines conducting research on the nervous system that some kind of coordinating network be set up, as detailed in a 1983 oral history interview with Miller sponsored by the Brain Research Institute of UCLA. By 1969, while Miller was chair of the Committee on Brain Science within the National Research Council, this urgency had become a clear mandate. "Like a crystal dropped into a supersaturated solution," as Miller characterized it, a "committee motion" proceeded quickly to the action of forming the Society for Neuroscience, with a membership of fifty thousand in the early twenty-first century. Miller, as always, exercised his uncanny ability to see to the heart of what needed to be done in organizations as well as in research. Unasked, he took the initiative to secure from the Sloan Foundation a grant of $20,000 to help cover the start-up costs of forming the society: legal fees of incorporation, membership recruiting, and public relations for educating legislators and the public as to the missions of the society. As a result, Miller is considered a key founding member. At the Society for Neuroscience's first meeting in 1970, he was voted president elect. It constituted for him one of the pinnacles of his career, along with being elected to the National Academy of Science in 1958, holding the office of APA president in 1960–1961, and receiving the National Medal of Science.

Learnable Voluntary Control of Autonomic Functions? In 1957 W. H. Gantt's translation of K. M. Bykov's book, *The Cerebral Cortex and the Internal Organs*, reported that autonomic responses in a wide variety of internal organ (*visceral*) systems, when elicited by their innately triggering stimuli, can then become elicitable by other stimuli that routinely closely precede and, thus, strongly predict these triggers. The well-known Pavlovian prototype for this classical conditioning is the learning of a dog to anticipatively salivate to the sound of a tone that he has come to associate as being followed immediately by meat powder to which he automatically salivates. The book's publication stimulated Miller to follow up on a long-standing hunch first recorded in print in 1951. He had entertained the possibility, against popular opinion, that autonomic responses in visceral motor systems are not limited to becoming learned reactions to stimuli but, if properly rewarded, can be trained—like ordinary "voluntary" responses—to become "intended" behaviors to obtain those rewards. For example, if one could learn how to consciously control internal body processes, the medical benefits would be enormous, and success would fulfill Hull's and his overarching hope to show an underlying relatedness of all laws of learning, spanning across voluntary, cognitive, and—now—autonomic domains of behavior.

Indeed, Alfredo Carmona with Miller showed in 1967 that thirsty dogs were able to increase or to decrease their autonomic response of salivation in order to obtain water rewards but, puzzlingly, displayed different postures during increases compared to decreases. Maybe just the postures were learned but somehow triggered the salivations. To rule this out, rats were treated with curare, which completely paralyzes the voluntary muscle system but leaves the autonomically controlled visceral muscle system unaffected. Then, the autonomic response of increasing (or, alternately, decreasing) the rats' heart rates was designated the specific response basis for their obtaining very rewarding brain stimulation.

Just as predicted, and reported in two companion articles to the Carmona study, the autonomic changes in heart-rate responding required for rewards did seem dramatically to occur. Over many studies from 1965 to 1972, even the general public, vis-à-vis *The New Yorker* and other media, became aware of the medical benefits this promised. But then Miller and Barry Dworkin in his laboratory began finding that these results mysteriously diminished until they could no longer be replicated even after repeated and varied attempts. When finally convinced of failure, Miller, though heartbroken, courageously took great pains to publicize it widely.

Despite disappointments in this line of research, it led to advances in technology to measure otherwise impossible-to-detect subtle changes in heart rate and other physiological responses. After finding that paralyzed rats failed to learn autonomic control, Miller shifted this technology to seeing whether people who had been paralyzed by gunshot wounds that severed their spinal cords could gain that control. They differed from the rats in being better candidates in terms of Miller and Dollard's four fundamentals necessary for effective instrumental learning: These patients had a high drive to try gaining control because their blood pressure was so low that whenever they sat or stood up they fainted. Unlike the rats, they were shown their own amplified heart rate and blood pressure readings, thus providing them biofeedback informational cues about their own performance, as Miller was invited to report in 1973. To this biofeedback information, the response they initially reported using—to try to change their readings—was to think emotional, often sexy, thoughts to which the desired blood pressure changes are normally reflexly connected. As these paralyzed patients became successful, they were gradually able to command these changes "directly." Whenever there was a desired response, even if too small an increment initially to be clinically relevant, the mere detectable fact of it was a reward, given the paralytics' high achievement motivation. But the summing of such increments mounted to clinically significant levels, and as they did, the rewards became enormous because not only could the paralytics now sit up without fainting but, as a result, they could now also attend plays and ball games. Nevertheless, how the patients achieved voluntary control of blood pressure via the autonomic nervous system was surprising; with a severed spinal cord the usual route of elevating blood pressure via the sympathetic component of the autonomic nervous system is also cut off. Parasympathetic (vagal) or blood-borne humoral factors are suspected or perhaps some subtle respiratory mediation still surviving paralysis, as reported in 1976 regarding vasomotor responses.

This and other studies using biofeedback also convincingly suggested the ability to bring autonomic responses under voluntary control, whether directly or indirectly. And as Miller loved to point out, toilet training, particularly the learning of control over the autonomic bladder sphincters, is a well-known—and rewarded—universal fact of life. Certainly, by 1985 the application of biofeedback methodology promoted by Miller and his associates had proved highly beneficial medically in treating a wide variety of problems, such as idiopathic scoliosis, enuresis, and migraine, problems involving both voluntary and autonomic response systems.

From the mid-1970s until a few years before his death in 2002, Miller's inquiries into biofeedback and learned behavior took on a new emphasis, that of their use to maintain homeostasis and minimize stress. This emphasis contributed substantially to the establishment not only of biofeedback as a discipline but also the fields of behavioral medicine and health psychology, all of which consider Miller a founding father.

Among Miller's last research contributions, 1993–1994, were his collaborations with Dr. Patricia Cowings and with Dr. Edward Taub. In particular, he took great pleasure in working with Taub in the development of constraint-induced movement therapy, a very effective treatment to rehabilitate stroke victims with motor impairment by overcoming their learned nonuse, which in turn also promotes neuroplastic changes in the brain that further enhance motor recovery. As a result, a fitting research epitaph to his entire career, devoted to understanding to what the laws of learning apply, can be the following statement: "The brain controls learned behavior but in turn learned behavior also controls the brain—a biofeedback cooperation."

Research Mentor and Educator. There were a number of research ventures in Miller's lab that do not fit nicely into the trajectory of his life characterizing this portraiture but which he strongly encouraged, supported, and included in his *Selected Papers*. For recommended readings there are his collaborations, among others, with: (1) David Egger on findings premonitory of the Rescorla-Wagner model, which now dominates studies in learning; (2) David Quartermain concerning memory consolidation as growing out of a study by Coons and Miller; and (3) studies devoted to understanding the signals for thirst with Don Novin, salt appetite with George Wolf and Edward Stricker, and hunger with Jack Davis, Eleanor Adair, Stan Tenen, David Booth, and Sarah Leibowitz. Among others whose research in his lab he fostered, were Sebastian P. Grossman for chemical coding of behavior discoveries published in 1960, E. E. Krieckhaus and George Wolf on latent learning in 1968, and Jay M. Weiss and Bruce S. McEwen for studies on stress, as cited in 1976.

Miller was considered a master of research design and communicator of the conceptual basis of scientific inquiry—so much so that in some respects that may be his greatest achievement, namely, helping psychology grow into a mature science. He always sought for parsimonious explanations of cause and effect but required that the hypotheses involved be rigorously defined in empirically testable ways that allow them to be confirmed or disconfirmed, ideally by a variety of measures. In his 1960 *Federation Proceedings* article he cautioned against "stopping as soon as a hypothesis is confirmed by a single test. [Especially in a] new field of investigation [such as the brain was in the 1950–1960s], it is essential to design careful behavioral tests of all conceivable alternatives." In an interview taped in 2000, he said an experiment should be designed not only to discover something but also to communicate it and that it would be best to design experiments so that the results would be rather obvious and would not demand elaborate data analysis. He warned investigators, while running experiments, to keep an eye out for unexpected findings because sometimes these are more important than the findings sought for. "And regarding things in an experiment that give you a lot of difficulty, it may be something fairly important or it wouldn't be an important difficulty. So, perhaps you may want to change your goal and decide that the difficulty is a more important variable to study than what you originally started out with." Indeed, as consulting editor of the *Journal of Experimental Psychology* for seven years, Miller passed on his research wisdoms widely. When he resigned, its chief editor, Arthur W. Melton, wrote: "It will be difficult, if not impossible, to replace you with another so keen at picking the flaws in logic or design" (Melton to Miller, 29 September 1956, unpublished letter).

During his professor emeritus years at Rockefeller, which began in 1980, he became quite alarmed by the dangers posed by the animal rights movement to research on treating illness and promoting health. Then, and after his return to Yale in 1985 as a research affiliate, he conducted vigorous efforts to educate the scientific and lay communities about the benefits of behavioral research on animals. He was an important figure in mobilizing the opposition of these communities to this threat.

Finally, as summarized in his last publication, *How to Prepare for Our Future of Totally Unexpected Opportunities*, he conducted vigorous efforts to communicate to the scientific and lay communities a basic understanding of the scientific method and the enormous benefits it has yielded and will continue to do, if well fostered. He served, thus, as an exemplary model for the more than 150 students he trained in research, many of whom became distinguished researchers themselves. In the year 2000 this was the theme of the final of his countless honors, the Award in Neuroscience Education, bestowed by the Association of Neuroscience Departments and Programs.

Miller was survived by a son, York, and daughter, Sarah Rose Mauch, children of his first wife, Marion Edwards Miller, who died 13 October 1997. He was also survived by his second wife, Jean Shepler Miller, whom he married on 21 July 1998 and who was a friend of the family and former music teacher to his children. To these partners he gave enormous credit and thanks: the first for protecting him from so much flotsam and jetsam of daily life—such as paying bills—so that he could concentrate

Miller

on his science, and the second for providing him so much comfort and tolerance in his few remaining years.

BIBLIOGRAPHY

Materials are held in the Neal E. Miller Papers collection at Manuscripts and Archives, Yale University Library.

WORKS BY MILLER

"The Influence of Past Experience upon the Transfer of Subsequent Training." PhD diss., Yale University, 1935.

With John Dollard, Leonard W. Doob, et al. *Frustration and Aggression.* New Haven, CT: Yale University Press, 1939.

With R. R. Sears, O. H. Mowrer, L. W. Doob, and J. Dollard. "I. The Frustration-Aggression Hypothesis." *Psychological Review* 48 (1941): 337–342.

With John Dollard. *Social Learning and Imitation.* New Haven, CT: Yale University Press, 1941.

"Experimental Studies of Conflict Behavior." In *Personality and Behavior Disorders: A Handbook Based on Experimental and Clinical Research*, edited by Joseph McVicker Hunt, 431–465. New York: Ronald, 1944.

Staff, Psychological Research Project (Pilot) [Miller, N. E. (Ed.)]. "Psychological Research on Pilot Training in the AAF." *American Psychologist* 1 (1946): 7–16.

"Studies of Fear as an Acquirable Drive: I. Fear as Motivation and Fear-Reduction as Reinforcement in the Learning of New Responses." *Journal of Experimental Psychology* 38 (1948): 89–101.

"Theory and Experiment Relating Psychoanalytic Displacement to Stimulus-Response Generalization." *Journal of Abnormal and Social Psychology* 43 (1948): 155–178.

With John Dillard. *Personality and Psychotherapy: An Analysis in Terms of Learning, Thinking, and Culture.* New York: McGraw-Hill, 1950.

With Clark J. Bailey and James A. F. Stevenson. "Decreased 'Hunger' but Increased Food Intake Resulting from Hypothalamic Lesions." *Science* 112 (1950): 256–259.

"Comments on Multiple-Process Conceptions of Learning." *Psychological Review* 58 (1951): 375–381.

With D. Kraeling. "Displacement: Greater Generalization of Approach than Avoidance in a Generalized Approach-Avoidance Conflict." *Journal of Experimental Psychology* 43 (1952): 217–221.

With E. J. Murray. "Displacement: Steeper Gradient of Generalization of Avoidance than of Approach with Age of Habit Controlled." *Journal of Experimental Psychology* 43 (1952): 222–226.

With E. J. Murray. "Displacement and Conflict: Learnable Drive as a Basis for the Steeper Gradient of Avoidance Than of Approach." *Journal of Experimental Psychology* 43 (1952): 227–231.

With M. L. Kessen. "Reward Effects of Food via Stomach Fistula Compared with Those of Food Via Mouth." *Journal of Comparative and Physiological Psychology* 45 (1952): 555–564.

With A. K. Myers. "Failure to Find a Learned Drive Based on Hunger; Evidence for Learning Motivated by 'Exploration.'" *Journal of Comparative and Physiological Psychology* 47 (1954): 428–436.

With J. M. R. Delgado and W. W. Roberts. "Learning Motivated by Electrical Stimulation of the Brain." *American Journal of Physiology* 179 (1954): 587–593.

"Experiments on Motivation; Studies Combining Psychological, Physiological, and Pharmacological Techniques." *Science* 126 (1957): 1271–1278.

"Objective Techniques for Studying Motivational Effects of Drugs on Animals." In *Psychotropic Drugs*, edited by Silvio Garattini and Vittorio Ghetti. Amsterdam: Elsevier, 1957.

With G. H. Bower. "Rewarding and Punishing Effects from Stimulating the Same Place in the Rat's Brain." *Journal of Comparative and Physiological Psychology* 51 (1958): 669–674.

"Motivational Effects of Brain Stimulation and Drugs." *Federation Proceedings* 19 (1960): 846–854. See pp. 850–851.

With H. Barry III. "Motivational Effects of Drugs: Methods which Illustrate Some General Problems in Psychopharmacology." *Psychopharmacologia* 1 (1960): 169–199.

"Learning and Performance Motivated by Direct Stimulation of the Brain." In *Electrical Stimulation of the Brain*, edited by Daniel E. Sheer. Austin: University of Texas Press, 1961. Contains advice as to the importance of taking a variety of measures before inferring the nature of an underlying state, particularly in brain research.

"Strengthening the Behavioral Sciences." *Science* 136 (1962): 233–241. Miller chaired the Behavioral Science subpanel of the President's Science Advisory Committee, which produced this report.

"Some Psychophysiological Studies of Motivation and of the Behavioural Effects of Illness." *Bulletin of the British Psychological Society* 17 (1964): 1–20.

With L. DiCara. "Instrumental Learning of Heart-Rate Changes in Curarized Rats: Shaping, and Specificity to Discriminative Stimulus." *Journal of Comparative and Physiological Psychology* 63 (1967): 12–19.

With A. Carmona. "Modification of a Visceral Response, Salivation in Thirsty Dogs, by Instrumental Training with Water Reward." *Journal of Comparative and Physiological Psychology* 63 (1967): 1–6.

Neal E. Miller: Selected Papers. Chicago: Aldine-Atherton, 1971.

"Biofeedback: Evaluation of a New Technique" [Invited editorial]. *New England Journal of Medicine* 290 (1974): 684–685.

With B. R. Dworkin. "Visceral Learning: Recent Difficulties with Curarized Rats and Significant Problems for Human Research." In *Cardiovascular Psychophysiology: Current Issues in Response Mechanisms, Biofeedback, and Methodology*, edited by Paul A. Obrist, A. H. Black, Jasper Brener, et al. Chicago: Aldine, 1974.

"Behavioral Medicine as a New Frontier: Opportunities and Dangers." In *Proceedings of the National Heart and Lung Institute Working Conference on Health Behavior, Basye, Virginia, May 12–15, 1975*, edited by Stephen M. Weiss. Bethesda, MD: U.S. Dept. of Health, Education, and Welfare, Public Health Service, National Institutes of Health, 1975.

Evans, Richard I. *The Making of Psychology: Discussions with Creative Contributors.* New York: Knopf, 1976. See chapter 14, pp. 169–183.

"Behavioral Medicine: Symbiosis between Laboratory and Clinic." *Annual Review of Psychology* 34 (1983): 1–31.

"Learning, Stress, and Psychosomatic Symptoms" [memorial paper in honor of Jerzy Konorski]. *Acta Neurobiological Experimentalis* 36 (1976): 141–156. Contains citations concerning Jay Weiss's and Bruce McEwen's research on stress.

With Wesley C. Lynch, Haruyo Hama, et al. "Instrumental Control of Peripheral Vasomotor Responses in Children." *Psychophysiology* 13 (1976): 219–221.

With T. G. Pickering, B. Brucker, et al. "Mechanisms of Learned Voluntary Control of Blood Pressure in Patients with Generalized Bodily Paralysis." In *Biofeedback and Behavior*, edited by Jackson Beatty and Heiner Legewie. New York: Plenum, 1977.

With B. S. Brucker. "A Learned Visceral Response Apparently Independent of Skeletal Ones in Patients Paralyzed by Spinal Lesions." In *Biofeedback and Self-Regulation*, edited by Niels Birbaumer and H. D. Kimmel. Hillside, NJ: Erlbaum, 1979.

With B. R. Dworkin. "Different Ways in which Learning Is Involved in Homeostasis." In *Neural Mechanisms of Goal-Directed Behavior and Learning*, edited by Richard F. Thompson, Leslie H. Hicks, and V. B. Shvyrkov. New York: Academic Press, 1980.

"Some Main Themes and Highlights of the Conference." *Health Psychology Suppl.* 2 (1983): 11–14. Supplement to the *Proceedings of the National Working Conference on Education and Training in Health Psychology, May 23–27, 1983, Arden House, Harriman, New York; Sponsored by the Division of Health Psychology of the American Psychological Association*, edited by George D. Stone. Hillsdale, NJ: Erlbaum, 1983.

Brain Research Institute. "Neal Elgar Miller, PhD—Interviewed 8 November 1983." Brain Research Institute, Neuroscience History Archive, Oral History Project Series CON Code MIL.

With D. Caroline Coile. "How Radical Animal Activists Try to Mislead Humane People." *American Psychologist* 39 (1984): 700–701.

"The Value of Behavioral Research on Animals." *American Psychologist* 40 (1985): 423–440.

With B. Dworkin, S. Dworkin, et al. "Behavioral Method for the Treatment of Idiopathic Scoliosis." *Proceedings of the National Academy of Sciences of the United States of America* 82 (1985): 2493–2497.

With B. R. Dworkin. "Failure to Replicate Visceral Learning in the Acute Curarized Rat Preparation." *Behavioral Neuroscience* 100 (1986): 299–314.

"Education for a Lifetime of Learning." In *Health Psychology: A Discipline and a Profession*, edited by George C. Stone, S. M. Weiss, J. D. Matarazzo, et al. Chicago: University of Chicago Press, 1987. Contains reflections on important statesmanly lessons learned by Miller in the course of doing research on pilot training in the Army Air Force in World War II. Note p. 11.

With G. C. Stone, S. M. Weiss, et al., eds. "Health Psychology in the Twenty-First Century." In *Health Psychology: A Discipline and a Profession*, edited by George. C. Stone, S. M. Weiss, J. D. Matarazzo, et al. Chicago: University of Chicago Press, 1987.

"Behavior to the Brain to Health." In *The Neurosciences: Paths of Discovery II*, edited by Fred Samson and George Adelman. Boston, MA: Birkhauser, 1992.

With Edward Taub, T. A. Novack, et al. "Technique to Improve Chronic Motor Deficit after Stroke." *Archives of Physical Medicine and Rehabilitation* 74 (1993): 347–354.

With Edward Taub, J. E. Crago, et al. "An Operant Approach to Rehabilitation Medicine: Overcoming Learned Nonuse by Shaping." *Journal of Experimental Analysis of Behavior* 61 no. 2 (1994): 281–293.

With Patricia S. Cowings, W. B. Toscano, et al. *Autogenic-Feedback Training as a Treatment for Airsickness in High Performance Military Aircraft: Two Case Studies.* NASA Technical Memorandum 108810. Moffett Field, CA: National Aeronautics and Space Administration, Ames Research Center, 1994.

"How to Prepare for Our Future of Totally Unexpected Opportunities." In *Mind and Brain Sciences in the 21st Century*, edited by Robert L. Solso. Cambridge, MA: MIT Press, 1997.

"Interview with Dr. Neal Miller." Yale University School of Medicine: MedMedia Services. Taped interview for showing at the annual meeting of the Association of Neuroscience Departments and Programs held in 2000 in New Orleans.

OTHER SOURCES

Bykov, Konstantin M. *The Cerebral Cortex and the Internal Organs.* Translated by W. H. Gantt. New York: Chemical Publishing, 1959.

Coons, Edgar E. "Motivational Correlates of Eating Elicited by Electrical Stimulation in the Hypothalamic Feeding Area." PhD diss., Yale University, 1964.

———, and J. A. F. Cruce. "Lateral Hypothalamus: Food Current Intensity in Maintaining Self-Stimulation of Hunger." *Science* 159 (1968): 1117–1119.

———. "Obituaries—Neal Elgar Miller (1909–2002)." *American Psychologist* 57 (2002): 784–786.

Grossman, S. P. "Eating or Drinking Elicited by Direct Adrenergic or Cholinergic Stimulation of Hypothalamus." *Science* 132 (1960): 301–302.

Hess, Walter Rudolf. *Das Zwischenhirn: Syndrome, Lokalisationen, Funktionen.* 2nd ed. Basel: Schwabe, 1954.

Jonas, Gerald. "Visceral Learning." *New Yorker*, 19 August 1973 and 26 August 1973.

Krieckhaus, E. E., and G. Wolf. "Acquisition of Sodium by Rats: Interaction of Innate Mechanisms and Latent Learning." *Journal of Comparative and Physiological Psychology* 65 (1968): 197–201.

McEwen, B. S., C. J. Denef, J. L. Gerlach, et al. "Chemical Studies of the Brain as a Steroid Hormone Target Tissue." In *The Neurosciences: Third Study Program*, edited by Francis Otto Schmitt and Frederic G. Worden. Cambridge, MA: MIT Press, 1974.

Mowrer, O. H. "A Stimulus-Response Analysis of Anxiety and Its Role as a Reinforcing Agent." *Psychological Reviews* 46 (1939): 553–566.

Olds, James, and Peter Milner. "Positive Reinforcement Produced by Electrical Stimulation of Septal Area and Other Regions of Rat Brain." *Journal of Comparative and Physiological Psychology* 47 (1954): 419–427.

Trowill, J. A. "Instrumental Conditioning of the Heart Rate in the Curarized Rat." *Journal of Comparative and Physiological Psychology* 63 (1967): 7–11.

Weiss, J. M. "Psychological Factors in Stress and Disease." *Scientific American* 226, no. 6 (1972): 104–113.

Edgar E. Coons

MILLER, STANLEY LLOYD

(*b.* Oakland, California, 7 March 1930; *d.* National City, California, 20 May 2007), *chemistry, prebiotic chemistry, origin of life, astrobiology.*

Miller's pioneering work was instrumental in the establishment of the scientific field devoted to the study of the emergence of life on Earth. In a series of breakthrough experiments in the early 1950s, he demonstrated for the first time the synthesis of biologically relevant organic compounds from simple building blocks under physical and chemical conditions presumed to exist on the primeval Earth. Since then, together with numerous colleagues and students, Miller has investigated the possible steps and chemical compounds involved in the emergence of life. His other research interests include the natural occurrence on Earth and other parts of the solar system of clathrates, or gas hydrates, a class of crystalline solids in which water molecules form cagelike structures around low-molecular-weight gases, most commonly methane. In the 1960s, Miller suggested a mechanism of general anesthetics with reference to possible clathrate hydrate formation.

Family Background and Professional History. Miller was born in Oakland, California, to Nathan Harry Miller and Edith Eileen Levy. His father was a lawyer and served as a deputy and later assistant district attorney in Oakland, working under Earl Warren, then the district attorney for Alameda County and later chief justice of the U.S. Supreme Court. His mother had been a teacher before marrying and later a homemaker. Miller's father, born in then czarist Russia, now Belarus, was the first in his large, Jewish immigrant family to go to college. Both Miller and his brother were encouraged to become lawyers or doctors. Miller's older brother Donald chose chemistry instead and Stanley followed suit, both joining the University of California (UC) at Berkeley, whose Department of Chemistry was among the best in the nation. Donald

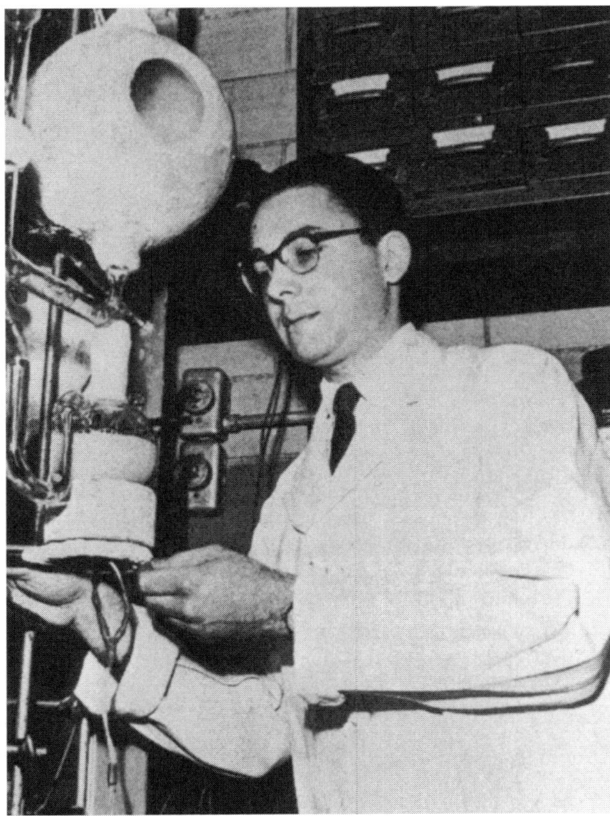

Stanley Lloyd Miller. SPL/PHOTO RESEARCHERS, INC.

received a PhD from the University of Illinois and spent most of his career as a senior chemist at the Lawrence Livermore National Laboratory.

Stanley Miller, who was an avid reader, attended public schools in Oakland and his decision to pursue a career in science was influenced both by his brother's choice and his own belief in the importance of science for society. Miller received a BS in chemistry from UC Berkeley in 1951 and a PhD, under the mentorship of Harold Urey, from the University of Chicago in 1954. In 1955 he was a F. B. Jewett Fellow at the California Institute of Technology, and from 1955 to 1960 a postdoctoral fellow, instructor, and assistant professor in the Department of Biochemistry, College of Physicians and Surgeons, Columbia University. Urey, who moved to the University of California, San Diego (UCSD), in 1958 and his colleagues, being impressed by Miller's outstanding work and achievements, invited him in 1960 to join the Chemistry Department. Miller was instrumental in shaping the new San Diego campus and its curriculum, becoming a full professor in 1968.

As an acknowledgment of his eminent contribution to the establishment of the origin-of-life field, Miller was the first scientist working in this area to be elected (in 1973) to the National Academy of Sciences. In 1983 he received the Oparin Medal, the highest recognition of the International Society for the Study of the Origin of Life, and was the president of this society from 1986 to 1989. He was an honorary councilor of the Higher Council for Scientific Research of Spain and a member in the Phi Beta Kappa and Sigma Xi organizations.

Following a series of strokes since 1999, Miller died in a hospital in National City, south of San Diego, at age 77. His scientific legacy was commemorated in numerous obituaries in the scientific and general press.

The Miller-Urey Experiment. In the fall of 1951, shortly after he began his graduate studies at the University of Chicago, Miller was captivated by a lecture given by Nobel laureate chemist and physicist Harold Urey. Based on his theory of the origin of solar systems, Urey suggested that the primordial terrestrial atmosphere was hydrogen rich, that is, of a reducing nature. He emphasized the relevance of the atmosphere's constituents to the synthesis of organic molecules and to the origin of life, urging experimental study of these issues (Urey, 1952).

Miller was engaged at that time with his thesis advisor, Edward Teller, the father of the hydrogen bomb, in an attempt to elucidate the mechanism of the synthesis of chemical elements in stars. However, this work did not show progress and when Teller left the University of Chicago abruptly to establish the Radiation Laboratory at the University of California, the not yet twenty-three-year-old Miller approached Urey. Overcoming his initial reluctance, Urey agreed in the fall of 1952 to let Miller perform an experiment simulating early Earth conditions in order to examine prebiotic chemical reactions and their products.

Unbeknownst to Urey, and brought to his attention only after his 1951 talk, his ideas on the nature of the early atmosphere matched the groundbreaking origin-of-life theory formulated in the 1920s and 1930s by the Russian biochemist Alexander Oparin. Oparin's ideas, together with a similar, though more limited, theoretical elaboration by the British geneticist and biochemist J. B. S. Haldane, were later referred to as the Oparin-Haldane hypothesis. Contending that the synthesis of organic compounds from constituents of the ancient atmosphere was a crucial step toward life, Oparin and Haldane further suggested that the chemical evolution of these simple organic molecules into more complex ones took place in the primitive ocean, forming the "primordial soup." Since an atmosphere rich in oxygen, similar to the present one, decomposes organic material, all these stages were proposed to be made possible by the existence of an atmosphere constituted of the reducing gases, ammonia (NH_3), methane (CH_4), free hydrogen (H_2), and water vapor.

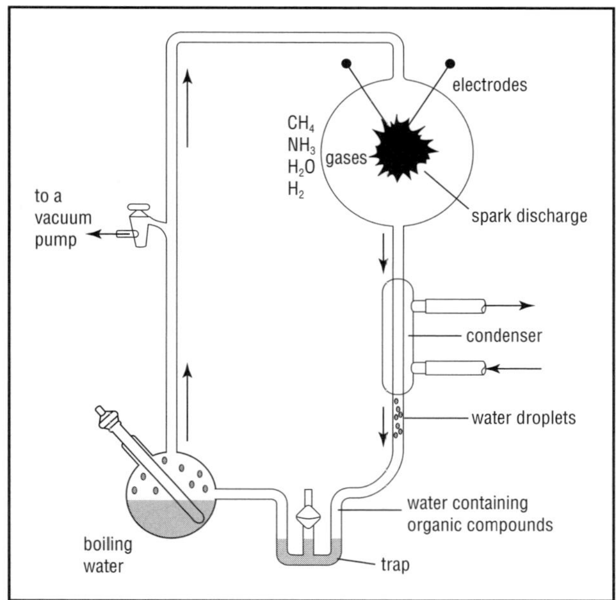

Primordial-Earth Atmosphere.

By hypothesizing the emergence of the first organisms from organic molecules synthesized in the prebiotic environment, Oparin and Haldane rejected the then-prevailing autotrophic notion that organic matter was built by early life from carbon dioxide and water. Adopting Oparin and Haldane's conception, the ensuing Miller-Urey experiment differed from previous attempts (conducted with no connection to the origin-of-life question) to synthesize organic compounds within the autotrophic tradition. Furthermore, by simulating a reducing atmosphere Miller's procedure differed from several experiments performed in the early 1950s, with the origin of life in mind, in which carbon dioxide instead of methane was used and which did not produce biologically relevant organic compounds in high yield.

Miller built a system of glass flasks and tubes in which water vapor was obtained by boiling the "ocean" in a reservoir of water. The vapor was transferred to a gas mixture containing methane, ammonia, and hydrogen, simulating the primordial atmosphere. Urey and Miller hypothesized that ultraviolet light and electric discharges might have been the principal primordial sources of energy in the synthesis of organic compounds. For technical and theoretical reasons electric discharges, simulating lightning, were chosen and applied via electrodes attached to the "atmosphere vessel." The continuous discharge caused the gases to interact and the products were then condensed and moved back to the "ocean," where some of them were dissolved.

In November 1952, Miller applied the described procedure to perform his most elaborate experiment. Analysis of the reaction products revealed that about 10 percent of the available carbon was converted into organic compounds, about 2 percent of which were amino acids, the building blocks of proteins. Miller determined that hydrogen cyanide (HCN) and formaldehyde (H_2CO) were the major organic products in the gas mixture and their interaction in the "ocean" led to the synthesis of amino acids. The results, published in the journal *Science* on 15 May 1953, caused great excitement in the scientific community, as well as in the popular press, and were later repeated and confirmed by other investigators.

Significantly, the results were not statistically random: only a small number of biologically relevant organic compounds in high yields were produced in the experiment out of the vast number of potential organic substances. Glycine and alanine, the most common amino acids in proteins, were the major products (Lazcano and Bada, 2003). Moreover, in work performed by Miller and other researchers in the 1970s it was found that the same amino acids and in the same relative quantities were obtained when the content of meteorites that reached Earth were analyzed, particularly the Murchison meteorite that fell in Australia in 1969. Since meteorites are considered to be relics of the formation of the solar system, their organic content could indicate that chemical processes similar to the Miller reactions were common in the solar system, including the prebiotic Earth.

In experiments by Miller and others that followed in the 1950s and 1960s, various mixtures of reducing gases and sources of energy were used to yield amino acids and other organic molecules. The chemist Juan Oró achieved the synthesis of the nitrogenous base adenine, an important component of the nucleic acids, DNA and RNA.

Miller's Further Contributions. Miller's groundbreaking prebiotic synthesis of organic compounds was based on the notion of a primordial reducing atmosphere. Oparin and then Urey founded this notion on the discovery of CH_4 and NH_3 in the atmospheres of Jupiter, Saturn, Uranus, and Neptune, and on the then-accepted assumption that Earth was formed from a hydrogen-rich dust cloud. Later models of the origin of the early atmosphere emphasized the volcanic release of gases from Earth's mantle, following the impact of meteorites and other bodies on Earth's surface during its formation. A gradually emerging picture depicts a complex atmosphere, resulting both from external impacts and internal processes in Earth's mantle. Carbon dioxide (CO_2), carbon monoxide (CO), nitrogen (N_2), water, methane, and hydrogen were probably all present in varying proportions.

Though the nature of the early atmosphere is still an unsettled question, explored through experiments and novel theoretical models, Miller went on to investigate the modified conception of the primordial atmosphere in his later work. Among his studies conducted since the 1980s, Miller achieved, in the early 2000s, the synthesis of amino acids and nucleic acid bases in a gas mixture that contained CO, CO_2, N_2, and H_2O, using high-energy protons as a high-energy source required in less reducing conditions.

Another related, and as yet unsettled, question pertains to the source of organic compounds on the early Earth. Based on the discovery of a variety of organic molecules in outer space, and on the analysis of the contents of comets and meteorites, it is widely accepted that massive amounts of organic materials and water were delivered to Earth by impacting bodies at least during its first half billion years. Many investigators regard this external delivery as the only source for organic material. Miller and others view it as a possible addition to organic synthesis that was carried out on Earth. Obviously, the relative importance of these two sources depended on the relative abundance of reducing gases in the atmosphere.

The site on Earth where life might have emerged is among the most contentious issues in the origin-of-life community. Since the late 1970s, an alternative research program contesting the primordial "soup" notion suggests the synthesis of bioorganic molecules and the emergence of life at the vicinity of hydrothermal vents on the ocean floor. According to this theory, mineral surfaces, reducing gases released from the ocean crust, and the availability of chemical energy in these sites provided a more suitable environment for organic synthesis and the emergence of life than the ocean.

Miller has long rejected the hydrothermal-vents hypothesis, claiming that the high temperatures of the vents are destructive to organic molecules. In a series of studies performed since the late 1980s, Miller showed that higher temperatures are not compatible with both amino acid and nucleic acid bases. In experiments performed in the 1990s and 2000s he extended the ocean notion and showed that prebiotic material could have been concentrated on beaches and drying lagoons that provide abundant mineral surfaces necessary for polymerization. However, this does not exclude a role for the ocean's soup as a source for the required building blocks.

The hydrothermal-vent-and-temperature debate led Miller to study the time window during which life could have emerged. He referred to the fact that the entire ocean passes through the deep-sea vents every ten million years, destroying in this process all the dissolved organic components. In various publications in the 1990s Miller thus claimed that living systems had to emerge within a geologically short period, maybe not more than ten million years, compatible with the destruction rate of their components. The general trend of narrowing the time window is a radical departure from the older notion of billions of years during which life could have emerged due to a "lucky accident."

Miller's Work on the RNA and Pre-RNA Worlds. Following the famous Watson-Crick discovery of the double-helical structure of DNA (published one month before the Miller 1953 paper) and the consequent rise of molecular biology, the origin-of-life problem began to be formulated in terms of genetic material, protein enzymes, and their interaction. For Miller, the most fundamental question facing researchers was the nature of the first genetic material that could have replicated, mutated, and evolved. Opinions on this question differ between the metabolic and genetic points of view, implicitly referred to by Oparin and Haldane, respectively, in the 1920s and 1930s. These two traditions that came into full bloom following the development of the origin-of-life field in the 1960s emphasize different aspects of the conception of life: "geneticists" view life first and foremost as a self-replicating molecular entity; "metabolists," as an organized system of interacting molecules maintaining its stability through metabolism. Miller has always fiercely opposed the metabolists, rejecting their contention that the early stages of natural selection and evolution in the emergence of life could have depended on the reproduction of a multimolecular, metabolizing system instead of the replication of a genetic molecule (Fry, 2000).

Miller, together with Leslie Orgel, a leading origin-of-life scientist, and many other "geneticists" became convinced that a watershed in life's emergence was the RNA-world—a hypothetical prebiotic stage in which RNA molecules functioned both as genetic material and as catalysts. The possibility of such dual function was indicated following the discovery in the 1980s of RNA enzymes, later called ribozymes. The RNA-world theory, strengthened by the discovery of ribozymes, seems to suggest a solution to a basic challenge facing the study of the origin of life: the chicken-and-egg relationship between nucleic acids and proteins, which depend on each other for their synthesis and function.

However, based on Miller's and other scientists' work, the RNA-world could not have been the first chemical "world" to emerge, owing to the complexity of RNA and its constituents. Since the early 1990s, Miller and colleagues began searching for a pre-RNA world, constituted of molecules that were easier to synthesize prebiotically, that could have replicated, and that could have later transformed into RNA.

Of the RNA nitrogen bases, purines are synthesized prebiotically more readily than pyrimidines. Miller demonstrated for the first time in the 1990s that high yields of the two pyrimidine bases, uracil and cytosine, can be achieved not in a dilute solution but under drying conditions. He also produced urazole, a modified uracil in which a five-membered ring replaced the six-membered one. Due to its chemical properties, urazole could have been a possible precursor of uracil. Another line of study involved the production of substituted uracils, to which various amino acids were attached. Assuming that such molecules could have been part of ribozymes, they would have greatly enhanced the catalytic activities of RNA enzymes.

Following numerous experiments under prebiotic conditions, Miller became convinced that ribose, the sugar component in RNA building blocks, could not have played a role in the first genetic polymers. Without enzymes, ribose cannot be synthesized in adequate quantity and purity. Moreover, both ribose and other sugars are highly unstable in aqueous solutions, even at low temperatures. Thus, Miller and others began experimenting with alternatives to the present-day ribose-phosphate backbone of RNA. Among the most serious candidates, originally suggested by Peter E. Nielsen, is peptide-nucleic-acid (PNA), a polymer that has a proteinlike backbone to which nitrogen bases are attached. Miller has shown that the units composing the PNA backbone can be easily synthesized in mildly reducing conditions. They can be concentrated and polymerized under conditions that simulate drying beaches and lagoons.

Miller the Exobiologist. From its inception, Miller's research on the origin of life was embedded in the wider context of the search for life on other planets. In the wake of the 1953 experiment, the astronomer Carl Sagan described his mission in science as extending Miller's results to astronomy. The results of the Miller-Urey experiment were interpreted in the 1950s and at later times as indicating the possibility of bioorganic synthesis in the primordial solar system and on other solar-system planets. After the founding of the National Aeronautics and Space Administration (NASA) in 1958, the young Miller was among the main contributors to the establishment of the field of "exobiology," later to be called astrobiology. Several of Miller's later experiments lent credence to the hypothesis that the potential for prebiotic chemistry exists beyond Earth. He and colleagues have shown that adenine, glycine, and alanine can be produced in solutions frozen for years, made of materials similar to the atmospheric constituents of the 1953 experiment. It seems that such synthesis might be possible under conditions prevalent on Jupiter's moon, Europa, and possibly on other jovian moons. In 1992, NASA established a "virtual" research center, NSCORT (NASA Specialized Center of Research and Training), including the research groups of Miller, Leslie Orgel, Jeffrey Bada, Gustaf Arrhenius, and Gerald Joyce at UCSD and the Scripps Institute of Oceanography. NSCORT investigators have since been active in the study of the origin of life on Earth and beyond.

Miller's Legacy. Creationists, strongly denounced by Miller for promoting ignorance about science, often rely on the empirical debates among origin-of-life scientists over specific prebiotic scenarios to discredit the very study of the emergence of life. However, in distinction to ongoing scientific controversies, contentions that life could have emerged on Earth only through a supernatural intervention are antiscientific in nature. Clearly, the empirical details of both the Oparin-Haldane hypothesis and the Miller experiments were reflections of their corresponding 1930s and 1950s scientific contexts that later underwent some changes. Nevertheless, the fundamental evolutionary philosophical and theoretical assumptions underlying Miller's endeavor continue to guide origin-of-life research.

Most importantly, Miller's 1953 study helped to establish a new experimental field by opening avenues of research into the origin of life. His work since 1953, embodying both the achievements and the open questions still facing the field, attests to the significance of his scientific legacy. Already as a young scientist, Miller was noted for his extraordinary persistence in pursuing the most difficult scientific problems. It was this persistence, in addition to his other professional assets, that accounted for Miller's groundbreaking contributions to the establishment and development of the study of the emergence of life on Earth.

BIBLIOGRAPHY

A Web site with an extensive list (though not covering all the years) of Miller's references is http://exobio.ucsd.edu/miller.htm.

WORKS BY MILLER

"A Production of Amino Acids under Possible Primitive Earth Conditions." *Science* 117 (1953): 528–529.

With Harold C. Urey. "Organic Compound Synthesis on the Primitive Earth." *Science* 130 (1959): 245–251.

"The Atmosphere of the Primitive Earth and the Prebiotic Synthesis of Amino Acids." *Origins of Life* 5 (1974): 139–151. On Murchison meteorite.

"Clathrate Hydrates in the Solar System." In *Ices in the Solar System,* edited by J. Klinger, 59–78. Dordrecht, Netherlands: Reidel, 1985.

With Antonio Lazcano. "How Long Did It Take for Life to Begin and Evolve to Cyanobacteria?" *Journal of Molecular Evolution* 39 (1994): 546–554.

With Antonio Lazcano. "The Origin of Life—Did It Occur at High Temperatures?" *Journal of Molecular Evolution* 41 (1995): 689–692.

With Michael P. Robertson. "Prebiotic Synthesis of 5-Substituted Uracils: A Bridge between the RNA World and the DNA-Protein World." *Science* 268 (1995): 702–705.

With Rosa Larralde and Michael P. Robertson. "Rates of Decomposition of Ribose and Other Sugars: Implications for Chemical Evolution." *Proceedings of the National Academy of Sciences of the United States of America* 92 (1995): 8158–8160.

"From Primordial Soup to Prebiotic Beach." Interview by Sean Henahan conducted in October 1996. Available from http://www.accesexcelence.org/WN/NM/miller.html.

With Matthew Levy, Karen Brinton, and Jeffrey L. Bada. "Prebiotic Synthesis of Adenine and Amino Acids under Europa-like Conditions." *Icarus* 145 (2000): 609–613.

With Kevin E. Nelson and Matthew Levy. "Peptide Nucleic Acids rather than RNA May Have Been the First Genetic Molecule." *Proceedings of the National Academy of Sciences of the United States of America* 97 (2000): 3868–3871.

With Kevin E. Nelson, Michael P. Robertson, and Matthew Levy. "Concentration by Evaporation and the Prebiotic Synthesis of Cytosine." *Origins of Life and Evolution of the Biosphere* 31 (2001): 221–229.

With Miyakawa Shin, Hiroto Yamanashi, Kensei Kobayashi, et al. "Prebiotic Synthesis from CO Atmospheres: Implications for the Origins of Life." *Proceedings of the National Academy of Sciences of the United States of America* 99 (2002): 14628–14631.

OTHER SOURCES

Fry, Iris. *The Emergence of Life on Earth: A Historical and Scientific Overview.* New Brunswick, NJ: Rutgers University Press, 2000.

Lazcano, Antonio, and Jeffrey L. Bada. "The 1953 Stanley Miller Experiment: Fifty Years of Prebiotic Organic Chemistry." *Origins of Life and Evolution of the Biosphere* 33 (2003): 235–242.

Urey, Harold C. "On the Early Chemical History of the Earth and the Origin of Life." *Proceedings of the National Academy of Sciences of the United States of America* 38 (1952): 351–363.

Iris Fry

MITCHELL, PETER DENNIS

(*b.* Mitcham, Surrey, United Kingdom, 29 September 1920; *d.* Glynn near Bodmin, Cornwall, United Kingdom, 10 April 1992), *biochemistry, chemiosmotic theory, bioenergetics.*

Mitchell pursued the development of theoretical approaches in biochemistry, culminating in the proposal and acceptance of his chemiosmotic theory. This theory helped forge the field of bioenergetics (the study of how energy is obtained, transformed, and used in living cells) by unifying several apparently disparate fields, and, in the estimation of some, produced a paradigm shift by introducing spatial directionality into biochemistry. He was awarded the Nobel Prize in Chemistry in 1978. Although his research program was formulated at the universities of Cambridge and Edinburgh, the testing and refinement of his theory was effected at his private, independent research laboratory, the Glynn Research Institute. Here he engaged in a double experiment to explore the potential of his chemiosmotic ideas as well as to see if world-class science could be done in such a small, private research establishment.

Origins and Early Education. Peter Mitchell was the second son of Christopher Mitchell, a distinguished civil engineer and administrator in the Ministry of Transport, and Kate (née Taplin) Mitchell. The Mitchell family was from Dorset, England, but descended from seventeenth-century French Huguenot immigrants. Peter Mitchell's uncle, Sir Godfrey Mitchell, built Wimpy Construction into one of the largest contracting firms in Europe; gifts of shares of Wimpy stock provided Mitchell with considerable financial freedom and funds for establishing and maintaining the Glynn Research Institute.

Mitchell's academic record at local grammar schools and his secondary education at Queen's College, Taunton, were not particularly distinguished. He excelled in mathematics and physics, but was otherwise an indifferent student, doing poorly in subjects such as history and geography that seemed to lack fundamental principles. At Queen's he found that he could reason from first principles to deduce on his own what he could otherwise find in textbooks, which made physics attractive, although not chemistry as it was then taught. This established a pattern that persisted throughout his life, in which he confidently developed his own understanding of a subject through reasoning rather than consulting standard texts or experts. He failed the scholarship entrance examination for Cambridge and it was only through the intervention of his headmaster, Christopher Wiseman, who recognized Mitchell's talent and potential, that Mitchell was admitted to Jesus College, Cambridge for the fall of 1939.

Education and Work at Cambridge, 1939–1955. Mitchell chose to study physics, chemistry, physiology, and biochemistry for his Tripos I (first two years) and then biochemistry for his Tripos II (third year). Again, Mitchell's performance was not stellar (second-class marks on his examinations) but he flourished in the Biochemistry Department, then probably the best in the world, under the encouragement of Frederick Gowland Hopkins, who perceived Mitchell's potential for research. Mitchell stayed on, as a graduate student, doing war-related research in the department under the supervision of James Danielli.

Mitchell was intellectually shaped by Hopkins's approach of dynamic biochemistry that emphasized understanding enzyme-catalyzed metabolism. Although biochemists viewed the cell as a "bag of enzymes," Mitchell noted that the way enzymologist Malcolm Dixon drew reactions could imply a directionality in the action of enzymes rather than a directionless, or scalar, catalytic process. Working with Danielli on the nature of cellular membranes and the movement of chemicals across them reinforced Mitchell's emerging idea that the directionality, or vectorial character, of transport across membranes was somehow connected with the directionality and spatial-temporal organization of biochemical processes more generally.

After the war and Danielli's departure for King's College London, Mitchell worked essentially unsupervised on his thesis research, working out the implications of his intuitions about biochemical organization. He submitted an unconventional thesis in 1948. It opened with a philosophical discussion about directional processes and the roles of static and dynamic elements in such processes. A theoretical section followed on the diffusion of substances in biological systems, in which Mitchell set out a mathematical formulation of his vectorial ideas. After a section on the nature of the bacterial surface there was a final section in which Mitchell's preliminary, but solid, experimental results on amino acid uptake by bacteria were presented. His examiners, Ernst Gale of the department and external examiner A. G. "Sandy" Ogston, rejected the thesis as being inchoate and incoherent.

Mitchell's friendship with David Keilin of the nearby Molteno Institute, who provided Mitchell with temporary space in his laboratory, was crucial in helping him through this setback. Keilin was angered by the committee's action and encouraged Mitchell to rewrite the thesis. Indeed, Keilin was something of a scientific and personal father figure to Mitchell; Mitchell's Nobel Prize lecture, "David Keilin's Respiratory Chain Concept and Its Chemiosmotic Consequences," reflected the intellectual debt Mitchell felt to Keilin's influence (Mitchell, 1979). In the event, the then head of department, Albert Chibnall, assigned Gale to supervise Mitchell's second effort, which involved research on the mechanism of action of penicillin. Mitchell's second thesis was more conventional and was accepted on 6 December 1950.

Although it turned out that Mitchell's proposed mechanism for penicillin action was incorrect, the thesis served to focus his thinking on phosphate transport into bacteria and how that was connected to the role of phosphate in intermediary metabolism. Mitchell began developing a research program on such phenomena, and although he continued thinking in the terms of his first thesis he did not state such notions explicitly except in a paper presented in Moscow in 1956, after he had left Cambridge. There he spelled out his ideas, described in the first thesis, on directionality and intracellular gradients (Mitchell, 1957a). In effect, these ideas provided an intuitive metaphor for nonequilibrium thermodynamic processes, which helped Mitchell organize his thinking in relation to cellular structure and the "flame" of metabolism.

After Mitchell completed his doctoral degree, the new head of the department, Frank Young, appointed him to a five-year position as a demonstrator. Mitchell worked in the Sub-Department of Microbiology, now headed by Gale, but founded by Marjorie Stephenson. She also helped found the Society for General Microbiology in 1944 and was one of the first two women to be elected to the Royal Society in 1945. When, in 1948 as president of the society, she was organizing the meeting for 1949 on the bacterial surface, she asked Mitchell, though still a graduate student, to give a major talk, in which he identified the osmotic barrier of bacteria with their cytoplasmic membrane. Further, he speculated that membrane proteins were not inert and unstructured, but acted as globular, precisely folded enzymes in facilitating transport (Mitchell, 1949).

Stephenson did not live to preside at this meeting, but before she died she intervened again in Mitchell's career in a way that had a lasting effect. She suggested that Jennifer Moyle, who was a research assistant in her laboratory, work with Mitchell. This began a formidable and productive collaboration that lasted, with one brief interruption, until Moyle's retirement in 1983. Both Mitchell and Moyle felt that Stephenson had real insight into their unique and complementary strengths, Mitchell as an imaginative and brilliant theorist and Moyle as a meticulous and superb experimentalist. Together they pursued a line of research on bacterial transport informed by Mitchell's increasingly more precise and articulated theoretical speculations and tested by Moyle's careful experimentation.

In a series of well-crafted publications on phosphate transport in bacteria, Mitchell and Moyle agued that metabolism (involving chemical work) and transport (involving osmotic work) were but two aspects of an underlying unitary process. Summarizing this work Mitchell wrote that "in complex biochemical systems, such as those carrying out oxidative phosphorylation … the osmotic and enzymic specificities appear to be equally important and may be practically synonymous" (Mitchell, 1954, p. 254). This was Mitchell's first mention of a possible link of oxidative phosphorylation and an osmotic (transport) type of process. Oxidative phosphorylation is the process in bacteria and mitochondria in which electrons, derived from nutrients, are passed through a complex set of membrane-bound proteins, known as the respiratory chain, to an oxygen molecule, with the concomitant synthesis of ATP (adenosine triphosphate). ATP then can provide energy to drive other processes in the cell. The process of cellular respiration just described should not be confused with the respiration, or breathing, of organisms. Cellular respiration is why oxygen is needed by all aerobic organisms.

Mitchell did not get along well with Young, and his contract at Cambridge was not renewed in 1955. However, Michael Swann, who knew Mitchell from Swann's time at Cambridge, offered Mitchell a position as director of a new Chemical Biology Unit in the Department of Zoology at the University of Edinburgh; Mitchell accepted on the condition that Moyle be hired to be his research associate.

Research at Edinburgh, 1955–1963. Mitchell's time at Edinburgh was perhaps his most creative. During it he brought his research program based upon a holistic theoretical approach to living systems to fruition and developed a detailed theory of vectorial metabolism, linking transport and metabolism, and applied it specifically to the problem of the mechanism of oxidative phosphorylation. In this new environment, where he independently directed his own subdepartment, Mitchell theorized with greater assurance, aided by the skilled experimental work of Moyle.

Mitchell and Moyle showed that the respiratory chain in bacteria was located in the cytoplasmic membrane and concluded that it might have a direct role in ion transport. Mitchell, in his 1957 paper "A General Theory of Membrane Transport from Studies of Bacteria," developed a notion of "ligand conduction" as the mechanism of transport. He argued that "enzymes are the conductors of bacterial membrane-transport—that metabolic energy is generally converted to osmotic work by the formation and opening of covalent links between translocators in the membrane and the carried molecules exactly as in enzyme-catalysed group-transfer reactions" (p. 136). Arguing from the necessarily vectorial nature of enzymes involved in transport, Mitchell and Moyle, in their 1958 paper "Group-Translocation: A Consequence of Enzyme-Catalysed Group-Transfer," presented a generalization that enzymes act to "transport" substrates vectorially through their active sites but that the consequence of this is only observable when the enzymes are plugged through a membrane. In their 1959 paper "Coupling of Metabolism and Transport by Enzymic Translocation of Substrates through Membranes" they proposed that such a

Mitchell

mechanism would couple metabolism and transport. This concept was further articulated in Mitchell's 1959 Biochemical Society symposium paper "Structure and Function in Micro-organisms" where he introduced the term *chemiosmotic* in which the osmotic link of compounds or ions being transported from one side of a biological membrane to the other involves a chemically linked group, or ligand, being conducted through a membrane enzyme (p. 91). He extended this notion of chemiosmotic linkages to cells more generally, including the mitochondrial membranes of more complex eukaryotic cells.

In August 1960 Mitchell summarized the work of the previous five years when he presented the opening lecture, "Biological Transport Phenomena and the Spatially Anisotropic Characteristics of Enzyme Systems Causing a Vector Component of Metabolism," at the Prague Symposium on Membrane Transport and Metabolism. In this lecture he articulated, at a general level, his theory based upon chemiosmotic principles.

Six weeks later, in Stockholm in a symposium session on "Specific Membrane Transport and its Adaptation," at the end of a paper reporting work of his graduate student B. P. Stephen, Mitchell speculated that the enzyme glucose-6-phosphate phosphatase, which they had shown to be located in the bacterial cytoplasmic membrane, could be considered as an example of chemiosmotic coupling. He proposed that the reaction could be reversed to synthesize, rather than hydrolyze, the glucose phosphate if there were a proton gradient across the membrane. Mitchell further speculated that similar considerations could apply to the synthesis of ATP in photosynthetic and oxidative phosphorylation.

Mitchell's application of his theoretical approach to the problem of the mechanism of oxidative phosphorylation had several key features as set forth in an abstract submitted mid-February 1961: (1) The respiratory-chain reactions in the membrane released protons vectorially to one side of the membrane and hydroxyl ions to the other side, thus generating a difference in proton concentration across the membrane (a pH gradient); (2) such a transmembrane pH gradient can arise only if the membrane is impermeable to protons; (3) ATP can be made by reversal of the ATPase (ATP synthase) reaction if there is a mechanism to utilize the energy in the pH gradient to drive the synthesis of ATP. Such reversal of the ATPase means that, instead of reacting ATP with water and releasing energy at the ATPase enzyme, water is removed from ADP and phosphate to make ATP using energy in the proton gradient, thus making the enzyme an "ATP synthase." In 1966 Mitchell provided a specific mechanism by which protons were transported across membranes. In a process he termed *ligand conduction* the transported proton was linked to an electron in a hydrogen atom bonded to another atom. This bound proton was called the ligand. When the molecule containing the liganded proton moved from one side of the membrane to the opposite side, the effect was to transport the proton across the membrane and to release it to bulk solvent on the other side (Mitchell, 1966). Mitchell also proposed a direct role of the proton in the ATP synthase active site.

Peter Dennis Mitchell. *Mitchell in the laboratory.* FROM ARCHIVE MATERIAL OF THE FORMER WYNN RESEARCH FOUNDATION LTD. HELD BY THE GLYNN LABORATORY OF BIOENERGETICS AT UCL.

The possibility of such proton translocation by the respiratory chain had already been suggested by several authors, including Robert Davies, Heinrich Lundegårdh, and Sir Rutherford Robertson; however, it still needed to be shown that such proton translocation occurred in bacteria, mitochondria, and chloroplasts. Proton impermeability of membranes was a novel suggestion and most biochemists at that time thought it unlikely. The mechanism by which Mitchell thought protons could make ATP by reversing the ATPase was novel. Davies had earlier speculated that a pH gradient could somehow catalyze ATP synthesis. However, no one had demonstrated that protons could indeed drive ATP synthesis.

During the fall of 1960 Mitchell conducted preliminary experiments demonstrating that bacterial membranes were indeed proton impermeable and in 1961 he extended the work to mitochondria. In January 1961 a paper (submitted August 1960) by Robert J. P. Williams of Oxford University, "Possible Functions of Chains of Catalysts," appeared in the premier issue of the new *Journal of Theoretical Biology,* in which Williams proposed intramembrane anhydrous proton gradients as the common intermediate between the respiratory chain and ATP synthesis. Before submitting his "Coupling of Phosphorylation to Electron and Hydrogen Transfer by a Chemiosmotic Type of Mechanism" paper to *Nature* (published in July 1961), Mitchell opened a correspondence with Williams on 24 February 1961, in part to see how similar their mechanisms were. This led to misunderstandings and controversies that continued past Mitchell's death (see Williams, 1993; also see Prebble and Weber, 2003, as well as Weber and Prebble, 2006). To Mitchell's satisfaction, though not to Williams's, Mitchell concluded the mechanisms were distinct and went forward with the publication of his proposal, without mention of Williams's paper or the correspondence.

Shortly thereafter Mitchell's ill health due to ulcers led him to take a leave and ultimately to resign from Edinburgh. He purchased a property with a beautiful but derelict Regency house, Glynn, near Bodmin in Cornwall and in 1962 began renovations of it, acting as master of works, to restore the building and remodel it to serve both as a research laboratory and family residence. Moyle came to join in the work and help set up the formal organization of Glynn Research Ltd. By fall 1964 research began at Glynn.

Research at Glynn, 1964–1997. Mitchell made the decision to continue the line of experimental work on membrane impermeability that he had begun at Edinburgh. With Moyle he devised experiments to test not only if the respiratory chain in mitochondria ejected protons but also to quantify how many protons were translocated per electron moving to an oxygen molecule at the end of the chain. As Mitchell's proposal had not attracted much serious attention in the field, it made sense for Mitchell's small research team to focus upon experimental testing of his approach. Fortunately Mitchell's proposal was amenable to empirical scrutiny in the 1960s with relatively simple equipment.

The small size of the group, the simplicity and elegance of the experiments, and the close connection of theory and experiment all became hallmarks of the Glynn style of science. Given that the prevailing paradigm of the field of oxidative phosphorylation was the chemical theory proposed in 1953 by E. C. "Bill" Slater (based upon the expectation that there should be chemical intermediates analogous to those seen in metabolism), Mitchell realized that he had to convince his colleagues to view the phenomenon in a radically different manner. So shifting the field, while working from a small and independent research facility, became the other aspect of the Glynn program.

Mitchell realized that the theorizing and experimenting at Glynn would need to leverage allies from the more traditional research laboratories, something Mitchell sought to do through active correspondence, frequent presentations at international meetings, and bringing scientists for consultations and extended visits to his beautifully situated institute. Indeed, the Glynn guest book reads as a who's who of the emerging field of bioenergetics.

One of the first visitors to Glynn was André Jagendorf, then at the McCollum-Pratt Institute in Baltimore, Maryland. Jagendorf had obtained data that chloroplasts upon illumination translocate protons, which fitted Mitchell's prediction, and he wanted to further understand the theoretical arguments. A year later Jagendorf showed that chloroplasts in the dark synthesized ATP when subjected to an artificial pH gradient of just the size Mitchell had predicted would be required. Additional evidence supporting aspects of the chemiosmotic approach was obtained by Brian Chappell and Anthony Crofts at Bristol University in their studies of ion transport in mitochondria. By 1968 Mitchell had supporting evidence for all three "pillars" of his proposal. These results meant that the chemiosmotic hypothesis could no longer be ignored and a storm of controversy broke out that persisted for a number of years. Meanwhile, Mitchell made revisions to his theoretical model of oxidative phosphorylation, presented in two volumes published by the Glynn Research Institute (Mitchell, 1966, 1968).

Mitchell's program at Glynn could be considered a success, and by 1973 most bioenergeticists acknowledged that a proton gradient was the energy-conserving link between the oxidation-reduction reactions of the respiratory chain and ATP synthesis. However, aspects of Mitchell's specific mechanisms were not so widely accepted. Paul Boyer at the University of California at Los Angeles had proposed a quite different alternative mechanism for the synthesis of ATP by ATPase, one involving protein conformational changes via indirect interaction with protons. In contrast, Mitchell's ATPase mechanism, as it was developed in the 1970s, based upon his ideas of ligand conduction, involved a direct use of protons in the active site. Similarly Mitchell in his 1966 reformulation of his model used ligand conduction to explain the proton to electron ratios he observed. However, many in the field doubted both the ratios Mitchell reported and his mechanistic explanation.

Starting in 1974 Al Lehninger from Johns Hopkins University and Mårten Wickström from the University of Helsinki presented results with ratios higher than those

Nobel Prize. *Peter Dennis Mitchell accepting the Nobel Prize from King Carl XVI Gustaf.* AP IMAGES.

observed by Mitchell and Moyle. This led to another controversy that lasted for over a decade. At stake were not just the experimental results but also Mitchell's ligand conduction mechanisms. In the middle of this controversy Mitchell was awarded the Nobel Prize in Chemistry in 1978 for his chemiosmotic theory of biological energy transfer even though mechanistic details were still in dispute.

Ultimately, by 1985 Mitchell had to concede that the higher ratios were correct, but he still sought to explain them by further development of his fundamental theory of ligand conduction. He also continued to argue for his direct, vectorial explanations of the higher numbers of protons (3 to 4) needed to synthesize ATP than his theory originally had predicted (2 protons per ATP). Indeed almost to his dying day Mitchell was refining his ATPase mechanism. Besides the confidence he always had in his intellectual abilities, he felt that his basic approach had been vindicated by his solution of the basic mechanism of oxidative phosphorylation.

In 1975 he successfully modified his theory to account for the proton/electron ratio for one part of the respiratory chain, that between the initial protein complex that oxidized NADH and the final protein complex, the cytochrome oxidase, that transferred electrons to oxygen to make water. He did this by assuming that the ligand conduction could be done by a mobile membrane-soluble molecule, known as coenzyme Q, which would ferry the extra protons across the membrane. This was an extraordinary feat of imagination going well beyond the experimental data available at the time. The Q cycle, as Mitchell called it, is essentially accepted today. Mitchell's attempts to repeat the Q-cycle feat with the ATPase and the cytochrome oxidase were not successful. Accumulated experimental results overwhelmingly support Boyer's conformational-coupling mechanism for the ATPase and Boyer was awarded a share of the Nobel Prize in Chemistry in 1997. What is presented in textbooks today as the mechanism of oxidative phosphorylation is best characterized as the Mitchell-Boyer mechanism.

From the mid-1970s on, the endowment of Glynn from the Wimpy shares was insufficient to fully sustain the operation of the Glynn Research Institute. Moyle retired in 1983 and in 1985 Mitchell retired as director of research, although he still headed the institute; Peter Rich, a bioenergeticist from Cambridge, became the research director. Rich obtained extramural funding to support the more instrument-intensive research that was mandated as the field matured. Aside from continuing his theoretical work, Mitchell sought to obtain funding to maintain Glynn as an institution. In this endeavor he met with limited success, and after his death in 1992, it became even harder to obtain support for Glynn per se, despite its illustrious record of success. Ultimately, in 1996 Rich transferred the research operations to University College London as the Glynn Laboratory of Bioenergetics. Thus what had been started as an attempt to do major research outside of university or government laboratories ended up absorbed back into the university system.

BIBLIOGRAPHY

A comprehensive bibliography of Peter Mitchell's publications can be found in Slater, 1994. There is an extensive archive of Mitchell's unpublished papers held at the University of Cambridge Library.

WORKS BY MITCHELL

"The Osmotic Barrier in Bacteria." In *The Nature of the Bacterial Surface,* edited by A. A. Miles and N. W. Pirie. Oxford: Blackwell Scientific, 1949.

"Transport of Phosphate though an Osmotic Barrier." *Symposia of the Society for Experimental Biology* 8 (1954): 254–261.

"A General Theory of Membrane Transport from Studies of Bacteria." *Nature* 180 (1957a): 134–136.

"The Origin of Life and the Formation and Organizing Functions of Natural Membranes." In *International Symposium on the Origin of Life on the Earth,* edited by A. Oparin et al. Moscow: House Academy of Science USSR, 1957b.

With Jennifer Moyle. "Group-Translocation: A Consequence of Enzyme-Catalysed Group-Transfer." *Nature* 182 (1958): 372–373.

With Jennifer Moyle. "Coupling of Metabolism and Transport by Enzymic Translocation of Substrates through Membranes." *Proceedings of the Royal Physical Society of Edinburgh* 28 (1959): 19–27.

"Structure and Function in Micro-organisms." In *The Structure and Function of Subcellular Components,* edited by Eric Mitchell Crook. Biochemical Society Symposia 16. Cambridge, U.K.: Cambridge University Press, 1959.

"Approaches to the Analysis of Specific Membrane Transport." In *Biological Structure and Function,* vol. 2, edited by T. W. Goodwin and O. Lindberg. London: Academic Press, 1961. The Stockholm symposium paper presented in September 1960.

"Chemiosmotic Coupling in Oxidative and Photosynthetic Phosphorylation." *Biochemical Journal* 79 (1961): 23P–24P. The abstract submitted mid-February prior to presentation at the Biochemistry Society meeting and published in July 1961.

"Coupling of Phosphorylation to Electron and Hydrogen Transfer by a Chemi-osmotic Type of Mechanism." *Nature* 191 (1961): 144–148.

"Biological Transport Phenomena and the Spatially Anisotropic Characteristics of Enzyme Systems Causing a Vector Component of Metabolism." In *Membrane Transport and Metabolism,* edited by Arnost Kleinzeller and A. Kotyk. Prague: Czechoslovak Academy of Sciences, 1962. The paper read by Mitchell in August 1960 at the Prague Symposium.

"Chemiosmotic Coupling in Oxidative and Photosynthetic Phosphorylation." *Biological Reviews* 41 (1966): 445–502. A shorter version of *Chemiosmotic Coupling in Oxidative and Photosynthetic Phosphorylation.* Bodmin, U.K.: Glynn Research Ltd., 1966.

Chemiosmotic Coupling and Energy Transduction. Bodmin, U.K.: Glynn Research Ltd., 1968.

"A Chemiosmotic Molecular Mechanism for Proton-Translocating Adenosine Triphosphatases." *FEBS Letters* 43 (1974): 189–194. A presentation of Mitchell's ATPase mechanism in which protons have a direct involvement.

"The Protonmotive Q Cycle: A General Formulation." *FEBS Letters* 59 (1975): 137–139. An early version of the Q cycle.

"David Keilin's Respiratory Chain Concept and Its Chemiosmotic Consequences." In *Les Prix Nobel en 1978.* Stockholm: Nobel Foundation, 1979. Also available from http://nobelprize.org/. Mitchell's Nobel Prize lecture, which provides an account of the development of the chemiosmotic theory and reviews its status as of that time.

With Roy Mitchell, John A. Moody, Ian C. West, et al. "Chemiosmotic Coupling in Cytochrome Oxidase: Possible Protonmotive O-Loop and O-Cycle Mechanisms." *FEBS Letters* 188 (1985): 1–7. In this paper Mitchell concedes that the ratio of protons ejected to electrons is nonzero but proposes how his fundamental ligand conduction mechanism could account for the results.

"Foundations of Vectorial Metabolism and Osmochemistry." *Bioscience Reports* 11 (1991): 297–346.

OTHER SOURCES

Orgel, Leslie E. "Are You Serious Dr. Mitchell?" *Nature* 402 (1999): 17. This article attempts to assess the historical significance of Mitchell's contribution to science. Orgel compares Mitchell's originality and impact with those of Copernicus and Darwin.

Prebble, John N. "The Philosophical Origins of Mitchell's Chemiosmotic Concepts." *Journal of the History of Biology* 34 (2001): 433–460.

———, and Bruce H. Weber. *Wandering in the Gardens of the Mind: Peter Mitchell and the Making of Glynn.* New York: Oxford University Press, 2003. This is, at present, the only full-length biography of Mitchell as well as an account of his Glynn Research Institute.

Saier, Milton. "Peter Mitchell and His Chemiosmotic Theories." *ASN News* 63 (1997): 13–21. This article also assesses Mitchell's contribution to science.

Slater, Edward C. "Peter Dennis Mitchell, 29 September 1920–10 April 1992." *Biographical Memoirs of Fellows of the Royal Society* 40 (1994): 282–305.

Weber, Bruce H. "Glynn and the Conceptual Development of the Chemiosmotic Theory: A Retrospective and Prospective View." *Bioscience Reports* 11 (1991): 577–647.

———, and John N. Prebble. "An Issue of Originality and Priority: The Correspondence and Theories of Oxidative Phosphorylation of Peter Mitchell and Robert J. P. Williams, 1961–1980." *Journal of the History of Biology* 39 (2006): 125–163.

Williams, Robert J. P. "Possible Functions of Chains of Catalysts." *Journal of Theoretical Biology* 1 (January 1961): 1–17. Submitted August 1960.

———. "The History of Proton-Driven ATP Formation." *Bioscience Reports* 13 (1993): 191–212.

———. "Bioenergetics and Peter Mitchell." *Trends in Biochemical Sciences* 27 (2002): 393–394.

Bruce Weber

MITSCHERLICH, EILHARD

(*b.* Neuende [Jeverland], Germany, 7 January 1794; *d.* Berlin, Germany, 28 August 1863), *chemistry, mineralogy, geology.* For the original article on Mitscherlich see *DSB,* vol. 9.

Mitscherlich came from a middle-class family in the tiny principality (Erbherrschaft) of Jever, which since the reign of Catherine the Great belonged to Russia. His father, also named Eilhard Mitscherlich, was a minister; his mother, née Maria Elisabeth Eden, was the daughter of a small art dealer. From 1804–1810 he attended high school (provincial school) at the town of Jever, where he was much influenced by one of his teachers, the historian F. C. Schlosser. On the advice of Schlosser in 1813 he matriculated at the University of Heidelberg to study Arabic and Persian.

In 1815 Mitscherlich moved to Paris to continue his studies in Eastern languages. After his hope to visit Persia as a member of a delegation that Napoléon Bonaparte had intended to send to the shah was frustrated, he began to study medicine in Göttingen, intending to become a physician on ships sailing to Asia. In Göttingen he also took courses in physics and in chemistry with Friedrich Stromeyer. In the spring of 1818 Mitscherlich decided to go to Berlin in preparation for an academic career in chemistry. There he was warmly supported by H. F. Link, a botanist, chemist, and expert in Eastern languages. He also befriended the mineralogist Gustav Rose, who taught him the basics of crystallography.

In December 1818, working in Link's laboratory at the Prussian Academy of Sciences, Mitscherlich discovered that the potassium, sodium, ammonium, and barium compounds of arsenic and phosphoric acid crystallize to give equivalent pairs with almost identical, that is, isomorphic, crystallographic forms. He also described the crystal forms of the vitriols of manganese, copper, iron, cobalt, zinc, nickel, and magnesium. From a crystallographic standpoint, these substances could be divided into groups, which Mitscherlich distinguished on the basis of their water of crystallization, the ratio between the oxygen of the oxide and that of the water of crystallization being 1:5 for manganese and copper and 1:7 for zinc, nickel, and magnesium. He published his discovery of isomorphism in the *Abhandlungen* of the Prussian Academy for 1818–1819, which was translated into French in 1820. In his paper he stated that "through crystallographic examination, the compositions of bodies will be determined with the same certainty and exactness as through chemical analysis."

Eilhard Mitscherlich. *Portrait of Eilhard Mitscherlich.* SHEILA TERRY/SCIENCE PHOTO LIBRARY.

This discovery revolutionized mineralogy, as the overwhelming majority of mineralogists of that day adhered to the theory formulated by R. J. Haüy that every specific chemical compound has its own specific crystal form. Against the opinion of many mineralogists, Mitscherlich also denied any difference in principle between "natural" minerals and "artificial" minerals.

Furthermore, the discovery of isomorphism was itself a useful addition to chemistry. Jöns Jakob Berzelius especially welcomed the discovery, as it proved helpful in the determination of atomic weights. When compounds of elements with known atomic weights crystallize isomorphically with compounds containing an element of unknown atomic weight, isomorphism suggests the number of atoms of the element in question within one multiple, from which the atomic weight can be determined. The discovery in some cases also allowed chemists to predict the composition of unknown compounds. In 1827 Mitscherlich proved this in the case of selenium, which had been discovered by Berzelius in 1817. Guided by the isomorphic crystallization with the corresponding sulfur compounds, he prepared both previously known selenous acid compounds and hitherto unknown selenic acid compounds. At the same time, he was able to provide correct formulas for the two oxides—SeO_2 and SeO_3—thereby offering impressive proof of the fertility of both chemical atomic theory and isomorphism.

In 1819 Mitscherlich met Berzelius, who was so impressed by the young man that he tried to convince the Prussian minister of education to award him the chair of chemistry at the University of Berlin, which was vacant after the death of M. H. Klaproth and which he himself had been offered. But Mitscherlich was thought to be too inexperienced for this prestigious position; instead the ministry gave him a fellowship to work under the guidance of Berzelius in Stockholm, where he stayed from 1819 until 1822. In Berzelius's laboratory in 1822 he discovered dimorphism (polymorphism) of compounds like sodium phosphate and sodium arsenate. On his return to Berlin, Mitscherlich was elected a member of the Prussian Academy with his own laboratory and a government apartment, where he resided after his marriage with his growing family. Of his five children, his son Alexander (1836–1918) is known as the inventor of a process for extracting cellulose from wood through boiling with calcium bisulfite.

In 1822 Mitscherlich was appointed professor of chemistry at the University of Berlin. He proved to be a good teacher, often illustrating his lectures with practical demonstrations. His *Lehrbuch der Chemie,* published in installments from 1829, became a standard textbook in practical chemistry. On several journeys to Sweden, to France (where he collaborated with A. J. Fresnel in investigating the alteration of the double refraction of crystals as a function of temperature), and to England, as well as by extensive correspondence, Mitscherlich also kept in contact with the European chemical community. While he always was on very good terms with his mentor Berzelius, he often felt unjustly attacked by Justus von Liebig both on a purely scientific level and on a personal level, when Liebig hotly defended his mentor Joseph-Louis Gay-Lussac against seemingly unfair remarks by Mitscherlich and when he strongly criticized the state of academic chemistry in Prussia.

In Berlin, while continuing to do research on isomorphic groups, he also tackled other problems in inorganic and organic chemistry. After having improved William Hyde Wollaston's reflective goniometer in 1823, Mitscherlich discovered the nonisotropic thermal dilation of crystals not belonging to the cubic system. At about the same time, he modified Jean-Baptiste-André Dumas's apparatus, which enabled him to measure vapor densities at high temperatures, and thus to determine the densities of bromine and other elements and compounds. His other accomplishments include the discovery of selenic acid (1827), the clarification of the composition of permanganates versus the manganates (1831), and a method to detect traces of phosphorus (1855). In organic chemistry he investigated benzene (since 1833) after he had obtained it independently of Michael Faraday by the dry distillation of benzoic acid, and he synthesized nitrobenzene, azobenzene, benzenesulfonic acid, diphenylsulfone, and *m*-sulfobenzoic acid. He also succeeded in distinguishing between the solid compound hexachlorocyclohexane and the liquid trichlorocyclohexane. His notion that benzene is the radical of aromatic substances lead to a controversy with Liebig, who still held benzoyl to be the radical of this class of substances. In 1834 Mitscherlich published an investigation of the formation of diethyl ether when alcohol is heated together with sulfuric acid. To explain this reaction he proposed a theory of chemical action by contact, which Berzelius then called "catalytic" action. Liebig strongly rejected that idea. Research on catalysis led Mitscherlich—independently of Louis Pasteur—to investigate the function of yeast, which he took to be a microorganism, in fermentation, which was ridiculed by Liebig. Mitscherlich also studied the inversion of sugar and in 1847 invented a saccharimeter, a polarimeter designed to facilitate the analysis of sugar solution, the principle of which continues to find application today.

After 1830 Mitscherlich's early interests in geology and petrology and especially volcanism became more prominent. His contribution to these sciences consisted more in patient field research in Germany, France, and Italy than in any new theories.

SUPPLEMENTARY BIBLIOGRAPHY

WORKS BY MITSCHERLICH

Lehrbuch der Chemie. 2 vols. Berlin: Mittler, 1829–1840, with several further editions, two French editions; translated into English under the title *Practical and Experimental Chemistry Adapted to Arts and Manufactures.* London: Whittaker, 1838.

Gesammelte Schriften von Eilhard Mitscherlich, Lebensbild, Briefwechsel, Briefwechsel und Abhandlungen. Edited by A. Mitscherlich. Berlin: Mittler, 1896.

OTHER SOURCES

Bugge, G. "Mitscherlich." In *Das Buch der großen Chemiker.* Berlin: Verlag Chemie, 1930.

Krätz, O. "Der Nachlass Eilhard Mitscherlichs in der Abteilung Chemie des Deutschen Museums." *Abhandlungen und Berichte des Deutschen Museums* 41, no. 3 (1973): 29–48.

Poggendorff, J. C. *Biographisch-literarisches Handwörterbuch der exacten Wissenschaften.* Vol. II. Leipzig, Germany: J.A. Barth, 1863.

Rose, G. "Zur Erinnerung an Eilhard Mitscherlich." *Zeitschrift der Deutschen Geologischen Gesellschaft* 6 (1864): 21–72.

Schütt, H.-W. *Die Entdeckung des Isomorphismus.* Hildesheim, Germany: Gerstenberg, 1984.

———. *Eilhard Mitscherlich: Baumeister am Fundament der Chemie.* Munich, Germany: Oldenbourg, 1992. Translated as *Eilhard Mitscherlich: Prince of Prussian Chemistry* by William E. Russey. Washington, DC: American Chemical Society, 1997.

Hans-Werner Schütt

MIZUSHIMA, SAN-ICHIRŌ (*b.* Tokyo, Japan, 21 March 1899; *d.* Tokyo, 3 August 1983), *physical chemistry, molecular structure.*

One of the pioneers in physical organic chemistry in Japan, San-ichirō Mizushima is internationally known for his investigations, from the mid-1920s, of the molecular structures of organic compounds with physical instrumentation, such as radio waves, Raman spectroscopy, infrared spectroscopy, and electron diffraction. Most notably, he elucidated internal rotation around a C-C single bond and discovered the "gauche" form of rotational isomers around 1940.

Early Life and University Education. Mizushima was born in Nihonbashi, Tokyo (Edo), the eldest son of an affluent merchant dealing with luxurious gold-woven textiles for kimonos, whose family business dates back to the eighteenth century. Destined to enter the family business, Mizushima received a sophisticated education at prestigious secondary and higher schools in Tokyo, especially in Western languages, as his family had business dealings with Western countries. He was therefore not particularly encouraged to follow a scientific career. The decline of his family business in his boyhood prompted him to seek another career, and Mizushima chose chemistry, his primary interest in elementary and secondary school, as his major. His choice of career should therefore be regarded as a product of Japanese science education at the elementary and secondary levels established in the mid-Meiji period in the 1890s, rather than as a reflection of his family background, which had often been the case in the early Meiji period in the 1870s. He entered the Department of Chemistry, the Faculty of Science of Tokyo Imperial University, in 1920, and graduated in 1923, when he became an assistant there to his former teacher, Japanese physical chemist Masao Katayama.

As Mizushima himself wrote in 1972, the Department of Chemistry at Tokyo Imperial University had a tradition in physical chemistry. Jōji Sakurai, virtually the founder of the department, had studied chemistry at University College London in England between 1876 and 1881 with Alexander William Williamson; he had assimilated his mentor's dynamic view of the atomic constituents of molecules and "physicalist" approach to chemistry, which emphasized the importance of studying physical properties of chemical substances with instrumentation used in experimental physics, before being appointed as one of the first Japanese chemistry professors at Tokyo in 1882. Sakurai argued, as early as the early 1880s, that chemistry in the future should be "chemical dynamics," that is, "the science of studying the changes caused by the vibration and motion of atoms," and that chemists would have to clarify the truths of chemistry from the viewpoint of physics to advance the science further. This agenda remained an elusive dream during Sakurai's short career as a research chemist during the 1880s and 1890s, but his strong presence provided a favorable condition for the development of physical chemistry in Tokyo's Department of Chemistry.

Mizushima's mentor, Katayama, had chosen physical chemistry as his area of specialization under Sakurai's influence. After graduating from the Department of Chemistry at Tokyo in 1900, Katayama did overseas study (then a prerequisite for Japanese academics for further promotion) at the University of Zürich, Switzerland, with the electrochemist Richard Lorenz and at the University of Berlin, Germany, with the physical chemists Walther Nernst and Max Bodenstein between 1905 and 1909. He was appointed the first professor of physical chemistry at the newly established Tōhoku Imperial University in Sendai, Japan, in 1911 and then succeeded Sakurai as the professor of physical chemistry at Tokyo in 1919. Influenced by Sakurai's pro-atomistic view—and being aware of the contemporary methodological arguments about the role of hypotheses in science, most notably the "energetics" of the German physical chemist Wilhelm Ostwald—Katayama positively adopted atomism as a working hypothesis and published an influential textbook of physical chemistry based on chemical thermodynamics in Japanese, *Kagaku Honron* (Fundamentals of chemistry), in 1914.

Mizushima

Katayama chose theoretical investigations in surface and colloid chemistry, based on his molecular interpretation of thermodynamics and later on the quantum theory, as his research field. His most important research outcome was "Katayama's equation" published in 1916, an equation describing the relationship between surface tension and the temperature of liquids, which he derived from the theory of corresponding states proposed by the Dutch physical chemist Johannes Diderik van der Waals. Katayama is said to have assigned to his students experimental investigations related to his theoretical considerations in surface and colloid chemistry. Indeed, according to Mizushima's recollection in his article published in *Kagakushi* in 1975, Katayama assigned a chemical investigation using radio waves to Mizushima around 1923, hoping that he might be able to "discover proper oscillations of colloidal particles whose frequencies should be within a range much lower than those of molecular internal vibrations" (p. 1). Mizushima could not discover what he had hoped for, but his investigation led to the first experimental support for the theory of electric moments involving dielectric constants developed by the Dutch-born physicist Peter Debye between 1912 and 1913.

Anomalous Dispersion and Absorption of Radio Waves and Dipole Moments. Debye's theory was concerned with an explanation of the change of the dielectric constants of polar substances with varying temperature as well as with varying frequency of external alternating electric field by postulating the existence of permanent dipoles within organic molecules. He proposed this theory in the context of the emergence of polar explanations of organic reactions and the growing interest in polarity within organic compounds in the 1900s and 1910s. According to this theory, in a static or slowly alternating external electric field, organic molecules with permanent dipoles would be oriented in the direction of the electric field causing an increase in dielectric constant, against their temperature-dependent thermal movements after "the time of relaxation" of molecules, which is proportional to the viscosity and the cube of radii of molecules and inversely proportional to the absolute temperature. As the period of alternating electric field would approach the time of relaxation, the orientation of the polar organic molecules could no longer follow the change of electric field. As a result, their contribution to the dielectric constant would disappear, and anomalous dispersion and dielectric loss (absorption of radio waves) would occur. For lack of experimental supports, however, this theory had failed to attract much attention on the part of chemists.

Mizushima's research on dispersion of radio waves (or "electric waves" as Mizushima put them in his papers in English, probably following the Japanese word for radio waves, *denpa*) by glycerin and monovalent alcohols reveals attributes that characterized his research style throughout his career: his ingenuity in constructing physical instrumentation by hand, his skill of networking for interdisciplinary collaborations, and his intellectual prowess in interpreting his experimental findings with available theories. With the technical support of his colleagues in electric engineering at Tokyo, Mizushima first constructed several oscillators emitting radio waves with different wavelengths of 3.08, 6.1, 9.5, and 50 meters and later of 58 centimeters. According to his recollection in 1975, "if I had been an electric engineer, I would then have endeavored to make radio waves of even shorter wavelengths. However, as I was an apprentice chemist, I came across the idea of measuring [dielectric constants of glycerin and alcohols] using available radio waves in continuously changing temperatures" (p. 1). He thus obtained temperature-dielectric constant and temperature-dielectric loss diagrams of glycerin and several monovalent alcohols in several wavelengths. Mizushima argued, based on his data, that Debye's dipole theory held well in all monovalent alcohols that he examined; he published his finding in English in the *Bulletin of the Chemical Society of Japan*, the newly inaugurated Western-language journal of the Nihon Kagaku-kai (Chemical Society of Japan), in 1926.

The idea of continuously changing temperatures proved a key in Mizushima's investigation leading to an experimental support of Debye's theory. However, the above quote suggests that, in doing so, he seems to have been guided not by theories but by his instinct as a physical chemist, for whom temperature control was a standard experimental procedure. The role of Debye's theory for Mizushima was to give a physical meaning to his measurement and to pave the way for the extensive subsequent measurements of the dipole moments of molecules. It is no wonder that Debye was pleased to read Mizushima's papers, arranged the publication of their summary in the prestigious *Physikalische Zeitschrift* in the following year, and explained Mizushima's findings in detail in his monograph, *Polare Molekeln* (Leipzig, Germany, 1929).

Mizushima was promoted to assistant professor at Tokyo in 1927, did overseas study between 1929 and 1931 at the University of Leipzig, Germany, with Debye, and was awarded a Rigaku Hakushi gō (doctorate of science) from Tokyo Imperial University in absentia in 1930. In Leipzig Mizushima spent the majority of his time learning quantum mechanics and its application to chemistry. As Debye's laboratory was then concerned with the investigation of the structures of gas molecules by means of gas-phase electron diffraction, it is likely that Mizushima came across the idea of investigating internal rotation around a C-C single bond in 1,2-dihalogenoethane during his overseas study by learning about the paper of Hermann Mark and Raimund Wierl in 1930.

Mizushima

They argued that the two chlorine atoms in this molecule are approximately in the *cis-* and *trans*-positions according to gas-phase electron diffraction, contrary to the assumption that the rotation around single bonds such as C-C was free, as had been thought since the establishment of stereochemistry by Jacobus Hendricus van't Hoff and J. A. Le Bel in the 1870s.

Internal Rotation and the Discovery of Rotational Isomerism. The key research question for Mizushima was therefore whether rotation around single bonds such as C-C was actually free or whether there were some stable forms. Mizushima started this project in 1932, soon after he returned from Germany. This time he chose to adopt emerging multiple techniques for the investigation of molecular structures such as Raman spectroscopy, infrared spectroscopy, and electron diffraction, as well as the measurement of dipole moments. For this purpose, Mizushima used his extended interdisciplinary networks with manufacturers of optical instruments and physicists at Tokyo Imperial University and the Rikagaku Kenkyūjo (Riken, the Institute of Physical and Chemical Research, established in 1917), where Katayama had held the additional post of researcher; Mizushima assumed the same office in 1934. As he broadened his research front, he felt the necessity to recruit students and to organize a research group. With the support of his former teacher and superior Katayama (Mizushima succeeded Katayama as full professor of physical chemistry in 1938), he was able to recruit advanced students for his research and to build a well-coordinated research group consisting of students of both Katayama and himself, such as Ken-ichi Higashi, Yonezō Morino, and Takehiko Shimanouchi.

The starting point was in his familiar territory, that is, the measurement of temperature changes in the dipole moment of 1,2-dichloroethane in solution with Higashi. Within a year, in 1932, they found that its dipole moment increased when measured at higher temperature or in solvents with higher dipole moment. According to Mizushima's interpretation, this finding suggested some sort of rotation around a C-C single bond within molecules. At the same time, Mizushima, with suggestions and technical advice from the spectroscopist and physicist at the Riken, Yoshio Fujioka, decided to adopt Raman spectroscopy and assigned the measurement of its Raman spectra to Morino.

Without prior research experience in spectroscopy of any kind, it took some time for Morino to master Raman spectroscopy. However, the technological situation in Japan in the 1930s was encouraging for starting such a research project because, as he later recalled in his obituary of Mizushima in 1983, "the advancement of domestic production of optical weapons such as periscope of submarines was strategically important for Japan at that time. An investigation of glass was well underway in the Nihon Kōgaku (Japan Optics Manufacturing Company, today's Nikon), and the technology of removing distortion of glass has just completed there" (p. 1286). Morino constructed handmade Raman spectrographs with the lenses and prisms provided by Masao Nagaoka, an engineer of the Nihon Kōgaku and lifelong friend of Mizushima from his secondary school days. After several attempts, Morino succeeded in 1934 in taking photographs of the Raman spectra of 1,2,-dichloroethane in the liquid state and in solutions. Later in 1936 he took photographs of the Raman spectra of this and other ethylene halides in the solid and liquid states, which showed that several Raman lines in the liquid state disappear on solidification.

Combining this result with the data of dipole measurements by Higashi and the theoretical calculation of normal vibration frequencies and intramolecular potential of this molecule by Morino and Shimanouchi, Mizushima inferred that 1,2-dichloroethane molecules occurred only in the symmetrical *trans*-form in the solid state, and that in the liquid state another rotational isomer existed. According to his interpretation, this new form was not the *cis*-form, but could be obtained from the *trans*-form by an internal rotation of about 120°; Mizushima's interpretation, together with the above-mentioned result of Morino's Raman spectra measurement, was first published in 1936 in his "home" journal as a Riken researcher, *Scientific Papers of the Institute of Physical and Chemical Research, Tokyo* in English, and then in the *Physikalische Zeitschrift* in German in the following year. Increasingly convinced of the existence of this new configuration by his similar researches with other compounds with C-C single bonds, Mizushima coined the term *gauche form* in 1940 to designate it with the help of the Japanese organic chemist and x-ray crystallographer, Isamu Nitta, professor of physical chemistry at Osaka Imperial University, Japan, and a close friend of Mizushima from school days; Mizushima began to use it in his publications in *Scientific Papers* in 1940 and in the U.S.-based *Journal of Chemical Physics* in 1941.

These interpretations were later confirmed by gas-phase electron diffraction of 1,2-dichloroethane molecules by Morino in collaboration with Shigeto Yamaguchi, a former student of Mizushima working at Riken, in 1943, which showed that around 20 percent of all molecules were in the gauche form at room temperature. Between 1946 and 1959, when Mizushima retired from the University of Tokyo (Tokyo Imperial University was renamed the University of Tokyo in 1947), the investigation of internal rotation in his laboratory was extended to other single bonds such as C-O, C-N, C-S, and S-S, using the above-mentioned techniques as well as thermal infrared spectroscopy and analysis measuring energy and entropy differences. By these extended researches his team confirmed that the gauche form existed not only in a C-C single bond, but also in a variety of single bond skeletons of both organic and inorganic compounds.

Mizushima's research on internal rotation gained international recognition after the end of World War II, especially in the United States. In 1951 he was invited by Cornell University to give the G. F. Baker Lectures in chemistry and by the University of Notre Dame, Indiana, to give the P. C. Reilly Lectures in chemistry; he thereafter gave special lectures at various universities in the United States as well as in Europe during summer vacations. Mizushima kept a particularly close relationship with the University of Notre Dame and held a visiting professorship there during the 1950s, partly because he and his wife, Tokiko (she was from the Shōda family and an aunt of Empress Michiko, consort of Emperor Akihito), were Roman Catholic. He was elected in 1955 a bureau member of the International Union of Pure and Applied Chemistry and held this position until 1967.

Structure of Proteins. Mizushima's discovery of the rotational isomers of 1,2-dichloroethane can arguably be regarded as one of the earliest examples of conformational analysis, which saw considerable development in the chemistry of alicyclic compounds and polymers in the 1950s. In addition, during World War II, Mizushima undertook several wartime researches, such as Raman spectroscopic analysis of paraffin in petroleum and polymers as the material of radar. After the war, Mizushima, in collaboration with Shimanouchi, who had research experiences in infrared spectroscopy and in the calculation of long-chain molecular vibrations, turned his attention to the structure of proteins, which was an unexplored area in physical chemistry of polymers.

Understandably, the starting point of the investigation of proteins by Mizushima and Shimanouchi was the *trans-* and gauche-form of rotational isomers of C-C and C-N single bonds, which constitute polypeptide chains. They postulated in 1947 the "B (Bent) form" and led students' works in Raman and infrared spectroscopy and in calculations of molecular vibrations of peptides and proteins to support this model. Unfortunately for Mizushima and Shimanouchi, their B model failed to gain international recognition, as the "α-helix" model proposed by Linus Pauling in 1951 soon prevailed in the fast-growing field of molecular biology and biochemistry. However, Mizushima and Shimanouchi accumulated experimental and theoretical know-how in protein chemistry by this project and trained a considerable number of students who later developed their careers in biological physical chemistry and molecular biology.

Mizushima retired from the University of Tokyo in 1959 at the age of sixty following the University of Tokyo custom of forced retirement taken up by Sakurai and other professors in 1919; he was succeeded by Shimanouchi. Mizushima moved to corporate research and was instrumental in establishing the Tokyo Research Institute of the Yahata Seitetsu (Yahata Steel Manufacturing Company) as director. He remained there for ten years.

Mizushima's research style as a physical chemist is characterized, first of all, by his interpersonal skills in recruiting young chemists and networking with scientists and engineers in different fields. His educational background of having attended prestigious secondary and higher schools in Japan and his connections with Tokyo Imperial University and Riken scientists and engineers counted much in setting up his electronic and spectroscopic investigations, even though he had had comparatively little research experience in these fields. Second, Mizushima's research consisted of frequent movements between experimental investigations and theoretical considerations. He eagerly assimilated Debye's theory of polar molecules and quantum mechanics to interpret his experimental results and to give coherence to the development of his research field. However, a theory was for Mizushima but "a summary of the nature." He was clearly more interested in finding experimental facts unpredictable by existent theories than the construction of a theory with known experimental facts.

Mizushima's way of managing laboratory spaces reflected his emphasis on the discovery of unpredicted experimental facts by means of exchange of ideas: As soon as he was appointed full professor, he allocated a large room next to his office for students and encouraged discussion between teachers and students and among students there. This room was designed so that Mizushima could enter his office only by passing through this large student room. Discussion in this room was seemingly unconstrained, but in fact was under the watchful eye of Mizushima, who was always hungry for new ideas and experimental data. Mizushima built a successful research school on a careful balance between freedom and constraint given to his students and associates.

BIBLIOGRAPHY

The Scientific Papers of Professor S. Mizushima: A Collection Presented by His Friends and Pupils on the Occasion of the Celebration of the Completion of His Thirty-Sixth Year as a Member of the Faculty of the University of Tokyo *(University of Tokyo, 1959) is a select collection of Mizushima's scientific papers; it contains a complete list of his scientific publications, a short biography, and useful surveys of his researches by his collaborators such as Higashi, Morino, and Shimanouchi.*

WORKS BY MIZUSHIMA

Structure of Molecules and Internal Rotation. New York: Academic Press, 1954. Mizushima's only monograph in English.

"A History of Physical Chemistry in Japan." *Annual Review of Physical Chemistry* 23 (1972): 1–14. Mizushima's personal view of the history of physical chemistry in Japan.

"Bunshi Kagaku (Kōzō Kagaku) no Hajimatta Koro" [On the early years of molecular science or structural chemistry]. *Kagakushi* 3 (August 1975): 1–3. Mizushima's recollection of his research on abnormal dispersion and absorption of radio waves.

"Hitoketa no Jikken" [Experiments of the first order]. *Kagaku to Kōgyō* 36 (1983): 727–728. Published posthumously, this article contains information on his collaborative research of internal rotation.

OTHER SOURCES

Baba Hiroaki, Tsuboi Masamichi, and Tazumi Mitsuo, eds. *Kaisō no Mizushima Kenkyūshitsu* [Mizushima Laboratory in reminiscences]. Tokyo: Kyōritsu Shuppan, 1990. Collected recollections by Mizushima's students. Useful for outlining the Mizushima school, especially during and after World War II.

Higashi Ken-ichi. "Denpa no ijō bunsan to kyūshū ni kansuru kenkyū" [[Mizushima's] Research on anomalous dispersion and absorption of radio waves]. *Tanpakushitsu Kakusan Kōso* 28 (1983): 1285–1286. An obituary in Japanese by his collaborator.

Kikuchi, Yoshiyuki. "The English Model of Chemical Education in Meiji Japan: Transfer and Acculturation." PhD diss., Open University, 2006. See Chapters 4–7 for an account of Sakurai.

Kuchitsu, Kozo. "Early Days of Gas Electron Diffraction Studies in Japan." *Structural Chemistry* 16 (2005): 29–32. An English article on Morino, which also mentions his collaboration with Mizushima.

Mizushima Keiichi, ed. *Mizushima San-ichirō: Sono Omoide* [San-ichirō Mizushima and his reminiscences]. Tokyo, 1984. Recollections by Mizushima's family members and personal friends. Useful source on his family background.

Morino, Yonezō. "Obituary: Takehiko Shimanouchi." *Journal of Raman Spectroscopy* 12 (1982): ii–iv. Also mentions Shimanouchi's collaboration with Mizushima.

———. "Mizushima San-ichirō Sensei to Bunshi Bunkō" [Professor San-ichirō Mizushima and molecular spectroscopy]. *Tanpakushitsu Kakusan Kōso* 28 (1983): 1286–1287. An obituary in Japanese by his collaborator.

Tamamushi Bunichi. "Kaimen Kagaku eno Michi: Takayama Masao Kyōju Seitan 100-shūnen ni chinande" [The way to surface chemistry: In memory of centennial birth of Professor Masao Katayama]. *Kagakushi* 8 (October 1978): 1–6. Personal account of Katayama's work by his student in surface chemistry.

Tsuboi Masamichi. "Mizushima San-ichirō Sensei no Kenkyū Sokuseki" [On the works of Professor San-ichirō Mizushima]. *Kagakushi* 22 (1995): 142–151. Survey of Mizushima's research by one of his students.

Yoshihara Kenji. "Kaiten iseitai no hakken: Mizushima San-ichirō Sekai wo meguru Gauche no Hankyō" [The discovery of rotational isomers: San-ichirō Mizushima and the reaction to the gauche form all over the world]. *Gendai Kagaku* 403 (October 2004): 14–19. Accessible guide to Mizushima's researches.

Yoshiyuki Kikuchi

MÖLLER, SOPHIE C(H)ARLOTTE JULIANE (LOTTE)

(*b.* Koblenz, Germany, 17 June 1893; *d.* Göttingen, Germany, 22 June 1973), *oceanography, continental hydrography, limnology.*

Möller counts as the first female professor of oceanography in Germany. She published the first analysis of the deep-sea circulation in the Indian Ocean. Blocked from a promising career in oceanography due to the rivalry of a colleague, she changed fields to hydrography and limnology.

Education. Lotte Möller was born in Koblenz on 17 June 1893. Her father was an auditor at the Prussian Ministry of Agriculture. When her family moved to Berlin, she first visited a private school and later changed to a public secondary school for girls in Berlin. In 1914, at age twenty, she finished the girls' high school with a pedagogical examination, which allowed her to teach at primary and secondary schools as well as to enroll at the philosophical faculty of the University at Berlin. Later she mentioned that school days as well as teaching had been hard to bear, due to her shy nature. During World War I she studied mathematics and geography (1914–1919). She was fascinated by the work of Albrecht Penck, director of the Institute and Museum of Marine Research at Berlin, who taught regional geography, while his colleague Alfred Merz taught limnology (the study of lakes). Max Planck, who would receive the Nobel Prize in 1919, stimulated her interest in physics and mathematics. During this period she also took part in geological courses and became familiar with fieldwork methods.

When male students had to join the army in 1916, Möller and her fellow female students took over Merz's temperature measurements at the Sakrower See. From October 1917 to November 1918 she worked in the laboratory of the Technical Department of Radio Equipment. When she was preparing for her thesis for the next examination, she participated in the investigation of the tides in the North Sea. Finally in 1920 she passed her state examination in geography with honors. After passing her second state examination in the spring of 1921, she continued to investigate the tides. At the same time she taught in several schools in Berlin. During summer she was able to carry out her own research and measurements aboard a ship in the southeastern part of the North Sea.

In February 1923 she was granted leave from school teaching to accept a job as *ausserordentliche Assistentin* (female assistant with a special contract) with Merz. Within a year she prepared her PhD thesis on the deviation of current measurements in the ocean (1924). In his report Merz stressed that her investigation was methodically exemplary. It allowed for the correction of systematic errors from previous measurements and for the analysis of historical data together with contemporary measurements.

Career at the University. Möller was very lucky to become Merz's regular assistant in 1925. (There were only twelve female assistants at the university in Berlin between 1913 and 1933.) She helped him prepare for the German Atlantic Expedition with the surveying ship *Meteor,* which was to investigate the southern Atlantic Ocean from 1925 to 1927. But for the first time she experienced discrimination due to her gender, because of the regulations that forbid females on ships of the German navy. For her male colleagues the expedition was a very good opportunity for working in an unexplored area, but Möller, who was thoroughly qualified, had to stay at home. Instead, in addition to her teaching and temperature research on the Sakrower See, she was in charge of organizing supplies for *Meteor* and analyzing the new data sent to Berlin.

A great privilege was bestowed on her when the German Marine Board offered her the opportunity to accompany the fleet aboard a steamer during a journey in the Mediterranean Sea in 1926, where she could carry out meteorological measurements. During the summer of 1927, she participated in a tourist cruise to the North Cape of Norway. On her way back, she stopped in Bergen (Norway) to work at the famous Geophysical Institute, the European center of oceanography. There she investigated internal waves in fjords.

After Merz's death in 1925 at the beginning of the *Meteor* expedition, Möller continued his scientific legacy and followed his last wish to publish the tables and diagrams of his hydrographical investigation of the Bosporus and the Dardanelles. Knowing the ideas and the way of thinking of her former supervisor, she added additional, previously missing figures and used his short notes to analyze the data. She always made clear what Merz had done and what had been her own conclusions. The work, published in 1928, culminated in a synthesis of the mean conditions of currents between the Black Sea in the northeast and the Mediterranean Sea in the southwest. Her work was of such enduring quality that it was still cited in the third edition of *Allgemeine Meereskunde,* by Gunter Dietrich and others, published in 1975.

In the same year, her commitment to the *Meteor* expedition was honored with the *Meteor* medal of the Emergency Society of German Science, which had financed the expedition.

Möller's older colleague Georg Wüst, who had been promoted from assistant to curator in 1928, felt deeply neglected because Merz had given his legacy by a formal will to her and not to him, although he also had been Merz's student. He did not want to stay in her shadow and made this very obvious. To get out of further quarrels with him, she withdrew from her analysis of the *Meteor* data and looked for another field of work. After long discussions with Albert Defant and Penck, she decided to change to continental hydrography, which was a new research area at German universities. She hoped never to have her work conflict with Wüst's again.

Supplanting from Oceanography. Before Merz left to lead the *Meteor* expedition, he had proposed themes for Möller's and Wüst's second (habilitation) theses required for attaining the rank of professor in Germany. While Wüst was the first German to pass a habilitation in oceanography in June 1929, Möller was only the fourth woman to finish the habilitation in Berlin a month later and became the first female oceanographer. Her thesis dealt with the circulation of the Indian Ocean on the basis of temperature and salinity measurements, and surface currents observations. She used her new methodology to correct systematic errors of older data. In that effort she incorporated deep-sea data from about twenty expeditions to the Indian Ocean dating back to the early 1870s. She presented maps of mean surface currents between 20° N and 20° S for each month of the year, which showed that the deep-sea circulation is dependent on the surface currents, which vary very strongly from season to season. Her results entered the American textbook by Harald Sverdrup and others, *The Oceans,* in 1942 and became one of the basic sources to describe the oceans around South Africa in 1950.

Penck wrote that Möller showed much more versatility than Wüst and noted that she was a very efficient oceanographer and very experienced in limnology. Although she had submitted a thesis on oceanographical research, she received a *venia legendi* (teaching authorization) for geography with special consideration of hydrography. This was to make it clear that she would not interfere with Wüst in the same area of research. Thus she became the first privatdozent to lecture on the hydrography of both running and standing waters.

At the institute she mainly was in charge of the practical course for students at the Sakrower See, where she had established a small field station in October 1927. This lake served as an interface between limnology and

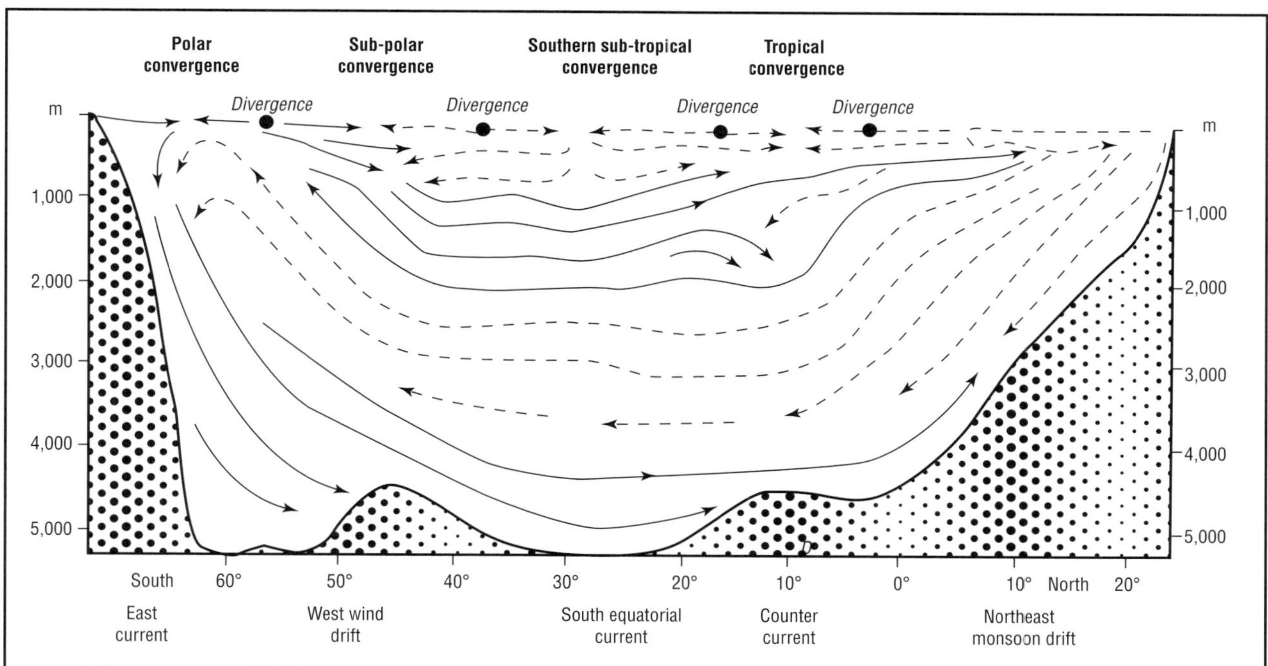

Figure 1. *Meridional component of the circulation in the West Indian Ocean during North winter.*

oceanography, and here she gained great achievements through the investigation of the physical, chemical, and other hydrographical parameters. She also lectured on hydrography in two courses and sometimes on polar oceans or on the North and Baltic seas.

In 1931 she published the results of different oceanographical investigations like water stratification, movement in straits, and hydrographic conditions in Norwegian fjords. An instruction for calculation of water level in the German Bay, prepared for the German Marine Board also in 1931, was followed by a general description of the tides in this area (1933).

She developed a fast and reliable method for synoptic and spatial registration of the waters, which she used in collaboration with the Reich Administration of Waterways to study lakes and catchments areas of rivers. Finally, her investigations resulted in the establishment of the Hydrographical Service and its Hydrographical Institutes. Additionally she continued working on the determination of the constants of seawater. From 1933 onward she investigated the "Frisches Haff," the lagoon in the Bay of Danzig, and integrated modern oceanographical methods with hydrography.

Career under the National Socialist Regime. After seizure of power by the National Socialist Party (NSDAP, or Nazis) on 30 January 1933, women had fewer opportunities to study and to do research as well as to work. At that time Möller was the only remaining female assistant out of six in the institutes of natural science. When Wüst joined the NSDAP on 20 April 1933, her colleagues recommended that she should do the same, so Wüst could not start a political lever against her. On 1 May 1933 she became a member, hoping that as a result she would keep her job. This decision did further her career. When others had to leave, she was permanently appointed in 1934 and became curator at the Institute of Marine Research. On 11 July 1935 her first appointment was *ausserordentliche Professorin* (female professor with a special contract) as the only woman among forty-seven male colleagues, and finally, on 25 May 1939, she was appointed *ausserplanmässige Professorin,* (additional female professor), while Wüst received an *ausserplanmässige Professur* (additional professorship). Due to her very good scientific reputation she was elected, with Penck's sponsorship, to the German Academy of Natural Scientists Leopoldina at Halle in 1940.

To support the Soviet Union campaign in 1941 Möller had to prepare maps of the tides at Helgoland for the Supreme Naval Command. An atlas of the hydrographic conditions of the Gulf of Biscay followed in the same year. When the new department of Continental Hydrography originally proposed in the 1930s was approved on 1 April 1942 to evaluate materials for war in the occupied Eastern territories, Defant wanted Möller to become head of the department and to receive a *beamtete ausserordentliche Professur* (permanently appointed professorship on a special contract). But due to fundamental considerations of the ministry responsible, the chair was not appointed to her, but was given to Wüst. Instead she became head of the new department and received Wüst's former position as group leader. For financial compensation, she got a paid teaching appointment for continental hydrography.

When a connection of the Russian waterways with the German Vistula-Dnieper channel was planned in occupied Poland, Möller led the preparation of a report on the Polish Bug–Pripyat region in 1942. Back home she was in charge of a research program on temperature and ice conditions of the rivers Spree and Havel for the Hydrographical Institute at Potsdam. The investigations were stopped when the instruments, the library, and the archive of the institute had to be evacuated to a salt mine close to Schönebeck-Elbe as a result of the increased air raids that had begun in 1943. Later Möller was called to the Nautical Department of the Supreme Naval Command to participate in the measurements of tides and currents.

New Start. After the war Möller was the only remaining civil servant in charge of the institute, but because of her membership in the NSDAP she was dismissed without notice on 29 December 1945. Möller left Berlin and moved to Göttingen in 1946, where she received a research commission from the academy for "Raumforschung und Landesplanung" (for Space Research and Regional Planning) to investigate the hydrographical conditions of Lower Saxony and completed a survey of the river basin of the Weser for the Directory of the Waterways. Her next publications dealt with the chemical composition of ground and surface waters in connection with the geological conditions of northwest Germany (1949, 1950), which were far ahead of her time.

In 1950 she applied for early retirement so she could spend more time on her scientific interests. The request was denied. In summer semester 1952 she received an unpaid teaching appointment at the university in Göttingen, but still continued her regional analysis of the geographical distribution of concentrations of dissolved substances of ground and surface waters. In 1956 she was appointed *ausserplanmässige Professorin* (female professor with a special contract) for geography and hydrography. In winter semester 1957–1958 she lectured on limnology at the university in Munich. She then retired from the professional world and, slowly losing her sight, spent her last years in Göttingen.

BIBLIOGRAPHY

A complete bibliography and catalog of archival material at the universities of Berlin, Göttingen, and Munich as well at the Leopoldina in Halle can be found in Brosin (1999).

WORKS BY MÖLLER

Die Deviation bei Strommessungen im Meere. Veröffentlichungen des Instituts für Meereskunde, new series A, 13. Berlin: E. S. Mittler und Sohn, 1924. Berlin PhD thesis.

Alfred Merz' Hydrographische Untersuchungen in Borporus und Dardanellen. Veröffentlichungen des Instituts für Meereskunde, new series A, 18. Berlin: E. S. Mittler und Sohn, 1928. This is Möller's analysis of Merz's data.

Die Zirkulation des Indischen Ozeans auf Grund von Temperatur- und Salzgehaltstiefenmessungen und Oberflächenstrombeobachtungen. Veröffentlichungen des Instituts für Meereskunde, new series A, 21. Berlin: E. S. Mittler und Sohn, 1929. Habilitation thesis.

Das Tidegebiet der Deutschen Bucht (Die Vertikalkomponente der Gezeiten). Veröffentlichungen des Instituts für Meereskunde, new series A, 23. Berlin: E. S. Mittler und Sohn, 1933.

"Stechlin-See und Sakrower See bei Potsdam." *Archiv für Hydrobiologie* 29 (1935): 137–156.

"Die chemische Beschaffenheit der Grund- und Oberflächengewässer Nordwestdeutschlands in Beziehung zu den geologischen Verhältnissen." In *International Association of Theoretical and Applied Limnology Proceedings.* Vol. 10, *Congress in Switzerland August 1948,* edited by Wilhelm Rodhe. Stuttgart, Germany: E. Schweizerbart'sche Verlagsbuchhandlung, 1949.

OTHER SOURCES

Brosin, Hans-Jürgen. "Lotte Möller (1893–1973) und die gewässerkundlichen Arbeiten am Institut für Meereskunde Berlin." *Historisch-meereskundliches Jahrbuch* 6 (1999): 19–34.

Dietrich, Günter, et al. *Allgemeine Meereskunde: Eine Einführung in die Ozeanographie.* 3rd ed. Berlin: Borntraeger, 1975.

Lüdecke, Cornelia. "Lotte Möller (1893–1974)—Erste Ozeanograhieprofessorin im deutschsprachigen Raum." *Koryphäe—Medium für feministische Naturwissenschaft und Technik* 35 (2004): 39–42.

Sverdrup, Harald Ulrik, Martin Howell Johnson, and Richard Howell Fleming. *The Oceans: Their Physics, Chemistry and General Biology.* Englewood Cliffs, NJ: Prentice Hall, 1942.

Cornelia Lüdecke

MONTE, GUIDOBALDO, MARCHESE DEL

(*b.* Pesaro, Italy, 11 January 1545, *d.* Pesaro, 6 January 1607), *mechanics, perspective, astronomy, mathematics.* For the original article on Guidobaldo del Monte see *DSB,* vol. 9.

Guidobaldo has often been viewed as a minor figure in the history of mechanics; Duhem described him as "sometimes in error, always mediocre" (Van Dyck, p. 373). Recent research has delved into his writings in greater detail and revealed his frequently ingenious approaches to contemporary problems in physical science and elucidated the historical importance of his work on perspective. This article is divided into two parts. The first emphasizes his work in mechanics and cosmology; the second deals primarily with his writings on perspective.

Mechanics. "Mechanics is no longer mechanics if it is separated from machines"; in current terms mechanics deals with *constrained material systems*. This is the program that Guidobaldo announces in the preface to his *Mechanicorum Liber* (Treatise on Mechanics), in which machines are the five simple machines of ancient engineering tradition, namely, the lever, the pulley, the wheel and axle, the wedge, and the screw.

The *Mechanicorum Liber* gives the appearance of an unbalanced text because 80 percent of its pages deal solely with levers and pulleys; this circumstance can be explained by the fact that Guidobaldo performed many experiments with levers and pulleys, constructing for this purpose true experimental apparatuses: special pulley systems "that turned with a puff of air," equal-armed levers with coinciding centers of gravity and points of suspension. For this particular type of lever Guidobaldo anticipates neutral equilibrium, and he demonstrates it on the grounds that whatever may be the position of the lever, the center of gravity always remains at the same height.

This subject occasioned a debate between Guidobaldo on one side and, on the other, Giordano, Niccolò Tartaglia, and Girolamo Cardano, who denied the state of neutral equilibrium and maintained that the lever would return spontaneously to the horizontal position. The dispute is a good example of scientific "rhetoric" in that Guidobaldo turns his opponents' own arguments against them. For example, in order for the lever to return spontaneously to the horizontal position, the highest part of the lever must "gravitate" more than the lower part, but this implies a displacement of the center of gravity, which is absurd because the position of the center of gravity does not change according to the inclination of the bodies. Therefore it is not true, as is commonly stated, that for Guidobaldo one must take into account the convergence of the weights on the balance toward the center of Earth: his thesis appears only as a rhetorical device in this dispute on equilibrium, and in fact Guidobaldo does not take it into account when he studies the problem in the early propositions of the *Mechanicorum Liber*. Guidobaldo shows that the properties of simple machines are reducible to the properties of the lever. For these simple machines he describes the relations among the weights, hoisting heights of the weights, the time elapsed, and the velocity, along with a physical magnitude that he calls variously "stress," "power," or "force," which in any case indicates something capable of producing or inhibiting the motion of a mechanical system. Guidobaldo enunciates a principle that in current terms can be expressed thus: in machines there is no saving of labor. From his technical experiments Guidobaldo extracted important data such as the clear identification of *string tension* and of the *constrained reaction of the supports* that govern the pulley systems.

One should note the parallel sociocultural action, so to speak, that Guidobaldo undertakes. First, on the philosophical plane, he joins the debate about the relation between art and nature; he shows clearly that machines neither deceive nor surpass nature, but they produce the same effects that nature itself would produce under the same conditions. Second, following the line of thought begun by his mentor Federico Commandino, Guidobaldo continues in the work of reestimation of both theoretical and applied mathematical disciplines within a cultural context that traditionally privileged philosophical, theological, juridical, and medical studies. Thus, Guidobaldo promotes mechanical science around the idea of a broad and highly esteemed presence of machines in the ancient world. He exalts as great "mechanicians" Hero of Alexandria, Ctesibius of Alexandria, and Pappus of Alexandria, and he contests Plato's criticisms of Eudoxus of Cnidus and Archytas of Tarentum for their conceptions of mechanics, which were more applicative than speculative. The highest place of all is occupied by Archimedes, regarded as the ideal figure of the technologist capable of fusing theory with practice, speculation with action.

As far as mechanics is concerned, Guidobaldo perceives an absolute continuity between Aristotle and Archimedes. The Aristotle that he examines is the Aristotle of the *Mechanical Problems*, in which Guidobaldo claims to have found in implicit form principles that Archimedes later formulated in a rigorous manner. His appreciation of Aristotle is not simply formal; the *Mechanicorum* contains not only the Archimedean approach to problems, which considers weights, centers of gravity, and distances from the fulcrum, but also the Aristotelean approach, which deals with weights, displacements, and "virtual" velocities, which today we would call the static and dynamic aspects of mechanics.

The above-mentioned debate over the neutral equilibrium of the lever, besides its polemic purposes, assumed for Guidobaldo a theoretical importance. In the context of his studies, the neutral equilibrium marks the delicate passage from immobility to movement. In machines, says Guidobaldo, the disruption of equilibrium, or rather the passage from supporting weights to moving them, occurs when the relation between resistance and power becomes less than the relation between the "virtual" displacement of power and that of resistance. But how much less? Guidobaldo speaks of this in a letter written in 1580 to Giacomo Contarini (1536–1595), a Venetian patrician

Monte

and an expert in fortifications. Guidobaldo concludes that "matter creates some resistance" when weights move, not when they are supported.

The first printed text on mechanics, the *Mechanicorum Liber* was a great success as evidenced by its translation into Italian four years later, which indicated an active interest on the part of technicians who did not know Latin but who needed to understand the principles of their end products in order to be able to improve them.

Cosmology. In the writings of Guidobaldo the subject of cosmology occupies a somewhat secondary position, which is in keeping with the general orientation of the scientific environment in Urbino, where there was scant interest in such questions. Guidobaldo, however, finds it natural to accept the geocentric image of the universe and he justifies it mechanically. In his commentary on the *Equiponderanti* (*Plane Equilibrium*) of Archimedes he establishes that the Earth, since it is a sphere, has a single center that exhibits both the geometric properties of symmetry and the mechanical properties of the center of gravity. Since according to Aristotle the Earth lies at the center of the universe, the center of gravity will also be at that point. To the objection that the Earth is formed of water and earth, "elements" that have different specific gravities, Guidobaldo responds by citing a proposition in *On Floating Bodies* in which Archimedes demonstrates that the surface of the waters has a spherical form with its center coincident with the center of the Earth. In a page of the *Meditatiunculae* (Little Meditations) he again approaches the question from a mechanical point of view; in fact, he recognizes that the displacement of bodies on the surface of the Earth makes the distribution of weights change, thus causing a displacement of the terrestrial center of gravity and consequently of the entire Earth, an old idea that can be found in Giovanni Buridano. Guidobaldo's booklet *De Motu Terrae* (Concerning the Earth's Motion) has been lost, but given these presuppositions it probably did not contain any different ideas.

The *Problemi astronomici* (Problems of Astronomy), published posthumously by his son Orazio, is a text dedicated exclusively to mathematical astronomy; not even in the chapter on comets does Guidobaldo give any opinions on the terrestrial or celestial nature of those bodies.

He was, however, compelled to speak out in 1604, when there appeared a supernova that called into question the physical doctrine that the heavens are incorruptible. The easiest solution was to classify it as a comet, but unlike comets, the supernova did not show an inherent movement with respect to the fixed stars. This fact was indeed confirmed by Johannes Kepler's observations, which were known to Guidobaldo very probably through Father Christopher Clavius. Guidobaldo accepted these observations insofar as they conformed to his own. Nevertheless, he remained in doubt about the star-comet alternative and was unable to decide whether the heavens could be "corruptible."

Guidobaldo on Perspective. In 1600 Guidobaldo published *Perspectivae Libri Sex* (Six Books on Perspective), which became a turning point in the history of the mathematical theory of perspective. Before Guidobaldo, Commandino, Egnazio Danti, and Giovanni Battista Benedetti had sought to understand the geometry behind perspective, and they had been successful in proving the correctness of certain perspective constructions. Guidobaldo, however, took a different approach, in which he based his considerations on general geometrical laws. He was the first to realize the importance of the perspective images of sets of parallel lines as the basis of constructions, and he created the concept of a general vanishing point. His accomplishments were so fruitful that it is appropriate to designate him the father of the mathematical theory of perspective.

Guidobaldo's inspiration to take up perspective most likely came from his teacher Commandino. Thus, of the two manuscripts on perspective that Guidobaldo left—presumably dating from the period 1588–1592—the oldest one reflects many of Commandino's ideas. The younger one, by contrast, contains new ideas that resulted in Guidobaldo's innovative treatment of perspective.

Before Guidobaldo, it was common knowledge among mathematicians and practitioners of perspective that the images of lines perpendicular to the picture plane converge in one point—later called the principal vanishing point—which is the orthogonal projection of the eye point upon the picture plane. Similarly, some writers were aware that the images of horizontal lines forming an angle of 45° with the picture plane converge at a point on the horizon—later called a distance point. Guidobaldo realized, and proved, that the images of a set of parallel lines that cut the picture plane π (Figure 1) all meet in a point, say V, which he called their *punctum concursus.* He proved that this convergence point, later called a vanishing point, is the point of intersection of the picture plane and the line among the parallel lines that passes through the eye point O. This insight gave Guidobaldo a means to determine the image of a line l that cuts the picture plane in a point A (Figure 1): Since the point A is situated in the picture plane it is its own image and hence lies on the image of l; furthermore the image of l, prolonged, passes through its vanishing point V; in other words the image of l is determined by the points A and V.

From the image of a line, Guidobaldo turned to determining the image of a given point; he did this by constructing the images of two lines passing through the

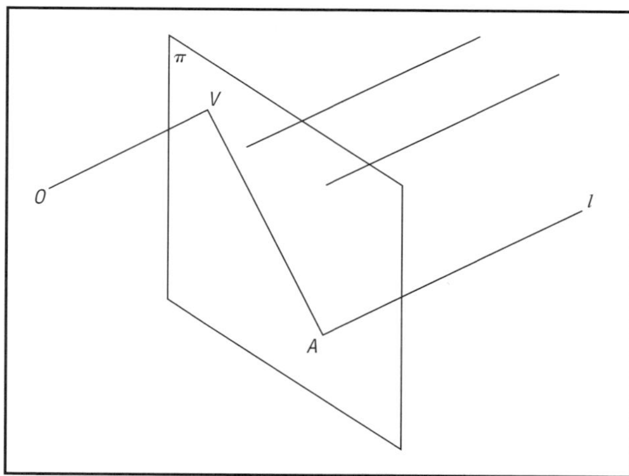

Figure 1. *The vanishing point V for line l and lines parallel to l.*

given point. He was so taken by this possibility that he presented no fewer than twenty-three different methods of constructing the image of a point.

All Guidobaldo's successors took over his concept of a vanishing point either directly from his work or from some of the authors inspired by him, among whom Simon Stevin and Samuel Marolois presumably were the most influential. A great part of the further development of the theory of perspective consisted of generalizations of Guidobaldo's ideas. Thus, later mathematicians introduced the concept of a vanishing line for a set of parallel planes cutting the picture plane. This line consists of the vanishing points of all the lines in the parallel planes—the horizon being a noticeable example of a vanishing line, namely of horizontal planes. Guidobaldo did not single out the concept of a vanishing line, but it occurs implicitly in his work. After Guidobaldo, inverse problems of perspective caught the interest of several of the leading mathematicians in the field of geometrical perspective. Guidobaldo had also touched on this topic, and he opened up a few other topics.

It is impressive how much Guidobaldo obtained by combining classical Greek geometry with his concept of vanishing points. His style of presentation, however, is remarkably inept because he included a lot of unnecessary theorems (for more details on *Perspectivae Libri Sex*, see Andersen, 2007).

Guidobaldo on Euclid and Proportions. As Paul Lawrence Rose wrote in the original *DSB* article, three manuscripts by Guidobaldo on proportions and on Euclid's *Elements* have been identified; however, at present the locations of only two of them are known. Guidobaldo's work on the theory of proportion, and in particular his generalization of Euclid's concept of composition of ratios, were treated by some scholars at the end of the last century.

SUPPLEMENTARY BIBLIOGRAPHY

WORKS BY GUIDOBALDO

I sei libri della prospettiva di Guidobaldo dei marchesi del Monte dal latino tradotti, interpretati e commentati [The six books on perspective by Marquis Guidobaldo del Monte, translated from the Latin with an interpretation and a commentary]. Edited by Rocco Sinisgalli. Rome: Bretschneider, 1984.

La teoria sui planisferi universali di Guidobaldo Del Monte [Theory on the planispheres of the universe by Guidobaldo del Monte]. Edited by Rocco Sinisgalli and Salvatore Vastola. Florence: Cadmo, 1994.

OTHER SOURCES

Andersen, Kirsti. *The Geometry of an Art: The History of the Mathematical Theory of Perspective from Alberti to Monge.* New York: Springer, 2007. See pages 237–265.

Bertoloni Meli, Domenico. "Guidobaldo Dal Monte and the Archimedean Revival." *Nuncius: Annali di storia della scienza* 7, no. 1 (1992): 3–34.

———. *Thinking with Objects: The Transformation of Mechanics in the Seventeenth Century.* Baltimore: Johns Hopkins University Press, 2006.

Biagioli, M. "The Social Status of Italian Mathematicians, 1450–1600." *History of Science* 27 (1989): 41–95.

Field, J. V. *The Invention of Infinity: Mathematics and Art in the Renaissance.* Oxford: Oxford University Press, 1997. See pages 171–177.

Galluzzi, Paulo. *Momento: Studi galileiani* [Moment: Galilean studies]. Rome: Edizioni dell'Ateneo & Bizzarri, 1979.

Gamba, Enrico. "Guidobaldo Del Monte matematico e ingegnere" [Guidobaldo del Monte, mathematician and engineer]. In *Giambattista Aleotti e gli ingegneri del Rinascimento* [Giambattista Aleotti and the engineers of the Renaissance], edited by A. Fiocca. Florence: Olschki, 1998.

———, and Vico Montebelli. *Le scienze a Urbino nel tardo Rinascimento* [The sciences in Urbino in the High Renaissance]. Urbino: QuattroVenti, 1988.

Giusti, Enrico, ed. *Euclides Reformatus: La teoria delle proporzioni nella scuola galileiana* [Euclid reformed: The theory of proportions in the Galilean school]. Turin: Bollati Boringhieri 1993. Includes the two booklets *In Quintum Euclidis Elementorum Librum* (On the fifth book of Euclid's *Elements*) and the *De Proportione Composita* (On compound proportion).

Marchi, Paola. *L'invenzione del punto di fuga nell'opera prospettiva di Guidobaldo dal Monte.* PhD diss., Università degli studi di Pisa, Italy, 1998.

Micheli, Gianni. "Guidobaldo del Monte e la meccanica" [Guidobaldo del Monte and mechanics]. In *La matematizzazione dell'universo: Momenti della cultura matematica tra '500 e '600* [The mathematicization of the universe: Episodes in mathematical culture between the sixteenth and seventeenth centuries], edited by Lino Conti. Assisi: Porziuncola, 1992.

Naylor, R. "The Evolution of an Experiment: Guidobaldo del Monte and Galileo's Discorsi Demonstration of Parabolis Trajectory." *Physis* 16 (1974): 323–346.

Renn, Jürgen, ed. *Galileo in Context*. Cambridge, U.K.: Cambridge University Press, 2001.

Van Dyck, M. "Gravitating towards Stability: Guidobaldo's Archimedean-Aristotelian Synthesis." *History of Science* 44 (2006): 373–407.

Enrico Gamba
Kirsti Andersen

MONTEIRO, ANTÓNIO A.

(*b.* Moçâmedes, Angola, 31 May 1907; *d.* Bahía Blanca, Argentina, 29 October 1980), *mathematics.*

Monteiro conducted his research in mathematics in four countries: Portugal, France, Brazil, and Argentina; his work also had an impact on the perception of modern mathematics in Spain. Monteiro's main contributions pertain to functional analysis, general topology, algebra and algebraic logic.

Early Life. António A. Monteiro was born on 31 May 1907 in Moçâmedes (later Namibe), Angola, then Portuguese West Africa. He was the son of a Portuguese army officer who was stationed there, and who was killed in action in 1915 when his son was only eight years old.

At the age of ten Monteiro entered the Lisbon Military College, graduating in 1925; he then joined the Faculty of Science of the University of Lisbon as a mathematics student. In 1929 he married Lídia Maria de Faria Torres and in the following year graduated as a *Licenciado* in mathematics.

With a scholarship from the Portuguese science research council, the *Instituto para a Alta Cultura*, (IAC) he moved to the Institut Henri Poincaré, where he was a student of Maurice Fréchet. Monteiro received a *Doctorat d'État es-Sciences Mathématiques* from the University of Paris in 1936. He worked on integral equations, a topic in the background of new developments in the theory of linear compact operators in Banach spaces.

His studies in France would later play an important role in the transmission of the French contemporaneous perceptions of mathematics to Portugal and later to Brazil and Argentina. While in France, he also became interested in the research developed in the United States, by Garrett Birkhoff on lattice theory and by Marshall Stone on Boolean algebras and general topology. Later, developments in the United States influenced deeply his views on research and on mathematics education.

Renovation of Mathematics in Portugal. Back in Portugal, Monteiro's research interests moved steadily in the direction of the more abstract areas of functional analysis and topology, some of which had been considered or even introduced by Fréchet. From the late 1930s he exhibited a unique gift for attracting colleagues and graduate students to join him in the areas of research in which he worked. In 1938 the *Academia de Ciências de Lisboa* awarded him the Artur Malheiros Prize for his work on the theory of infinite sets.

From 1938 Monteiro gave a series of mathematical seminars on abstract analysis at the Faculty of Sciences; from 1942, these continued at the *Centro de Estudos Matemáticos de Lisboa*, an institution sponsored by the IAC. Also in 1942, a similar research institute was created in Porto under the direction of his life-long friend Ruy Luís Gomes. The two institutes coordinated their research work and exchanged lecturers and students; this was a novelty in the mathematical Portugal of these years.

Following his return to Lisbon from Paris, in 1936, Monteiro gave careful consideration to the development of the institutional side of his discipline. In 1937 he launched the first exclusively mathematical research journal ever to appear in his country, *Portugaliae Mathematica*. He also recognized the difficulty of raising mathematical standards at the university while the secondary school mathematics education remained at a low level; in 1940 he contributed to the creation of *Gazeta de Matemática*, a journal aimed at raising the level of teachers and students in the final years of Portuguese secondary schools. An outstanding group of young Portuguese mathematicians emerged from Monteiro's seminars; with their help and enthusiasm he supported the creation of the *Sociedade Portuguesa de Matemática* (SPM), of which he was elected the first secretary in 1940. Since then, the SPM has become a focal point for mathematicians and mathematics teachers in his country.

Move to Argentina. A highly principled man with deep democratic convictions, Monteiro soon found himself in opposition to the oppressive regime of António de Oliveira Salazar, who ruled Portugal for more than thirty-five years, from 1932 to 1968. As a result of his independent attitude, his situation became untenable and he was finally forced to emigrate. In 1945 he moved to the University of Brazil, in Rio de Janeiro; there he continued with his own research work and the training of research students. One of them, Leopoldo Nachbin, became a leading mathematician, later a professor at the University of Rochester. The journal Monteiro founded in Rio de

Janeiro in 1948, *Notas de Matemática*, was published in the early twenty-first century by an international publishing house.

In 1949, through the invitation of Julio Rey Pastor, Monteiro moved to Argentina, where he lived for over thirty years until his death in 1980. Initially he joined the University of Cuyo; the doctoral dissertation of Antonio Diego, the first of a group of brilliant students he trained there, was later published in book form by Gauthier-Villars in Paris. His passage through that university was also marked by the creation of the *Departamento de Investigaciones Científicas*, a mathematics research institute advocated by Rey Pastor, and a UNESCO-sponsored Latin American symposium on pure mathematics. At the time Monteiro continued working on lattice theory, trying to use the notion of filter, introduced by Henri Cartan in Paris in 1937, to discuss arithmetic properties of topological spaces. He was interested in finding mathematical objects that, in a general topological space, played a role analogous to that of integers in the field of real numbers. Early results were first communicated at the above mentioned UNESCO meeting, and in more detail in a long paper on the subject he sent to the Fréchet Jubilee in Paris, in 1950. Again through the influence of Rey Pastor, Monteiro was made director of the Mathematical Institute of a new *Universidad Nacional del Sur*, established in Bahía Blanca, Argentina, in 1955. In less than ten years his institute became one of the leading mathematical centers of Latin America, specializing in the modern chapters of mathematics. Through his work on lattice theory, in the 1950s Monteiro became interested in problems of the algebra of logic, a topic which would become the central focus of his research from the 1960s; he and his collaborators explored also its connections with theoretical computing.

In 1961 the *Universidad de Buenos Aires*, the largest university in Argentina, made him a visiting professor for a year, as part of an inducement to attract him to stay there on a more permanent basis. His lectures in Buenos Aires had a profound impact on young research students and resulted in the opening of new areas of research in mathematics at that university. At the end of his appointment Monteiro returned to his institute in Bahía Blanca.

By the 1970s Monteiro was already regarded in Argentina as one of its finest intellectuals. In 1969–1970 a fellowship from the National Research Council of Argentina enabled Monteiro to spend a year doing mathematics research in Europe. In 1972 he retired from the *Universidad Nacional del Sur*, which conferred on him, for the first time, the title of emeritus professor. In 1974 the *Unión Matemática Argentina* awarded him, as it had awarded Rey Pastor before him, the title of Honorary Fellow; this was in recognition of his original mathematical research and of his singular contribution to its development in Argentina.

A Brief Return to Lisbon. When democracy returned to Portugal its science research council, the *Instituto Nacional de Investigação Científica*, invited Monteiro to return to Lisbon. He visited Portugal from 1977 to 1979, after a thirty-two year exile. In Lisbon he was awarded the prestigious Gulbenkian Prize for Science and Technology for 1978 for his work on multi-valued logic. He died in Bahía Blanca, after his return to Argentina, on 29 October 1980.

Impact of Monteiro's Mathematical Work. The Portuguese government awarded him, posthumously, the Military Grand Cross of the Order of Saint James; the *Sociedade Portuguesa de Matemática* dedicated an entire volume of *Portugaliae Mathematica* to honor his memory. The International Congress of Mathematicians, in its 2006 meeting in Madrid, devoted a session to commemorating Monteiro's centenary. His complete works, edited by Eduardo L. Ortiz and Alfredo Pereira Gomes, were published in 2007 by the Gulbenkian Foundation and the Humboldt Press, London, in an edition jointly sponsored by the Académie des Sciences, Paris, and the Academies of Science of Argentina, Brazil, Portugal, and Spain.

BIBLIOGRAPHY

WORKS BY MONTEIRO

Sur l'additivité des noyaux de Fredholm. (Thése présentée a la Faculté des Sciences de l'Université de Paris pour obtenir le Grade de Docteur ès-Sciences Mathématiques, [Série A, No. 1643, No. d'ordre: 2509]), Paris, 1936.

With Alfredo Pereira Gomes. *Introdução ao estudo da noção de função contínua.* Lisboa: Deposita'rio: Livraria Sa'da Costa, 1944.

"Sur l'arithmétique des filtres premiers." *Comptes Rendus des Seances de l'Académie des Sciences*, Paris, 225 (1947): 846–848.

"Filtros e ideais." *Notas de Matemática* (1948): 1–57, 1–131.

"L'arithmétique des filtres et les espaces topologiques." In *Segundo Simposium de Matemáticas.* Buenos Aires: UNESCO, (1954): 129–162.

"Généralisation d'un théorème de R. Sikorski sur les algèbres de Boole." *Bulletin des Sciences Mathématiques* 89 (1965): 65–74.

"Sur les algèbres de Heyting symétriques." *Portugaliae Mathematica* 39 (1980): 1–237.

The Works of António A. Monteiro, 8 vols. Edited by Eduardo L. Ortiz and Alfredo Pereira Gomes. London: Humboldt Press and Lisbon: The Gulbenkian Foundation, 2007. This edition also contains a collection of manuscript notes left by Monteiro and edited by his son Prof. Luiz Monteiro with a group of his collaborators at the UNS's Mathematical Institute.

OTHER SOURCES

Cignoli, Roberto. "La obra matemática de António Monteiro." In *II Encontro Luso-Brasileiro de Historia da Matemática*, edited by Sergio Nobre. São Paulo, Brazil, 1997. A clear account of Monteiro's mathematical work.

Gomes, Alfredo Pereira. "O regreso de António Monteiro a Portugal de 1977 a 1979." *Portugaliae Mathematica* 39 (1985): 33–41. Special issue in honor of António Monteiro.

Luís Gomes, Ruy and Luis Neves Real. "António Aniceto Monteiro e o C.E.M. do Porto (1941/1944)." *Portugaliae Mathematica* 39 (1985): 9–14. Special issue in honor of António Monteiro.

Monteiro, Luiz. "Profesor Dr. António A. R. Monteiro y su actividad en la Universidad Nacional del Sur." In *II Encontro Luso-Brasileiro de Historia da Matemática*, edited by Sergio Nobre. São Paulo, Brazil, 1997.

Nachbin, Leopoldo. "The Influence of António A. Ribeiro Monteiro in the Development of Mathematics in Brazil." *Portugaliae Mathematica* 39 (1985): 15–17. Special issue in honor of António Monteiro.

Ortiz, Eduardo L. "Professor Antonio Monteiro and Contemporary Mathematics in Argentina." *Portugaliae Mathematica* 39 (1985): 19–32. Special issue in honor of António Monteiro.

———. "Transferencias de Matemática Pura y Física Teórica de Portugal a Argentina en 1943–58: Beck, Monteiro y Ruy Gomes." In *Um dia com o Centro de Estudos Matemáticos do Porto,* edited by Maria do Céu Silva, et al. Porto, Portugal: Centro de Matemática da Universidade do Porto, 2001.

———. "António A. Monteiro and the Practice of Mathematics." In *The Practice of Mathematics in Portugal*, edited by Luís Saraiva and Henrique Leitão. Coimbra, Portugal: Por ordem da Universidade, 2004. Monteiro's ideas on mathematics research and education.

Ribeiro, Hugo. "Actuação de António Aniceto Monteiro em Lisboa entre 1939 e 1942." *Portugaliae Mathematica* 39 (1985): 5–7. Special issue in honor of António Monteiro.

Silva da Silva, Circe Mary. "António Aniceto Ribeiro (1907–1980) no Brasil." In *II Encontro Luso-Brasileiro de Historia da Matemática*, edited by Sergio Nobre. São Paulo, Brazil, 1997.

Sousa Amaral, Elza Maria Alves de. "António A. R. Monteiro—Um matemático Português no Brasil." In *II Encontro Luso-Brasileiro de Historia da Matemática*, edited by Sergio Nobre. São Paulo, Brazil: 1997.

Eduardo L. Ortiz

MONTEREGIO, JOANNES DE

SEE **Regiomontanus, Johannes**.

MORENO, FRANCISCO PASCASIO

(*b.* Buenos Aires, Argentina, 31 May 1852; *d.* Buenos Aires, 22 November 1919), *anthropology, geology, paleontology, geography.*

Moreno, who can be considered one of the first anthropologists of Argentina, worked intensively to collect materials in that country and to make them known through preservation in local museums. Moreno spent several years in Europe, where he was inspired by major natural history museums to promote the building of a national establishment of that kind in Argentina. At the start of the twentieth century he was appointed by the Argentine government to act as an expert (*perito*) in the border conflict between Argentina and Chile. His late years were devoted to politics, public education, and the development of scientific and natural resource policies.

Social Context. Francisco P. Moreno was born in Buenos Aires, where he attended primary school. His English-Creole family—the Moreno Thwaites—were active in Buenos Aires commercial, financial, and insurance circles, as well as local politics. His father, Francisco Moreno (1819–1888), was one of the founding members of the influential Club del Progreso, secretary of the Buenos Aires Commerce Stock Market, director of the Buenos Aires Province Bank, member of the Argentine parliament (1854), and a member of the board of Argentine railroads. Francisco Pascasio and his brother did not attend university; rather they worked in the family's insurance companies. The family also possessed sheep ranches in Buenos Aires, where the Moreno sons started their first natural history and archaeology collections, later stored in their private residence. Francisco Pascasio pursued this activity in his adult years. Moreno's scientific self-education relied on handbooks for amateur scientific travelers, such as David Kaltbrunner's *Manuel du Voyageur* published in Zürich in 1879. Thanks to his family connections—especially the friendship of his father with the minister of government of the Province of Buenos Aires—he became part of Argentine learned societies and political networks, where he negotiated state support for his scientific endeavors (Quesada, 1924–1925). He received an honorary doctorate from the University of Córdoba in 1877 and the Royal Geographical Society Founder's Medal in 1907 for extensive explorations in the Patagonian Andes.

Anthropological Collections. The interest of young Moreno in amassing collections of natural history and archaeology drew the attention of prominent members of Buenos Aires political and intellectual circles. Becoming a member of the Sociedad Científica Argentina (Argentinean Scientific Society), established in 1872, he acted as director of the society's museum (1875). Moreno was an extensive traveler: subsidized by his father and Sociedad Científica, in the years 1873–1877 he explored the valleys of Patagonia and the Argentinian Northwest, where he continued to collect natural history and archaeological objects, recording the natural resources of the regions. He pioneered in Argentina the use of both anthropometric instruments created by French anthropologists and Paul Broca's instructions for the collection of calibrated anthropometric data.

In 1877 he presented his collections to the Province of Buenos Aires for the purpose of establishing an archaeological and anthropological museum and to be appointed as its perpetual director. The museum was inaugurated in August 1878. In the years that followed, Moreno's rhetoric, little by little, became plagued by arguments that tied science to fatherland, and exploration traveling to the country's rights over Patagonian territories. In 1879 he was appointed by the national government to lead the Southern Territories' Exploring Commission, sent to the rivers Negro and Deseado, in the Patagonian plateau. Instead, he left the expedition to explore the Patagonian Andes, where he was taken prisoner by the Manzaneros' chief Shaihueque.

The national government considered Moreno a deserter of a public mission. For that reason the minister of government suggested he leave Argentina to acquire real scientific education at the École d'Anthropologie in Paris, in order to become a professional scientist and to skip the dangers of enthusiasm and self education, elements that Moreno celebrated as the core of his scientific endeavors. In Paris he acted as an Argentine correspondent in the frame of the extensive international network articulated by Broca's successor Paul Topinard for completing the collection of skeletons and crania of the École d'Anthropologie. In the late 1870s he contributed in providing evidence to the idea sustained in Paris that in the Americas, as in Europe, the native race was characterized by dolichocephalism, the brachycephalic race having arrived lately from the West.

La Plata Museum. Returning to Argentina in 1881, Moreno lobbied for the formation of a monumental national museum in Buenos Aires, which by different circumstances was established as a provincial institution in the city of La Plata, a short distance from Buenos Aires. The Museo de La Plata, Argentina, established in 1884, was the first in South America to have a building especially designed for the requirement of a museum. Devoted to the study of "American man" and evolution in South America, the museum envisioned a continental scope; to achieve its goals Moreno employed different strategies to collect objects that encompassed geology, zoology, paleontology, botanic, archaeology, and societies that, at the time, were perceived to be in the process of "extinction." In the late 1870s and the 1880s several campaigns against native peoples from Patagonia and Chaco were carried out as governmental or private initiatives to erase "savagery" from lands to be included in the market economy. Either to preserve information about "vanishing races" or to record the changes experienced by native peoples in the process of becoming "civilized," expeditions were dispatched to the localities where that process was taking place. As a result, the Museo de La Plata repositories continue to represent, in the early twenty-first century, one of the sources for researching the preindustrial period of native peoples inhabiting present-day Argentina and the Southern Cone (Sheets-Pyenson, 1988; Lopes and Podgorny, 2000). This position was not always assured: administrators of the budget of the Province of Buenos Aires were not always sympathetic to Moreno's requirements, and he had to redefine the mission of the Museo de La Plata several times in order to justify its continuing existence.

Geological and Geographical Expeditions. During his expeditions of the late 1870s in the Southern Andes, Moreno explored Lake Nahuel Huapí and Río Santa Cruz. In doing so he named several lakes, such as the Lake San Martín.

A concern with the question of the distribution and origin of mammals as posed by Florentino Ameghino (1854?–1911) in the late 1880s had been responsible for shifting the interest of the museum's expeditions toward Patagonia vertebrate paleontology. Naturalist travelers were dispatched to Chubut, Santa Cruz, Tierra del Fuego, and Isla de los Estados to collect fossil mammalians, reptiles, and birds. These collections represent an outstanding contribution to the knowledge of a previously unknown fossil fauna. Museo de La Plata employees also surveyed different regions of the country and published geologic profiles of the Argentine Andes. The research expeditions also revealed a great number of lower forms of vertebrates, including numerous marsupialia, some of which—according to Moreno—were closely related to the mammals of the Pleistocene fauna of Australia.

When Moreno was appointed in 1896 as geographical *perito* (expert) in the border conflict with Chile, following the policy settled in the Treaty of 1881, he explored the Andean regions with a team of geologists. Maps, photographs, plans, and geologic profiles complemented a complete geographical and physiographic description of Patagonia that resulted from the expedition under Moreno's leadership. One of Moreno's most important accomplishments was the observation of the fact that in the Patagonian Cordillera the interocean *divortium aquarum* in many places does not overlap with the highest peaks of the Andes. Moreno also recognized two glacial events in Patagonia (Camacho, 2000). During those years, he also propagated the idea of the ancient connection between the new uplifted lands of the southern part of the American continent and the other lands of the Southern Hemisphere—Africa and Australia (Camacho, 2000; Moreno, 1899). In 1899 Moreno proposed in London that experienced geologists from the Royal Geographical Society, the Royal Society, and the British Museum, with other scientific institutions, should carry out the systematic examination of the Argentine country in order to investigate south American fossiliferous strata (Moreno, 1899).

Scientific and Educational Policies. In 1906 Moreno resigned the directorship of the Museo de La Plata. He was elected national deputy for 1910–1913. In this capacity he proposed several projects, such as the construction of railroads in Patagonia (1910); the acquisition of Ameghino's collections and library for the national museum (1911); the creation of a national scientific service (for topographic, hydrographical, geologic, and biological surveys, 1912); and the establishment of national parks (1912) (Ludueña, 1995). Moreno cooperated in the organization of the Congreso Científico Internacional Americano (Buenos Aires, 1910). He acted as vice president of National Council for Education, devoting much work to the protection of working-class children, and to the dismantling of the National Museum of Pedagogy, which was led by socialist teachers. Moreno was also active in the introduction to Argentina of the Boy Scouts movement in 1911. Most of Moreno's articles were published in the *Revista* and *Anales* of the Museo de La Plata, publications he established in 1890.

Public Dimension of Moreno. Moreno died in Buenos Aires in November 1919, in a country divided by the so-called social issue (*cuestión social*) that generated the most diverse reactions among the Argentine upper class, such as the creation in January 1919 of Liga Patriótica, a permanent citywide militia that upheld "fatherland and order." Moreno's funeral was a public event attended by the president of the Liga Patriótica, who turned Moreno into a hero of the Argentine Right movements.

This adoption of Moreno by the Argentine Right was fulfilled in the 1930s and 1940s. Since then, Moreno has been presented to the public as the sentry of Patagonia. In this frame, those elements that during Moreno's life were criticized by his contemporaries—enthusiasm, self-education, and amateurism—became the key elements for Moreno's future biographers, such as Aquiles Ygobone (1953) and Carlos A. Bertomeu (1949). This kind of biography that emphasized the patriotic value of Moreno's travels continues to be very popular even in the early twenty-first century. Instead of a reliable source for the historian of science they constitute a corpus that still requires further study to enable a full understanding of the history of ideology in Argentina.

BIBLIOGRAPHY

WORKS BY MORENO

"Cementerios y paraderos prehistóricos de la Patagonia." *Anales científicos argentinos* 1 (1874): 2–13.

"Sur des restes d'industrie humaine préhistorique dans la République Argentine." *Compte-rendu du Congrès international d'anthropologie et d'archéologie préhistoriques.* Stockholm: Norstedt & Söner, 1876.

El estudio del hombre Sud-Americano. Buenos Aires: La Nación, 1878.

Viaje a la Patagonia Austral, 1876–1877. Buenos Aires: La Nación, 1879.

"Voyages en Patagonie." *Bulletin de la Société de Géographie de l'Est* 2 (1880): 534–571.

"Antropología y arqueología. Importancia del estudio de estas ciencias en la República Argentina." *Anales de la Sociedad Científica Argentina* 12 (1881): 160–173, 193–207.

"Patagonia. Resto de un antiguo continente hoy sumergido. Contribuciones al estudio de las colecciones del Museo Antropológico y Arqueológico de Buenos Aires. Conferencia del 15 de Julio de 1882." *Anales de la Sociedad Científica Argentina* 14 (1882): 97–137.

"El Museo de La Plata, rápida ojeada sobre su fundación y desarrollo." *Revista del Museo de La Plata* 1 (1890): 1–30.

Esploración arqueológica de la Provincia de Catamarca: Primeros datos sobre su importancia y resultados. La Plata, Argentina: Tall. del Museo, 1891.

"Notas sobre algunas especies de un género aberrante de los Dasypoda (Eoceno de la Patagonia) conservadas en el Museo de La Plata." *Revista del Museo de La Plata* 2 (1891): 57–63.

With Alcide Mercerat. "Catálogo de los Pájaros Fósiles de la República Argentina conservados en el. Museo de La Plata." *Anales del Museo de La Plata* 1 (1891): 7–71.

"Reconocimiento de la región andina de la República Argentina. Apuntes preliminares sobre una excursión a los territorios del Neuquén, Río Negro, Chubut y Santa Cruz hecha por las secciones Topográfica y geológica bajo a dirección de F. P. Moreno, director del Museo." *Revista del Museo de La Plata* 8 (1898): 99–372.

"Note on the Discovery of *Miolania* and of *Glossotherium* (*Neomylodon*) in Patagonia." *Nature* 1556, no. 60 (1899): 395–398.

OTHER SOURCES

Bertomeu, Carlos A. *El perito Moreno, centinela de la Patagonia: Estudio biográfico.* Buenos Aires: El Ateneo, 1949.

Camacho, Horacio. "Francisco P. Moreno y su contribución al conocimiento geológico de la Patagonia." *Saber y Tiempo* 9 (2000): 5–32.

"Embodied Institutions. La Plata Museum as Francisco P. Moreno's Autobiography." 34th Cimuset Conference in Brazil, Río de Janeiro, 2006. Río de Janeiro: Mast, 2007.

Hosne, Roberto. *Francisco Moreno: Una herencia patagónica desperdiciada.* Buenos Aires: Emecé, 2005.

Lopes, Maria Margaret, and Irina Podgorny. "The Shaping of Latin American Museums of Natural History." *Osiris* 15 (2000): 108–118. An accessible overview of the history of the Museo de La Plata.

Ludueña, Felipe. *Labor parlamentaria del Perito Doctor Francisco P. Moreno.* Buenos Aires: Secretaría Parlamentaria. 1995.

Luna, Félix. *Francisco P. Moreno.* Buenos Aires: Planeta, 2001.

Moreno, Eduardo V. *Reminiscencias de Francisco P. Moreno. Versión propia.* 2nd ed. Buenos Aires: Editorial Universitaria de Buenos Aires, 1979.

———. *Perito Moreno's Travel Journal: A Personal Reminiscence.* Buenos Aires: El Elefante Blanco, 2002.

Moreno Terrero de Benites, Adela. *Recuerdos de mi abuelo Francisco Pascasio Moreno: "El perito Moreno."* Buenos Aires: s.n., Tall. Gráf. La Tradición, 1988.

Podgorny, Irina. "Bones and Devices in the Constitution of Paleontology in Argentina at the End of the Nineteenth Century." *Science in Context* 18, no. 2 (2005): 249–283. The most accessible discussion in English.

———. "La derrota del genio. Cráneos y cerebros en la filogenia argentina." *Saber y Tiempo* 5, no. 20 (2006): 63–106.

Quesada, Ernesto. "Doctor Francisco P. Moreno: 1852–1919. Fundador y primer director del Museo: Homenaje a su memoria en representación del Instituto Histórico y Geográfico del Brasil." *Revista del Museo de La Plata* 28 (1924–1925): 9–16. The most reliable biographical note on F. P. Moreno.

Sheets-Pyenson, Susan. *Cathedrals of Science: The Development of Colonial Natural History Museums during the Late Nineteenth Century.* Montreal: McGill-Queen's University Press, 1988. A good overview for the general reader.

Ygobone, Aquiles. *Francisco P. Moreno. Arquetipo de argentinidad. Contribución al estudio e investigación histórica, geográfica, económica y social del País.* Buenos Aires: Orientación Cultural, 1953.

Irina Podgorny

MORGAN, THOMAS HUNT

(*b.* Lexington, Kentucky, 25 September 1866; *d.* Pasadena, California, 4 December 1945), *embryology, genetics.* For the original article on Morgan see *DSB,* vol. 9.

The original *DSB* article presented Thomas Hunt Morgan as a specialist in embryology and genetics. Garland E. Allen painted Morgan as a man "known to his friends, colleagues, and students as a man of quick mind, incisive judgment, and sparkling humor" (p. 515). The reader sees a Morgan who won a Nobel Prize for his work in genetics, but also the study of heredity as a logical and consistent part of a more complex Morgan excited about natural history and organisms generally. Allen introduced Morgan's most important students, but the emphasis remained on Morgan and his ideas and methods. The picture was consistent with that presented in formal obituaries and earlier biographical sketches, though Allen was much more aware of the larger context in which Morgan worked than most previous authors.

In his much longer biography of Morgan published two years later, Allen developed this picture further and added some additional themes that he pursued in other work in more detail. Chapter 3 of *Thomas Hunt Morgan: The Man and His Science* (1978) laid out the idea of a "revolt from morphology" that had formed a foundation for his textbook, *Life Science in the Twentieth Century.* Thus, Morgan became the exemplar for a broad interpretation of trends in the history of biology.

Work at Bryn Mawr. Importantly, the years that Allen characterized in terms of the "revolt" and that he tied to Morgan's endorsement of the experimental embryological program of "Entwicklungsmechanik" were also the years that Morgan was on the faculty at Bryn Mawr College. Allen acknowledged the significance of this appointment at a leading women's college in a couple of pages, but later scholarship by Margaret Rossiter and Helen Lefkowitz Horowitz has carried exploration of the role of women in science, and the role of Bryn Mawr and Martha Carey Thomas in particular, much further.

The fact that Morgan and fellow leading biologists Edmund Beecher Wilson and Jacques Loeb each began his career at Bryn Mawr in the last two decades of the nineteenth century deserves more attention. Despite the limited archival materials in the scientists' collections concerning this early period, there may well be instructive materials available at Bryn Mawr or in collections of outstanding students there. Researchers have little understanding of what Morgan, Wilson, and Loeb gained from Bryn Mawr, though it is clear that Morgan gained a wife. Lilian Vaughan Sampson Morgan became Morgan's collaborator on many projects, and a researcher in her own right.

It is known what scholarly work Morgan carried out at Bryn Mawr, but there is little about his teaching or interactions with students in his lab. One can hope for future insight along these lines to illuminate the way science was carried out in that time and place and to learn more about what the growing study of women in science reveals about scientific careers more generally. Because the building of a collaborative team became a central feature of Morgan's research approach, and because Morgan did work with such outstanding young women as Nettie Maria Stevens during his Bryn Mawr days, one can only

Thomas Hunt Morgan. *Thomas Hunt Morgan with a microscope.* © BETTMANN/CORBIS.

speculate about whether he began to learn such lessons there and carried them with him.

Morgan as Naturalist. In 1904, Wilson recruited Morgan to join him at Columbia University where Morgan remained until he was again lured away, this time at age sixty-two, to the California Institute of Technology (Caltech). In his full biography, Allen portrayed Morgan as a passionate and energetic researcher driven by questions and pursuing productive methodologies. Allen's Morgan was never a single-minded geneticist, but rather a naturalist always fascinated by questions about development, evolution, heredity, and the way that all those forces work together. From the 447-page biography, the reader learns about the details of Morgan's 22 books and more than 370 published papers. Allen worked through the diverse lines of research that Morgan pursued, sketching the driving questions, the ideas, the organisms studied, and Morgan's results and interpretations. His was a first-rate biography consistent with the highest scholarly standards of the time.

Allen concluded his study by making clear that this is not an example of the "great man" view of history, where science and other successes are driven by one great man after another, each doing great things. It was important to Allen not to focus on the Nobel Prize–winning work, nor on the Caltech lab where Morgan worked from 1928 until his death in 1945, but rather all aspects of the whole career of the whole man. As Allen explained

> It is in the qualities of the interaction of human and intellectual spheres that Morgan has contributed much to our understanding not only of genetics, but also of the process of science. Morgan was a product of his times, perhaps more than he would have been willing to admit. But he left his imprint on modern biology; he influenced the subsequent course of work in the field in a way that made it quite different from what had gone before. A lucid experimentalist himself, he also possessed that special personal quality that enabled him to work cooperatively. It is in this way, more perhaps than in his technical finds, that he represented the most profound wave of the future. (1978, pp. 399–400)

As a Marxist, Allen saw it as important to emphasize the social and institutional contexts, and to demonstrate that what matters for the processes of science is the social interactive accumulation of contributions. For Allen, this meant not only that Morgan's own contributions were replaced and interpreted by others, but that Allen's own interpretations would be replaced as well. He explained that he saw his biography as only a beginning, as raising more questions than it answered. "My hope," Allen wrote,

> is that it will help to focus some of the important questions for other historians of biology to pursue in depth. Topics such as the relationship between embryology and genetics, the growth of eugenics and theories of the genetic basis of human and animal behavior, the development of population genetics, and genetics and biochemistry are but a few areas which have only been touched upon, but not developed, in the present volume. If this book serves any long-lasting function, it will be more in the questions it asks, than the answers it provides. (p. xiii)

Allen's portrait of Morgan has had lasting impact, and is likely to remain the most important starting point for study of Morgan for some time. Yet his study did stimulate further questions and explorations, just as he wished, and those have provided a richer understanding of the history of science and of Thomas Hunt Morgan as a part of that scientific enterprise. Some of the studies that expand the understanding of Morgan and of the history of science include Robert E. Kohler's emphasis on the material culture of the Morgan lab at Caltech, Jane Maienschein's examination of Morgan's epistemology, and Frederic L.

Holmes's look at Morgan in the context of the history of genetics and biochemistry.

Other biographical studies, such as Ian B. Shine and Sylvia Wrobel's *Thomas Hunt Morgan: Pioneer of Genetics* (1976) or an essay by Eric Kandel, have emphasized Morgan's contributions to genetics, and have largely set aside the connections of those studies with other areas of biology. These serve their purpose, but in emphasizing the emergence of genetics, they miss the connectedness across areas of evolution, development, and heredity that Allen's approach revealed and that helps illuminate the complexity of both life and the science that seeks to understand the phenomena of life.

Kandel's 1999 essay, "Thomas Hunt Morgan at Columbia University: Genes, Chromosomes, and the Origins of Modern Biology," was intended to highlight one of Columbia's great men for the *Columbia Magazine.* Yet rather than seeing Morgan as a biologist, concerned with a range of questions about life, Kandel gave the impression that Morgan cared only about genes and suggested that Morgan was in search of the gene, which he identified in the "year of discovery," 1910. As Kandel put it, the great breakthrough of twentieth-century biology was

> the discovery that the gene, localized to specific positions on the chromosome, was at once the unit of Mendelian heredity, the driving force for Darwinian evolution, and the control switch for development. This remarkable discovery can be traced directly to one person and to one institution: Thomas Hunt Morgan and Columbia University. (p. 2)

Such exaggerations are typical because posterity often looks back at what are considered great ideas and great successes by great men. While understandable in the context, they are highly problematic because they give mistaken impressions of how science works. Morgan was not single-mindedly looking for "the gene," and indeed he rejected the Mendelian theory of heredity and the theoretical and unverifiable "gene" until late 1910. Even then, as Maienschein has demonstrated, his epistemological commitments required a high standard of evidence in favor of theoretical claims. And as Holmes explained in the first chapter of his *Reconceiving the Gene,* Morgan's understanding of what a gene might be changed over time and was complex at any rate.

Furthermore, study of genetics did not bring together study of heredity, evolution, and development during Morgan's lifetime. Morgan continued to struggle to see how genetic inheritance might connect with embryology. When the young Boris Ephrussi wrote to Morgan that his 1934 *Embryology and Genetics* did not, in fact, bring the two fields together, Morgan responded that the book did indeed include both and that he had not promised to show how they are connected. It was too early to understand how genetics and development intersect. Therefore, the picture is much more complex than the linear progress toward discovery of fact that Kandel presented.

Morgan as Lab Director. The most important revisionist look at Morgan's place in the history of science has been Robert E. Kohler's *Lords of the Fly:* Drosophila *Genetics and the Experimental Life* (1994). As the title suggests, this is a study of the fly and the layers of what is became popular to call the "material culture" of scientific study of this fruit fly that became so important to the understanding of genetics. Kohler explained clearly that he sought to examine the fly room as a particularly instructive example of "the nature of experimental life"—particularly instructive because of the focus on a famous community that had had important results certified as successful. As Kohler noted, "Few laboratory creatures have had such a spectacularly successful and productive history as *Drosophila.*" He saw Morgan's fly room, first at Columbia and then at Caltech, as "an archetypical experimental community" (p. 1). Kohler did not intend to write a biographical study of one man, nor an intellectual tracing of one man's or even one scientific school's ideas. Instead, he sought to illuminate science by looking at an exemplary laboratory and all the people and interactions and practices within it. What also emerged from Kohler's book was a revised picture of Morgan and his contributions.

Whereas Allen's Morgan was a fine man, inspiring to his students and successful in putting together collaborative teams, Kohler's Morgan was more the representative of an older generation whose team of younger students carried out many of the intellectual and most of the technical innovations in the lab. Allen's Morgan had disagreements with others and taught students such as Hermann J. Muller who had disputes with their advisor. But the lab remained largely a happy and productive place in Allen's study.

Perhaps the differences arose partly because Allen concentrated more on the earlier Columbia years while Kohler looked more closely at the Caltech years. But the differences are not just minor matters of emphasis or focus. For Allen, Morgan's contributions were intellectual and social. Morgan built up a remarkably successful lab, and Morgan's group carried out outstanding scientific work there. Once Allen had detailed that work, however, Kohler could shed light on the cracks in the system. He shows that a collaborative team in science, where so much hinges on who gets the credit, is likely to experience disputes or at least uneasiness over credit. His readers see that while Morgan provided intellectual drive, he contributed relatively little technical innovation concerning how to study the fly, or how to get at the genes and their structure and function and effects.

Kohler beautifully laid out the work in the fly room, and the interactions of the "boss and boys" (p. 62), in ways that raise questions about what it meant to work as a team, to mentor younger students, to work together for so long in such different ways. Remember that Morgan was already near official retirement age by the time he moved to Caltech, yet he continued his research almost until his death. Kohler discussed how the relationships changed, and how the dynamics of the fly room evolved.

Through Kohler's study, the researcher comes to understand "the experimental life" in new ways. Kohler provided an outstanding complement to Allen's more traditional focus on the leading man full of ideas and questions. Together, these studies depict a picture of Morgan as a complex scientist in an increasingly complex scientific community and set of practices. Together, they raise new questions that suggest that even more additions and revisions of an understanding of Morgan can be expected in the future. They also show that in producing scientific biography of the twentieth century and later, the individual scientist must be placed in the larger context not only of social and institutional constraints but of choices and material culture and laboratory practices. Ideas, technology, organisms and their sometimes errant real life behaviors, scientists, and assumptions all work together to shape and define science—and to define the contributions and biographical interpretations of any one contributor.

SUPPLEMENTARY BIBLIOGRAPHY

WORK BY MORGAN

Embryology and Genetics. New York: Columbia University Press, 1934.

OTHER SOURCES

Allen, Garland E. *Life Science in the Twentieth Century.* New York: Wiley, 1975; Cambridge, U.K.: Cambridge University Press, 1978.

———. *Thomas Hunt Morgan: The Man and His Science.* Princeton, NJ: Princeton University Press, 1978.

Holmes, Frederic Lawrence. *Reconceiving the Gene: Seymour Benzer's Adventures in Phage Genetics,* edited by William C. Summers. New Haven, CT: Yale University Press, 2006.

Horowitz, Helen Lefkowitz. *The Power and Passion of M. Carey Thomas.* Urbana: University of Illinois Press, 1999.

Kandel, Eric R. "Thomas Hunt Morgan at Columbia University: Genes, Chromosomes, and the Origin of Modern Biology." *Columbia Magazine* (Fall 1999). Available from http://www.columbia.edu/cu/alumni/Magazine/Legacies/Morgan/.

Kohler, Robert E. *Lords of the Fly:* Drosophila *Genetics and the Experimental Life.* Chicago: University of Chicago Press, 1994.

Maienschein, Jane. "T. H. Morgan's Regeneration, Epigenesis, and (W)holism." In *A History of Regeneration Research: Milestones in the Evolution of a Science,* edited by Charles Dismore. Cambridge, U.K.: Cambridge University Press, 1991.

———. *Transforming Traditions in American Biology, 1880–1915.* Baltimore, MD: Johns Hopkins University Press, 1991.

Rossiter, Margaret. *Women Scientists in America: Struggles and Strategies to 1940.* Baltimore, MD: Johns Hopkins University Press, 1982.

Shine, Ian B., and Sylvia Wrobel. *Thomas Hunt Morgan: Pioneer of Genetics.* Lexington: University of Kentucky Press, 1976.

Jane Maienschein

MORGENSTERN, OSKAR (*b.* Görlitz, Germany, 24 January 1902; *d.* Princeton, New Jersey, July 26, 1977), *economics, forecasting, theory of games, defense economics, accuracy of observations.*

Morgenstern was one of the two founders of the theory of games, along with John von Neumann. This seminal work provided the social sciences with the precise mathematical tools to describe strategic decision-making. He is also known for his early work on economic forecasting and on the limits of economic behavior.

Morgenstern was trained as a member of the Austrian school of economics but was far more open to new ideas than were most of its members. It was founded by Karl Menger as a school of economic thought stressing individualism. He received the degree of Doctor Rer. Pol. from the University of Vienna in 1925. With a Laura Spellman Rockefeller Fellowship, he subsequently studied at the Universities of London, Paris, and Rome, and then at Harvard University in Cambridge, Massachusetts, and Columbia University in New York City. He later noted that one of his important memories of this time was a visit to Francis Edgeworth shortly before he died. Edgeworth was one of his heroes and a precursor to the invention of cooperative game theory.

In 1929 Morgenstern returned to the University of Vienna as a privatdozent. Two years later he succeeded Friedrich Hayek as director of the Austrian Institute for Business Cycle Research in Vienna, where he concentrated on the study of speculation and economic prediction and employed Abraham Wald at the institute. Morgenstern had a great eye for talent and was willing to hire Wald, an unknown, poor Rumanian Jew whose talents in the application of mathematics to economics and statistics soon became apparent. In 1935 Morgenstern became a professor of economics at the University of Vienna. He was also a participant in Karl Menger's

Morgenstern

influential Vienna Circle. Morgenstern was an advisor to the Austrian National Bank from 1932 to 1938 and to the Ministry of Commerce from 1936 to 1938. In 1936 he became a member of the Committee of Statistical Experts of the League of Nations.

Princeton and Game Theory. Although not Jewish, Morgenstern in 1938 was deemed to be politically unacceptable, and he therefore left Austria for the United States, where he was appointed as a lecturer in economics at Princeton University in New Jersey. He became an associate professor in 1941 and a full professor in 1944, the year he became a U.S. citizen.

Morgenstern's 1935 article, "Perfect Foresight and Economic Equilibrium," prompted the mathematician Edward Cech to have him look at the 1928 article by John von Neumann on two-person zero-sum games. How one predicts the behavior of others and how this influences one's own behavior is critical to game theory analysis and to economic forecasting. The von Neumann article offered a formalization of this idea. He finally met von Neumann in Princeton, where they became good friends as well as colleagues. Together, they wrote *Theory of Games and Economic Behavior* (1944), which not only launched game theory but provided the basis for the theory of choice under uncertainty.

In the best sense of the term, Morgenstern must be regarded as a great entrepreneur in the development of economics in general and game theory in particular. There has always been considerable skepticism concerning his role in the development of game theory. An unverified story has a mathematician ask von Neumann, "What was Oskar Morgenstern's contribution to the Theory of Games?" Von Neumann is said to have replied: "Without Oskar, I would have never written the *Theory of Games and Economic Behavior*." This anecdote appears to reflect the fact that although Morgenstern's mathematical abilities were quite limited, when he recognized an important idea that could be mathematized, he persisted in finding mathematical collaboration.

Other Activities. In 1948 he headed up the Econometrics Research Program at Princeton, sponsored primarily by the U.S. Office of Naval Research. Morgenstern was a founder of both the *Naval Research Logistics Quarterly* and the *International Journal of Game Theory*. He was deeply concerned with application as well as with theory, which led him to help found a highly successful consulting group known as Mathematica, Inc.

Morgenstern also wrote an influential book, *On the Accuracy of Economic Observations* (1950); this work reflected his strong feelings about the use of misplaced accuracy in economics. Morgenstern continued working on a variety of themes, notably promoting and extending the von Neumann multi-sector growth model in "A Generalization of the von Neumann Model of an Expanding Economy" (1956), with John G. Kemeny and Gerald L. Thompson. He also wrote on national defense and on finance, in particular the testing of the emerging random walk hypothesis in *Predictability of Stock Market Process* (1970), with Clive W. J. Granger.

Assessments of Morgenstern's Contributions. The reception of Morgenstern and von Neumann's book on the theory of games was mixed, and it took many years for it to work its way into mainstream economics, despite some favorable early reviews. For example, an instance of lordly disregard is attributed to Joseph Schumpeter, who supposedly remarked that the *Theory of Games and Economic Behavior* was written by a mathematician who knew no economics and an economist who knew nothing whatsoever. Another, verified comment on Morgenstern's contributions was made by Richard Bellman. In reply to a question about what Morgenstern's contributions to economics were, Bellman replied, "Wald and von Neumann." In fact, if all that Morgenstern had done was to be the catalyst to get Wald and von Neumann to work on basic problems in economics, that would have been considerably more than most economists accomplish in a lifetime.

Outside the L'Académie française (French National Academy), whose membership is limited to forty, is a statue, referred to as the forty-first chair. It serves to remind all that national academies and prizes are not merely the product of the institutions of the society but are operated by committees whose bias is toward safety and peer acceptance. Morgenstern had all of the characteristics destined for a forty-first chair. His mathematics were poor and his methodology was weak, but against this his imagination was considerable and his ability to select large problems and to spot and promote unconventional talent was great. He would have honored the Nobel Prize.

It has been observed that progress in science proceeds from funeral to funeral. Neither Morgenstern nor von Neumann lived long enough to see the enormous impact of the theory of games. Too many people had to die before the profession as a whole was able to accept the depth of the sea change that had taken place. In the early twenty-first century this change combined with a far deeper understanding of networks and information. The overall change proceeded at a faster pace, but the start-up costs were considerable. Jacob Viner, a distinguished economist at Princeton and a contemporary of Morgenstern, commented that he could not see how game theory could be of any use whatsoever in economics when it could not even solve chess, which was so much simpler than any economic problem. The point that the scientific

Oskar Morgenstern. RALPH MORSE/TIME LIFE PICTURES/GETTY IMAGES.

underpinnings of economics were being developed painstakingly was completely missed by most of the faculty at Princeton (and elsewhere) at that time.

Much of the theory of games changed the nature of the use of mathematics and logic in the social sciences. Combinatorics became important. The development of the axioms for a utility function defined up to a linear transformation set the stage for many further applications of the axiomatic method to problems in economic theory.

Observations on the speed of progress and change are not unique to the theory of games in the development of economic theory. The great work of Antoine Cournot, *Recherches sur les principes mathématiques de la théorie des richesses* (1838; *Researches on the Mathematical Principles of the Theory of Wealth,* 1963), was essentially ignored for many years and then subject to attack by the mathematician Joseph Bertrand. The misunderstanding of Bertrand, however, can be cleared up easily by using the modern theory of games. Cournot had chosen quantity as a strategic variable. Bertrand argued that price was more natural. Either or both would produce reasonable economic models. New approaches are easy to misinterpret or to ignore. Cournot's work, the great precursor of games in strategic form solved for their noncooperative equilibria, spent far longer a time in purgatory than did the *Theory of Games and Economic Behavior*

The great precursor to cooperative game theory was Edgeworth's *Mathematical Psychics* (1881). This, too, hardly swept the fields of economic thought for many years. But as is well known in 2007, the glimmerings of the combinatorics of cooperative game theory and the concept of the core were already in this book.

Morgenstern, Cournot, Edgeworth, and von Neumann all lived comfortable upper-middle- to upper-class lives. Von Neumann, the mathematician, was phenomenal, and his work was primarily in areas where the collegial perception of the importance of new work is almost instantaneous. Therefore, his recognition as a major figure in applied mathematics came nearly immediately. Even without the theory of games, his career would have been deemed extraordinary. However, the three economists—Morgenstern, Cournot, and Edgeworth—had to face a different context for academic judgment. Full understanding of the impact of their work came slowly. None of them lived long enough to hear popular accolades; all of them, though, managed to survive long enough to receive the positive feedback that counted. That was the recognition of a handful of peers whose opinions they respected.

The success of game theory since the 1950s and 1960s has far outstripped the expectations in the of even the most optimistic of game theorists of those decades. Game theory has evolved into an independent academic subject with insights particularly in the social sciences, but also in biology, computer science, and mathematics. It will play a role in the overall development of a viable theory of organization. Oskar Morgenstern did not live to see its immense spread and acceptance, but his vision and ability to understand what he and von Neumann had started was considerable.

The acceptance of new ideas is often slow. The development of science is a social process. The individual professionals all come with highly different personalities. There does not appear to be any ideal. Some would welcome the thought that great productivity, intelligence, and originality would be accompanied with generosity and social graces. There is, unfortunately, little evidence that these various gifts are highly correlated.

Morgenstern's Virtues. Morgenstern combined reasonably superior conventional intelligence with great drive, great originality, and skepticism, together with honesty and intrinsic decency. He was highly sensitive to the realities of his environment and not overly upset about what to others might appear a hostile climate. Although Morgenstern had a fair number of students, he did not actively construct a school, as others have done. Yet many of his students, and even the short-term visitors to his research projects, can look back and recognize that knowledge and understanding are moved forward in many different ways. Many of them also may recollect that he was concerned that their own professional careers not be damaged by their trust in working for an individual who did not stand in the center of the current profession but was gambling on the shape of the horizon.

The laserlike intellect of a von Neumann is direct and overwhelming. But Morgenstern's curiosity, application, insight, and willingness to be many miles ahead of the troops in unexplored territory enabled him to provide von Neumann with direction, motivation, and insight in application of game theory to economics that the latter might not have otherwise obtained.

Possibly the descriptor that best sums up Oskar Morgenstern's insight and skills comes from a Spanish word as used in Argentina. It is *rastrodero,* which can be translated as "pathfinder" or "tracker." The translation does not, however, do justice to the full meaning, which implies being alone in the wilderness, yet having enough experience and self-sufficiency to be comfortable in the unknown.

Morgenstern's personality combined a veneer of Germanic "Herr Professor" formalism with a sense of humor and personal concern for his students. In the study at his elegant home at Princeton was a portrait of the last king of Saxony, whom, he noted was his grandfather. He died of cancer in Princeton in 1977, survived by his wife, Dorothy (née Young), whom he married in 1948, and their two children, Karl and Karen.

BIBLIOGRAPHY

WORKS BY MORGENSTERN

Wirtschaftsprognose: Eine Untersuhung ihrer Voraussetzungen und Möglichkeiten. Vienna: Julius Springer, 1928.

"Perfect Foresight and Economic Equilibrium." *ZfN* (Zeitschrift fur National Oekonomie) (1935): 171.

With John von Neumann. *Theory of Games and Economic Behavior.* Princeton, NJ: Princeton University Press, 1944.

On the Accuracy of Economic Observations. Princeton, NJ: Princeton University Press, 1950.

With John G. Kemeny and Gerald L. Thompson. "A Generalization of the von Neumann Model of an Expanding Economy." *Econometrica* 24, no. 2 (April 1956): 115–135.

The Question of National Defense. New York: Random House, 1959.

With Clive W. J. Granger. *Predictability of Stock Market Prices.* Lexington, MA: Heath Lexington Books, 1970.

"Thirteen Critical Points in Contemporary Economic Theory: An Interpretation." *Journal of Economic Literature* 10, no. 4 (December 1972): 1163–1189.

With Gerald L. Thompson. *Mathematical Theory of Expanding and Contracting Economies.* Lexington, MA: Lexington Books, 1976.

OTHER SOURCES

Cournot, Augustin A. *Researches into the Mathematical Principles of the Theory of Wealth.* Translated by Nathaniel T. Bacon. New York: Macmillan, 1897. A translation of the original 1838 French work.

Edgeworth, Francis Y. *Mathematical Psychics: An Essay on the Application of Mathematics to the Moral Sciences.* 1881. Reprint, London: London School of Economics, 1932.

Martin Shubik

MORRISON, PHILIP

(*b.* Somerville, New Jersey, 7 November 1915; *d.* Cambridge, Massachusetts, 22 April 2005), *nuclear physics, quantum electrodynamics, cosmic radiation, theory of quasars, high-energy astrophysics and cosmology, science education.*

Morrison was one of the most fascinating and colorful characters in twentieth-century physics. Historical accident brought him into the development of the atomic bomb in the United States. He became centrally involved in the project and saw firsthand the devastation it caused in Japan. This experience led him to become a fervent opponent of any further development of atomic weapons. He was a founding member of the Federation of American Scientists, and throughout his life was an eloquent spokesman for international arms control. From 1946 to 1964 he was a physics faculty member at Cornell University, with a specialization in nuclear physics. He also began working in astrophysics; in this connection he helped originate the search for radio communications from distant civilizations—the project that became known as SETI (Search for Extraterrestrial Intelligence). In 1965 he joined the Physics Department at the Massachusetts Institute of Technology (MIT), and remained with that department until his death. Morrison was an inspiring and creative teacher of university students, but, beginning in the 1960s, he also became deeply involved in precollege science education, especially for young children and the general public. He used film and television in addition to his unique talents as speaker and writer. Besides these manifold activities he served for nearly twenty years (beginning in 1966) as the book review editor for *Scientific American* magazine. Morrison was married twice: in 1938 to Emily Kramer (divorced, 1961) and in 1964 to Phylis Singer, who died in 2002.

Early Years. When Morrison was two years old his family moved to Pittsburgh, Pennsylvania. His childhood education began at home, because at the age of about three he contracted poliomyelitis. His exceptional talents soon became evident. According to a personal memoir, his ability to read was self-taught. In 1920, shortly before he was five, his father, a retail merchant, brought home a crystal radio, which inspired the young Morrison with a love of more general scientific tinkering, although still with a big emphasis on radio. At age eight he entered second grade in the city schools and remained in that system through high school. In 1932 he entered the Carnegie Institute of Technology as a prospective radio engineer, but he found physics and physicists to be more congenial, and in 1936, after his BS degree, he entered the University of California at Berkeley as a graduate student in theoretical physics. He obtained his PhD in 1940 under the supervision of J. Robert Oppenheimer; his thesis was in the field of electrodynamics. The United States was still in the throes of the Great Depression, and jobs in academia for new graduates were hard to find. For Morrison, always an activist, the situation was not made easier by his leadership of fellow graduate students in a campaign for better pay. He did, however, obtain teaching positions, first for two years at San Francisco State College and then for a shorter period at the University of Illinois (Urbana-Champaign).

But great events—the discovery of nuclear fission and the onset of World War II—changed Morrison's life decisively. He has described how, in the summer of 1939, he and his fellow graduate students at Berkeley began sketching on the blackboard their conceptions of the possible design of a fission bomb. Independently of them, their senior colleagues, headed by Oppenheimer, were professionally engaged in studying these same possibilities. Morrison soon became directly involved.

The Manhattan Project. The Manhattan Project was the name given to America's atomic bomb program when it was officially established in August 1942 under the direction of U.S. Army Lieutenant General Leslie R. Groves. In late 1942 Morrison was invited to join the project by Robert F. Christy, previously a fellow graduate student at Berkeley. Christy himself had been recruited to work in the project as a theoretical nuclear physicist in the Metallurgical Laboratory at the University of Chicago, where the world's first nuclear reactor achieved criticality under the direction of Enrico Fermi in December of that year.

Morrison was quickly persuaded to join the effort, his first task being to experiment with subcritical assemblies that would guide the design of the major power reactors that would produce plutonium for bombs. He continued to work at the Chicago laboratory as a self-styled "neutron engineer" for more than a year. He also spent some time at the Argonne Park Laboratory near Chicago, where Fermi built the first high-power reactor, paving the way for the major plutonium plants at Hanford, Washington.

While at Argonne, Morrison and a colleague (Karl Cohen) wrote letters proposing ways of learning whether plutonium production might be going on in Germany. They thought that clues to the existence of reactors might exist in slight temperature rises in rivers used to provide their cooling water, or in weak radioactivity from the water. These proposals reached General Groves, and he enlisted Morrison as a kind of informal advisor on technical intelligence. The result was that Morrison made a number of visits to Groves's headquarters in Washington, D.C., where he helped in the analysis of information being collected in Germany by the Alsos scientific mission that accompanied the American forces as they moved eastward.

In the spring of 1943 the laboratory that became the scientific headquarters of the Manhattan Project had been set up at Los Alamos, New Mexico, under Oppenheimer. Morrison was one of a number of people who were added to Los Alamos in the summer of 1944, following a crisis that had just arisen. The crisis was the discovery that plutonium made in the big reactors had a very high rate of spontaneous fission, due to the accumulation of the plutonium isotope Pu-240. This invalidated the assumption that a plutonium bomb could be like the simple gun design adopted for a uranium-235 bomb. The firing of one lump of plutonium into another along a gun barrel was far too slow; neutrons liberated through spontaneous fission during this process would probably cause a premature detonation resulting in a feeble explosion (a "fizzle"). A completely different plan was needed. The solution was an implosion device, in which a core of plutonium was surrounded by an array of chemical explosives that would violently compress the fissile material for a few millionths of a second. During this brief time an "initiator" would supply a burst of neutrons to detonate the nuclear explosion. A special subgroup, composed of Morrison and his partner, Marshall Holloway, was given the task of designing the plutonium core of the bomb ("the pit") and had the responsibility of procuring, fabricating, and testing all the components inside this volume except for the initiator itself.

The resulting plutonium bomb was tested in July 1945 at Alamogordo, New Mexico. Morrison acquired some renown as the person who took care of the precious sphere of plutonium as it was transported from Los Alamos to Alamogordo. (He famously described the plutonium sphere, with its internally generated warmth from alpha-particle radioactivity, as feeling rather like a small cat.) He also took part in the final assembly of the test bomb on its tower in the New Mexico desert.

Morrison

Hiroshima, Nagasaki, and After. Morrison was a member of the small group that traveled to Tinian Island in the Marianas (which had been captured from the Japanese in 1944) to prepare two bombs for delivery: the "Little Boy" (uranium) and the "Fat Man" (plutonium). Morrison's responsibility was with the latter, which was dropped on Nagasaki. He helped assemble it, and three days later he flew over the ruined city. On 6 September he walked through Hiroshima and spoke with Japanese officials and with some old professional colleagues. Then, in December 1945, he testified before the U.S. Senate Special Committee on Atomic Energy (chaired by Brien McMahon) and presented an unforgettable picture of the devastating effects of atomic warfare. One of the committee members remarked: "I should like to say to … Mr. Morrison that he is the most eloquent witness that I have ever heard since I have been around Congress" (p. 249).

In August 1945, just after the end of World War II, Morrison helped found the Association of Los Alamos Scientists, which was formed to promote international control of atomic energy. Early in 1946 the group published an influential book, *One World or None,* a collection of essays by leading scientists. It had a foreword by Niels Bohr, and the first main article was by Morrison, describing the total helplessness of Hiroshima in face of the overwhelming force of one atomic bomb, and the imagined situation if New York City were to suffer a similar fate. In the same year Morrison drafted the aims of the recently established Federation of American Scientists, and served as its first president until 1949. He and his colleagues were deeply concerned about the failure of the public and public officials to understand the immensity of the challenge that nuclear weapons had brought to world politics.

With his passionate concern for world peace and his energy and skill as a communicator, Morrison worked tirelessly on behalf of nuclear disarmament. In the process he ran afoul of some hostile reactions, especially in the Joseph McCarthy era of American politics. In 1938 he had joined the Young Communist League and in 1939 the Communist Party of the United States. Like many idealistically minded people with leftist leanings he later severed his connection with communism. In 1953, however, he was called before the Senate Committee on the Judiciary, where he readily admitted his early Communist Party membership but declined to name anyone else. This occurred during his time at Cornell University, where two successive presidents of that institution, in part because of pressure from influential persons, asked him to tone down his activism. Although he complied, his concern for the issues was unabated; it continued throughout the Cold War, and was revived in the 1970s after his move to MIT. Its last major expression was in the book *Reason Enough to Hope,* coauthored with Kosta Tsipis and published in 1998.

Physics Research. Despite the many other claims on his time and energy, Morrison maintained an active commitment to research through most of his career. Before joining the Manhattan Project he already had a strong preparation in theoretical physics with an initial concentration on nuclear physics. This carried into his early years at Cornell University and, by his own estimation in later life, one of his best research projects (conducted with his student Jerome Pine) was an experimental investigation of the radiogenic production of helium isotopes in rocks. Soon, however, a special interest in high-energy particles led him into astrophysics. In 1954 he coauthored a paper on the origin of cosmic rays, a subject on which he wrote an article for *Reviews of Modern Physics* (1957) and a similar but much longer review published in *Handbuch der Physik* in 1961. Until this time he had published mainly in *Physical Review;* thereafter his papers were to be found mostly in such publications as the *Astrophysical Journal.* Between 1954 and 1996 he wrote about fifty articles, many of them in collaboration with students or colleagues, including Kenneth Metzner, Hong-Yee Chiu, James Felten, Leo Sartori, Kenneth Brecher, Franco Pacini, Mineas Kafatos, William Ingham, Alberto Sadun, Munib Abdulwahab, and Dana Roberts. The topics ranged widely, but many were concerned with the generation or scattering of electromagnetic radiation by astronomical objects. In these fields, Morrison valued most highly his papers on the connection between cosmic-ray intensity and solar activity, and on his calculation that neutrinos play a much bigger role in taking energy away from hot degenerate objects than do electrons.

Morrison and Science Education. In 1956 Professor Jerrold Zacharias at MIT proposed a project to revolutionize the teaching of high school physics by reducing rote learning and giving students a better insight into how one learns firsthand about the physical world. He brought together a group of college and high school teachers to address the problem; the group was named the Physical Science Study Committee. Morrison was one of the first to join this effort, and wrote the first drafts for important parts of the resulting textbook. Soon, however, he transferred his main attention to presecondary science education. In 1960 he was one of the organizers of what became known as the Elementary Science Study (ESS) and he became the chairman of its steering committee. The target population consisted of children and teachers at the elementary school level; the primary emphasis was on observation and experiment. The center of the project was the Education Development Center (originally Educational Services Inc.) in Watertown, Massachusetts, but participant teachers came from across the United States.

In 1965 the reach of ESS became international in two different respects. That year marked the beginning of a

Philip Morrison. *Philip Morrison teaching an engineering class.* GJON MILI/TIME LIFE PICTURES/GETTY IMAGES.

collaboration with the U.S. Peace Corps program; the ESS provided training for Peace Corps instructors who worked with elementary schools in several foreign countries. Also, a more specific collaboration was set up with the African Primary Science Program, which was started in 1965. Morrison helped to advance this program by attending a meeting in Ghana. He and his wife Phylis also participated in a workshop in Ghana in 1967.

At this period of his life Morrison became quite a world traveler in the cause of general science education. One contribution, aimed specifically at young people, was his series of Christmas Lectures at the Royal Institution, London, in 1966, with the title "Gulliver's Laws: The Physics of Large and Small." A special mark of Morrison's international influence was the hanging of a portrait at the Science Center in New Delhi, recognizing his role in stimulating the establishment of science centers throughout India.

Of course, at both Cornell University and MIT Morrison was involved in the teaching of normal undergraduate and graduate courses, but he had a special interest in the introductory level. At Cornell, together with Professor Donald F. Holcomb, he created a general physics course that evolved into a textbook: *My Father's Watch* (1974). At MIT he joined Professor John G. King in teaching an electromagnetism course based on take-home experiment kits. This, too, led to a lively book: *Zap!: A Hands-on Introduction to Electricity and Magnetism* (1991).

SETI. This biography is not the place to attempt a detailed account of the SETI project, but Philip Morrison's own role in it demands attention, for it was the fundamental one of proposing the project in the first place (together with his partner Giuseppe Cocconi). Their seminal letter in *Nature* in 1959 explored the feasibility of detecting possible transmissions from planets of other solar systems. The background to it was a paper "On Gamma-Ray Astronomy" that Morrison published in the journal *Nuovo Cimento* in 1958. Morrison and Cocconi were not radio astronomers, and they first considered making observations at gamma ray wavelengths. But they came quickly to the conclusion that microwaves would be a much more practical choice, with the famous hydrogen line at 1,420 megahertz as the logical vehicle for transmission by a scientifically sophisticated civilization elsewhere in the galaxy. Morrison was clear that the emphasis should be on "listening"; transmission from Earth was far beyond the available resources.

In 1960 the radio astronomer Frank Drake began a search of his own using the National Radio Astronomy Observatory in Green Bank, West Virginia. Morrison himself did not take part in any observations, but twenty years later, and again forty years later, he reviewed the state of the search, which by the year 2000 involved very large numbers of "listeners"—without, as yet, any signals.

Morrison as Writer and Public Educator. Morrison's extraordinary talent for communication, both written and oral, made him an ideal person to interpret science for the general public. One of his major contributions to this was his long service as reviewer for the *Scientific American.* During those twenty years he wrote close to 1,500 reviews and read several times that number of books. The collection *Philip Morrison's Long Look at the Literature* (1990) contains a hundred pieces chosen by him, and attests to his ability to present and explain the essence of a multitude of different scientific topics.

In 1968, in collaboration with the architect and designer Charles Eames, he made a short film titled *Powers of Ten.* This was inspired by a small book, *Cosmic View: The Universe in Forty Jumps,* created by a Dutch teacher, Kees Boeke, in 1957. The film was remade in a much more refined form in 1977 and was followed in 1982 by an illustrated book enriched with many details, with text written jointly by Philip and Phylis Morrison.

In 1987 Philip Morrison presented a six-part national television series, *The Ring of Truth,* about the bases of human scientific understanding of the universe. The essential content of the series was captured and preserved in a lavishly and imaginatively illustrated book of the same title, written (like *Powers of Ten*) by Philip and Phylis Morrison working as a team.

Philip Morrison's last major work (1995) of scientific popularization was a collection of his earlier articles dealing with basic scientific theories, astronomy, SETI, education, the nuclear age and its politics, and a final section, "Friends and Heroes." He titled the collection *Nothing Is Too Wonderful to Be True*—a remark taken directly from the notebooks of the great nineteenth-century physicist Michael Faraday.

Inspiring Eloquence and Intellect. The above bare account does not adequately recognize the immense personal impact that Morrison made on thousands of individuals. He inspired audiences around the world with his eloquence, and was treasured by his numerous friends. At a symposium held at MIT in 1976 to celebrate his sixtieth birthday, the eminent physicist Victor Weisskopf said of him: "Nobody else has better demonstrated, or rather embodied, what it means to the human soul to perceive or recognize a new scientific discovery or a new theoretical insight." That quality pervaded his approach to all of his interests and survived until the end of his days.

Honors and Awards. Morrison's achievements and his varied contributions to science, education, and society were recognized in many ways. He was a Fellow of the American Physical Society and a member of the National Academy of Sciences. In 1964 he was given the Oersted Medal of the American Association of Physics Teachers for his outstanding contributions to physics education. In 1985 he received MIT's Killian Faculty Achievement Award, and in 1987 the Andrew Gemant Award of the American Institute of Physics "for his contributions to the cultural, artistic or humanistic dimension of physics." In 1988 he received the AAAS-Westinghouse Award for his contributions to the public understanding of science.

BIBLIOGRAPHY

Valuable biographical information can be found in transcripts of oral interviews conducted by Owen Gingerich and Robert Norris under the auspices of the Center for History of Physics (American Institute of Physics), archived at the Center for History of Physics of the American Institute of Physics, College Park, MD. Personal memoirs collected by Herbert Lin in September 2005 following a Morrison memorial symposium at MIT are available at http://www.memoriesofmorrison.org.

WORKS BY MORRISON

"If the Bomb Gets Out of Hand." In *One World or None,* edited by Dexter Masters and Katherine Way. New York: McGraw-Hill, 1946.

With Jerome Pine. "Radiogenic Origin of the Helium Isotopes in Rock." *Annals of the New York Academy of Sciences* 62 (1955): 69–92.

With Hans A. Bethe. *Elementary Nuclear Theory.* New York: Wiley, 1956.

"On Gamma-Ray Astronomy." *Nuovo Cimento* 7 (1958): 858–865.

With Giuseppe Cocconi. "Searching for Interstellar Communications." *Nature* 184 (1959): 844–846.

"The Origin of Cosmic Rays." In *Handbuch der Physik* [Encyclopedia of physics]. Vol. 46.1, *Kosmische Strahlung I* [Cosmic rays I], edited by Siegfried Flügge. Berlin: Springer-Verlag, 1961.

With Emily Morrison, eds. *Charles Babbage and His Calculating Engines.* New York: Dover Publications, 1961.

"Resolving the Mystery of the Quasars?" *Physics Today* 26 (March 1973): 23–29.

With Donald F. Holcomb. *My Father's Watch.* Englewood Cliffs, NJ: Prentice-Hall, 1974.

With Phylis Morrison and the Office of Charles & Ray Eames. *Powers of Ten.* New York: Scientific American Books, 1982.

With Phylis Morrison. *The Ring of Truth.* New York: Random House, 1987. Companion book to their television series, *The Ring of Truth.* 6 videocassettes. Alexandria, VA: PBS Video, 1987.

Philip Morrison's Long Look at the Literature. New York: W. H. Freeman, 1990.

With Phylis Morrison and John G. King. *Zap!: A Hands-on Introduction to Electricity and Magnetism.* Woolwich, ME: KT Associates, 1991.

Nothing Is Too Wonderful to Be True. Woodbury, NY: AIP Press, 1995. Thanks are due to Elizabeth Cavicchi for locating the source of this title in entry no. 10040 (19 March 1849), *Faraday's Diary,* vol. 5, edited by Thomas Martin. London: G. Bell & Sons, 1934.

"Recollections of a Nuclear War." *Scientific American* 273 (August 1995): 42–46.

With Kosta Tsipis. *Reason Enough to Hope.* Cambridge, MA: MIT Press, 1998.

OTHER SOURCES

Boeke, Kees. *Cosmic View: The Universe in 40 Jumps.* New York: J. Day, 1957. The book that inspired *Powers of Ten.*

Hawkins, David. *Project Y: The Los Alamos Story.* Los Angeles and San Francisco: Tomash, 1983.

Perlman, David. "Philip Morrison—Scientist with Social Conscience." *San Francisco Chronicle,* 27 April 2005: B7. Obituary.

Rhodes, Richard. *The Making of the Atomic Bomb.* New York: Simon & Schuster, 1986.

Sartori, Leo, and Kosta Tsipis. "Philip Morrison." *Physics Today* (March 2006): 83. Obituary.

Schweber, Silvan S. *In the Shadow of the Bomb.* Princeton, NJ: Princeton University Press, 2000.

Smith, Alice Kimball. *A Peril and a Hope: The Scientists' Movement in America, 1945–47.* Chicago: University of Chicago Press, 1965.

U.S. Senate Special Committee on Atomic Energy. *Hearings on S. Res. 179, pt. 2,* 79th Cong., 1st sess., 6 December 1945. Morrison's testimony is on pp. 233–253.

A. P. French

MORSE, MARSTON

MORSE, MARSTON (*b.* Waterville, Maine, 24 March 1892; *d.* 22 June 1977, Princeton, New Jersey), *mathematics, differential geometry, calculus of variations, functions of several variables.*

An American mathematician, Morse was an early and influential member of the Institute for Advanced Study at Princeton, New Jersey. He is particularly associated with the theory of functions of several variables on manifolds and on the calculus of variations.

Early Life and Career. Morse was the son of Howard Calvin Morse, a farmer and realtor, and Ella Phoebe Marston. He was a student at Coburn Classical Institute in Waterville, Maine. At age eighteen he entered Colby College, also in Waterville. Morse graduated from Colby College in 1914 and took his PhD from Harvard University in 1917. He then joined the American Expeditionary Force in World War I and was awarded the Croix de Guerre with Silver Star for bravery under fire. On his return to the United States he taught at Cornell University in Ithaca, New York, and then briefly at Brown University in Providence, Rhode Island, before joining the faculty at Harvard University at Cambridge, Massachusetts, in 1926. He became a professor at the newly established Institute for Advanced Study in Princeton in 1935 and retired from there in 1962 as professor emeritus, but he continued to conduct research for the rest of his life. His war work in World War II on terminal ballistics earned him a Meritorious Service Award, which he received from President Franklin Roosevelt in 1944.

After the war Morse was active in the creation of the National Science Foundation and served on its first board from 1950 to 1954. A deeply religious man, he converted to Catholicism and was the Vatican's representative at the Atoms for Peace Conference of the United Nations in 1952. He received honorary degrees from more than twenty universities, and among other distinctions he was awarded the associate membership of the French Academy of Sciences and the corresponding membership of the Italian National Academy of the Lincei. His strong attraction to these countries, deepened by his religious convictions, made these awards particularly pleasing to him. He was also a fine pianist with a particular, but by no means exclusive, affinity for the works of Johann Sebastian Bach.

The Morse Inequalities. Morse's long and productive mathematical career drew particular impetus from the work on Henri Poincaré. Therefore, he contributed to the growing subject of topology always with an eye to its origins and uses in dynamics, analysis, and differential geometry and in later years was somewhat opposed to the elaborate algebraic structures created by the new generations of topologists. As he put it in a lecture in 1949: "Always the foundation and never the Cathedral." In an early work, "Recurrent Geodesics on a Surface of Constant Negative Curvature," he took up a topic raised by Poincaré and Jacques Hadamard and studied surfaces of constant negative curvature bounded by closed geodesics. The question he answered was: what geodesics lie entirely in the surface (and do not end on one of the boundaries)? His answer, in more modern terminology, was given as a word in the generators of the fundamental group of the surface, and Morse's later work with Gustav Hedlund in 1944, "Unending Chess, Symbolic Dynamics and a Problem in Semigroups," marks the earliest occurrence of what has come to be called symbolic dynamics. Using this

Morse

technique, Morse was able to characterize the geodesics that lie entirely in the surface as a limit of recurrent but nonperiodic geodesics and to show that there are uncountably many of them.

In 1925 Morse published his first paper, "Relations between the Critical Points of a Real Function of *n* Independent Variables," on the distribution of the critical points of a function on a manifold. (These are the points where all its first derivatives vanish.) The simplest example is the height function on a torus. One can think of the torus as an inner tube of a bicycle wheel in the vertical position. The height function has critical points at the top and bottom of the torus and at the highest and lowest points where the torus (the inner tube) meets the wheel. At these points the derivatives vanish, but the matrix, H, of their second derivatives is nondegenerate. Morse called such functions nondegenerate, and his first result was that a nondegenerate function on a manifold has a finite number of critical points. Furthermore, the critical points are of various kinds. In the case of the torus, the first distinction is between the points at the top and bottom, where the surface is locally bowl shaped, and the other two points, where the surface is locally saddle shaped. A more refined distinction, also valid on a manifold of any dimension, depends on the number of negative eigenvalues of the matrix H (which varies from critical point to critical point). Morse called the number of negative eigenvalues of the matrix H at a critical point the index of the point and defined the number m_k to be the total number of critical points with k negative eigenvalues, and he showed that these numbers were related to the dimensions of the homology groups of the manifold by a series of inequalities (today called the Morse inequalities). In the case of the torus, the Morse numbers are $m_0 = 1, m_1 = 2, m_2 = 1$ (working from the lowest to the highest critical point). In this case the Morse numbers coincide exactly with the dimensions of the homology groups.

The Morse inequalities are extremely useful in determining the homology of a manifold and therefore, in certain cases, the manifold itself. For example, only a sphere can have just two critical points, a fact crucial to John W. Milnor's remarkable discovery that the seven-dimensional sphere can have nonstandard differentiable structures.

Morse's inspiration for this work was George D. Birkhoff's paper "Dynamical Systems with Two Degrees of Freedom" of 1917. Morse's proof of his theorems was based on the idea of deforming the manifold by letting it flow along the lines of steepest descent for the given function. As is easily seen in the torus case, this concentrates the surface more and more at its critical points. A separate argument then establishes what can happen in homological terms in a neighborhood of each critical point. This is done nowadays with the machinery of algebraic topology; Morse gave more intuitive arguments of considerable profundity using the language of topology as established by Oswald Veblen at the time.

The Calculus of Variations. Remarkable as these results are, Morse intended them as results on the way to a global theory of the calculus of variations. His paper, "The Foundations of a Theory of the Calculus of Variations in the Large in *m*-Space," published in the *Transactions of the American Mathematical Society* in 1929, and his book, *The Calculus of Variations in the Large,* published in 1934, go a considerable way in this direction, but the much greater difficulties of the subject (by comparison with Morse theory) give his results a less conclusive feel that is appropriate to the opening up of a new subject. He found important results regarding the index of an extremal curve, but this concept of an index, which generalizes the concept of an index of a critical point of a function, now leads to an infinite sequence of numbers. This is indicative of a number of difficulties in the general theory that arise because it is intrinsically infinite dimensional.

The continuing importance of Morse's work was demonstrated by the fact he that gave two invited addresses at International Congresses of Mathematicians. One was at Zürich, Switzerland, in 1932, titled "Calculus of Variations in the Large." The other was at Cambridge, Massachusetts, in 1950, titled "Recent Advances in Variational Theory in the Large."

BIBLIOGRAPHY

Both Morse's Selected Papers, *edited by Raoul Bott (New York: Springer-Verlag, 1981), and his* Collected Papers *(Singapore: World Scientific, 1987), carry a complete bibliography of his work.*

WORKS BY MORSE

"Recurrent Geodesics on a Surface of Constant Negative Curvature." *Transactions of the American Mathematical Society* 22, no.1 (1921): 18–100. Also in *Selected Papers,* pp. 21–37.

"Relations between the Critical Points of a Real Function of *n* Independent Variables." *Transactions of the American Mathematical Society* 27, no. 3 (1925): 345–396.

"The Foundations of a Theory of the Calculus of Variations in the Large in *m*-Space." *Transactions of the American Mathematical Society* 31 (1929): 379–404.

The Calculus of Variations in the Large. New York: American Mathematical Society, 1934.

With Gustav Hedlund. "Unending Chess, Symbolic Dynamics and a Problem in Semigroups." *Duke Mathematical Journal* 11, no. 1 (1944): 1–7. Also in *Selected Papers,* pp. 583–589.

With Stewart S. Cairns. *Critical Point Theory in Global Analysis and Differential Topology.* New York: Academic Press, 1969.

Selected Papers. Edited by Raoul Bott. New York: Springer-Verlag, 1981.

Collected Papers. Singapore: World Scientific, 1987.

OTHER SOURCES

Birkhoff, George D. "Dynamical Systems with Two Degrees of Freedom." *Transactions of the American Mathematical Society* 18 (1917): 199–300.

Bott, Raoul. "Marston Morse and His Mathematical Works." *Bulletin of the American Mathematical Society*, n.s., 3 (1980): 907–950.

Pitcher, Everett. "Marston Morse." *Biographical Memoirs of the National Academy of Sciences* 65 (1994): 222–260. Also available from http://books.nap.edu/openbook.php?record_id=4548&page=222.

Jeremy Gray

MOSCHOPOULOS, MANUEL (*b.* c. 1265, Crete [?]; *d.* after 1430), *mathematics.*

Moschopoulos, a Byzantine scholar, was a nephew of Nicephoros Moschopoulos, Metropolitan of Crete. He was a student of Maximus Planudes who wrote to the uncle an enthusiastic letter about the young man. Some letters of his dated between 1295 and 1316 have been preserved.

Manuel Moschopoulos was mainly a philologist and a grammarian. He left numerous work on classical authors: editions of classical texts, a dictionary of Attic words, a paraphrase of the first two books of the *Iliad,* a paraphrase of *Works and Days* of Hesiod, grammatical exercises, and a *Discourse against the Latins.*

Around 1305–1306, he was involved in a plot and spent some time in jail. According to the letters written in his prison, it seems that he took part in a conspiracy against the emperor Andronic II, but it is difficult to discover the precise reason of Moschopoulos's misfortune.

His unique scientific work consists of a *Treatise on Magic Squares* written at the request of his friend Nicolas Rhabdas. The question is how to organize numbers from 1 to n^2 in a square, in such way that the sum of numbers in each row, column, or diagonal is always equal to

$$m = \tfrac{1}{2} n (n^2 + 1)$$

with n being the number of cells of the side of the square.

This kind of exercise occurs in Arabic writings from the ninth century and passed to the Latin world, but Moschopoulos's treatise did not show any hint of Arabic or Latin influence. In the Arabic world and the Latin Middle Ages, those squares were commonly associated with magical practices. This is the reason why one usually speaks of magic squares. Moschopoulos ignored the magical side of the subject and simply referred to *squared numbers* or *numbers in a square.* It was a pure arithmetical exercise.

The author thus explained methods for constructing such squares. It is a construction that varies according to the parity of the number n, which can be odd (3, 5, 7 ...), even-even (4, 8, 12 ...) or odd-even (6, 10, 14 ...). This last case was not developed in the treatise, in spite of the announcement made by Moschopoulos. The origin of Moschopoulos's treatise is not clear. There existed no Greek writing on the matter before Moschopoulos's work and no Arabic treatise can be identified as the source of Moschopoulos. He may have learned something on the subject with help of oral explanations given by a traveler or a scholar having been in Persia. At the end of the thirteenth century and in the beginning of the fourteenth century, Persian astronomical and astrological treatises were imported from Constantinople, and it would not be surprising if the magic squares had excited the curiosity of an unknown amateur of mathematical games who brought them to Byzantium.

BIBLIOGRAPHY

Descombes, René. *Les carrés magiques. Histoire, théorie et technique des carrés magiques de l'Antiquité aux recherches actuelles.* Paris: Vuibert, 2000.

Sesiano, Jacques. "Hestellungsverfahren magischer Quadrate aus islamicher Zeit." *Suddhoffs Archiv* 64 (1980): 187–196; 65 (1981): 251–265; 71 (1987): 78–89; 79 (1995): 193–226.

———. *Un traité médiéval sur les carrés magiques.* Lausanne, Switzerland: Presses polytechniques et universitaires romandes, 1996.

———. "Les carrés magiques de Manuel Moschopoulos." *Archive for History of Exact Sciences* 53, no. 5 (1998): 377–397.

———. "Le traité d'Abū' l-Wafā' sur les carrés magiques." *Zeitschrift für Geschichte der arabisch-islamichen Wissenschaften* 12 (1998): 121–244.

———. *Les carrés magiques dans les pays islamiques.* Lausanne, Switzerland: Presses polytechniques et universitaires romandes, 2004.

———. "Magic Squares for Daily Life." In *Studies in the History of the Exact Sciences in Honour of David Pingree,* edited by Charles Burnett, Jan P. Hogendijk, Kim Plofker, et al., 715–734. Leiden, Netherlands: Brill, 2004.

Ševčenko, Ihor. "The Imprisonment of Manuel Moschopoulos in the Year 1305 or 1306." *Speculum* 27 (1952): 133–157.

Tannery, Paul. "Le traité de Manuel Moschopoulos sur les carrés magiques." In *Mémoires scientifiques IV,* 27–60. Toulouse, France, 1920. Greek text with French translation.

———. "Manuel Moschopoulos et Nicolas Rhabdas." In *Mémoires scientifiques IV,* 1–19. Toulouse, France, 1920.

Anne Tihon

MOSER, JÜRGEN K. (*b.* Königsberg, Germany (later Russia), 4 July 1928; *d.* Zürich, Switzerland, 17 December 1999), *mathematics, analysis, celestial mechanics.*

Moser won a Wolf Prize, awarded by the Wolf Foundation in 1994–95, "for his fundamental work on stability in Hamiltonian mechanics and his profound and influential contributions to nonlinear differential equations." He was one of the founders of KAM (Kolmogorov-Arnold-Moser) theory and of Nash-Moser theory. His book, *Stable and Random Motions in Dynamical Systems: With Special Emphasis on Celestial Mechanics* (1973), helped redefine celestial mechanics.

A profound mathematical analyst, Moser did deep work in a variety of fields of mathematics, both pure and applied. These included dynamical systems, especially small divisor problems and relations with celestial mechanics; functional analysis, especially Nash-Moser theory; partial differential equations, especially regularity questions and Harnack inequalities; complex geometry; completely integrable systems; and variational calculus.

Early Years. Moser's father was a neurologist. His parents managed to prevent his being enrolled in an "elite" school for future Nazi leaders at the age of ten, but he was drafted to fight on the eastern front at the age of fifteen. After surviving the war and escaping from the Russian zone of postwar Germany, he enrolled in Göttingen in 1947, where he studied mathematics under Franz Rellich.

Later, Moser worked with Carl Ludwig Siegel, one of whose interests was celestial mechanics. Siegel's book, *Vorlesungen über Himmelsmechanik,* was based on notes that Moser took of Siegel's lectures. A revision of this book by Moser, *Lectures in Celestial Mechanics,* appeared under the joint authorship of Siegel and Moser. Siegel suggested that Moser work on Birkhoff's problem related to the stability of the solar system.

Stability of the Solar System. Have the orbits of the planets remained approximately the same since the formation of the solar system from four billion to five billion years ago? Isaac Newton's theory predicts that a planet, in the absence of other planets, would move on an elliptical orbit around the sun. It also predicts that these elliptical orbits change slowly over time under the gravitational influence of the other planets. It was observed in the eighteenth century that perturbations of the orbits of the planets were large enough that the solar system might become unstable in a relatively short time, compared to the age of the solar system. Toward the end of the eighteenth century, Joseph-Louis Lagrange and Pierre-Simon Laplace showed that all the observed perturbations could be explained by first and second order perturbation theory on the basis of Newton's law of gravitation. Such perturbations were quasi-periodic. This showed that the observed perturbations were consistent with the stability of the solar system.

First and second order perturbation theory provided only the beginning terms of an infinite series of periodicities. Karl Weierstrass observed that if this series converged, then the solar system (or, rather, Newton's model of it) would be stable. He suggested to Gösta Mittag-Leffler that the problem of proving convergence should be sponsored as a prize by the king of Sweden. Henri Poincaré won the prize for his paper "Sur le problème des trois corps et les équations de la dynamique."

Poincaré did not actually solve the problem; rather, the prize was awarded for the paper's wealth of ideas. He did, however, find an argument that strongly suggested the existence of random motions ("chaos" in the sense of chaos theory). Such random motions are incompatible with the convergence of all the series that arise, although they are compatible with some, even most.

KAM Theory. In 1954 Andrey Kolmogorov published "On the Conservation of Conditionally Periodic Motions for a Small Change in Hamilton's Function." This was the first progress toward proving stability. His theorem states that in a small Hamiltonian perturbation of an integrable system satisfying a nondegeneracy condition, most invariant tori survive. An integrable system is one in which all invariant solutions are quasi-periodic, that is, can be expressed as convergent infinite sums of periodic functions. Every quasi-periodic solution lies on an invariant torus and passes arbitrarily close to every point of the torus infinitely often.

Saying that an invariant torus survives means that in the perturbed system, there is an invariant torus near the original invariant torus, and every solution in it is quasi-periodic with the same frequencies as the solutions in the unperturbed torus. Saying that most invariant tori survive means that the invariant tori in the perturbed system fill out most of the phase space—that is, their complement has small measure ($2d$-dimensional volume, where d is the number of degrees of freedom).

Quasi-periodic motions are very regular. Thus, the union of the invariant tori exhibits no chaos. On the other hand, the complement of this set generally does exhibit chaos, as Poincaré's argument and later extensions of it show.

Planetary motion may be regarded as a small perturbation of an integrable system, provided that the masses of the planets are small enough in relation to the mass of the sun. The integrable system in this case is the limiting case when the masses of the planets vanish. Unfortunately, Kolmogorov's theorem does not apply, because his nondegeneracy condition is not satisfied. Nonetheless, in the

Jürgen Moser. COURTESY OF TMNA.

early 1960s there were high hopes of extending Kolmogorov's method to the problem of stability of planetary motions. In fact, Vladimir I. Arnold, Moser, and much later, Michael Herman and Jacques Féjoz, obtained results along these lines, thus realizing these hopes, although the extension was much harder than anticipated.

In his prize paper, Poincaré studied the restricted three-body problem extensively. This is the case where one mass vanishes (so it moves under the influence of the other two masses but does not influence them) and the other two masses move in circular orbits about each other. It is further assumed that all three masses move in a plane. Poincaré showed that the study of such a system can be largely reduced to the study of the dynamics of an area preserving transformation of an annular region in the plane. This led Poincaré and, later, George D. Birkhoff in the early twentieth century, to study the dynamics of area-preserving transformations in great depth.

In his paper, "On Invariant Curves of Area-Preserving Mappings of an Annulus" (1962), Moser solved the fundamental problem posed by Birkhoff in his study of area-preserving transformations of surfaces. This concerned the stability of a fixed point P. Moser's theorem states that there exist arbitrarily small invariant neighborhoods of P, under suitable hypotheses on the transformation. His proof was inspired by the work of Kolmogorov but also relied on a normal form theorem of Birkhoff and a very profound analytic technique originally developed by John Nash to solve the isometric embedding problem. Moser followed up this paper with three papers in 1966 and 1968, one of them written jointly with William H. Jefferys, regarding the restricted three-body problem and a problem concerning confinement in a magnetic bottle. Together with a deep result of Arnold (the stability of a planetary system in the plane with only two planets, both of extremely small mass), these were the first stability results in celestial mechanics.

Although all of these results closely resemble Kolmogorov's original result, it does not seem that Kolmogorov's original method can be used to obtain them without the profound improvements introduced by Moser and Arnold. Moser's improvement used Nash's method, which enabled him to deal with the case when the given data are highly differentiable, instead of analytic, as in the Kolmogorov case. This is usually taken as the main significance of Moser's improvement. Nonetheless, for the solution of Birkhoff's problem, Moser's improvement seems necessary even when the transformation is analytic. This is because Moser's solution depends on Birkhoff normal form, which presents the given transformation as a small perturbation of an integrable system. The perturbation is small in the C^4 topology, which is good enough for the application of Moser's method, but not for the application of Kolmogorov's method, which would require that the perturbation be small in the C^ω topology. Likewise, the extra robustness of Moser's method seems to be required for the problems in celestial mechanics and the problem of magnetic confinement that he solved.

Nash-Moser Theory. Both Kolmogorov's stability theorem and Nash's isometric embedding theorem depend on deep extensions of the classical implicit function theorem. Kolmogorov's proof used Newton's iteration scheme. Nash's involved smoothing of functions. In his solution of Birkhoff's problem and in "A New Technique for the Construction of Solutions of Nonlinear Differential Equations" (1961) Moser combined these two techniques.

In lectures at Pisa in 1966, Moser showed that Newton iteration with smoothing can be used to prove infinite dimensional implicit function theorems in many circumstances where classical methods fail. These ideas were later developed into abstract implicit function theorems by Francis Sergeraert and Richard S. Hamilton. Such abstract implicit function theorems are known as Nash-Moser theory. The paper of Féjoz, "Démonstration du 'théorème d'Arnold' sur la stabilité du système planétaire (d'après Herman)," which generalized Arnold's theorem on planetary stability to an arbitrary number of planets in arbitrary dimensions, relies heavily on such abstract implicit function theorems.

More Analysis. In addition to his contributions to KAM theory and Nash-Moser theory, Moser made major contributions to other fields of mathematical analysis. In 1961 Moser generalized the classical Harnack inequality in the theory of linear elliptic partial differential equations. Moser's result assumed less regularity on the coefficients than the classical result. A key estimate obtained independently by Ennio De Giorgi and Nash in their solutions of Hilbert's nineteenth problem follows easily from Moser's result. De Giorgi and Nash had given elaborate (and different) proofs of this estimate about three years earlier. Moser also deduced a generalization of Bernstein's theorem (concerning minimal surfaces in three-dimensional space) to arbitrary dimensions.

In 1971 Moser proved a sharp form of an inequality due to Neil Trudinger and used it to determine which even functions on the two spheres are the Gauss curvature of a metric conformal to the standard metric. In 1974, Shiing-Shen Chern and Moser determined local invariants of real hypersurfaces of real codimension one in a complex number space of arbitrary dimension. In the 1980s Moser created a theory of foliations and laminations of codimension one on a torus of arbitrary dimension whose leaves are minimals of a nonlinear variational problem (for example, minimizing area). Under suitable hypotheses, he proved the existence of laminations and the persistence of foliations (similar to KAM theory).

Positions. Moser was a professor at the Courant Institute of Mathematical Science of New York University from 1960 to 1980, and director of the Courant Institute from 1967 to 1970. He was president of the International Mathematical Union from 1983 to 1986. He was director of the Research Institute for Mathematics of the Swiss Federal Institute of Technology from 1980 until his retirement in 1995.

He died of prostate cancer. He was survived by his wife, two daughters, a step-son, and six grandchildren.

BIBLIOGRAPHY

Chern and Hirzebruch, eds., Wolf Prize in Mathematics, *vol. 2 (cited below) contains a complete bibliography of Moser's mathematical works.*

WORKS BY MOSER

"A New Technique for the Construction of Solutions of Nonlinear Differential Equations." *Proceedings of the National Academy of Sciences of the United States of America* 47 (1961): 1824–1831.

"On Invariant Curves of Area-Preserving Mappings of an Annulus." *Nachrichten Akademie Wissenschaften Göttingen Mathematische-Physikalische Klasse* 11 (1962): 1–20.

With William H. Jefferys. "Quasi-Periodic Solutions for the Three-Body Problem." *Astronomical Journal* 71 (1966): 568–578.

"A Rapidly Convergent Iteration Method and Nonlinear Partial Differential Equations, I and II." *Annali Scuola Normale Superiore Pisa* 20 (1966): 265–315, 499–535. The Nash-Moser theory.

"Lectures on Hamiltonian Systems." *Memoirs of the American Mathematical Society* 81 (1968): 1–60. Includes a discussion of a containment problem for magnetic field lines.

"Quasi-Periodic Solutions of the Three-Body Problem." *Bulletin Astronomique* 3 (1968): 53–59.

Stable and Random Motions in Dynamical Systems: With Special Emphasis on Celestial Mechanics. Annals of Mathematics Studies 77. Princeton, NJ: Princeton University Press, 1973.

With Carl Ludwig Siegel. *Lectures on Celestial Mechanics.* Translation by Charles I. Kalme of *Die Grundlehren der Mathematische Wissenschaften* 187. New York and Heidelberg, Germany: Springer-Verlag, 1971.

OTHER SOURCES

Chern, Shiing-Shen, and Friedrich Hirzebruch, eds. *Wolf Prize in Mathematics.* Vol. 2. River Edge, NJ: World Scientific Publishing, 2001.

Féjoz, Jacques. "Démonstration du 'théorème d'Arnold' sur la stabilité du système planétaire (d'après Herman)." *Ergodic Theory and Dynamical Systems* 24 (2004): 1521–1582.

Hasselblatt, Boris, and Anatole Katok. "The Development of Dynamics in the 20th Century and the Contribution of Jürgen Moser." *Ergodic Theory and Dynamical Systems* 22 (2002): 1343–1364. A very extensive discussion of Moser's mathematical work in dynamics.

Kolmogorov, Andrey N. "On the Conservation of Conditionally Periodic Motions for a Small Change in Hamilton's Function." *Doklady Academiia Nauk SSSR* 98 (1954): 527–530 (in Russian). English translation, Casati and Ford, eds., *Stochastic Behavior in Classical and Quantum Hamilton Systems* (Volta Memorial Conference Como, 1977). Lecture Notes in *Physics* 93 (1997): 51–56.

Lax, Peter D. "Jürgen Moser, 1928–1999." *Ergodic Theory and Dynamical Systems* 22 (2002): 1337–1342. Moser's life and personality by a close friend, together with an impressionistic appreciation of his work.

Mather, John N., Henry P. McKean, Louis Nirenberg, et al. "Jürgen K. Moser (1928–1999)." *Notices of the American Mathematical Society* 47 (December 2000): 1392–1405. A brief discussion of Moser's life, together with an extensive discussion of his mathematical work and a bibliography.

Poincaré, Henri. "Sur le problème des trois corps et les équations de la dynamique." *Acta Mathematica* 13 (1890): 1–227.

Siegel, Carl Ludwig. *Vorlesungen über Himmelsmechanik.* Berlin, Göttingen, and Heidelberg: Springer-Verlag, 1956.

John N. Mather

MOTT, NEVILL FRANCIS (*b.* Leeds, United Kingdom, 30 September 1905; *d.* Cambridge, United Kingdom, 8 August 1996), *condensed-matter physics, metals, amorphous semiconductors, glasses.*

For the whole of a working life of over sixty years, Mott was the unquestioned leader of English condensed-matter physicists. At the universities of Bristol and Cambridge in England his intuitive appreciation of promising research fields attracted a circle of students and colleagues. His prolonged and searching analysis of electrical conduction in disordered systems earned him a Nobel Prize in Physics in 1977 that he shared with John H. Van Vleck and Philip W. Anderson. He was knighted in 1962 and made a Companion of Honour in 1995.

Early Years at Cambridge. Mott's parents, Charles Francis Mott and Lilian Mary Reynolds, had both worked as research students of J. J. Thomson, Cavendish Professor of Physics at Cambridge University, and he grew up expecting a life in physics, with Cambridge as the center of choice. He studied mathematics at St. John's College, Cambridge, graduating in 1927, at the very time that Werner Heisenberg, Erwin Schrödinger, and others in continental Europe were revolutionizing physics with the development of quantum mechanics. With no local experts at hand, except the reclusive Paul Dirac, he taught himself German so as to read about the new techniques from the original papers. A half year with Niels Bohr in Copenhagen was immensely valuable, and he returned having solved several problems in atomic physics and satisfied himself that a career in theoretical physics was feasible. He predicted that when alpha particles were scattered by helium nuclei, the identity of the two particles, together with the fact that they obeyed Bose statistics, would cause twice as many to be observed at a deflection of forty-five degrees than would be expected from Ernest Rutherford's classical theory. Verification of the prediction elicited Rutherford's praise and confirmed his career decision. A paper reconciling the wave picture of α-particle emission with the sharply localized tracks observed in cloud-chamber photographs is still cited as a valuable contribution to the interpretation of quantum mechanics.

In 1930, after returning to Cambridge from a one-year lectureship at Manchester, England, Mott married Ruth Eleanor Horder. They had two daughters, Elizabeth and Alice. His wife, Ruth, a classical scholar and harpsichordist, complemented Mott's enduring friendship for all his colleagues and students by the welcome she gave to their wives and families. Their contented life together ended only with his death.

Nevill Francis Mott. AP IMAGES.

The Move to Bristol. Mott's commitment to nuclear physics ended in 1933 when he accepted, still only twenty-eight years old, the offer of a professorship in theoretical physics at Bristol University. A fine new laboratory had just been built and Arthur M. Tyndall, the talented head of the department, had begun to gather a research team. On arrival, Mott found staff members already engaged in problems concerning metals: Herbert Skinner was measuring with precision the spectra of x-rays from light elements, while Clarence Zener and Harry Jones had begun theoretical studies of metallic conduction. Mott's enthusiastic leadership welded these and others into a group that later could be recognized as one of the earliest pioneering groups of solid-state physics. Until

Mott

the outbreak of World War II, its members were largely involved with electrons in metals, though after Ronald Gurney's arrival in 1936 their interests expanded to include electrical conduction and other properties involving defects and impurities in otherwise nonconducting crystals and in semiconductors.

Such problems, though they were being studied experimentally by Robert W. Pohl and his students in Göttingen, were not to the taste of many leading continental theorists—Wolfgang Pauli dismissed them as "dirty physics." Nevertheless the foundations had been laid, in more ideal form, by Arnold Sommerfeld and his younger followers, especially Hans Bethe, Felix Bloch, and Rudolf Peierls; following Schrödinger's formulation of quantum mechanics, they had shown how electrons could move as freely through a crystal lattice as light waves through glass, though their behavior is modified by the atomic structure. The electron wavelength is comparable to the spacing of atoms so that something akin to Bragg reflection of x-rays affects the dynamics strongly, and in each direction of motion there are forbidden, as well as allowed, bands of energy. Since, according to the Pauli exclusion principle, each permitted state may be occupied by only one electron, there may be solids in which the electrons are sufficient to fill a particular allowed band, with none left over. As a small electric field cannot change the state of electrons in filled bands, such solids are insulators. In other solids, the metals, there are partially filled bands and a current is produced easily. In the lowest state of the metal, at absolute zero, all states up to a certain maximum energy, the Fermi level, are filled; this energy is large enough that at ordinary temperatures, few electrons are thermally affected and the sharp distinction between filled and empty states is only slightly blurred. Between insulators and metals there are the semiconductors, where the forbidden range of energy above the top filled band is sufficiently small that some electrons may be thermally excited into the next empty (conduction) band to produce an electrical conductivity that gets better as the temperature is raised.

Bloch's original exposition of this viewpoint assumed, against all probability, that the strong Coulomb interactions between electrons were not significant; it might be expected that they would collide and exchange energy so frequently as to vitiate, through the action of the Heisenberg uncertainty principle, the idea of a well-defined Fermi level. This is a question that Skinner attacked experimentally with his delicate studies of x-ray spectra; the sharp boundary to the spectrum at the high-energy end indicated an equally sharp cutoff to the energy spectrum of the electrons in the light metals he used. In consultation with Mott and Jones, he concluded that an excited electron just above the Fermi level could not readily be scattered by the other electrons; each could only do so if it found a vacant state into which to move—another consequence of the exclusion principle—and the shortage of available states would make the scatterings very improbable. The assumption of independent particles is therefore a good starting point.

The first of Mott's major books from Bristol, *The Theory of the Properties of Metals and Alloys* (1936), for which Jones was coauthor, starts from here and attempts bravely to explain how different crystal structures and electron concentrations give each metal its peculiar character. Not everything has stood up to subsequent experiment and analysis, but it was the first book in English to apply quantum mechanics to metals and was very influential in introducing this branch of physics to the next generation of researchers. It also illustrates a characteristic of the new Bristol school, the fusing of experiment with theory, each team member keeping steadily in mind the general physical picture and, wherever possible, subordinating minor details to the overall grasp of processes. This attitude can be recognized in all Mott's work from then on. He may indeed, as he said, have regretted not having studied mathematics more deeply as a student, but his colleagues, especially the experimenters, did not count this a fault.

Insulators and Semiconductors. The Coulomb interaction between electrons, which apparently plays a minor role in metals, becomes a major issue in the imperfect insulating crystals that interested Mott and Gurney and were the subject of the next important book from the Bristol school, *Electronic Processes in Ionic Crystals* (1940). To a great extent they had to rely on experimental results from elsewhere, especially from Pohl's group, whose investigations of color centers in the alkali halides supplied their first topic. A vacant halide site in the crystal behaves as a positive charge, attracting an electron into a hydrogen-like orbit. Because of the relative permittivity of the crystal, and the lattice field that lowers the electron's effective mass, it is only loosely bound and is a strong absorber of visible light; this gives the crystal its characteristic deep color.

Mott and Gurney then turned to matters of technical importance, the photographic process and semiconducting rectifiers, to the understanding of which they made significant innovations. They paid particular attention, in their discussion of the action of light on silver bromide, to the effects of gross overexposure. A small crystal of silver bromide eventually becomes totally opaque, seemingly being converted into a grain of metallic silver. Unlike the alkali halides, silver bromide is an ionic conductor—an interstitial silver ion may wander, albeit slowly, through the lattice. When an incident photon dislodges an electron from a silver atom, both electron and ion begin to migrate. The faster-moving electron attaches itself to any speck of silver it finds, and the charged speck attracts the interstitial silver ion so that in due course the speck is larger by one atom. Mott and Gurney pointed out that there is no space for growth of the speck within a perfect lattice, but the surface of the bromide crystal or microcracks are suitable sites. When, later, the prevalence of dislocations was appreciated, they were seen also to play an important part in the process. All this, however, involves far more photons than are needed when the photographic plate is to be developed. They comment at some length on what development involves, but at the time of writing there were many outstanding mysteries. The value of their contribution is not that it completed, but that it initiated, a sound understanding of a difficult subject.

The treatment by Mott and Gurney of semiconducting rectifiers must be seen in the light of what was then known. Only later, through the work of Karl Lark-Horovitz and his colleagues working at Purdue University in Indiana during the war, were germanium and silicon purified to such a degree that there was no doubt they were semiconductors. Until then the only semiconductor rectifiers in use were the cat's whisker rectifiers of early radio sets (already superseded by thermionic diodes) and the power-handling rectifiers made by oxidizing the surface of a copper sheet and pressing metallic contacts against the outer oxide surface layer. It was copper oxide, along with other compounds, that Alan Wilson had in mind when he explained semiconductors as insulators with only a very small energy gap, so that thermal excitation sufficed to produce conduction electrons and leave conducting holes in the otherwise filled valence band. In addition, impurities may behave as excess positive charges (donors) with a weakly bound electron that can readily be excited into the conduction band, or as negative charges (acceptors) with a weakly bound hole—that is to say, an electron can readily be attracted from the valence band.

Mott's theory of the copper oxide rectifier, formulated independently by Walter Schottky, relies on the impurity sites associated with an excess of oxygen in the oxide layer to equalize the Fermi energy in the copper and its oxide. When, however, two metals are joined, equalization is achieved by a double layer of charge at the junction, and electrons are copiously available to provide charges. In copper oxide, on the other hand, only the sparse defects can serve, and when they give up their weakly bound charges to leave an insulating layer, it is too thick to allow passage of a current. In this layer there is a potential gradient that only thermally excited electrons can surmount. A potential difference applied from outside can either increase the gradient and inhibit electrical conduction, or, in the reverse sense, lower it and enhance the conductivity. This explanation of the rectifying process accords well with experiment and can be taken over with minor adjustment to describe the modern semiconducting p-n junction.

Postwar Bristol and Cambridge. Like its predecessor, Mott and Gurney's book broke new ground and would have had as great an immediate impact but for the outbreak of war and cessation of academic research. In 1945 Mott returned to Bristol, assured of soon succeeding Arthur M. Tyndall as head of the department. The prewar team had largely disbanded, but new staff soon renewed the old harmony of theory and experiment, albeit with a shift of emphasis to dislocations and their role in metallic deformation, work-hardening, and fatigue. Mott was in charge—along with Frank Nabarro, Charles Frank, and others, including Jacques Friedel, Mott's future brother-in-law—of a formidable team whose achievements somewhat overshadowed his own, occupied as he was with heavier departmental duties. Among the group's many outputs, Frank's theory of the leading part played by dislocations in crystal growth is outstanding for originality and elegance. Mott's twenty years at Bristol were for him the happiest of a long and happy life. When, in 1954, he was invited to succeed Sir Lawrence Bragg as Cavendish Professor in Cambridge, it was only reluctance to disappoint his still-living parents that persuaded him to accept.

The strength of metals was still very much in Mott's mind in 1954 when he moved to the Cavendish chair of physics at Cambridge and found an active group similarly engaged. Peter Hirsch's direct observation, in an electron microscope, of moving dislocations pleased him, but his concern to make changes in the department, along with his involvement with the Pugwash Conferences on Science and World Affairs and with other public issues, reduced his personal research for some years. During his time at Cambridge, Bragg had given enthusiastic support to Max Perutz and John Kendrew in their heroic determination of protein structure, and more guarded support to Francis Crick and James Watson's elucidation of the double helix of DNA. These researches had established the Cavendish (as the department of physics is generally known) at the center of the new science of molecular biology; Mott, though persuaded of the importance of this subject, quickly saw that the laboratory did not have space for both its group and the solid-state theoreticians he was determined to assemble. In the event, having been rehoused (with his help) in a new laboratory of its own, the molecular biology group grew enormously beyond anything the Cavendish could have coped with.

Outside physics, Mott saw a real need to make substantial changes in the university, especially in the organization of science courses for students, which ranged from mathematics to medicine; aided by other science professors, he made great progress. In the belief that it would give him a foothold beyond the Cavendish, he accepted the mastership of Gonville and Caius College (1959–1966) but eventually became impatient with the internal maneuverings of the fellows and resigned. By that time, however, he had attained an authority among the university's scientists that led to his chairing a committee on the development of high-level industrial research in the city of Cambridge. The committee's recommendations, and the seed corn supplied by the richest college, Trinity, overcame the city's reluctance and resulted in the creation of Cambridge Science Park, which has since served as a model for many similar ventures in the United Kingdom.

The Mott Transition. During this period Mott continued thinking about electrons in solids. He had never forgotten how J. H. de Boer and E. J. W. Verwey, at a Bristol meeting in 1937, pointed out that the electrons in nickel oxide, NiO, were too few to completely fill the energy bands as described by the independent-electron theory; yet NiO was an insulator. Peierls had immediately pointed to the Coulomb interaction as the reason, and it was already appreciated that this interaction depended strongly on electron density. Rather paradoxically, it is in dilute electron gases that the effect is most pronounced; thus, electrons can move freely enough, and almost independently, to conduct electricity in a solid or liquid metal, but in the vapor of the same material, mercury, for example, they are strictly confined to their atoms. Returning to this problem in Cambridge, Mott realized that dilute impurities in semiconductors provided an almost ideal model. Hellmut Fritzsche and coworkers in Chicago had produced, by slow neutron bombardment, carefully controlled mixtures of donor and acceptor centers in otherwise highly purified crystals of germanium; transmutation of germanium to arsenic creates a donor, and of germanium to gallium an acceptor. These two are in a fixed proportion determined by the cross section of germanium for the two transmutations, but the total number is controllable by the neutron dosage.

It is convenient at this point to pretend that the donors outnumber the acceptors, so that the account may proceed more easily, without significant change, in terms of electrons rather than holes. At zero temperature all the acceptor levels are filled and a fraction of the donors are deprived of electrons. Electrical conduction in such a system can take place only by quantum mechanical tunneling of an electron from an occupied to an unoccupied site. In a real material the inevitable tiny variations of environment make for variations of energy level on otherwise identical sites. As a result the temperature must be raised to permit thermally assisted transfer between sites. This mechanism, hopping conduction, involves transitions between neighbors or, at lower temperatures, more distant sites. For the latter process Mott used rather simple arguments (later verified more rigorously by others) to show that the conductivity should vary as $\exp(-C/T^{1/4})$; this prediction was borne out by experiment and later shown to be relevant to conduction in amorphous films of germanium and silicon.

As the density of centers increases, for example by heavier neutron dosage, it must be expected that hopping conduction will be replaced by metallic conduction as the electron states become delocalized in a narrow donor impurity band, but the physics involved has proved highly controversial. In Mott's view, at a certain critical concentration there would be an abrupt transition, like a phase change. A low concentration of free electrons would form a weak screen around positive charges, reducing the Coulomb attraction of a bound electron and facilitating the hopping, so that more free electrons would be available. At some concentration the process would become inherently unstable; all electrons on donor sites would become free, forming a half-filled band with weak metallic properties. Mott did not present his reasoning with mathematical rigor but, typically for his innovative ideas, with a certain reliance on intuition. His estimated critical concentration, however, was in excellent agreement with experiment, and what was soon known and widely discussed as the Mott transition became, if not an article of faith, at any rate an attractive hypothesis.

At about the same time as the birth of the Mott transition, Philip W. Anderson, working at Bell Telephone Laboratories in New Jersey, was conceiving an alternative point of view and, following a different tradition, presenting it in such a difficult and detailed mathematical form as to delay its immediate discussion, let alone enthusiastic acceptance. He showed that randomly distributed scattering centers, which at low concentrations limit the free path of electrons in metals without preventing their motion, at higher concentrations may confine them to localized states and prevent conduction at zero temperature without invoking Coulomb interactions between electrons. For intermediate degrees of disorder the localized states lie near the extremities of electron bands; if the Fermi level shifts from extended to localized states, the material changes from a conductor to an insulator. Mott early appreciated the importance of the Anderson transition and the consequent development of the concept of mobility edges in amorphous semiconductors. The new ideas from Mott and Anderson led to an outpouring of learned papers from solid-state theorists.

From about 1966, Mott found himself in a position to leave departmental and outside problems in other willing hands and devote himself to attempts to resolve the controversies he, along with Anderson and others, had started. He retired as department head in 1971 but remained in the department for another twenty-five years until two days before his death, never losing his enthusiasm for physics. He was awarded the Nobel Prize in Physics in 1977, along with Anderson and Van Vleck, for fundamental theoretical studies of magnetic and disordered systems. In his Nobel Prize address he paid tribute to Anderson's contributions—a typically generous acknowledgment of a development that considerably influenced his views on disordered systems. Unlike many late Nobel laureates he continued to publish until the end; more than 100 of his papers, of at least 320 in total, appeared after 1977. They covered a range of related problems in disordered systems—liquid metals, solutions of alkali metals in liquid ammonia, and especially amorphous semiconductors and glasses. With Mott at the center of a large and fluctuating group that included Edward A. (Ted) Davis and Michael Pepper, and with many other laboratories joining in the elucidation of these difficult problems, a vast literature developed and was reduced to order in the last of his collaborative books, Mott and Davis's *Electronic Processes in Non-crystalline Materials* (1971, 1979), the two editions of which had wide circulation in several languages.

The Last Years. The discovery in 1986, by J. Georg Bednorz and K. Alexander Müller, of high-temperature superconductivity initiated an explosion of research into which Mott was willingly drawn. With A. S. Alexandrov he developed, and championed in the face of many mutually incompatible alternative theories, an explanation in terms of spin-polaron pairs. None of the then-contending theories had, at Mott's death in 1996, found general support; nor had they ten years later, at the time of this writing. Whatever the permanent value of Mott's proposals, it was heartening to all who knew him to see the survival at so late a date of the intellectual excitement that had driven him from his earliest days.

In 1998 Davis edited *Nevill Mott: Reminiscences and Appreciations,* a collection of ninety essays by Mott's friends and colleagues that gives an overview of his wide-ranging interests and powers of invention but, above all, shows the devotion he inspired in all who could penetrate the apparently austere shell that quite thinly enclosed a warm, amusing, and generous man.

BIBLIOGRAPHY

Unpublished letters and manuscripts are in the archives of the University of Cambridge. A microfiche listing published papers is to be found in Biographical Memoirs of Fellows of the Royal Society, London *44 (1998).*

WORKS BY MOTT

"The Wave Mechanics of a-Ray Tracks." *Proceedings of the Royal Society of London,* series A, 126 (1929): 79–84.

With H. S. W. Massey. *The Theory of Atomic Collisions.* Oxford: Clarendon Press, 1933.

With H. Jones. *The Theory of the Properties of Metals and Alloys.* Oxford: Clarendon Press, 1936.

With R. W. Gurney. "The Theory of the Photolysis of Silver Bromide and the Photographic Latent Image." *Proceedings of the Royal Society of London,* series A, 164 (1938): 151–167.

"The Theory of Crystal Rectifiers." *Proceedings of the Royal Society of London,* series A, 171 (1939): 27–39.

With R. W. Gurney. *Electronic Procesess in Ionic Crystals.* Oxford: Clarendon Press, 1940.

With W. D. Twose. "The Theory of Impurity Conduction." *Advances in Physics* 10 (1961): 107–163.

"Conduction in Non-Crystalline Materials III: Localized States in a Pseudogap and Near Extremities of Conduction and Valence Bands." *Philosophical Magazine* 19 (1969): 835–852.

With E. A. Davis. *Electronic Processes in Non-crystalline Materials.* 2nd ed. Oxford: Clarendon Press, 1979.

Editor. "The Beginnings of Solid State Physics." *Proceedings of the Royal Society of London,* series A, 371 (1980): 3–177. A collection of articles about the history of solid-state physics.

A Life in Science. London: Taylor and Francis, 1986. A short autobiography.

With A. S. Alexandrov, eds. *Sir Nevill Mott: 65 Years in Physics (Selected Papers).* Singapore: World Scientific, 1995.

OTHER SOURCES

Anderson, Philip W. "Absence of Diffusion in Certain Random Lattices." *Physical Review* 109 (1958): 1492–1505.

Davis, E. A., ed. *Nevill Mott: Reminiscences and Appreciations.* London: Taylor and Francis, 1998.

Hoddeson, Lillian, Ernest Braun, Jürgen Teichmann, et al., eds. *Out of the Crystal Maze: Chapters from the History of Solid State Physics, 1900–1960.* New York: Oxford University Press, 1992. The first attempt to write a comprehensive history of solid-state physics.

Pippard, A. Brian. "Sir Nevill Francis Mott, C.H." *Biographical Memoirs of Fellows of the Royal Society* (London) 44 (November 1998): 313–328.

Brian Pippard

MUELLER, FERDINAND JAKOB HEINRICH VON

(*b.* Rostock, Germany, 30 June 1825; *d.* Melbourne, Australia, 10 October 1896), *botany, geography.*

Born and educated in Germany, Ferdinand Jakob Mueller became Australia's most distinguished scientist and the leading authority on the Australian flora, with more than one thousand publications, including numerous books, to his credit. His work, primarily in descriptive and economic botany, remains fundamental to Australian plant science. A noted explorer of areas of Australia previously unvisited by Europeans, he became a major promoter

Mueller

of expeditions into unexplored regions of inland Australia, New Guinea, and Antarctica. He played a central role in the formation of important Australian scientific institutions. A leading figure in the acclimatization movement, he was among the first to recognize the damage being done to the Australian environment by European settlers and to call for more sustainable land management.

Early Career: Germany and Australia. Mueller was apprenticed to a pharmacist in Husum, Schleswig-Holstein, in 1840. Required to assemble an herbarium, he developed a passion for botany, spending every spare moment botanizing and establishing links with other enthusiasts. To complete his pharmacy qualifications, he enrolled at Kiel University in 1845, attending lectures in chemistry, geology, and some medical subjects, as well as in botany. He passed the *Staatsexamen* in pharmacy in March 1847. Inspired by reading Alexander von Humboldt's travels, and by mingling with the elite of German science at the 1846 congress of German scientists and medical doctors (*Versammlung Deutscher Naturforscher und Ärzte*), held in Kiel, Mueller dreamed of becoming a scientific traveler. Both his father Friedrich Müller, a customs officer at Rostock, and his mother Louise Müller, née Mertens, from Tönning in Schleswig-Holstein, had died from tuberculosis while he was a child. When the same disease carried off his older sister in 1845—five other siblings had died in infancy—he became fearful for his health and that of his two surviving sisters, and decided to seek a drier climate. Australia, botanically rich but still little known scientifically, was an attractive destination for a would-be Humboldtian naturalist. Shortly before he and his sisters sailed in July 1847, he submitted his doctoral thesis at Kiel University; it was a survey of the flora of southern Schleswig, effectively a catalog of his impressive herbarium assembled during the previous seven years.

At first, Mueller settled in South Australia, finding work in an Adelaide pharmacy and botanizing at every opportunity. Naturalized as a British subject in 1849, he anglicized his name from Müller. He ranged as far afield as Mount Gambier, in the southeast, and northward to the Flinders Ranges and the desert country near Lake Torrens, and sent a large collection of plants to the Hamburg botanist Otto WilhelmSonder, who functioned for many years as, in effect, his European agent. He also sent descriptions of many items he thought represented new species. He recognized, however, that without an adequate botanical library or access to authenticated specimens, his identifications must be tentative, and he relied on Sonder to check his analyses before publishing them. Two papers in *Linnaea* resulted, one with Sonder as coauthor. Sonder also arranged for sections of Mueller's collection to be described by experts on particular families, resulting in a series in *Linnaea* under the heading "Plantae Muellerianae" that made Mueller's name known among European botanists.

Government Botanist. In August 1852, Mueller moved to Melbourne, intending to set up a pharmacy. However, Victoria's scientifically inclined governor, Charles Joseph La Trobe, impressed by Mueller's botanical knowledge, created the new position of government botanist and appointed Mueller to it on 26 January 1853. He occupied this position until his death.

Mueller immediately embarked on a series of arduous journeys that took him into almost every corner of Victoria, much of it rugged terrain previously unvisited by Europeans, to survey the flora of a colony settled less than twenty years earlier. Mueller aimed to identify potentially valuable indigenous plants, and he played an important role in promoting the industrial usefulness of eucalypts in particular. From his journeys he formed a substantial herbarium that provided the basis for magisterial accounts of Victoria's flora.

From mid-1855, Mueller took leave to serve as botanist on the North Australian Exploring Expedition led by Augustus Charles Gregory. In the course of eighteen months, Mueller traveled more than 3,000 kilometers (1,850 miles) on horseback in northern Australia with Gregory, and assembled an enormous collection of plants, many new to science. Under his contract, his primary collection went to Kew Gardens in England, but Mueller was allowed to keep a duplicate collection. Not content, as most previous colonial collectors had been, for metropolitan botanists to describe his material, he sent his own descriptions to London with the specimens. Some were published in the *Proceedings* of the Linnean Society, but the volume of material he sent overwhelmed Kew's resources, and most of his descriptions were returned to him. Increasingly confident of his mastery of the Australian flora, Mueller thereupon launched his own publication, *Fragmenta Phytographiae Australiae*, which became his principal vehicle for publishing descriptions of new species; ninety-four issues appeared between 1858 and 1882.

Throughout this period and beyond, Mueller continued botanical fieldwork in Victoria, and he also visited Western Australia, Tasmania, and southern New South Wales. Now, however, he rarely ventured beyond the frontiers of European settlement, instead encouraging explorers to collect on his behalf specimens that he then described. He also encouraged settlers to collect for him. Sometimes he acquired whole collections, including his friend Sonder's enormous herbarium, containing at least a quarter of a million specimens and extremely rich in type specimens—including many from Australia—which he

Mueller

purchased from Sonder's widow in 1883. By collection and purchase, the Melbourne herbarium expanded very rapidly under his direction to become one of the world's great herbaria, and the paramount collection of Australian forms.

Collaboration with Bentham. From the moment Mueller decided, while still in South Australia, not to return to Germany, he dreamed of writing a definitive Australian *Flora*. He was the obvious person to do the Australian volumes for a series of British colonial floras proposed by Kew in the late 1850s. The English botanists insisted, however, that he would need to study the specimens at Kew and in other European collections from which many Australian species had been named. Mueller had long planned such a visit but, despite repeated urging from William Hooker and his son Joseph, he did not go, and authorship was eventually given to the Englishman George Bentham instead. Bentham, however, who never set foot in Australia, relied on Mueller's assistance, which was formally acknowledged on the title page of all seven volumes of Bentham's *Flora Australiensis*.

Over almost twenty years, Mueller systematically loaned his vast and ever-growing Australian collections to Bentham, after first publishing the new species. His collections became "authenticated" as a result of Bentham's work, and their return gradually transferred taxonomic control over Australian materials from England to Australia. Mueller's proposed supplement to *Flora Australiensis* was never published, but his *Systematic Census of Australian Plants* (1882; 2nd ed., 1889) cited the many new descriptions that he and others had published subsequent to the appearance of relevant volumes of Bentham's work. *Eucalyptographia* (1879–1884) offered a masterly, magnificently illustrated account of the ubiquitous Australian genus that Bentham, recognizing the deficiencies of his own treatment, had urged Mueller to write.

By the standards of his time, Mueller was very much a taxonomic "lumper" rather than a "splitter," frequently treating differences in form that most other botanists would have regarded as sufficient to define a new species as variations induced by "climatic or geological circumstances." The number of plant species was, he believed, greatly overrated. Convinced that only by careful examination of the variability of species in a variety of habitats could the true limits to species be set, he sought specimens from as many locations as possible. His own extensive knowledge of living plants led him, during the writing of *Flora Australiensis*, to engage in some vigorous differences of opinion with Bentham, who adopted a wholly herbarium-based approach. Bentham, being author, of course prevailed.

Implicit in Mueller's argument was his view, to which he staunchly adhered even after the appearance of Charles Darwin's *Origin of Species*, that species are fixed and immutable. The observed variability on which Darwin had erected his theory, was, Mueller argued, entirely within the boundaries of species; the notion that species themselves varied was an artifact of incorrect boundaries—more exactly, of too many boundaries—having been drawn. Though Mueller undoubtedly saw Darwinism as a threat to religious beliefs, his objection was a scientific one, as he carefully emphasized whenever he discussed the matter, whether in letters or in print. Mueller recognized that his views had become unfashionable among English-speaking naturalists but nevertheless felt duty-bound to speak out, from a scientific standpoint, against a doctrine "calculated to shake the pillars on which the consolation of so many rests" (1998–2006, vol. 2, p. 279). The introduction to *Vegetation of the Chatham Islands* (1864) contains his most considered statement. Consistent with his anti-Darwinian views, in his numerous publications on fossil plants, he recognized the extinction but not the evolution of forms.

Mueller did not regard genera and families in the same light as species. Far from being fixed, they were in his view merely "strongholds around which we arbitrarily array [species] to facilitate generalization, to ease the search and to aid the memory" (1864, p. 8). Their limits must always reflect the differing viewpoints of individual observers. In arranging genera, Mueller from his early days in Schleswig-Holstein was an adherent of the natural system of Antoine-Laurent de Jussieu, and later Augustin-Pyrame de Candolle. Robert Brown's *Prodromus Florae Novae Hollandiae* (1810), inevitably the starting point for his study of the Australian flora, reinforced his commitment to this approach. Mueller did not, however, follow these authorities unthinkingly in every particular. While rejecting on the basis of his Australian experience some modifications to the Candollean system proposed by Bentham in *Flora Australiensis*, he developed rearrangements of his own, chiefly in distributing the "unnatural" Monochlamydeae into other divisions. His scheme was subsequently adopted in other major nineteenth-century works on the Australian flora as more "truly natural" than rival systems.

Mueller gave absolute precedence to priority in the naming of species, leading him, in his *Systematic Census*, to abandon some widely used names in favor of names which, while published first, had become neglected. For this he was heavily criticized by Bentham and his colleagues at Kew, who were sometimes willing to abandon strict priority, and who dismissed laboring over priorities as useless "philological" work. Mueller was unrepentant, and his views eventually prevailed in the international code of nomenclature.

Royal Botanic Garden Melbourne. Shortly after Mueller returned to Melbourne from northern Australia in mid-1857, directorship of the Melbourne botanic garden was added to his responsibilities as government botanist. Soon he found himself also in charge of the colony's zoo, housed in the garden from 1858 to 1861. He proved an energetic administrator, overseeing an extensive series of capital works, and exchanging seeds and plants with gardens in many other parts of the world. As a result of these exchanges, the number of plant varieties in the garden increased from fifteen hundred to around seventy-five hundred. Mueller's large-scale distribution of plants and flowers within the colony brought him into conflict with local nurserymen, and he was also criticized by those who did not share his view of the garden as predominantly a scientific and educational resource, and wished to see it developed as a public pleasure space. Eventually, in 1873, his enemies triumphed and he was dismissed—or, rather, the position of director of the garden was abolished. Though he continued as government botanist, this was a devastating blow to Mueller both personally and because he believed that access to living specimens in the garden was vital to his scientific work. Even twenty years later, merely to mention his eviction would still bring tears to his eyes.

Mueller was a lifelong enthusiast for acclimatizing useful species, plant or animal, in new parts of the world, and he regarded plant acclimatization as a major function of any worthwhile botanic garden. His vast program of exchanges of seeds and plants with other gardens around the world was intended not merely to embellish the Melbourne garden but to provide the basis for large-scale distributions from the garden of potentially useful exotic varieties. In common with his contemporaries, Mueller had little notion of nature as a fragile ecological structure that needed protecting; on the contrary, he sought to fill gaps in the creation with appropriate and useful foreign species. He even looked forward to establishing "cold-enduring plants and herbs" in Antarctica and the sub-Antarctic islands, to open the way for eventual settlement of the region. His *Select Extra-Tropical Plants Readily Eligible for Industrial Culture or Naturalisation*, first published in 1876 under a slightly different title, became his most widely published work, appearing in German, French, and posthumous Portuguese translations, and in English in Indian and American as well as several Australian editions. Mueller helped establish many exotic species in Australia, some of them extremely useful. Others, however, quickly ran out of control and became notorious weeds. At the same time, Mueller was vigorously exporting Australian species elsewhere. *Eucalyptus globulus* was a particular favorite for regions with a suitable climate, both as a fast-growing source of timber and, because of its extraordinary transpiration rate, to help drain swampy areas. Largely as a result of his efforts, this species became naturalized in many parts of the world.

In his early years, Mueller enthusiastically advocated exploitation of Victoria's forests. In later years, however, as he observed their widespread destruction, he began calling for sustainable management of what was left. Where notable species were threatened with extinction, he became a preservationist, calling for permanent reservation of areas where these species flourished. The successful public campaign that followed is generally seen as the start of the national parks movement in Victoria.

Mueller was closely associated with almost every significant Australian exploring initiative in the second half of the nineteenth century. He maintained a close relationship with the German geographical publishing house of Justus Perthes, publisher of *Petermann's geographische Mittheilungen*, keeping the founder of the journal, August Petermann, and his successors abreast of the exploration of inland Australia and furnishing them with up-to-date data for incorporation in their maps. Chiefly as a result of Mueller's activities, these maps became recognized as the best available maps of Australia. Explorers grateful for Mueller's support bestowed names of his choosing on geographical features that they encountered, and the publication of these on Perthes's maps helped ensure that they stuck.

In the 1880s and 1890s, Mueller led an Australian campaign promoting the scientific exploration of Antarctica. Though he and his colleagues failed to achieve this objective, they were instrumental in reawakening international interest in the region and thus contributed indirectly to the remarkable efflorescence of Antarctic exploration that occurred soon afterward. They also succeeded in establishing Antarctic exploration as a task for scientists rather than old-style explorers seeking merely to traverse new territory.

Throughout his working life, in addition to his enormous output of scientific publications, Mueller maintained a vast correspondence that kept him in touch with fellow scientists elsewhere. He also supplied botanical, zoological, mineralogical and ethnographical materials to institutions around the world. He was elected to more than one hundred scientific societies, including the Leopoldina (1857), the Royal Geographical Society (1858), the Linnean Society (1859), the Royal Society of London (1861), and the Paris Academy of Sciences (1895).The Royal Society awarded him one of its two Royal Medals for 1888. The king of Württemberg granted him his "von" in 1867 and made him a hereditary baron (*Freiherr*) four years later, the British knighted him in 1879, and other nations bestowed some twenty other knighthoods and many lesser honors on him. A small, wiry man, Mueller never married, though he became

Mueller

engaged on at least two occasions. Following his death, the Australasian Association for the Advancement of Science created its Mueller Medal to recognize important Australian contributions to science. His name is also commemorated in at least two genera, many species, and several geographic features, and in the title of the scientific journal published by the Melbourne Herbarium, *Muelleria.*

BIBLIOGRAPHY

For lists of Mueller's publications, see Churchill et al. and Home et al., eds., cited below. Mueller's massive files of incoming correspondence, exploration diaries, and working notes disappeared, presumably destroyed, some years after his death. However, significant numbers of letters and other papers survive at the Royal Botanic Gardens Melbourne, the Public Record Office Victoria, Kew Gardens, Gotha, and elsewhere. The Royal Botanic Gardens Melbourne holds photocopies of many letters held in other repositories.

WORKS BY MUELLER

Plants Indigenous to the Colony of Victoria. Melbourne: Government Printer, 1862–1865.

Vegetation of the Chatham Islands. Melbourne: Government Printer, 1864.

Descriptive Notes on Papuan Plants. Melbourne: Government Printer, 1875–1890.

Select Extra-Tropical Plants: Readily Eligible for Industrial Culture or Naturalisation, with Indications of Their Native Countries and Some of Their Uses (1876). 9th ed. Melbourne: Government Printer, 1895.

Introduction to Botanic Teachings at the Schools of Victoria, through References to Leading Native Plants. Melbourne: Government Printer, 1877.

The Native Plants of Victoria, Succinctly Defined. Melbourne: Government Printer, 1879.

Systematic Census of Australian Plants, with Chronologic, Literary and Geographic Annotations. Melbourne: M'Carron, Bird, 1882.

Eucalyptographia: A Descriptive Atlas of the Eucalypts of Australia and the Adjoining Islands. Melbourne: Government Printer, 1879–1884.

Key to the System of Victorian Plants. Melbourne: Government Printer, 1886–1888.

Description and Illustrations of the Myoporinous Plants of Australia. Melbourne: Government Printer, 1886.

Iconography of Australian Species of Acacia and Cognate Genera. Melbourne: Government Printer, 1887–1888.

Iconography of Australian Salsolaceous Plants. Melbourne: R. S. Brain, Government Printer, 1889–1891.

Home, R. W., and Sara Maroske. "Ferdinand von Mueller and the French Consuls." *Explorations: A Bulletin Devoted to the Study of Franco-Australian Links* 18 (1997): 3–50. Mueller's correspondence with successive French consuls in Melbourne.

Regardfully Yours: Selected Correspondence of Ferdinand von Mueller. 3 vols. Edited by R. W. Home, et al. Bern, Switzerland: Lang, 1998–2006. Revised versions of lists of Mueller's plant names and of his publications are included in volume 1. Volume 3 includes a list of Mueller's many honors, memberships, and other awards.

Voigt, Johannes H., ed. *Die Erforschung Australiens: Der Briefwechsel zwischen August Petermann und Ferdinand von Mueller, 1861–1878.* Gotha, Germany: Justus Perthes, 1996. Mueller's correspondence with August Petermann.

OTHER SOURCES

Churchill, D. M., T. B. Muir, and D. M. Sinkora. "The Published Works of Ferdinand J. H. Mueller (1825–1896)." *Muelleria* 4 (1978): 1–120, and "Supplement." *Muelleria* 5 (1984): 229–248. List of works.

Cohn, Helen, and Sara Maroske, "Relief from Duties of Minor Importance: The Removal of Baron von Mueller from the Directorship of the Royal Botanic Gardens." *Victorian Historical Journal* 67 (1996): 103–127.

Daley, Charles. "Baron Sir Ferdinand von Mueller, K.C.M.G., M.D., F.R.S., Botanist, Explorer, and Geographer." *Victorian Historical Magazine* 10 (1924): 23–75.

Gillbank, Linden. "Alpine Botanical Expeditions of Ferdinand Mueller." *Muelleria* 7 (1992): 473–489.

Home, R. W., ed. *The Scientific Savant in Nineteenth-Century Australia.* Canberra: Australian Academy of Science, 1997 (*Historical Records of Australian Science* 11, no. 3 [June 1997]: 281–454).

———, Sara Maroske, A. M. Lucas, and P. J. Lucas. "Why Explore Antarctica?: Australian Discussions in the 1880s." *Australian Journal of Politics and History* 38 (1992): 386–413.

Lucas, A. M. "Baron von Mueller: Protégé Turned Patron." In *Australian Science in the Making,* edited by R. W. Home. Cambridge, U.K.: Cambridge University Press, 1988.

———. "Letters, Shipwrecks, and Taxonomic Confusion: Establishing a Reputation from Australia." *Historical Records of Australian Science* 10 (1995): 207–221.

———. "Assistance at a Distance: George Bentham, Ferdinand von Mueller, and the Production of *Flora australiensis.*" *Archives of Natural History* 30 (2003): 255–281.

———, P. J. Lucas, Thomas A. Darragh, and Sara Maroske. "Colonial Pride and Metropolitan Expectations: The British Museum and Melbourne's Meteorites." *British Journal for the History of Science* 27 (1994): 65–87.

———, Sara Maroske, and Andrew Brown-May. "Bringing Science to the Public: Ferdinand von Mueller and Botanical Education in Victorian Victoria." *Annals of Science* 63 (2006): 25–57.

Maroske, Sara. "Science by Correspondence: Ferdinand Mueller and Botany in Nineteenth-Century Australia." PhD diss., University of Melbourne, 2005.

———, and Andrew Brown-May. "Breaking into the Quietude: Re-reading the Personal Life of Ferdinand von Mueller." *Public History Review* 3 (1994): 36–63.

———, and Helen M. Cohn. "'Such Ingenious Birds': Ferdinand Mueller and William Swainson in Victoria." *Muelleria* 7 (1992): 529–553.

Muir, T. B. "An Index to the New Taxa, New Combinations, and New Names Published by Ferdinand J. H. Mueller."

Muelleria 4 (1979): 123–168. Index to the plant names introduced by Mueller.

Powell, J. M. "A Baron under Siege: Von Mueller and the Press in the 1870s." *Victorian Historical Journal* 50 (1979): 18–35.

Voigt, Johannes H., and Doris M. Sinkora. "Ferdinand (von) Müller in Schleswig-Holstein; or, The Making of a Scientist and of a Migrant." *Historical Records of Australian Science* 11 (1996): 13–33.

Willis, Margaret. *By Their Fruits: A Life of Ferdinand von Mueller, Botanist and Explorer.* Sydney: Angus and Robertson, 1949. The best separately published biography available to date, but cannot always be relied on.

R. W. Home

MUGNIER, CECILE

SEE **Vogt, Cecile and Oskar**.

MÜLLER, FERDINAND JAKOB HEINRICH VON

SEE **Mueller, Ferdinand Jakob Heinrich von**.

MÜLLER, JOHANNES (VON KÖNIGSBERG)

SEE **Regiomontanus, Johannes**.

MULLIKEN, ROBERT SANDERSON

(*b.* Newburyport, Massachusetts, 7 June 1896; *d.* Alexandria, Virginia, 31 October 1986), *quantum chemistry, molecular orbital theory, molecular structure.*

Mulliken is counted as one of the founders of theoretical quantum chemistry, along with Linus Pauling. Mulliken, instrumental in the definition of basic concepts and methods to study molecular structure and spectra, as well as in the shaping of its language and nomenclature, was awarded the Nobel Prize in Chemistry in 1966 for his "fundamental work concerning chemical bonds and the electronic structure of molecules by the molecular orbital method." Working within the boundary of two scientific disciplines, Mulliken left his imprint in an area that during his lifetime gradually shifted from physics to chemistry. From experiment he moved toward theory, as his contributions also brought mathematics and computers into the realm of chemical practice.

Education and Career. The son of Samuel Parsons Mulliken, an organic chemist from the Massachusetts Institute of Technology (MIT), Robert, like his father, attended MIT, receiving an undergraduate degree in chemistry in 1917. After graduation, he accepted a wartime job as a junior chemical engineer for the U.S. Bureau of Mines, and he conducted research on poison gases at the American University in Washington, D.C. Following World War I, he worked as a chemist at the New Jersey Zinc Company until 1919, when he opted for university life and enrolled at the University of Chicago in order to work with the physical chemist William Draper Harkins. In 1921 he earned his PhD in chemistry with a dissertation on the partial separation of mercury isotopes by evaporation (and other methods). He stayed one more year as a National Research Council Fellow, working on an extension of his former research in the attempt to obtain bigger isotope separations with mercury by using improved equipments and methods. In the process, he built the first "isotope factory," an apparatus that took advantage of the slightly different behaviors of isotopes during evaporation and diffusion through a membrane.

Mulliken still held a National Research Council Fellowship when he moved in 1923 to the Jefferson Physical Laboratory at Harvard University. In 1926 he became an assistant professor of physics at New York University. He became an associate professor of physics at the University of Chicago in 1928, where he stayed until his death, with a dual appointment at Florida State University as a Distinguished Research Professor of Chemical Physics from 1964 to 1971. The year after his return to Chicago in 1929, he married Mary Helen Von Noé; they became the parents of two daughters. Mulliken became a full professor in 1931 and was elected as a member of the National Academy of Sciences in 1936.

During World War II, Mulliken collaborated on the Manhattan Project as the director of the Information Division of the Plutonium Project at the Metallurgical Laboratory at the University of Chicago. While he valued first and foremost his scientific work, which he pursued until the end of his life, he also viewed science as having a renewed role in a society facing new challenges during and after the war. In 1955 he served as scientific attaché at the U.S. Embassy in London. From 1956 to 1961 he was Ernest DeWitt Burton Distinguished Service Professor of Physics, and he was the Distinguished Service Professor of Physics and Chemistry at the University of Chicago from 1961 to 1985. Mulliken received several medals and awards from the American Chemical Society—the G. N. Lewis Gold Medal, the Theodore William Richards Gold Medal, the Peter Debye Award, the John Gamble Kirkwood Award, and the J. Willard Gibbs Medal—before being awarded the Nobel Prize.

Molecular Physics, Electrons, and Molecular Spectra. Since his high school days, Mulliken was intrigued by the role that electrons played in the architecture of matter. In 1913, the year of the publication of a new hybrid model of the atom by the Danish physicist Niels Bohr, Mulliken presented at his high school graduation ceremony an essay titled "Electrons: What They Are and What They Do." The elucidation of the role played by electrons in the structure, behavior, and spectra of molecules became a central and recurrent theme in his scientific life.

In the years when atomic physics was coming of age and increasing in importance as a topic at the forefront of research for European scientists, American physicists chose instead to concentrate on molecular physics. Mulliken moved to Harvard University and joined a group of physicists, including Edwin Crawford Kemble and Raymond Thayer Birge, that exemplified this trend. Molecules, not atoms, became their main target. The experimental work on isotope separation prepared Mulliken to move smoothly into spectroscopy, and specifically into the analysis of molecular spectra, starting with diatomic molecules and looking for evidence of the existence of different isotopes in their spectra (isotope effect).

Mulliken assisted Kemble and Birge in the preparation of their 1926 comprehensive report on the spectra of diatomic molecules for the National Research Council, written together with Walter F. Colby and Francis Wheeler Loomis. More complicated than the spectra of elements, band spectra (then the current designation for molecular spectra) were classified on the basis of three types of contributions associated with the three different components of the energy of a molecule (due to nuclear rotations, nuclear vibrations, and electronic motions). By implication, an isotope effect in the spectra could be the result of three contributions: rotational, vibrational, and electronic. Mulliken began to look for evidence of vibrational contributions in visible and ultraviolet spectra. His experimental work enabled him to identify a new molecular fragment—nitric oxide (NO)—and to suggest the existence in molecules of an energy at a temperature of zero degrees Kelvin (zero point energy), a concept that was soon to find a theoretical justification within the framework of the new quantum mechanics.

Mulliken then shifted to the consideration of the electronic distribution in molecules. He found evidence that diatomic molecules with the same number of electrons shared similar spectroscopic properties with the element in the periodic table having the same number of electrons. This analogical behavior has occurred in one form or another for scientists such as Rudolf Mecke and Hertha Sponer in Germany, as well as Birge in the United States, and became the starting point for the development of a classificatory scheme for diatomic molecules in order to group them into different families. Subsequently, this classifying scheme led to the suggestion that similar electronic structures were associated with corresponding systems of energy levels.

The two years Mulliken spent at New York University were particularly productive. An active group of students gathered around him, working along the lines of his new research program. At the same time, he became recognized as an international leader on the classification of band spectra.

This was a period in which quantum mechanics emerged, wave and matrix mechanics were formulated and proved mathematically equivalent, and the Copenhagen interpretation of the behavior of the miscroscopic realm, grounded on Bohr's complementarity principle and Heisenberg's uncertainty principle, came into view. Mulliken began a lifetime friendship with Friedrich Hund, the German theoretical physicist who introduced quantum mechanics into the study of molecular structure. Even though molecular rotations and vibrations had been studied by Mulliken and others within the framework of the old quantum theory, Hund used quantum mechanics to show that the electronic quantum states of a diatomic molecule could be interpolated between two limiting cases: the situation in which the two atoms are separated, and the opposite situation in which their two nuclei are considered to be united into one. This work gave theoretical support to Mulliken's former hypothesis that electronic quantum numbers could change drastically in the process of molecule formation, and to his subsequent successful attempt to assign individual quantum numbers to electrons in molecules.

Mulliken's work on the interpretation of spectra of diatomic molecules ended with the preparation of three classic review articles (1930–1932) in which he introduced his famous correlation diagrams, which enabled one to visualize the state of a molecule in relation to the separated atoms and the united atom descriptions. The correlation diagrams were considered by the physicists John Hasbrouck Van Vleck and Albert Sherman, in their famous 1935 review paper, to play a role relative to diatomic molecules equivalent to that played by Mendeleev's periodic table for atoms. The visualization of the properties of diatomic molecules went hand in hand with Mulliken's effort to secure an international agreement on notation for diatomic molecules, which he managed successfully to accomplish in 1930. In 1955, an agreement on notation was also secured for polyatomic molecules.

Molecule Formation and Chemical Bonding. The assignment of quantum numbers to electrons in molecules (1928–1932), as suggested by the study of their electronic

Robert S. Mulliken. *Robert S. Mulliken in laboratory.* © BETTMANN/CORBIS.

spectra, was directly linked to Mulliken's initial analysis of the conditions of molecule formation in diatomic molecules. This led to the proposal of a novel approach to the question of molecule formation and chemical bonding, abandoning the notion of chemical bonds and valence, and dispensing with the conceptual framework of classical valence theory. Mulliken set forward a theoretical scheme in which molecule formation was analyzed in terms of each electron's motions in the field of two or more nuclei as well as that of other electrons, in what he called molecular orbitals. To counteract the established view of a molecule as an aggregate of atoms, Mulliken contended, in the same manner as Gertrude Stein, that "a molecule is a molecule is a molecule." He refused to reduce a molecule to an aggregate of atoms, and instead built it from nuclei and electrons. Mulliken's new approach to valence theory, which came to be known as the molecular orbital (MO) theory, was the result of a painstaking analysis of band spectra data. Starting as a largely phenomenological theory based on the extension of Bohr's building-up principle to molecules, according to which the molecules were pictured as being formed by feeding electrons into orbits (or orbitals) that encircled all nuclei, it soon became integrated into the framework of quantum mechanics, through the participation of other scientists. In addition to Hund, Erich Hückel, and Gerhard Herzberg, from Germany, the British entered the field. In 1929 John E. Lennard-Jones suggested the physical simplification that consisted of representing molecular orbitals by a linear combination of atomic orbitals, a step that in itself proved fundamental to the mathematical development of MO theory within the framework of quantum mechanics.

Mulliken's extension of the idea of molecular orbitals to small polyatomic molecules (1932–1935) brought about several important new results. Whereas the physicist John Clarke Slater had shown that group theory was not essential to the analysis of atomic spectra, Mulliken demonstrated that it was indispensable in dealing with polyatomic molecules. As molecular symmetry varies with electronic state, group theoretical methods proved to be an indispensable tool in the classification of the states of highly symmetrical molecules like benzene. Mulliken also developed a quantum theory of the double bond along the lines suggested by Hückel and introduced a scale of absolute electronegativities (1934), which was intended to be a reply to Pauling's scale of relative electronegativities.

The Genesis and First Decades of Quantum Chemistry: Mulliken versus Pauling. Mulliken's proposal to attack the problem of molecule formation was opposed by Linus Pauling, who had put forward an alternative method to study molecular structure and chemical bonding. Contrary to Mulliken's approach, Pauling's valence bond (VB) approach was based on a resonance theory of the chemical bond, which was meant to extend classical structural theory. It thus envisioned molecules as aggregates of atoms bonded together along privileged directions.

Originated in the joint work on the hydrogen molecule by the German physicists Walter Heitler and Fritz London (1927), the method was extended to other molecules by Slater (1931) and, especially, by Pauling himself, who based his semiempirical approach on ideas such as hybridization of atomic orbitals to form bond orbitals that possessed directional character and resonance among several valence-bond structures. He came to believe that bonds are formed as a result of the overlapping of two atomic orbitals, and that the stronger bond is formed by the atomic orbital overlapping the most with a certain atomic orbital in the other atom. The bond direction is defined as the direction in which the concentration of individual bond orbitals is highest. The strength and directional character of bonds is thus explained as a result of the overlapping of individual bond orbitals, which is

Mulliken

itself a reflection of a greater density of charge concentrated along a particular direction. Under certain conditions, during bond formation, atomic orbitals must be combined and the new hybridized orbitals—which are formed as linear combinations of atomic *s*, *p*, and *d* orbitals—are particularly suited for bond formation. Pauling came to believe that bonds are formed as a result of the overlapping of two bond orbitals, and that the stronger bond is formed by the bond orbital overlapping the most with a certain bond orbital in the other atom. The bond direction is defined as the direction in which the concentration of individual atomic orbitals is highest. The strength and directional character of bonds is thus explained as a result of the overlapping of individual atomic orbitals, which is itself a reflection of a greater density of charge concentrated along a particular direction. Furthermore, in those compounds for which no single structure seemed to represent adequately all its properties, Pauling suggested that the molecule could be represented as a hybrid of two or more conventional forms of the molecule—a situation that he dubbed "resonance among several valence-bond structures." Introduced in "The Nature of the Chemical Bond" series (1931–1933), these ideas were further developed and presented to a wider audience in the famous book, *The Nature of the Chemical Bond* (1939).

The differences in outlook of Pauling's and Mulliken's proposals, which Mulliken himself characterized as reflecting two opposite points of view—Pauling's following "the ideology of chemistry," his own departing from it (Mulliken, 1935)—may well account, together with factors such as personality, rhetorical skills, and communication strategies, for the immediate and widespread success of VB theory when compared to MO theory. Although Pauling and Mulliken thought differently on how the newly developed quantum mechanics could, in practice, be applied to the problem of the chemical bond, they shared a common outlook on how to construct their theoretical schemata, on the character of the constitutive features of their theories, on what the relation of physics to chemistry should be, and on the discourse they developed to legitimate their respective theories.

Seen from this vantage point, the genesis and development of quantum chemistry as an autonomous subdiscipline was dependent on those scientists who, like Mulliken, were able to realize that what had started as an application of physics was becoming an integral part of chemistry. According to Charles Alfred Coulson's words in a symposium commemorating fifty years of valence theory (1969), those who managed to escape successfully from the "thought forms of the physicist" (Coulson, 1970, p. 259) by implicitly or explicitly addressing issues such as the role of theory in chemistry and the methodological status of empirical observations helped to create a new space for chemists to go about practicing their discipline.

The Internationalization of Quantum Chemistry. Throughout a period extending to the late 1950s, the VB method dominated quantum chemistry for reasons that were not entirely due to its superiority. In sharp contrast with Mulliken, who was neither a persuasive writer nor an eloquent teacher, Pauling's ability to present the theory of resonance as an extension of former chemical theories, and to show its explanatory power when dealing with a broad range of chemical phenomena involving ground state properties, especially in small molecules, accounted for the initial popularity of the VB method. Furthermore, endorsing explicitly two main aspects of chemical tradition, Pauling emphasized model building and visualizability as constitutive features of his chemical theory of the bond, a choice that proved decisive to its adoption.

The ascendancy of the MO theory accompanied the downfall of the VB theory. It was largely associated with the contributions of Coulson, an advocate of the MO theory whose rhetorical and pedagogical skills equaled those of Pauling. In a sense, Coulson's textbook *Valence* (1952) played the role of a book that Mulliken never wrote, since it counterbalanced the approach followed in Pauling's *The Nature of the Chemical Bond.* The MO theory also proved easily adapted to the classification of the excited states of molecules—one of the realms of molecular spectroscopy—and above all, suitable for computer programs.

Beginning in the mid- and late 1930s, when quantum chemistry was already delineated as a distinct subdiscipline, the contributions of a group of British theoreticians proved rather decisive. Lennard-Jones, D. R. Hartree, and Coulson were the best-known members of this group. In different ways, they were all strongly influenced by Mulliken's legacy. Of the three, Coulson was the most vocal and the person whose work encompasses all those trends characteristic of what has been called the "British approach" to quantum chemistry (Simões and Gavroglu, 1999; Simões, 2003). If the "German approach" inaugurated by London, Heitler, Hund, and Hückel stressed the application of first principles of quantum mechanics to chemistry, and if the "American approach" of Pauling, Mulliken, Van Vleck, and Slater was characterized by a pragmatism together with a creative disregard for the strict obeisance to the first principles of quantum mechanics, the British perceived the problems of quantum chemistry first and foremost as calculational problems, and by devising novel calculational methods they tried to bring quantum chemistry within the realm of applied mathematics. For the members of this group, Coulson in particular, to make a discipline more rigorous meant to incorporate applied mathematical techniques that would serve in practical situations to offer solutions. They would become constitutive to the discipline itself. But, simultaneously, Coulson's pedagogical activities pushed forward the idea that chemists with no mathematical training could follow the discipline's trends.

After the war, molecular physics quickly lost ground in relation to other emerging specialties within physics, such as nuclear and particle physics. Mulliken returned to his former work. Supported by the Rockefeller Foundation and the Office of Naval Research, as well as other granting agencies, Mulliken's group, named after 1952 the Laboratory of Molecular Structure and Spectra, continued to produce high-quality work on the experimental and theoretical study of molecular structure and spectra. Among Mulliken's postwar contributions, the following works stand out: the development of a charge-transfer interpretation of spectra of donor-acceptor molecular complexes; the calculation of spectral intensities and the explanation of the selection rules that characterize transitions in molecular spectra; the theory of hyperconjugation (pseudo-triple bond) in organic molecules; the "magic formula," an attempt to quantify Pauling's criterion of maximum overlapping by defining bond strength in terms of the overlap integral (the integral over all space of the product of two atomic orbitals, each coming from different atoms); and the concept of population analysis, in which the concept of overlap population (the electron population between atoms) was put forth as the best measure of the strength of a chemical bond.

Mulliken became a pivotal player in launching quantum chemistry as a genuinely international enterprise. In this new phase, the organization of meetings and conferences became crucial to the discipline's consolidation. At home, Mulliken participated in a meeting organized by the Division of Physical and Inorganic Chemical Society honoring G. N. Lewis (1947), where he delivered a review paper assessing the past and present state of development of the application of quantum mechanics to problems of molecular structure and spectra. Believing that the time was ripe for a "new emphasis on the use of semi-empirical methods" in quantum chemistry and molecular spectroscopy, he offered a classification and description of available methods, contrasted the VB and the MO approaches, pointing out their advantages and drawbacks, and concluded that in the realm of molecular spectroscopy, in which there still exists a vast body of empirical data on the spectra of complex molecules rather unsystematically or poorly organized, there were "rich possibilities" for theoretical interpretations (Mulliken, 1947).

The next year, both Mulliken and Pauling were invited speakers and guiding stars at the 1948 Paris Colloque de la Liaison Chimique, jointly organized by the Centre National de la Recherche Scientifique (CNRS) and the Rockefeller Foundation. The first to be held in France after the war, this conference was the meeting point of practically all active quantum chemists. Besides Mulliken and Pauling, Coulson, J. D. Longuet-Higgins, L. E. Sutton, Lennard-Jones, and M. Polanyi stood among those attending the meeting. Marking the beginning of quantum chemistry in France, the strategy of its local promoters was to move the discussion to complex problems of quantum biochemistry. In the meeting, they probed the possibilities of the VB and the MO methods, but gradually shifted to the MO method, developing the technique of "molecular diagrams" and managing to reinforce the recourse to visual imagery in the framework of MO theory.

At about the same time, the successful utilization of digital computers in quantum chemistry to compute wave functions and energy levels was prepared by a program discussed and agreed upon at the Shelter Island Conference (1951), organized by Mulliken and considered to be a "watershed" in his autobiography (Mulliken, 1989). The program aimed at obtaining formulas for the "troublesome" integrals needed for the integration of Schrödinger's equation, and then making them available to the community of quantum chemists in standardized tables.

The outcome of this conference reinforced the move of Mulliken's group away from semiempirical calculations toward wholly theoretical (ab initio) calculations. Active participants of this group included C. C. Jo Roothan, Klaus Ruedenberg, and Bernard J. Ransil. In semiempirical calculations the computation of molecular properties was carried out by setting up a theoretical framework; then, at certain points, integrals that were difficult to compute were replaced by experimentally determined quantities. The adaptation to molecular problems of the scheme of the self-consistent-field approximation, which had been widely used for atomic problems, implemented the program outlined at the shelter island conference. The use of computers to calculate the time-consuming integrals of the increasingly sophisticated versions of the MO method also opened the way to the investigation of molecules that were otherwise inaccessible to experimentation. At the experimental level, computers in many instances replaced laboratory experiments as sources of new data.

By 1959 a conference on molecular quantum mechanics was convened in Boulder, Colorado, to debate the impact of computers in quantum chemistry, with Mulliken again at center stage as a member of its steering committee. The splitting of the community into two groups—ab-initionists and those advocating semiempirical methods, essentially dependent on diverging views concerning the use of large-scale electronic computers—

was assessed by Coulson as pointing to deep, perhaps irreconcilable, divisions among the practitioners of quantum chemistry.

As in all scientific disciplines, quantum chemistry evolved through time, its practice being shaped by its founders and their immediate followers. In a 1998 paper in *Nature,* the 1981 Nobel laureate Roald Hoffmann summarized poetically the different sorts of inputs in affirming its tradition: "American and British chemists had secured a place for quantum mechanics in chemistry, through the charismatic exposition of Linus Pauling, the quieter and deep reflections of Robert Mulliken, and the elegant, perceptive teaching of Charles Coulson" (1998, p. 750). As exemplified by Mulliken's career, the ability to "cross boundaries" between disciplines was, perhaps, the most striking and permanent characteristic of those who, like Mulliken himself, consistently contributed to the development of quantum chemistry.

BIBLIOGRAPHY

Mulliken's papers, correspondence, and other manuscript materials are deposited in the Joseph Regenstein Library of the University of Chicago. Letters and an interview with Mulliken, conducted by Thomas S. Kuhn in 1964, are held in the Archives for the History of Quantum Physics in the American Institute of Physics and in the American Philosophical Society.

WORKS BY MULLIKEN

"Electronic Structure of Polyatomic Molecules and Valence. VI. On the Method of Molecular Orbitals." *Journal of Chemical Physics* 3 (1935): 375–378.

"Quantum-Mechanical Methods and the Electronic Spectra and Structure of Molecules." *Chemical Reviews* 41 (1947): 201–206.

"The Path to Molecular Orbital Theory." *Pure and Applied Chemistry* 24 (1970): 203–215. One of Mulliken's recollections.

"Spectroscopy, Molecular Orbitals, and Chemical Bonding." In *Nobel Lectures in Chemistry 1963–1970,* 131–160. Amsterdam: Elsevier, 1972.

Selected Papers of Robert S. Mulliken. Edited by D. A. Ramsay and Jürgen Hinze. Chicago: University of Chicago Press, 1975. Selection of Mulliken's most important papers on molecular structure and spectra.

Robert S. Mulliken: Life of a Scientist, an Autobiographical Account of the Development of Molecular Orbital Theory with an Introductory Memoir by Friedrich Hund. Edited by Bernard J. Ransil. Berlin: Springer-Verlag, 1989. Mulliken's autobiography, edited posthumously.

OTHER SOURCES

Assmus, Alexi. "The Americanization of Molecular Physics." *Historical Studies in the Physical and Biological Sciences* 23 (1992): 1–34.

Butler, Loren. "Robert S. Mulliken and the Politics of Science and Scientists, 1939–1946." *Historical Studies in the Physical and Biological Sciences* 25 (1994): 25–45.

Coulson, Charles Alfred. "Recent Developments in Valence Theory." *Pure and Applied Chemistry* 24 (1970): 257–287.

Gavroglu, Kostas, and Ana Simões. "The Americans, the Germans and the Beginnings of Quantum Chemistry: The Confluence of Diverging Traditions." *Historical Studies in the Physical and Biological Sciences* 25 (1994): 47–110.

Hoffmann, Roald. "Kenichi Fukui (1918–1998)." *Nature* 391 (1998): 750.

Longuet-Higgins, Hugh Christopher. "Robert Sanderson Mulliken." *Biographical Memoirs of the Fellows of the Royal Society* 35 (1990): 329–354.

Löwdin, Per-Olov, and Bernard Pullman, eds. *Molecular Orbitals in Chemistry, Physics and Biology: A Tribute to Robert S. Mulliken.* New York: Academic Press, 1964. A commemorative volume assessing Mulliken's contributions to quantum chemistry.

Park, Buhm Soon. "The 'Hyperbola of Quantum Chemistry': the Changing Practice and Identity of a Scientific Discipline in the Early Years of Electronic Digital Computers, 1945–1965." *Annals of Science* 60 (2003): 219–247.

Simões, Ana. "Chemical Physics and Quantum Chemistry in the Twentieth-Century." In *Modern Physical and Mathematical Sciences,* vol. 5, edited by Mary Jo Nye, 394–412. Cambridge, U.K.: Cambridge University Press, 2003.

———, and Kostas Gavroglu. "Quantum Chemistry *qua* Applied Mathematics. The Contributions of Charles Alfred Coulson (1910–1974)." *Historical Studies in the Physical Sciences* 29 (1999): 363–406.

Ana Simões

MURRAY, HENRY ALEXANDER (*b.* New York, New York, 13 May 1893; *d.* Cambridge, Massachusetts, 23 June 1988), *psychology, personality theory, the study of lives.*

Murray was a founder of personality psychology who emphasized "personology" or the study of lives in his most influential book, *Explorations in Personality* (1938). He was also a pioneer in personality assessment, and co-inventor of the Thematic Apperception Test (TAT). As director of the Harvard Psychological Clinic beginning in 1928, and professor in Harvard's Psychology and then Social Relations department until 1962, Murray trained, inspired, and provoked many who would shape personality psychology in the decades to come.

Childhood and Education. Henry A. Murray was born in New York City on 13 May 1893. His father, Henry Alexander Murray Sr., was a banker; he and Murray's mother, Fannie Morris Babcock, were listed in the Social

Murray

Register. Their early houses were just off Fifth Avenue on West 49th and West 51st Streets, and were demolished in the 1930s to make way for Rockefeller Center. Murray described his childhood in his autobiography as that of "the average, privileged American boy."

Murray had warm relations with his father, and thus did not personally resonate to Sigmund Freud's account of Oedipal hostilities of a boy toward his father. Murray was the middle of three children, with an older sister, Virginia, born in 1890 and a younger brother, nicknamed "Mike," born in 1897. Murray felt that his mother favored his older sister and younger brother, and as a child he came to "the grievous (and valid) realization that he could count on only a third-best portion of his mother's love" (1967, p. 298). This left him with a "marrow of misery and melancholy" that he suggests sensitized him to the sufferings of others, particularly women, and may have influenced his later career choices of medicine and psychotherapy. This underlying melancholy was "repressed by pride and practically extinguished in everyday life by a counteracting disposition of sanguine and expansive buoyancy," yet he was left with "an affinity for the darker, blinder strata of feeling," which drew him to tragic themes in literature and psychology. In psychology, his interest was not in the psychophysics of perception, but in following a "bent of curiosity toward all profound experiences of individual men and women" (Murray, 1981 [1959], p. 8).

Murray attended prep school at Groton and then Harvard College from 1911 to 1915. He majored in history but was not a diligent student, and was proudest of being the captain of the Harvard crew team. He was also active in many social organizations, elected during his junior year to lead the Phillips Brooks House Association, a social service organization for Harvard students. His only exposure to psychology in college was two lectures by Hugo Münsterberg on the senses, which sent him looking for the nearest exit. He later joked to his biographer in 1970 that he had "majored in the three Rs—Rum, Rowing, and Romanticism" (Robinson, 1992, p. 27).

The day after the final crew race against Yale, Murray became engaged to Josephine Rantoul, an attractive, outgoing woman from an upper-class Boston family, with an interest in social service. They were married in 1916 and lived together until her death in 1962; they had one daughter, Josephine, born in 1921, who later became a physician. Intellectually, Murray came alive in medical school at the Columbia College of Physicians and Surgeons, graduating at the top of his class with a medical degree in January 1919. Murray wanted to pursue the underlying sciences in more depth, so he obtained a master's degree in biology at Columbia in 1920, and a PhD in physiological chemistry from Cambridge University in 1927. He began a surgical internship at Presbyterian Hospital in New York City in the fall of 1920. Paul Robeson came into Presbyterian on a stretcher with a torn thigh muscle from football. Murray assisted in the surgery, and was assigned to look after the patient. Murray introduced him to a woman in the pathology lab, Essie Cardozo Goode, whom Robeson soon married. Murray and his wife stayed friends with the Robesons for years; attended Robeson's performances in *Emperor Jones*, *All God's Children*, and *Othello*; and held receptions for them at their home.

In 1921 Franklin D. Roosevelt was admitted to the hospital with an attack of infantile paralysis. George Draper, Murray's influential teacher of case conferences in medical school, was assigned the case, and Murray, as intern, drew the patient's blood nearly every day for six weeks, and talked about common experiences at Groton and Harvard. In Murray's recollections, the future president was "very talkative" and didn't seem at all depressed. In later years Murray was introduced to Eugene O'Neill, and had him over for the evening, with O'Neill talking about his father's drinking and family turmoil, and Murray about Jungian themes. Murray felt inarticulate in relation to O'Neill, and when O'Neill asked him for medical advice in 1927, Murray referred him to a friend from medical school.

After completing his surgical internship in 1922, Murray accepted a fellowship at the Rockefeller Institute for Medical Research, studying biochemical and medical changes in chicken embryos, leading eventually to twenty-one papers authored or co-authored in physiological or medical journals. While working at the Rockefeller Institute, he was struck by the theoretical opposition between two of its most eminent staff, Jacques Loeb, who advocated an extreme form of mechanism, and Alexis Carrel, who favored a form of vitalism or holism. How, Murray asked, can one account for such conflicting interpretations of the same phenomena? It seemed useful to consider science as "the creative product of an engagement between the scientist's psyche" and the world. This prepared Murray for reading Carl Gustav Jung's *Psychological Types* (1923), which "came to him as a gratuitous answer to an unspoken prayer" (Murray, 1981 [1967], p. 56).

This led to two enduring interests, "the question of varieties of human beings … and the question of what variables of personality are chiefly involved in the production of dissonant theoretical systems" (p. 56). These questions were part of Murray's intellectual entry into psychology, to be complemented by a more tumultuous emotional path to psychology—through literature, love, and his meetings with Jung.

Murray

Expanding Psychology to Include Persons and Lives. When Forrest Robinson proposed writing a biography of Murray in 1970, Murray replied that there was little to tell, except for a forty-year secret love affair that had revolutionized his life. Christiana Morgan was born in 1897 to a wealthy Boston Brahmin family, her father a professor at Harvard Medical School. She attended finishing school, served as a nurse in World War I, married Will Morgan in 1919, and bore a son in 1920. She met Murray at a Wagner opera in New York City; several months later at a dinner she asked Murray what he thought about Jung as compared to Freud. Murray said he didn't know, but hearing her enthusiasm, he read Jung's *Psychological Types* (1923) as soon as it was published.

While working on a PhD in biochemistry at Cambridge University, and having started to fall in love with Christiana, Murray visited Jung over spring vacation, 1925. "On the crest of a wave I visited Dr. Jung in Zurich supposedly to discuss abstractions; but in a day or two to my astonishment enough affective stuff erupted to invalid a pure scientist. This was my first opportunity to weigh psychoanalysis in a balance; and I recommend it as *one* method of measuring the worth of any brand of personology. Take your mysteries, your knottiest dilemmas, to a fit exponent of a system and judge the latter by its power to order and illumine your whole being. This assuredly is a most exacting test, to apply the touchstone of your deep perplexity to a theory, to demand that it interpret what you presumably know best—yourself. But then, what good is a theory that folds up in a crisis?" (Murray, 1981 [1940], pp. 293–294)

Henry Murray. AP IMAGES.

Harvard Psychological Clinic. The Harvard Psychological Clinic was established in 1926, and Murray was hired as a research fellow in abnormal psychology to assist Dr. Morton Prince, founder and director of the clinic. Prince became ill, and Murray succeeded him in 1928 as director, with Prince dying the following year. Murray had a vision of psychology and a vision of the role of the clinic, which is sketched in "Psychology and the University" (1981 [1935]). "There is reason to believe that in coming years the university which contributes most to the advancement of learning and the cultivation of the human spirit will be the one which develops and sustains the greatest school of psychology" (p. 337).

Psychology can be defined "as the science which describes people and explains why they perceive, feel, think, and act as they do" (1981, p. 338). In Murray's view, no science of this kind yet existed. He critiqued the kinds of questions pursued in the academic psychology of his day as "bound to the ideology of introspectionism," or introspections on responses to different physical stimuli (vision, hearing, tactile sensations). From these psychophysical investigations into sensation and perception, which Murray sometimes called "eye, ear, nose and throat psychology," consideration of "man as a human being has somehow escaped" (1981, p. 339).

In an often repeated passage, Murray wrote in 1935 that "The truth which the informed are hesitant to reveal and the uninformed are amazed to discover is that academic psychology has contributed practically nothing to the knowledge of human nature. It has not only failed to bring light to the great, hauntingly recurrent problems, but it has no intention, one is shocked to realize, of attempting to investigate them. Indeed—and this is the cream of a wry jest—an unconcerned detachment from the natural history of ordinary mortals has become a source of pride to many psychologists" (1981 [1935], p. 339). Murray's hope was that the Harvard Psychological Clinic could be a place for building connections between "the old academic psychology and the new dynamic psychology" (Robinson, 1992, p. 148).

Murray

One new technique developed at the Harvard Psychological Clinic was the Thematic Apperception Test (TAT). The TAT is a series of ambiguous drawings, such as a boy looking at a violin on the table before him, or a man turning away from a woman lying on a bed. Subjects were asked to tell a story about the pictures, what is going on, what led up to the picture, and what may happen in the future. The objective was to draw out people's fantasies, an important part of their unconscious life. Fantasies are important as they can be related to feelings and emotions, to formative experiences, to overt action, to neurotic symptoms, or to creative work. Morgan drew some of the TAT pictures, and she is listed as first author on the original paper (1935), perhaps to draw her more into the work of the Clinic.

Murray was powerfully influenced by psychodynamic theory (Freud and Jung), and was affected by William James, the Gestaltists, Kurt Lewin, Clyde Kluckhohn, and others. He felt that Freudians emphasized sex and aggression, while Murray proposed a larger set of needs, including both viscerogenic or biological needs, such as needs for food, water, sex, and harm avoidance; and psychological needs, such as for acquisition, superiority, achievement, recognition, dominance, autonomy, affiliation, nurturance, play, and so on.

Murray believed that psychodynamic psychologists were looking at some of the right questions, but with inadequate methods, whereas academic psychologists were sometimes more scientifically rigorous but investigating trivial problems. *Explorations in Personality* (1938) was an effort to integrate these two worlds, and to explore the uses of multiple scientific methods for "personology" or the study of lives, a kind of "experiential psychology." His team of co-authors included many who went on to influential careers in psychology, including Robert White, Donald MacKinnon, Nevitt Sanford, Saul Rosenzweig, Jerome Frank, Erik Homburger (later Erikson) and others. In his autobiography, Murray said that in some quarters he was "thought of not as an author so much as an author of authors, a diversity of them, none bound to his ideas" (1981 [1967], p. 71).

When Murray came up for tenure at Harvard in 1936, although the manuscript for *Explorations in Personality* was in draft, it had not yet been published. The meeting was held at the house of the Harvard President, James Bryant Conant. One of Murray's supporters, Gordon Allport, argued that Murray was the intellectual descendant of William James and important in maintaining a humanistically oriented psychology at Harvard. Another committee member, neuropsychologist Karl Spencer Lashley, had recently been hired at Harvard; the chair of psychology, Edwin G. Boring, argued that Lashley was the best psychologist in the world. Lashley had a strong opposition to psychoanalysis, and strongly opposed the appointment. He said that James had done "more harm to psychology than any man that ever lived," and threatened to resign if Murray was given tenure (Robinson, 1992, p. 225). Lashley saw this as a clash between "the older humanistic and philosophical psychology" (Murray) versus the new more exact and biological approach to psychology (Lashley). The tenure vote was split three to three. As a compromise, Murray was given two five-year non-tenured appointments.

Murray, angered at this critical tenure review by men whose opinion he did not overly respect, went on leave from 1937 until the fall of 1941. After a year in Europe, he returned to the United States to work on his biography of Herman Melville, taking Melville through age thirty-three, when he finished *Pierre.* With the attack on Pearl Harbor on 7 December 1941, the world changed, and Murray's conception of himself and his work in the world also changed. Fighting against Nazism and winning World War II became of greatest immediate importance, while exploring the unconscious had a lower priority.

In response to a request from the Office of Strategic Services (OSS), predecessor to the Central Intelligence Agency, Murray finished by October 1943 a 227-page psychological study of Adolf Hitler, "Analysis of the Personality of Adolph [sic] Hitler, with Predictions of His Future Behavior and Suggestions for Dealing with Him Now and After Germany's Surrender." Much of this was later published, without adequate acknowledgement of Murray's role, by Walter C. Langer as *The Mind of Adolf Hitler: The Secret Wartime Report* (1972).

Once the Hitler study was completed, Murray went to Washington, D.C. to eventually lead a program selecting recruits for the OSS intelligence service. This multiform assessment drew on procedures from the Harvard Psychological Clinic and used a variety of tests of intelligence, mechanical ability, group problem solving, debating ability, and physical strength. The candidates were rated on eleven different variables, discussed in a diagnostic council, and sketched in a biographical profile, as reported in *The Assessment of Men* (Murray, et al, 1948).

Personality in Society and Culture. Murray was changed by World War II. The "deep-diving" exploration of the unconscious with Morgan, trying to go beyond upper-class conventions, was no longer as central in his life as it had been, and he turned more to the ways in which personality is interwoven with society and culture. How could another world war be prevented? His thoughts turned to world government, and the need perhaps for a "new mythology" or a new cultural framework to integrate opposing cultural systems and reduce the likelihood of future international conflicts.

Murray

Murray's two five-year appointments would have ended in 1947, but Murray resigned from Harvard in June 1945. Behind the scenes, even though not formally on the faculty, he was involved in the formation of Harvard's new interdisciplinary Department of Social Relations, founded in January 1946. He completed the manuscript for *Assessment of Men* (1948) on the U.S. Office of Strategic Services study he had headed, and he co-edited *Personality in Nature, Society, and Culture* (Kluckhohn and Murray, 1948, revised 1953), which became an important collection of readings in the new Social Relations department. This included the famous line, "Every man is in certain respects (a.) like all other men, (b.) like some other men, (c.) like no other man." (In later statements, this was rephrased in terms of "persons.") Individuals are like "all other persons" due to similar features in the biological endowments of all humans, in their physical environments, and in their social and cultural worlds. Being like "some other persons" can be affected by membership in different nations, tribes, and social classes. Similarities can also be shaped by having different types of psychopathology, or between the wealthy and the poor in different societies.

Finally, there are the ways in which a person is like no other person. An individual's ways of perceiving, feeling, needing, thinking, and behaving are not exactly duplicated by others. This singularity is produced by unique biological endowments interacting with particular environments, and unique sequences of interaction between developing persons and their environments. Analysis of these similarities and differences and their causes could engage social and clinical psychologists, sociologists, and cultural anthropologists in interdisciplinary inquiry for years to come.

Morgan did not want Murray to return to Harvard after World War II, but to devote more time to finishing an account of their relationship, which they had both been working on. She wrote that his work on Melville could be a preparation for writing about their relationship. He never published a book-length biography of Melville, but did write a 90-page introduction plus notes to Melville's *Pierre* (1949), a novel that Morgan and Murray felt uncannily reflected their experience.

Murray did return to Harvard in 1948, as a lecturer with tenure in Social Relations; he was promoted to full professor in 1950, and remained there until his retirement in 1962. His conceptual work often refers obliquely to the power of "creative dyads," but it was not clear what he was referring to, until he told this part of his story to Forrest Robinson, as related in *Love's Story Told: A Life of Henry A. Murray* (1992). Murray's wife, Josephine, died in 1962, and Morgan drowned near a beach where they were vacationing in the Caribbean in 1967, perhaps from medical problems, alcohol, or suicide. Murray was not able to openly tell their story during his lifetime, and it may have cost them dearly.

Murray entered a second marriage, which gave him a new life, with psychologist Nina Chandler Fish in 1969. She was familiar enough with the dyad to avoid that pattern and seek another way of life together. A number of scholars tried to help Murray with his unfinished publications, including Eugene Taylor, and several "Morsels" on Melville were published in the 1980s.

In 1970, when approached by prospective biographer Robinson, Murray provided nearly one hundred interviews, with the agreement that the book would be published posthumously. Murray died in 1988, and his biography was published in 1992. The biography proved immensely controversial. It illuminated much about Murray's relationship with Morgan, and his connections to Jung and Melville. This is a complex story, sometimes tragic, and much remains to be understood about how Murray's life is related to his work in personality theory, personality assessment, and the history of psychology and social relations at Harvard (Runyan, 1994, 2006).

Murray's Legacy. Murray made major contributions as a founder of personality psychology, a leader in personality assessment, director of the Harvard Psychological Clinic, and a scholar of Herman Melville. With his background of an MD and a PhD in biochemistry, he sought to expand the bounds of scientific psychology so that it could include the study of persons and lives. Many were influenced by Murray, either personally or by his work.

Michigan State University started a series of Henry A. Murray lectures beginning in 1978, and that same year, the annual Henry A. Murray award for contributions to personality psychology and the study of lives was established and given through the Society of Personality and Social Psychology of the American Psychological Association.

Murray was inspired by James, as well as by Jung, Freud, Melville, and others. In turn, Murray's vision inspired many who went on to develop personality psychology. The first generation includes Robert White, who wrote *The Abnormal Personality* (1948) and *Lives in Progress* (1952) and followed Murray as director of the Harvard Psychological Clinic; Donald MacKinnon, who became the founding director of the Institute of Personality Assessment and Research at the University of California, Berkeley in 1949; Nevitt Sanford, who co-authored *The Authoritarian Personality* (1950) and founded the Wright Institute; Gardner Lindzey, who edited the *Handbook of Social Psychology* (1954) and co-authored *Theories of Personality* (1957); and Erik Erikson, author of

Murray

Childhood and Society (1950), *Young Man Luther* (1958), and *Gandhi's Truth* (1969).

Personality psychology is constituted of at least three strands of work: the measurement and correlation of traits or individual difference, the study of individual lives, and the experimental study of psychological processes. Murray has had a significant influence on at least the first two of these traditions.

In *Paradigms of Personality Assessment*, Jerry S. Wiggins (2003) reviews the history of personality assessment in five traditions: psychodynamic, interpersonal, personological, multivariate, and empirical (Minnesota Multiphasic Personality Inventory, MMPI). He argues that Murray has had more influence on personality assessment across all of these traditions than any other single individual, including Freud.

In the study of needs and motivation, David McClelland was a leader in studying achievement motivation, which could be assessed through scoring TAT responses. McClelland's students, David Winter and Dan McAdams, studied power motivation and affiliation motives respectively. McAdams (2006) developed a conceptual framework for integrating the three levels of traits, characteristic adaptations including motives and goals, and life stories.

Rae Carlson famously asked, "Where is the person in personality research?" (1971), pointing out how infrequently personality psychology journals include studies of individual lives. The situation has improved somewhat since then, with William M. Runyan (1982) and Alan C. Elms (1994) providing overviews of the study of lives, and with the *Journal of Personality* doing special issues on the study of individual lives in 1988 and 1997.

A later generation of psychologists working in the study of lives, all influenced by Murray or his work, include Elms, McAdams, Abigail Stewart, Irving Alexander, Nicole Barenbaum, James Anderson, Ian Nicholson, William Todd Schultz, George Atwood, and Runyan, with selections in *Psychobiography and Life Narratives* (McAdams and Richard L. Ochberg, 1988), and the *Handbook of Psychobiography* (Schultz, 2005).

BIBLIOGRAPHY

WORKS BY MURRAY

Papers of Henry Murray. Cambridge, MA: Pusey Library, Harvard University.

With others. *Explorations in Personality: A Clinical and Experimental Study of Fifty Men of College Age.* New York: Oxford University Press, 1938. A founding book in personality psychology. A 70th anniversary edition was published by Oxford University Press in September 2007, with a preface by Dan McAdams.

"What Should Psychology Do about Psychoanalysis?" *Journal of Abnormal and Social Psychology* 35 (1940).

With OSS Assessment Staff. *Assessment of Men.* New York: Rinehart, 1948.

Editor and author of Introduction. Melville, Herman. *Pierre, or the Ambiguities.* New York: Hendricks House, 1949.

Editor, with Clyde Kluckhohn and David M. Schneider. *Personality in Nature, Society, and Culture,* 2nd rev. ed. New York: Knopf, 1953.

"Preparations for the Scaffold of a Comprehensive System." In *Psychology: A Study of a Science,* Vol. 3, edited by Sigmund Koch. New York: McGraw-Hill, 1959.

"Henry A. Murray." In *A History of Psychology in Autobiography,* Vol. V, edited by Edwin G. Boring and Gardner Lindzey. New York: Appleton-Century-Crofts, 1967.

Endeavors in Psychology: Selections from the Personology of Henry A. Murray. Edited by Edwin S. Shneidman. New York: Harper & Row, 1981. Includes Murray's most important articles and chapters.

OTHER SOURCES

Anderson, James W. "The Life of Henry A. Murray: 1893–1988." In *Studying Persons and Lives,* edited by Albert I. Rabin et al. New York: Springer, 1990.

Barenbaum, Nicole. "Henry A. Murray: Personology as Biography, Science, and Art." In *Portraits of Pioneers in Psychology,* Vol. VI, edited by Gregory A. Kimble, Michael Wertheimer, and Charlotte White. Washington, DC: American Psychological Association, 2006.

Carlson, Rae. "Where is the Person in Personality Research?" *Psychological Bulletin* 75 (1971): 201–219.

Douglas, Claire. *Translate this Darkness: The Life of Christiana Morgan.* New York: Simon & Schuster, 1993. A feminist and Jungian biography of Murray's partner.

Elms, Alan C. *Uncovering Lives: The Uneasy Alliance of Biography and Psychology.* New York: Oxford University Press, 1994.

Robinson, Forrest G. *Love's Story Told: A Life of Henry A. Murray.* Cambridge, MA: Harvard University Press, 1992. A major biography.

Runyan, William McKinley. *Life Histories and Psychobiography: Explorations in Theory and Method.* New York: Oxford University Press, 1982.

———. "Coming to Terms with the Life, Loves, and Work of Henry A. Murray." *Contemporary Psychology* 39 (1994). Review of Robinson's 1992 biography.

———. "Psychobiography and the Psychology of Science: Understanding Relations between the Life and Work of Individual Psychologists." *Review of General Psychology,* 10, no. 2 (2006): 147–162.

Schultz, William Todd, ed. *Handbook of Psychobiography.* New York: Oxford University Press, 2005.

Smith, M. Brewster, and James W. Anderson. "Henry A. Murray (1893–1988)." *American Psychologist* 44, no. 8 (1989): 1153–1154.

William McKinley Runyan

N

NAMIAS, JEROME (*b.* Bridgeport, Connecticut, 19 March 1910; *d.* La Jolla, California, 10 February 1997), *meteorology, climatology, oceanography, popular science.*

With the exception of British colonial meteorologist Gilbert Walker (1868–1958), no long-range forecaster achieved greater prominence and influence during the twentieth century than Jerome Namias. He helped legitimate climate prediction and laid the foundations for its institutionalization as a "Big Science" after 1970. Namias began his career as a leading disciple of the Bergen School of meteorology. In the course of thirty years as head of the U.S. Weather Bureau's Extended Forecast Section, his efforts greatly increased the useful range of forecasts in the United States, from less than a week to an entire season. His investigations of air-sea interactions played a vital role in the incorporation of the open ocean and teleconnections into climate forecasting. Like Walker, Namias encouraged environmental scientists to conceive of climate variability in global terms, though he was an outspoken skeptic of the influence that the El Niño phenomenon exercised over North America.

Apostle of the Bergen School. Jerome Namias grew up in the industrial city of Fall River, Massachusetts. On his father's side, he came from a family of Sephardic Jews who fled Spain in the 1490s and then bounced around the Atlantic World. His father, Joseph, immigrated to the United States and eventually provided optometry services to New England textile factory workers. Jerome became a weather enthusiast in high school, but a series of personal problems almost prevented him from becoming a professional of any sort. When his father fell ill, Jerome turned down a four-year scholarship to Wesleyan University in order to stay home and support his family. One year after finishing high school, Jerome contracted tuberculosis, but he made the most out of his long convalescence: he took a series of correspondence courses, including a college-level meteorology course from American Meteorological Society (AMS) founder Charles F. Brooks, a dedicated supporter of amateur involvement in atmospheric science. This course revived Jerome's interest in the weather, and he began searching for employment by writing letters to prominent meteorologists, just as the United States plunged into the Great Depression.

His boldness paid off. H. H. Clayton hired Namias to move to Washington, D.C., to compile data for the Smithsonian's World Weather Records, an important organ for the worldwide diffusion of global weather observations. Namias also assisted Clayton with the use of solar observations to predict long-range weather changes. Always the autodidact, Namias struggled through the publications of the Bergen School of meteorology on his own time. As Robert Marc Friedman has shown (1989), this classic research school founded by Norwegian geophysicist Vilhelm Bjerknes used hydrodynamic concepts such as the polar front to revolutionize mid-latitude forecasting after World War I. Namias wrote a letter to Bjerknes's Swedish disciple Carl-Gustaf Rossby at the Massachusetts Institute of Technology (MIT) "politely questioning" two statements in Rossby's monograph *Thermodynamics Applied to Air-Mass Analysis* (1932). Rossby arranged for this promising recruit to take graduate coursework at MIT in meteorology, even though Namias lacked an undergraduate degree. Rossby apprenticed Namias to German scientist

Karl Lange, MIT's specialist on aerological soundings. Namias used upper-air observations of the passage of cold fronts through the Boston area to publish his first two scientific monographs in 1934. That same year, Namias followed in the footsteps of another Rossby disciple, Horace Byers, by taking a short-lived position as an airline forecaster for Transcontinental and Western Air (TWA). After losing this job to Depression-era cutbacks, Namias spent a few months seeking an undergraduate degree at the University of Michigan before again falling ill. In his autobiography, Namias expressed amazement that he had achieved so much as a scientist with so little formal education.

An infusion of federal funds to study the dust bowl drought enabled Rossby to bring Namias back to MIT as his full-time research assistant in 1936. This sparked a lifelong interest in climate anomalies. Following Bergen School orthodoxy, Namias rejected statistical, climatological approaches to long-range forecasting favored by Walker and Clayton, and instead embraced "qualitative physical reasoning" and the analysis of synoptic maps. Namias eventually developed his own, highly subjective approach to atmospheric problems, emphasizing empirical case studies of large-scale developments. As Richard Somerville explains (2003), Namias became a "grand master" of these techniques and stuck with them, through thick and thin, while the rest of the profession embraced numerical modeling.

Namias achieved his first important breakthrough analyzing the thermodynamics associated with the humidity content of interacting air masses. "Isentropic analysis" provided an invaluable tool for predicting precipitation associated with thunderstorms, particularly in summer (1938). Rossby, meanwhile, developed his celebrated theory of long waves in the westerlies. Namias used another new mapping technique, differential analysis, to extrapolate upper-level barometric conditions over the North Pacific and North Atlantic from surface observations. When Rossby saw the initial hemispheric map Namias produced for Christmas Day, 1940, "he got very excited. The long waves were vivid.... He set to work scribbling right on the map to compute the motion of those waves according to his equations.... Those first computations, on the side of the map triggered a whole new chain of thinking in the 1940s," particularly in extended-range forecasting (quoted in Basu, 1984, p. 200).

Namias played an equally important role spreading these new ideas and techniques. In 1934–1935, under Rossby's supervision, he wrote a series of articles for the AMS *Bulletin* that explained the basics of air mass analysis. Namias later compiled these in a textbook widely used by training programs during World War II. After the war, the head of the U.S. Weather Bureau, Francis W. Reichelderfer—another early U.S. convert to the Bergen School—

Jerome Namias. *Namias in his Weather Bureau office.* **AP IMAGES.**

sent Namias on extended missions to forecasting centers in Scandinavia, the United States, and eventually Australia, New Zealand, and Mexico, to make sure they stayed abreast of new research and mapping techniques. The mass media frequently looked to Namias to explain weather phenomena to the public, both in print and on television. "Thank God for the 'Jet Stream,'" Namias recalled, because it provided a straightforward way to explain the new ideas emerging from World War II, and soon became a household phrase ("Autobiography," 1986, p. 20). In these ways, Namias played an important role in the worldwide colonization of meteorological practice by the Bergen School.

The Politics of Long-Range Forecasting. In May 1940, Namias moved back to Washington to establish an Extended Forecast Section at the U.S. Weather Bureau that would make operational use of these new ideas. In those days, forecasts more than a couple of days in advance were considered "long-range" and subject to considerable doubt. During World War II, the Extended Forecast Section worked closely with military officers to produce five-day forecasts for Allied forces based on "mean circulation methods." Namias received a commendation for forecasting a lull in surf conditions that enabled the 8 November 1942 invasion of North Africa.

The abnormal winter of 1949–1950 inspired Namias to shift his focus toward longer-term changes in the weather. As this season unfolded, he tracked the slow, steady progression of the North Pacific anticyclone from a position east of Hawaii to the Yukon. He soon recognized that the location and intensity of this "center of action" determined an abrupt flip-flop of weather conditions during late winter. He and his longtime collaborator Phil Clapp also directed their attention to the so-called index cycle, a quasi-periodic shift of four-to-six-week duration in the prevailing westerlies during winter. By 1953, they figured out how to relate this cycle to centers of action and could produce operational thirty-day forecasts. These discoveries were also important for debunking Irving Langmuir's claim that his cloud-seeding experiments were responsible for producing weekly weather cycles in the eastern United States.

Too much success could have drastic political consequences. During the mid-1950s, Namias and his collaborators developed a technique using wind patterns associated with the Bermuda high to locate regions of particular hurricane vulnerability. Namias's thirty-day hurricane advisory for June 1957 turned out to be devastatingly correct. Hurricane Audrey, a category four storm, struck the Gulf Coast and killed 390 people in the exact region Namias had identified as most vulnerable. Two Gulf State senators with influence over Weather Bureau appropriations put a stop to these advisories so they would not have a negative impact on coastal tourism.

This blow to Namias's ambitions did not cause him to shy away from forecasts of even longer range. In 1968, after a decade of experimentation, the Extended Forecast Division initiated ninety-day forecasts driven by Namias's new insights into the role that air-sea interactions and atmospheric teleconnections played in sustaining climate anomalies. Despite poor initial results, Namias's seasonal advisories acquired significant political influence. They reputedly affected the Nixon and Ford administrations' decisions in favor of exporting grain to the Soviet Union and against fuel rationing during the Arab oil embargo. Namias "became the guru of long-range forecasting" when a rare "synergy" of large-scale conditions enabled him to forecast the exceptionally cold, snowy winter of 1976–1977 in the eastern United States. The press gave him front-page coverage when he cautiously (and accurately) predicted a break in the extended drought affecting the Far West during the winter of 1977–1978. During this period, Namias also became one of the first scientists to describe even longer-term climate "regimes" lasting up to a decade.

Which Center of Action? In 1957–1958, strange weather affected almost the entire Pacific Basin. Oceanographer John Isaacs—another prominent scientist of Namias's generation with little formal training—organized an interdisciplinary symposium at Rancho Santa Fe, California, in June 1958 to discuss this "extraordinary year." He invited Namias to fly to Southern California to explain mid-latitude atmospheric anomalies. Afterward, Namias confided to Isaacs, "I have a feeling that this meeting will usher in a new era of concentrated thought and development relating to climate anomalies in the ocean and atmosphere" (Cushman, 2004, p. 140). Namias made this a self-fulfilling prophecy. He focused the rest of his career on air-sea interactions and worked more and more closely with marine scientists on the Pacific Coast. Three life-changing incidents accelerated this shift: the death of his close friend and collaborator Harry Wexler in 1962 from a heart attack, followed by his own heart attack and a serious auto accident in 1963–1964. He delayed leaving U.S. Weather Bureau headquarters completely until 1971, however, so he could support the artistic career of his wife (and Wexler's sister-in-law) Edith Paipert.

Namias relished leaving Washington's bureaucratic wrangling for an academic post at the Scripps Institution of Oceanography, a position he held from 1968 until he suffered a career-ending stroke in 1989. Yet he could not leave politics behind. Scientists now recognize 1957–1958 as marking the beginning of modern El Niño research in the United States, but this was not preordained. During the late 1960s, Namias became deeply engaged in a debate regarding the "source area of anomalies" in the Pacific Basin. He was predisposed to see the North Pacific as the most important center of action affecting downstream weather patterns in the United States. After all, he had spent three decades studying the behavior of mid-latitude westerlies and plotting thousands of polar projection maps. (These maps graphically pushed the tropics to the margins of his worldview.) Jacob Bjerknes, the son of Vilhelm and a major contributor to polar front theory, became convinced during the 1950s that tropical processes drove climate variation in the Pacific Basin. During the 1960s, he published three fundamental papers linking the El Niño phenomenon to these changes. Their remarkably friendly debate came to a head during the planning stages of what became known as the North Pacific Experiment (NORPAX). Namias used his prestige in Washington to ensure that the North Pacific garnered most of the attention from this classic Big Science project. Scientists later criticized Namias for his "tropical skepticism" when it became clear that Bjerknes had been basically correct. That said, Namias gave far more credence to tropical teleconnections than most scientists from this era. In a 1976 article inspired by the 1972–1973 El Niño event—one of the first studies that also incorporated an analysis of the "inverse El Niño" (now known as La Niña)—he found unambiguous "evidence for a contemporary relationship

Namias

between Northern Hemisphere westerlies and variations in equatorial [sea-surface temperatures]." Nevertheless, he found it "almost impossible to prove cause and effect" and favored the explanation that subtropical wind anomalies caused this variation (Namias, 1976, pp. 130, 134). After the 1982–1983 "super Niño" turned this phenomenon into an international obsession, Namias contributed some wise words of prudence, still worth hearing: "Unfortunately, El Niños, like everything else, including human beings, all vary and no two are exactly alike." Even though they possessed "enough common characteristics to be tantalizing," he doubted whether they could provide a clear guide to seasonal forecasting, at least in North America (Namias, 1985, p. 173).

In the short term, tropical skepticism undoubtedly influenced U.S. government patronage for climate research and almost nipped El Niño studies in the bud. During an earlier era, the Bergen School's triumph had an even broader, negative impact on climatological research. Namias's caution and dedication to a set of tried-and-true techniques underpinned his success and prestige as a long-range forecaster. Over the long term, his ability to deliver usable long-range forecasts helped attract enormous institutional support for climate research, first at the Scripps Institution of Oceanography, then at national and international levels. Only an apostle of the Bergen School—with a little prodding from El Niño—could have accomplished so much to legitimate climate forecasting during the postwar era.

BIBLIOGRAPHY

Papers, 1932–1990. (MC 20) Archives of the Scripps Institution of Oceanography, University of California, San Diego. With a guide by Dawnelle Ricciardi.

WORKS BY NAMIAS

Subsidence within the Atmosphere. Harvard Meteorological Studies, no. 2. Cambridge, MA: Blue Hill Meteorological Observatory of Harvard University, 1934.

With C.-G. Rossby. *Structure of a Wedge of Continental Polar Air Determined from Aerological Observations.* Meteorological Course, Professional Notes, no. 6. Cambridge, MA: Massachusetts Institute of Technology, 1934.

"Thunderstorm Forecasting with the Aid of Isentropic Charts." *Bulletin of the American Meteorological Society* 19, no. 1 (1938): 1–14.

An Introduction to the Study of Air Mass and Isentropic Analysis. 5th ed. Milton, MA: American Meteorological Society, 1940. Originally published in the *Bulletin of the American Meteorological Society* (1934–1935).

Extended Forecasting by Mean Circulation Methods. Rev. ed. Washington, DC: U.S. Weather Bureau, 1947. Originally published as a confidential wartime document in 1943.

"The Index Cycle and Its Role in the General Circulation." *Journal of Meteorology* 7, no. 2 (1950): 130–139.

"The Jet Stream." *Scientific American* (October 1952): 26–31. Example of science popularization.

Thirty-Day Forecasting: A Review of a Ten-Year Experiment. Meteorological Monographs, vol. 2, no. 6. Boston: American Meteorological Society, 1953.

"Seasonal Fluctuations in Vulnerability to Tropical Cyclones in and off New England." *Monthly Weather Review* 83, no. 8 (1955): 155–162.

"Recent Seasonal Interactions between North Pacific Waters and the Overlying Atmospheric Circulation." *Journal of Geophysical Research* 64 (1959): 631–646. His first major study of air-sea interactions.

"A Five-Year Experiment in the Preparation of Seasonal Outlooks." *Monthly Weather Review* 92, no. 10 (1964): 449–464. On 90-day forecasts.

"Long-Range Weather Forecasting: History, Current Status, and Outlook." *Bulletin of the American Meteorological Society* 49, no. 5 (1968): 438–470. Invaluable historical overview.

"Some Statistical and Synoptic Characteristics Associated with El Niño." *Journal of Physical Oceanography* 6, no. 2 (1976): 130–138. A rare statistical study.

With Robert R. Dickson. "North American Influences on the Circulation and Climate of the North Atlantic Sector." *Monthly Weather Review* 104, no. 10 (1976): 1255–1265. Introduces concept of decadal climate regimes.

"Multiple Causes of the North American Abnormal Winter, 1976–77." *Monthly Weather Review* 106, no. 3 (1978): 279–295.

With Daniel R. Cayan. "El Niño: Implications for Forecasting." *Oceanus* 27, no. 2 (1984): 41–47.

"Remarks on the Potential for Long-Range Forecasting." *Bulletin of the American Meteorological Society* 66, no. 2 (1985): 165–173.

"Autobiography." In *Namias Symposium,* edited by John O. Roads. Scripps Institution of Oceanography Reference Series, 86-17. La Jolla, CA: Scripps Institution of Oceanography, 1986. Essential source; includes comprehensive bibliography and ten articles evaluating Namias's contributions to specific scientific problems.

"Summer Earthquakes in Southern California Related to Pressure Patterns at Sea Level and Aloft." *Journal of Geophysical Research* 94 (1989): 17671–17679. Example of Namias's occasional willingness to study risky topics.

OTHER SOURCES

Basu, Janet Else. "The Making of a Scientist: Jerome Namias, Pioneering the Science of Forecasting." *Weatherwise* 37, no. 4 (1984): 190–194, 199–201.

"The *Bulletin* Interviews: Dr. Jerome Namias." *WMO Bulletin* 37, no. 3 (July 1988): 157–169.

Cushman, Gregory T. "Choosing between Centers of Action: Instrument Buoys, El Niño, and Scientific Internationalism in the Pacific, 1957–1982." In *The Machine in Neptune's Garden: Historical Perspectives on Technology and the Marine Environment,* edited by Helen M. Rozwadowski and David K. van Keuren, 133–182. Sagamore Beach, MA: Science History Publications, 2004.

———. "The Struggle over Airways in the Americas, 1919–1945: Atmospheric Science, Aviation Technology, and Neocolonialism." In *Intimate Universality: Local and Global Themes in Weather and Climate History,* edited by James R. Fleming, Vladimir Jankovic, and Deborah Coen, 175–222. Sagamore Beach, MA: Science History Publications, 2006.

Friedman, Robert Marc. *Appropriating the Weather: Vilhelm Bjerknes and the Construction of a Modern Meteorology.* Ithaca, NY: Cornell University Press, 1989.

Roads, John O. "Jerome Namias, March 19, 1910–February 10, 1997." *Biographical Memoirs of the National Academy of Sciences* 76 (1999): 243–267.

Somerville, Richard C. J. "Climate and Atmospheric Science at Scripps: The Legacy of Jerome Namias." *Oceanography* 16, no. 3 (2003): 93–97.

Gregory T. Cushman

NASH, JOHN FORBES, JR.

(*b.* Bluefield, West Virginia, 13 June 1928), *game theory, Nash equilibrium, bargaining, differential geometry, Riemannian manifolds, nonlinear differential equations.*

Nash won a Nobel Prize for formulating the idea of a Nash equilibrium and proving that such equilibria always exist in finite games. He also founded modern bargaining theory and made substantial contributions in differential geometry. His unexpected recovery from a long-standing schizophrenic illness in time to be awarded his Nobel Prize made him something of a folk hero, celebrated in both a book on his life and an Oscar-winning movie.

The highs and lows of the life of John Nash are out of the range of experience of most human beings. As an undergraduate, he initiated the modern theory of rational bargaining. His graduate thesis formulated the idea of a Nash equilibrium, which is now regarded as the basic building block of the theory of games. He went on to solve major problems in pure mathematics, using methods of such originality that his reputation as a mathematical genius of the first rank became firmly established. But at the age of thirty he fell prey to a serious schizophrenic illness. Irrational delusions precipitated a variety of self-destructive behaviors that wrecked his career and his marriage. With only occasional remissions, his illness persisted for many years, during which time he languished in obscurity, cared for by his ex-wife, Alicia, in spite of everything. By the early 1990s, he was no longer delusional, although this fact was not widely appreciated. Fortunately, his recovery was brought to the attention of the Nobel committee who were deciding to whom to award prizes for game theory, which had by degrees totally transformed the face of economic theory while Nash was out of action. Their award of the 1994 Nobel Prize in Economics to Nash (along with John Harsanyi and Reinhard Selten) was instrumental in making him something of a cultural hero in his old age, celebrated in Sylvia Nasar's best-selling biography, and in the movie, *A Beautiful Mind,* in which Nash as a young man is played by the appropriately good-looking Russell Crowe. Nash himself seems to think that the mental instability that is popularly thought to accompany genius may be a price worth paying. As he says of Zoroaster, without his "madness," he would perhaps only have been another of the faceless billions who have lived and died on this planet.

Nash Bargaining Solution. Nash intended to follow in his father's footsteps and become an engineer, but the chemical engineering courses at Carnegie Tech (now Carnegie Mellon University) did not hold his attention, and he finally registered as a mathematics major. He took only one course in economics, but he reports that this was enough to inspire the idea that is nowadays referred to as the Nash bargaining solution. The originality of this work can be measured by the fact that the tradition among economists at this time was that the bargaining problem is indeterminate unless one has psychological information about the relative "negotiating skills" of the bargainers. For example, in the case of the classic problem of Divide-the-Dollar, in which a dollar can be split between two players if and only if they agree on who should get how much, economists felt unable to say anything at all.

John von Neumann and Oskar Morgenstern's path-breaking *Theory of Games and Economic Behavior* endorsed this position as late as 1944, arguing that nothing more can be said beyond the fact that a rational bargain will be individually rational and Pareto efficient. The former simply means that both bargainers get as much from their agreed outcome as they would from refusing to agree at all. The latter means that nothing is wasted, in the sense that no other outcome is available that both bargainers prefer. In Divide-the-Dollar, any split of the dollar satisfies both criteria.

In 1950, Nash argued to the contrary that the problem of rational bargaining under complete information (when both bargainers' preferences are common knowledge) is determinate—although he did not disavow a "negotiating skills" interpretation until a later paper of 1953. His approach was based on von Neumann and Morgenstern's 1944 proof that, under plausible assumptions, a rational decision maker will act as though maximizing the expected value of a function that assigns a real number called a utility (or a payoff) to each possible outcome. If this utility function is concave, the decision maker is said to be risk averse, since he then prefers a physical mixture of half of any two outcomes to a lottery in which he gets each of these two outcome with probability one

Nash

John Forbes Nash, Jr. © REUTERS/CORBIS.

half. With two players, any outcome can be identified with a pair (u_1, u_2). Nash therefore abstracted a bargaining problem to be a pair (X, d), in which the feasible set X is a convex, compact set whose points represent all possible bargaining outcomes, and the disagreement point d is a point inside X that corresponds to the result of a disagreement. The shape of the set X and the location of the point d within X are determined by the extent to which each player is averse to taking risks.

Nash proposed a set of axioms for the rational outcome of such a bargaining problem. They admit a unique solution that is called the Nash bargaining solution of the problem. It is the point (u_1, u_2) in X at which the Nash product $(u_1 - d_1)(u_2 - d_2)$ is maximized (subject to $u_1 > d_1$ and $u_2 > d_2$). If the players have identical attitudes to taking risks, the Nash bargaining solution of Divide-the-Dollar corresponds to a fifty-fifty split, but if we make one player more risk averse than the other, his share of the dollar will decrease.

The following are informal variants of Nash's axioms:

Axiom 1. The outcome is individually rational and Pareto efficient.

Axiom 2. The outcome is independent of the calibration of the bargainers' utility scales.

Axiom 3. If the bargainers sometimes agree on the payoff pair s when t is feasible, then they never agree on t when s is feasible.

Axiom 4. In symmetric situations, both bargainers get the same.

The second axiom recognizes that the choice of an origin and a unit for a utility scale is arbitrary, as in the case of a temperature scale. The fourth axiom is less a rationality assumption than a decision to confine attention to symmetric bargaining procedures. (In its absence, the Nash product is replaced by $(u_1 - d_1)^a (u_2 - d_2)^b$, where $a > 0$ and $b > 0$ are constants whose ratio characterizes the relative bargaining power of the two bargainers in an asymmetric procedure. The resulting bargaining outcome is said to be a generalized or asymmetric Nash bargaining solution.) The third axiom, which compares rational agreements in different bargaining problems, is an informal version of a principle called the Independence of Irrelevant Alternatives. For example, a committee of the prestigious Econometric Society was deciding which of A, B, or C to invite to give a fancy lecture. B was quickly eliminated, but it took a long time to agree that the invitation should go to A rather than C. Someone then pointed out that B could not make the event anyway. This observation provoked a renewal of the debate that ended up with the invitation going to C. This is a violation of the Independence of Irrelevant Alternatives, which says that the choice between A and C should be independent of the availability of B, who is an "irrelevant alternative" because he will not be chosen even if available.

In 1953, Nash extended his result to the case when a predetermined disagreement point d is not given, but each player has a number of strategies that might be used in the event of a disagreement. If each player can make an irrevocable threat to use some mixture of these strategies if the bargaining breaks down, Nash showed that the situation reduces to a game that can be solved by an appeal to von Neumann's minimax principle. This result has limited application in practice because of the difficulty of making threats that are genuinely irrevocable.

Nash Program. Nash was born in 1928, the same year in which John von Neumann created the subject of game theory by proving his minimax theorem. Not much notice was taken of this major creative step until von Neumann and Morgenstern published *The Theory of Games and Economic Behavior* in 1944. This book is divided into two very distinct parts, which are nowadays regarded as the origins of noncooperative and cooperative game theory respectively. In the noncooperative half of the book, the authors offered a general formulation of a game and analyzed the case of two-person, zero-sum games—the case to which the minimax theorem applies—in detail. In the cooperative half of the book, they observed that when the players in a game can sign binding preplay agreements that govern their future behavior, then the detailed strategic structure of the game becomes irrelevant. They then exploited this insight to study the problem of coalition formation in games with many players, but their results are nowadays often thought only to be fully applicable in zero-sum cooperative games.

Nash's 1950 axiomatic characterization of his bargaining solution was received by those who took note of it as a new approach to cooperative game theory. His axiomatic methodology became the standard tool in this area among the small school of mathematicians who followed up his ideas in the 1960s. However, Nash's alternative defense of his bargaining solution was largely overlooked until considerably later.

His alternative defense consisted of a brief analysis of an explicit noncooperative bargaining model. In this Nash Demand Game, each of the two players simultaneously makes a binding commitment to a take-it-or-leave-it utility demand. If the pair of demands lies in the feasible set X of the bargaining problem, then each player receives his demand. Otherwise, each player receives his payoff at the disagreement point d. Anticipating his 1951 paper, Nash observed that any Pareto-efficient, individually rational outcome of the bargaining problem corresponds to a Nash equilibrium. He was therefore faced with an equilibrium selection problem. Which of this infinite class of Nash equilibria should be regarded as the solution of the game? To deal with this problem, Nash introduced an element of doubt about the precise nature of the feasible set into his model. He replaced X by a smooth probability density function that differs from 1 or 0 only in a small band containing the frontier of X. Under mild conditions, the Nash equilibria of this smoothed Nash Demand Game are then all close to the Nash bargaining solution of the original bargaining problem.

A typically laconic sentence in Nash's 1951 paper on Nash equilibria proposes using the study of such noncooperative negotiation models more generally. In consequence, the idea that the range of applicability of cooperative solution concepts should be explored by investigating the type of noncooperative negotiation models that implement them has become known as the Nash program. A big success in this program came in 1982, when Ariel Rubinstein showed that bargaining models in which the players can exchange demands forever until an agreement is reached have a unique subgame-perfect equilibrium, provided that the players both discount the unproductive passage of time at a positive rate. (Selten defines a subgame-perfect equilibrium to be a pair of strategies that is not only a Nash equilibrium in the whole game, but also induces Nash equilibria in all subgames, whether reached in equilibrium or not.) When the interval between successive demands in Rubinstein's model approaches zero, it turns out that the unique subgame-perfect outcome converges on a generalized Nash bargaining solution in which the bargaining powers a and b are the reciprocals of the respective rates at which the two players discount time (Binmore, 1987). Impatience therefore joins risk aversion as a characteristic that inhibits bargaining success. This result is commonly thought to represent a striking vindication of both the Nash bargaining solution and the Nash program in general.

Nash Equilibrium. After completing his undergraduate degree, Nash received offers of fellowships from both Harvard and Princeton. It was fortunate that he chose to go to the mathematics department at Princeton after receiving an encouraging letter from Albert Tucker, who became his thesis advisor. His fellow students, notably John Milnor and Lloyd Shapley, were a brilliant group that flourished in the hothouse atmosphere that followed the mass emigration of European mathematicians from oppression in their own countries. Harold Kuhn remained a loyal friend through Nash's long illness, and was later to prove instrumental in bringing Nash's recovery to the attention of the Nobel committee.

Nash's short thesis began by defining the notion of a Nash equilibrium for a noncooperative game. An n-player game can be idealized as a bundle of strategy sets and a payoff function. Each player independently chooses a strategy from his or her strategy set. The payoff function then maps the resulting strategy profile to a vector of real numbers that specifies who gets what payoff when the strategy profile is used in the game. A Nash equilibrium is a profile of strategies, one for each player, in which each player's strategy is a best reply to the strategies chosen by the other players. Nash went on to show that all finite games have at least one Nash equilibrium if mixed strategies are allowed. (Even before von Neumann, Émile Borel had formulated the notion of a pure strategy as a plan of action for a player that specifies his behavior under all possible contingencies in a game. He also drew attention to the importance of mixed strategies, in which a player selects a pure strategy using a carefully chosen random device. Mixed strategies become relevant when it is important to keep your opponent guessing.) It is for this work that Nash was awarded a Nobel Prize in 1994.

There are two factors that make Nash equilibria important in game theory. The first depends on the notion of a rational solution of a game. A book that offers advice on how to play a game when it is common knowledge that all the players are rational would need to recommend the play of a Nash equilibrium in order to be authoritative. If it recommended the play of a strategy profile that is not a Nash equilibrium, then at least one player would elect not to follow the book's advice if he believed that the other players would. The book would then fail to be authoritative.

The second reason that Nash equilibria are important is evolutionary. If players are repeatedly drawn at random from a very large population to play a particular game, then the strategies that they are planning to use will vary over time if they keep adjusting their behavior in the direction of a better reply to whatever is currently being played in the population at large. Such an adjustment process can only cease to operate when the population reaches a Nash equilibrium. (With this interpretation, a mixed equilibrium can be realized as a polymorphic equilibrium, in which different players in the population all plan to play a pure strategy, but these pure strategies need not be the same.)

Nash referred to the second interpretation as "mass action" in his thesis, but the editors of *Econometrica,* where his thesis was published in 1951, asked for this section to be removed. However, it is nowadays generally acknowledged that it is the evolutionary interpretation that explains the very considerable predictive power of Nash equilibrium for economic data obtained in laboratory experiments with experienced human subjects who are sufficiently well paid. For similar reasons, Nash equilibrium is also important in explaining biological data. (An evolutionarily stable strategy [ESS], as introduced by John Maynard Smith and George Price [1972], is simply a refinement of a symmetric Nash equilibrium.) The title of Richard Dawkins's *Selfish Gene* explains the biological success of the idea of a Nash equilibrium in a nutshell. One can use the rational interpretation of a Nash equilibrium to predict the outcome of an evolutionary process, without needing to follow each enormously complicated twist and turn that the process might take.

The reason why some papers prove to be culturally pivotal is a matter for historians of science. The idea of an equilibrium is certainly not original to Nash's 1951 paper. It is implicit in David Hume's famous *Treatise on Human Nature* of 1739, and explicit in Augustin Cournot's 1838 work on the market games played between two rival manufacturers (for which reason a Nash equilibrium is sometimes called a Cournot-Nash equilibrium). Von Neumann was also aware that the strategy profiles that satisfy his minimax principle for two-person, zero-sum games are necessarily Nash equilibria for this special class of games. Nor was Nash's use of a fixed-point theorem to prove his existence theorem unprecedented. Von Neumann had made a similar use of the Brouwer fixed-point theorem to prove his minimax theorem. Shizuo Kakutani was moved to prove his generalization of the Brouwer theorem after hearing von Neumann lecture on the subject. However, what cannot be contested is that it was Nash's work that eventually converted the economics profession to game theory, albeit after a gestation period of more than a quarter of a century. Nowadays, the idea of a Nash equilibrium is regarded as the basic tool of microeconomic theory, and all its recent successes, notably the design of big-money auctions in the telecom industry and elsewhere, can be traced back to Nash's 1951 paper.

Nash was not shy about taking his ideas to the big names in the academic world. He famously proposed a scheme for reinterpreting quantum physics to Albert Einstein, who responded by suggesting that he first learn some physics. It is unfortunate that Nash got similar treatment from John von Neumann, when he showed him his existence theorem. Von Neumann apparently dismissively observed that he saw how the result could be proved using a fixed-point theorem.

Why did von Neumann not see the significance of Nash's theorem? One possibility is that von Neumann recognized that the best-reply criterion is only a necessary condition for a strategy profile to count as the rational solution of a game, but that the equilibrium selection problem would need to be solved—as von Neumann had implicitly solved it for two-person, zero-sum games—before one could claim to have a sufficient condition for the rational solution of a general game. Perhaps von Neumann would have taken more interest if he had considered the evolutionary implications of Nash equilibria, or if he had been aware of Nash's application (with Lloyd Shapley) of the idea to three-player poker models. However, uninformed enthusiasts do Nash no favors when they make von Neumann's atypical lack of insight on this occasion a reason for belittling von Neumann's own achievements in game theory. It is similarly no criticism of Isaac Newton that he stood on the shoulders of giants.

Nash Embedding. After completing what eventually turned out to be one of the most successful theses ever written, Nash spent time on and off at RAND in Santa Monica, California. RAND is a private foundation set up at the onset of the Cold War with the Soviet Union, for the purpose of maintaining the input from scientists and mathematicians that had proved very valuable at some pivotal points in World War II. A mythology has grown up that attributes an absurdly unrealistic influence on political and military strategy to game theorists at this time, especially those associated with RAND, but Nash himself seems to have contributed nothing of military value at all. He therefore deserves none of the coals of fire heaped, for example, on the head of von Neumann—supposedly the inspiration for title character in the movie *Dr. Strangelove*—for being thought to have created game theory for evil purposes.

Although Nash had such a large impact on economic theory, he never thought of becoming an economist. He was anxious to make his mark as a creative mathematician. The idea that first brought him the kind of recognition he was seeking was that the apparently very general shapes to which mathematicians refer when speaking of manifolds are fundamentally no more general than the shapes determined by polynomial equations, provided that one operates in a Euclidean space of high enough dimension. Even to propose such a conjecture was thought to be a wild venture by mathematicians of the time. In spite of such skepticism, Nash turned down the offer of a permanent position at RAND in order to return to Princeton in 1950, where he worked on his idea with Donald Spencer, who proved to be an invaluable aid to Nash as he sought to put his intuitions into the form of an acceptable mathematical proof—a task that he always found difficult. Nash published the completed paper under the title "Real Algebraic Manifolds" in 1952. Its second theorem asserts that:

> Theorem. *A closed differential manifold always has a proper algebraic representation in the Euclidean space of one more than twice its number of dimensions.*

Certain problems in differential geometry can therefore be reduced to counting the number of solutions to polynomial equations (Artin and Mazur).

Nash was disappointed at not being offered a position at Princeton, but accepted the offer he received from the Massachusetts Institute of Technology (MIT), to which he relocated in 1951. Although the Mathematics Department at MIT boasted Norbert Wiener, it had not yet acquired the prestige it currently enjoys, and Nash was one of a number of young men hired with the deliberate intention of putting the department on the map. The atmosphere seems to have been almost absurdly competitive, and Nash's endeavors to assert his superiority in this new environment made him popular neither with his colleagues nor his students, who doubtless felt that he should put up or shut up. However, it is hard to believe that Nash really proved one of the major mathematical theorems of the twentieth century in response to a testy challenge from a colleague, as he joked when first presenting the work in 1955. His earlier work would naturally have focused his attention on the problem that had been considered by Georg Friedrich Bernhard Riemann long before.

The question is whether the abstract shapes called Riemannian manifolds are really as abstract as they were thought to be. Nash argued that they are really nothing more than submanifolds of an ordinary flat space, but a proof of this claim would need to show how to construct a sufficiently smooth embedding of any given Riemannian manifold in a Euclidean space of sufficiently high dimension. Nash astonished the mathematical community by describing such a construction in his paper "The Imbedding Problem for Riemannian Manifolds," which was published in the *Annals of Mathematics* in 1956. Its final theorem asserts that:

> Theorem. *Any Riemannian n-manifold with C^k positive metric, where $k > 2$, has a C^k isometric embedding in a Euclidean space of $(3n^3+14n^2+11n)/2$ dimensions.*

The proof incorporates a result that J. Schwartz refers to in his influential *Nonlinear Functional Analysis* as the "hard" implicit function theorem. This theorem applies, for example, to functions from one Banach space to another, even when their Gateaux derivatives may be unbounded as linear operators and have an unbounded linear inverses. (See also Moser [1961] and Lang [1962].)

This work opened a window on the properties of nonlinear partial differential equations, which subject Nash pursued in 1956 while ostensibly on leave at the Advanced Institute at Princeton, but spending much of his time at the Courant Institute in New York. He returned to MIT the next year with novel results on local existence, uniqueness, and continuity. In spite of previous frictions, his MIT colleagues were generous in the help they gave Nash in putting his ideas into a publishable form. The paper appeared in 1958 with the title "Continuity of Solutions of Parabolic and Elliptic Equations." However, Nash was disappointed to find that some of the results of this paper had been anticipated by Ennio de Giorgi, who had been working independently on similar problems. This coincidence, which he still feels may have lost him his chance at a Fields Medal, together with the failure of his next project—which was a wildly ambitious attempt to rewrite the foundations of quantum theory—is thought to have been partly instrumental in precipitating the breakdown that followed.

Breakdown. Nash was a bookish loner as a boy. He became more obviously eccentric when he began to mix in academic circles, the subject of comment even by colleagues whose own behavior would be regarded as decidedly odd by normal standards. His adolescence seems to have been delayed or extended, so that he remained sexually ambivalent, fiercely competitive, and overly anxious to impress into his late twenties. His schizophrenia was presaged by his apparent unawareness of his responsibilities, notably toward his students at MIT and the illegitimate child he fathered in 1953. The bright spot in his personal life came with his marriage to Alicia, whom he married in 1957. However, Nash's life began to fall apart in 1958, when he reports that the same intuition that had

John Forbes Nash. *Nash speaks during a news conference at the University in Princeton, New Jersey, 1994.* AP IMAGES.

served him so well in solving mathematical problems began to feed him delusions that led to his becoming increasingly dysfunctional. Nothing is gained by itemizing the self-destructive behaviors that led to his being forcibly hospitalized on several occasions. With occasional remissions, matters continued in this way until 1970, when Alicia—whom he had divorced for her part in his hospitalizations—took him in to prevent his becoming homeless. He then famously survived as a phantom haunting the Princeton campus, engaged in arcane research comprehensible to nobody but himself. Only in the early 1990s did his old Princeton acquaintances begin to notice signs of a recovery that is apparently unusual in such serious cases as his. Nash believes that he eventually learned to distinguish between his rational and irrational intuitions using the power of his intellect. To the extent that this is true, there is therefore a message of hope for those similarly afflicted.

Nobel Laureate. In 1993, a symposium on game theory was held of the kind that the Nobel committee for economics sometimes use to help them decide to whom to award a prize in a particular area. Most of the game theorists who attended assumed that Nash's illness ruled him out as a candidate. (It is not clear why the fact that someone is thought to be ill should disbar him from an academic honor, but it had even proved difficult to get Nash nominated as a fellow of the Econometric Society some years earlier, although the vote when taken was overwhelmingly favorable.) However, word of Nash's recovery got to the committee in time for it to be possible for him to be awarded the 1994 Nobel Prize along with John Harsanyi and Reinhard Selten, who developed his ideas in the context of games with incomplete information and games with a dynamic structure. (Reports of dissent in the committee and resentment elsewhere would seem to overdramatize the actual events, although it is perhaps a pity that the Nobel citation should have left his work on bargaining unmentioned.)

John and Alicia Nash are now remarried, and take pleasure in the modicum of fame that the book and movie about their lives has brought them. Nash's switchback career therefore ends on an upbeat note, although few would agree with his own assessment that his intellectual achievements were an adequate compensation for all the accompanying pain and suffering.

BIBLIOGRAPHY

WORKS BY NASH

"The Bargaining Problem." *Econometrica* 18 (1950): 155–162.

With Lloyd Shapley. "A Simple Three-Person Poker Game." In *Contributions to the Theory of Games,* edited by Harold Kuhn and Albert Tucker. Annals of Mathematics Studies, no. 24. Princeton, NJ: Princeton University Press, 1950. Reprinted in *Essays on Game Theory.*

"Non-Cooperative Games." *Annals of Mathematics* 54 (1951): 286–295.

"Real Algebraic Manifolds." *Annals of Mathematics* 56 (1952): 405–421.

"Two-Person Cooperative Games." *Econometrica* 21 (1953): 128–140.

"The Imbedding Problem for Riemannian Manifolds." *Annals of Mathematics* 63 (1956): 20–63.

"Continuity of Solutions of Parabolic and Elliptic Equations." *American Journal of Mathematics* 80 (1958): 931–954.

Essays on Game Theory. Cheltenham, U.K.: Edward Elgar, 1996.

"Autobiography." In *The Essential John Nash,* edited by Harold Kuhn and Sylvia Nasar. Princeton, NJ: Princeton University Press, 2002.

OTHER SOURCES

Artin, M., and B. Mazur. "On Periodic Points." *Annals of Mathematics* 81 (1965): 82–99.

Binmore, Ken. "Nash Bargaining Theory II." In *Economics of Bargaining,* edited by Ken Binmore and P. Dasgupta. Cambridge, U.K.: Cambridge University Press, 1987.

Cournot, A. *Researches into the Mathematical Principles of the Theory of Wealth.* London: Macmillan, 1929. First published 1838.

Dawkins, Richard. *The Selfish Gene.* Oxford: Oxford University Press, 1976.

Hume, David. *A Treatise on Human Nature,* edited by L. A. Selby-Bigge. Revised by P. Nidditch. Oxford: Clarendon Press, 1978. First published 1739.

Kuhn, Harold, and Sylvia Nasar, eds. *The Essential John Nash.* Princeton, NJ: Princeton University Press, 2002.

Lang, S. *Introduction to Differentiable Manifolds.* New York: Wiley, 1962.

Maynard Smith, John, and G. Price, "Logic of Animal Conflict." *Nature* 246 (1972): 15–18.

Milnor, J. *Differentiable Topology.* Princeton, NJ: Princeton University Press, 1958.

———. "The Game of Hex." In *The Essential John Nash,* edited by Harold Kuhn and Sylvia Nasar. Princeton, NJ: Princeton University Press, 2002.

Moser, Jurgen. "A New Technique for the Construction of Solutions of Nonlinear Differential Equations." *Proceedings of the National Academy of Sciences of the United States of America* 47 (1961): 1824–1831.

Nasar, Sylvia. *A Beautiful Mind.* New York: Faber and Faber, 1998.

Rubinstein, Ariel. "Perfect Equilibrium in a Bargaining Model." *Econometrica* 50 (1982): 97–109.

Schwartz, J. *Nonlinear Functional Analysis.* London: Gordon and Breach, 1969.

Selten, Reinhard. "Reexamination of the Perfectness Concept for Equilibrium Points in Extensive-Games." *International Journal of Game Theory* 4 (1975): 25–55.

Shapley, Lloyd. "A Value for n-Person Games." In *Contributions to the Theory of Games,* vol. 2, edited by Harold Kuhn and Albert Tucker. Annals of Mathematics Studies, no. 28. Princeton, NJ: Princeton University Press, 1953.

von Neumann, John. "Zur Theorie der Gesellschaftsspiele." *Mathematische Annalen* 100 (1928): 295–320.

von Neumann, John, and Oskar Morgenstern. *The Theory of Games and Economic Behavior.* Princeton, NJ: Princeton University Press, 1944.

Ken Binmore

NEEDHAM, DOROTHY MOYLE (*b.* London, England, 22 September 1896; *d.* Cambridge, England, 22 December 1987), *biochemist, social activist, historian of science.*

Needham was a pioneer of muscle biochemistry in the United Kingdom, who contributed to the big question of how chemical reactions produce heat and especially work that is characteristic of muscle. In 1921 she confirmed the intercoversion of glycogen and lactic acid, as postulated by Otto Meyerhoff, a foremost muscle physiologist and 1922 Nobel colaureate (Needham, 1950) while utilizing methods developed by her PhD advisor, Frederick G. Hopkins, the founder of British biochemistry (D. M. Needham & Foster, 1921). During the 1920s she published on the metabolism of several acids in muscle, thus contributing to an understanding of interlocking pathways of aerobic and anaerobic carbohydrate breakdown. She was also worked on cyclic phosphate transfer in muscle contraction, as well confirming, in 1939, with collaborators that myosin, the contractile protein of muscle, behaved as the anzyme ATPase (adenosine triphosphatase), a landmark finding that established for the first time a direct correlation of structure and function. Needham also published major books in the history of muscle biochemistry (1932, 1971). She also collaborated on a documentary history of biochemistry (D. M. Needham & Teich, 1992) that covered two centuries of original research.

Early Years. Dorothy Moyle Needham was part of a generation of women who obtained formal scientific education at Cambridge University, while benefiting from new opportunities opened by World War I. Born in London as one of three children of John Thomas Moyle, a clerk in the Patents' Office or a civil servant, and Ellen Daves Moyle, she began her studies at Girton College in 1915, as a student of the Natural Science Tripos. Her choice of Girton, the older and more militant of the two women's colleges at the time at Cambridge, was influenced by her maternal aunt, Agnes Daves, headmistress of the high school Dorothy had attended , and a living example of the value of education and independence for women, at a time of ongoing suffrage struggle. That decision was further reinforced by the granting of the vote to women in 1918, as well as the perception of that generation of British women that marriage might not be an option, due to heavy male casualties in World War I.

Needham's choice of chemistry was rare at the time for women, with relatively few students in the Women's Colleges studying, let alone specializing, in science. Marie Curie's solo Nobel Prize for Chemistry in 1911 (eight years after she shared the Nobel Prize for Physics with her husband Pierre and senior physicist Henri Becquerel), as well as Curie's service in World War I as an operator of x-ray ambulance units, may have inspired Needham's choices; she too would later collaborate with a husband in the same field and would contribute to the war effort during World War II. Of course, Girton had a tradition of excellence for women. In 1887 Agnata Ramsey had earned the highest marks in classics, prompting a congratulatory letter from Queen Victoria; Ramsey subsequently married the master of Trinity College, thus setting a model of combining scholarly excellence and marriage, which Needham, along with other educated women at Cambridge, would emulate and adapt to their own circumstances. Such role models, the teaching of chemistry at Girton by Miss M. B. Thomas (which Needham felt was superior to that offered by the Department of Chemistry at Cambridge University), and the growing acceptability of employment for women during and after World War I were key forces that shaped Dorothy Moyle Needham's professional choices.

After passing part II of the tripos, specializing in chemistry, in 1919, she began graduate studies in biochemistry with Frederick G. Hopkins. Hopkins's prominence at the time as the creator of the new field of biochemistry, as well as his gentle, self-effacing, demeanor (stemming in part from the long-term marginality of his hybrid field in the prevailing disciplinary power structure of the scientific establishment) and his quiet but staunch support of socialist agendas for greater egalitarianism among classes, races, and genders, attracted socialists and other varieties of progressive men, minorities, colonials, and especially women. Indeed, Hopkins's former collaborator turned the first secretary of the Medical Research Council (MRC) (1919–1933) Sir Walter Morley Fletcher commented in his correspondence on the prominence of "clever Jews and talkative women" in Hopkins's lab. Out of his five hundred research associates from many countries in the period between 1919 and 1947, 12 percent were women (J. Needham and Baldwin, 1949). At a time (1921) when Cambridge University had decided, for a second time in two decades, not to grant formal degrees to women (remaining the last university to do so, in 1948), Hopkins encouraged many women, including his daughter Barbara, to both become biochemists and marry colleagues; he even celebrated their marriages within his institute by writing poems.

Needham's scientific path was thus influenced by her most judicious choice to specialize in biochemistry, a new field of growing opportunities, by her early association with the rising fortune of Hopkins, and a post–World War I relaxation of previous, rigid (Victorian and Edwardian) standards of social control for women. After twenty-five painful years of marginality as lecturer at Cambridge University's Department of Physiology, Hopkins had finally begun to receive formal recognition as a professor and head of his own institute, the Sir William Dunn Institute of Biochemistry and Nutrition. He was knighted in 1925 for science advisory service in World War I on nutrition, shared the Nobel Prize in Physiology and Medicine in1929 for codiscovering vitamins as necessary growth factors, and became president of the Royal Society (1931–1936). Under these most fortuitous circumstances, Needham was able to continue her research in Hopkins's department from 1919 until her retirement in 1963. At her entry in 1919, her colleagues included two other distinguished women biochemists, Muriel Wheldale Onslow, a pioneer of biochemical genetics (who can be seen in a famous photo of Hopkins and his eight research associates in 1916, half of whom were women, no doubt due to the war), and Marjory Stephenson. Needham and Stephenson, a founder of microbial biochemistry, were among the first women to be elected to the Royal Society after World War II. (Wheldale Onslow died in 1932.)

Research on Muscle Metabolism. In the early 1920s, Needham worked under Hopkins on aerobic synthesis of the muscle fuel glycogen for the Food Investigation Board of the Department of Scientific and Industrial Research (DSIR), receiving for this work the "title" of MA in 1923 and of PhD in 1926. (Women were not able to receive formal degrees in the Senate House until 1948; hence they received "titles" stating that the holder of the "title" would have had a BA or MA degree had that holder been a man.) She also received the Gamble Prize, in 1924, for an essay on "the correlation of the structure, function, and chemical composition in different types of striated muscle," a topic that defined her research interest for the rest of her life. From 1925 to 1928 she held a Beit Memorial Fellowship, a prestigious postdoctoral research fellowship that enabled her to continue with research on muscle metabolism, while taking part in the pioneering work on the role of adenosine triphosphate (ATP) in muscle contraction, a role discovered by Herbert Lohmann in Germany in 1928. She summarized this research in a book, *Biochemistry of Muscle* (1932), which she was repeatedly asked to update, especially after the mid-1950s. Eventually, she did so, while including both historical and contemporary material, but only after she retired from active research in 1963.

The resulting comprehensive book, *Machina Carnis: The Biochemistry of Muscular Contraction in Its Historical Development* (1971), covered in its twenty-four chapters many landmarks in muscle research, including the discovery of ATP in 1928; the discovery of ATPase activity of myosin by Vladimir A. Engelhardt and Militsa N. Ljubimova in 1939; the discovery of tropomyosin by Kenneth Bailey in 1946; and the discovery of the sliding filament mechanism by Hugh Huxley and Jean Hanson in 1953. Emphases upon the processes providing energy for the contraction of muscles, the structure of diverse muscle tissues, theories of muscle contraction, and dead and diseased muscle are part of a more inclusive treatment of more general biochemical topics such as cellular respiration, oxidative phosphorilation, and glycolysis.

During World War II, Needham participated in research useful to the war effort, as part of a group working for the Ministry of Supply, which focused on the effects of chemical weapons (especially mustard gas) on skin and bone-marrow metabolism. After the war she collaborated on research in protein and enzyme biochemistry (1944, 1951) while concluding her four decades of

Needham

research in muscle biochemistry with a study of the proteins of smooth muscle in the uterus (1962).

In parallel with her research, Needham participated in the Department of Biochemistry's teaching, giving both lectures and laboratory supervision, including for several PhD theses. In 1945 she was awarded an ScD by Cambridge University and was among the first women to be elected to the Royal Society, in 1948, having been preceded only by her biochemist colleague Stephenson and crystallographer Kathleen Lonsdale, who were elected in 1947.

At the time of her death in 1987, at age ninety-one, Needham was collaborating on a sourcebook for the history of biochemistry in collaboration with the historian of biochemistry Mikulas Teich, who completed the book after her death. *A Documentary History of Biochemistry, 1770–1940* (1992) involved the selection, translation, annotation, and historical contextualization of landmark biochemical papers for almost two centuries. It remains an indispensable tool for historians of biochemistry, who otherwise might not have been able to appreciate original texts in biochemistry, written in a variety of European languages, or to get a firsthand glimpse into interwar Cambridge biochemistry.

Dorothy Needham was also active in numerous social causes, often as a partner in a collaborative couple. As a Cambridge University scientist educated at a Cambridge college, she knew the importance of college fellowship in university life and hence helped to found two new colleges at Cambridge University for research women who had no college appointments: New Hall in 1946, and Lucy Cavendish College in 1962. With the women's liberation movement, she was rediscovered by older colleges and was elected to fellowship by both Girton, her college as a student, and Gonville and Caius, where she participated in many college activities for a decade (1966–1976) as the master's wife and collaborator.

Partner in a Collaborative Couple. Dorothy Needham's research, as well as her career pattern and public persona as an activist woman scientist, were defined not only by her early association with Hopkins as a uniquely enlightened scientist and the most important personality in British biochemistry; of comparable importance were the collaborative opportunities afforded by her marriage in 1924 to a biochemist colleague, Joseph Needham. Joseph Needham's prolific activities in many fields inevitably affected Dorothy, who was often asked by Joseph to join his diverse research or social activities.

However, the Needhams were able to forge a flexible partnership that enabled each partner to pursue a personal line of research while collaborating with each other whenever such a collaboration was possible and productive. They were part of a post–World War I generation of avant-garde scientists who sought to redefine marriage along the more egalitarian notions that prevailed in the aftermath of women's suffrage in the 1910s and the rise of socialism in the interwar period. Many of the Needhams' colleagues thus explored new marital patterns, such as marriages to older and more educated women, open marriages, and on the whole more egalitarian marriages than ever before. However, the Needhams were relatively rare in carving a stable social identity as a distinguished scientist and activist collaborative couple, an identity that both enabled and constrained their scientific work and personal life.

In scientific terms, the Needhams could use each other not only as a sounding board, but also as a collaborator, especially when there was time pressure or funds were lacking to hire research associates. For example, Dorothy took part in Joseph's research in both biochemical embryology and protein structure throughout the 1930s, in addition to her own ongoing research in muscle biochemistry. Though Dorothy worked on the British war effort during World War II, she also joined Joseph in China for almost two years during 1944–1945, while serving as a chemical advisor to the Sino-British mission that he directed in China in the period 1942–1946. That mission provided scientific and technical assistance to Chinese scientists, then under siege by the Japanese occupation of China's coastal parts, and also shaped Joseph Needham's decision to transfer his postwar research effort to the comparative history of Chinese science.

Though the Needhams no longer collaborated scientifically after the war, when Joseph devoted himself to a new historical undertaking, Dorothy remained helpful to him for his lecturing duties as reader of biochemistry, until the mid-1960s (when he became master of Gonville and Caius), by providing and updating material, something that only a practicing biochemist could do. Along these lines, Dorothy's work on her comprehensive book *Machina Carnis* (1971) benefited from her husband's scholarly experience with the history of science.

Dorothy Needham's professional status was nevertheless adversely affected by her status as a woman scientist married to a colleague. While Joseph had early job security, from the age of twenty-four, when he both completed his PhD and was elected to fellowship by Gonville and Caius College, Dorothy's research was to rely on research grants ("soft money"), mostly from governmental sources such as DSIR, the MRC and the Agricultural Research Council (ARC) in the United Kingdom, and the U.S. National Institutes of Health (NIH). This form of support worked out during Hopkins's life, especially because successive MRC secretaries, such as Walter Fletcher in the 1920s and Edward Mellanby in the 1930s

Needham

and 1940s, were among Hopkins's admirers, as well as during Joseph's research period, when she was often needed as a collaborator.

However, Dorothy's lack of a formal position and salary also led to difficult situations in the early 1950s, when the MRC declined to renew her modest grants on the ground that temporary grants should not become a permanent form of support. While a university fund provided relief for three years, she was initially denied research grants by the Royal Society because its president, Lord Adrian, believed that married women had no need for a salary of their own. Eventually, she was able to get research grants from the ARC. Because by that time Joseph was no longer active in biochemical research, Dorothy's predicament—as a woman scientist whose marital status was used to deny her either a regular salary or an independent grant, despite scientific distinction as a Fellow of the Royal Society and departmental service of three decades—became only too clear in the 1950s. Ironically a period when funding of science became particularly abundant, science policy in the 1950s was slow to benefit women scientists, especially when they could no longer be treated as collaborators of their husbands.

However, both Needhams reaped the benefits of being an activist couple in the social and political sphere. As the only couple marching in DSc gowns in Cambridge University processions (since 1945), and after 1948, when Dorothy was among the first women to be elected to the Royal Society (Joseph had been elected in 1941), as the only F.R.S. couple in Cambridge, the Needhams were aware that they symbolized a rare success to both collaborate and retain independent careers. Theirs was a remarkable predicament because it signaled the compatibility of career and family life for both men and women, at a time most women were forced to choose one over the other.

The Needhams also cultivated a joint identity as a socially and politically active couple (Werskey, 1978, traces about a dozen such couples at Cambridge in the 1930s) who both shared many causes—for example, both sat on the Cambridge Trade Council as representatives of the Association of Scientific Workers—but also each retained a unique constellations of social activities. Thus, while Dorothy ran on a Labour Party ticket to the Cambridge Town Council, Joseph became secretary of the Cornford-Maclaurin Fund, which aided families of the fallen in the Spanish Civil War. They each had a wide range of humanitarian and charitable causes, including for Dorothy: Amnesty International; Animals' Vigilantes; Anti-Nuclear Campaign; Cambridge Welfare and Preservation Societies; Cambridge University's Newcomers Club; El Salvador Committee for Human Rights; Friends of the Earth; Medical and Scientific Aid for Vietnam, Laos and Kampuchea; Medical and Scientific Committee for Soviet Jewry; and the Movement for the Ordination of Women.

The Needhams enjoyed many important and influential friendships with other couples, for example, with the British historians Charles and Dorothea Singer, and the French biochemists Louis and Sarah Rapkine; as well as individual friendships with scientists and other colleagues, including members of the Biotheoretical Gathering. This "scientific Bloomsbury" of the 1930s, in which the Needhams were the only scientist couple, saw Dorothy often admonishing Joseph for jumping to theoretical conclusions prior to conducting experimental work, or declining the generous offer of their close friends, the Woodgers, to assist them in having children, by the "radical" methods of that time.

Now that Dorothy Needham's archival papers are cataloged, at Girton College's Library of Cambridge University in Cambridge, U.K., historians may be able to get more complete answers to questions such as her role in muscle biochemistry, her role in college life (especially the founding of two new women's colleges), the workings of a collaborative marriage in science and social activism over half a century, and her own way toward a major accomplishment in the history of science.

BIBLIOGRAPHY

WORKS BY NEEDHAM

With Dorothy Lilian Foster. "A Contribution to the Study of the Interconversion of Carbohydrate and Lactic Acid in Muscle." *Biochemical Journal* 15 (1921): 672–680.

Biochemistry of Muscle. London: Methuen, 1932.

With J. Needham and C. H. Waddington. "Physico-chemical Experiments on the Amphibian Organizer." *Proceedings of the Royal Society* B 114 (1934): 393–422.

With Mary Dainty, et al. "Studies on the Anomalous Viscosity and Flow-Birefringence of Protein Solutions." *Journal of General Physiology* 27 (1944): 355–399.

With Joseph Needham, eds. *Science Outpost Papers of the Sino-British Science Cooperation Office in China, 1942–1946.* London: Pilot Press, 1948.

With Joseph Needham. "Sir F. G. Hopkins' Personal Influence and Characteristics." In *Hopkins and Biochemistry,* edited by Joseph Needham and Ernest Baldwin, 111–122. Cambridge, U.K: Cambridge University Press, 1949.

"Myosin Adenosinetriphosphate in Relation to Muscle Contraction." In *Metabolism and Function, a Collection of Papers Dedicated to Otto Meyerhof on the Occasion of His 65th Birthday,* edited by David Nachmansohn, 42–59. Amsterdam: Elsevier, 1950.

With Louis Siminovitch and Sarah M. Rapkine. "On the Mechanism of the Inhibition of Glycolysis by Glyceraldehyde." *Biochemical Journal* 49 (1951): 113–124.

"Contractile Proteins in the Smooth Muscle of the Uterus." *Physiological Reviews* 42, supp. 5 (1962): 89–96.

Machina Carnis: The Biochemistry of Muscular Contraction in Its Historical Development. Cambridge, U.K.: Cambridge University Press, 1971.

With Mikulas Teich. *A Documentary History of Biochemistry, 1770–1940.* Rutherford, NJ: Fairleigh Dickinson University Press, 1992.

OTHER SOURCES

Abir-Am, Pnina G. "The Biotheoretical Gathering, Transdisciplinary Authority and the Incipient Legitimation of Molecular Biology in the 1930s: New Perspective on the Historical Sociology of Science." *History of Science* 25 (March 1987): 1–70.

———. "Collaborative Couples Who Strove to Change the World: The Social Policies and Personal Tensions of the Russells, the Myrdals, and the Mead-Batesons." In *Creative Couples in the Sciences,* edited by Helena M. Pycior, Nancy G. Slack, and Pnina G. Abir-Am, 267–281. New Brunswick, NJ: Rutgers University Press, 1996.

Bradbrook, Muriel C. *"That Infidel Place": A Short History of Girton College, 1869–1969* . Cambridge, U.K.: Girton College, 1984. See especially chapter five, "The Girton Girl: Social Images from Within and Without," pp. 91–120.

Huxley, H. E. "A Personal View of Muscle and Motility Mechanisms." *Annual Review of Physiology* 58 (1996): 1–19.

Kamminga, Harmke, and Mark W. Weatherall. "The Making of a Biochemist." *Medical History* 40, nos. 1–2 (1996a,b): 269–292, 415–436.

Mason, Joan. "The Women Fellows' Jubilee." *Notes and Records of the Royal Society of London* 49, no. 1 (January 1995): 125–140.

Needham, Joseph. *Order and Life.* New Haven, CT: Yale University Press, 1936; Cambridge, MA: MIT Press, 1968; dedicated to members of the Biotheoretical Gathering, including Dorothy Needham.

———. "The Making of a Honorary Taoist" (under pseudonym of Henry Holorenshaw). In *Changing Perspective in the History of Science,* edited by Mikulas Teich and Robert Young, 1–20. London: Heinemann, 1973.

Needham, Joseph, and Ernest Baldwin, eds. *Hopkins and Biochemistry.* Cambridge, U.K.: Cambridge University Press, 1949.

Needham, Joseph, and David E. Green, eds. *Perspectives in Biochemistry: 31 Essays Presented to Sir Frederick Gowland Hopkins on the Occasion of His 75th Birthday.* Cambridge, U.K.: Cambridge University Press, 1938.

Szent-Gyorgyi, Andrew G. "The Early History of the Biochemistry of Muscle Contraction." *Journal of General Physiology 123* (2004): 631–641.

Teich, Mikulas. "Dorothy Moyle Needham, 22 September 1896–22 December 1987." *Biographical Memoirs of Fellows of the Royal Society* 49 (2003): 351–366.

Werskey, Gary. *The Visible College: A Collective Biography of British Scientists and Socialists of the 1930s.* London: Allen Lane, 1978.

Pnina G. Abir-Am

NEEDHAM, JOSEPH

(*b.* London, England, 9 December 1900; *d.* Cambridge, England, 24 March 1995), *scientist, international activist, historian of science.*

Needham was a visionary and an innovative scientist, social activist, and historian, whose seven decades of scholarship shaped many fields of knowledge. Needham's scientific research pioneered the recasting of the traditional relationships between physicochemical sciences and biology that revolutionized the life sciences in the second half of the twentieth century, while focusing in particular on the interdisciplinary field of biochemical embryology. He was also a prolific author, having published about one hundred scientific papers and more than two dozen books on science; the relationship of science with philosophy, religion, ideology, and politics; and the history of Chinese and Western science. Needham was an intellectual leader of progressive causes, most notably the anti-Fascist cause during the 1930s, and the cause of international cooperation in science, especially in the framework of UNESCO, during the 1940s. The second half of Needham's life, 1950–1995, was devoted to a pioneering study of the history of Chinese science that fostered a crucial sense of intellectual parity between East and West while inspiring numerous international scholars. Needham inspired and encouraged collaborating scientists from many countries who flocked to Cambridge to work with him during his bench heydays, as well as generations of scholars in the history of life sciences, the history of Chinese science, or the history of international scientific exchanges, who sought him out since the 1970s.

Needham was born in London, England, where his father, also called Joseph Needham, practiced medicine on Harley Street. His mother, Alicia Adelaide Montgomery, was a composer of songs. He was an only child who was much influenced by the incompatible temperaments of his parents, and by his education at Oundle School, a progressive school in Northamptonshire, which he did not particularly enjoy but which gave him a lasting legacy in the form of inspiring history lessons, a visionary outlook, and technical skills.

Visionary and Innovative Scientist. Needham intended to follow in his father's footsteps and train in medicine. However, he gravitated toward biochemistry in graduate school (1921–1924) under the influence of his college tutor at Cambridge University, the notable chemist William H. Hardy. Needham trained under Sir Frederick Gowland Hopkins, the founder of this discipline, who became a much-loved father figure (Needham's father died in 1920). Needham embarked upon an academic career, becoming reader, or "second in command," in the Department of Biochemistry at Cambridge University. The decision to trade medicine for biochemistry was facilitated by his election to fellowship in his college, Gonville and Caius, which meant a sinecure for life with both job security and intellectual independence as a scholar.

Needham's broad, polymathic interests (philosophical, historical, political, religious, literary) and his responsiveness to rising issues of social justice led him to gradually gravitate away from mainstream biochemistry and focus instead on radical, interdisciplinary, and collaborative ventures designed to replace the prevailing scientific hierarchies with a new, egalitarian order based on parity between biology and the physical sciences, as well as greater equality among classes, races, and genders. Needham credited his broad vision and his courage to pursue utopian projects and entertain nonconformist social views to the influence of his high school headmaster, the visionary educator Frederick W. Sanderson, and the latter's friend and frequent visitor at the school, the utopian writer Herbert G. Wells, as well as the satirical playwright George Bernard Shaw (Needham, 1973).

Needham's formerly mild interest in social reform was reinforced in the mid-1920s by his colleague and friend, the French biochemist Louis Rapkine, who introduced him to Marxism, though this interest was to take an activist form only after 1931. Until then, in addition to his professor, Hopkins, the main influence upon Needham was his encounter with the zoologist turned philosopher of biology Joseph Henri Woodger of the University of London, following his review of Woodger's book *Biological Principles* (1929). Woodger introduced Needham to the philosophy of biology, which Woodger understood as a system of empirically valid and conceptually clear logical propositions, along logical empiricist lines. Needham's intense correspondence with Woodger and other philosophers of biology, most notably Ludwig von Bertalanffy, led him to elaborate on the major debate at the heart of biology, the so-called mechanist-vitalist debate that polarized scientists between those who asserted the sufficiency of physicochemical methods in biology and those who asserted the irreducibility of biology to physics and chemistry. Needham updated this centuries-long debate in view of the scientific findings of the late 1920s (mainly the quantum revolution in physics and its holistic view of the atom as a system) and the new tools of the philosophy of science, such as the distinction between methodology and metaphysics.

As already evident in his first paper ("The Philosophical Basis of Biochemistry," 1925), Needham, much as his mentor Hopkins, was preoccupied with bridging the contradictory doctrines of mechanism and vitalism for relevance to the foundations of biology in general and biochemistry in particular, and he seized upon the potential of the philosophy of science in providing a solution to this problem. Needham's solution was to develop an intermediary position, while aiming to retain the best features of mechanism and vitalism, by restricting the former to the lower status of a heuristic methodology, while conferring upon the latter the higher status of a metaphysics, yet one which does not intervene in scientific practice.

However, Needham's obsessive quest to reconcile opposites—a quest attributed to his childhood desire to reconcile his incompatible parents, or an analytically minded social conservative father and an artistically minded bohemian mother (Needham, 1973)—and hence his unique ability to tolerate and compartmentalize contradictions exposed Needham to Woodger's constant criticism. These philosophical concerns were soon to be superseded by Needham's discovery of a new vocation, that of exhaustive scholarship in combining historical and contemporary detail in science. In order to demonstrate the compatibility of mechanism and organicism for defining the philosophical status of biochemistry, and especially for his own research in biochemical embryology, Needham plunged into a massive exploration of the mutual relevance of biochemistry and embryology since antiquity and until his own time.

The resulting three-volume book, *Chemical Embryology* (1931), not only displayed Needham's remarkable ability to cope with a vast number of sources, both recent and ancient (the first volume was soon reprinted as *A History of Embryology,* 1934) but also revealed his naïveté regarding the prospects of interdisciplinary research at the time. Needham's 1931 book was praised for its erudition but criticized for being an unsatisfactory hybrid, neither biochemical enough nor embryological enough. An update published a decade later, *Biochemistry and Morphogenesis* (1942), better avoided an earlier perception that he was aiming at reducing morphology, the "most biological" discipline, to its chemical aspects, a perception responsible for antagonism among classical biologists.

Like many others, Needham experienced 1931 as a turning point. On the scientific side, he embarked upon the biochemical chase for the "organizer" or inducer of embryonic organs, while following up with several collaborators the molecular prospects of a key discovery at the heart of embryology. This was one of the most ambitious research programs at the time, extending beyond disciplinary boundaries, while anticipating the line of revolutionary research associated with mRNA in the 1950s. On the sociopolitical side, Needham's exposure to two international congresses held in London at a time of great upheaval greatly influenced him toward adopting a dialectical materialist orientation and to become active in socialist causes.

The first such meeting, held at the Science Museum in London in July 1931, was the Second International Congress for the History of Science (ICHS). Needham was one of eight speakers at the session on "The Recasting of the Relationships between Physics and Biology," which included the biologists Joseph H. Woodger, John S. Haldane, Edward S. Russell, and Lancelot Hogben; the physicists Lancelot L. Whyte and John D. Bernal, both of Cambridge University; and a Soviet delegate, Boris Zavadovsky, who argued in favor of new, egalitarian, relationship between physics and biology from dialectical materialist premises. Needham was impressed by the latter's arguments and soon seized upon dialectical materialism as a philosophical system that was able not only to bridge opposites in science but also to introduce an ethics of justice in social affairs. Of similar influence were the speeches of other members of the Soviet delegation, most notably its head, Nikolai Bukharin, the chief Soviet ideologue, and Boris Hessen, whose paper "The Social and Economic Roots of Newton's Principia" introduced what became known as the externalist approach to the history of science. The Second ICHS thus stimulated Needham, among others, to adopt a socialist viewpoint in both science and society.

The Centennial of the British Association for the Advancement of Science (BAAS), the most well-attended BAAS meeting ever, with delegations flowing from all corners of the British Empire, held in September 1931 at the Royal Institution in London, among other venues, was another Congress that lent its weight to influencing public opinion in science and its foundations. Needham's much-admired mentor, Hopkins, delivered a keynote address to the Physiological Section of BAAS, in which he labeled biology in general and biochemistry in particular as the "science of life," and hence the science of the future, as opposed to physics, which he portrayed as a "science of death" due to its war involvements. The BAAS president, General Jan Smuts, himself a philosopher, also argued in favor of parity between biology and physics, in the name of popular philosophies of emergent evolution, with which Needham too had sympathized and was to further develop in his prestigious Spencerian Lecture at Oxford University in 1937 (reprinted in Needham, 1946).

The influence of these congresses stemmed not only from their international standing and size but also from their timing. Held amidst the shocking collapse of the gold standard, hunger marches of unemployed miners, the fall of the second Labour government, and the king's appeal for a national unity coalition, these international science meetings embodied all the contradictions that a sensitive young scientist-philosopher-historian such as Needham could perceive. He was not alone in thinking that major social, political, and scientific change was just around the corner.

The convergence of such historical factors led Needham to engage in "collective action" by participating in an informal group, the "Biotheoretical Gathering," a group of philosophically minded scientists intent on exploring the prospects of interdisciplinary research, once the epistemological parity of biology and the physical sciences had been acknowledged in such major international venues. The group included scientists from Cambridge, Oxford, and London universities who met twice per year; they maintained rapport by correspondence, until the outbreak of World War II, which dispersed its members worldwide. Their collective research projects envisioned a new, innovative, and interdisciplinary, conceptual and social space that can be seen as the first systematic discourse in molecular biology.

Though all of Needham's partners in this informal group contributed theoretical and empirical ideas—most notably the biocrystallographer Bernal, the biomathematician Dorothy M. Wrinch, the physicochemical morphologist and epigeneticist Conrad H. Waddington, among others—researchers owe their knowledge of this group to Needham's role as a devoted coordinator and "scribe" who wrote and kept the minutes of this group's fascinating meetings. After World War II, Needham's and Bernal's preoccupations turned to science policy in the late 1940s and to the history of science in the 1950s and beyond. Wrinch and Waddington continued to work in different forms of theoretical biology, while Woodger became a full-time philosopher of biology. Though their collective forum was not reconvened after World War II in its prewar form, some of their ideas regarding the problem of protein structure and function were pursued by a new generation of scientists, for example, Max Perutz, John Kendrew, Francis Crick, John Randall, and Rosalind Franklin, who became instrumental in launching molecular biology in the post–World War II era. Needham took part in a critical phase in the history of the molecular revolution in biology, both as a visionary scientist-actor and as the metascientist creator of archival records from the 1930s.

Author. Between 1925 and 1946, Needham authored not only scientific papers and large-scale synthetic books on the relationship between biochemistry and embryology, most notably the above mentioned *Chemical Embryology* (1931), *Order and Life* (1936), and *Biochemistry and Morphogenesis* (1942), but also a variety of essays, often assembled into edited collections on science's relationship to philosophy, history, religion, and politics. For example, Needham's *Time, the Refreshing River* (1943) and *History Is on Our Side* (1946) include essays and addresses from the 1930s that engage the burning issues of the day, most notably the fight against Fascism, the role of Marxism in social evolution, the place of religious experience, the philosophy of emergent evolution, and the importance of science in war and peace. He was unusual among other

Joseph Needham. DAVID LEVENSON/GETTY IMAGES.

politically active scientists, especially on the Left, in insisting on the compatibility of Marxism with religion, and in writing extensively on science and religion.

Needham was so prolific an author in part because he learned at the young age of eight to write directly on the typewriter; because he found in writing a medium of expression best suited to someone of shy and bookish dispositions; and because he understood the importance of his proximity to Cambridge University Library and lived all his life next door to it. His ability to maximize his use of time was further reflected in his habit to invite his visitors to meals, whether breakfast or dinner, so as not to waste his precious scholarly time. By the time his seventieth anniversary Festschrift was published in 1973 (Teich and Young, eds.), Needham had published almost thirty books, including several edited collections of essays by others. The eightieth Festschrift, published in 1982 (Hu, ed.) required significant additions to his bibliography. It is plausible to assume that Needham's influence was exercised primarily via his prolific writings.

Of special importance are the two volumes Needham coedited in honor of Hopkins in 1938 and 1949. These volumes capture the history of biochemistry from the perspective of the collective memory of those who worked with Hopkins until his death in 1947 and are a unique resource for historians wishing to understand the rise of the first British school of biochemistry, the contributions of women, minority, and overseas scientists, the reasons for its decline in the post–World War II era, or the rise of an internationally famous Laboratory of Molecular Biology outside the Cambridge University structure. Needham's initiatives as prolific editor thus complement his authorial ones in establishing the presence of a unique voice concerned with social conscience, a sense of intellectual equality across race, gender, and class, and a quest for justice, tolerance, and open-mindedness to other cultures.

Social Activist. During the 1930s, Needham was active in several progressive causes, ranging from serving on the Cambridge Trade Council, together with his wife, Dorothy Moyle Needham, as delegates of the Association of Scientific Workers, to being chairman of the Socialist League, a Labour Party group, and serving as treasurer of the Cornford-McLaurin Fund (which assisted relatives of the fallen in the Spanish civil war). Though Needham lacked the oratorical powers of John B. S. Haldane or Bernal, unlike them and many other scientists on the Left who followed the erratic agendas of the Communist Party of Great Britain or the Comintern, Needham was able to prioritize the activity of help to victims of Fascism and to limit his infatuation with Marxism to philosophical rhetoric. Needham was considered to be one of top five Leftist public intellectuals in the 1930s (Werskey, 1978); he delivered his message via extensive writings, which provided a moderate form of intellectual leadership in a historical time of great need.

Science Statesman in the International Arena. During the 1940s, Needham served as scientific director of the Chinese-British mission in unoccupied China and as a liaison with European organizations of international science cooperation that planned the United Nations Educational, Scientific, and Cultural Organization (UNESCO) at the end of World War II. From 1942 to 1946 he oversaw a British effort to help unoccupied China maintain its scientific activity despite the hardship of the Japanese occupation of parts of China. Needham's mission employed ten British and sixteen Chinese, who distributed scientific books and equipment, "imported" from India by Royal Air Force planes "commuting" over the Himalayas, to remote sites all over vast China. He thus came to be perceived as a friend of Chinese scientists in their greatest hour of need and was recognized with widespread gratitude and various honors, including membership in the Academia Sinica. Needham used his diplomatic mission in China during World War II to become acquainted with people, books, manuscripts, and technical devices that he would later integrate in his multivolume study of science in China. Needham's wartime experience in China served as a blueprint for his later role in the period of 1946–1948 as director of UNESCO's Natural Science Division. He was also responsible for

Needham

adding scientific concerns (the "S") to UNESCO's initial cultural and educational mandates.

Scholar of the History of Chinese Science. The second half of Needham's life was devoted to a pioneering study of the history of Chinese science and its comparative relationship to Western science. His monumental, multivolume studies, *Science and Civilization in China* (1954), fostered a crucial sense of intellectual parity between East and West. This work is of a unique magnitude, with twenty volumes in print, while covering a wide variety of subjects including astronomy, alchemy, and chemistry, botany, agriculture, metallurgy, and numerous other subjects.

It is tempting to accept Lu Gwei-Djen's somewhat teleological account (1982) of Needham's biography, namely that all the versatile experiences accumulated by Needham until he turned to his monumental and comparative study of Chinese science had an eventual purpose—to serve as building blocks in this unprecedented and most amazing undertaking of seeking to cover a vast civilization while doing so from a comparative perspective and from an outlook of intellectual parity. Despite methodological and historiographical debates surrounding Needham's undertaking (Habib & Raina, 1999), the work continues to serve as a reference point to all scholars of Chinese or any other non-Western science.

However, Needham's vision of East-West parity, and his persistence in implementing it over half a century, will continue to inspire future scholars. Safely enshrined at the Needham Research Institute in Cambridge, U.K. (http://www.nri.org.uk), with an endowment contributed by both governmental and private donors, Needham's life work has gone a long way since his initial impulse to escape the absolutism of Western religion led him to pursue the greener pastures of Taoist moderation and relativism. He was fortunate to live long enough to see his one-time dream of East-West cultural parity materialize and contribute to world harmony.

Mentor of International Scholars. Needham understood the importance of mentoring younger scholars and was invariably helpful with valuable tips needed for coping with the complexities of academic life at Cambridge University, a life he knew only too well for seven decades. Among the international scholars Needham cultivated were Mikulas Teich, a historian of biochemistry who arrived in the United Kingdom as a refugee from the Soviet invasion of Prague in 1968, and who shaped, together with leading British historians of science such as Robert Young and Roy Porter, many historiographic fronts, as well as Gary Werskey, Donna Haraway, and Pnina Abir-Am, whose PhD theses included chapters on Needham's work in the interwar period. Other scholars, too many to enumerate, benefited from Needham's mentorship, while contributing to his multivolume enterprise, *Science and Civilization in China.*

Yet another key aspect of Needham's unique persona that must be mentioned, and indeed better researched, is his productive collaboration with his two wives, Dorothy Mary Moyle Needham, whom he married in 1924, and Lu Gwei-Djen, whom he married in 1990, following Dorothy's death in 1987. Both women took their PhD in biochemistry at Cambridge University, with Lu arriving there in 1937 to work in Dorothy Moyle Needham's laboratory. Though both women maintained independent careers, they also collaborated significantly with Joseph Needham, while making indispensable contributions to his two major projects in science and in history of science, respectively.

For example, Joseph Needham's ability in the 1930s to conduct a demanding research project in physicochemical morphology at a time he was also engaged in teaching, writing large books, lecturing, and leading social activism depended on Dorothy Moyle Needham's experimental skills, her constant presence in the laboratory, and her willingness to put her work aside during the collaboration on the "organizer." Moyle Needham remained all her life in the Department of Biochemistry at Cambridge, where she focused on the biochemistry of muscle contraction; she was among the first women to be elected to the Royal Society, in 1948, and was a Fellow of New Hall, a women's college established in Cambridge after World War II. Joseph Needham's election to the Royal Society in 1941 was thus endebted to Dorothy Moyle Needham's steady collaboration during the 1930s.

Similarly, Lu conducted research in the United States and Europe in the 1940s and 1950s, joining Needham as a long-term collaborator and project associate director for three decades in the 1960s. She became a foundation Fellow of Robinson College, the first coeducational college in Cambridge, which Needham was instrumental in establishing. At the same time, Needham's vast undertaking in the history of Chinese science is inconceivable without the contributions of Lu Gwei-Djen, who not only stimulated his forays into the unknown territory of Chinese science and civilization, as early as 1937, but who also served as an ongoing resource of Chinese language, culture, and contacts, until she formally joined his project as a collaborator.

By the standards of postwar era Needham appears to have been more egalitarian regarding class, race, and gender than most members of his generation. His collaborative authorship with each wife reflected the socialist ideals of intellectual and marital partnership, though it seems that he was the partner who most benefited from such

Needham

cross-gender collaborative ventures, undertaken as they were, under conditions of patriarchy, in the absence of children-based families, as well as in the golden shadow of Cambridge University privileged lifestyle as a don, and later master, of an ancient and prestigious college.

Needham's vast work and challenging personal life will no doubt continue to attract attention from historians of science. His meticulous habit of leaving clearly written traces will greatly help in discerning the origins of such unique visions and passions as bridging biochemistry and embryology, science and religion, science and ideology, Europe and China, or East and West.

BIBLIOGRAPHY

Needham's personal papers (and correspondence) are available for consultation at the Cambridge University Library, The Manuscripts Room, West Road, Cambridge, U.K. A paper catalog is available there; an online catalog is available at http://wwwa2a.org.uk/html/NCUAS, as is the case with all cataloged collections of British scientists who are Fellows of the Royal Society. The most complete bibliography is the one included in Needham's 80th anniversary volume, compiled by Lu Gwei-Djen in Explorations in the History of Science and Technology in China, *Special Number in Honor of J. Needham's eightieth birthday, edited by Tao-Ching [also spelled Daojing] Hu, pp. 703–720. Shanghai: Shanghai Chinese Classics Publishing House, 1982.*

WORKS BY NEEDHAM

"The Philosophical Basis of Biochemistry." *Monist 35* (1925): 27–48.

Chemical Embryology. 3 vols. Cambridge, U.K.: Cambridge University Press, 1931.

Order and Life. New Haven, CT: Yale University Press, 1936; Cambridge, MA: MIT Press, 1968.

With David E. Green, eds. *Perspectives in Biochemistry: 31 Essays Presented to Sir Frederick Gowland Hopkins on the Occasion of His 75th Birthday.* Cambridge, U.K.: Cambridge University Press, 1938.

Time, the Refreshing River. London: Allen & Unwin, 1943.

History Is on Our Side, a Contribution to Political Religion and Scientific Faith. London: Allen & Unwin, 1946.

With Ernest Baldwin, eds. *Hopkins and Biochemistry.* Cambridge, U.K.: Cambridge University Press, 1949.

Science and Civilization in China. Cambridge, U.K.: Cambridge University Press, 1954–present; early volumes authored alone; later volumes coauthored with collaborators; more than 20 volumes are now in print; titles can be viewed on the Web site on the Needham Research Institute, Cambridge, available from http://www.nri.org.uk/science.html.

"Preface" to *Science at the Cross Roads,* pp. vii–x, by Nikolai Bukharin et al. 2nd ed. London: Frank Cass, 1971. The first edition was published in 1931, in London, by Kniga, within 10 days of the 2nd Congress, and had no preface.

With Lu Gwei-Djen. *Science in Traditional China.* Cambridge, MA: Harvard University Press, 1981.

"The Making of a Honorary Taoist" (under pseudonym of Henry Holorenshaw). In *Changing Perspective in the History of Science,* edited by Mikulas Teich and Robert Young, 1–20. London: Heinemann, 1973.

OTHER SOURCES

Abir-Am, Pnina G. "Recasting the Disciplinary Order in Science: A Deconstruction of Rhetoric on 'Biology and Physics' at Two International Congresses in 1931." *Humanity and Society 9* (November 1985): 388–427.

———. "The Biotheoretical Gathering, Transdisciplinary Authority and the Incipient Legitimation of Molecular Biology in the 1930s: New Perspective on the Historical Sociology of Science." *History of Science* 25 (March 1987): 1–70.

———. "The Philosophical Background of Joseph Needham's Work in Chemical Embryology, 1925–1942." In *Conceptual History of Modern Embryology,* edited by S. Gilbert, 159–180. New York: Plenum Press, 1991.

Allen, Garland A. "Inducers and 'Organizers': Hans Spemann and Experimental Embryology." *History and Philosophy of Life Sciences* 15 (1993): 229–236. Essay review of Hamburger, 1988.

Bayertz, Kurt, and Roy Porter, eds. *From Physico-theology to Bio-technology: Essays in the Social and Cultural History of Biosciences, A Festschrift for Mikulas Teich's 80th Birthday.* Amsterdam: Rodopi, 1998.

Habib, S. Irfan, and Dhruv Raina, eds. *Situating the History of Science: Dialogues with Joseph Needham.* Oxford: Oxford University Press, 1999.

Hamburger, Viktor. *The Heritage of Experimental Embryology.* New York: Oxford University Press, 1988.

Haraway, Donna J. *Crystals, Fabrics, and Fields, Metaphors of Organicism in 20th Century Development Biology.* New Haven, CT: Yale University Press, 1976.

Hsu, Elisabeth, ed. *Innovation in Chinese Medicine. Festschrift in Commemoration of Lu Gwei-djen.* Cambridge, U.K.: Cambridge University Press, 2001.

Hu Tao-Ching [also spelled Daojing], ed. *Explorations in the History of Science and Technology in China,* Special Number in Honor of J. Needham's eightieth birthday. Shanghai: Shanghai Chinese Classics Publishing House, 1982.

Kamminga, Harmke, and Mark W. Weatherall. "The Making of a Biochemist." *Medical History* 40, nos. 1–2 (1996a, b): 269–292, 415–436.

Lu Gwei-Djen. "The First Half-Life of Joseph Needham." In *Explorations in the History of Science and Technology in China,* edited by Tao-Ching [also spelled Daojing] Hu, 1–38. Shanghai: Shanghai Chinese Classics Publishing House, 1982. Volume in honor of J. Needham's eightieth birthday.

Stephenson, Marjory. "Frederick Gowland Hopkins, 1861–1947." *Biochemical Journal* 42 (1948): 161–170.

Teich, Mikulas. "From 'Enchyme' to 'Cytoskeleton': The Development of Ideas on the Chemical Organization of Living Matter." In *Changing Perspectives in the History of Science,* edited by Mikulas Teich and Robert M. Young, 439–471. London: Heineman, 1973.

Neel

———. "How It All Began? From the Enlightenment in National Context to Revolutions in History." *History of Science* 51 (2003): 335–343.

Teich, Mikulas, and Robert M. Young, eds. *Changing Perspectives in the History of Science.* London: Heinemann, 1973. A Festschrift volume dedicated to Needham's seventieth birthday.

Teich, Mikulas, and Roy Porter, eds. *The National Question in Europe in Historical Context.* Cambridge, U.K.: Cambridge University Press, 1993.

———. *The Industrial Revolution in National Context.* Cambridge, U.K.: Cambridge University Press, 1996.

Teich, Mikulas, Roy Porter, and Bengt Gustafsson, eds. *Nature and Society in Historical Context.* Cambridge, U.K.: Cambridge University Press, 1997.

Werskey, Gary. "Introduction" to *Science at the Cross Roads,* by Bukharin et al., pp. xi–xxix. 2nd ed. London: Frank Cass, 1971. The first edition was published in 1931 by Kniga in London.

———. "Understanding Needham." Introduction to Needham's *Moulds of Understanding, a Pattern of Natural Philosophy,* edited by Gary Werskey, 13–28. London: Allen & Unwin, 1976.

———. *The Visible College: A Collective Biography of British Scientists and Socialists of the 1930s.* London: Allen Lane, 1978.

Pnina G. Abir-Am

NEEL, JAMES VAN GUNDIA (*b.* Hamilton, Ohio, 22 March 1915; *d.* Ann Arbor, Michigan, 1 February 2000), *human genetics, radiation genetics, human mutation research, population genetics, genetics and public policy.*

Neel was a founding member of the American Society of Human Genetics and played a critical role in the scientific and institutional development of human and medical genetics in the United States; he directed the program assessing the genetic effects of radiation on the offspring of survivors after the use of the atomic bomb in 1945; he created the Department of Human Genetics at the University of Michigan in 1956, one of the first such departments in the United States, and he chaired it for twenty-five years. An interdisciplinary thinker, with an interest in the relevance of genetic data to public policy, his work often addressed the biological and cultural future of the human species. His 1960s work with the anthropologist Napoleon Chagnon among the Yanomami Indians in Venezuela became the subject of a major international controversy shortly after his death.

Early Life. James Van Gundia Neel (known as Jim) was born into a middle-class household in March 1915. When he was ten years old his father, Hiram Alexander Neel, died of pneumonia, and his mother, Elizabeth Minette Van Gundia Neel, moved with her three children from Detroit to Wooster, Ohio. For financial reasons a college education was not assured, but a scholarship to the College of Wooster made it possible and at Wooster he had the opportunity to study with the *Drosophila* geneticist Warren Spencer. Spencer's teaching shaped Neel's intellectual interests and professional future. In 1935 he went immediately from his undergraduate studies at Wooster to the University of Rochester, where he became the first American graduate student of the recent German émigré Curt Stern, another critical figure in the development of human genetics in the United States. (Neel's obituary of Stern is cited below.)

Neel's 1939 thesis at Rochester looked at temperature effects on gene expression. Using flies with abnormal patterns of bristles (hairlike appendages), he was able to characterize mathematical relationships between body size, bristle number, and known mutant gene forms. Even as he was completing this project, however, Neel was thinking of human genetics. As a graduate student he had taken three medical school courses (including anatomy) and had convinced Stern to offer a graduate seminar in human genetics. (Stern later wrote a textbook of human genetics, partially inspired by the keen interest of his student.) Neel did not immediately turn to human studies upon the completion of his PhD, however. On Stern's advice, and with some reluctance, he accepted a position as an instructor in biology at Dartmouth College, going there in the fall of 1939. He stayed at Dartmouth two years.

In the fall of 1941 he was awarded a National Research Council fellowship to study at Columbia University with the prominent geneticists Theodosius Dobzhansky and Leslie Clarence Dunn. There Neel completed his first major scientific publication on a highly mutating line of flies (1942). It was also at Columbia that he made the decision to earn a medical degree: if he was going to study human heredity, he reasoned, he should understand human disease, abnormality, physiology, and anatomy. Concerned about the impending U.S. entry into World War II, he also believed that a physician could do more to help his country than a geneticist. He applied to the University of Rochester medical school just before the Japanese attack on Pearl Harbor of 7 December 1941, and he became a student there in the summer of 1942.

In October 1942, in Rochester, he met Priscilla Baxter, a recent graduate of the Smith School of Architecture in Cambridge, Massachusetts, then working as a mechanical designer at the Stromberg-Carlson Company. In May 1943 they were married, and they later had three children.

All medical students not exempted from service for physical reasons were given military commissions during

Neel

the war. Due to the accelerated wartime pace of medical education, Neel completed his medical education at Rochester in September 1944, and became an assistant resident in medicine at Strong Memorial Hospital. Neel was the only member of the early group of scientific human geneticists in the United States to choose to earn both an MD and a PhD. Some influential students of human heredity in this period, such as Victor McKusick, were skilled clinicians with no formal training in laboratory genetics; others, such as H. J. Muller, were experienced Drosophilists who extrapolated from their work with flies to comment about human heredity. But Neel was both a physician and a geneticist, and his work reflected his commitments to both the laboratory and the clinic.

In 1945 Neel accepted a position at the University of Michigan at Ann Arbor, where he was to remain for the rest of his life. In 1947 he was one of the key participants in the creation of the American Society of Human Genetics, which formally came into being in 1948. He wrote the first paper to be published in the new society's journal, the *American Journal of Human Genetics,* and he served the society as a member of the board of directors (1948–1950 and 1968–1970), vice president (1952–1953 and 1955–1957), and president (1953–1954).

One of his first major contributions to human genetics elucidated the nature of the inheritance of a complex genetic disease, sickle-cell anemia. Early work on thalassemia during his medical school days had alerted him to the possible importance of carrier states that result in a milder form of the full-blown disease. In 1948, he began working with African American populations in Detroit to understand an apparently similar genetic system. In his 1949 paper in *Science,* Neel demonstrated that the two forms of the disease, one mild, one disabling, reflected either heterozygosity or homozygosity for a single gene. Sickle-cell anemia, he demonstrated, was a classic Mendelian trait in which the heterozygous form had phenotypic effects, and the homozygous form constituted full-scale sickle-cell disease. Neel's paper appeared in the same issue of *Science* in which sickle-cell anemia was characterized by Linus Pauling and his coworkers as a "molecular disease," after they showed that the hemoglobin molecule in patients with the disease is characteristically elongated, thus producing the sickling of the cells.

In 1954 Anthony Allison demonstrated that sickle-cell trait, the heterozygous condition, conferred early immunity to a form of malaria endemic in Africa. This explained why the trait, and also the disease, were so common in populations historically living in malarial regions: those with sickle-cell trait had a survival advantage at an early age. Neel thus contributed significant insights to the understanding of a disease that remains the most compelling human example of what is called overdominance, or the heterozygote advantage, the condition in which a heterozygous genotype has a higher relative fitness than either homozygous form.

Atomic Bomb Studies. Before the atomic bombs were dropped on Hiroshima and Nagasaki, Japan, on 6 and 9 August 1945, plans for studies of their physical effects on buildings and urban structures were already in place. But plans for studies of their biomedical effects on survivors were sketchy at best, partly because many of those involved in planning the use of these weapons did not expect that anyone heavily irradiated would survive the bombings.

Radiation was known to have biological effects, including genetic effects, as H. J. Muller had demonstrated with his studies of irradiated fruit flies in 1927, and some of those involved in the project to build the atomic bomb, code-named the Manhattan Engineering District, had been exposed to levels of radiation that produced illness or even death. (The physicist Louis Slotin died from the effects of a 1946 radiation burst at Los Alamos.) Secret research on the biological effects of radiation had been undertaken in several places during the war, including at the University of Rochester, where Neel was then a medical student, and Neel was vaguely aware that some secret work relating to radiation was underway there. Just after the bombings, he told a colleague who had been involved in the Manhattan Engineering District unit at Rochester that he would be interested in assessing the genetic effects of the bombs on survivors in Japan. This comment, apparently somewhat casual, eventually led to his appointment to carry out an exploratory visit to Japan as a medical corps lieutenant in November 1946.

By the spring of 1947, Neel was planning and directing the genetics study of what came to be known as the Atomic Bomb Casualty Commission (ABCC). He began a lifelong affiliation with the scientific study of the survivors, which continued long after his full-time work in Japan ended. Michigan was his base, but he returned to Japan regularly and continued to publish on the atomic bomb survivors and on other Japanese populations. The ABCC was a long-term, interdisciplinary U.S. study of the health of the atomic bomb survivors and their offspring, organized and overseen by the National Academy of Sciences, and funded by the new Atomic Energy Commission. With American, British, Australian, and Japanese staff at laboratories in Hiroshima, Nagasaki, and a "control" city, Kure, the ABCC examined survivors every year or so, tracking their illnesses and attempting to determine their risks as a result of exposure to radiation.

Neel's genetics study involved examining every baby born to atomic bomb survivors, looking for abnormalities

Neel

of structure or function, and determining whether these abnormalities were the result of mutation. The method involved comparing survivors with a statistically matched group of offspring from parents who had not been exposed to the atomic bombings. This would be a difficult assignment under any circumstances, in postwar Japan made even more difficult by virtue of the sometimes-strained social relationships between local residents and the occupying Allied forces, and the sensitivity of the questions addressed by the genetics research. Many Japanese expressed anger over the use of the atomic bombs by the United States, and the studies conducted primarily by American scientists and physicians were the subject of intermittent controversy for three decades. In 1975 the ABCC was renamed the Radiation Effects Research Foundation, and reorganized as a joint Japanese-U.S. program with more balanced funding and participation.

Neel's genetics work in Japan, much of it carried out with his coauthor, the geneticist William J. (Jack) Schull, who joined him in Japan and in Ann Arbor in 1949, was both empirically rich and frustratingly inconclusive. In papers and reports spanning almost fifty years, Neel, Schull, and their colleagues attempted to construct compelling quantitative data about radiation risk for heritable mutations. As new technologies appeared—computing, electrophoresis, molecular genetics, and gene mapping—they were applied to the Japanese materials. But genetic effects remained elusive and unclear, and as several observers have noted, the most striking result of fifty years of work on these questions is that there is in no instance a statistically significant effect of parental exposure, in any of their studies (Schull et al., 1981). While compelling evidence of elevated cancer risk in the affected population emerged quickly, evidence for genetic effects was never clear or robust. The data from Japan at times even seemed to suggest that human beings were less sensitive to the mutagenic effects of radiation than were mice or flies, the primary experimental organisms used in radiation experiments (Neel and Schull, 1956; Neel and Lewis, 1990).

The work on the survivors produced data that were widely recognized as the most important available on the genetic effects of radiation in human beings, and that played an important role in the global, long-term assessment of radiation risk and the establishment of radiation protection standards. Neel and others involved in the study knew when it began that they would be looking not for unique radiation effects, but only for a possible slight increase in the types of defects that would normally appear in any population. They also knew that the numbers might be too low to yield statistically significant genetic results. They were convinced, however, that it was important to undertake the study regardless, because of the high public stakes in accurate scientific data about radiation risk.

In his 1994 autobiography, Neel identified the attempt to understand the genetic effects of radiation as one the most significant points of intersection between the science of genetics and societal concerns, and as the most comprehensive project in genetic epidemiology ever undertaken (p. 246). Certainly it was an unusual opportunity to test theories about mutation against the realities of human exposure to a known mutagenic agent.

The Thrifty Genotype and Amerindian Work. In the late 1950s, Neel's interests in human evolution led him to consider how environmental changes could transform a genetic trait from an advantage to a disease. His 1962 paper on diabetes mellitus as a "thrifty genotype" remains a key source for work in genetic epidemiology and is still frequently cited. It outlined one of his most provocative lines of research.

In that paper, Neel proposed that some modern diseases that seem to be obviously disadvantageous might have facilitated survival at one time in human evolution. In other words, an evolutionary strength could become, under different circumstances, a disease. His key example was non-insulin-dependent diabetes, a disease that even by 1960 was becoming a public health problem in the industrialized world. Neel suggested that the quick insulin trigger in this form of diabetes was a practical asset to people living on feast-or-famine regimes. With a near-starvation diet, the ability to conserve glucose is a major asset. If the pancreas secretes insulin quickly in response to elevated blood sugar, then glucose loss is minimized, which would be important to people with intermittently severe dietary restrictions. But with the rise of urbanized and industrialized societies, and an overabundance of access to food, this quick response became problematic. Neel and other observers made the comparison to sickle-cell anemia: perhaps the gene facilitating quick insulin response was most advantageous in the heterozygous form, a circumstance that would preserve the gene in the general population and explain the rising risk of diabetes in prosperous, well-fed populations. Since 1962, Neel's thrifty genotype has been invoked frequently to explain the epidemics of obesity and non-insulin-dependent diabetes in populations all over the world.

In 1962, the same year that he published on the thrifty genotype, Neel traveled to Brazil to carry out his first fieldwork with isolated populations in South America. Neel may have been interested in South American Indians before 1955, but his relationship to Francisco Salzano played a critical role in the initiation of actual field research in Brazil, which then led to other studies in Panama, Costa Rica, and Venezuela. Salzano, a *Drosophila* geneticist then at the University of Rio Grande do Sul, came to Neel's laboratory with a Rockefeller Foundation grant to study human heredity. One of his projects during his year in Ann Arbor was to prepare a summary paper on studies of Amerindian groups, and this paper, published in 1957, suggested some of the inadequacies of earlier studies, which generally dealt only with comparative blood grouping. Human population genetics research, Salzano and Neel agreed, should be much broader, encompassing studies of disease pressure, social practices of reproduction, diet, and environmental risks. The selection pressures shaping the lives and health of isolated populations, Neel proposed, provided some insight into the circumstances of human evolution.

Neel commonly invoked the threat of "civilization" as an urgent justification for his Amerindian studies. He said that the relatively few remaining primitive populations of the world were so rapidly being disrupted that his generation was almost surely the last to encounter any such groups in relatively undisturbed condition. He was also attracted to the "vanishing world" of the Amerindian, interpreting the grueling fieldwork that he undertook in remote and difficult-to-reach locations as a test of his own character.

For about thirty years, Neel and his colleagues and students from Ann Arbor carried out work in a large number of Yanomami villages, and with about twenty other tribes in South and Central America. The work was supported by the Atomic Energy Commission, which had also been paying for the work in Japan, on the premise that isolated populations, living in environments relatively free of industrial pollutants, could provide data about the elusive "natural" mutation rate of human populations. One result was the collection of about fifteen thousand blood samples, which revealed an unexpectedly high level of genetic variation in such isolated populations. Human genetic diversity, Neel's work suggested, was maintained even in small groups, presumably by practices of kinship and marriage among local villages. Neel also proposed that the physiology of these remote groups was rapidly changing. The most isolated populations had radically lower blood pressure and glucose levels and very different patterns of infectious disease ecology, when compared with more urban populations.

In 1970 the work in Venezuela became the subject of one of the most widely used teaching films in the discipline of anthropology: *The Yanomamo: A Multidisciplinary Study*, a film favored by anthropologists to introduce generations of college students to fieldwork. Neel features prominently in the forty-five-minute film, as both narrator and participant. He tells the story of a trip to a village, the diets and habits of its inhabitants, and the research undertaken there. Accompanying him, and featured in the film, is the young cultural anthropologist Napoleon Chagnon, who began his work in the Amazon while he was a graduate student at the University of Michigan.

The Controversy over the Yanomami. Neel had the distinction of becoming, only a few months after his death, the focus of a major international controversy. It was sparked by the journalist Patrick Tierney's book, *Darkness in El Dorado: How Scientists and Journalists Devastated the Amazon* (2000), in which Tierney proposed that Neel, Chagnon, and other scientists working with isolated populations had engaged in unethical and even murderous behavior. Tierney claimed that Neel had intentionally used a "virulent" and outdated form of vaccine during a 1968 field trip to study the Yanomami living along the Orinoco River. Neel allegedly wanted to produce a measles outbreak that would provide a field test of his theories about the differential survival under disease pressure of those with male dominance genes.

Compelling evidence that the epidemic began before Neel reached the field, and that he provided rapid and responsible medical care to those affected, was very soon made public. Tierney's claims about the vaccine itself were also quickly refuted by an appeal to scientific reports and documents from 1968, and by testimony from contemporary immunologists familiar with the vaccine used. Colleagues who had worked closely with Neel in South America testified to his humane treatment of those he studied, as did his own meticulous field notes, correspondence, and other archival materials. Public criticism of Neel was rapidly tempered, but the controversy itself, later focusing much more on Chagnon, continued to unfold. Organizations such as the National Academy of Sciences and the American Anthropological Association produced major reports about it, and it became the impetus for a widening debate about the proper treatment of populations under study around the world. An influential and respected researcher, the winner of numerous honors and awards, Neel became perhaps most famous for his role in this controversy some seven months after his death.

Geneticist Who Emphasized Environment. Throughout his career Neel was markedly productive, publishing more than 650 articles and 10 books. These included a widely used textbook of human genetics, written with Schull (1954), an autobiography (1994), and several book-length reports about his work with populations in Japan (1956, 1965, 1991). He was a major force in shaping the field of human genetics through his teaching, his mentoring of postdoctoral students, and his public role in society. His honors included the Lasker and Allen Awards, the National Medal of Science, and membership in the National Academy of Sciences.

Unlike a later generation of scientists interested in human genetics, Neel was resolutely convinced that genetic health depended not on mining disease genes, but on improving the human environment. He sought to understand heredity as a guide to understanding how the environment should be organized so as to facilitate human health. In a 1974 lecture Neel observed that there was growing evidence that malnutrition in the early years of life affects intelligence. He proposed that if it is true that better nutrition improves intellectual performance, then any nation would have much more to gain from feeding its children well than it could possibly gain from conquering a dozen genetic diseases. The claim was an implicit criticism of the growing emphasis in human genetics on identifying disease genes, an emphasis that grew only more intense with the rise of the biotechnology industry and the Human Genome Project.

Neel was a complicated twentieth-century figure, a scientist who was interested in addressing major, and often sensitive, questions about evolution, human population genetics, and the human future. He became a human geneticist in the wake of eugenics, even writing an early paper based on data about the inheritance of red hair that he collected at the Eugenics Records Office in Cold Spring Harbor, New York. By the time of his death in 2000, the "complete" human genome had been mapped and genomic medicine was a social and political reality. His life thus spanned a period of dramatic and important scientific change, during which the field he chose became central to public support of the biological sciences and to the biotechnology industry. He was in some ways resistant to these changes, less interested in mapping genes than in understanding gene-environment interactions.

BIBLIOGRAPHY

Neel's papers, including a complete bibliography of his publications, are held primarily at the American Philosophical Society in Philadelphia. Other materials relevant to his work are held in the ABCC collection at the Houston Academy of Medicine–Texas Medical Center Library, in the Bentley Historical Library at the University of Michgan at Ann Arbor, and in the archives of the National Academy of Sciences in Washington, DC.

WORKS BY NEEL

"A Study of a Case of High Mutation Rate in *Drosophila Melanogaster.*" *Genetics* 27 (1942): 519–536.

"The Inheritance of Sickle Cell Anemia." *Science,* n.s., 110 (1949): 64–69.

With William J. Schull. *Human Heredity.* Chicago: University of Chicago Press, 1954.

With William J. Schull. *The Effect of Exposure to the Atomic Bombs on Pregnancy Termination in Hiroshima and Nagasaki.* National Academy of Sciences–National Research Council Publication 461. Washington, DC: National Academy of Sciences–National Research Council, 1956.

"Diabetes Mellitus: A 'Thrifty' Genotype Rendered Detrimental by 'Progress'?" *American Journal of Human Genetics* 14 (1962): 353–362.

With William J. Schull. *The Effects of Inbreeding on Japanese Children.* New York: Harper and Row, 1965.

"Our Twenty-Fifth." *American Journal of Human Genetics* 26 (1974): 136–144.

With William J. Schull and Masanori Otake. "Genetic Effects of the Atomic Bombs: A Reappraisal." *Science* 213 (1981): 1220–1227.

"Curt Stern, 1902–1981." *Annual Review of Genetics* 17 (December 1983): 1–11.

With Susan E. Lewis. "The Comparative Radiation Genetics of Humans and Mice." *Annual Review of Genetics* 24 (1990): 327–362.

With William J. Schull. *The Children of Atomic Bomb Survivors: A Genetic Study.* Washington, DC: National Academy Press, 1991.

Physician to the Gene Pool. New York: John Wiley, 1994.

OTHER SOURCES

Crow, James F. "Jim Neel—Some Memories." *Mutation Research* 543 (2003): 93–96.

Lindee, M. Susan. *Suffering Made Real: American Science and the Survivors at Hiroshima.* Chicago: University of Chicago Press, 1994.

———. "Voices of the Dead: James Neel's Amerindian Studies." In *Lost Paradises and the Ethics of Research and Publication,* edited by Francisco M. Salzano and A. Magdalena Hurtado. Oxford: Oxford University Press, 2004.

Morton, Newton E. "Darkness in El Dorado: Human Genetics on Trial." *Journal of Genetics* 80 (2001): 45–52.

———. "Recollections of James Neel." *Mutation Research* 543 (2003): 97–104.

Pauling, Linus, Harvey A. Itano, S. J. Singer, and Ibert C. Wells. "Sickle Cell Anemia: A Molecular Disease." *Science* 110 (1949): 543–548.

Salzano, Francisco M. "The Blood Groups of South American Indians." *American Journal of Physical Anthropology* 15 (1957): 555–579.

———. "James V. Neel and Latin America—Or How Scientific Collaboration Should Be Conducted." *Genetics and Molecular Biology* 23, no. 3 (2000): 557–561.

Santos, Ricardo Ventura. "Indigenous Peoples, Postcolonial Contexts and Genomic Research in the Late 20th Century: A View from Amazonia." *Critique of Anthropology* 22, no. 1 (2002): 81–104.

Schull, William J. "James Van Gundia Neel, March 22, 1915–February 1, 2000." In *Biographical Memoirs,* vol. 81. Washington, DC: National Academy of Sciences, 2002.

Tierney, Patrick. *Darkness in El Dorado: How Scientists and Journalists Devastated the Amazon.* New York: W.W. Norton, 2000.

Weiss, Kenneth M., and R. H. Ward. "Obituary. James V. Neel, MD, PhD (March 22, 1915–January 31, 2000): Founder

Effect." *American Journal of Human Genetics* 66 (2000): 755–760.

M. Susan Lindee

NESMEJANOV, ALEKSANDR NIKOLAEVICH

(*b.* Moscow, Russia, 9 September (28 August old Russian style) 1899; *d.* Moscow, U.S.S.R., 17 January 1980), *chemistry, organometallic chemistry.*

Nesmejanov specialized in developing methods of synthesis and studying properties of organometallic compounds; developing new organic syntheses based on reactions of β-chlorvinylketones and polyhalogenated aliphatic compounds; understanding the dual reactivity and stereochemistry of electrophilic substitution; and developing methods to create artificial foods.

Early Research. His father, Nikolai Vasilyevich Nesmejanov, a graduate of the law faculty of Moscow University, was a principal at an orphanage. His mother, Luidmila Danilovna Nesmejanova , who was also involved in teaching, had a talent for painting and decorative arts. Under his mother's influence Nesmejanov was attracted to botany and natural sciences in general since childhood. In 1908, he entered a private gymnasium (secondary school), while studying Latin and Greek with his father in the evenings. In 1917, he started his university studies in the Physics and Mathematics Faculty of Moscow University. He worked all through his university years: as a night guard in the Chemistry Faculty and as a laboratory assistant in the Military Pedagogical Academy. In 1922, Nesmejanov graduated with a degree in physical chemistry, and accepted Nikolay D. Zelinsky's offer of a position in the Department of Organic Chemistry to prepare for a doctoral degree.

Zelinsky gave his protégé a topic for his first scientific research, a study of the derivatives of cyclopropane. After a few years of investigation, Nesmejanov created his own task: to find esters of complex acids of type $HHg^{II}I_3$ and $HPb^{II}I_2$.

Nesmejanov's interest in mercury compounds was connected to his experience in a chemical pesticide laboratory where he served as a technician in the late 1920s. As is well known, many mercury compounds were used to protect seeds from pests. Nesmejanov was forced to work in appalling conditions—there was one desk and a single fume hood for the entire laboratory. Evenings he spent fighting rats. According to his assistant, Nesmejanov worked in the lab "very bravely: for example, he heated a bulb of organic material over an open flame, … however if solvent vapors caught fire he always managed to extinguish it, by blowing on it" (Makarova, 1988, p. 192).

It was known that attempts to combine, for example, CH_3I and HgI_2 directly came to nothing. The young scientist then decided to decompose phenyldiazonium salts of the abovementioned complex acids. Successful decomposition of $[C_6H_5N_2]HgI_3$ in 1929 led to development of a new general synthetic approach in organic chemistry: obtaining organometallic compounds by decomposing double diazonium salts with metal halides ("Nesmejanov's diazomethod"). This method allowed for introduction of a metal atom into a predetermined position in an organic molecule. With aid of this technique scientists were able to synthesize many organometallic compounds, which in turn served as parent substances for preparing various classes of hetero-organic compounds (i.e., compounds with metal-carbon bonds).

During the 1935–1948 period, Nesmejanov and his students investigated many ways of interconverting various organometallic compounds, particularly mutual transitions between organomercurials and organic compounds of main group metals such as magnesium, zinc, cadmium, aluminum, thallium, and tin. The wide array of experimental data that was assembled during the course of these investigations led to a relationship between the position of an element in the periodic table and its ability to form organic derivatives.

Nesmejanov also studied geometrical isomerism in organometallic derivatives of ethylene. He was able to produce β-chlorvinyl derivatives of elements such as mercury, antimony, tin, and tantalum in a pure state. This work led to one of the most important rules of stereochemistry, that of retention of stereochemical configuration in processes of electrophilic and radical substitution at the carbon atom of the carbon–carbon double bond.

Nesmejanov also paid particular attention to the properties and structures of addition products of transition metal salts and nonmetal halogenides to unsaturated organic compounds. He proved that such products are true hetero-organic compounds (i.e., they have metal–carbon bonds).

From 1950 to 1959, Nesmejanov conducted a series of field studies of β-chlorvinylketones chemistry (together with Nikolai K. Kochetkov and Margarita I. Rubinskaya), and of organophosphorus, organofluorine and organomagnesium compounds. In 1960, he discovered the phenomenon of metallotropy: the reversible transfer of an organomercury unit between hydroxy and nitroso groups in *para*-nitrosophenol.

In addition to issues concerning organic synthesis, Nesmejanov spent a lot of time on the theory of organic chemistry. For example, it was known that metals and

Nesmejanov

their salts could add to multiple carbon-carbon bond, for example

$$HC\equiv CH + HgCl_2 \rightarrow ClCH{=}CHHgCl.$$

Nesmejanov called the resulting compounds quasi-complex compounds. A key characteristic of such compounds was their dual reactivity, i.e. their ability, when bound with different, and sometimes even with the same reagents, to produce products of different structural types. For example:

$$ClCH{=}CHHgCl + HBr \rightarrow ClCH{=}CH_2 + HgClBr,\ ClCH{=}CHHgCl + 3KJ \rightarrow C_2H_2 + KHgl_3 + 2KCl.$$

Theoretically, one of the reasons for such behavior of the quasi-complex compounds could be the existence of an equilibrium between organometallic and additive compounds of acetylene with mercuric chloride:

$$ClCH{=}CHHgClC_2H_2{\cdot}HgCl_2$$

However, the investigations conducted by Nesmejanov and his collaborators demonstrated that β-chlorvinyl derivatives of heavy main group metals are actually organometallic compounds, containing multiple carbon-carbon bonds. Then in 1949 Nesmejanov offered a theory according to which dual reactivity of such compounds was due to σ,σ-conjugation between the carbon-mercury bond and carbon-chlorine bond, i.e. by the shift of electronic density of the following type:

$$ClHg{-}HC{=}CH{-}Cl$$

From 1950 to 1959, Nesmejanov together with Nicolai K. Kochetkov conducted a series of experiments dedicated to the reactivity of β-chlorvinylketones, which found application as convenient primary substances for the synthesis of aliphatic, aromatic, and heterocyclic compounds, particularly pyrazoles, pyrilium derivatives of pyridine salts, and so on. Furthermore, in these years Nesmejanov together with Rachel H. Freidlina studied reactions of polyhalogenated aliphatic compounds (particularly those containing the groups $Cl_3{-}CH_2{-}$, $CCl_3CH{=}C<$ and $CCl_2{=}CH{-}$, which enabled the development of new syntheses of compounds such as ω-chlorocarboxylic acids and α-aminoacids.

Nesmejanov's interest in synthesis of artificial foods developed primarily in the second half of 1950s and was connected with finding easier means of synthesizing α-aminoacids and α,α- dichloroalkenes of the type $CCl_2{=}CHR$.

In the 1960s to 1970s, experiments with artificial foods became a key aspect of his work. The main problem he hoped to solve was to obtain food-grade protein without killing animals. The scientist stopped eating meat when he was nine years old, and at twelve he became a whole-hearted vegetarian, eliminating fish from his diet. He firmly believed in humane treatment of animals and not killing them. During the first stage of his experiments, he hoped to synthesize essential amino acids that one could add to broth and other dishes and later to develop peptides and then complete proteins.

Nesmejanov believed that it was possible to utilize heap food waste, such as casein from milk. As the experiments proceeded in full-gear, he said to his colleagues: "I think it's worth starting with something that would stun society and break the wall of distrust around synthetic foods" (Slonimskii, 1999, p.10). When he was asked to clarify, he dreamily answered: "For example, start with caviar!" Indeed, in 1964, the Institute of Hetero-organic Compounds developed the first samples of artificial caviar from milk, and then they developed technology that obtained caviar from casein, protein and broken eggs, as well as other waste. His laboratory developed a synthetic black caviar that for a while was sold in Soviet grocery stores. Nesmejanov was very pleased with the results, but being a dedicated vegetarian, did not eat the caviar because it contained gelatin.

In the 1960s, Nesmejanov and his collaborators prepared ferrocerone, the first drug of the ferrocene series used to treat iron deficiency.

Administrative and Political Work. Beginning in the 1940s, Nesmejanov spent progressively more time on administrative tasks. From 1945 to 1948 he served as dean of the Chemistry Faculty of Moscow University, and from 1948 to 1951 as the rector of the university. From his initiative stemmed construction of new buildings for the university in the Lenin (later Vorob'ev) Hills. After the creation of the Institute of Organic Chemistry in 1934, Nesmejanov ran the institute's Laboratory of Organometallic Compounds, and in 1939 he was elected a corresponding member of the Academy of Science and president of the Institute of Organic Chemistry, over which he presided until 1954, when he organized an Institute of Hetero-organic Compounds. In 1943, he was elected an academician of the Academy of Sciences of the U.S.S.R., and from 1946 to 1948, he held the position of academician-secretary of the Department of Chemical Sciences of the Academy of Science. In 1951, Nesmejanov was appointed president of the Academy of Sciences of the U.S.S.R., in which post he served until 1961. During his presidency fifteen new institutes were created, including Institutes of Biological Physics (1952), Radio Technology and Electronics (1953), and Scientific Information (1952), the latter publishing a multiseries peer-reviewed journal (analogous to the American *Chemical Abstracts*)

Nesmejanov

concerning all major branches of science. (In 1956, this institute was reorganized into the All-Union Institute of Scientific and Technological Information.) Besides these, numerous other institutes were created that focused on economic and sociopolitical as well as scientific topics.

As a president of the Academy of Sciences within a totalitarian system, Nesmejanov often ended up in difficult situations. For example, starting in 1946, a Soviet chemist, Gennadi V. Chelintsev, published papers, and in 1949 a book, in which he discussed his "new structural theory," with which he challenged traditional "mechanistic" quantum chemistry. Nesmejanov strongly criticized Chelintsev's ideas. This dispute revolved around the quantum chemical theory of resonance, proposed by Linus Pauling in 1930s, which was rejected by Chelintsev as contrary to Marxist dogma, but that was initially defended by Nesmejanov. In 1949 in No. 3 of the Soviet journal *Voprosu philosophii* [Problems of philosophy], two articles were published that were very critical of Pauling's theory, one by Vladimir M. Tatevsky and Michael I. Shakhparonov, the other by Oleg A. Reutov. In both articles the theory of resonance was criticized only from an ideological standpoint. This theory was charged with "idealism" on the grounds that representing the same compound by several resonance structures violates the principle that each chemical compound should be represented by one formula. In 1949, a third article condemning Pauling's theory appeared, and this time the author was Yuri A. Zhdanov (son of Joseph Stalin's close friend, Andrey A. Zhdanov), who was then the head of the Science Department of the Central Committee of the Communist Party.

In 1950, Nesmejanov joined in criticism of the resonance theory. During a meeting of the Academic Council of the Institute of Organic Chemistry (February 1950), he called for further criticism of the theory and also made sure to challenge those instances in his own work that could have been interpreted as supportive of Pauling's theory. This theory was proclaimed "physically baseless, and ideologically sinful" (1950, p. 442).

The campaign against the theory of resonance turned out to be absolutely fruitless both in scientific and administrative respects, unlike the campaign of 1948 against genetics when many people's lives were destroyed by Lysenko. After the resonance case among chemists the biggest price was paid by Yakov K. Syrkin and Mirrah E. Dyatkina, who were fired from the Institute of Physical Chemistry, although rehired not too long after. Other "suspects" (Michael V. Vol'kenstein and Andrey I. Kirpianov) survived virtually unscathed, and Nesmejanov became the president of the Academy of Science in 1951. While the campaign against genetic studies led to annihilation of an entire branch of science in the USSR and to serious prosecution of scientists, the "anti-resonance" campaign on the other hand, touched on very specific theory and was nothing more than a superficial ritual that did not leave a deep imprint on the development of quantum chemistry in the Soviet Union, particularly because from the 1950s many chemists turned to the method of the molecular orbitals, which did not require the use of the theory of resonance.

At the same time Nesmejanov had a difficult relationship with Trofim D. Lysenko, who actively challenged genetics but was supported by the Soviet leaders Stalin and Nikita S. Khrushchev. Unlike the instance with the resonance theory, here Nesmejanov held his ground and refused to agree to any compromises supporting investigations on genetics in the USSR. "I listened to an entire course on genetics of the biology department in my student years," he remembered, "and G. Mendel's name in my mind stood next to that of John Dalton … I was too much of an optimist and was convinced that Lysenko and Lysenkoism would be an accidental and short-lived episode. I had no idea that this 'episode' would last thirty years" (1999, pp. 135–136.)

In April 1960, Khrushchev, under Lysenko's influence, reproached Nesmejanov for certain supposed shortcomings of the Academy of Sciences, specifically the study of some "silly midges" (fruit flies). "I got up," remembered Nesmejanov, "and to everyone's horror, announced that the study of these very midges is of vital importance to many branches of science. That was an unheard of (public!) speech contradicting Khrushchev's view. Then I said: 'Undoubtedly, there is an option to replace the president [of the academy], to find an Academician more suitable for this role. I am convinced, for example, that Mstislav V. Keldysh would do much better with these tasks.'—'I think so too,' replied Khrushchev" (1999, p. 264). Shortly afterwards Nesmejanov was invited to the Kremlin where he was told that the leadership of the Communist Party had decided to appoint academician Mstislav V. Keldysh to the post. Nesmejanov had no choice but to resign.

Nesmejanov took his forced resignation from the post of president of the Academy of Science of U.S.S.R. rather lightly. The day after his resignation, almost all of the members of the academic council of the Institute of Hetero-organic Compounds, came over to his office to give him moral support. When he saw them at the door Nesmejanov asked in surprise: "What happened?" Then Martin I. Kabachnik said: "We gathered here to show solidarity, but do not know what to do next." Nesmejanov smiled: "What to do? Let's have a drink! After all I was reborn!" With that he went to the cupboard and got out a bottle of cognac and glasses. Having left a high post he was now able to dedicate himself to directing scientific

Nesmejanov

experiments (primarily in the area of artificial foods) and to teaching.

Nesmejanov was awarded six Orders of Lenin (first in 1945, last in 1979), an Order of the Red Banner of Labor (1949), and a gold medal named for of M.V. Lomonosov (1961). He was a Laureate of the State (1943) and received the Lenin Prize of the U.S.S.R. (1966). At the direction of soviet leader Leonid I. Brezhnev, who held scientists in high respect (if they did not meddle in political matters as Andrei D. Sakharov did), the 1966 Lenin Prize and the 1979 Order of Lenin were given as sort of "rehabilitation" for his dismissal under Khrushchev. The spectrum of Nesmejanov's interests was quite varied: he knew history well, wrote poems, and painted.

BIBLIOGRAPHY

WORKS BY NESMEJANOV

"Eine neue Methode zur Synthese von aromatischen quecksilberorganischen Salzen." *Berichte der Deutschen Chemischen Gesellschaft* 62 (1929): 1010–1018.

"Eine neue Methode zur Darstellung von symmetrischen aromatischen quecksilberorganischen Verbindungen." *Berichte der Deutschen Chemischen Gesellschaft* 62 (1929): 1018–1020.

"Über Doppelsalze von Phenyl-Diazoniumjodid mit Quecksilberjodid und über die Bildung von Diphenyljodoniumsalzen bei der Zersetzung dieser Doppelsalze." *Zeitschrift für Anorganische und Allgemeine Chemie* 178 (1929): 300–308.

"Die Reaktion von quecksilberorganischen Verbindungen mit Salzen des zwei-wertigen Zinns als Methode zur Darstellung von zinnorganischen Verbindungen." *Berichte der Deutschen Chemischen Gesellschaft* 63 (1930): 2496–2504.

"Aromatische Zinnverbindungen mit Halogen im Benzolkern." *Berichte der Deutschen Chemischen Gesellschaft* 64 (1931): 628–636.

With E. I. Kan. "Di-β-Naphthyl Mercury." *Organic Syntheses* 12 (1932): 46–47.

"β-Naphthylmercuric Chloride." *Organic Syntheses* 12 (1932): 54–56.

"Über die Synthese von quecksilber-organischen Verbindungen mit negativen Substituenten mittels der Diazo-Methode." *Berichte der Deutschen Chemischen Gesellschaft* 67 (1934): 130–134.

"Über die unmittelbare Synthese von Säure-fluoriden aus Säuren und die Herstellung von Formylfluorid." *Berichte der Deutschen Chemischen Gesellschaft* 67 (1934): 370–373.

"Carbonyls of the VI Group Metals in the Periodic System." *Comptes Rendus des Séances de l Académie des Sciences URSS* 26, no. 1 (1940): 54–59.

"Structure of Addition Products of Metal Halides and Unsaturated Compounds." *Comptes Rendus des Séances de l Académie des Sciences URSS* 29, no. 8–9 (1940): 567–570.

With Rachel H. Freidlina. "Addition of Iodine Trichloride to Acetylene and the Structure of β-Chlorovinyl Iodochloride." *Doklady Akademii Nauk SSSR,* Series A, 31, no. 9 (1941): 892–894.

"Otvet G.V. Chelintsevu" [Reply to G.V. Chelintsev]. *Izvestiya Akademii nauk SSSR. Otdeleniye khimicheskikh nauk,* no. 5 (1950): 544.

"O «kontaktnukh» khemicheskikh svyazakh i «novoy structurnoy teorii»" [On "contact" chemical bonds and the "new structural theory"]. *Izvestiya Akademii nauk SSSR. Otdeleniye khimicheskikh nauk,* no. 2 (1952): 200.

"Réactivité double et tautomerie." In *XIVe Congrès international de chimie pure et appliquée: Conférences principales et conférences des sections. Zürich, 21.–27. VII. 1955.* Basel: Birkhäuser Verlag, 1955.

With Lubov' G. Makarova and T. P. Tolstaya. "Heterolytic Decomposition of Onium Compounds (Diphenylhalogenonium and Triphenyloxonium Salts)." *Tetrahedron* 1 (1957): 145–157.

"Die Anwendung der Telomerisationsreaktion zur Synthese von ω-Aminocarbonsäuren und die Herstellung neuer Polyamidfasern auf ihren Basis." *Chemistry & Technology* 9, no. 3 (1957): 139–150.

Izbrannuye trudu [Selected Works]. 4 vols. Edited by Aleksandr V. Topchiev. Moscow: Izdatel'stvo Akademii nauk SSSR, 1959.

Na kacheliakh XX veka [On a Swing of the Twentieth Century.] Moscow: Nauka, 1999.

OTHER SOURCES

Graham, Loren. *Science and Philosophy in the Soviet Union.* New York: Knopf, 1972.

Hunsberger I. M. "Theoretical Chemistry in Russia." *Journal of Chemical Education* 31, no. 9-10 (1954): 504-514.

Kabachnik, Martin I., ed. *Aleksandr Nikolaevich Nesmejamov: Uchenui i chelovek* [Aleksandr Nikolaevich Nesmejanov: Scientist and Individual]. Moscow: Nauka, 1988.

Kursanov, D. M., M. G. Gonikberg, B. M. Dubinin, et al. "The Present State of Chemical Structural Theory." *Journal of Chemical Education* 29, no. 1 (1952): 1-13.

Makarova, Lubov' G. [no title]. In *Aleksandr Nikolaevich Nesmejamov: Uchenui i chelovek* [Aleksandr Nikolaevich Nesmejanov: Scientist and Individual], edited by Martin I. Kabachnik. Moscow: Nauka, 1988.

"Na uchenom sovete Instituta organichesloi khimii" [In Academic Council of the Institute of the Organic Chemistry]. *Izvestiya Akademii nauk SSSR. Otdeleniye khimicheskikh nauk,* no. 4 (1950): 438–444.

Reutov, O. A. "O knige G. V. Chelintseva 'Ocherki po teorii organicheskoy khimii'" [On the Book by G.V. Chelintsev "Essays on the Theory of Organic Chemistry"]. *Voprosu Filosofii* [Problems of Philosophy] no. 3 (1949): 309–317/.

Slonimskii, Grigorii L. "Memoirs on Aleksandr Nesmejanov." *Khimia i jizn-XXI* vek [Chemistry and Life—XXInd century], no. 9 (1999): 10.

Tatevskii V. M., and M. I. Shakhparonov. "About a Machistic Theory in Chemistry and its Propagandists." *Journal of Chemical Education* 29, no. 1 (1952): 13-14.(Original publication: Tatevskii V. M., and M. I. Shakhparonov. "Ob odnoy makhistskoi teorii b eyo propadandistakh."

Voprosu Filosofii [Problems of Philosophy] no. 3 (1949): 176–192.

Tsupkin, Gennadii A., ed. *Aleksandr Nikolaevich Nesmejanov: organizator nauki* [Aleksandr Nikolaevich Nesmejanov: Manager of Science.] Moscow: Nauka, 1996.

Igor S. Dmitriev

NEUBERG, CARL ALEXANDER (*b.* Hanover, Germany, 29 July 1877; *d.* New York, New York, 30 May 1956) *chemistry, biochemistry, dynamic biochemistry.*

Neuberg, a German-Jewish pioneer in dynamic biochemistry, gained international recognition through his elucidation of the biochemical reactions of alcoholic fermentation in which he discovered a number of different enzymes such as carboxylase and of intermediates such as fructose-6-phosphate (Neuberg ester). In 1906 Neuberg founded *Biochemische Zeitschrift,* the second journal of the young discipline of biochemistry, and he also became the founding director of the Kaiser-Wilhelm-Institut für Biochemie (Kaiser Wilhelm Institute of Biochemistry) in Berlin in 1925. In 1934 he was forced out of his position by Nazi legislation. After emigrating from Germany in 1939, he tried unsuccessfully to find appropriate working conditions in various other countries. In 1941 he found refuge in the United States, where he was able to conduct research in unpaid academic positions, earning his money as a consultant to industry.

Early Life and Career. Carl Neuberg was the first child of Julius Sandel Neuberg, a Jewish cloth and leather merchant in Hanover, and his wife Alma Niemann; he had two younger sisters. In 1892 the family moved to Berlin, where Carl Neuberg attended a *humanistisches Gymnasium* (high school with focus on the classical languages) in Berlin and graduated with distinction in March 1896.

Neuberg then studied chemistry in Berlin and Würzburg and at the Technische Hochschule (Technical University) in Charlottenburg. In addition to his chemical studies, he attended courses in mathematics, philosophy, and physics. Conducting experiments for his doctoral thesis at Emil Fischer's Institute of Chemistry at the University of Berlin under the supervision of Alfred Wohl, Neuberg obtained his PhD in 1900. Emil Fischer, Nobel laureate in chemistry of 1902, was one of most prominent organic chemists of his time, with pathbreaking work in, among other things, the chemistry of proteins and carbohydrates. He was known for stressing exact experimentation. Alfred Wohl, a specialist in carbohydrate chemistry, directed Neuberg's interest to the chemistry of organic compounds containing three carbon atoms. The first part of Neuberg's thesis dealt mainly with two of these compounds, acrolein and glycerinaldehyde, the latter substance playing a major role in Neuberg's wartime research 14 years later. The two other parts of his thesis, researched with the analytical correctness required of Emil Fischer's students, consisted of the application of analytical methods to characterize esters of boric acid and the purification of osazone.

In 1899, before finishing his dissertation, Neuberg was appointed a chemical assistant at the Pathological Institute of the university hospital "Charité" in Berlin. The institute was founded in 1856 and from 1893 to 1902 headed by Rudolf Virchow. Neuberg worked in the institute's chemical department under Ernst Salkowski, a clinical analytical chemist, and was responsible for teaching medical students various aspects of physiological chemistry. In 1903 Neuberg became a Privatdozent (private lecturer) at the University of Berlin. There, in 1906 at the age of twenty-eight, he was appointed an *außerplanmäßiger,* or extraordinary professor, which meant he had the right to teach at a university but had no paid permanent position. When he left the Charité in 1909, Neuberg had published around 120 papers, mostly concerning carbohydrate and fatty acid chemistry, but also on the characterization of alcohol, aldehyde, and ketone reactions. He had also completed some studies on the chemistry of malignant tumors.

As a Jewish scientist, however, his chances of appointment to one of the few full professorships in physiological chemistry in Germany were nearly nonexistent. Therefore, Neuberg, despite his ambition and growing reputation in the field, accepted in 1909 the offer of the physiologist Nathan Zuntz, the director of the Institut für Tierphysiologie (Institute of Animal Physiology) at the Landwirtschaftliche Hochschule Berlin (Agricultural College in Berlin). Zuntz wanted Neuberg to become head of the institute's chemical department.

In 1911 Neuberg edited a comprehensive volume titled *Der Harn sowie die übrigen Ausscheidungen und Körperflüssigkeiten von Mensch und Tier* (Urine as well as other excretions and bodily fluids in man and animal), which soon became a standard work in analytical medical chemistry, published by Julius Springer's publishing house. The majority of its contributors were, like Neuberg, Jewish university teachers in Berlin, among them Wilhelm Caspari, Ludwig Halberstaedter, Adolf Loewy, Julius Morgenroth, Artur Pappenheim, and Carl Posner.

When August Wassermann was appointed director of the newly founded Kaiser-Wilhelm-Institut für experimentelle Therapie (Kaiser Wilhelm Institute for Experimental Therapy) in Berlin in 1913, Neuberg became head of the institute's chemical department, a position in which he remained until Wassermann's death in 1925. Early on, the Kaiser-Wilhelm-Gesellschaft (Kaiser Wilhelm Society) made efforts to establish an Institut für Biochemie (Institute for Biochemistry) for Neuberg. In 1917 a preliminary institute was founded with Neuberg officially as director; it remained, however, affiliated to Wassermann's institute. The plans for a new building seemed to materialize only when through Neuberg's connections the Goldenberg-Oetker-Stiftung, a foundation, donated two million Reichmark in 1919. The money was given to the Kaiser Wilhelm Society for the establishment of a Kaiser Wilhelm Institute for Biochemistry, which they did in 1920. But the donated money lost its value through the great inflation in the early 1920s, and so the building could not be constructed. Neuberg had to wait until Wassermann's death before he became the director of his own Kaiser Wilhelm Institute for Biochemistry in the old building of the Institute of Experimental Therapy. He also became provisional head of the rest of that institute, a small department of immunochemistry that was closed down in 1936.

Family and Values. Carl Neuberg was deeply rooted in German culture. He was strongly attached to imperial Germany and especially loyal to Kaiser Wilhelm II, whom he met during the inauguration ceremony of the Kaiser Wilhelm Institute for Experimental Therapy. A photograph of this meeting hung above his desk even during his exile in New York much later. This loyalty, however, did not bring him into conflict with his Jewishness. Despite his strong assimilation to German culture and politics, he was proud of the high esteem in which intellectual and ethical values were held in Jewish tradition, and he was well versed in the Bible and Jewish history and was fluent in Latin, Greek, and Hebrew. He would not convert to Christianity for opportunistic reasons, such as having a better chance to receive a professorship. Neuberg became a member of the Central-Verein deutscher Staatsbürger jüdischen Glaubens (Central Association of German Citizens of Jewish Faith), founded in 1893 in response to anti-Semitism in Germany. The association fought for full citizenship rights of German Jews.

In 1907 Neuberg married Helene "Hela" Lewinski. They had two daughters, Irene and Marianne. Hela died from leukemia in 1929. Their elder daughter Irene studied biochemistry, conducted her graduate studies in her father's laboratory and at the Institut Pasteur in Paris, and received her PhD from the University of Berlin in 1932. After 1933 Irene and Marianne emigrated and eventually settled in the United States, where Irene first lived in New York and later moved to California.

Research on Fermentation. Neuberg's most brilliant and lasting achievements were in the biochemistry of alcoholic fermentation. By the mid-nineteenth century, it was widely accepted that alcoholic fermentation and other fermentations were catalyzed by living organisms, such as yeast. However, there remained a bitter dispute about the mechanism underlying fermentation, which was finally resolved in 1897 by the chemist Eduard Buchner. Buchner demonstrated that, contrary to a widespread assumption shared by Louis Pasteur, alcoholic fermentation was not dependent on whole yeast cells but took place also in cell-free extracts from yeast. Buchner concluded that these extracts contain a fermentation enzyme, zymase, and that fermentation is a purely chemical process. This discovery, for which Buchner was awarded the Nobel Prize in Chemistry in 1907, marks the beginning of biochemical research on enzymes and a new approach to studies on alcoholic fermentation. Subsequently Neuberg was among the first to examine and clarify the metabolic complexity hidden behind Buchner's zymase.

Around 1910, the elucidation of intermediate biochemical pathways in cells began with biochemical studies on the degradation of sugar, glycolysis, and fermentation. In the process of glycolysis, glucose—containing six carbon atoms—is degraded to pyruvate, containing three carbon atoms. In alcoholic fermentation, which occurs in the absence of oxygen, sugar is degraded via pyruvate to carbon dioxide (containing one carbon atom) and alcohol (ethanol, containing two carbon atoms). Given his expertise in the field of three-carbon-compounds, Neuberg was able to pioneer studies on the elucidation of both glycolysis and alcoholic fermentation, by creating chemical methods to examine steps and compounds of metabolic pathways and by shedding light on the sequence of reactions leading to alcoholic fermentation.

In 1911 he reported, at a meeting of the Deutsche Physiologische Gesellschaft (German Physiological Society), that contrary to a widespread assumption, yeast was able to ferment pyruvate in the presence of hydrogen peroxide and iron salts. He thus confirmed a suggestion by Otto Neubauer and Konrad Fromherz that pyruvate might be an intermediate in ethanolic fermentation. Neuberg showed that pyruvate is decarboxylated into carbon dioxide and acetaldehyde, which is then further reduced to ethanol. These results for the first time showed a splitting up of the reactions of sugar degradation into different steps and proved wrong the mode of action Eduard Buchner had suggested for his zymase; Buchner thought that a single enzyme would catalyze the whole sugar degradation process. Neuberg and his colleague Lázló Karczag recommended in 1911 that the enzyme they had discovered, catalyzing the process of pyruvate oxidation, be named carboxylase.

Following a suggestion of Alfred Wohl that a pathway be found which would arrange these intermediates,

Neuberg in 1913 developed his first fermentation diagram (Neuberg schema). He wrote it as a working hypothesis for the first edition of the textbook *Handbuch der Biochemie des Menschen und der Tiere* (*Manual of Biochemistry of Men and Animals*) published by the Gustav Fischer Verlag and edited by Carl Oppenheimer. In his diagram, which Neuberg spread in advance of publication among his colleagues as a preprint of his chapter in the book, he suggested the production of pyruvate and glycerol through degradation of a hexose (a sugar containing six carbon atoms, as in glucose) through intermediate steps. The fermentation diagram was generally accepted by the scientific community. The fact that later research revealed some flaws, such as the assumption of methylglyoxal as an intermediate, did not depreciate the general value of the scheme as the first biochemical sequence showing the degradation of a sugar to alcohol in a certain specific stepwise order.

Neuberg's discovery of the production of glycerol by fermentation and his introduction of a new method into fermentation analysis, the trapping method, turned out to be of great importance for industry and the military. When he tested the addition of sodium bisulfite on pyruvate degradation, Neuberg found a considerable amount of glycerol emerging besides acetaldehyde and carbon dioxide. The removal of acetaldehyde by bisulfite affects the chemical equilibrium of the reaction chain and thus promotes the formation of glycerol derivatives. This method became known as the acetaldeyde trapping method. It enabled Neuberg to elucidate steps of alcoholic fermentation, interpreting the results—as it turned out, correctly—as a question of available hydrogen acceptors. The method also allowed the production of the glycerol substitutes perglycerine and perkaglycerine.

Wilhelm Connstein and Karl Lüdecke modified the trapping method for industrial use in glycerol production. It is an example of the impact of basic chemical research on industrial chemistry. The process provided a nearly unlimited source of glycerol derivatives during World War I in Germany, when shortages of fatty acids stopped common glycerol production at the same time that large amounts of it were needed to produce nitroglycerine for explosives, brake fluids, and other lubricants for military use. Using Neuberg, Connstein, and Lüdecke's method of production, several hundred tons of glycerol were produced by three different chemical companies in Germany during the war; because of the war, however, the researchers did not publish their method until 1918.

The relationship of Neuberg's work with the chemical industry affected Neuberg's life in two different ways. First, during World War I, he was asked to carry out frontline inspections in order to examine the properties of the brake fluids produced by his method. For his some seven missions he received the status of combatant, which later, when the Nazis came to power, enabled him to avoid being dismissed as a Jew in 1933. Second, one of the three chemical companies producing glycerol, Goldenberg, Geromont, and Company, was headed by a second cousin of Neuberg. After World War I, the Goldenberg-Oetker-Stiftung, a joint foundation of that company and the industrialist Dr. August Oetker, donated the profits of glycerol production, two million Reichmark, to the Kaiser Wilhelm Society. As was mentioned above, this donation obliged the society to found a new Kaiser Wilhelm Institute for Biochemistry, headed by Neuberg.

Neuberg's war service did not prevent him from continuing his work on fermentation during the war. He tested chemically synthesized three- and four-carbon-compounds as a starting point for fermentations and found many of them underwent fermentation with different end-products. He set up two more diagrams of fermentation, first for the degradation of sugar into certain amounts of alcohol, acetic acid, glycerol, and carbon dioxide, and second, for the degradation of sugar under different conditions into equal amounts of pyruvate and glycerol. In 1918 he succeeded in preparing a hexose-monophosphate that was later found to be fructose-6-phosphate as an intermediate of fermentation. Fructose-6-phosphate was subsequently named Neuberg ester. Like the discoveries of fructose-biphosphate by Arthur Harden and William John Young and glucose-6-phosphate by Robert Robison, Neuberg's discovery was of great biochemical importance because it unraveled a further component of the glycolysis, the glucose degradation pathway. In addition to carboxylase, Neuberg discovered a number of other enzymes. Later he studied reduction processes of various sugars in plants.

Neuberg's discovery of carboxylase and his fermentation diagram became the basis for understanding the biochemical processes of alcoholic fermentation. They marked a turning point in the history of biochemistry and had a profound impact on its development. They motivated many biochemists, who would otherwise have continued work on the isolation and investigation of cell constituents, to shift their focus to the elucidation of metabolic pathways and to isolating and characterizing the enzymes responsible for the reactions.

***Biochemische Zeitschrift* (Biochemical Journal).** By October 1906, Carl Neuberg had completed his editing of the papers that appeared in the first volume of his newly founded journal, *Biochemische Zeitschrift*, published with the Julius Springer publishing house. By choosing this title, he became one of the first researchers in Germany to use the term *Biochemie* instead of *Physiologische Chemie*. The plans for a new journal of biochemistry—around thirty years after *Zeitschrift für Physiologische Chemie* was founded by Felix Hoppe-Seyler—had already been made two years earlier. Neuberg and Ferdinand Springer, head of the Springer publishing house, had convinced five well-known biochemists (at the time usually called physiological chemists)—among them Eduard Buchner (Nobel Prize in Chemistry, 1907), Paul Ehrlich (Nobel Prize in Physiology or Medicine, 1908) and Nathan Zuntz—to serve as editors of the first edition. Their names on the cover of the journal were followed by Neuberg's as the acting editor and those of forty-one scientists from twelve countries as contributors. During the following years, the *Biochemische Zeitschrift* gained a high international reputation among biochemists and was one of the publisher's best-selling journals. As was true with some other journals at the time, Neuberg as the acting editor (despite being only at the beginning of his career) decided by himself which articles would be published. Helped by his wife, Helene, he edited over 8,500 articles in 230 volumes of his journal until 1930.

In 1933, after the Nazis came to power, Wolfgang Grassmann, a student of Richard Willstätter's, became co-editor of the journal. When Neuberg was dismissed by the Kaiser Wilhelm Society in 1934, Grassmann became its sole editor and Neuberg's name no longer appeared on the title page. After the war, Neuberg's name was reinstated. Interestingly, the dates of his period as sole editor, were wrongly stated to end in 1932 instead of 1933, implying that he left before the dismissal of Jewish scientists by Nazi laws.

Dismissal and Emigration. In accordance with a Nazi civil service law, almost all Jewish scientists were dismissed from universities in April 1933 and, shortly after, from the Kaiser Wilhelm Institutes, Neuberg was still exempted from dismissal because of his combatant status in World War I. However, when in 1934 a Nazi mechanic at the institute whom Neuberg had tried to dismiss because of his disturbing political activities, denounced Neuberg for defaming Adolf Hitler as behaving like an "Elefant im Porzellanladen" (a bull in a china shop), the Kaiser Wilhelm Society forced Neuberg to retire. Neuberg remained provisional head until his successor, Adolf Butenandt, was appointed in May 1936. Neuberg was not allowed to continue his work at the Kaiser Wilhelm Institute, but he found work at the private laboratory of a bread factory in Berlin. The reasons why he remained in Germany although both his daughters were already living in the United States are unclear.

Neuberg fled to the Netherlands in August 1939 just a month before World War II began. After an odyssey of one and a half years, during which he spent three months at the University of Amsterdam and eight months at the Hebrew University in Jerusalem and traveled to the United States via Iraq, Iran, India, and New Guinea, Neuberg arrived in New York City in February 1941. He became affiliated for a short while with the Brooklyn Polytechnic Institute and the New York Medical College, and later on worked as a consultant to industry. Neuberg resumed contact with a number of his former colleagues in Germany. But in spite of spending some time as guest researcher at the Technical University of Munich in 1952, he refused to accept an invitation to return as researcher on a long-term basis to the Max Planck Institute for Biochemistry in Tübingen.

Neuberg was a prolific writer. He published around nine hundred papers and wrote six books. The many honors he received included his fellowships of the academies of science in Göttingen in Germany, Copenhagen in Denmark, Leningrad in the Soviet Union, and New York, along with his eight honorary doctorates, the Emil Fischer Medal of the Gesellschaft Deutscher Chemiker (German Chemical Society), and the Carl Neuberg Medal of the New York Academy of Sciences. He died of pneumonia on 30 May 1956 in New York at the age of seventy-eight.

Carl Neuberg was one of the greatest biochemists of his generation. By elucidating basic compounds of sugar degradation and alcoholic fermentation, he became a pioneer of research in intermediate metabolism. In addition, the methods that he developed remained important in biochemistry for decades. Neuberg, together with the Nobel laureates Otto Warburg and Otto Meyerhof, made Germany the international leader in biochemistry before the Nazis came to power.

BIBLIOGRAPHY

Neuberg's papers are in the American Philosophical Society in Philadelphia.

WORKS BY NEUBERG

"Die Kohlenhydrate." In: *Handbuch der Biochemie des Menschen und der Tiere,* edited by Carl Oppenheimer. Vol. 1. Jena, Germany: Fischer, 1909: 159–225.

Der Harn sowie die übrigen Ausscheidungen und Körperflüssigkeiten von Mensch und Tier. Edited by Carl Neuberg. Berlin, Germany: Julius Springer, 1911.

With Lázló Karczag. "Über zuckerfreie Hefegärungen. IV. Carboxylase, ein neues Enzym der Hefe." *Biochemische Zeitschrift* 36 (1911): 68–75.

"Die Gärungsvorgänge und der Zuckerumsatz der Zelle." In *Handbuch der Biochemie des Menschen und der Tiere,* extension of Vol. 1, edited by Carl Oppenheimer. Jena, Germany: Fischer, 1913.

With E. Reinfurth. "Natürliche und erzwungene Glycerinbildung bei der alkoholischen Gärung." *Biochemische Zeitschrift* 92 (1918): 234–266.

OTHER SOURCES

Auhagen, Ernst. "Carl Neuberg." *Biochemische Zeitschrift* 328 (1956): 322–324.

Barnett, James A. "A History of Research on Yeasts 5: The Fermentation Pathway." *Yeast* 20 (2003): 509–543.

Björk, Ragnar. "Inside the Nobel Committee on Medicine: Prize Competition Procedures 1901–1950 and the Fate of Carl Neuberg." *Minerva* 39 (2001): 393–408.

Conrads, Hinderk, and Brigitte Lohff. *Carl Neuberg—Biochemie, Politik und Geschichte: Lebenswege und Werk eines fast verdrängten Forschers. Geschichte und Philosophie der Medizin.* Stuttgart, Germany: Franz Steiner Verlag, 2006.

Engel, Michael. "Enzymologie und Gärungschemie: Alfred Wohls und Carl Neubergs Reaktionschemata der alkoholischen Gärung. Der 'chemische Gesichtspunkt' als Kennzeichen der Berliner Schule." *Mitteilungen der Fachgruppe für Geschichte der Chemie der Gesellschaft deutscher Chemiker* 12 (1996): 3–29.

Gottschalk, Alfred. "Prof. Carl Neuberg." *Nature* 178, no. 4536 (6 October 1956): 722–723.

Nachmansohn, David. *German-Jewish Pioneers in Science, 1900–1933: Highlights in Atomic Physics, Chemistry, and Biochemistry.* Berlin, Germany: Springer-Verlag, 1979.

Nord, F. F. "Carl Neuberg, 1877–1956." *Advances in Carbohydrate Chemistry* 13 (1958): 1–7.

Ute Deichmann
Simone Wenkel

NEWELL, ALLEN (*b.* San Francisco, California, 19 March 1927, *d.* Pittsburgh, Pennsylvania, 19 July 1992), *computer science, artificial intelligence, cognitive psychology.*

Newell was a founder of artificial intelligence (AI) and a pioneer in the use of computer simulations in psychology. In collaboration with J. Cliff Shaw and Herbert A. Simon, Newell developed the first list-processing programming language as well as the earliest computer programs for simulating human problem solving. Over a long and prolific career, he contributed to many techniques, such as protocol analysis and heuristic search, that later became part of psychology and computer science. Colleagues remember Newell for his deep commitment to science, his care for details, and his inexhaustible energy.

Education. Newell was the second and youngest son of Jeanette Le Valley Newell and Robert R. Newell, a professor of radiology at Stanford Medical School. At age sixteen, Allen Newell fell in love with Noël McKenna, a fellow high school student. They were married four years later and had a son, Paul.

Although he admired his father, whom he described as a "complete man," Newell did not grow up planning to be a scientist. After completing one quarter at Stanford University, at the end of World War II, he was drafted into the navy. His father, Robert Newell, belonged to a team of scientists involved in the study of the Bikini Atoll nuclear tests, and Robert asked that his son Allen be assigned to assist the team. Allen's contribution was to write maps of the radiation distribution over the atolls. This exciting endeavor ignited Newell's interest in science. Back from the navy, he reenrolled in Stanford University, where he majored in physics. Still fascinated with radiation, he spent much of his college time working on x-ray microscopy as a research assistant.

As a freshman, Newell took a course in which George Polya, a distinguished mathematician, covered his book *How to Solve It* (1945); Newell was so fascinated that he took many more courses with him. Polya's book concerns *heuristics*—plausible methods for solving problems. Unlike *algorithmic* methods, which are always guaranteed to solve every solvable instance of a problem, heuristic methods may or may not lead to the best solution. But for many problems, algorithms are either unavailable or impractical. In such cases, heuristic methods are needed. Heuristic methods were to play a critical role in Newell's later research.

In 1949, Newell went from Stanford to Princeton, to pursue graduate studies in mathematics. As a research associate for Oskar Morgenstern, he worked on stochastic models of logistic problems and on game theory, which had recently been invented by Morgenstern with John von Neumann. But pure mathematics was not for Newell. By the end of his first year, he left Princeton for a job at RAND Corporation in Santa Monica, California. RAND was a recently founded think tank, devoted to research with military applications and funded mainly by the U.S. Air Force. As a member of RAND's Mathematics Division, Newell was free to pursue research that interested him. He could also collaborate with the many talented scientists who worked at RAND, as well as dozens of external consultants who visited every summer.

RAND Corporation. RAND provided Newell with several formative experiences. With Joseph B. Kruskal, he coauthored two reports in which they applied formal game-theoretic methods to organization theory. He spent six weeks in Washington, DC, visiting the Munitions Board, which was responsible for logistics at the Pentagon. Upon his return, Newell wrote a report proposing a research program for the "science of supply." He also designed and conducted experiments on decision making in small groups, experiments along the lines of those by Fred Bales, a Harvard social psychologist and RAND consultant. Eventually, Newell joined an ambitious team of psychologists devoted to the experimental study of human organizational behavior.

Besides Newell, the group consisted of William C. Biel, Robert Chapman, and John L. Kennedy. They built and studied a full-scale simulation of an Air Defense Early Warning Station, whose crew had to observe radar signals and decide whether to send planes to investigate them. The simulation was aimed at understanding the crew's interactions with radar screens, interception aircraft, and each other. The technique for doing so, which involved tape-recording and analyzing the crew's phone conversations, prefigured Newell's later work on human "thinking-aloud" protocols. This research led to a training program for the Air Defense Command and to the creation of the System Development Corporation to implement it. For security reasons, the group published little. Nevertheless, for this work, Biel, Chapman, Kennedy, and Newell shared the 1979 Alexander C. Williams Jr. Award from the Human Factors Society.

Within the group, Newell was in charge of simulating air traffic radar displays, which had to be realistic and continuously evolving in time. To do so, he enlisted the help of Cliff Shaw, a RAND programmer who became a long-term collaborator. Newell and Shaw programmed an IBM Card-Programmed Calculator to generate the successive radar displays, based on data from actual flight patterns, which gave them early experience using computing machines for non-numerical tasks—an activity that became paramount to Newell's research.

The 1950s decade was the heyday of cybernetics, information theory, and automata theory. The first modern computers were being built, and a hot new idea was the analogy between mental and computational processes. The analogy was initially proposed by Warren S. McCulloch and Walter Pitts. It was quickly adopted and developed by Norbert Wiener, John von Neumann, and other scientists, whose work would have an impact on Newell.

In 1936, Alan M. Turing had proposed a formal model of computation that became the foundation of theoretical computer science. In 1943, McCulloch and Pitts argued that neurons were simple logic devices such that mental processes could be explained by computations performed by the brain. In the late 1940s, several laboratories, including one at RAND, began building modern digital computers—"electronic brains," as they became popularly known. In 1948, Norbert Wiener's *Cybernetics* offered a vision for a new science of minds and machines, and the publication of Claude Shannon's mathematical theory of information generated considerable excitement. Turing argued in 1950 that computers could be programmed to behave as intelligently as humans (although Newell did not learn of this until much later). Ross Ashby offered an influential synthesis of these ideas in his book *Design for a Brain* (1952). In 1949, William Grey-Walter built mechanical turtles that plugged themselves into electrical outlets when their batteries ran low; a version of them could be seen crawling around RAND offices. By the early 1950s several people took steps towards artificial intelligence (AI): Turing and Shannon sketched designs for chess-playing computers; Arthur Samuel programmed a computer to play checkers; and Oliver Selfridge and G. P. Dinneen wrote computer programs to do pattern recognition and learning. During his five years of residence at RAND, Newell absorbed these new ideas, which were ushering in the information-processing revolution and the birth of AI.

Another man attracted by this new culture of information processing and automata was Herbert Simon, who was then an established social scientist at Carnegie Institute of Technology (later Carnegie Mellon University), in Pittsburgh, Pennsylvania. Simon was a consultant for Newell's group at RAND, and the two became lifelong friends. In 1954, Newell decided to move to Pittsburgh and write a PhD dissertation under Simon. Before leaving RAND, Newell attended a seminar by Selfridge on his work with Dinneen on computer learning and pattern recognition. Impressed with Selfridge's demonstration that a computer could exhibit such intelligent behavior, Newell had what he described as a "conversion experience": He envisioned programming computers to act as intelligent agents. He decided to devote all his energies to the task of understanding the human mind by simulating it. This remained the primary focus of his research for the rest of his life.

Computers as Intelligent Agents. Newell immediately began working on his new research program. During the following four months, he wrote a computer program designed to play chess in a way that resembled human playing. The program was a step toward Newell's characteristic methodology of *cognitive simulation*: drawing ideas from psychology in programming and understanding the mind by building one. With Simon, he later argued that a program that simulates a cognitive process constitutes a rigorous theory of the process, and that psychological theories should be accompanied by computer simulations. Newell did not manage to implement his first chess program, but some of his ideas came to fruition in a later chess program (1958).

In 1955, while remaining affiliated with RAND, Newell moved to Carnegie Tech. He defended his dissertation in 1957 and became institute professor in 1961. He never moved again—he stayed at Carnegie Tech even during sabbaticals. The last five years of the 1950s saw Newell—together with Shaw (still at RAND) and

Newell

Allen Newell. BILL PIERCE/TIME LIFE PICTURES/GETTY IMAGES.

Simon—producing the work on AI that propelled the Carnegie-RAND group to international fame: Logic Theorist, General Problem Solver, list processing, and protocol analysis.

Logic Theorist (LT) was designed to discover proofs of the logical theorems contained in Chapter 2 of Alfred N. Whitehead and Bertrand Russell's *Principia Mathematica* (1910–1913). LT represented axioms and theorems by symbolic structures (called *states*) and modified them by applying suitable operators. But LT did not attempt every combination of symbols and operators—there was not enough speed and memory for that. Also, its method was not designed to find proofs in the most efficient way possible. Rather, LT's heuristic method attempted to mimic human discovery: It started with the theorem to be proved, and then it searched for axioms and operators from which to derive the theorem. It managed to prove thirty-eight out of fifty-two theorems.

LT was simulated by hand in December 1955 and produced the first mechanical proof of a theorem on 9 August 1956. It was the only running program presented at the Dartmouth Conference of 1956—the first conference explicitly devoted to AI—and it was the first mechanical theorem-prover. It was part of an ambitious research program of simulating human thinking, and it came with a novel way to program computers.

At the time, there were no high-level programming languages. Computers were programmed in a language very close to the 1s and 0s manipulated by the processor. This made it difficult to define non-numerical symbolic structures, such as the logical formulae manipulated by LT. Furthermore, computer memories were very small, which made it difficult to use computers for tasks, such as heuristic search, that required a varying and unpredictable amount of memory. To overcome these and other obstacles, Newell and his collaborators invented the first list-processing language. A list is like a simple associative memory, in which one symbol has a link to another, which links to another, and so on. In list processing, the lists—the symbols and links—are created and modified to generate structures of (in principle) unlimited length and complexity. Many of the ideas introduced with list processing became fundamental to computer science. One of the Dartmouth organizers, John McCarthy, went on to write Lisp, an improved list-processing language that became standard in AI.

To develop and test models of human thinking, data were needed. Neuroscience was not advanced enough to provide them, and introspection was considered unreliable. Mainstream experimental psychologists recorded only behaviors and reaction times during simple tasks, without asking subjects for clues as to what they were thinking. To Newell and Simon, these traditional data sources seemed insufficient to understand human problem solving. Hence, they revived introspection in the form of *protocol analysis.* They asked subjects to think aloud while doing their logical derivation or other task, and they recorded their subjects' speech. They devised procedures for both extracting information about thought processes from the protocols and testing the validity of the protocols. Protocol analysis provided the main ground for testing the accuracy of Newell and Simon's simulations, and it expanded the range of evidence available to psychologists.

In 1957, by analyzing the protocol of a subject doing logic derivations, Newell and Simon discovered a general heuristic method for solving problems. They dubbed it *means-ends analysis*: A subject compares the current state of the problem with a goal state (the *ends*), finds the difference between them, searches in memory for operators that might reduce this kind of difference (the *means*), and applies them to the current state. The process is repeated until either all differences are eliminated—and the

Newell

problem is solved—or the subject gives up. In the latter case, the available resources (operators, time, etc.) have been used, but the problem remains unsolved.

Means-ends analysis became the core of a theory of human problem solving and of General Problem Solver (GPS), a program that was more powerful and general than LT and other AI programs at the time. Unlike LT, which specialized in logical theorems, GPS could solve problems in different domains. All it needed was a way to represent the domain, operators for manipulating the representations, and information about which operators could reduce which differences. To some extent, GPS could even construct new operators from a set of primitives and learn which operators reduced which differences. After GPS, means-ends analysis became widely used in AI.

Sometimes, GPS would get lost in the search for a solution to a subproblem, digging itself into a processing hole without exit. The Carnegie-RAND group thought this pitfall might be addressed by writing into each operator the conditions for its correct application. In this way, operators could be applied to relevant situations without requiring searches that risked being endless. Each instruction would take the form of an "if-then" statement—"if things are so and so, then do such and such"—and would be applied automatically if and only if its conditions were satisfied. The result of each operation would be deposited in a central memory storage, or working memory, on which all operators could write. Instructions of this if-then form are called *productions* and constitute *production systems*, a general programming style invented by logician Emil Post (1943) and adapted to computer science by Robert Floyd (1961). Newell took production systems to heart as a potent new way of programming. He developed a succession of production system languages, which he and others used to build AI systems.

Unified Theories of Cognition. From the 1960s, Newell participated in many collaborative research projects in computer science. One of the most significant projects led to a technique for comparing computer architectures. Architecture is the set of fixed mechanisms and organizing principles of a computer. Together with the software that runs on it, a computer's architecture explains its behavior. In 1968, Newell agreed to help Gordon Bell write a textbook on computer architectures (first edition, 1972; revised edition, with Dan Siewiorek, 1981).

In order to classify and compare different computer architectures, Newell and Bell distinguished different *levels* of analysis—descriptions of computers and their behavior containing different amounts of detail—and devised general languages for two important levels. One was the system level, which is constituted by the main components of a computer, such as processors, memories, and links between them. The other was the instruction level, which is constituted by the primitive operations performed by a processor and the set of primitive instructions that drive them. Newell and Bell's language for the instruction level, ISP (Instruction Set Processor) later made it possible for different computers to simulate each other. As long as one computer had an ISP description and another could run an interpreter for ISP, the second computer could simulate the first by running its ISP description.

Another important project developed by Newell led to a theory of human-computer interaction. In 1970, the Xerox Palo Alto Research Center—a center on digital technology—was formed in Palo Alto, California. Newell, a consultant for the center, proposed to study the way that users interact with computers. So, in 1974, Stuart Card and Thomas Moran—two of Newell's students—moved to Palo Alto. Together with Newell, they collected a wide range of psychological data and theories—such as Fitts's Law, the power law of learning, and models of human typing—and unified them into a general model of routine cognitive skills that could be used by designers of computer interfaces (published in 1983).

The model described the human cognitive architecture, which was assumed to include perceptual, motor, and cognitive processors as well as memories to store data. The model estimated the main functional characteristics of the components, such as the time required for a processor's cycle and the size of the memories. The model was also associated with a methodology for analyzing a computer user's routine task by separating the task into the basic processes necessary to perform it. Using this methodology, a designer could approximately predict the time it would take a user to perform a certain routine task, such as typing a piece of text or using the mouse to reach a target. Modeling the routine cognitive skills of human beings required a synthesis of many psychological data and theories. This provided a blueprint and some impetus for Newell's final and most ambitious project: a theory of the widest possible range of psychological phenomena, a unified theory of cognition.

Newell saw the science of psychology as fragmented: Practitioners specialized in a narrow range of phenomena, such as some aspect of perception, memory, or reasoning; perhaps they even developed a specialized theory to explain the phenomena. But starting in the 1970s, Newell argued that psychologists could aim higher. Newell saw minds and computers as *knowledge systems*, namely, systems that may be understood in terms of the content of their beliefs and goals. At the knowledge level—the most abstract level of analysis for intelligent systems—behavior is predicted and explained by assuming that the system pursues goals in light of its beliefs. According to Newell, knowledge systems are implemented—always imperfectly—by *physical symbol systems*, that is, systems that generate behavior by executing programs on symbolic structures. From his extensive experience with artificial computers, he knew that computers could be understood in terms of their architecture (the fixed mechanisms) plus their programs (the software). Newell argued that the human mind could be understood in the same way, provided that psychologists go beyond their narrow specializations and bring existing psychological data and theories to bear on the nature of the human cognitive architecture.

As a vehicle for his unified theory of cognition, Newell chose Soar, a production systems architecture for general intelligence that he and his students John Laird and Paul Rosenbloom began working on around the early 1980s. The core of Soar as a unified theory is a general-purpose problem solver. To a first approximation, it is a production systems version of GPS. The system learns by *chunking*, a notion that takes George Miller's classic notion of an information chunk (1956) and extends it to procedural learning: After it solves a problem, Soar creates a new instruction in the form of a production, which summarizes what needs to be done to solve that problem. The next time it encounters that problem, Soar may use this new production, without having to solve the problem anew. Thus, Soar's chunking explains some types of learning.

In developing his unified theory, Newell took into account as many architectural constraints as possible: from neuroscience (size and speed of components), psychology (behaviors and reaction times), and computer science (features of symbol processing). He and his collaborators developed their theory into explanations of many psychological phenomena at many temporal scales, from simple behaviors, such as pressing a button when a light goes on, to solving difficult problems, such as cryptarithmetic puzzles. Although Newell's unified theory aims at bridging levels and satisfying multiple constraints, Newell did not attempt to explain how the architecture he proposed may be implemented in the human brain.

Newell subsumed much of his previous work—on problem solving, human-computer interaction, and computer architectures—within Soar as a unified theory. In addition, many important psychological phenomena and some influential mid-range theories (such as Philip Johnson-Laird's theory of mental models) found a place within Soar. Newell worked on Soar until his death from cancer in 1992 at the age of sixty-five. After that, work continued in several laboratories around the world. Soar made possible the creation of virtual human beings, such as synthetic pilots that behaved as much as possible like human pilots.

Newell led the development of computer science, AI, and cognitive science as both disciplines and institutions, and his peers recognized his role in research and service. His long list of honors includes: the Harry Goode Memorial Award of the American Federation of Information Processing Societies (1971); the A. M. Turing Award of the Association of Computing Machinery (1975, with Herbert Simon); founding president of the American Association for Artificial Intelligence (1980); the Distinguished Scientific Contribution Award of the American Psychological Association (1985); and in 1992, one month before his death, the National Medal of Science.

BIBLIOGRAPHY

WORKS BY NEWELL

"Allen Newell Collection." Carnegie Mellon University Archives. Available from http://diva.library.cmu.edu/Newell/. Newell's Nachlass.

With Hugh S. Kelly, Fred M. Tonge, Edward A. Feigenbaum, et al. *Information Processing Language-V Manual.* 2nd ed. Englewood Cliffs, NJ: Prentice-Hall, 1964.

With Herbert Simon. *Human Problem Solving.* Englewood Cliffs, NJ: Prentice-Hall, 1972.

With Daniel P. Siewiorek and C. Gordon Bell. *Computer Structures: Principles and Examples.* New York: McGraw-Hill, 1982.

With Stuart Card and Thomas P. Moran. *The Psychology of Human-Computer Interaction.* Hillsdale, NJ: LEA, 1983.

Unified Theories of Cognition. Cambridge, MA: Cambridge University Press, 1990.

"Précis of *Unified Theories of Cognition.*" *Behavioral and Brain Sciences* 15 (1992): 425–492. With commentaries by many cognitive scientists and a response by Newell.

With Paul S. Rosenbloom and John E. Laird, eds. *The Soar Papers: Research on Integrated Intelligence*, vol. 2. Cambridge, MA: MIT Press, 1993.

OTHER SOURCES

Boden, Margaret. *Mind as Machine: A History of Cognitive Science.* Oxford: Oxford University Press, 2006. Devotes many pages to Newell's work and its historical role.

Feigenbaum, Edward A., and Julian Feldman, eds. *Computers and Thought.* New York: McGraw-Hill, 1963. Reprints some of Newell, Shaw, and Simon's early AI papers.

Laird, John E., and Paul S. Rosenbloom. "The Research of Allen Newell." *AI Magazine* 13, no. 4 (1992): 17–45.

Michon, John, and Aladin Akyurek, eds. *Soar: A Cognitive Architecture in Perspective.* Norwell, MA: Kluwer Academic, 1992.

Simon, Herbert A. "Allen Newell: 1927–1992." *IEEE Annals of the History of Computing* 20, no. 2 (1998): 63–76.

Steier, David, and Tom M. Mitchell, eds. *Mind Matters: A Tribute to Allen Newell.* Mahwah, NJ: LEA, 1996.

Gualtiero Piccinini

NEWELL, HOMER EDWARD, JR. (*b.* Holyoke, Massachusetts, 11 March 1915; *d.* Alexandria, Virginia, 18 July 1983), *mathematics, physics, astrophysics, space science.*

Homer E. Newell Jr. served for nearly thirty years as a leader in the space science community, first at the Naval Research Laboratory and later as a key official in the National Aeronautics and Space Administration (NASA). He is best known for his service as the NASA associate administrator for space science during the Apollo era of the 1960s. But even before the creation of NASA in 1958, Newell played a key role in efforts to develop the space science community and to use the rapidly advancing technology of rocketry and electronics to study the upper atmosphere and space. He retired from NASA in 1973, along with many other Apollo era leaders, and continued to serve on science study boards and to write and lecture on the subject until his death a decade later.

Early Professional Experiences. Educated at Harvard University, where he earned both bachelor and master of arts degrees, he then went to the University of Wisconsin, where he received a PhD in mathematics in 1940. While away from his native New England, Newell met, courted, and married Mary Janice May Hurd of Madison, Wisconsin (known to all as Janice) in February 1936. They eventually had four children, Judith, Sue, Jennifer, and Andrew.

Upon completing his PhD, Newell accepted a position as an instructor in the Mathematics Department of the University of Maryland, and he moved his family to Kensington, Maryland. Newell worked at the university for only two years, and through the bulk of World War II served as an aerial navigation instructor for the Civil Aeronautics Administration. This fulfilled his military obligation, maximized the use of his talents, and kept him near his growing family. Indeed he stayed in government service the remainder of his career. In 1944 Newell moved to the Naval Research Laboratory (NRL) in suburban Washington, D.C. During his tenure with NRL he served as theoretical physicist, mathematician, section head, head of the Rocket Sonde Branch, and acting superintendent of the Atmosphere and Astrophysics Division.

The Early Space Science Program. Beginning in 1945, the NRL organized a rocket research component to explore the possibilities of this new technology developed by various nations, especially Germany with its V-2 program. Named the Rocket Sonde Research Section, NRL viewed this organization as necessary to the long-term future of national defense. Germany had demonstrated with its V-2s that this technology held potential for the United States, and all of the federal organizations engaged

Homer Newell. COURTESY OF NASA.

in research into high-speed flight scrambled to develop the capability. In addition to NRL, the army brought back for study not only captured V-2s but also some of the scientists and engineers who had developed these weapons, most notably Wernher von Braun and several associates from Peenemünde, who made a point of surrendering to the Americans so they might continue their work after the war. As another example, the National Advisory Committee for Aeronautics (NACA) created the Pilotless Aircraft Research Division (PARD) at its Langley Research Center, Hampton, Virginia, devoting its efforts to the study of stability and maneuverability of high-speed weapons, especially guided missiles.

Newell joined the NRL Rocket Sonde Research Section immediately, and in 1946 was named to head it. He commented in his 1980 memoir that the members of this section were inexperienced and somewhat naive at first. He wrote:

> No one in the section was experienced in upper atmospheric research, so the section immediately entered a period of intensive self-education. Members lectured each other on aerodynamics, rocket propulsion, telemetering—whatever appeared to be important for the new tasks ahead. The author gave a number of talks on satellites and satellite orbits. Indeed, the possibility of going immediately to artificial satellites of the earth as research platforms was considered by the group, which assimilated carefully whatever information it could obtain from military studies of the time. The conclusion was that one could

Newell

indeed begin an artificial satellite program and expect to succeed, but that the amount of new development required would be costly and time consuming. (p. 33)

Newell's purpose in this effort had more to do with science than engineering, however, and he guided the section away from efforts to reach orbit as a near term goal. Instead he emphasized the development of small and less complex "sounding rockets" designed to reach the upper atmosphere, where scientists could use instrument packages to measure cosmic rays and other physical phenomena of interest. As he wrote in his memoir, "scientists could not hope to have their instruments aloft for some years to come and, anyway, were not likely to get their hands on the necessary funds. The Rocket Sonde Research Section accordingly shelved the satellite idea and turned to sounding rockets" (p. 34).

In the context of scientific exploration of the upper atmosphere Newell first demonstrated on a broad stage one of his chief skills, the scientist as entrepreneur. The bespectacled, balding scientist had the ability to persuade divergent people with divergent interests and priorities to agree on fundamental steps and to execute them. This proved one of his most important talents throughout his later career. He repeatedly fashioned coalitions of scientists, engineers, and military and government officials to support various initiatives that at first seemed impossible. For example, he proved central to efforts to persuade the army's Jet Propulsion Laboratory (JPL), which wanted to develop rockets for national security purposes, to allow scientists to place scientific instruments atop them. Newell accepted JPL's condition that these efforts be utilitarian science that either directly supported the larger defense mission or was a natural by-product of it. Beyond that, he persistently advocated the role of science and oversaw efforts to place on some of the army's test vehicles instruments that provided data about the upper atmosphere, solar and stellar ultraviolet radiation, and the aurora. This became a very successful scientific program that was carried out with limited fanfare and funding. As a result, scientists taking part in this program used JPL's WAC-Corporal rocket, and later the Department of Defense's captured V-2s, as well as follow-on missiles, for scientific research throughout the 1940s and 1950s.

The breakthrough in Newell's, and several of his colleagues', campaign for science on military rockets came on 16 January 1946 when several physicists and astronomers interested in cosmic-ray, solar, and atmospheric research gathered at NRL along with representatives of the military services to discuss possible cooperation. "It was plain from the deliberations that a number of groups," he recalled in his memoir, "both in universities and in the military would be interested in taking part in a program of high-altitude rocket research" (p. 34). This meeting led to the creation of the V-2 Upper Atmosphere Panel to oversee this effort in February 1946 to "develop a scientific program, assign priorities for experiments to fly on the V-2s, and to advise the Army Ordnance Department on matters essential to the success of the program" (Megerian). In March 1948 it became the Upper Atmosphere Rocket Research Panel and in 1957 the Rocket and Satellite Research Panel. It prioritized the use of these vehicles to study solar and stellar ultraviolet radiation, the aurora, and the nature of the upper atmosphere. As a result, the panel served as the "godfather" of the infant scientific field of space science. This successful collaboration led to numerous important scientific results, including measurement of the ionosphere, solar radiation, cosmic radiation, micrometeorites, and sky brightness, as well as biomedical research and photography of Earth from space.

Newell played a key role in these activities throughout the pre-*Sputnik* period. Initially chaired by Ernst Krause, whom Newell worked for at NRL, the panel later had James Van Allen as chair and thereafter Newell. He and the other members of this panel put the V-2s to good scientific use. For example, between 1946 and 1951 sixty-seven captured V-2s were test launched, most with some scientific payload aboard. The panel also oversaw development of new sounding rockets and continued to control the nation's sounding rocket program until NASA Headquarters took over this function in 1958. After the formation of NASA, several members of the panel, including Newell, joined NASA and applied the experience they had gained to the organization and management of NASA's space science program.

At the same time, Newell was involved as the space science coordinator for the Naval Research Laboratory's Viking rocket program. Built by the Glenn L. Martin Company, the first Viking launched from White Sands on 3 May 1949, while the twelfth and last Viking took off on 4 February 1955. The program uncovered significant scientific information about the upper atmosphere and took impressive high-altitude photographs of Earth. All of these were sounding rockets, and their science experiments were coordinated through the Upper Atmosphere Rocket Research Panel.

IGY Space Science Program. Although space science went back to the early twentieth century and advanced significantly using balloons and atmospheric flights before the development of rocketry, it received an immeasurable boost from the International Geophysical Year (IGY) of July 1957 through December 1958. As early as 1950 a small group of scientists that included Newell began discussing among themselves the possibility of using Earth-circling satellites to obtain scientific information about the planet. In 1952, urged on by these same American scientists, the International Council of Scientific Unions (ICSU) proposed the IGY, a cooperative scientific endeavor to study solar-terrestrial relations during a period of maximum solar activity. In all, 67 nations agreed.

In October 1954, at the behest of Newell and his colleagues, ICSU challenged nations to use their missiles being developed for war to launch scientific satellites to support the IGY research program. In July 1955 largely the same enclave of American scientists convinced President Dwight D. Eisenhower that the United States should respond to the ICSU call for participation in the IGY by launching a scientific satellite. Eisenhower's decision called for existing organizations within the Department of Defense to develop and launch a small scientific satellite, "under international auspices, such as the International Geophysical Year, in order to emphasize its peaceful purposes[;] … considerable prestige and psychological benefits will accrue to the nation which first is successful in launching a satellite … especially if the USSR were to be the first to establish a satellite" (NSC 5520). The result was Project Vanguard, carried out under the supervision of the NRL, with Newell in a key position to oversee the development of the scientific payload. The proposed launch vehicle combined the older Viking first stage, an Aerobee sounding rocket second stage, and a new third stage with a 3.5-pound scientific satellite payload.

While Vanguard was in development, the Soviet Union launched *Sputnik 1* on 4 October 1957 and utterly changed the nature of space science. This satellite was the Soviet entry into the IGY program, and its success spelled crisis in the United States. Within weeks accelerated efforts for American space flight had been placed in motion. Almost in desperation the NRL attempted the launch of the first Vanguard mission on 8 December 1957; it led to a spectacular explosion and fire on the launchpad on national television. To catch up, on 31 January 1958 the U.S. Army's Ballistic Missile Agency used a Redstone rocket to place the first American satellite, *Explorer 1,* into orbit. This satellite discovered what came to be known as the Van Allen belts of radiation, and a terrestrial magnetosphere.

Like many others, Newell helped to develop the response to *Sputnik.* The event led directly to several critical efforts aimed at "catching up" to the Soviet Union's space achievements. Among these:

- a full-scale review of both the civil and military programs of the United States (scientific satellite efforts and ballistic missile development);
- establishment of a presidential science advisor in the White House, who had responsibility for overseeing the activities of the federal government in science and technology;
- creation of the Advanced Research Projects Agency in the Department of Defense, and the consolidation of several space activities under centralized management;
- establishment of the National Aeronautics and Space Administration to manage civil space operations; and
- passage of the National Defense Education Act to provide federal funding for education in the scientific and technical disciplines.

A direct result of this crisis, NASA began operations on 1 October 1958, absorbing the NACA intact: its eight thousand employees, an annual budget of one hundred million dollars, three major research laboratories—Langley Aeronautical Laboratory, Ames Aeronautical Laboratory, and Lewis Flight Propulsion Laboratory—and two smaller test facilities. NASA quickly incorporated other organizations into the new agency. These included the space science group of the Naval Research Laboratory in the District of Columbia, including Homer Newell; the Jet Propulsion Laboratory managed by the California Institute of Technology for the army; and the Army Ballistic Missile Agency in Huntsville, Alabama. Eventually NASA created several other centers, and by the early 1960s had ten located around the country.

Establishment of Space Science at NASA. Homer Newell enthusiastically transferred to NASA immediately after its creation in October 1958 to assume responsibility for planning and development of the new agency's space science program. Working under Dr. Abe Silverstein, who headed NASA's Office of Space Flight Program, Newell's first task involved developing a science program for NASA. He recognized that the National Aeronautics and Space Act of 1958 gave NASA broad authority to oversee all space science activities in the United States. The act gave NASA responsibility for "the expansion of human knowledge of phenomena in the atmosphere and space" (section 102[c][1]). Another passage set a goal for space science: "The preservation of the role of the United States as a leader in aeronautical and space science and technology" (section 102[c][5]).

Newell also received from NASA administrator T. Keith Glennan a clear statement of his task. It outlined the objectives for NASA's space flight experiments, and stated that the research program would be national in scope based on recommendations from educational and research institutions, industry, and federal laboratories. A key player in this process would be the Space Science Board (SSB) of the National Academy of Sciences, but

NASA would establish the priorities for experiments and projects, not the SSB. Newell once again demonstrated his capability as a scientific entrepreneur by forging a strong relationship with the SSB that preserved NASA's suzerainty while ensuring useful SSB involvement. Among other things, he used the board to provide broad oversight of NASA's space science program and conduct many summer studies to develop long-range strategies for space science.

Newell also established a Space Science Steering Committee of other senior NASA officials and appointed several scientific subcommittees to provide technical support. Broadly based, these subcommittees had some of the most prestigious scientists in the nation, as well as many representatives from other NASA organizations. They took control of efforts to develop programs of research in their specific fields, reviewed proposals for experiments on any scientific mission, and established priorities. In spite of some rocky disturbances early in NASA's history, Newell built close relationships between members of the scientific community and the engineering community that dominated NASA. By the early 1960s he had created a relatively stable and collegial, cobbling together a NASA/university/industry/research installation partnership to execute a broad range of scientific activities in the 1960s. By fostering a diversity of opinion from all interested parties in this process, Newell ensured that decisions were not only better than could be obtained by any one person, but also that they constituted a broad consensus. He also encouraged the scientists and engineers to communicate effectively so that a mission was ready for development and that the program office had chosen the best possible experiments. Newell's success was reflected in the decision of the new NASA Administrator, James E. Webb, in November 1961 to appoint him associate administrator of a newly created Office of Space Science. Thereafter Newell reported directly to Webb, but continued to operate in essentially the same way.

Webb also gave Newell responsibility for oversight of NASA's launch vehicles for robotic missions. He assigned JPL and the Goddard Space Flight Center, Greenbelt, Maryland, to him, and asked him to take responsibility for relations with the university community. By the end of 1961, therefore, Newell had under his direct control the entire assets, institutions, and facilities needed to conduct NASA's space science program. This approach to space science continued approximately unchanged until 1974, when NASA Administrator James C. Fletcher reorganized NASA in the aftermath of Apollo and following the retirement of Newell.

Apollo Science. In 1961 President John F. Kennedy, responding to perceived challenges to U.S. leadership in science and technology, announced a lunar landing effort that would place an American on the Moon before the end of the decade. Kennedy unveiled this commitment, called Project Apollo, before Congress on 25 May 1961 in a speech on "Urgent National Needs," billed as a second State of the Union message. Though it was not created as a science program, Newell worked tirelessly to ensure that a healthy science component existed in the Apollo program. He succeeded largely through diligence and not a little conference room brawling.

It was never easy, however; Newell had constantly to negotiate the differences in priority between engineers interested in landing astronauts on the Moon and returning them safely versus scientists seeking to advance scientific ends. Newell commented specifically on this problem in his 1980 memoir:

> For space science one of the most difficult problems of leadership, both inside and outside NASA, concerned the manned spaceflight program. Underlying the prevailing discontent in the scientific community regarding this program was a rather general conviction that virtually everything that men could do in the investigation of space, including the moon and planets, automated spacecraft could also do and at much lower cost. This conviction was reinforced by the Apollo program's being primarily engineering in character. Indeed, until after the success of *Apollo 11,* science was the least of Apollo engineers' concerns. Further, the manned project appeared to devour huge sums [of money], only small fractions of which could have greatly enhanced the unmanned space science program. (p. 290)

The scientists viewed the amount spent on human space missions as excessive and by reducing that part of NASA's budget the funding could go to robotic missions. The expansive costs of human spaceflight might be more effectively utilized for scientific purposes by sending only robots. They perceived inefficiency, redundancy, and enormous costs to keep astronauts alive as waste, and with only a small percentage of that funding they believed they could accomplish so much.

This was very much an issue of an individual scientist's angle of vision. James A. Van Allen, the dean of astrophysics and a respected voice on behalf of science, worked with Newell for years but always opposed human spaceflight, including Apollo, because of the high costs that he believed could be used more productively to send out robotic explorers. In addition to other arguments, Newell appealed to the scientific community's pragmatism. He often made the case to his scientist colleagues that everyone gained by having the much larger human spaceflight activity essentially serving as political cover for the much smaller space science program. If not for human

Newell

spaceflight, he asserted, Congress, the public, the media, and those representing competing interests would raid the space science budget. As it was, therefore, the human spaceflight budget would be the target. This served to quell the criticisms of many scientists who recognized that spaceflight was not a zero-sum game and that a reduction in the human spaceflight budget would not result in a corresponding increase in funding for space science.

Under Newell's leadership, scientists exploited the opportunity to place more than seventy-five experiments on the various Apollo missions, and in the case of the last landing mission, to have one of their own, geologist Harrison Schmitt, undertake fieldwork on the Moon. The science packages deployed on the Moon led eventually to an impressive array of more than ten thousand scientific papers and a major reinterpretation of the origins and evolution of the Moon. As reported in *Science* in the issue of 30 March 1973, near the time of Newell's retirement from NASA, "Man's knowledge of the moon has been dramatically transformed during the brief 3½ years between the first and last Apollo landing" (Hammond, p. 1313).

Planetary Science. In addition to the human spaceflight programs, Newell also presided over an aggressive effort to send scientific probes to the Moon and planets, as well as observatories placed in Earth orbit. During the 1960s the U.S. space program began an impressive effort to gather information on the solar system using ground-, air-, and space-based equipment. Although the most significant findings of this investigation would not come until the 1970s, perhaps the "golden age" of planetary science, studies of the planets captured the imagination of many people from all types of backgrounds like nothing else save the Apollo lunar missions. For all the genuine importance of magnetospheric physics and solar studies, meteorology and plate tectonics, it was photographs of the planets and theories about the origins of the solar system that appealed to a much broader cross section of the public. As a result NASA had little difficulty in capturing and holding a widespread interest in this aspect of the space science program.

A centerpiece of Newell's planetary science program was the Mariner series of probes, originated in the early part of the decade to investigate the nearby planets. Built by Jet Propulsion Laboratory scientists and technicians, satellites of this program proved enormously productive. The United States claimed the first success in planetary exploration during the summer of 1962 when *Mariner 2* was launched toward Venus. In December it arrived at the planet, probing the clouds, estimating planetary temperatures, measuring the charged particle environment, and looking for a magnetic field similar to Earth's magnetosphere (but finding none). In July 1965 *Mariner 4* flew by Mars, taking twenty-one close-up pictures, and *Mariner 5* visited Venus in 1967 to investigate the atmosphere. *Mariner 6* and *Mariner 7,* launched in February and March 1969, each passed Mars about five months later, studying its atmosphere and surface to lay the groundwork for an eventual landing on the planet. Among other discoveries from these probes, they found that much of Mars was cratered almost like the Moon, that volcanoes had once been active on the planet, that the frost observed seasonally on the poles was made of carbon dioxide, and that huge plates indicated considerable tectonic activity. Proposals for additional Mariner probes were also considered but because of budgetary considerations did not fly during the decade. These space probes, as well as others, accumulated volumes of data on the near planets and changed many scientific conceptions that had long held sway.

While Newell was pleased with these accomplishments, all was not rosy with the politics of planetary exploration. In the summer of 1967, even as the technical abilities required to conduct an adventurous space science program were being demonstrated, Newell and the planetary science community suffered a devastating defeat in Congress and lost funding for a soft-lander to Mars. No other NASA effort except Project Apollo was more exciting than the Mars program in the middle part of the decade. The planet had long held a special attraction to Americans, so much like Earth and possibly even sustaining life, and the lander would have allowed for extended robotic exploration of the Red Planet. A projected $2 billion program, the lander was to use the Saturn V launch vehicle being developed for Apollo. The problem revolved around the lack of consensus among scientists on the validity of the Mars initiative. Some were excited but others thought it was too expensive and placed too many hopes on the shoulders of one project and one project manager. Without that consensus and with other national priorities, such as spending for Great Society social programs, combating urban unrest, and the military in Vietnam, the Mars lander was an easy target in Congress.

From this defeat Newell and the scientific community learned a hard lesson about the pragmatic, and sometimes brutal, politics associated with Big Science. They realized that strife within the discipline had to be kept within the discipline in order to put forward a united front against the priorities of other interest groups and other government leaders. While imposing support from the scientific community could not guarantee that any initiative would become a political reality, without it a program could not be funded. They also learned that while a $750 million program found little opposition at any level, a $2 billion project crossed an ill-defined but very real threshold triggering intense competition for those dollars. Having learned these lessons, as well as some

Newell

more subtle ones, the Newell contingent regrouped and went forward in the latter part of the decade with a trimmed-down Mars lander program, called Viking, that was funded and provided astounding scientific data in the mid-1970s.

Later Years. In 1967 NASA administrator James Webb extended Newell's responsibilities by naming him as the agency's associate administrator, the position from which he retired on 31 December 1973. After his retirement Newell spent the next decade serving on advisory committees and writing and lecturing widely on space science. He died of a stroke at his Alexandria, Virginia, home on 18 July 1983.

Representative Edward Boland inserted into the *Congressional Record* a statement about Newell's life and accomplishments, singling out his belief that the "scientific exploration of space should be under civilian rather than military auspices. He was also a staunch supporter of the free exchange between nations of data collected by rockets and satellites. This policy was at the heart of the International Geophysical Year of 1957–58." To the last Newell had asserted the importance of space science. He told a reporter from the *Washington Times* in 1982 that he "believes that the Reagan administration is not spending enough money or energy on space science and exploration." He continued, "We start something—go great guns—yet leave the whole thing unfinished. There's research still to be done. You wish it could be done!"

BIBLIOGRAPHY

WORKS BY NEWELL

High Altitude Rocket Research. New York: Academic Press, 1953.

Vector Analysis. New York: McGraw-Hill, 1955.

Space Book for Young People. New York: Whittelsey House, 1958.

Sounding Rockets. New York: McGraw-Hill, 1959.

Window in the Sky: The Story of Our Upper Atmosphere. New York: McGraw-Hill, 1959.

Express to the Stars: Rockets in Action. New York: McGraw-Hill, 1961.

Guide to Rockets, Missiles, and Satellites. New York: Whittelsey House, 1961.

Beyond the Atmosphere: Early Years of Space Science. NASA Special Publication 4211. Washington, DC: National Aeronautics and Space Administration, Office of Management, Scientific and Technical Information Program, 1980.

OTHER SOURCES

Beattie, Donald A. *Taking Science to the Moon: Lunar Experiments and the Apollo Program.* Baltimore, MD: Johns Hopkins University Press, 2001.

Boland, Edward P. "Dr. Homer E. Newell Jr., Associate Administrator of NASA, 1967–1973," *Congressional Record,* daily edition, 29 July 1983, p. E 3994. Also U.S. Congress. Boland (MA). "Dr. Homer E. Newell Jr., Associate Administrator of NASA, 1967–1973." *Congressional Record,* permanent edition, 98th Cong., 1st sess., 129, part 16 (29 July 1983): 21780–21781.

Bulkeley, Rip. *The Sputniks Crisis and Early United States Space Policy: A Critique of the Historiography of Space.* Bloomington: Indiana University Press, 1991.

Green, Constance McLaughlin, and Milton Lomask. *Vanguard: A History.* Washington, DC: Smithsonian Institution Press, 1971.

Hammond, Allen L. "Lunar Science: Analyzing the Apollo Legacy." *Science,* n.s., 179 (1973): 1313–1315.

Lowman, Paul D., Jr. "T Plus Twenty Five Years: A Defense of the Apollo Program." *Journal of the British Interplanetary Society* 49 (1996): 71–79.

Megerian, George K. "Minutes of V-2 Upper Atmosphere Research Panel Meeting." V-2 Report no. 1, 27 February 1946 (unpublished). NASA Historical Reference Collection, NASA History Office, Washington, DC.

Murray, Bruce. *Journey into Space.* New York: W.W. Norton, 1989.

National Security Council, NSC 5520. "Draft Statement of Policy on U.S. Scientific Satellite Program," 20 May 1955 (unpublished). NASA Historical Reference Collection, NASA History Office, Washington, DC.

Naugle, John E. *First among Equals: The Selection of NASA Space Science Experiments.* NASA Special Publication 4215. Washington, DC: National Aeronautics and Space Administration, Office of Management, Scientific and Technical Information Program, 1991.

"Space Planner; Homer Edward Newell Jr.," *New York Times,* 13 April 1959, p. 18.

Spitzer, Lyman, Jr. "Astronomical Advantages of an Extra-Terrestrial Observatory." *Astronomy Quarterly* 7 (September 1946): 19–20.

United States Congress. *National Aeronautics and Space Act of 1958* (Public Law 85-568, 29 July 1958). *U.S. Statutes at Large* 72 (1958): 426–438.

United States National Committee for the International Geophysical Year 1957–1958. "Minutes of the First Meeting, Technical Panel on Earth Satellite Program, October 20, 1955" (unpublished). NASA Historical Reference Collection, NASA History Office, Washington, DC.

Van Allen, James A. *Origins of Maqnetospheric Physics.* Washington, DC: Smithsonian Institution Press, 1983.

Varricchio, Louis. "Inconstant Moon—A Brief History of U.S. Lunar Science from 1840 to 1972" (unpublished paper). NASA Historical Reference Collection, NASA History Office, Washington, DC.

Ward, Kathryn. "Physicist Homer Newell." *Washington Times,* 8 July 1982.

Roger D. Launius

Newell

NEWELL, NORMAN DENNIS (*b.* Chicago, Illinois, 27 January 1909; *d.* Leonia, New Jersey, 18 April 2005), *paleontology, earth history, sedimentary geology, education.*

As an invertebrate paleontologist, Newell was internationally known for his work on classification, morphology, and evolution of fossil bivalve mollusks. In a broader perspective, he recognized the episodic nature of life's history and called attention to its major turning points and mass extinctions. A pioneer in the field of paleoecology, he applied his research on modern reefs and associated sediments to interpretations of their counterparts in the rock record. He was an authority on Permian and Triassic stratigraphy, and argued for worldwide fall in sea level as a cause of late Permian extinctions.

Boyhood. Soon after Newell's birth, his dentist father moved the family to the small town of Stafford, Kansas, where Norman spent his boyhood. Although Virgil Bingham Newell did not live to see Norman enter college, the father's strong interest in natural history clearly influenced his son's career choice. The elder Newell had retained his textbooks from a college geology course and had Norman poring over them by the age of ten. Two years later the pair traveled to Colorado to look for fossils. On this trip Norman saw his first rock ledges and collected his first fossil.

Education. When he finished high school in Stafford, Newell's mother, Nellie (Clark) Newell, fulfilled her pledge to his father to see that Norman went to college. She accompanied him to Lawrence, the site of the University of Kansas, where she acquired a house and rented rooms to help finance his tuition. Norman, already an accomplished clarinetist, helped pay his way by playing in local dance bands. At the University of Kansas Newell majored in geology and received both BS (1929) and AM (1931) degrees. During these years, he had close contact with Geology Department head and state geologist Raymond Moore. Moore's forceful personality and single-minded determination to excel left a lasting impression. An especially valuable experience was a summer field course in which Moore took nine students in an open truck on a round-trip geological traverse between Lawrence and Los Angeles.

In addition to the student-professor relationship, several specific actions by Moore were important in shaping Newell's career. As state geologist, Moore gave Newell part-time work as an undergraduate and continued to employ him following graduation. Newell earned his master's degree during his first years with the state survey. Moore, whom Newell later referred to as his foster father, then recommended him for a graduate fellowship at Yale where, after two years of residence, he was awarded a doctorate in 1933.

Three people were especially influential during Newell's years at Yale. Professor Carl O. Dunbar, a renowned invertebrate paleontologist and stratigrapher, supervised his graduate program. Although retired, the eminent earth historian Charles Schuchert was still active and a source of friendly advice. In fact, Schuchert helped make Newell's New Haven days financially feasible by employing his wife Valerie to catalog specimens. The third memorable individual was an older graduate student, J. Brookes Knight (1888–1960), whose personality and intense interest in fossil mollusks greatly impressed Newell. It was at Knight's suggestion that he chose bivalve mollusks, then termed pelecypods by American paleontologists, as his field of specialization. A Sterling Fellowship subsidized a postdoctoral year at Yale, during which Newell accomplished most of the research embodied in the first of his influential paleontological monographs.

Professional Advancement. Newell's first professional employment was as a geologist with the Kansas State Geological Survey (1929–1937). During this interval, interrupted by three years of study at Yale, Newell published geologic maps and reports on eastern Kansas counties. Still benefiting from state geologist Moore's tutelage, Newell gained practical field experience in detailed classification and correlation of strata.

In 1934, while still employed by the state survey, Newell was appointed to the University of Kansas geology faculty. This dual appointment continued until 1937 when Moore gave his protégé another career boost. The U.S. State Department had appointed Moore to be an official delegate to the International Geological Congress to be held that year in the Soviet Union. When the university chancellor, no friend of Moore, refused to release him for that purpose, Moore appointed Newell to take his place. At the congress the twenty-eight-year-old Newell became acquainted with many foreign paleontologists and stratigraphers. He recognized the importance of being part of an international network of scientists with kindred interests, and he actively maintained such contacts throughout his career.

Upon his return, Newell accepted an associate professorship at the University of Wisconsin where he taught until 1942. Soon after America's entry in World War II, the State Department recommended him to the Peruvian government to participate in that country's survey of petroleum resources, an assignment that lasted for three years.

In 1945 Newell joined the staffs of two New York City institutions: Columbia University, as professor of geology, and the American Museum of Natural History, as

Newell

curator. This arrangement proved ideal and Newell's career flourished in an environment that combined excellent research support at the museum with teaching and supervision of graduate students at the university. His dual responsibilities continued until his formal retirement in 1977 when he was awarded emeritus status in both positions. If anything, retirement only whetted his appetite for research. The last of his annual field seasons involved work in Utah, Nevada, and Idaho when he was eighty-one. At age ninety he was still working many hours each week at the museum.

Scientific Accomplishments. Newell's reputation as a leading authority on taxonomy, morphology, and evolution of fossil bivalve mollusks began with publication in 1937 of a now-classic monograph on late Paleozoic representatives of the superfamily Pectinacea. This report was decades ahead of its time in integrating biological and paleontological information (e.g., muscle anatomy) and concepts (e.g., population variability) when interpreting morphology and relationships of fossil shells. Innovations in this work include original observations on ligament structure and on shell microstructure and mineralogy. The treatment of fossils as once-living organisms, an approach now taken for granted, was unusual at a time when invertebrate paleontologists were trained by geology faculties with the goal of using fossils to determine the relative age of their host strata.

Although Newell continued to describe new species to the end of his life, it can be argued that his most influential taxonomic work took place in the 1960s. The highlights were the publication in 1965 of his comprehensive classification of the Bivalvia and his major role, both as editor and contributor, in producing volumes one and two of the Bivalvia section of the *Treatise on Invertebrate Paleontology.* These two books appeared in 1969 and served for decades as primary references in their field.

Unlike many paleontologists whose dedication to a particular taxonomic specialty commands all their attention, Newell had an unusually broad perspective on the fossil record. He shared his insights in papers that motivated his colleagues to find patterns in the record of speciation and extinction and to consider their causes in a biological context. In this respect, he helped transform invertebrate paleontology from its passive descriptive and applied aspect before World War II to a subsequent mutually beneficial partnership with the life sciences.

In several papers, Newell emphasized the episodic nature of the fossil record and the major turning points that he termed revolutions in the history of life. He called attention to the association in earth history of marine mass extinctions with worldwide changes in sea level and became well known for his advocacy of lowered sea level as the best explanation for the times of global mass extinctions of marine life. In this concept, withdrawal of the seas from the continents would impact shallow marine communities by loss of habitat space. As the subject of mass extinction attracted increased attention, Newell's hypothesis took its place in a lengthening list of proposed causes, each eventually considered by the scientific community to have some merit but to be unsatisfactory as the sole explanation.

During the 1950s Newell became a recognized leader in the emerging fields of paleoecology and carbonate sedimentology. He understood before most of his colleagues that interpretations of fossil reefs and ancient limestones would benefit from knowledge of modern environments where reefs are growing and carbonate sediments are accumulating. This vision caused him to organize teams of graduate students and colleagues for parallel work in the Bahamas and West Texas. The former activity produced a series of widely cited publications on carbonate sediments and marine ecology of the Grand Bahama Banks. These reports were part of the "first wave" of research by geologists from industry and academe that made the Bahamas a model for interpreting the origin of ancient limestones. The fieldwork in West Texas and the adjacent part of New Mexico resulted in a 1953 coauthored book on the Permian reef complex of the Guadalupe Mountains. The influence of that book on successive generations of geologists studying the Permian strata of that area cannot be overestimated.

Newell's interest in the Permian period, the last part of the Paleozoic era of earth history, did not begin or end with the West Texas project. As a stratigrapher, he had a career-long dedication to rocks of that age and to the superjacent Triassic strata. This stratigraphic interval has a particular fascination for earth historians because the Permo-Triassic boundary coincides with a major change in the fossil record that defines the passage from Paleozoic to Mesozoic eras. The late Permian mass extinctions are recognized as the most devastating on record, yet the Permo-Triassic boundary in many parts of the world is within a sequence of strata lacking evidence of dramatic physical events. Newell's first investigations concerning these topics dealt with the pertinent strata in the Rocky Mountains. Nearly two decades elapsed before he returned to the general problems posed by gaps in the stratigraphic record and, in particular, to the widespread hiatus at the Permo-Triassic boundary. From then on he was a frequent contributor to the long-term international debate concerned first with criteria for defining that boundary in the rock record and finally with selecting a locality for the world reference section.

Although not typical of his career activity, Newell's three years in Peru during World War II resulted in several

Newell

important scientific publications. Furthermore they illustrate his diverse talents as a field geologist and his career-long ability to turn apparently disadvantageous situations into opportunities. Much of his fieldwork was carried out under rigorous conditions in mountainous terrain where little geological work had been done. The best known of his reports, a 1949 Geological Society of America memoir on the geology of the Lake Titicaca region, established a foundation on which later specialists on geology of this part of the Andes could build.

Other Accomplishments. In the early 1970s Newell recognized that growing scientific illiteracy in the body politic was providing a willing audience for antievolutionists. He was among the first to take the problem seriously and, through a series of articles, took an active role in arousing the scientific community to the threat to science education. Not content with preaching to the choir, he devoted considerable time and effort to the writing of a 1982 book that would help the concerned layman make sense of the controversy.

When Newell arrived in New York in 1945, he organized a professional training program in invertebrate paleontology which involved cooperation between his two employers—Columbia University and the American Museum of Natural History. Some forty advanced degrees were granted in the program, many of them to exceptional individuals who became distinguished professors and museum paleontologists. In the former category, examples of his doctoral students are Alfred G. Fischer, Stephen Jay Gould, Bernhard Kummel, J. Keith Rigby, and Francis G. Stehli. Museum paleontologists include Roger L. Batten, Alan H. Cheetham, Niles Eldredge, Thomas R. Waller, and Ellis L. Yochelson.

Newell was not a charismatic lecturer, but many of the distinguished doctoral students he mentored eulogized him as a teacher. This was not for his classroom performance but for the manner in which he had influenced their lives. They were lastingly impressed by the characteristics observable in his day-to-day professional activity: a dedication to his science, a sharply focused pursuit of his current research program, and an ability to recognize and transcend weaknesses in conventional paleontological practices. Stephen Jay Gould, arguably Newell's most famous student, was lavish in his praise of Newell's influence on his career. Newell's comment in response to one of Gould's encomiums is revealing: "Steve honors me by calling me his teacher, but my role was primarily to encourage him and to point out promising opportunities" (1994, p. 25).

In his role as curator at the American Museum of Natural History, Newell served at various times as department head and as dean of the council of the scientific staff. Newell was active in many professional societies, serving as president of the Society for the Study of Evolution (1949), the Paleontological Society (1960–1961), and the Society of Systematic Zoology (1972–1973).

Personal Characteristics. Newell was by nature a field geologist with that breed's zest for scientific adventure and fundamental drive to collect data firsthand. For him, the next day (or season) of fieldwork was enthusiastically anticipated as an opportunity for exciting discoveries.

Although he often pointed out the significance to his career of having been in the right place at the right time and of the support received from others, several personal traits were critical to his success: superior intellect, strong self-discipline, basic self-confidence, and ambition. Little time was wasted on indecision, and a strong sense of priorities kept him from distractions and from bogging down in detail. Nevertheless the numerous visitors who interrupted his days at the museum received a cordial and gracious reception as did those who enjoyed the hospitality offered at the Newell household. In these social occasions he was convivial but never flamboyant. He was neither one to tell jokes nor to respond to them with a belly laugh, yet he had a dry, often self-deprecating sense of humor that surfaced unexpectedly on many occasions. In both writing and speaking, his manner of expression was incisive, parsimonious, and characterized by a dignified vocabulary and an absence of clichés.

He married Valerie Zirkle in 1928 while a student at the University of Kansas. Following her death in 1972, he married Gillian Wormall in 1973. For the rest of his life, Norman and Gillian were inseparable. She was an enthusiastic participant in all phases of his scientific work, and sustained him during his final years of declining health. Newell had no children.

Honors and Awards. Newell received the Mary Clarke Thompson Medal (National Academy of Sciences, 1960), Distinguished Service Alumni Award (University of Kansas, 1961), Medal of the University of Hiroshima (1964), Hayden Award in Geology and Paleontology (Philadelphia Academy of Sciences, 1965), Verrill Medal (Yale Peabody Museum, 1966), Gold Medal for Achievement in Science (American Museum of Natural History, 1978), Paleontological Society Medal (1979), Raymond C. Moore Medal (Society of Economic Paleontologists and Mineralogists, 1980), Scientific Freedom and Responsibility Award (American Association for the Advancement of Science, 1987), Penrose Medal (Geological Society of America, 1990), Special Award (American Association of Petroleum Geologists, 1996), Geological Society of Peru Medal (1997), and Legendary Geoscientist Award (American Geological Institute, 2004). He was elected to the American Philosophical Society (1971), the American Academy of Arts and Sciences (1979), and the National Academy of Sciences (1979).

BIBLIOGRAPHY

A complete bibliography of Newell's publications is included in the finding aid to the Norman Newell papers held in the library archives at the American Museum of Natural History in New York City.

WORKS BY NEWELL

Late Paleozoic Pelecypods: Pectinacea. State Geological Survey of Kansas, vol. 10, part 1 (1937). The first of his major paleontological monographs.

"Phyletic Size Increase, an Important Trend Illustrated by Fossil Invertebrates." *Evolution* 3 (1949): 103–124. An early effort to find patterns in the invertebrate fossil record.

Geology of the Lake Titicaca Region, Peru and Bolivia. Boulder, CO: Geological Society of America, 1949. A pioneering work on Andean geology.

With J. Keith Rigby, Arthur John Whiteman. and John Samuel Bradley. "Shoal-Water Geology and Environments, Eastern Andros Island, Bahamas." *Bulletin of the American Museum of Natural History* 97 (1951): 1–29. The first results of Newell's work on modern carbonate sediments.

With J. Keith Rigby, Alfred George Fischer, Arthur John Whiteman, John E. Hickox, and John Samuel Bradley. *The Permian Reef Complex of the Guadalupe Mountains Region, Texas and New Mexico.* San Francisco: W. H. Freeman, 1953. A classic study, organized and led by Newell, of a famous fossil reef.

"Catastrophism and the Fossil Record." *Evolution* 10 (1956): 97–101.

"Classification of the Bivalvia." *American Museum Novitates* 2206 (1965): 1–25. This classification was used in the 1969 *Treatise on Invertebrate Paleontology.*

"Revolutions in the History of Life." In *Uniformity and Simplicity,* edited by Claude C. Albritton, Jr. Boulder, CO: Geological Society of America Special Papers, no. 89, 1967.

With Leslie R. Cox and 23 others. *Treatise on Invertebrate Paleontology,* Part N, *Mollusca 6, Bivalvia,* vols. 1 and 2. Boulder, CO: Geological Society of America, 1969. When Cox died during preparation of these volumes, Newell assumed major responsibility for bringing them to completion.

With Donald W. Boyd. "Oyster-like Permian Bivalvia." *Bulletin of the American Museum of Natural History* 143 (1970): 217–282. Over several decades, Boyd coauthored numerous publications with his former professor.

"Special Creation and Organic Evolution." *Proceedings of the American Philosophical Society* 117 (1973): 323–331. The first of several articles in which he decried the resurgence of creationism.

Creation and Evolution: Myth or Reality? New York: Columbia University Press, 1982. An attempt to explain the controversy to nonscientists.

"Mass Extinction: Unique or Recurrent Causes?" In *Catastrophes and Earth History: The New Uniformitarianism,* edited by William A. Berggren and John A. Van Couvering. Princeton, NJ: Princeton University Press, 1984.

"Response [to Presentation of the Penrose Medal]." *Geological Society of America Bulletin* 103 (1991): 571–573. He voices his concern regarding several aspects of contemporary society.

"A Salute to Stephen J. Gould." *Kirtlandia* 48 (1994): 25–28. Includes Newell's appraisal of his role in Gould's education.

With Donald W. Boyd. "Pectinoid Bivalves of the Permian-Triassic Crisis." *American Museum of Natural History Bulletin* 227 (1995): 1–95. Many new species are described, but many of the phylogenetic conclusions are unconvincing.

With Christopher A. McRoberts. "Marine Myalinidae (Bivalvia: Pterioida) from the Permian of West Texas." *American Museum Novitates* 3469 (2005): 1–15. Newell's last paper appeared three weeks before his death.

OTHER SOURCES

Gould, Stephen Jay. "Reply [to Presentation of the David S. Ingalls, Jr. Award for Excellence]." *Kirtlandia* 48 (1994): 29–30. A famous Newell student expresses his appreciation to his mentor.

Pearce, Jeremy. "Norman Newell, 96, Scientist Who Studied Dying Species." *New York Times,* 23 April 2005. A representative obituary.

Donald W. Boyd

NEWTON, ISAAC (*b.* Woolsthorpe, England, 25 December 1642; *d.* London, England, 20 March 1727), *mathematics, dynamics, celestial mechanics, astronomy, optics, natural philosophy.* For the original article on Newton, see *DSB,* vol. 10.

Since I.B. Cohen's entry in the original *DSB* (1974), careful study and analysis of Newton's manuscripts has revised our understanding of all aspects of his life and work. In the first part of this Postscript, George Smith describes recent historical work on Newton's mathematics, optics, and mechanics. In the second section, William Newman discusses the new research on Newton's alchemy and matter theory.

New Collections of Newton's Papers. I. B. Cohen noted in the original *DSB* (1974) that three volumes remained to be published in both *The Mathematical Papers of Isaac Newton,* edited by D. T. Whiteside (vols. VI–VII, covering the period from 1684), and *The Correspondence of Isaac Newton* (vols. V–VII, covering from 1709). Cohen also noted that much work remained to be done on Newton's unpublished manuscripts, some of which has now been carried out. As much studied as Newton had been at the time of Cohen's comprehensive entry, the publication of these volumes, together with Volume 1 of *The Optical Papers of Isaac Newton* (ed. A. E. Shapiro, 1984) and R. S. Westfall's intellectual biography, *Never at Rest* (1980), has led to a deeper understanding of Newton's scientific work, especially concerning his own view of that work. The advances are summarized below in the sequence Cohen followed: mathematics, optics, and the *Principia.*

Mathematics. The last three volumes of *The Mathematical Papers* have provided a much richer picture of the geometrical mathematics that Newton had settled on during the 1680s. Whiteside's annotations in Volume VI covering the mathematics of Book 1 of the *Principia* bring out the relation between the geometry with limits that Newton employed there and the Leibnizian symbolic calculus that subsequently came to dominate "Newtonian" mechanics. Still more important are the more than five hundred pages in Volume VII that present Newton's never completed *Geometria* of the early 1690s. The goal of this work was to start from the foundations of elementary classical geometry, ultimately developing with full rigor the fluxional methods of Newton's calculus, but within a strictly geometrical framework. This work shows that Newton's preference for geometric over symbolic mathematics involved more than geometry's claim to higher standards of rigor or his predilection for the wisdom of the ancients. In his *Arithmetica Universalis* he had already derived algebraic methods out of elementary arithmetic, establishing their rigor so far as these methods go. Newton, however, did not see how limits could be added to symbolic mathematics in a fully rigorous manner, while geometry (as his *Geometria* was going to show) allowed limits to be added rigorously; and the constructions of synthetic geometry have a claim to exactness that the incommensurability of irrational numbers prevented symbolic mathematics from matching when symbols are taken to stand in for numbers, as they are in *Arithmetica Universalis*, rather than for geometric magnitudes.

Volume VIII of *Mathematical Papers* primarily concerns the controversy with Leibniz over priority to the calculus, examined in detail in A. R. Hall's *Philosophers at War* (1980). Newton without question was the first to develop what, following Leibniz, we now call the calculus, but Leibniz developed it independently, in the process coming to promote symbolic methods as preferable to geometry, primarily because they make discoveries much easier. One has to wonder how different the history of mathematics might have been if Newton had found a publisher for his extensive treatise *De Methodis Serium et Fluxionum* in 1672, before Leibniz had made his discoveries.

Optics. Newton's *Optical Lectures* of 1670–1672 (*Optical Papers*, vol. I) supplement the original *DSB* account of his work in optics in two ways. First, they reveal that the extensive experiments described in his published papers on colors in the 1670s and Book I of the *Opticks* comprise only a fraction of the total experiments he performed on refraction. The further experiments generally served to cross-check the results of the principal experiments or to pave the way to them. The full range of experiments thus shows how meticulous an experimenter Newton was. Second, the *Lectures* contain a passage showing that, long before the *Principia,* he viewed mathematical principles as crucial to scientific knowledge:

> Indeed, since an exact science of them [colors] seems to be one of the most difficult that philosophy is in need of, I hope to show—as it were, by my example—how valuable mathematics is in natural philosophy. I therefore urge geometers to investigate nature more rigorously, and those devoted to natural science to learn geometry first.... [W]ith the help of philosophical geometers and geometrical philosophers, instead of the conjectures and probabilities that are being blazoned about everywhere, we shall finally achieve a natural science supported by the greatest evidence. (*Optical Papers*, vol. I, p. 87)

Although A. E. Shapiro is still preparing the second volume of the *Optical Papers*, his *Fits, Passions, and Paroxysms* (1993) has already described Newton's struggle to produce the theory presented in Books II and III of the *Opticks* of such periodic phenomena as "Newton's rings" and Grimaldi's "fringes." In addition to complicating the commonplace conception of Newton as a proponent of a corpuscular theory of light, Shapiro's book displays once more Newton's commitment to having the empirical world decide questions.

Principia. I. B. Cohen's "A Guide to Newton's *Principia,*" which accompanies his and Anne Whitman's new translation, has updated his original *DSB* account of the book. The combination of this "Guide" with Whiteside's explanatory notes in Volume VI of *Mathematical Papers* has made the recondite details of the *Principia* much more accessible. Recent research that builds on the work of Cohen and Whiteside has also added new dimensions to some long-standing disputes generated by the book, the most important of which will be summarized here.

Although Newton undoubtedly found absolute space an indispensable heuristic for conceptualizing absolute motion, efforts by physicists to reformulate Newtonian theory in a relativistic space-time framework have made clear that the empirical science of the *Principia* does not presuppose it. It presupposes a Euclidean three-dimensional affine space, with time separate. As Corollaries 5 and 6 to the Laws of Motion make clear, the book cannot

Newton

provide means for distinguishing rest from absolute uniform motion in a straight line, or even absolute accelerated motion in which all accessible bodies are undergoing the same acceleration in a straight line. What it does claim is that the forces that cause them enable absolute, real changes of motion, especially curvilinear changes, to be distinguished from relative, merely apparent changes of motion. The Newtonian assumptions in conflict with Einstein's theory, besides Euclidean space, involve always in principle being able first to settle any question about the simultaneity of two events and, second, to distinguish between uniformly accelerated free-fall and inertial motion. This partial rapprochement with Einstein, first developed by Howard Stein in 1968, has been laid out more recently in Robert DiSalle's *Understanding Space-Time.*

In Book 1, Newton seems in places to gloss over the difference between discrete forces, or impulses, and continuously acting forces. His use of proportions rather than equations allows him to avoid dimensional inconsistencies in doing so, but questions still arise about his employing motions governed by impulses to reach conclusions about motions governed by continuous forces. Bruce Pourciau has shown that Newton was making an implicit assumption that can be proved, but not by methods known to him: *every motion generated by a centripetal force acting uninterruptedly for a given time is the limiting case of motions generated by centripetal impulses.* Some have also argued that Newton's laws of motion were formulated strictly for discrete forces without his ever justifying their application to continuous forces. Pourciau has now shown that the second law, as Newton conceived it, holds for both discrete and continuous forces. In a manuscript first published in Volume 6 of *Mathematical Papers* (p. 539ff), Newton explained that his measure of the "change of motion" referred to in the law is the distance after a given time between where the given body is and where it would have been had it proceeded inertially; under this measure (with the "evanescent" increments of time of Lemma 10 serving in the case of nonuniform continuous forces), Newton's law applies to both types of force.

The importance to the *Principia* of some less discussed parts of Book 1 has now become clearer. Newton introduced a second method for inferring rules of force from motions in the second edition, employing curvature: force varies as $v^2/(r\sin\alpha)$, where α is the angle between the tangent to the trajectory and the radius vector to the center of force, in contrast to the familiar v^2/r for uniform circular motion that he and Huygens had independently discovered decades earlier. Michael Nauenberg and Bruce Brackenridge have shown that Newton was already in full command of, and in places took important advantage of, these curvature methods in the first edition. The scope and power of the results on precessing orbits in Section 9 have been spelled out, primarily in papers by S. R. Valluri and colleagues. And Section 10 on constrained motion has now been shown to make a crucial contribution to the book. Newton's "Moon Test," showing terrestrial gravity extends to the Moon, employs Huygens's pendulum measure of surface gravity. This measure presupposes uniform gravity acting along parallel lines, in *prima facie* conflict with Newton's inverse-square centripetal gravity. Section 10 legitimates this measure by showing that it, and Galilean gravity generally, hold in the limit at the surface of a uniformly dense sphere or spheroid as its radius becomes indefinitely large—in much the manner of Einstein's proof that Newtonian gravity holds in the static weak-field limit of his new theory of gravity.

All but the last two sections of Book II concern motion in resisting media. The conclusion that Newton wanted to draw has always been clear: the absence of any sign of such forces in the motions of the planets and comets shows that the celestial regions are free of the sort of fluid required by Descartes' and Leibniz's vortex theories of celestial motion. To show this, Newton had to show that the density and hence inertia of any fluid medium gives rise to forces of resistance. What has now become clearer is how much of the effort of Book II is devoted to disaggregating the contribution to resistance made by the inertia of the fluid from the contributions made by its viscosity and friction between it and a moving body. In the first edition Newton had hoped that pendulum-decay experiments could directly disaggregate the inertial resistance, but the results fell short of his standards, leading him to add vertical-fall experiments in the next two editions. The data from these vertical-fall experiments were of very high quality, but they did not directly disaggregate the inertial contribution, leaving a lacuna in his reasoning later exposed by d'Alembert.

Newton's claim to having "deduced" the law of gravity from phenomena of orbital motion in Book 3 has been the subject of much analysis over the last thirty years. Howard Stein and Dana Densmore have called attention to the one real lacuna in this "deduction" (Proposition 5, Corollary 1, as originally noted by Roger Cotes while he was editing the second edition); William Harper has shown how well the other steps in the reasoning stand up to scrutiny; and George Smith has emphasized how Newton was employing approximative reasoning throughout, with his Rules of Reasoning then providing the license to *take* (Newton's word) the law to be exact.

Two further advances have been made with the rest of Book 3. Newton revised Propositions 19 and 20 on the variation of surface gravity with latitude and the figure of the Earth twice, reaching three different conclusions in the three editions. We now see why Newton viewed them as so important. Christiaan Huygens recognized that these are the only (then) empirically accessible results in the

Principia that presuppose gravity between every two particles of matter. In replying to the book in his *Discourse on the Cause of Gravity* (1690), he devised an *experimentum crucis* around these results and announced that he had evidence from pendulum-clock measurements at sea refuting Newton. This also clarifies why these propositions became so important during the 1730s and 1740s. Finally, Curtis Wilson and others have clarified how large a gap remained between Newton's quantitative efforts on the lunar orbit and later eighteenth-century work, as has D. E. Cartwright for the gap in the case of the tides.

SUPPLEMENTARY BIBLIOGRAPHY

WORKS BY NEWTON PUBLISHED AFTER 1974

Certain Philosophical Questions: Newton's Trinity Notebook, edited by J. E. McGuire and M. Tamny. Cambridge, U.K.: Cambridge University Press, 1983.

The Correspondence of Isaac Newton, vols. V–VII, edited by A. R. Hall and L. Tilling. Cambridge, U.K.: Cambridge University Press, 1975, 1976, 1977.

Isaac Newton's Papers and Letters on Natural Philosophy. 2nd ed. Cambridge, MA: Harvard University Press, 1978.

The Mathematical Papers of Isaac Newton, vols. VI–VIII, edited by D. T. Whiteside. Cambridge, U.K.: Cambridge University Press, 1974, 1976, 1981.

The Optical Papers of Isaac Newton, vol. 1, edited and translated by A. E. Shapiro. Cambridge, U.K.: Cambridge University Press, 1984. The first of two projected volumes.

Philosophical Writings, edited by A. Janiak. Cambridge, U.K.: Cambridge University Press, 2004. Newton's philosophical writings in English translation.

The Preliminary Manuscripts for Isaac Newton's 1687 Principia, *1684–1686.* Cambridge, U.K.: Cambridge University Press, 1989.

The Principia, *Mathematical Principles of Natural Philosophy: A New Translation*, translated by I. B. Cohen and A. Whitman. Berkeley, Los Angeles, and London: University of California Press, 1999.

OTHER SOURCES PUBLISHED AFTER 1974

Biographical and Bibliographical

Gjertsen, Derek. *The Newton Handbook.* London and New York: Routledge & Kegan Paul, 1986.

Hall, A. Rupert. *Isaac Newton, Adventurer in Thought.* Oxford: Blackwell, 1992.

Hall, A. Rupert, ed. *Isaac Newton, Eighteenth-Century Perspectives: A Collection of Early Biographical Memoirs.* Oxford: Oxford University Press, 1999.

Harrison, John. *The Library of Isaac Newton.* Cambridge, U.K.: Cambridge University Press, 1978.

Wallis, Peter, and Ruth Wallis. *Newton and Newtoniana, 1672–1975: A Bibliography.* London: Dawsons, 1977.

Westfall, Richard Samuel. *Never at Rest: A Biography of Isaac Newton.* Cambridge, U.K.: Cambridge University Press, 1983.

Collections of Studies

Bechler, Zev, ed. *Contemporary Newtonian Scholarship.* Dordrecht, Boston, and London: D. Reidel, 1982.

Buchwald, Jed, and I. Bernard Cohen, eds. *Isaac Newton's Natural Philosophy.* Cambridge, MA: MIT Press, 2001.

Cohen, I. Bernard, and Richard S. Westfall. *Newton: Texts, Backgrounds, and Commentaries, A Norton Critical Edition.* New York and London: W. W. Norton, 1995.

Cohen, I. Bernard, and George E. Smith, eds. *The Cambridge Companion to Newton.* Cambridge, U.K.: Cambridge University Press, 2002.

Dalitz, Richard H., and Michael Nauenberg, eds. *The Foundations of Newtonian Scholarship.* Singapore: World Scientific, 2000.

Durham, F., and R. D. Puddington, eds. *Some Truer Method: Reflections on the Heritage of Newton.* New York: Columbia University Press, 1990.

Fauvel, John, Raymond Flood, Michael Shortland, and Robin Wilson, eds. *Let Newton Be! A New Perspective on His Life and Works.* Oxford and New York: Oxford University Press, 1988.

Harman, P. M., and Alan E. Shapiro. *The Investigation of Difficult Things: Essays on Newton and the History of the Exact Sciences.* Cambridge, U.K.: Cambridge University Press, 1992.

King-Hele, D. G., and A. R. Hall, eds. *Newton's* Principia *and Its Legacy.* Proceedings of a Royal Society Discussion Meeting of 30 June 1987. London: The Royal Society, 1988.

Theerman, P. and A. F. Seef, eds. *Action and Reaction.* Newark, Delaware: University of Delaware Press, 1993.

Mathematics

Guicciardini, Niccolò. *The Development of Newtonian Calculus in Britain, 1700–1800.* Cambridge, U.K.: Cambridge University Press, 1989.

———. *Reading the Principia: The Debate on Newton's Mathematical Methods for Natural Philosophy from 1687 to 1736.* Cambridge, U.K.: Cambridge University Press, 1999.

Hall, A. Rupert. *Philosophers at War: The Quarrel Between Newton and Leibniz.* Cambridge, U.K.: Cambridge University Press, 1980.

Pourciau, Bruce. "The Preliminary Mathematical Lemmas of Newton's *Principia.*" *Archive for History of Exact Sciences* 52 (1998): 279–295.

Optics

Hall, A. Rupert. *And All Was Light: An Introduction to Newton's Opticks.* Oxford: Clarendon Press, 1993.

Schaffer, Simon. "Glass Works: Newton's Prisms and the Use of Experiment." In *The Use of Experiment: Studies in the Natural Sciences*, edited by David Gooding, Trevor Pinch, and Simon Schaffer, pp. 67–104. Cambridge: Cambridge University Press, 1989.

Shapiro, Alan E. *Fits, Passions, and Paroxysms: Physics, Method, and Chemistry and Newton's Theories of Colored Bodies and Fits of Easy Reflection.* Cambridge, U.K.: Cambridge University Press, 1993.

Newton

———. "The Evolving Structure of Newton's Theory of White Light and Color: 1670–1704." *Isis* 71 (1980): 211–235.

———. "The Gradual Acceptance of Newton's Theory of Light and Color," *Perspectives on Science* 4 (1996), pp. 59-104.

———. "Newton's Experimental Investigation of Diffraction for the *Opticks*: A Preliminary Study." In *The Foundations of Newtonian Scholarship,* edited by R. H. Dalitz and M. Nauenberg, pp. 29–56. Singapore: World Scientific, 2000.

———. "Newton's Optics and Atomism." In *The Cambridge Companion to Newton,* edited by I. B. Cohen and G. E. Smith, pp. 227-255. Cambridge, U.K.: Cambridge University Press, 2002.

The Principia

Bertoloni Meli, Dominico. *Equivalence and Priority: Newton versus Leibniz.* Oxford: Clarendon Press, 1993.

———. *Thinking with Objects: The Transformation of Mechanics in the Sevententh Century.* Baltimore, MD: The Johns Hopkins University Press, 2006.

Brackenridge, J. Bruce, and Michael Nauenberg. "Curvature in Newton's Dynamics." In *The Cambridge Companion to Newton,* edited by I. B. Cohen and G. E. Smith, pp. 85–137. Cambridge, U.K.: Cambridge University Press, 2002.

Cartwright, David Edgar. *Tides: A Scientific History.* Cambridge, U.K.: Cambridge University Press, 1999.

Chandrasekhar, S. *Newton's Principia for the Common Reader.* Oxford: Clarendon Press, 1995.

Cohen, I. Bernard. *The Newtonian Revolution.* Cambridge, U.K., and New York: Cambridge University Press, 1980.

DiSalle, Robert. *Understanding Space-Time: The Philosophical Development of Physics from Newton to Einstein.* Cambridge, U.K.: Cambridge University Press, 2006.

Greenberg, Daniel L. *The Problem of the Earth's Shape from Newton to Clairaut.* Cambridge, U.K.: Cambridge University Press, 1995.

Harper, William. "Isaac Newton on Empirical Success and Scientific Method." In *The Cosmos of Science: Essays of Exploration,* edited by John Earman and John D. Norton, pp. 55–86. Pittsburgh: University of Pittsburgh Press, 1997.

———. "Howard Stein on Isaac Newton: Beyond Hypotheses?" In *Reading Natural Philosophy: Essays in the History and Philosophy of Science and Mathematics* , edited by D. B. Malament, pp. 71–112. Chicago: Open Court, 2002.

Nauenberg, Michael. "Newton's Early Computational Method for Dynamics." *Archive for History of Exact Sciences* 46 (1994): 221–252.

Pourciau, Bruce. "Newton's Argument for Proposition 1 of the *Principia.*" *Archive for History of Exact Sciences* 57 (2003): 267–311.

———. "The Importance of Being Equivalent: Newton's Two Models of One-Body Motion." *Archive for History of Exact Sciences* 58 (2004): 283–321.

———. "Newton's Interpretation of Newton's Second Law." *Archive for History of Exact Sciences* 60 (2006): 157–207.

Schliesser, Eric, and G. E. Smith. "Huygens's 1688 Report to the Dutch East India Company on the Measurement of Longitude at Sea and the Evidence It Offered Against Universal Gravity." *Archive for History of Exact Sciences,* forthcoming.

Smeenk, Christopher, and G. E. Smith. "Newton on Constrained Motion: A Commentary on Book 1 Section 10 of the *Principia.*" *Archive for History of Exact Sciences,* forthcoming.

Smith, George E. "The Newtonian Style in Book II of the *Principia.*" In *Isaac Newton's Natural Philosophy,* edited by J. Z. Buchwald and I. B. Cohen, pp. 249–313. Cambridge, MA: MIT Press, 2001.

———. "How Did Newton Discover Universal Gravity?" In *Beyond Hypothesis: Newton's Experimental Philosophy.* Proceedings of a Conference at St. John's College, Annapolis. *The St. John's Review* XLV (1999): 32–63.

———. "From the Phenomenon of the Ellipse to an Inverse-Square Force: Why Not?" In *Reading Natural Philosophy: Essays in the History and Philosophy of Science and Mathematics,* edited by D. B. Malament, pp. 31–70. Chicago: Open Court, 2002.

———. "The Methodology of the *Principia.*" In *The Cambridge Companion to Newton,* edited by I. B. Cohen and G. E. Smith, pp. 138–173. Cambridge, U.K.: Cambridge University Press, 2002.

Stein, Howard. "Some Philosophical Prehistory of General Relativity." In *Minnesota Studies in the Philosophy of Science,* vol. VIII, *Foundations of Space-Time Theories,* edited by J. Earman, C. Glymour, and J. Stachel, pp. 3–49. Minneapolis: University of Minnesota Press, 1977.

———. "'From the Phenomena of Motions to the Forces of Nature': Hypothesis or Deduction?" *PSA 1990.* Proceedings of the 1990 Biennial Meeting of the Philosophy of Science Association, vol. 2, pp. 209–222. East Lansing: Philosophy of Science Association, 1991.

———. "Newton's Metaphysics." In *The Cambridge Companion to Newton,* edited by I. B. Cohen and G. E. Smith, pp. 256–307. Cambridge, U.K.: Cambridge University Press, 2002.

Valluri, Sree Ram, Curtis Wilson, and William Harper. "Newton's Apsidal Precession Theorem and Eccentric Orbits." *Journal for the History of Astronomy* 28 (1997): 13–27.

Valluri, S. R., P. Yu, G. E. Smith, and P. A. Wiegart. "An Extension of Newton's Apsidal Precession Theorem." *Monthly Notices of the Royal Astronomical Society* 358 (2005): 1273–1284.

Whiteside, D. T. "The Prehistory of the *Principia* from 1664–1686." *Notes and Records, The Royal Society* 45 (1991): 11–61.

Wilson, Curtis. "The Newtonian Achievement in Astronomy." In *Planetary Astronomy from the Renaissance to the Rise of Astrophysics, Part A: Tycho Brahe to Newton,* edited by R. Taton and C. Wilson, pp. 233–274. Cambridge, U.K.: Cambridge University Press, 1989.

———. "Newton on the Moon's Variation and Apsidal Motion: The Need for a Newer 'New Analysis.'" In *Isaac Newton's Natural Philosophy,* edited by J. Z. Buchwald and I. B. Cohen, pp. 139–188. Cambridge, MA: MIT Press, 2001.

———. "Newton and Celestial Mechanics." In *The Cambridge Companion to Newton* , edited by I. B. Cohen and G. E. Smith, pp. 202–206. Cambridge, U.K.: Cambridge University Press, 2002.

George E. Smith

The Significance of Newton's Alchemical Research. In the original *DSB* (1974), I.B. Cohen wrote that it was it was "difficult to determine whether to consider Newton's alchemy as an irrational vagary of an otherwise rational mind, or whether to give his hermeticism a significant role as a developmental force in his rational science" (*DSB*, vol.10, p. 82). Since the publication of these words, scholarly developments have substantially reduced the viability of Cohen's first alternative. The topic of alchemy has yielded up much of its erstwhile mystery to scrutiny and it is clear that the subject was not only a reasonable field of endeavor in its day, but a veritable *cause célèbre.* Alchemy, or to use the largely synonymous early modern term, *chymistry,* included not only *chrysopoeia* (transmutation of base metals) but a host of more attainable pursuits, such as the making of medicines, dyes and pigments, alcoholic beverages, and colored glasses, and the metallurgical purification and reduction of ores. In short, the imposition of a modern distinction between *alchemy* and *early chemistry* is an anachronism.

Chymistry was also the source of diverse theories of material composition, including an important corpuscular theory of matter to which Newton and his older contemporary and acquaintance Robert Boyle were heirs. Having its roots in medieval alchemy, this corpuscular theory had no difficulty accommodating the transmutation of one metal into another by the replacement and rearrangement of particles at the micro-level. It is no mark of irrationality, then, that Newton and Boyle were committed seekers of the philosophers's stone, and that such luminaries as John Locke and Gottfried W. Leibniz were all deeply interested in the *aurific* art. The age of gold was also the age of gold-making.

It is much harder to reply to Cohen's second alternative. Although Newton's alchemical work was certainly not an "irrational vagary," it does not follow automatically that his chymistry contributed in any major way to Newton's more famous scientific discoveries. Despite two major books by Betty Jo Teeter Dobbs on Newton's alchemy that have appeared along with a number of articles devoted to the subject, as well as Richard Westfall's magisterial biography, *Never at Rest,* the verdict is still out. Both Dobbs and Westfall were at various times inclined to see Newton's alchemy as having contributed in a major way to his mature theory of gravitation, and more generally to his conviction that forces could operate at a distance. There is no direct evidence for this view in any of the documents submitted by Dobbs or Westfall for scrutiny, however, and on the few occasions when Newton did describe the causes of gravity in an explicitly alchemical context, he explained the falling of bodies by mechanical means, not as a result of force at a distance. This is particularly the case in Newton's important early manuscript "Of Nature's Obvious Laws & Processes in Vegetation" (Smithsonian Institution, Dibner MS. 1031B), where Newton postulated a material ether that forces bodies downward and is also responsible for chymical properties such as cohesion. In later works, such as Query 31 of the *Opticks,* Newton did import chymical powers in the form of a *vis fermentativa* whose ultimate source is the Flemish chymist Joan Baptista Van Helmont, but this "fermentative force" is quite distinct from gravitational attraction. Finally, it should be obvious that Newton had more immediate sources than alchemical literature to draw upon for the idea of immaterial forces acting on matter. In particular, he was the beneficiary of several centuries of research on the immaterial attraction exercised by magnets, beginning with Petrus Peregrinus in the thirteenth century and proceeding through the works of many seventeenth-century figures ranging from William Gilbert to Johannes Kepler. In a word, the idea that Newton derived his theory of universal gravitation from alchemy has become something of a canard.

But it does not follow from this, of course, that Newton's chymistry had no connection with his more famous scientific endeavors, or that it wielded no influence upon them. One promising area lies in Newton's early work on the analysis and synthesis of white light by means of prisms. From his earliest researches, Newton seems to have held the private conviction that light was composed of tiny corporeal bodies—corpuscles. Because Newton also viewed matter more generally as corpuscular, it is therefore not surprising that he recorded his fundamental optical discoveries alongside chymical phenomena and experiments in his early manuscripts, such as his *Certain Philosophical Questions* and the laboratory notebook now kept in Cambridge University Library under the shelfmark Additional 3975.

Although Newton's earliest efforts to break white light into its spectral colors by means of prisms seem to have had non-chymical sources, his decision to recombine those colors and hence recreate the light that he started with is highly suggestive of early modern chymistry. It is the largely chymical manuscript CU add. 3975 that contains the first record of Newton's resynthesis of white light after his having analyzed it into its spectral colors, and the same codex contains Newton's notes on Robert Boyle's famous *redintegration* (resynthesis) of various materials from their components after they had been subjected to analysis. It is highly likely that the form of demonstration

Isaac Newton. **SCIENCE SOURCE/PHOTO RESEARCHERS, INC.**

employed by Newton, analysis followed by resynthesis, owed a significant debt to Boyle and to the tradition of alchemy as a whole, which had been expressly viewed as the "art of analysis and synthesis" since the beginning of the seventeenth century. Boyle's important reintegration of saltpeter had received public notice when he published his *Certain Physiological Essays* (1661) and his *Origine of Formes and Qualities* (1666). Hence the resynthesis of compounds was a subject very much *au courant* in the scientific circles traveled by Newton at the very time when he was making his fundamental optical discoveries, and one that was sure to appeal to the young savant.

Newton's Chymical Theory. Whereas there was significant bleed-through from Newton's chymistry to his other scientific endeavors, it is equally important to determine the nature of his chymistry as a whole, without judging it merely in relation to his physics. The chymical *nachlass* that Newton left unpublished (now being published on the *Chymistry of Isaac Newton* website) consists of about a million words of text that can be divided into four rough categories—synopses, transcriptions, and running commentaries on existing alchemical texts; cross-referencing and lexicographical tools such as Newton's *Index chemicus*; laboratory notebooks such as CU add. 3975 and 3973; and treatises, or rather clusters of ideas arranged in the form of commonplace entries, such as "Of Nature's Obvious Laws & Processes in Vegetation." Of these four types of text, only the last provides a straightforward entry into Newton's theory of chymistry. Hence the remaining remarks will focus on the main texts of this sort, namely "Of Nature's Obvious Laws" and the hitherto unstudied Latin text also found in Smithsonian MS. Dibner 1031B that begins with the phrase "Humores minerales continuo decidunt" ("Mineral humidities continually fall down"). In these texts Newton presented a theory that the world is a vast living being, which continually inhales and exhales a subtle, vital, ethereal material. Within the earth this material provides the *Urstoff* from which minerals and metals are formed. On the surface of the earth, the same material accounts for the generation, growth, and sustenance of life.

It is clear that the material principle alluded to by Newton was his reworking of an idea derived from the *sal nitrum* theorists, a major school within early modern alchemy. The main figure associated with this movement was Michael Sendivogius, a Polish courtier, alchemist, and mining consultant in the employ of the Hapsburg emperor Rudolf II. Sendivogius's *Novum lumen chemicum* (1604) and *Tractatus de suphure* (1616) argue that there is a volatile niter (also referred to as philosophical mercury) that circulates between the core of the earth and the sun. This fiery cosmic principle serves as the source of life on earth, and like Newton's ether, it is involved in the subterranean generation of minerals and metals.

Curiously, Newton explicitly distanced himself from the *sal nitrum* theorists in his 1675 *Hypothesis of Light.* He presented a theory, however, that is otherwise remarkably similar to the one proposed in "Of Natures Obvious Laws." After describing an aereal, volatile spirit that accounts for flame and vital activity in the *Hypothesis*, Newton said "I mean not the imaginary volatile saltpeter" [Turnbull, *Correspondence of Isaac Newton*, 1959, vol. 1, p. 365]. A. Rupert Hall has pointed out that Newton may have preferred the version of the *sal nitrum* theory found in Sendivogius's work to contemporary English versions that had been influenced by Cartesianism. This could be the case, but a careful reading of Newton's "Humores minerales," the Latin text also found in Smithsonian MS. 1031B, reveals that Newton's own theory of metallic generation was not entirely identical to that usually expressed by the *sal nitrum* school.

In its most common form, the volatile niter theory viewed subterranean processes in terms of the sublimation and condensation of mineral vapors. Within the earth, the

Newton

volatile niter was supposed to combine with sulfur and various impurities to yield the metals by reiterate vaporization and condensation. If one consults Newton's "Humores minerales," however, it is immediately obvious that he introduced another process into the generation of metals, namely solution. Writing under the influence of the German alchemist Johannes Grasseus, Newton laid out an elaborate subterranean process. According to this theory, minerals are dissolved by underground acidities, which then analyze the minerals into their mercurial and sulfurous constituents and carry them downwards toward the center of the earth. The downwards-falling solution then encounters fumes that are rising upwards, and combines with them, which accounts for the generation of further metals from the initial dissolved minerals. The subterranean process of solution by naturally occurring acids therefore became an integral part of Newton's theory, and the volatile niter of the *sal nitrum* theorists was nowhere openly mentioned by name. Nonetheless, "Humores minerales" concluded in a way quite similar to the niter theory's insistence on a general, universal spirit. The text ended by saying "These two spirits [i.e. mercury and sulfur] above all wander over the earth and bestow life on animals and vegetables. And they make stones, salts, and so forth."

As one can see from the texts in Smithsonian MS. Dibner 1031B, Newton used chymistry as the source for something like what physicists in the early twenty-first century call a "theory of everything," namely a physical theory that unifies and accounts for all known natural phenomena. Although Newton's alchemically-based theory did not belong to the realm of mathematical physics, it too tried to account for widely diverse phenomena, including organic life, the origin of heat and flame, the mechanical cause of gravitation, cohesion, the generation of metals and minerals, and so forth, by making an appeal to an ethereal medium. Perhaps because of the marvelous properties that Newton ascribed to the single ethereal medium behind such phenomena, some scholars have seen Newton's interest in alchemy as arising above all from his religious sensibilities. In a qualified fashion this can be granted, because Newton's science as a whole was undoubtedly conditioned by his deep religious convictions. Rather than seeing Newton's chymistry as somehow more religiously oriented than his physics, however, one should view it as arising from the same desire to penetrate behind the appearances and to arrive at the most general possible explanation of reality. In the hands of Newton, both chymistry and physics were tools for arriving at fundamental truths about Nature and its operations.

SUPPLEMENTARY BIBLIOGRAPHY

The totality of Newton's chymical nachlass *is being published on line in diplomatic and normalized versions with translations of the Latin as part of* The Chymistry of Isaac Newton*, edited by William R. Newton, available from http://www.dlib.indiana.edu/collections/newton/.*

WORKS BY NEWTON

Dobbs, Betty Jo Teeter. *The Foundations of Newton's Alchemy: or, "The Hunting of the Greene Lyon."* Cambridge, U.K.: Cambridge University Press, 1975. Several of Newton's chymical writings have been edited and translated as appendices to this work and *The Janus Faces of Genius.*

———. *The Janus Faces of Genius: The Role of Alchemy in Newton's Thought.* Cambridge, U.K.: Cambridge University Press, 1991.

McGuire, J. E., and Martin Tamny. *Certain Philosophical Questions: Newton's Trinity Notebook.* Cambridge, U.K.: Cambridge University Press, 1983. Some chymical material is already found in Newton's student notebook, *Certain Philosophical Questions.*

OTHER SOURCES

Dobbs, Betty Jo Teeter. "Newton Manuscripts at the Smithsonian Institution." *Isis* 68 (1977): 105–107.

———. "Newton's Copy of *Secrets Reveal'd* and the Regimens of the Work." *Ambix* 26 (1979): 145–169.

———. "Newton's Alchemy and his Theory of Matter." *Isis* 73 (1982): 511–528.

———. "Newton's 'Clavis': New Evidence on its Dating and Significance." *Ambix* 29 (1982): 190–202.

———. Review of *Contemporary Newtonian Research,* edited by Zev Bechler. *Isis* 74 (1983): 609–610.

———. "Conceptual Problems in Newton's Early Chemistry: A Preliminary Study." In *Religion, Science, and Worldview: Essays in Honor of Westfall, Richard S,* edited by Margaret J. Osler and Paul L. Farber, pp. 3–32. Cambridge, U.K.: Cambridge University Press, 1985.

———. "Newton and Stocism." *The Southern Journal of Philosophy (Supplement)* 23 (1985): 109–123.

———. "Alchemistische Kosmogonie und arianiasche Theologie bei Isaac Newton." *Wolfenbütteler Forschungen* 32 (1986): 137–155.

———. "Newton's Alchemy and his 'Active Principle' of Gravitation." In *Newton's Scientific and Philosophical Legacy,* edited by Paul B. Scheuer and Guy Debrock, pp. 55–80. Dordrecht, Netherlands: Kluwer, 1988.

———. "Newton's *Commentary* on *The Emerald Tablet* of Hermes Trimegistus: its Scientific and Theological Significance." In *Hermeticisim and the Renaissance: Intellectual History and the Occult in Early Modern Europe,* edited by Ingrid Merkel and Allen G. Debus, pp. 182–191. Washington, D.C.: The Folger Shakespeare Library, 1988.

———. "Newton's Rejection of a Mechanical Aether for Gravitation: Empirical Difficulties and Guiding Assumptions." In *Scrutinizing Science: empirical Studies of Scientific Change,* edited by Arthur Donovan, Lary Laudan, and Rachel Laudan, pp. 69–83. Dordrecht, Netherlands: Kluwe, 1988.

———. *Alchemical Death & Resurrection: The Significance of Alchemy in the Age of Newton.* Washington, D.C.: Smithsonian Institution Libraries, 1990.

———. "Newton as Alchemist and Theologian." In *Standing on the Shoulders of Giants: A Longer View of Newton and Halley,* edited by Norman J. W. Thrower, pp. 128–140. Berkeley: University of California Press, 1990.

———. "'The Unity of Truth': An Integrated View of Newton's Work." In *Action and Reaction: Proceedings of a Symposium to Commemorate the Tercentenary of Newton's 'Principia,'* edited by Paul Theerman and Adele F. Seeff, pp. 105–122. Newark, NJ: University of Delaware Press, 1993.

———. "Newton as Final Cause and First Mover." *Isis* 85 (1994): 633–643.

———, and Margaret C. Jacob. *Newton and the Culture of Newtonianism.* Atlantic Highlands, NJ: Humanities Press, 1995.

Figala, Karin. "Zwei Londoner Alchemisten um 1700: Sir Isaac Newton und Cleidophorus Mystagogus." *Physis* 18 (1976): 245–273.

———. "Newton as Alchemist." *History of Science* 15 (1977): 102–137.

———. "Die exakte Alchemie des von Isaac Newton." *Verhandlungen der Naturforschenden Gesellschaft in Basel* 94 (1984): 157–227.

———. "Newton's Alchemy." In *The Cambridge Companion to Newton,* edited by I. Bernard Cohen and George E. Smith, pp. 370–386. Cambridge, U.K.: Cambridge University Press, 2002.

———, J. Harrison, and Ulrich Petzoldt. "De Scriptoribus Chemicis: Sources for the Establishment of Isaac Newton's (Al)Chemical Library." In *The Investigation of Difficult Things,* edited by P.M. Harman and A. E. Shapiro, pp. 135–179. Cambridge, U.K.: Cambridge University Press, 1992.

———, and Ulrich Petzoldt. "Alchemy in the Newtonian Circle: Personal Acquaintances and the Problem of the Late Phase of Isaac Newton's Alchemy." In *Renaissance and Revolution: Humanists, Scholars, Craftsmen, and Natural Philosophers in Early Modern Europe,* edited by Judith V. Field and Frank A. J. L. James, pp. 173–192. Cambridge, U.K.: Cambridge University Press, 1993.

Golinski, Jan. "The Secret Life of an Alchemist." In *Let Newton Be!,* edited by John Fauvel, pp. 147–167. Oxford, U.K.: Oxford University Press, 1988.

Hall, A. Rupert. *Isaac Newton, Adventurer in Thought.* Oxford, U.K.: Blackwell, 1992.

———. "Isaac Newton and the Aerial Nitre." *Notes and Records of the Royal Society of London* 52 (1998): 51–61.

———. "Pitfalls in the Editing of Newton's Papers." *History of Science* 40 (2002): 407–424.

Lederer, Thomas. "Leben, Werk und Wirkung des Stralsunder Fachschriftstellers Johann Grasse (nach 1560–1618)." In *Pommern in der Frühen Neuzeit,* edited by Wilhelm Kuhlmann and Horst Langer, pp. 227–237. Tübingen, Germany: Max Niemeyer, 1994.

McGuire, James E. "Neoplatonism and Active Principles: Newton and the *Corpus Hermeticum.*" In *Hermeticism and the Scientific Revolution,* edited by Robert S. Westman and James E. McGuire, pp. 93–142. Los Angeles: Clark Memorial Library, University of California, 1977.

Newman, William R. "Newton's *Clavis* as Starkey's *Key.*" *Isis* 78 (1987): 564–574. The "Clavis," a work ascribed by Dobbs to Newton and published in *The Foundations of Newton's Alchemy,* has subsequently been proven to be by George Starkey.

———. *Gehennical Fire: The Lives of George Starkey, an American Alchemist in the Scientific Revolution.* Cambridge, MA: Harvard University Press, 1994. revised ed. Chicago: University of Chicago Press, 2003.

———, and Lawrence M. Principe. "Alchemy v. Chemistry: The Etymological Origins of a Historiographic Mistake." *Early Science and Medicine* 3 (1998): 32–65.

———. "The Background to Newton's Chymistry." In *The Cambridge Companion to Newton,* edited by I. Bernard Cohen and George E. Smith, pp. 358–369. Cambridge, U.K.: Cambridge University Press, 2002.

———. *Atoms and Alchemy: Chymistry and the Experimental Origins of the Scientific Revolution.* Chicago: University of Chicago Press, 2006a.

———. "From Alchemy to 'Chymistry.'" In *The Cambridge History of Science: Early Modern Science,* vol. 3, pp. 497–517. Cambridge, U.K.: Cambridge University Press, 2006b.

Priesner, Claus, and Karin Figala. *Alchemie: Lexikon einer hermetischen Wissenschaft.* Munich, Germany: C. H. Beck, 1998.

Principe, Lawrence M. "The Alchemies of Robert Boyle and Isaac Newton: Alternate Approaches and Divergent Deployments." In *Rethinking the Scientific Revolution,* edited by Margaret J. Osler, pp. 201–220. Cambridge, U.K.: Cambridge University Press, 2000.

———, and William R. Newman. "Some Problems with the Historiography of Alchemy." In *Secrets of Nature: Astrology and Alchemy in Early Modern Europe,* edited by William R. Newman and Anthony Grafton, pp. 385–431. Cambridge, MA: MIT Press, 2001.

Spargo, Peter E., and C. A. Pounds. "Newton's 'Derangement of the Intellect': New Light on an Old Problem." *Notes and Records of the Royal Society of London* 34 (1979): 11–32.

———. "Newton's Chemical Experiments: An Analysis in the Light of Modern Chemistry." In *Action and Reaction: Proceedings of a Symposium to Commemorate the Tercentenary of Newton's 'Principia,'* edited by Paul Theerman and Adele F. Seeff, pp. 123–143. Newark, NJ: University of Delaware Press, 1993.

———. "Investigating the Site of Newton's Laboratory in Trinity College, Cambridge." *South African Journal of Science* 101 (2005): 315–21.

Westfall, Richard S. "Isaac Newton's *Index Chemicus.*" *Ambix* 22 (1975a): 174–185.

———. "The Role of Alchemy in Newton's Career." In *Reason, Experiment and Mysticism in the Scientific Revolution,* edited by M. L. Righini Bonelli and William R. Shea, pp. 189–232. New York: Science History Publications, 1975b.

———. "The Influence of Alchemy on Newton." In *Science, Pseudo-Science and Society,* edited by Marsha P. Hanen,

Margaret J. Osler, and Robert G. Weyant, pp. 145–169. Waterloo, Canada: Wilfred Laurier University Press, 1980a.

———. *Never at Rest: A Biography of Isaac Newton.* Cambridge, U.K.: Cambridge University Press, 1980b.

———. "Alchemy in Newton's Library." *Ambix* 31 (1984): 97–101.

William Newman

NICE, MARGARET MORSE (*b.* Amherst, Massachusetts, 6 December 1883; *d.* Chicago, Illinois, 26 June 1974), *ornithology, animal behavior, ecology.*

Nice is best known for her work in field ornithology. She also played a leading role in introducing to American ornithologists and behavioral biologists the work of the European ethologists Konrad Lorenz and Nikolaas Tinbergen. Her life experiences reflect how the cultural expectations of her day imposed obstacles to women of talent who aspired to be contributors to science.

Early Life and Studies. Margaret Morse Nice was the fourth of seven children of Anson Daniel Morse, a professor of history at Amherst College, and Margaret Duncan Ely Morse. As a youth, she displayed an enthusiasm for the outdoors and for nature study, both of which seem to have been encouraged by her parents. This support had its limits, however, as they were disinclined to think that their daughters should become anything other than mothers and homemakers. The parents were nonetheless happy to send Margaret in 1901 to nearby Mount Holyoke College in South Hadley, Massachusetts. There she gained a familiarity with modern languages that would later serve her well as an ornithologist, but she was uninspired by the instruction she received in zoology; she felt that her classes in that subject bore little relation to her interest in living animals in the wild. She did not decide to attend graduate school until after encountering Clifton F. Hodge, a biologist at Clark University in Worcester, Massachusetts, who persuaded her that it was possible to be a zoologist who was more interested in studying the lives of animals than dissecting animal bodies.

Margaret Morse enrolled at Clark University as a graduate student in 1907. She found Hodge and the developmental psychologist, G. Stanley Hall, to be highly stimulating teachers. She undertook research on the food of the bobwhite, thinking that this could become the subject of a doctoral dissertation. Her graduate career was cut short, however, by her marriage in 1909 to fellow graduate student Leonard Blaine Nice. She took on the roles of wife and then mother. The first of her five children (all daughters) was born in 1910. Nice later acknowledged having some regrets for not completing her PhD work, and she objected when, even after gaining fame for her own researches, she was identified as a "housewife" rather than as a "trained zoologist."

Her husband's career as an academic physiologist took the family to Boston in 1911 and then successively to Norman, Oklahoma (in 1913); Columbus, Ohio (in 1927); and Chicago, Illinois (in 1936). Caring for a growing family left Margaret Nice with little time for research, but she made the best that she could of her situation. She observed systematically her first child's acquisition and use of words. The findings she published in 1915 were counted as a master's thesis eight years later by Clark University, and she was awarded a master's degree in psychology, backdated to 1915.

Nice had become a bird-watcher as a child, and she had chosen a bird study for her research as a graduate student. She returned to the study of birds in earnest in 1919, provoked by a proposed change in the Oklahoma state game laws that would have led to the shooting of young mourning doves. Her investigations of the nesting times of mourning doves led her back to the study of birds in the wild and to a desire to know all the birds of the region. Her efforts culminated in her publication, with her husband, of *The Birds of Oklahoma* (1924). Upon moving to Ohio in 1927, her initial impulse seems to have been to come to know all the birds of her new surroundings. Over time, however, she came to concentrate her attentions on the life histories of birds of a single species, the song sparrow (*Melospiza melodia*).

Song Sparrow Research. Nice's song sparrow studies exploited recent innovations in the practice of bird banding. Banding had begun around the turn of the twentieth century as an aid to the study of bird migration. In the late 1910s, bird-watchers started trapping birds and putting distinctive, colored bands on birds' legs as means of identifying individual birds in the field. Nice exploited this technique to the fullest. She trapped and banded her first song sparrow in the spring of 1928. The following year she conducted an intensive study of two song sparrow pairs. She subsequently expanded her efforts, making a census of all the song sparrows in Interpont, a forty-acre floodplain near her home in Columbus. By 1935 she had banded a total of 870 song sparrows. She recorded the behavior of individual birds throughout their lives, kept track of family lineages, located the territories that individual birds occupied from year to year, and studied the birds' mating, migration, song production, and more. Focusing on the detailed life histories of all the individuals in a local population over the course of many seasons, this study was unprecedented. From Nice's perspective the work had an additional attraction: She could happily

Margaret Morse Nice. *Margaret Morse Nice, 1944.* AP IMAGES.

report at the end of her eight-year project that she had killed no birds and collected no eggs in the course of her studies. Her activities as an investigator had tended toward the bird's protection rather than its destruction.

Prominent among Nice's concerns in her song sparrow research was the idea that males occupy and defend territories, an idea made current by the English ornithologist H. Eliot Howard through his studies of British warblers and his book, *Territory in Bird Life* (1920). Howard himself had not banded the birds he studied. Nice, in contrast, banded her subjects and followed in detail the way the males birds established and defended their territories, courted females, and so forth. She described the respective behavior patterns of invaders and defenders during territorial encounters. She also paid special attention to the role of birdsong in territorial behavior and to the development of territorial song in the individual. In addition she explored the relation of territorial defense to questions of population. She concluded that in the song sparrow, territorial behavior serves to prevent overcrowding.

Contacts and Influence. By attending meetings of ornithological societies in the United States and Europe, Nice came to know the world's leading ornithologists. At the 1931 meeting of the American Ornithologists' Union, she met the young German ornithologist Ernst Mayr, who was working at the American Museum of Natural History in New York City. He was impressed by her work and put her in touch with Erwin Stresemann, the editor of the German *Journal für Ornithologie*, which was the most distinguished ornithological journal in the world at the time. Nice's first extended account of her song sparrow work appeared in Stresemann's journal, in German, in 1933 and 1934 under the title "Zur Naturgeschichte des Singammers." She elaborated on her work in later articles, and most importantly in two monographs titled "Studies in the Life History of the Song Sparrow," published thanks to Mayr's help in the *Transactions of the Linnaean Society of New York* (1937, 1943).

Nice's scientific contacts, her own work as a field ornithologist, and her facility with modern languages provided her with a broad view of contemporary advances in ornithology. In 1934 she began reviewing current ornithological literature on bird behavior, ecology, and life histories for the journal *Bird-Banding.* From then until 1942, when ill health caused her to curtail her work, she wrote hundreds of abstracts on the latest work in the field. In the mid-1930s she signaled to American ornithologists the importance of the work of the young Austrian naturalist Konrad Lorenz, whom she had met in Oxford in 1934 at the Eighth International Ornithological Congress. She in turn influenced Lorenz's own thinking, at least indirectly, for it was she who put Lorenz in contact with the American psychologist Wallace Craig, whose ideas profoundly affected Lorenz's understanding of instinct. Concluding that the work of Lorenz and his Dutch colleague, Nikolaas Tinbergen, provided the most promising foundation for studying wild birds under natural or seminatural conditions, Nice spent a month in 1938 in Lorenz's home in Austria learning Lorenz's techniques of raising and studying young nestlings. The second volume of her song sparrow study, focusing on behavioral questions, reflected her commitment to the views of the European ethologists.

Nice's most important contributions to ornithology were in the area of scientific practice. Through her systematic trapping, banding, and observing of birds in the wild, she made visible the scientific possibilities of life history studies. She is additionally noteworthy for the major role she played in the network of communication among twentieth-century ornithologists interested in field studies and behavior, despite the fact that she never held an academic position. European ornithologists also appreciated the active role she played after World War II in arranging for CARE packages to be sent to ornithologists in need of food, clothing, and other daily necessities. Throughout her career she was a forceful spokesperson for conservation. She was the first woman to be made president of a major American ornithological society, the Wilson Ornithological Club, in 1938–1939. That organization, now the Wilson Ornithological Society, began in 1997 awarding annually the Margaret Morse Nice Medal to an individual or individuals distinguished by "a lifetime of contribution to ornithology."

BIBLIOGRAPHY

The bulk of Nice's manuscript correspondence and other papers are at the Cornell University Library. The best published source for a bibliography is her Research Is a Passion with Me, *cited below. Additional items relating to her editorial work for* Bird-Banding *and the* Wilson Bulletin *are held by the Wilson Ornithological Society.*

WORKS BY NICE

"The Development of a Child's Vocabulary in Relation to Environment." *Pedagogical Seminary* 22 (1915): 35–64.

With Leonard Blaine Nice. *The Birds of Oklahoma.* Norman: University of Oklahoma, 1924.

"The Theory of Territorialism and Its Development." In *Fifty Years' Progress of American Ornithology, 1883–1933,* by the American Ornithologists' Union. Lancaster, PA: American Ornithologists' Union, 1933.

"Zur Naturgeschichte des Singammers." *Journal für Ornithologie* 81 (1933): 552–595; 82 (1934):1-96.

"Studies in the Life History of the Song Sparrow. I. A Population Study of the Song Sparrow." *Transactions of the Linnaean Society of New York* 4 (1937): 1–247. Nice's most important work.

"The Social Kumpan and the Song Sparrow." *Auk* 56 (1939): 255–262.

"Studies in the Life History of the Song Sparrow. II. The Behavior of the Song Sparrow and Other Passerines." *Transactions of the Linnaean Society of New York* 6 (1943): 1–328.

"Development of Behavior in Precocial Birds." *Transactions of the Linnaean Society of New York* 8 (1962): 1–211.

Research Is a Passion with Me. Edited by Doris Heustis Speirs. Toronto: Consolidated Amethyst Communications, 1979. Nice's autobiography, containing an extensive but not wholly complete bibliography of her published writings.

OTHER SOURCES

Ainley, Marianne Gosztonyi. "Field Work and Family: North American Women Ornithologists, 1900–1950." In *Uneasy Careers and Intimate Lives: Women in Science, 1789–1979,* edited by Pnina G. Abir-Am and Dorinda Outram. New Brunswick, NJ: Rutgers University Press, 1987.

Furumoto, Laurel, and Elizabeth Scarborough. "Placing Women in the History of Comparative Psychology: Margaret Floy Washburn and Margaret Morse Nice." In *Historical Perspectives and the International Status of Comparative Psychology,* edited by Ethel Tobach. Hillsdale, NJ: L. Erlbaum, 1987.

Mayr, Ernst. "Epilogue: Materials for a History of American Ornithology." In *Ornithology from Aristotle to the Present,* by Erwin Stresemann, edited by G. William Cottrell, translated by Hans J. Epstein and Cathleen Epstein. Cambridge, MA: Harvard University Press, 1975.

Mitman, Gregg, and Richard W. Burkhardt Jr. "Struggling for Identity: The Study of Animal Behavior in America, 1930–1945." In *The Expansion of American Biology,* edited by Keith R. Benson, Jane Maienschein, and Ronald Rainger. New Brunswick, NJ: Rutgers University Press, 1991.

Trautman, Milton B. "In Memoriam: Margaret Morse Nice." *Auk* 94 (1977): 430–441.

Richard W. Burkhardt Jr.

NIFO, AGOSTINO (*b.* Sessa Aurunca, Italy, c. 1469; *d.* Sessa Aurunca 18 January 1538), *medicine, natural philosophy, psychology, zoology.* For the original article on Nifo see *DSB,* vol. 10.

Research since the original *DSB* entry shows that Nifo's medical thought is marked by a shift from the astrological medicine of the early works to an updated humoral Galenism in the later *De ratione medendi.* In zoology Nifo's special contribution is a voluminous commentary on Aristotle's treatises on animals, which tries to combine syllogistic formalizations, humanistic philology, and naturalistic information.

Theory of *Regressus.* One aspect of Nifo's theory of scientific method, which is cursorily mentioned in the original entry, deserves more explanation. In his first commentary on Aristotle's *Physics* (1506), Nifo summarized a theory of *regressus* which is typical of early sixteenth century (and which would provide a basis for subsequent discourses on methods, such as those of Jacopo Zabarella). According to this theory, which Nifo ascribed to recent authors (*iuniores*), there are four modes of knowledge (or *notitiae*): (i) knowledge of the effect through the senses; (ii) a first discovery of the cause through a *demonstratio quia* (cf. Aristotle, *Posterior Analytics* I 13); (iii) subsequently, this cause is conceptually processed via a logical and linguistic treatment (labelled as *negotiatio intellectus*) that gives it the form of the middle term in a syllogism and makes it viable for (iv) a demonstration *propter quid* of the effect. The process of *negotiation*—possibly akin to the Platonic methods of composition and division—has the role of transforming the cause from being something in the real world to being a part of the scientific demonstration.

Medicine. In his early medical writings, Nifo endorsed a deterministic view of astrological medicine (a theoretical view shared by many Renaissance physicians). For instance, in his *De diebus criticis* (1504) he claimed that the relationship between the courses of fevers and the movements of heavenly bodies legitimate strong criteria of diagnosis and therapy which are based on strict astrological calculations. Similarly, in his *De nostrarum calamitatum causis* (1505) he linked epidemic cycles to the quadrangolations of constellations and to the comets. However, in his later *De ratione medendi* (completed in 1528, but published posthumously, Naples, 1528) Nifo gave no role to astrological medicine, and favored an up-to-date version of Galenic humoral (or complexionary) medicine: Diseases are reduced to a bad balance of the four humors (or bodily fluids: blood, phlegm, yellow bile, and black bile). Bearing in mind the contemporary debate on the scientific method, Nifo underscored the relevance on the application of the *demonstratio coniecturalis* (see the original entry on Nifo in *DSB* 10) as a method to reduce symptoms to their proper causes and to choose the most effective therapy.

Throughout the whole work Nifo aimed at giving an ordinate exposition of the main medical theories and procedures. Of particular relevance were the criteria for a differential diagnosis of smallpox (*variolae*) and measles (*morbilli*) (pp. 142–143) or the distinction between *cancerosi abscessus* (of humoral origin) and *venenosi abscessus* (of infective origin) (pp. 45–46). Nifo was also the author of a medical treatise on the lues (*De morbo Gallico,* Naples 1534) where a detailed analysis is given of glandular alterations in syphilis.

Zoology. In his bulky commentaries on Aristotle's zoological treatises (*Expositiones* on *Historia animalium, De partibus animalium,* and *De generatione animalium,* completed in 1534 in Salerno, but published posthumously: Venice 1546) Nifo tried to keep together, within the format of the medieval scholastic commentary, several disparate practices. These included such practices as literary erudition, syllogistic formalizations of Aristotle's arguments, humanistic philology (e.g. references to the original Greek text), and naturalistic information.

Nifo, who lived in an age of travels and geographical explorations, in the preface observed that the new discoveries of exotic animals do not really challenge the epistemic framework of Aristotle's zoology, in other words, a system of ultimate species and genera that allows the explanation of every possible single occurrence, including the new. For whatever animal is born or discovered "can only be aquatic or terrestrial; if aquatic, it will be fish or crustacean or gastropod or cephalopod; and if fish, it will be oviparous or viviparous, like cetaceans" (*Praefatio,* fol. 4r). These classifying schemes enable scholars to gather any novel information within a structured natural system "through the ultimate genera and through their proper predicates and through the causes of those predicates" (*Praefatio,* fol. 4r).

In the subsequent commentary each sentence of Aristotle's text is surrounded by a mass of annotations, ranging from philosophical, philological and naturalistic remarks, to virtually everything noteworthy written by previous commentators and authors (Galen, John Philoponus, Michael of Ephesus, Averroes, Albert the Great, etc.). Nifo's *Expositiones* on Aristotle's zoology are not a step toward early modern science, but an extreme attempt to keep together late medieval scholasticism, flavors of humanist philology, and novel pieces of information on animals.

SUPPLEMENTARY BIBLIOGRAPHY

As Edward Mahoney noted in the original DSB *entry, "there is no collected edition of Nifo's works." Thus, one must essentially rely on sixteenth-century editions. The following works constitute the few exceptions.*

WORKS BY NIFO

Niphi, Augustini. *Expositiones in Aristotelis libros metaphysices. Dilucidarium metaphysicarum disputationum.* Frankfurt, Germany: Minerva, 1967. This is an anastatic reprint of Venice 1559.

Lohr, Charles H. *Latin Aristotle Commentaries. II. Renaissance Authors.* Florence: Olschki 1988, 282–287. This text gives a list of Nifo's commentaries on Aristotle, either printed or surviving as unpublished manuscripts.

Sobre la belleza y el amor. Spanish translation and notes by F. Socas, Seville, Spain: Universidad de Sevilla,1990.

De pulchro et amore I, De pulchro liber, Du beau et de l'amour I, Le livre du beau, critical edition, French translation and notes by Boulègue L. Paris: Les Belles Lettres, 2003.

OTHER SOURCES

Ashworth, Earline Jennifer. "Agostino Nifo's reinterpretation of Medieval Logic." *Rivista Critica di Storia della Filosofia* 31 (1976): 355–374.

Cranz, Ferdinand Edward. "The Renaissance reading of *De anima*." In *Platon et Aristote à la Renaissance*, edited by Jean-Claude Margolin and Maurice de Gandillac, pp. 359–376. Paris: Vrin, 1976.

De Bellis, Ennio. *Nicoletto Vernia e Agostino Nifo. Aspetti storiografici e metodologici.* Galatina, Italy: Congedo Editore, 2003. Collected essays.

———. *Bibliografia di Agostino Nifo.* Florence: Olschki, 2005. This work contains a bibliography of the editions of Nifo's works and a bibliography of the secondary literature.

Gargani, Aldo G. *Hobbes e la scienza.* Turin, Italy: Einaudi 1971. Pages 32–38 are on Nifo's theory of scientific demonstration and its possible influence on Hobbes.

Garofano-Venosta, Francesco. "Il *De ratione medendi* di Agostino Nifo." *Pagine di Storia della Medicina* 15 (1971): 59–74.

Hissette, Roland. "Note sur l'édition princeps (1497) des *Destructiones destructionum d'Averroès avec Expositio* d'Agostino Nifo." *Bulletin de Philosophie Médiévale* 46 (2004): 55–60.

Jardine, Nicholas. "Galileo's Road to Truth and the Demonstrative Regress." *Studies in the History and Philosophy of Science* 7 (1976): 277–318.

Kuhn, Heinrich C. "Die Vervandlung der Zerstörung der Zerstörung. Bemerkungen zu Augustinus Niphus' Kommentar zur *Destructio Destructionum* des Averroes." In *Averroismus im Mittelalter und in der Renaissance*, edited by Friedrich Niewöhner and Loris Sturlese. Zürich, Switzerland: Spur, 1994.

Lautner, Peter. "Status and Method of Psychology according to the Late Neoplatonists and their Influence during the Sixteenth Century." In *The Dynamics of Aristotelian Natural Philosophy from Antiquity to Seventeenth Century*, edited by Cornelis Leijenhorst, Christoph Luethy, and J. M. M. H. Thijssen. Leiden: Brill 2002.

Mahoney, Edward P. "Pico, Plato, and Albert the Great: The Testimony and Evaluation of Agostino Nifo." *Medieval Philosophy and Theology* 2 (1992): 165–192.

———. *Two Aristotelians of the Italian Renaissance: Nicoletto Vernia and Agostino Nifo.* Ashgate, U.K.: Aldershot 2000. Collected essays.

Perfetti, Stefano. "Metamorfosi di una traduzione. Agostino Nifo revisore dei *De animalibus* gaziani." *Medioevo. Rivista di Storia della Filosofia Medievale* 22 (1996): 259–301. Shows how Nifo modified Gaza's humanist translation, by reintroducing elements from William of Moerbeke's thirteenth-century literal translation.

———. "Three Different Ways of Interpreting Aristotle's *De Partibus Animalium*: Pietro Pomponazzi, Niccolò Leonico Tomeo and Agostino Nifo." In *Aristotle's Animals in the Middle Ages and Renaissance*, edited by Carlos Steel, Pieter Beullens, and Guy Guldentops. Leuven, Belgium: Leuven University Press, 1999.

———. *Aristotle's Zoology and its Renaissance Commentators (1521–1601).* Leuven, Belgium: Leuven University Press, 2000. A whole chapter (pp. 85–124) deals with Nifo's commentaries on Aristotle's zoological works.

Pine, Martin. *Pietro Pomponazzi: Radical Philosopher of the Renaissance.* Padova, Italy: Antenore, 1986. At pp. 153–162 the author gives a summary of Nifo's *De immortalitate animae*, written against Pomponazzi.

Zambelli, Paola. "I problemi metodologici del necromante Agostino Nifo." *Medioevo. Rivista di Storia della Filosofia Medievale* 1 (1975): 129–171. An article on Nifo's reflections on borderline matters, such as necromancy and demonology.

Stefano Perfetti

NOVIKOFF, ALEX BENJAMIN

(*b.* Semyonevka, Ukraine, 28 February 1913; *d.* New York, New York, 9 January 1987), *histochemistry, cell biology.*

Among biologists, Novikoff is known foremost for his contributions to the discovery and characterization of several cell organelles—lysosomes, peroxisomes, microperoxisomes, and the Golgi body—as well as helping to pioneer the field of cell biology. Among a wider audience, he is notable as a victim of the excesses of the anti-Communist movement in mid-twentieth-century America. Novikoff's early associations with Marxism led to productive conceptual interpretations in biology but also to his being targeted by political demagogues.

Growing into Academics and Political Activism. Novikoff was born in the Ukraine. However, his family, hoping to escape poverty there, soon emigrated to the United States. They eventually settled in the Brownsville section of Brooklyn, New York, among other immigrants. Novikoff's father worked for his brother-in-law as a salesman in the garment industry. Novikoff excelled in school, even in his early years. At home he exhibited an interest in nature, keeping many small animals, skinning and dissecting the corpses, and even boiling a dead cat to study its skeleton. He eventually skipped four grades, graduating high school at age fourteen. The family, steeped in a Jewish heritage of valuing intellectual achievement, pinned its hopes (and its limited financial resources) on his pursuing a career in medicine. When he graduated Columbia University in 1931 (at age eighteen), however, new shifts in institutional sentiment limited opportunities for Jews. Despite promising credentials, Novikoff was not admitted to several medical schools. The experience left him bitter and helped fuel his uncompromising advocacy for justice.

Following the advice of his mentors, Novikoff instead entered graduate school in zoology in 1931, also at Columbia University. To finance his study, he began teaching at the newly formed Brooklyn College. For several years, he commuted twice daily between the two campuses and their respective contexts. So began a lifelong pattern, recognized by colleagues, of his being "tirelessly and utterly devoted to his work." At Columbia, Novikoff pursued experimental embryology and, beginning in 1932, spent several summers doing research at the Woods Hole Marine Biological Laboratory. From Arthur Pollister he gained an enthusiasm for cells. In 1936, at age twenty-three, he published his first scientific paper, followed in the next two years by three more. Meanwhile, at Brooklyn College, Novikoff did not take well to the stratification of junior and senior faculty. In 1935, he joined the growing Communist Party, an expression of his progressive idealism, his interest in Karl Marx's scientific perspectives toward society, and the party's focus on local labor issues. That simple act haunted him for the next three decades. Soon he was helping to write and distribute the communist newsletter on campus and defending the rights of younger staff. Novikoff was able to work on little sleep, and he continued his prodigious efforts. As he commuted, he wrote up his thesis and in 1938 received his PhD.

Weathering Repercussions. With his new degree, Novikoff was due for promotion at Brooklyn College. However, he had irritated many departmental colleagues and annoyed the administration with his activities for the teachers' union. Novikoff's credentials, even with many additional letters lauding his scientific work, seemed insufficient. Only after a year of public politicking was the new position approved. Antagonism toward the union sharpened.

Novikoff married in 1939 and began to drift away from party activities. His research continued, and by 1940 he had published nine papers. That same year a wave of conservatism swept through the state, and legislative committees targeted the communist affiliations of the teachers' union. The new college president, no friend of the union, did not intervene. Novikoff was investigated. Ultimately, no action was taken. Still, seeds of doubt were sown—and preserved in filed reports.

When the United States entered World War II, Novikoff wanted to serve in the military and sought a medical commission. Yet the mere suspicion of unspecified activities now dogged him. His application was denied, once in 1942 and again in 1943, based on vaguely documented doubts about his loyalty. Later, in 1948, Novikoff was hired by the U.S. Army to consult on two films about enzymes and carbohydrate metabolism. Again, questions about his loyalty surfaced and, although his work was purely biological and largely already completed, his appointment was terminated.

After an exciting postdoctoral fellowship on cells and cancer at the University of Wisconsin (1946–1947)—and five more papers—Novikoff was hired for a permanent position at the University of Vermont Medical College. Over the next several years he successfully secured grants and continued active publication. By 1953, however, the anti-communist movement flared again. Novikoff's personal associations in the late 1930s again became the subject of scrutiny, now at the federal level. Ultimately, Novikoff invoked the Fifth Amendment to refrain from "naming names." Because of leverage by the governor of Vermont and public opinion inflamed by the press—and despite faculty recommendations to the contrary—Novikoff, at age forty, was dismissed. He had failed, the official documents alleged, to exhibit "the qualities of responsibility, integrity and frankness that are fundamental requirements of a faculty member." Ironically, thirty years later, in 1983, the university's president, in acknowledging the incident and awarding Novikoff an honorary degree, would salute Novikoff"s "integrity and courage."

In searching for new options, Novikoff learned of plans for a new medical college to honor Albert Einstein: a Jewish institution that would in part accommodate those excluded from other schools. Novikoff wrote to Einstein. That led, in 1955, to his founding appointment at the new Albert Einstein College of Medicine, which became his home for the next three decades. In 1962 he received a lifetime career grant—$25,000 annually for twenty-five years—from the National Cancer Institute. Still, Novikoff was excluded from government review panels until 1972. He was elected to the National Academy of

Sciences in 1974. His Federal Bureau of Investigation file, closed by then, contained 822 pages.

Discovering Lysosomes. Ironically perhaps, the last research Novikoff published before his dismissal at the University of Vermont has come to be counted among his most significant. Novikoff had analyzed enzymatic activity in different parts of the cell. At the time, cells were typically broken and the parts separated by weight by centrifuging them at successively higher speeds and collecting each fraction. The standard protocol generated four fractions. Novikoff created ten, allowing for a more fine-scaled analysis. He measured the level of seven strategically selected enzymes in each fraction. He was then able to modify his fractions into six groups, effectively sorted by particle size and corresponding enzyme activity. As would become clear much later, Novikoff had mapped characteristic markers to six major cell organelles—two not yet known.

Novikoff's work came to the notice of Christian de Duve at the University of Louvain, who was particularly interested in one fraction. While investigating the effect of insulin on the enzyme glucose-6-phosphatase in rat liver cells, de Duve had encountered puzzling changes in the level of acid phosphatase activity. He had then isolated the effect to one fraction of the cell and, in 1952, proposed that it signaled an unknown membrane-bound particle. Novikoff's 1953 work on acid phosphatase seemed to confirm that interpretation. The two met in New York City and discussed their results in Central Park. By 1955 de Duve had identified five other enzymes in the same fraction. All broke molecules apart and so he called the prospective new organelles *lysosomes* (for *lyse*, to cleave).

De Duve's proposal was unusual because previously all organelles had first been identified visually. Perhaps his biochemical data did not reflect a real particle? De Duve thus invited Novikoff to collaborate toward generating micrographic evidence. Novikoff spent six weeks in Belgium the summer before he was to begin work at Albert Einstein College of Medicine. De Duve's lab provided the cell fractions, but had no electron microscope. At the end of each day Novikoff took the samples, iced in a thermos bottle, from Louvain to Paris by train and worked late into the night to produce the images, returning the next day to repeat the routine. The stunning results were announced the following spring: they had successfully visualized lysosomes—and thereby credibly demonstrated their existence.

Werner Straus, working independently at the same time, further established a primary enzymatic role of lysosomes as intracellular digestion. De Duve continued for many years to characterize how lysosomes functioned. Novikoff adapted a lead-based stain for use with acid phosphatase, which helped critically in further visualizing and interpreting lysosomes. His synoptic chapter on lysosomes in a 1961 textbook was instrumental in establishing their relevance among a wider audience. Novikoff went on to study the form of the lysosome in diverse cell types and tissues and in pathological conditions (such as in fatty liver, tumors, or nephrosis): This relatively unglamorous work importantly revealed context. (The cells included an induced hepatoma, now named for Novikoff.) "It is largely due to Novikoff's bold and imaginative use of morphological techniques," de Duve noted later in a 1969 retrospective, "that lysosomes have come to be recognized in a broader biological context." Novikoff's detailed scrutiny also revealed a close relationship between the lysosome and other organelles: the Golgi apparatus and endoplasmic reticulum (ER). He named the special hybrid structure GERL. It gave clues to how lysosomes formed. De Duve shared a Nobel Prize for his work in 1974, and Novikoff, overlooked in the award, wrote generously about de Duve's achievements for *Science* magazine.

Pioneering Cell Biology. Novikoff contributed substantially to the early development of cell biology in other ways, as well. For example, his 1953 cellular enzyme analysis included urate oxidase (uricase), which seemed to fractionate with acid phosphatase. De Duve thus began including it in his own studies. However, it was John F. Thomson and Florence J. Klipfel, in 1957, who observed that it sedimented with the familiar enzyme catalase, which breaks down hydrogen peroxide. By the mid-1960s du Duve's lab had characterized them both as part of a second suite of enzymes in yet another new organelle: the *peroxisome.* Soon, it was linked to structures (named microbodies) already identified microscopically in kidney cells by Johannes Rhodin in 1954. More extensive study of peroxisomes was facilitated by a stain (alkaline diaminobenzidine, or DAB) codeveloped by Novikoff and Sidney Goldfischer in 1969, which effectively visualized the activity of catalase in electron micrographs. Novikoff systematically surveyed peroxisomes as he had lysosomes, and in 1972, working with his second wife (and former lab technician) Phyllis, discovered a unique type, the *microperoxisome.*

Novikoff's most enduring contributions were technical and critical, not conceptual. As noted, he developed important stains for studying lysosomes and peroxisomes. Another important stain, developed in 1961, also with Goldfischer, was for nucleosidediphosphatase, an important marker for the Golgi body. This also provided the first information about that organelle's enzymatic properties. Novikoff was equally adept at finding flaws in widely used techniques. His important critiques included the Wachstein-Meisel procedures (1967), the interference of enzymes by lead in the Gomori technique (1970); and diffusion artifacts from diaminobenzidine cytochemistry (1972, 1980). He was an active participant in debates, strongly probative, yet also gracious and conceding when shown to be wrong.

Novikoff summarized his expansive knowledge in a 1970 textbook, *Cells and Organelles*, coauthored with Eric Holtzman, a former student. It was intended in part to present the achievements of cell biology, the understanding of the parts of the cell, as a complement to the molecular bias of James Watson's 1965 *Molecular Biology of the Gene*. The text was framed by opening and closing chapters on research methods and history, aimed toward encouraging others into research. One reviewer described it as "extraordinarily fine" and "at once exciting, scholarly, concise, and penetrating." It was used extensively and went through two subsequent editions.

Finally, Novikoff assumed many leadership roles. Among them, he was second president of the American Society for Cell Biology. He also served on several editorial boards, most notably for the *Journal of Histochemistry and Cytochemistry* from 1955 into the 1980s.

Working with a Marxist Perspective. Novikoff's brief participation in the Communist Party, as noted above, adversely affected his career. But his exposure to Marxism also helped contribute productively to the content and practice of his science. His conceptual outlook, interpretations of evidence, and professional conduct were all shaped in part by Marxist perspectives.

The traces are perhaps clearest in several publications from 1945. After nearly four years without publishing anything, Novikoff wrote a synoptic theoretical paper, "The Concept of Integrative Levels and Biology," for *Science*. It was a programmatic call against the extremes of both vitalism and mechanistic reductionism. Biologists, he claimed, needed to understand both parts and wholes. In particular, Novikoff rejected vague organizing principles at higher levels of organization, stressing instead "the material interrelationships" of different levels. Also, in denying privilege to either atomism or organicism, he advocated a "dialectical approach." Here he echoed the explicit Marxist language of dialectical materialism.

Accordingly, Novikoff profiled biochemistry as both essential to and limited in understanding cells. Likewise, he underscored how development transformed simple cell functions, at one level, into physiology at another level. But the ultimate aim of Novikoff's analysis was human society. He criticized thinkers, such as the English philosopher Herbert Spencer (1820–1903), who appealed to a misleading organism-society analogy that biologized culture, and he cautioned that conflating levels of organization led to "erroneous and dangerous social conclusions." He pointedly targeted the justification of fascists (namely, the Nazis), who alleged that "man's biology decides his social behavior." Novikoff claimed that people needed to understand distinctly sociological principles to keep society "free and democratic." He further referred, in a Marxist vein, to "the economic basis of social relations" and to the technological (materialist) roots of change. Here, in essence, was a biological framework, guided by Marxist principles, for interpreting social political action.

Novikoff's portrayal of evolution also reflected Marx's views on history and progress through a series of revolutions. Even the opening sentence stated, "the concept of integrative levels of organization is a general description of the evolution of matter through successive and higher orders of complexity and integration." At the same time, Novikoff warned against assumptions of an ill-defined progressive organizing trend, again echoing Marxist materialism. Novikoff noted the special features of humans, such as their ability to control their environment and thus, in a sense, to guide their own destiny. He also alluded to the plasticity of human intelligence, implying the potential for cultural change. The explicit lesson was that "social progress rests upon the planned activity of men," not nature. He quoted his fellow biologist Julian Huxley: "Purposes in life are made, not found." Finally, Novikoff noted that "man possesses a unique head and hand," invoking Marx's view of the parity of intellectual and manual labor. In all, Novikoff presented a view of the levels of biological organization—and its implications—that was strongly guided by Marxist principles of social change and scientific humanism.

In the same year, 1945, Novikoff wrote *Climbing Our Family Tree*, his first of two books for children. Writing about science for a young audience was largely unprecedented, and the work became an innovative landmark in children's literature. Writing the book itself thus expressed a kind of socialist outlook that deemed all ages as equally important audiences, and it was published by a communist press in New York City.

Novikoff's topic was evolution. The book presented the history of life as largely progressive, explaining and celebrating major evolutionary innovations, such as the transition to land or homeothermy, again commensurate with Marx's view of progress through revolutions. The culminating section, "Man's Freedom," described the same concepts about social organization that appeared in the "Integrative Levels" paper in *Science*: human independence from the environment and the roles of tools and of planning in social change. It closed poetically with a socialist ideal: "Men, working with each other, can become ever more free—ever more human."

Novikoff's second book for children, *From Head to Foot*, described human physiology. In addition to surveying the major systems, it introduced some great scientists and their historical discoveries and books, giving a sense of science as an active, exciting—and human—endeavor. Novikoff again closed portraying socialist ideals: "Man's complicated brain and nervous system, his body which can adapt itself so easily to different surroundings, his ability to plan, work, and use tools, give him a chance to work together with his fellows and deliberately improve his society until it suits him, until it gives everybody a good life."

The perspectives so evident in these early writings persisted as a context in Novikoff's later work. First, Novikoff was sensitized to look for differences and complexity among the parts, even in well-integrated structures. For example, in his 1953 study of cell fractions, he stressed the heterogeneity of enzyme activity in the different parts of the cell. Initially, he interpreted those differences as variations in the known organelles, the mitochondria and microsomes (ribosomes). Later, with more data, he accepted de Duve's claim that the unusual distributions indicated instead a new, undocumented organelle. The theme of heterogeneity reappeared in a 1959 paper, in which Novikoff profiled how the cells in a section of liver tissue, always assumed to be uniform, exhibited significant variation. Novikoff also clearly appreciated that the less prominent organelles, such as the lysosome or peroxisome (which he studied so thoroughly), were just as significant as any other, when viewed as part of the integrated whole.

Second, Novikoff continued to balance reductionist and more holistic perspectives. Much of his work involved the reductionist's aim of localizing biochemical functions to parts within cells. But he also did not lose sight of context. He studied how lysosomes and peroxisomes (as units) differed in widely various cellular conditions. In a similar way, he cautioned others about how cells differed in context: in tissue cultures versus in organic tissue. Parts and wholes were on a par. In his 1970 text, for example, after describing the many cell organelles (parts), he gave just as much coverage to the many cell types made from recombining them into different wholes.

Marxist and socialist perspectives also seemed to shape how Novikoff practiced science. He shared credit generously. When invited to comment on his 1961 *Proceedings of the National Academy of Sciences* (*PNAS*) paper as a "citation classic," for example, he acknowledged the key contributions of six others in a brief half-page article. Novikoff was utterly without pretension. Once when interns and residents at Albert Einstein College of Medicine went on strike, he joined the picket lines. Viewing science as a community of equals, he engaged in conversation—or debate—with any colleague, regardless of stature, to the pleasant surprise of many students. His posture of valuing "dialectics" promoted the critical analysis of ideas.

Novikoff's science was richly—and fruitfully—influenced by Marxist perspectives. Ironically, such real, but hardly subversive influences were never the focus of those who targeted Novikoff for Communist activities. Ultimately, Novikoff's career, as one colleague noted, indicated that a passion for social justice and for one's own work need not be inconsistent with good science.

BIBLIOGRAPHY

Novikoff's complete papers (c. 1930–1985) are archived at the University of Vermont, University Archives, Record Group 74, Boxes 197–224.

WORKS BY NOVIKOFF

Climbing Our Family Tree. New York: International Publishers, 1945.

"The Concept of Integrative Levels and Biology." *Science* 101 (1945): 209–215.

From Head to Foot: Our Bodies and How They Work. New York: International Publishers, 1946.

With Estelle Podber, Jean Ryan, and Elsie Noe. "Biochemical Heterogeneity of the Cytoplasmic Particles Isolated from Rat Liver Homogenate." *Journal of Histochemistry and Cytochemistry* 1(1953): 27–46.

With Henri Beaufay, and Christian de Duve. "Electron Microscopy of Lysosome-rich Fractions from Rat Liver." *Journal of Biophysical and Biochemical Cytology* 2 (Supp.) (1956): 179–184. First visualization of lysosomes.

With Sidney Goldfischer. "Nucleosidediphosphatase Activity in the Golgi Apparatus and Its Usefulness for Cytological Studies." *Proceedings of the National Academy of Science USA* 47, no. 6 (1961): 802–810. Valuable staining method. "Citation classic" in 1985.

"Lysosomes and Related Particles." In *The Cell*, edited by Jean Bracher and Alfred E. Mirsky, Vol. 2. New York: Academic Press, 1961. Review establishing the identity of lysosomes.

With Sidney Goldfischer. "Visualization of Peroxisomes (Microbodies) and Mitochondria with Diaminobenzidine." *Journal of Histochemistry and Cytochemistry* 17 (1969): 675–680. Staining of catalase for peroxisomes.

With Eric Holtzman. *Cells and Organelles.* New York: Holt, Rinehart and Winston, 1970. Popular textbook of cell biology.

With Phyllis M. Novikoff. "Peroxisomes in Absorptive Cells of Mammalian Small Intestine." *Journal of Cell Biology* 53 (1972): 532–560. Identification of microperoxisomes.

OTHER SOURCES

de Duve, Christian. 1969. "The Lysosome in Retrospect." In *Lysosomes in Biology and Pathology*, Vol. 1, edited by John T. Dingle and Honor B. Fell. Amsterdam: North Holland Publishing Company.

Holmes, David R. *Stalking the Academic Communist: Intellectual Freedom and the Firing of Alex Novikoff.* Hanover, NH:

Published for University of Vermont by University Press of New England, 1989.

Douglas Allchin

NOZICK, ROBERT (*b.* Brooklyn, New York, 16 November 1938; *d.* Cambridge, Massachusetts, 23 January 2002), *political philosophy, epistemology, metaphysics, theory of rational decision.*

Nozick is probably best known for his philosophy of libertarianism in political philosophy and his idea of the "minimal state." He also made significant contributions in the areas of epistemology and the theory of rational decision in philosophy, as well as metaphysics, philosophy of mind, philosophy of religion, and ethics.

After obtaining his BA degree (1959) at Columbia University in New York City, he earned his MA degree (1961) and PhD (1963), both at Princeton University in New Jersey. He then taught at Princeton and at Rockefeller University in New York City before coming in 1969 to Harvard University in Cambridge, Massachusetts, where he became university professor and also served as chair of the Philosophy Department. Some of his most important works include *Anarchy, State, and Utopia* (1974), which won the National Book Award; *Philosophical Explanations* (1981); *The Examined Life: Philosophical Meditations* (1989); *The Nature of Rationality* (1993); and *Invariances: The Structure of the Objective World* (2001).

According to Nozick's libertarianism, the only just kind of state is a minimal one, in which rights of individuals are primary and the role of the state is limited to the protection of these rights, such as protection against violence, theft, and breach of contracts. His *Anarchy, State, and Utopia* advocates limited government, individual liberty, and the importance of private property. This book critiques the liberalism of his Harvard colleague, John Rawls, and Rawls's idea of redistributive justice (the idea that the state should be allowed to and should reallocate wealth in order to promote more equal distribution and to aid the disadvantaged); thus, Nozick, famously, opposed the idea of a welfare state.

In his *Philosophical Explanations*, Nozick argues for the epistemological view that belief is knowledge just in case the belief in question "tracks the truth"; basically, that is, belief is knowledge just (only) in case the believer would have belief in the proposition in question if and only if the proposition in question were true. This is intended to be an answer to some versions of skepticism about the possibility of actual knowledge and as an "externalist" alternative to more traditional "internalist" views of knowledge (according to the latter of which, basically,

Robert Nozick. **MARTHA HOLMES/TIME LIFE PICTURES/GETTY IMAGES.**

a knower must be aware of the factors that constitute warrant for the belief in question). His *Philosophical Explanations* also develops his "closest continuer" theory of personal identity, a metaphysical issue.

Nozick's most famous contribution to the theory of rational decision is his 1969 article, "Newcomb's Problem and Two Principles of Choice," which introduced Newcomb's problem to philosophers. In this decision problem, there are two boxes before the decision maker: one transparent, which clearly contains one thousand dollars, and the other opaque, which is known to contain either one million dollars or nothing. The choice is between taking the contents of only the opaque box—*act A*—and taking the contents of both boxes—*act B.* So far, it seems that the obviously correct choice is B. But now suppose that the agent is fully (or highly) confident of the following about how the contents of the opaque box were determined: there is a very rich and very accurate predictor (of choices in just this kind of situation) who earlier placed the one million dollars in that box if and only if the predicted act was A—thus almost always rewarding those who choose A (reward equals one million dollars) and not so richly rewarding those who choose B (reward equals one thousand dollars). The agent could reason in either of these two ways: (1) if I choose A, then, since the predictor is so accurate, I will probably walk away with one million dollars, where choosing B would probably give me only one thousand dollars, so I should choose A; or (2) the rich predictor has already made the prediction and put, or did not put, the one million dollars in the opaque box, and either way I get one thousand dollars more with B than with A, so I should choose B. Nozick develops his own solution to the puzzle—involving whether or not there is a cause-effect relation between acts and states of affairs. This introduction of the puzzle has spawned a voluminous literature in the philosophy of rational choice.

In addition to the National Book Award, Nozick was also honored by, among other things, becoming a fellow of the American Academy of Arts and Sciences and by delivering the John Locke Lectures at Oxford University. He also was active very in practical ways, having, for example, participated in the preparation of a brief to the U.S. Supreme Court urging the protection of individual rights in the matter of whether one should be allowed to have a doctor's help in ending one's own life, assuming mental competence and terminal illness.

BIBLIOGRAPHY

WORKS BY NOZICK

"Newcomb's Problem and Two Principles of Choice." In *Essays in Honor of Carl G. Hempel*, edited by Nicholas Rescher et al. Dordrecht, Netherlands: D. Reidel Publishing, 1970.

Anarchy, State, and Utopia. New York: Basic Books, 1974.

Philosophical Explanations. Cambridge, MA: Harvard University Press, 1981.

The Examined Life: Philosophical Meditations. New York: Simon and Schuster, 1989.

The Nature of Rationality. Princeton, NJ: Princeton University Press, 1993.

Invariances: The Structure of the Objective World. Cambridge, MA: Harvard University Press, 2001.

OTHER SOURCES

Albert, Max, and Ronald A. Heiner. "An Indirect-Evolution Approach to Newcomb's Problem." *Homo Oeconomicus* 20 (2003): 161–191.

Feser, Edward. *On Nozick.* Belmont, CA: Wadsworth, 2003.

Paul, Jeffrey, ed. *Reading Nozick: Essays on Anarchy, State, and Utopia.* Totowa, NJ: Rowman and Littlefield, 1981.

Schmidt, Christian. *Newcomb's Problem: A Case of Pathological Reality?* Montreal: Groupe de recherche en épistémologie comparée, Université du Québec à Montréal, 1995.

Schmitz, David, ed. *Robert Nozick.* New York: Cambridge University Press, 2002.

Sobel, Jordan Howard. *Taking Chances.* New York: Cambridge University Press, 1994.

Ellery Eells

NOZOE, TETSUO

(*b.* Sendai, Japan, 16 May 1902, *d.* Tokyo, Japan, 4 April 1996), *organic chemistry, chemistry of nonbenzenoid aromatic compounds.*

A leading Japanese organic chemist, Nozoe discovered *hinokitiol*, a seven-membered aromatic compound, and based on this discovery developed a new area of chemistry known as nonbenzenoid aromatic compounds.

Early Life and Education. Tetsuo Nozoe was born in Sendai, one of Japan' s largest cities, located in northern Honshu, on 16 May 1902. His father, Ju-ichi, was born in Nagasaki prefecture in Kyushu, as the third son of Sukeuchi Kinoshita, in 1865, just three years before the Meiji Restoration, which marked the beginning of the modernization of Japan. When he was seventeen, Ju-ichi was adopted by a Nagasaki family, Yasouzaemon Nozoe, and sent to Tokyo to study at the Law College of the Imperial University, then the only university in Japan. In 1890, while still a student, he married twenty-year-old Toyo, the sixth daughter of his adopted family. When Ju-ichi graduated from the Imperial University in 1893, he became a lawyer and moved to Sendai, a central city in northern Honshu, the largest island in Japan, with his family. There, he became involved in politics, serving as chairman of the Municipal Assembly, and as a member of the House of Representatives for one term.

Tetsuo was the sixth of eleven children; he had seven brothers and three sisters. He first became interested in chemistry while in his early teens in junior high school thanks to a chemistry teacher, who inspired him to begin to do some experiments at home. In 1920 he entered Dai Ni Koto-gakko at Sendai (which literally means the second high school), one of the elite national all-male liberal arts colleges; most graduates went on to one of the imperial universities. Even though his parents wanted him to be a medical doctor and he initially took a premedical class, Tetsuo soon decided to study chemistry and entered the Department of Chemistry of the College of Science at Tohoku Imperial University in 1923.

Tohoku Imperial University was founded in 1907 as the third imperial university, after Tokyo (1886) and Kyoto (1897). With a research-oriented mission and liberal admission policy, the university opened its doors not only to graduates of elite all-male liberal arts colleges, from which Tetsuo graduated, but also to those who graduated from technical colleges as well as teachers colleges, including women's teachers colleges.

The first professors in the Department of Chemistry included the distinguished chemists Masataka Ogawa, Masao Katayama, and Toshiyuki (Riko) Majima. Ogawa discovered a new chemical element, which he called "nipponium" (which was first incorrectly designated as the 43rd element but only recently shown to be rhenium). Katayama, a professor of physical chemistry, was a close acquaintance of Tetsuo's mother; they were members of the same Christian church. Although Katayama transferred to Tokyo Imperial University before Nozoe entered Tohoku Imperial University, it was perhaps upon Katayama's advice that Tetsuo decided on this university. There, Majima, a well-regarded professor of organic chemistry, became Nozoe's mentor and was to play a decisive role in his life.

Nozoe's Mentor: Riko Majima Born in 1874 in Kyoto, Riko Majima graduated from the Department of Chemistry of the College of Science at Tokyo Imperial University in 1899. After a four-year stay in Europe, from early 1907 to early 1911, he became a professor of organic chemistry at the newly established Tohoku Imperial University in March 1911. He was especially famous for the study of urushiol (a catechol [o-dihydrobenzene] derivative), the main component of the sap of the Japanese lacquer tree (*Rhus verniciflua* Stokes, *urushi-no-ki* in Japanese). The sap produced a black glossy varnish known as "japan" and japan ware was an important export product. From the very beginning of research on organic chemistry in Japan in the late 1870s, Japanese chemists often studied local natural products using methods newly developed in Europe. Majima, as well as Nozoe, followed this line of research. After discovering urushiol, Majima devised a new synthesis of the indole ring and started to study indole derivatives. As a leader of the first generation of research organic chemists, he contributed greatly to the establishment of organic chemistry laboratories in higher education and research institutes in Japan. Nozoe first studied the synthesis of indole derivatives under Majima.

Work in Formosa. After graduating in March 1926, Nozoe stayed on as Majima's assistant. However, at the end of June, Nozoe left Sendai for Formosa (now Taiwan) to become a researcher at the Monopoly Bureau in Taipei, the capital of Formosa, helped by Majima's strong recommendation. As one of Majima's most talented students, Nozoe was certainly a well-qualified candidate for a professorship at a planned new imperial university in Formosa. However, there may have been other reasons behind Majima's help and recommendation. In 1920 Tetsuo's father was elected a member of the Parliament (House of Representatives) after a heated general election against a local political leader, Ikunosuke Fujisawa, who later became the minister of Commerce and Industry and served as speaker of the House of Representatives. However, Tetsuo's father lost his seat in the following election in 1924 to Fujisawa. The defeat was a terrible blow to Ju-ichi Nozoe, who died in 1927 at the age of sixty-one, and his family began to experience financial difficulties. This may partly explain why all five surviving brothers (the other three having died young), including Tetsuo himself, worked overseas: two elder brothers as engineers for overseas trading companies, one as a principal of an agricultural college in Manchuria, and the other as a banker in Manchuria.

Nozoe arrived in Taipei on 2 June 1926. After the Sino-Japanese War in 1895, Formosa had become a Japanese colony. In 1930 the population of the island was 4.6 million, of which 229,000 were Japanese. Japanese was the official language. Nozoe was employed at the Camphor Research Laboratories of the Monopoly Bureau for the first year and for the next two years at the Department of Chemical Industry of the Central Research Institute, both of which were institutes of the Formosan Government-General in Taipei. He worked under Kinzo Kafuku, a graduate of the Chemistry Department of Tokyo Imperial University and a leading chemist in Formosa since 1912. In 1927, a year after his arrival, Nozoe married Kyoko Horiuchi, Kafuku's niece and a daughter of a director of an agricultural experimental station of the Formosan Government-General. The couple had one son and three daughters, all born in Formosa. Their son, Shigeo, born in 1931, followed his father's path by studying chemistry at Tohoku University, where he later became a professor at the College of Pharmacy.

In 1928 Taihoku Imperial University (Taihoku is the Japanese name for Taipei) was established, and Kafuku became a professor of chemistry in the College of Science and Agriculture. Nozoe was appointed as Kafuku's associate professor the following year. Taihoku Imperial University was the second Japanese imperial university in its colonies after Keijo Imperial University at Keijo (now Seoul), founded in 1925. Nozoe's main research interest was the study of natural products, especially those found in Formosa. Nozoe started actively studying the structures of saponins, glycosides with a distinctive foaming characteristic, and sapogenins, derivatives of the triterpenoid groups and nonsugar components of sapogins, isolated from local fruits (*Barringtonia asiatica* and *B. racemosa*). In 1936 he submitted a dissertation to the newly established Osaka Imperial University, where Professor Majima had become dean of the College of Science, and received a doctor of science degree. The following year, Nozoe predicted the correct structures for oleanolic acid and hederagenin, well-known sapogenins, using ultraviolet absorption spectroscopy. In 1937, upon Kafuku's return to Japan, Nozoe replaced him as a full professor at the university.

Nozoe also studied constituents of wool wax and those of other animal skin waxes and discovered a series of unusual branched chain fatty acids, lanolinic acids, and agnolinic acids (1939). However, World War II interrupted his studies. Aware of the profound advancements in these areas during and soon after the war, Nozoe did not resume these studies.

Discovery of Hinokitiol. Nozoe's most widely known research in Formosa was that on the chemical constituents of *taiwanhinoki* (*Chamaecyparis obtusa var. formosana,* now *C. taiwanensis*), a native conifer found in high mountainous areas. Some researchers in Japan were interested in the tree's acidic components because of the tree's resistance to wood-decaying fungi. Nenokichi Hirao, a chemist at a pharmaceutical company in Kobe, had reported the formation of a dark-red pigment from these components and had named it *hinokitin* in 1926. Nozoe obtained a phenolic compound, $C_{10}H_{12}O_2$, as the alkaline salt by shaking an ethereal solution of hinokitin with an aqueous alkaline solution (see Figure 1). The new compound was named *hinokitiol* and was first reported in 1936 in a special issue of the *Journal of the Chemical Society of Japan* to celebrate Professor Majima's sixtieth birthday. Nozoe also proved that hinokitin, which was sublimable *in vacuo* and soluble in organic solvents, was an iron complex of hinokitiol, $(C_{10}H_{11}O_2)_3Fe$, some of the earliest evidence for the presence of an iron complex in a natural compound.

Since the content of hinokitiol in *taiwanhinoki* is very low (0.1–0.2%), and even though he had found that *hiba* (*Thujopsis dolabrata* var. *hondae*), grown in northern Japan, also contained hinokitiol and became an important source of hinokitiol after the war, the source of hinokitiol remained a problem then. Shigehiro Katsura, a newly appointed professor of medicine transferred from Tohoku Imperial University, began in about 1938 to investigate the chemotherapy of tuberculosis and showed significant antibacterial activity in hinokitiol and *l*-rhodinic acid, both of which were extracted from *taiwanhinoki.* At Nozoe's request, the Taipei factory of the Takasago Perfumery Company (renamed the Takasago Chemical Company in 1939) collected stumps of *taiwanhinoki* left in the mountains and obtained the hinoki oil. The Takasago Perfumery Company was founded in 1920 in Tokyo by Tadaka Kainosho, a graduate of the Chemistry Department of Kyoto Imperial University. The company built a factory in Taipei to extract the by-products of manufactured camphor, which was indigenous to Formosa. Masayasu Kainosho, the second son of the founder of the company, had studied under Nozoe at Taihoku Imperial University and worked for the company in Taipei after graduating in 1940. Masayasu separated hinokitiol and *l*-rhodinic acid from hinoki oil. Nozoe obtained about 10 grams of hinokitiol, sufficient for a structural study that demonstrated that the compound was a seven-membered cyclic α-enolone with an isopropyl group. When Nozoe visited mainland Japan for the last time before the war, in 1940, he proposed an erroneous formula for hinokitiol, $C_{10}H_{14}O_2$, which contained two hydrogen atoms more than required by the correct structure. However, after his return to Formosa, unusual stability toward both acid (concentrated sulfuric acid) and alkaline solution (50% aqueous potassium hydroxide) that he found, along with a reconfirmation of the elemental analyses of hinokitiol, its acetate, and its methyl ether showed the correct molecular formula to be $C_{10}H_{12}O_2$. After the war hinokitiol, extracted from *hiba* in Japan, was used commercially as antibacterial for cosmetics, wood preservative, termite disinfestant, paint, wax and coatings.

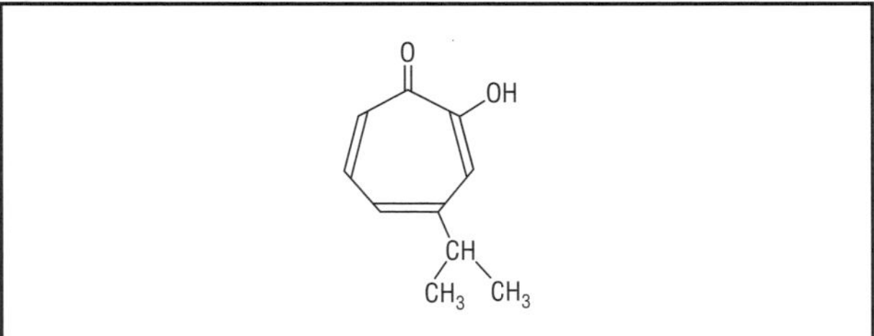

Figure 1. *Structure of hinokitiol.*

Because of the war, European chemical journals became unavailable in Formosa around 1937, and by 1941 the American chemical journals could not be obtained. Fortunately, Nozoe managed to obtain a copy of Linus Pauling's *The Nature of the Chemical Bond* (1939), probably one of the last academic publications imported into Formosa before the war with the United States began. After reading the book, Nozoe arrived at the idea that hinokitiol could be a new type of aromatic compound stabilized by resonance, involving an intramolecular hydrogen bond. Even though it turned out later that hinokitiol existed not as a resonance hybrid but as a pair of tautomers that interconverted through intramolecular hydrogen bonding, this idea was the first step that opened the new research area of nonbenzoniod aromatic compounds. Nozoe presented his ideas at the local Formosan branch of the Society of the Chemical Industry in 1941 for the first time, but the audience remained skeptical about his seven-membered structure.

Japan's plunge into World War II with the attack on Pearl Harbor on 7 December (8 December in Japan time) 1941 forced Nozoe to abandon fundamental research and pursue wartime practical research instead. Because of the continuous heavy bombing in Taipei, especially after 1943, the university had to evacuate the campus, and

Nozoe decided to move his laboratory to a mountainside about 20 kilometers (12 miles) from the city. However, on the very day they completed the evacuation and were ready to resume research, the war ended (15 August 1945). It then took a year to move the laboratory back to its original location.

Research in Taiwan after the War. After World War II, Formosa was returned to the Republic of China, and Taihoku Imperial University was renamed Taiwan National University. When the war ended, about 488,000 Japanese, including 166,000 military personnel, were living in Formosa. The last governor-general, Rikichi Ando, organized their return to Japan shortly before the Japanese colonial government in Formosa was officially abolished on 31 May 1946, with the exception of approximately 26,000 specialists, whom China kept. Nozoe had his son Shigeo return to Japan first. Nozoe hoped to follow Shigeo, but had to stay on with his wife and daughters, and he worked as a professor of chemistry at Taiwan National University under the orders of the Chinese government.

During the last years of the war, the Takasago Chemical Company mass-produced hinoki oil from *taiwanhinoki* as a gasoline substitute as well as a mineral processing oil. After the war, Nozoe found a large amount of hinokitin, the reddish brown mud iron complex compound of hinokitiol, discarded in the backyard of the factory. Suddenly, by chance, Nozoe had a very large amount of hinokitiol, several kilograms of crystals, soon after the war, when everything was in short supply. In the summer of 1946, Nozoe finally began his research on hinokitiol with all the members of his laboratory at the university.

Since he regarded hinokitiol as a compound with a novel aromatic system, he examined various substitution reactions: halogenation, nitration, azo coupling and so on. The results of his group's research at National Taiwan University were published in 1951–1952 after Nozoe returned to Japan.

In 1947 a Taiwanese uprising (called the "228 Incident") was forcibly put down by Chiang Kai-shek's Kuomintang government, and many Taiwanese intellectuals lost their lives. This political chaos in Taiwan offered Nozoe an opportunity to leave the country. He thus managed to return to Japan at the end of May 1948. His alma mater, Tohoku University, offered him a position.

Research on Hinokitiol at Tohoku University. At Tohoku University, Nozoe was first appointed temporary lecturer in July 1948. He was initially treated as a suspicious agent of some sort, which was not uncommon during the Cold War period for national officials, including teachers in national universities, but by December he was appointed professor of organic chemistry.

At the end of that year, Nozoe was invited to Osaka University to talk at a special seminar of the Department of Chemistry about his study on hinokitiol in Taiwan. In February of the following year, he was invited to give the same lecture at the University of Tokyo. This lecture was printed as "Studies on Hinokitiol" in *Yakugaku*, a pharmacy review journal in Japanese published by the Japanese Pharmaceutical Society. In the article, Nozoe gave an explanation, based on the variety of its reactions, of his 4-isopropltropolone structure for hinokitiol. He also suggested possible future directions for research on seven- and five-membered unsaturated cyclic systems. The article shows that he was able to follow the developments in this area of research in the West soon after his return from Taiwan.

In 1945 Michael J. S. Dewar, later a leading theoretical chemist, was a postdoctoral fellow at Oxford with Robert Robinson studying stipitatic acid, a mold product whose structure was in dispute. Dewar proposed a new kind of aromatic structure with a seven-membered ring for which he coined the term *tropolone* (cycloheptarienolone). At the end of 1948, Nozoe received, from Professor Shigehiko Sugasawa at the College of Pharmacy of the University of Tokyo, a copy of a letter from Holger Erdtman, professor of organic chemistry at the Royal Institute of Technology in Stockholm, together with a reprint of Erdtman's paper on the structure of thujaplicins, published in *Nature* in 1948. Sugasawa had once worked under Robinson at Oxford along with Erdtman, and Erdtman had isolated three isomeric monoterpenoids (named the α-thujaplicin, β-thujaplicin, and γ-thujaplicin) from *Thuja plicata* (Western red cedar). After corresponding, Erdtman and Nozoe found hinokitiol to be identical to B-thujaplicin, and to have the tropolone structure. Erdtman was only twenty days older than Nozoe, and they became lifelong friends.

When a symposium, "Tropolone and Allied Compounds," was organized by the Chemical Society of London in November 1950, Erdtman mentioned Nozoe's work on hinokitiol as a pioneering contribution to tropolone chemistry, thus helping Nozoe's research gain recognition in the West. Nozoe was able to publish his work on hinokitiol and its derivatives in *Nature* in 1951 thanks to J. W. Cook, chairman of the symposium.

At Tohoku University, Nozoe resumed his studies on the reactions of hinokitiol and its derivatives. He concentrated on electrophilic substitutions of the natural product. He succeeded in synthesizing tropolone as well as hinokitiol and its isomers in 1950 and 1951. The results were published in English in the *Proceedings of the Japan Academy* thanks to Professor Majima, a member of the Japan Academy since 1926. Majima's support and understanding greatly helped early recognition of Nozoe's work

Tetsuo Nozoe. *Professor Nozoe with members of his laboratory at Taipei University, 1947.* COURTESY OF PROFESSOR SHIGEO NOZOE.

in Japan. Nozoe received various awards, such as the Majima Award for Organic Chemistry of the Chemical Society of Japan (1944), the Japan Academy Award (1953), and the Order of Culture (1958), the most prestigious medal for one' s contribution to culture in Japan. He was only the second chemist recipient of the Order of Culture in postwar Japan, after Majima, who himself received the award in 1947.

In 1953 Nozoe was invited to lecture on troponoid chemistry at the 14th International Union of Pure and Applied Chemistry Congress in Stockholm. This was the first time he had been abroad. Before the war, it had been common practice for Japanese intellectuals to study in Europe or the United States for a few years before becoming a professor at an imperial university, but Nozoe had not had such a chance. Taking this opportunity, he visited various leading organic chemists in Europe and the United States during his five months of leave. After this, he took every opportunity to visit or invite chemists from all over the world to discuss topics of mutual interest. From his first trip abroad, he started to collect autographs, comments, tributes, and good wishes from famous chemists he encountered. He recorded them in his nine-volume notebook diaries; the surviving volumes are now kept in the Tohoku University Archives.

Nozoe's articles on the synthesis of tropolone appeared at almost the same time as those of William Von Eggers Doering in the United States and J. W. Cook and R. D. Haworth in the United Kingdom on the same subject. The synthesis of tropone, the parent ketone compound, was accomplished by William G. Dauben (1951), Doering (1951), and Nozoe (1952). In 1954 Doering synthesized the positively charged tropylium ion by the bromination of tropilidene, confirming the theory of aromatic character proposed in 1931 by Erich Hückel.

After the syntheses of tropone and tropolone, Nozoe concentrated his efforts on clarifying their chemical reactivity. He extended his research by cooperating with physical chemists in Japan to study various physical properties to gain a firm footing in aromatic chemistry. It must be noted that Nozoe was one of the first organic chemists in Japan to actively employ those physical approaches, such as electronic theory and physical instrumentation, that transformed organic chemistry after World War II elsewhere but were uncommon for organic chemistry in Japan at that time.

Since the azulene system contains the seven-membered ring system of troponoids, Nozoe started to study the conversion of troponoids to azulenoids soon after he returned to Sendai in 1948. He developed efficient syntheses of heteroazulenes and variously functionalized azulenes.

During the 1960s, Japan experienced unprecedented growth and expansion of its economy, as well as its institutions of higher education, especially the faculties and departments of science and technology. Thanks to Nozoe's efforts, a second chemistry department was established at Tohoku University in 1962. When Nozoe retired in 1965 at the age of sixty-three, the mandatory retirement age at the time, he made a financial donation for the establishment of a professorship for troponoid chemistry at the university and worked as the first professor on the post he created for two more years at Sendai until March 1968.

Work in the International Community. After his complete retirement from Tohoku University, Nozoe moved to Tokyo and continued laboratory work with a young research assistant and a secretary, offered by the Research Institute of the Kao Soap Company in Tokyo. He did his research in cooperation with small groups of professors all over Japan. Nozoe studied the reaction mechanism of azulenoids synthesis from troponoids and the design of new azulene syntheses. In the last years of his life, he was interested in the structural elucidation of the oxidation products of azulenes. The results were summarized in a thirty-page article, published posthumously. On 4 April 1996, just one month before his ninety-fourth birthday, Nozoe died of cancer in a hospital, a day after finishing proofreading his last paper.

During the second half of his life, Nozoe had contributed immensely to international meetings and congresses on organic chemistry, especially on nonbenzenoid aromatic chemistry. These activities helped greatly with the construction of international networks for the postwar generation of Japanese chemists.

Nozoe participated in the organizing committee of the 4th International Union of Pure and Applied Chemistry Symposium on the Chemistry of Natural Products, held in Kyoto in 1964 and coinciding with the Tokyo Olympics. It was the first large-scale international congress on chemistry in Japan and symbolized the postwar recovery of Japan in the academic world. In 1965 Nozoe cochaired, with John D. Roberts of the California Institute of Technology, the first Japan-U.S. Cooperative Seminar on Physical Organic Chemistry in Kyoto, where five U.S. chemists and fourteen Japanese chemists discussed their research for an entire week.

In 1970 the first International Symposium on the Chemistry of Nonbenzenoid Aromatic Compounds was held in Sendai. This meeting had been initially proposed by Ronald Breslow, a professor of chemistry at Columbia University, nine years earlier to commemorate Nozoe's retirement. The symposium was so successful that it was decided to hold such an international meeting every three to four years. Nozoe participated through 1995.

In 1961 Nozoe had published a 700-page reference book in Japanese, titled *Nonbenzenoid Aromatic Compounds*, one of twenty-five volumes in the *Comprehensive Organic Chemistry* series. He also published a textbook on organic chemistry in two volumes with some of his former students. In his last days, he planned to publish a comprehensive book in English, which covered the development of research on seven-membered aromatic compounds. He had collected more than 6,000 references on the subject and had drawn up a voluminous table of contents, but his plan was not realized in his lifetime; all of his students had already retired, and the new generation of chemists was too busy with their own research to compile such a comprehensive book on a research area that was no longer as active. Tetsuo Nozoe was nevertheless one of the fortunate chemists who helped to create a new field of chemistry and who lived long enough to see its full growth, during a period when chemistry research in Japan had finally achieved international recognition.

BIBLIOGRAPHY

Nozoe Tetsuo Kyoju Ronbun Mokuroku-shu (Collection of Papers of Professor Tetsuo Nozoe) *[in Japanese], published by Nozoe Tetsuo Kyoju Go-taikan Kinen-kai (Commemoration Committee for Professor Nozoe's retirement), 1966.*

WORKS BY NOZOE

"Studies on Hinokitiol." *Yakugaku* [Science of drugs] (in Japanese) 3 (1949): 174–198.

With S. Seto, Y. Kitahara, M. Kunori, and Y. Nakayama. "On the Synthesis of Tropolone (Cycloheptatrienolone)." *Proceedings of the Japan Academy* 26, no. 7 (1950): 38–42.

With S. Seto, K. Kikuchi, T. Mukai, S. Matsumoto, and M. Murase. "On the Synthesis of Hinokitiol (*m*-Isopropyltropolone)." *Proceedings of the Japan Academy* 26, no. 7 (1950): 43–46.

"On the Substitution Products of Tropolone and Allied Compounds." *Nature* 27 (1951): 1055–1060.

"Chemistry of Natural Tropolone and Allied Compounds (Main Lecture at XVIth Int. Congr. Pure and Applied Chemistry, Paris, 1957)." *Experientia* (Basel), Supp. VII (1957): 306–327.

"Tropones and Tropolones." In *Non-benzenoid Aromatic Compounds*, edited by D. Ginsburg. New York: Interscience, 1959.

With K. Takase, H. Matsumura, T. Asao, K. Kikuchi, and S. Ito. "Non-benzenoid Aromatic Compounds." In *Dai-Yuki*

Nozoe

Kagaku [Comprehensive organic chemistry] (in Japanese), vol. 13, edited by M. Kotake. Tokyo: Asakura-Shoten, 1960.

"Tropylium and Related Compounds." In *Progress in Organic Chemistry*, vol. 5, edited by J. W. Cook. London: Butterworths, 1961.

"Recent Advance in the Chemistry of Troponoids and Related Compounds in Japan." *Pure and Applied Chemistry* 28 (1971): 239–280.

"Cyclohepta[*b*][1,4]benzoxazine and Related Compounds: Some Novel Aspects in Heterocyclic Chemistry (A Review)." *Heterocycles* 30 (1990): 1263–1306.

"Seventy Years in Organic Chemistry." In *Profiles, Pathways, and Dreams: Autobiographies of Eminent Chemists*, edited by J. I. Seeman. Washington, DC: American Chemical Society, 1991.

With H. Takeshita. "Chemistry of Azulenoquinones and Their Analogues." *Bulletin of the Chemical Society of Japan* 69 (1996): 1149–1178.

Nozoe, Tetsuo, ed. *Organic Chemistry* [in Japanese], 2 vols. Tokyo: Hirokawa Shoten, 1970–1972.

OTHER SOURCES

Asao, Toyonobu, Sho Ito, and Ichiro Murata. "Tesuo Nozoe (1902–1996)." *European Journal of Organic Chemistry* (2004): 899–928.

Hitosuji no Michi: Tsuioku Nozoe Tetsuo Sensei [One way: For the memory of professor Tetsuo Nozoe] (in Japanese). Nozoe Tetsuo Sensei Tsuito Jigyo-kai [Commemoration committee for passing away of Professor Nozoe], Tokyo, 1997.

Takashima, Shinji, and Public Relations Department of Hinoki Shinyaku, Ltd. *Hinokitiol Monogatari* [The story of hinokitiol] (in Japanese). Tokyo: Hinoki Shinyaku, 1996.

Masanori Kaji

O

OAKLEY, KENNETH PAGE (*b.* Amersham, Buckinghamshire, United Kingdom, 7 April 1911; *d.* Oxford, United Kingdom, 2 November 1981), *geology, paleontology, anthropology.*

Oakley is best known for his role in dismantling the Piltdown forgery. The fossil cranium, jaw, and teeth supposedly discovered in a quarry in Piltdown, Sussex (England), had significantly influenced the British anthropological community's outlook on human evolution. Oakley's pioneering work in the advancement of reliable dating techniques set the final blow to the chimera of a modern human skull and an orangutan jaw, and was invaluable for the much-needed setting-straight of the fossil hominid record at the time. Oakley's work on relative and absolute dating represents a milestone in the history of paleoanthropology. His other interests were archaeology and folklore, with a primary focus on the culture of fossil hominids from a paleontological viewpoint. He carried out fieldwork in eastern and southern Africa.

Geological Survey and British Museum. He was born the son of Tom Page Oakley, a physician and onetime headmaster of Amersham Grammar School. He was educated at Halloner's Grammar School and studied geology and anthropology at University College London. Shortly after earning his BSc in 1933 he joined the Geological Survey (1934). In 1935, he was appointed assistant keeper of paleontology in the Department of Geology of the British Museum of Natural History in South Kensington, London. Three years later he received his PhD for his work on Silurian Pearl Bearing Bryozoa (Polyzoa). His early scientific papers concentrated on corals, sponges, and bryozoa, and included the regional guide to the Central England District in the British Regional Geology Series. In 1941 he married Edith Margaret Martin; they had two sons.

Oakley's career in the British Museum was significantly interrupted only by World War II, during which he served in the Geological Survey. However, his work there on natural sources of phosphate for fertilization triggered an interest in mineralogy that would prove central to his scientific contributions to the problem of dating. After the war, Oakley was made senior principal scientific officer (1947) at the British Museum. In 1954, he became director of the Anthropological Sections of the Departments of Geology and Zoology, and the following year he was promoted to senior principal scientific officer.

Oakley wrote *The Succession of Life through Geological Time* (1948) and *Man the Tool-Maker* (1949). Such British Museum handbooks were seen as expositions of orthodox thinking and, since they were written for a lay public, they were meant to provide an overview of the fundamentals in a clear and simple style. The first-mentioned volume presented an account of the major steps in the evolution of the animal and plant kingdoms, and it also served as a guide to the exhibits on the succession of life in the museum's Gallery V. The description of each geological period was split into several subdivisions: name, duration, geographical conditions, life in the sea, and life on land. These were summarized in a chart of the geological timescale.

Oakley's latter volume represented a guide to the early human artifacts displayed in the Central Hall at the British Museum (Department of Geology), for which he was largely responsible. In nine sections, *Man the Tool-Maker*

Oakley

dealt with human antiquity, the origins of tool making, the question of raw materials, technology, an outline of the cultural sequence in relation to geology, the evolution of Paleolithic cultures, implements associated with fossil hominids, and considerations of some of the attributes of "man the tool-maker." The booklet thus provided an introduction to Stone Age history and technology from a paleontologist's point of view (the larger Paleolithic collections of the Bloomsbury Museum pertained to the Department of British Antiquities). It was meant to be complementary to Wilfrid Edward Le Gros Clark's museum publication, *History of the Primates* (1949), which treated the biological aspects of human evolution. As such, Oakley regarded it as indispensable in providing a full picture of humans as social animals, who distinguished themselves from the rest of the animal kingdom through culture. As toolmakers, humans had acquired a marked capacity for conceptual thought (as opposed to the perceptual thinking of other primates).

Oakley's views on the evolution of culture were summarized in a table attached to the appendix. The main division of cultures was based on the presence or absence of hand axes, which seemed to be associated with two evolutionary lineages, with the "handaxe peoples" (Swanscombe and Upper Paleolithic "races") more closely related to *Homo sapiens* than the "flake-tool users" of Eurasia (Pithecanthropids, Neanderthaloids). Oakley described the development, migrations, and blending of these cultural stems in each of the three continents of the Old World. This was correlated to the development, migrations, and intermixture of hominid stems established on the basis of genetic principles, particularly blood-group data. All in all, although the book was seen as a textbook, it is not an easy read, as it presupposes knowledge in physical anthropology and genetics. Some of the orthodoxy of the views associated with the museum handbooks might be visible in Oakley's description of living and fossil "races;" for example, the South African Bushmen were seen as the degenerate descendants of the "big-brained Boskop race."

In other respects, Oakley's work was far from orthodox, and his development of dating techniques came at an opportune moment in the history of paleoanthropology. Remains of so-called Piltdown Man had been discovered by the local solicitor and amateur geologist Charles Dawson and others in a gravel pit at Piltdown in Sussex, England. During the years of 1911 and 1912, several cranial fragments and the right half of a mandible containing molar teeth were reportedly unearthed. While the mandible was apelike, the braincase was modern looking. It therefore seemed that already at the Pliocene-Pleistocene boundary there had existed a human type with essentially modern skull size. Piltdown thus supported the widespread assumption that the expansion of the brain had preceded the acquisition of a fully upright posture in the course of human evolution.

This put into question the ancestral status of the already known fossil hominids such as *Pithecanthropus erectus* (today *Homo erectus*) from Java, consisting of a femur, calvaria, and some teeth discovered by the Dutch physician Eugène Dubois at Trinil in 1891 and 1892. *Pithecanthropus* seemed to date from about the same period as Piltdown Man, but was less modern in brain anatomy. Piltdown also worked against the acceptance of the small-brained australopithecines, which began to be discovered in southern Africa from the mid-1920s onward, as anything but fossil apes. The forgery was eventually removed from the fossil record in part because of revolutionary inventions in dating technology that were driven by Oakley, who began to work on a chemical technique of relative dating in 1947.

Relative Dating and Debunking Piltdown. Oakley's war-related work on the distribution of phosphates led to his engagement with the problem of dating fossil human remains. Inspired by the work of the French mineralogist A. Carnot (1893), which built on insights of fluorine accumulation in bone and tooth that had begun to be gained earlier in the century, Oakley examined the uptake of fluorine by bone and confirmed that the amount of fluorine was correlated with the length of time it had been buried. Fluorine is absorbed from groundwater or moist sediments through irreversible ionic interchange with hydroxyl, transforming hydroxyapatite $[Ca_{10}(PO_4)_6.(OH)_2]$ into fluorapatite $[Ca_{10}(PO_4)_6.F_2]$.

However, since the uptake of fluorine depends on many variables, including the amount of fluorine in the groundwater, the numbers could not be calibrated against an absolute timescale. Rather, they provided what Oakley referred to as relative dating. Relative dating through the determination of the chemical composition of human remains in comparison with the chemical composition of other bones from the same deposit could answer the often vexing question of whether the human bones were original to that deposit or intrusive, for instance, due to the human habit of burying their dead, through which bones are brought into earlier deposits (Oakley, 1948a).

In 1932, Louis S. B. Leakey discovered the Kanam jaw and several teeth (*Homo kanamensis* after Leakey) at Lake Victoria in western Kenya. The *Homo sapiens*–like remains of supposedly Early Pleistocene age supported Leakey's belief that the human ancestral line went as far back as the Miocene and did not include the australopithecines. As such, he hailed Kanam Man as the earliest known human ancestor (Leakey, 1934). However, Leakey did not appear to have followed the careful excavation procedures required of a field scientist, which damaged

Kenneth Page Oakley. *Kenneth Page Oakley surrounded by models of pre-historic man.* © HULTON-DEUTSCH COLLECTION/CORBIS.

both his and Kanam Man's reputation. In January 1947, Oakley attended the first Pan-African Congress on Prehistory in Nairobi, Kenya, where Leakey's Kanam Man was discussed. Subsequently, Oakley submitted the Kanam find to the fluorine technique, but the results were inconclusive due to the high background fluorine of the Kenyan material.

Nonetheless, Oakley remained convinced of the method's value, and a breakthrough came the following year with the application of the fluorine technique to the controversial Galley Hill remains (1888), which had been used in support of the idea of a great antiquity of modern human morphology. In particular, the powerful anatomist Sir Arthur Keith, the onetime conservator of the Museum of the Royal College of Surgeons, had built his presapiens theory on this and other European finds of uncertain age, and saw in Galley Hill one of the proofs for long independent evolution of the modern human "races."

In a coauthored paper, Ashley Montagu, professor of anthropology at Rutgers University, New Brunswick (New Jersey), demonstrated that morphologically, the Galley Hill skull and mandible possessed no features which could not be matched in the contemporary population of Britain. While this would not have thwarted Keith's concept of a great age of relatively modern human anatomy, Oakley carried out a comparative fluorine analysis of the Galley Hill skeleton and Swanscombe skull, which had been found in similar geological circumstances in gravels at Swanscombe, East Kent, England (1935). He concluded that, contrary to the Swanscombe specimen, which was shown to be original to the Middle Pleistocene gravels of the Thames terrace, the Galley Hill skeleton was probably an intrusive burial of no great antiquity—i.e., Holocene (Oakley and Montagu, 1949).

Subsequently, Oakley was able to remove several specimens from the list of Paleolithic European remains or at least cast doubt on their place in it. Among these were

Oakley

the Fontéchevade skulls (modern-looking cranial remains from the Charente, France, discovered by Germaine Henri-Martin in 1947), which Oakley demonstrated to be younger than Swanscombe; the Moulin-Quignon jaw (Abbeville, France, 1863), already established as a fraud by some of the pioneers of human antiquity in the nineteenth century, confirmed by Oakley to be truly intrusive in the Middle Pleistocene gravel from which it had supposedly been taken; and the so-called Lloyd skull from the Thames Valley, London, which Oakley demonstrated to be in all likelihood of a later date than the associated Pleistocene fauna (Oakley, 1951).

In collaboration with the Department of the Government Chemist, Oakley then subjected the Piltdown remains to relative dating by fluorine content analysis. The results suggested that the cranium and jaw belonged to a single individual, which had been questioned by some anthropologists from the time of their discovery, but also that the find was much younger than claimed. The low fluorine content of the bones and teeth attributed to Piltdown showed that they did not belong to the Lower Pleistocene group of animal bones from the site (Oakley and Hoskins, 1950). However, many anthropologists took Oakley's result as reason to distrust the technique rather than the age of the fossils. Nonetheless, an ape-man chimera in England seemed even less likely at a younger date, so that Oakley's work prompted Joseph Sidney Weiner (1915–1982), then reader of physical anthropology at Oxford University, to instigate a full-scale reinvestigation into the site and its remains.

This included not only fluorine-content analysis, but also the determination of organic content in the form of nitrogen. The nitrogen of bones and teeth is part of the protein collagen that forms the organic matrix on which the phosphatic mineral matter has been deposited in growth. The collagen fibrils usually denature over time and nitrogen is constantly lost. Relative nitrogen dating had been carried out on the Cro-Magnon skeletons discovered by Édouard Lartet at Aurignac (Haute-Garonne, southern France) in 1860. Since Lartet's judgment that the human bones were contemporaneous with the Pleistocene fauna from the cave was disputed, he had samples of both analyzed for nitrogen content. While it had long been known that the "animal matter" of bones decreases with the time they spend underground, this was probably the first instant of the nitrogen test being used for a comparative analysis. Lartet was proven correct by the results, which were, however, not generally regarded as conclusive.

The combination of the methods of relative dating of fluorine and nitrogen demonstrated that the age of the Piltdown jaw and cranium differed. This finding corroborated Weiner's discovery that they had been deliberately stained and the teeth artificially remodeled to give the impression of great age and humanlike abrasion. The report dismissed the Piltdown jaw as that of a modern ape fraudulently treated to match the skull (Weiner, Oakley, and Clark, 1953). Further systematic inquiry made clear that the cranium also had been planted at the site and was not a genuine fossil, that indeed the entire Piltdown assemblage was forged (Weiner, 1955, and Oakley, Weiner, et al., 1955).

At the time of the final dismantling of the Piltdown forgery, the weird association of orangutan jaw and human skull had been worked with by anthropologists for several decades. Getting rid of it demanded a coordination of efforts. As Oakley put it,

> [a]lthough it was the application of the "fluorine test" to the Piltdown specimens in 1949 that triggered off the extensive investigations which eventually led to this result, the removal of all doubt about its correctness was due to teamwork on a scale probably unprecedented in solving a single problem. Thus a whole battery of physical and chemical techniques was brought to bear on the Piltdown problem before complete proof was obtained that the Piltdown skulls I and II and all the mammalian fossils recovered from Site I and Site II were part of an elaborate forgery. Some 25 scientists deserve credit for their contributions to this work. (1980, p. 52)

At the time of the Piltdown investigation, however, radiocarbon dating was not considered a possible test of the Piltdown remains because it would have meant destroying the specimens in order to obtain the quantity of carbon needed. In contrast to fluorine and nitrogen dating, radiocarbon dating is an absolute, or chronometric, dating technique that assigns a specimen an age in years. Only in 1959, when the radiocarbon-dating technique had been refined and smaller samples were sufficient, did a radiocarbon analysis provide a Holocene date for both cranium and mandible (Oakley and de Vries, 1959).

Oakley's involvement in the debunking of the Piltdown forgery turned him into a name in the scientific communities the world over. It also helped to establish anthropology as a subject in the British Museum, and in 1959, the Subdepartment of Anthropology was created as a consolidation of the Anthropological Sections; it was attached to the Department of Palaeontology. In fact, Oakley had hoped for the foundation of a separate Department of Anthropology, but it did not materialize. He did succeed, however, in securing new staff with an interest in human variability and paleoserology, in establishing important collections of casts and artifacts, and in greatly expanding the existing collections of comparative material.

Oakley

Frameworks. Oakley's pioneering work on fossil dating culminated in *Frameworks for Dating Fossil Man* (1964b). The book is divided into two parts: the first dealing with stratigraphic dating and the second with archaeological dating, that is, the use of artifacts as index fossils and the succession of cultures and events in Europe, Africa, and Asia. Among the stratigraphic dating sources are evidence of glaciers, fossil pollen, bones of extinct animals, and deep-sea cores. These were brought in association with Paleolithic cultures. In the second part Oakley followed the general postsynthesis trend of accepting only two genera in the Hominidae, *Homo* and *Australopithecus*, the acceptance of the latter into the hominid line having been catalyzed by the exposure of the Piltdown forgery, among other things. From his vantage point of geological as well as archaeological training, he also provided the ecological background essential to understanding early hominid behavior. The work ends with a listing of the then known fossil hominids and their dating in terms of the various frameworks developed throughout the book.

In the course of time, Oakley and others developed an entire system of relative dating, combining the analysis of fluorine and nitrogen of bone, antler, or dentine, with the determination of uranium contents. The uranium content—uranium is also absorbed from groundwater by the apatite of bone or tooth—could be assessed by a radiometric assay, which meant exposing a sample to a Geiger counter screened in a lead chamber and counting its B-radiations per minute. This method had the advantage of the specimen not being damaged, if it could fit into a 4 by 3 by 2 centimeter space.

Oakley also introduced a terminology for different kinds of dating (at the Wenner-Gren Symposium in New York in 1952). The first level of relative dating consisted of determining the chemical composition of human remains in comparison with the chemical composition of other bones from the same deposit to find out whether the human bones were intrusive or contemporaneous (called R.1 dating). Once contemporaneity was established, a human fossil bone could be associated with paleontological, geological, or archaeological markers from the same deposit, thereby allocating the specimen to a stage in the local sequence of deposits, faunas, and/or cultures (called R.2 dating). While referring a human bone to a certain cultural environment such as the Aurignacian was R.2 dating, its placement within worldwide and wide-scale systems, such as the sequence of cold and interstadial phases in the European Pleistocene, was considered R.3 dating.

Similarly, absolute dating methods could consist in the direct measurement of the carbon-14 radioactivity of the bone under consideration (invented in the 1950s by Willard Frank Libby), which Oakley termed A.1, or the age of the source deposit could be determined through measurement of its potassium-argon ratio (if it contained potassium) and associated bones, shells, or charcoal could be radiocarbon dated (A.2). Furthermore, the source bed might be correlated to a deposit of known age (A.3), or the age in years of the source bed might be inferred from knowledge of climatic fluctuations (A.4) (Oakley, 1964a, 1964b).

The prospect of reliable dating techniques seemed even more important to paleoanthropology than getting rid of the Piltdown fossils that had come to stand squarely in almost all hominid phylogenies. Triggered by the success of the dating techniques with regard to the Piltdown material, the Wenner-Gren Foundation granted Oakley financial support for applications of the combination of fluorine, uranium, and nitrogen dating procedures to approximately one thousand skeletal parts from Europe, Africa, the Americas, Asia, Australia, Indonesia, Malaysia, and the Pacific Islands. This was done in cooperation with museum curators, scientists, and laboratories. A slip-index databank containing information on the dating and the name of the responsible analyst and laboratory was compiled at the British Museum (Oakley, 1980).

Oakley's dating efforts were also associated with another of his great achievements during the stewardship of the Subdepartment of Anthropology, that is the compilation of the *Catalogue of Fossil Hominids* with Bernard Grant Campbell and Theya Ivitsky Molleson that was financially aided by the Wenner-Gren foundation (1967, 1971, 1975). It is still a valuable reference work. Due to the great progress made in fossil discoveries, in analysis of associated fauna and industries, and in stratigraphy and dating methods since the *Catalogue des hommes fossiles* by Henri Victor Vallois and Hallam Leonard Movius in 1953, the new catalog was greeted with much welcome. Specialists were responsible for individual entries on fossils from particular regions. Where available, each specimen was accompanied by information on place and date of discovery and name of discoverer, on the geological nature of the deposit, its stratigraphic age, and on faunal and archaeological contexts. Furthermore, essential literature, present repository, and availability of molds, as well as reference designation (museum registration number) and anatomical inventory were provided. A novelty with respect to its predecessor was the inclusion of information on relative and absolute dating according to the specific framework of types of dating developed by Oakley.

It is not a surprise that the scientist who helped to remove the Piltdown obstacle to a redrawing of the human family tree had already been honored in many ways during his lifetime. After all, with the Piltdown chimera gone and the acceptance of the australopithecines as hominids, bipedalism rather than brain expansion came to be viewed as early hominid adaptation, and Africa rather than Asia was confirmed as the most likely cradle of humankind. Oakley received the Wollaston Fund Award in 1941, and the Prestwich Medal of the Geological Society in London in 1963. In 1953 he was elected Fellow of the Society of Antiquaries, and in 1957 he became a Fellow of the British Academy of Science. He was president of the Anthropological Section of the British Association for the Advancement of Science in 1961. Oakley continued to publish after his retirement from the British Museum in 1969 due to multiple sclerosis, leaving behind a publication list of over one hundred items, among them his last book, *The Decorative and Symbolic Uses of Vertebrate Fossils* (1975).

BIBLIOGRAPHY

WORKS BY OAKLEY

With J. Desmond Clark, L. H. Wells, and J. A. McClelland. "New Studies on Rhodesian Man." *Journal of the Royal Anthropological Institute of Great Britain and Ireland* 77, no. 1 (1947): 7–32.

"Fluorine and the Relative Dating of Bones." *Advancement of Science* 4 (1948a): 336–337.

With Helen M. Muir-Wood. *The Succession of Life through Geological Time.* London: British Museum (Natural History), 1948b. 7th ed. 1967.

Man the Tool-Maker. London: British Museum (Natural History), 1949. 6th ed. Chicago: University of Chicago Press, 1976.

With Montague Francis Ashley Montagu. "A Re-Consideration of the Galley Hill Skeleton." *Bulletin of the British Museum (Natural History), Geology Series* 1, no. 2 (1949): 25–48.

With C. R. Hoskins. "New Evidence on the Antiquity of Piltdown Man." *Nature* 165 (1950): 379–382.

"The Fluorine-Dating Method." *Yearbook of Physical Anthropology* 5 (1951): 44–52.

With Joseph S. Weiner and Wilfrid Edward Le Gros Clark. "The Solution of the Piltdown Problem." *Bulletin of the British Museum (Natural History), Geology Series* 2 (1953): 141–146.

With Joseph Weiner, et al. "Further Contributions to the Solution of the Piltdown Problem." *Bulletin of the British Museum (Natural History), Geology Series* 2 (1955): 225–287.

With H. de Vries. "Radiocarbon Dating of the Piltdown Skull and Jaw." *Nature* 184, no. 4682 (1959): 224–226.

Frameworks for Dating Fossil Man. Chicago: Aldine, 1964a. 2nd ed. 1966. 3rd ed. London: Weidenfeld & Nicolson, 1969.

"The Problem of Man's Antiquity: An Historical Survey." *Bulletin of the British Museum (Natural History), Geology Series,* 9, no. 5 (1964b): 83–155.

With Bernard Grant Campbell. *Catalogue of Fossil Hominids. Part. I: Africa.* London: British Museum (Natural History), 1967.

"The Date of the 'Red Lady' of Paviland." *Antiquity* 42 (1968): 306–307.

With Bernard Grant Campbell and Theya Ivitsky Molleson. *Catalogue of Fossil Hominids. Part II: Europe.* London: British Museum (Natural History), 1971.

The Decorative and Symbolic Uses of Vertebrate Fossils. London: Oxford University Press, 1975.

With Bernard Grant Campbell and Theya Ivitsky Molleson. *Catalogue of Fossil Hominids. Part III: Americas, Asia, Australasia.* London: British Museum (Natural History), 1975.

"Relative Dating of the Fossil Hominids of Europe." *Bulletin of the British Museum (Natural History), Geology Series* 34, no. 1 (1980): 1–63.

OTHER SOURCES

Carnot, A. "Recherches sur la composition générale et la teneur en fluor des os modernes et des os fossiles des différents âges." *Annales de Mineralogie Paris* 3 (1893): 155–195.

Clark, Wilfrid Edward Le Gros. *History of the Primates: An Introduction to the Study of Fossil Man.* London: Printed by order of the Trustees of the British Museum, 1949.

Leakey, Louis S. B. *Adam's Ancestors: An Up-to-Date Outline of What Is Known about the Origin of Man.* London: Methuen, 1934.

Molleson, Theya. "K. P. Oakley." *RAIN* 48 (1982): 15–16.

Vallois, Henri Victor, and Hallam Leonard Movius. *Catalogue des hommes fossiles.* Algeria: Publication of the Nineteenth International Geological Congress, 1953.

Weiner, Joseph Sidney. *The Piltdown Forgery.* London: Oxford University Press, 1955.

Marianne Sommer

OCCHIALINI, GIUSEPPE PAOLO STANISLAO

(*b.* Fossombrone, Italy, 5 December 1907; *d.* Paris, France, 30 December 1993), *cosmic ray physics, Geiger-Müller counters, counter-controlled cloud chamber, nuclear emulsions, particle physics, space physics.*

Occhialini, one of the leading figures in twentieth-century physics, conducted cosmic ray studies and performed work in particle, and space physics. He was a consummate experimentalist and was involved in electron-positron pair production and pion discoveries.

Occhialini, nicknamed "Beppo," was the son of Etra Grossi and Raffaele Augusto Occhialini. His father was a well-known physicist who was appointed to the University of Pisa in 1911. The young Giuseppe attended elementary school in Pisa. In 1917 he and his mother moved to Florence, where he frequented the Ginnasio and the Liceo Scientifico. In November 1925, under pressure from his father, he undertook scientific studies at the University of Florence. He did so without enthusiasm, for his romantic nature disposed him toward a liberal arts career.

Arcetri Day. Occhialini graduated in physics from the University of Florence in 1929, with an (unpublished) dissertation on spectroscopy under his father's supervision. He joined the Institute of Physics (of the University of Florence) in 1930 as a voluntary research assistant, which led to a permanent appointment the following year. Like the Institute of Physics of the University of Rome (Istituto di fisica di via Panisperna) where Enrico Fermi and his group were working, the Florence Institute of Physics enjoyed the revival of physics research that took place in Italy after World War I. Antonio Garbasso, both a scientist and a politician, directed the Florence institute, located on the Arcetri Hill where Galileo Galilei spent his last years. In Rome, Orso Mario Corbino played a similar double role as a senator and as the director of the Institute of Physics at the University of Rome. Both men were leading actors in the organization of scientific research in Italy.

The years in Florence were very important for Occhialini's early formation. He belonged to a small, congenial group of young and brilliant physicists, including the charismatic Enrico Persico, Bruno Rossi, and Gilberto Bernardini. Persico's seminar introduced Occhialini and the others to the mysteries of the new quantum physics and to the thriving atomic and nuclear physics. Bernardini and Rossi began research on the emission of slow electrons by radioactive sources, a relatively original topic at the institute. Occhialini's earliest research paper (1930), supervised by Rossi, pertained to a related subject.

Occhialini's paper presented a new magnetic spectrograph for beta rays, based on a principle by Rossi. Designed to work for weak radioactive sources such as rubidium and potassium, the apparatus involved a Geiger-Müller counter, a facing aluminum surface on which the source was spread, and a deflecting magnet. This was one of the Florence group's first applications of the counter recently invented in 1928 by Hans Geiger and Walther Müller. Being in a precarious financial situation, the Florence laboratory favored this inexpensive device, which worked both for beta and gamma rays.

Occhialini's scientific career and activities at the Arcetri laboratory underwent a radical change in 1929 when Walter Bothe and Werner Kolhörster published their famous experiment in which single cosmic ray events were detected by means of two Geiger-Müller counters used in coincidence. This setup was far superior to an ionization chamber, which could detect only global ionization caused by a large number of particles over a long duration. Rossi quickly understood the opportunity the new configuration offered for investigating the physical properties of local cosmic radiation, and he launched his own program in this field.

Cosmic radiation, discovered at the beginning of the century by the Austrian physicist Victor Hess, had already been the subject of important investigations by the American physicist Robert Millikan. Millikan's program required extensive resources, including balloons equipped with electroscopes and ionization chambers; observations were made outdoors at sea level, at high altitude on California mountaintops, and in the upper atmosphere. In order to account for the wealth of results, Millikan proposed what he called the "birth cry theory," a set of more or less scientific conjectures about the origin and nature of cosmic radiation. In particular, he believed that primary cosmic rays could be only hard gamma rays.

Occhialini and his Florentine colleagues had a different conception of cosmic rays. They were aware that Bothe and Kolhörster supported the interpretation that primary rays were charged particles. The Florentine group was to confirm this latter hypothesis by improving the counter technique. In their experiment, Bothe and Kolhörster placed two Geiger-Müller counters one above the other a small distance apart and recorded the simultaneous pulses (coincidences) caused by the passage of individual particles through both counters. They observed the coincidences by connecting the wires of the two counters to two separate electroscopes. They obtained only double coincidences, and the method was very cumbersome. In order to improve upon this technique, Rossi devised a clever valve circuit that easily recorded coincidences of any order. It was mainly from this work that Occhialini acquired the expertise that he later brought to Cambridge.

Cavendish Laboratory. Occhialini joined the Cavendish Laboratory at Cambridge University in England in July 1931, at age twenty-four, thanks to a fellowship from Italy's National Research Council (CNR). His mission was to learn the technique of cloud chambers from Patrick M. S. Blackett. The Cavendish Laboratory had long been one of the world's premier centers for experimental physics. Under Ernest Rutherford's direction, it currently housed many outstanding young physicists interested in radioactivity and atomic physics. James Chadwick was working on a program that led him to the neutron, and James Cockcroft and Ernest Walton were on their way to discovering the first artificial disintegration of an atomic nucleus. Occhialini enjoyed the friendly community that discussed science, politics, and philosophy in academic clubs at the Cavendish Laboratory and elsewhere in Cambridge. Among them was the Kapitsa Club, founded by the Russian physicist Peter Kapitsa in 1922. Membership was restricted and the main concern was experimental physics. Occhialini thus joined a group of prestigious figures including Cockcroft, Ralph Fowler, and Walton as well as Blackett, Paul Dirac, and Nevill Mott.

The Italian fellowship offered to Occhialini was to enable him to spend three months in Cambridge; as it

Occhialini

turned out, Occhialini's stay spanned three enthusiastic years, with very little further support from CNR or Rutherford. Occhialini's mentor, Blackett, was a world authority in cloud chambers, acquired from a long series of studies by C. T. R. Wilson at the end of the nineteenth century on the condensation of moist air and the reproduction of atmospheric phenomena. Wilson's method materialized the path of ionizing agents, being based upon a property of ions in which they serve as centers for the formation of droplets in a supersaturated vapor. When a charged particle passes through a vessel containing a gas saturated with vapor, ions are formed along the whole of the trajectory. Under sudden increase of the volume (sudden expansion), vapor condenses around whatever ions are present in the chamber. A cloud of minute droplets then shows the trajectory of the charged particle. This array of droplets may be recorded photographically for quantitative work.

When Occhialini arrived in Cambridge, Blackett was using an automatic cloud chamber that was very convenient for the study of nuclear disintegration processes. However, the device was not well adapted for the cosmic ray studies he wished to initiate with Occhialini. Since the expansions were done at random, cosmic ray tracks were found in only a very small fraction of the photographs. Blackett and Occhialini hit upon the idea of triggering the expansion of the chamber with two Geiger-Müller counters placed above and below it. The cosmic particles took their own photograph, so to speak.

In 1932 Blackett and Occhialini observed the massive production of what they came to identify as electron-positron pairs. Their photographs showed showerlike multiple tracks diverging from a region over the chamber (see Figure 1), half of which had the magnetic curvature, range, and ionization that corresponded to positively charged particles with mass comparable to that of an electron. In the ensuing publication, they identified the new particle as the antielectron predicted by Dirac's relativistic theory of the electron. They also suggested a possible mechanism for the production of the showers, based on initial collision and nonionizing links. A few months earlier, Carl Anderson, Millikan's assistant at the California Institute of Technology, had already reported the existence of new low-mass positive particles in an untriggered cloud chamber, without referring to Dirac's theory. Anderson received the Nobel Prize in 1936 for this discovery. Blackett received the same honor in 1948 "for the development of the Wilson cloud chamber and his discoveries therewith in the fields of nuclear physics and cosmic rays." Occhialini was not mentioned in the citation.

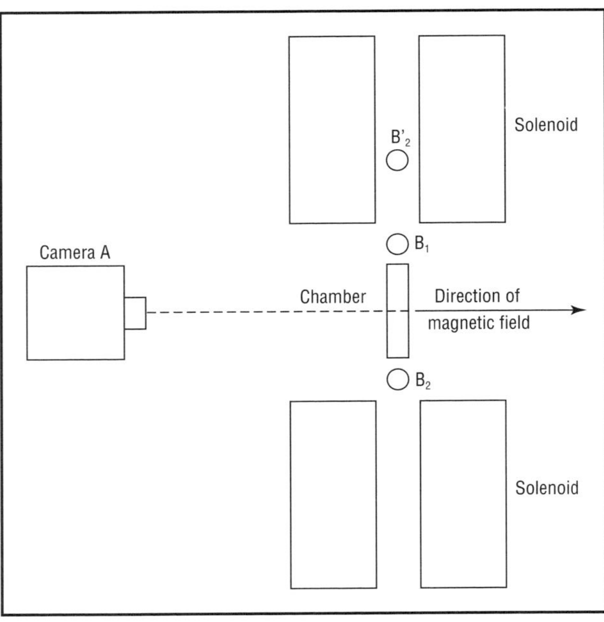

Blackett's and Occhialini's experimental set-up. B_1 and B_2 indicate the positions of the counters.

From Italy to Brazil. Occhialini returned to Italy in 1934 and resumed work thanks to a permanent professorship at the University of Florence. Unfortunately the Arcetri institute was no longer what it had been. Garbasso had passed away; Rossi had been appointed to Padua and Persico to Torino. Owing to the rise of Fascism, the political climate had become unbearable to Occhialini. He was a liberal and had become markedly anti-Fascist, although he had adhered to the Fascist Party in the 1920s. In 1936, during Italy's invasion of Ethiopia and involvement in the Spanish civil war, he had to remain in the party in order to save his job, but it was a tormenting decision.

In 1937 Occhialini accepted a professorship in Brazil offered by the Italian government and perhaps mediated by his father. He joined the University of São Paulo, which had just been created in 1934. The physics department was under the direction of Gleb Wataghin, an Italian-naturalized physicist born in Ukraine. With Wataghin, whom he had already met during a visit to the Cavendish Laboratory, Occhialini worked to develop Brazilian scientific activity. Primarily as experimentalists and secondarily as theoreticians, they launched cosmic ray physics in Brazil. This was a suitable research topic for a country such as Brazil, as it had been for Italy, because it required only small laboratories.

The intellectual and scientific atmosphere in South America was not the same as in Europe; in Brazil, scientific research was still in the process of becoming institutionalized. However, Occhialini had a real opportunity there to extend his scientific career. He held several chairs at the University of São Paulo, in general and experimental

Occhialini

physics. Not surprisingly, he built a triggered cloud chamber with his students and directed counter-based absorption experiments, both in the laboratory and outdoors. His leadership at an international symposium on cosmic rays held in Rio de Janeiro in 1941 testified to the excellence of this work. He extended his earlier work on the beta radioactivity of rubidium.

In August 1942 Brazil entered World War II. The Italian-run group at the University of São Paulo dissolved, and Wataghin resigned the direction of the physics institute. Occhialini remained in Brazil, although he could not take a position against Fascist Italy because his father was living there and there was a risk of reprisals. Information is scant concerning Occhialini's life in Brazil during the war, probably because he tried to keep a low profile as a foreigner living in an enemy country. It is rumored that he went into hiding in the Itatiaia Mountains near São Paulo. After the Italian armistice in September 1943 he spent time at the biophysics laboratory headed by Carlos Chagas Jr. at the University of Brazil and lectured at the University of São Paulo. Occhialini's interest focused on techniques of photography and plate processing.

The Bristol Period. At the end of 1944 Occhialini left Brazil and returned to England, invited by Blackett to join the British team working with Americans on the atomic bomb. However, he was barred from participating in that military research owing to his Italian nationality. Instead he was assigned to collaborate with Cecil F. Powell, again thanks to Blackett's help. In 1944 Powell still was a relatively unknown physicist, a pacifist who had strong left-wing views. He was engaged in experimental work, detecting and measuring the energy of nuclear particles through the utilization of photographic emulsions. Powell belonged to the H. H. Wills Physical Laboratory in Bristol, which was constructed in 1927 through generous funding by the Wills tobacco family. During the war period this laboratory was located in a bombarded neighborhood, but research continued to be carried on in a highly scientific atmosphere despite the insufferable conditions.

Photographic emulsions used by Powell in his n-p scattering studies (the detection and measure of nuclear particles) had major drawbacks: their thickness and sensitivity to ionizing particles needed to be increased. Through a fruitful collaboration with C. Waller of Ilford Ltd., Occhialini and Powell succeeded in preparing special emulsions with a greatly increased proportion of the heavy elements silver and bromine, which became a powerful tool for the study of elementary particles. Meanwhile the Bristol group had been enlarged by the arrival of Cesare Lattes and Ugo Camerini. These two young and brilliant former Occhialini students from the University of São Paulo specialized in cloud chambers and cosmic ray studies. Very soon Occhialini and Lattes realized that the new concentrated emulsions could be effectively used for the detection and study of cosmic rays.

Giuseppe Occhialini. AIP EMILIO SEGRE VISUAL ARCHIVES, SEGRE COLLECTION.

In the spring of 1946 Occhialini participated in a speleological expedition in France. He took a stack of the new Ilford C2 plates—which were only 2 inches by 1 inch and 50 μm thick—to the Pic du Midi, whose altitude was 2,867 meters, and exposed the plates for about one month to cosmic radiation. Occhialini, Lattes, Powell, and Hugh Muirhead (Powell's young student) realized from plate processing and scanning in Bristol between autumn 1946 and spring 1947 that they were involved in the discovery of a new particle. As a matter of fact, the Bristol physicists—making use also of Lattes's observations from plates exposed at the Chacaltaya Mountains in the Bolivian Andes—obtained evidence of the existence of a pi-meson, the particle associated with the force between protons and neutrons inside the nuclei. They also observed events showing a pi-meson coming to rest in the emulsion and decaying into a mu-meson, discovered ten years before, also in cosmic rays.

So with Powell, as with Blackett, Occhialini was involved in the development of a new experimental technique leading to a scientific discovery. In 1947 Powell and Occhialini prepared together an atlas titled *Nuclear Physics in Photographs.* In 1950 Powell received the Nobel Prize for "the development of the photographic method of studying the nuclear process and his discoveries regarding mesons with this method." Occhialini was not mentioned in the citation.

In 1948 Occhialini moved to the Free University in Brussels. There he married Constance "Connie" Charlotte Dilworth, a physicist from Bristol. They formed a research group on cosmic rays detected by emulsions, which, like electric counters years before, were an inexpensive experimental technique. The Occhialinis increased the sensitivity of the emulsions, and they performed a method for processing emulsions as thick as 600 μm, with which very long particle tracks could be recorded.

Back to Italy. In 1949 Occhialini moved to Genoa, where his father directed the physics institute at the university. He immediately formed a research group and trained students. There, as in Brussels, he continued developing nuclear emulsions for the study of cosmic rays. In 1951 his daughter Etra Mary Giovanna Occhialini was born. Augusto Occhialini died in the same year. The family moved to Milan in 1952, where Occhialini was offered a professorship in advanced physics at the university.

Occhialini played a major role in the revival of Italian physics in the postwar period. He and his wife stayed in touch with Powell in Bristol and developed collaborations with other countries. The G-stack project—a European collaboration to expose large numbers of plates of nuclear emulsions (37 x 27 x 15 cm) to cosmic rays with the expectation of detecting K-meson decay—was one of Occhialini's great scientific and organizational contributions of the 1950s. With the efficient support of the rector of the University of Milan, Giovanni Polvani, part of the Genoa group moved to Milan, where Occhialini assembled another research group on cosmic rays and nuclear emulsions. In the same period, at the request of UNESCO, Occhialini went to Brazil to help to create a laboratory for studying cosmic rays in Chacaltaya. In Europe, the foundation of the European Organization for Nuclear Research (CERN) in 1954 led physicists to favor accelerators over cosmic rays as a source of high-energy particles. The Milan group soon began using this new source.

At the end of the 1950s Occhialini and his wife wanted to return to their work with cosmic rays. Invited by Rossi, they spent a year at the Massachusetts Institute of Technology in order to familiarize themselves with the American space research program and astrophysical studies of cosmic rays. Rossi had become an expert on the physics of the ionosphere and the magnetosphere as well as on cosmic x-rays and gamma rays. Back in Europe the Occhialinis began studying the properties of the cosmic ray components from the Sun and from other bodies in the galaxy. They created a research group at the University of Milan, applying the new space technology in cosmic ray studies and high-energy astrophysics. They also played a fundamental role in the establishment of European scientific collaborations and in the development of the European Space Research Organisation (ESRO), an institution created at the beginning of the 1960s, later to become the European Space Agency (ESA). The Milan group directed by Occhialini took a fundamental part in the COS-B project, a second-generation space instrument conceived exclusively for gamma-ray astronomy. It was launched in 1975 and supplied the first gamma map of the galaxy.

Occhialini retired in 1983. In 1993, the year of his death, he was elected an honorary member of the European Physical Society. It was the last among a long list of honors from learned societies and academies: he was awarded the Charles Vernon Boys Prize of the Council of the Physical Society (London) for distinguished work in experimental physics in 1950; became a member of the Accademia dei Lincei in 1958 (and recipient of the Sella and Einaldi Einaudi prizes of this academy in 1934 and 1949) and foreign member of the Royal Society in 1974; and was the recipient of the Wolf Prize, "for his contributions to the discoveries of electron pair production and of the charged pion," in 1979.

BIBLIOGRAPHY

An extensive bibliography is in the Occhialini archive in the Istituto di Fisica Generale Applicata of the University of Milan, and in Leonardo Gariboldi's "The Reconstruction of Giuseppe Occhialini's Scientific Bibliography" (see below). See also the list of publications held in the Occhialini archive with Occhialini's own indications of the publications he considered most important

WORKS BY OCCHIALINI

With Patrick M. S. Blackett. "Photography of Penetrating Corpuscular Radiation." *Nature* 130 (1932): 363.

———. "Some Photographs of the Tracks of Penetrating Radiation." *Proceedings of the Royal Society of London* A 139 (1933): 699–720, 722, 724, 726.

With Patrick M. S. Blackett and James Chadwick. "New Evidence for the Positive Electron." *Nature* 131 (1933): 473.

———. "Some Experiments on the Production of Positive Electrons." *Proceedings of the Royal Society of London* A 144 (1934): 235–249.

With Cecil F. Powell, Derek L. Livesey, and L. V. Chilton. "A New Photographic Emulsion for the Detection of Fast Charged Particles." *Journal of Scientific Instruments* 23, no. 5 (1946): 102–106.

With Cecil F. Powell. *Nuclear Physics in Photographs.* Oxford: Clarendon Press, 1947. Occhialini's only book.

With Cecil F. Powell, Derek L. Livesey, and L. V. Chilton. "Processes Involving Charged Mesons." *Nature* 159 (1947): 694–697.

With Cesare M. G. Lattes and Cecil F. Powell. "Observations on the Tracks of Slow Mesons in Photographic Emulsions, Part 1." *Nature* 160 (1947): 453–456.

———. "Observations on the Tracks of Slow Mesons in Photographic Emulsions, Part 2." *Nature* 160 (1947): 486–492.

With Constance C. Dilworth and Ron M. Payne. "Processing Thick Emulsions for Nuclear Research." *Nature* 162 (1948): 102–103.

With B. Bhowmik et al. "The Interaction and Decay of K-Mesons in Photographic Emulsion, Part 1: General Characteristics of K-Interactions and Analysis of Events in Which a Charged π-Meson Is Emitted." *Il Nuovo Cimento* 13, no. 4 (1959): 690–729.

"Occhialini, Giuseppe." *Scienziati e Tecnologi Contemporanei* 2 (1974): 322–324; Milan: Mondadori, 1974. A short autobiography that is included in the Occhialini archive.

OTHER WORKS

Bignami, Giovanni F. "Giuseppe Paolo Stanislao Occhialini." *Biograpical Memoirs of the Fellows of the Royal Society of London* 48 (2002): 331–340. A detailed account.

Gariboldi, Leonardo. Tesi di Dottorato Di Ricerca, "Giuseppe Paolo Stanislao Occhialini (1907–1993): A Cosmic Ray Hunter from Earth." PhD diss., Universita Degli Studi di Milano, Facolta du Scienze Politiche, 2004–2005. Information on Occhialini's scientific life.

———. "The Reconstruction of Giuseppe Occhialini's Scientific Bibliography." In *Atti del XXIII Congresso Nazionale di Storia della Fisica e dell'Astronomia,* edited by Pasquale Tucci, Augusto Garuccio, and Maria Nigro. Bari, Italy: Prima editione, 2004.

Redondo, Pietro, et al., eds. *The Scientific Legacy of Beppo Occhialini.* Berlin, Heidelberg, and New York: Societa Italiana di Fisica; Bologna-Springer-Verlag, 2006.

Russo, Arturo. "Vita di uno sperimentatore." *Sapere* 4 (1996): 62–69.

Telegdi, Valentine L. "Giuseppe Occhialini." *Proceedings of the American Philosophical Society* 146, no. 2 (2002): 218–222.

Martha Cecilia Bustamante

OCHOA, SEVERO

OCHOA, SEVERO (*b.* Luarca [province of Asturias], Spain, 24 September 1905; *d.* Madrid, Spain, 1 November 1993), *biochemistry, enzymology, molecular biology.*

Ochoa's contributions to modern biology were significant and involved many problems central to twentieth-century biochemistry, including bioenergetics, enzymology, intermediary metabolism, and the foundation of molecular biology. Through a series of fortunate contingencies, he was able to follow biochemistry's disciplinary migration from Germany to Britain and, ultimately, to the United States. His diverse career bridged the flourishing of biochemistry during the twentieth century's middle decades—a period that Marianne Grunberg-Manago called "The Golden Age of Intermediary Metabolism" (1997, p. 353)—and helped establish early concepts of molecular biology. In her Ochoa obituary, Grunberg-Manago accurately summarized Ochoa's career as "a résumé of the history of contemporary biochemistry and the foundation of molecular biology."

Early Life and Education. Ochoa, named after his father, was one of seven children. His father, a lawyer and businessman, died when Ochoa was seven years old. His mother, the former Carmen Albornoz, moved the family to Málage on the Mediterranean coast "in search of a milder climate." Ochoa completed his *baccalauréat* in 1921 at a local Jesuit private high school. Inspired by the Nobel Prize–winning neurobiologist, Santiago Ramón y Cajal, he developed an interest in the natural sciences, especially biology. In 1923 he began medical studies at Madrid University; he did not intend to practice medicine, but chose this course of study because it was the best route to the study of biology. Ramón y Cajal had retired from working with students, and Ochoa was mentored by the "young, bright, and inspiring teacher, Juan Negrín." Negrín trained at the University of Leipzig, and he (as Ochoa described) "opened wide, fascinating vistas to my imagination, not only through his lectures and laboratory teaching, but through his advice, encouragement, and stimulation to read scientific monographs and textbooks in languages other than Spanish" (Ochoa, 1980, p. 2).

Negrín, who was interested in reactions of creatine, phosphocreatine, and creatinine, introduced Ochoa to experimental research and encouraged him and another student, José Valdecasas, to use his laboratory. The medical school lacked a research facility; thus Ochoa lived and worked at an institution that he described as the equivalent of an Oxford or Cambridge college. The environment was a rich intellectual experience; the Spanish dramatist and poet Federico García Lorca, the painter Salvador Dalí, and the film director Luis Buñuel were also working or studying at "La Residencia."

To learn laboratory practice, Negrín suggest that Valdecasas and Ochoa attempt to isolate creatinine (a biological "waste product" of phosphocreatine) from urine. After initial difficulties, the two succeeded, and a few months later they developed an easy micromethod to measure creatinine levels in muscle. In 1927, to improve his English skills, Ochoa spent the summer in Glasgow

Ochoa

with D. Noel Paton, Regius Chair of Physiology, working on creatine metabolism, where he further refined the assay procedure. Returning to Madrid, Ochoa and Valdecasas submitted their work to the *Journal of Biological Chemistry,* which rapidly accepted the paper (Ochoa, 1980, p. 4), thus beginning Ochoa's biochemistry career.

In summer of 1928, his bachelor of medicine completed, Ochoa began to think about going abroad for further training. At the time, biochemists were increasingly interested in the metabolic role of phosphocreatine. Ochoa's previous work on creatine and creatinine led to an interest in Otto Meyerhof's work on the chemical processes of muscle contraction. In 1929 Ochoa began work in Meyerhof's laboratory at the Kaiser Wilhelm Institute for Biology in Berlin-Dahlem. The institute was rapidly becoming an international center for biochemistry, with distinguished scientists such as Meyerhof, Otto Warburg, and Carl Neuberg, and was fertile ground for the expansion of Ochoa's scientific growth. After a brief visit to Madrid to take required examinations for the MD degree, Ochoa returned to Meyerhof's lab, which had moved from Berlin to Heidelberg. His work with Meyerhof was by and large confirmatory of earlier work, Ochoa claimed, and indeed he published little during this period.

While his work in Heidelberg may have been largely "confirmatory," Ochoa found the Meyerhof laboratory to be a "hot bed" of new biochemical ideas. In 1930 Einar Lundsgaard traveled from Denmark to Heidelberg to personally demonstrate that Meyerhof's ideas about energy generation, for which he received the 1922 Nobel Prize in Physiology and Medicine, were wrong and that phosphocreatine was involved in muscle contraction. Fritz Lipmann, who was in Meyerhof's lab at the time, commented that Lundsgaard's work was a "truly great discovery … [that] changed our concepts of metabolic energy transformation" (1969, pp. 246–247). Both Lundsgaard's demonstration and Meyerhof's acceptance of his error impressed Ochoa.

In late 1930 Ochoa returned to Madrid, where he and Francisco Grande Covián collaborated to study the role of adrenal glands in muscle contraction, which eventually became his MD thesis. After completing his medical education, Ochoa married Carmen García Cobián and in 1931 began postdoctoral study at the National Institute for Medical Research (NIMR) in London, directed by Sir Henry Dale. His research involved glyoxalase, an enzyme that catalyzes the conversion of methylglyoxal to lactic acid. The enzyme was important, because biochemists speculated that methylglyoxal might be an intermediate in glucose oxidation to lactic acid. Studying glyoxalase influenced Ochoa's career in two ways. First, the work was at the forefront in the rapidly evolving study of intermediary metabolism (i.e., the sequence of chemical reactions whereby foodstuffs are converted to compounds that are biologically useful for energetic and synthetic purposes). Second, the project initiated what became a lifelong interest in enzymology.

After two years in London, Ochoa returned to Madrid and began to study glycolysis in heart muscle. In 1935 the University of Madrid Medical School created a new Institute for Medical Research, and Ochoa became director of the Physiology Section. Unfortunately, within months the Spanish civil war erupted, and the Ochoas decided to leave Spain; in September 1936 they began what he later called the "wander years."

Wander Years. Once he decided to leave Spain, Ochoa contacted Meyerhof, who found him a place at Heidelberg. Ochoa noted that scientifically Meyerhof's laboratory had changed radically since his 1930 visit. In 1930 the primary focus was on physiology; "one could see muscles twitching everywhere" (Ochoa, 1980, p. 8). In 1936 the laboratory work was biochemical and focused on glycolysis and fermentation. The lab was beginning to purify and characterize enzymes that catalyzed these processes in muscle or yeast extracts.

Although the Meyerhof lab was scientifically vigorous, Ochoa observed that Meyerhof was in a precarious position; his family had left Germany, and Meyerhof himself planned to leave for Paris. Ochoa wryly noted that he had left one troubled country for another. Meyerhof arranged, through his friend Archibald Vivian Hill, for Ochoa to obtain a six-month Ray Lankester Investigator fellowship at the Marine Biological Laboratory (MBL) in Plymouth, England, which began in July 1937.

Ochoa's brief time at the Plymouth MBL was productive and happy, except for concerns about relatives still in Spain. He continued work begun in Meyerhof's lab on the metabolic role of "cozymase" (which came to be known as nicotinamide adenine dinucleotide, NAD), which he isolated in pure form. Support staff was not readily available, and Ochoa's wife, who had no prior laboratory training, helped on a variety of projects. Her assistance on NAD distribution in invertebrate muscle was such that the two coauthored a *Nature* paper (1937). More important, for Ochoa's long-term career, was a friendship with William Ringrose Gelston Atkins, who helped him secure a Nuffield Foundation fellowship. In December 1937 the Ochoas departed for Oxford, where Ochoa began a rich collaboration with Rudolph Albert Peters, who was Whitley Chair of Biochemistry.

During the 1920s Peters had established the concept that the B vitamin complex consisted of individual chemicals with specific physiological properties. His work increasingly focused on vitamin B_1 (thiamine) and its role in alleviating neurological beriberi symptoms. When

Ochoa

Ochoa joined his laboratory Peters was beginning work on the chemical mechanism of thiamine action, a goal in which Ochoa played a central role. Over the next two years Ochoa and Peters successfully isolated various enzymes and demonstrated the role of thiamine (in addition to various other cofactors) in enzyme action (Thompson and Ogston, 1983).

Ochoa understated his relationship with Peters when he described it as "a very happy and productive one." During the two years in Oxford, Ochoa published more than eighteen papers, eleven coauthored with Peters, two of which (Ochoa and Peters, 1938; Ochoa, et al., 1939) are seminal to Ochoa's career. Both papers explored connections between various cofactors and pyruvate metabolism in brain tissue. In addition to confirming many aspects of intermediary metabolism, the work established the role of both vitamin B_1 and "adenine nucleotides" (i.e., now known as adenosine triphosphate or ATP) as cofactors in pyruvate oxidation. Marianne Grunberg-Manago has suggested that the ATP involvement led to Ochoa's later interest in oxidative phosphorylation (1997, p. 353). More importantly, the two papers demonstrated both Ochoa's developing biochemical skills and his ability in the rapidly evolving field of enzymology.

Unfortunately, warfare again intervened; and the "happy and productive" period was short-lived as the laboratory's focus increasingly shifted to war support. Because of Ochoa's status as an alien, he was excluded from this work and increasingly began to consider a move to the United States. He wrote to Carl and Gerty Cori in St. Louis and was readily accepted to work in their Washington University laboratory. In August 1940 the Ochoas "sailed for the New World, not without sadness, but full of hope and expectations" (Ochoa, 1980, p. 9).

The move to the United States was, arguably, the most important event in Ochoa's career, so a reasonable question might arise about why the Coris were so willing to accept him into their lab. However, by 1939 Ochoa's resume must have been impressive. He had worked with two Nobel Prize recipients, and his Oxford work demonstrated his biochemical maturity. In 1938 Dale, recipient of the 1936 Nobel Prize in Physiology or Medicine, wrote a letter supporting Ochoa's application for a lectureship in biochemistry at University College, Dundee. Dale noted that Ochoa was "a man of exceptional promise in Biochemical research … a keen, enterprising, and well-qualified research worker in Biochemistry" (Dale, 1938). Clearly such letters would carry great impact in a lab even as sophisticated as that of Carl and Gerty Cori.

Although Ochoa had studied enzyme actions since his NIMR work, the previous work mostly involved crude, cell-free extracts. The Cori lab focus, however, was on purified enzymes free of potentially contaminating reactions. Although the Coris were not the first to study metabolism by isolating purified enzymes, Hugo Theorell called their in vivo synthesis of glycogen using crystalline enzymes an "astounding feat" (1947).

Severo Ochoa. SCIENCE SOURCE/PHOTO RESEARCHERS, INC.

For Ochoa, the St. Louis lab was both exciting and frustrating. Excitement arose from enzymology's central role in the research as well as the stream of visitors, such as Herman Kalckar and Earl Sutherland, and graduate students such as Sidney Colowick, who brought in new ideas and techniques. Frustration arose from his research work. Cori suggested that Ochoa attempt to study fructose conversion to glucose, which both men thought "ought to have been a cinch" (Ochoa, 1980, p. 10). Unfortunately, the problem was far more refractory and was not resolved for many years. Although he had been in the Cori lab for less than two years, apparently the research difficulties were sufficiently frustrating that

Ochoa decided to once again move, a decision that ultimately led to his career's major work.

Career Stability and "The Golden Age of Intermediary Metabolism." During his brief time at Oxford, Ochoa developed a strong friendship with Robert Stanley Goodhart, a New York University (NYU) nutritionist. Goodhart persuaded Ochoa to move to NYU, which he did in early 1942. His appointment as a Department of Medicine research associate began a long career at NYU, which Ochoa described as both "fruitful and happy." At age thirty-seven, Ochoa was now an independent investigator with his own graduate and postdoctoral students.

Although his initial NYU appointment was in medicine, two years later he moved to the Department of Biochemistry as assistant professor (his first faculty position). In another two years he was named chair of pharmacology. Ochoa noted that he was only the second biochemist to chair an American Medical School pharmacology department. However, he decided that he "was in good company" because "Cori was the first" (Ochoa, 1980, p. 11). Ochoa spent nine "exciting and productive" years (1946–1954) in pharmacology; in the summer of 1954 he was made chair of biochemistry, a position he held for twenty years until his retirement at age sixty-nine.

Ochoa's scientific career was varied and complex; he published more than five hundred papers on a variety of topics. Several general themes, which can be merely highlighted in this entry, run through his work. As noted earlier, Ochoa developed an early interest in enzymes, and at NYU he established one of the most powerful enzymology laboratories in the world. His enzymology work focused on processes of oxidative phosphorylation, CO_2 fixation, and enzymes involved in the tricarboxylic acid (TCA) cycle. Ochoa was a major contributor to elucidating the detailed steps of the TCA cycle (Kresge, et al., 2005). However, his work on oxidative phosphorylation led to what some biochemists believe to be his major contribution, RNA synthesis and the genetic code.

Oxidative Phosphorylation. From his undergraduate work on creatine phosphate, Ochoa was interested in cellular energetics, which arguably was one of the twentieth century's most difficult and contentious biochemical problems. While at Oxford he demonstrated that biological oxidations were "coupled" to phosphorylation reactions, often forming ATP. At NYU he demonstrated that the ratio of oxygen consumed to phosphate bonds formed (the P/O ratio) was three, the standard value soon adopted by other investigators (Ernster, 1993).

Shortly after completing this work, Ochoa abandoned the area of energetics to begin an enzymology program that achieved international distinction. The shift in research focus was apparently pragmatic. Grunberg-Manago observed that: "After completing this work on the P/O ratio, it appeared to Severo that the mechanism of oxidative phosphorylation was not likely to be understood without further knowledge of the enzymatic reactions involved in oxidation and particularly those coupled to phosphorylation" (1997, p. 354). Ochoa believed that if he was to understand energetics, he needed to understand the underlying enzymology.

CO_2 Fixation and the TCA Cycle. When Ochoa made this research shift, the central pathway for carbohydrate oxidation—and source of cellular energy—the TCA (or Krebs) cycle, had been sketched out and biochemists were beginning to fill in the details. In 1937 Hans Adolf Krebs and W. H. Johnson established that carbohydrates were oxidized to a two-carbon "active acetate" intermediate, which "condensed" with oxaloacetic acid to form a six-carbon tricarboxylic acid, citrate. Citrate was then sequentially oxidized to two molecules of CO_2 and oxaloacetate, which repeated the cycle. Ochoa decided to focus on an early suspected reaction, the conversion of isocitrate to α-ketoglutaric acid.

Previous work demonstrated that citrate was converted to isocitrate via cis-aconitate; the reactions leading to α-ketoglutarate, however, were only hypothetical, and "oxalo-succinic acid" was a postulated intermediate. Ochoa started with oxalo-succinic acid and observed α-ketoglutarate formation. Thus, he concluded that oxalo-succinic acid was indeed a reaction intermediate; decarboxylation of this compound led to CO_2 and α-ketoglutarate. The process, he believed, was as follows (note that, in modern use, TPN_{ox} and TPN_{red} are referred to as NADP and NADPH):

$$\text{Isocitric acid} + TPN_{ox} \rightleftarrows \text{oxalosuccinic acid} + TPN_{red} \text{ (Reaction 1)}$$

$$\text{Oxalosuccinic acid} \rightleftarrows \alpha\text{-ketoglutaric acid} + CO_2 \text{ (Reaction 2)}$$

Ochoa then made an interesting intellectual leap. By the 1940s, Harland Goff Wood and Chester Werkman had established that CO_2-fixation was not exclusive to plants and specialized bacteria (called the "Wood-Werkman Reaction") (Singleton, 1997). The reaction, however, had no mechanism. Ochoa reasoned that if the decarboxylation process in Reaction 2 was reversible, CO_2 would be "fixed," thereby providing a mechanism to explain the Wood-Werkman reaction. The easiest way to test this hypothesis was to use isotopic carbon as a tracer, but at the time Ochoa's lab lacked the ability to use isotopes (Grunberg-Manago, 1997, p. 355).

In October 1944 Ochoa purchased a Beckman DU spectrophotometer using a $1,200 American Philosophical Society grant. Ochoa thought that he might use the instrument to measure CO_2-fixation via the reverse of

Reactions 1 and 2 by measuring TPN_{ox} production when the enzymes were incubated in the presence of α-ketoglutarate and CO_2. However, he viewed the hypothesis as "too good to be true" and procrastinated doing the experiment until persuaded to do so by his good friend Efraim Racker. When he ran the experiment and the spectrophotometer indicated TPN_{ox} production, Ochoa was so excited he ran out of the room calling for everyone to "come and watch this." No one came, and Ochoa realized that the time was past 9 p.m. (Ochoa, 1980, p. 15). The experiment, which confirmed an important aspect of the TCA cycle, was Ochoa's first with a spectrophotometer. Nevertheless, he rapidly "became a virtuoso of coupled spectrophotometric assays of oxidative enzymes" (Grunberg-Manago, 1997, p. 355) and influenced generations of biochemists.

In 1948 Ochoa began to work on what he called "the most elusive enzyme of the citric acid cycle." The enzyme, referred to as the "condensing enzyme," catalyzed the reaction of oxaloacetate, a four-carbon dicarboxylic acid, with "active acetate," an unknown two-carbon compound, to form the six-carbon tricarboxylic citric acid. He assigned a new postdoctoral student, Joseph Stern, who had trained with Krebs, to work on the problem.

Stern's early attempts to study the enzyme in animal tissues were unsuccessful; thus, in a move that Grunberg-Manago (1997, p. 355) calls "characteristic of Severo," he turned to a bacterial system. Ochoa, Stern, and another student combined extracts from *Escherichia coli* and pig heart that synthesized citrate from acetyl phosphate and oxaloacetate but also required small amounts of coenzyme A (CoA). From this system, the group crystallized the condensing enzyme, the first crystalline TCA cycle enzyme.

Further work demonstrated that the *E. coli* extract contained an enzyme, transacetylase, which catalyzed acetyl CoA formation from acetyl phosphate and CoA. This observation confirmed Feodor Lynen's prediction that acetyl CoA was the "active acetate" in the TCA cycle. Ochoa's lab joined with Lynen's lab to demonstrate that the condensing enzyme catalyzed the reversible reaction (Ochoa, 1980, p. 17):

Oxalosuccinic acid + Acetyl CoA ⇄ CoA + Citrate (Reaction 3)

The two studies discussed here provided major descriptions for two major sections of the TCA cycle. Further work in Ochoa's lab helped to clarify other portions of the cycle while showing how the cycle was part of the broader intermediary metabolism scheme (Grande and Asensio, 1976, p. 4). Arguably, Ochoa completed the work that Krebs began. Based on this work alone, Ochoa would be considered a major figure in the history of biochemistry.

RNA Synthesis and the Genetic Code. In 1954 Ochoa returned to the oxidative phosphorylation problem and began looking for enzymes capable of converting ADP to ATP. Like most biochemistry labs at the time, the Ochoa lab now worked with radioisotopes, and Ochoa decided to approach the problem by looking for reactions that incorporated radioactively labeled phosphate $^{32}PO_4^{=}$ ($^{32}P_i$) into ATP. A new postdoctoral student from Paris, Grunberg-Manago, picked up the problem (Ochoa, 1980, p. 18).

Using bacterial extracts from *Azobacter vinelandii,* Grunberg-Manago quickly demonstrated an active exchange reaction between $^{32}P_i$ and ATP and partially purified the activity. In early experiments, she had used amorphous ATP. She later repeated the experiment with crystalline—and thus purer—ATP, and the reaction no longer worked. She discovered that the amorphous ATP was contaminated with ADP; this observation led her to believe that the reaction she observed was:

ADP ⇄ AMP + $(PO)_4^{=}$ (Reaction 4)

Ochoa did not believe Grunberg-Manago's initial data and offended her by saying that "it was impossible." Later, "regretting his first reaction," Ochoa came to Grunberg-Manago's lab, where she was easily able to convince him that ADP was indeed the reaction substrate. As Grunberg-Manago noted, Ochoa became "very excited, because no known enzyme was able to catalyse such an exchange." Within a short time Grunberg-Manago had characterized the reaction further and demonstrated that other nucleotide diphosphates (i.e., UDP, CDP, GDP, and IDP) were substrates in addition to ADP (Grunberg-Manago, 1997, p. 359).

Up to this point, Grunberg-Manago had studied the process as an "exchange" reaction; she incubated bacterial extracts with $(^{32}PO)_4^{=}$ and nucleotide diphosphate and looked for radioactivity incorporated into the nucleotide. Consequently, the true products in Reaction 3 were ambiguous. In the summer of 1954 she began a series of experiments to more precisely characterize the enzymatic reaction. In one set of experiments she had difficulty isolating the product, which seemed to be of high molecular weight. Further work demonstrated that the product was a nucleotide polymer identical to ribonucleic acid, and that the true reaction was:

$(XMP)_n$ ⇄ n XDP + n $(PO)_4^{=}$ (Reaction 5) [where X is a nucleotide base (adenine, uracil, etc)].

Grunberg-Manago and Ochoa debated what to call the new enzyme. Ochoa, hoping that it might be involved in polynucleotide synthesis, wanted to name the enzyme "RNA synthetase." Grunberg-Manago, however, thought the activity involved RNA degradation and favored calling it phosphorylase. Ochoa yielded, saying "Marianne, because I like you very much, I will adopt the name you suggested," and the enzyme was called "polynucleotide phosphorylase" (Grunberg-Manago, 1997, p. 360). Regardless of name, the enzyme was the first in vitro synthesis of a large molecular weight biological compound and launched Ochoa's research in a new direction.

The period between 1951 and 1961 was one of the most exciting in biological research. Consider that during the decade Alfred Hershey and Martha Chase confirmed that DNA was indeed the genetic material, James D. Watson and Francis Crick demonstrated DNA's structure, Matthew Meselson and Franklin Stahl demonstrated the nature of DNA replication, Arthur Kornberg isolated DNA polymerase, and the role of messenger RNA (mRNA) was clarified. By 1961 François Jacob and Jacques Monod were able to sketch out what became known as the "central dogma" of modern biology: that is, that information flows from DNA to RNA to protein (Thieffry and Sarkar, 1998). An organism's genotype resided in its DNA; protein was responsible for expressing the organism's phenotype. As the discipline of molecular biology began to evolve out of biochemistry, research focus shifted to understand the mechanisms driving those processes; a central problem of this research program was to understand the nature of the "genetic code." How was information contained in four DNA nucleotides converted into a functional sequence of twenty amino acids in a protein? Polynucleotide phosphorylase played an important role in answering that question.

In 1959 Marshall Nirenberg and coworkers at the National Institutes of Health (NIH) began experimental attempts to understand how DNA information was expressed as protein function. Nirenberg synthesized RNA molecules consisting of a single base (e.g., poly-U was an RNA molecule made up entirely of the nucleoside uridine). This synthetic mRNA was introduced in an *E. coli* protein synthesis system containing a mixture of amino acids, one of which contained a radioactive label. Incorporation of the labeled amino acid into protein indicated that the base in the polynucleotide coded for that amino acid. At the 1961 International Congress of Biochemistry in Moscow, Nirenberg and Heinrich J. Matthai reported that a poly-U mRNA was translated into polyphenylalanine; thus, the RNA code for phenylalanine was uracil (or thymine in DNA).

Peter Lengyel and Joseph Speyer, in Ochoa's lab, started to work with cell-free protein synthesis systems in early 1961. Their hypothesis was that synthetic polyribonucleotides, of known base composition, generated with polynucleotide phosphorylase would act as mRNA and incorporate amino acids into protein depending upon the polyribonucleotide base composition (Ochoa, 1980, p. 20). The hypothesis was highly successful, and very shortly the Ochoa and Nirenberg labs were engaged in a tight, and highly competitive, race to solve the genetic code.

Initially, Nirenberg was unaware of the competition. He had given a talk on his work (accounts of this incident differ as told by Ochoa and Nirenberg) and was in the process of answering audience questions. He was surprised when Peter Lengyel from Ochoa's laboratory told the audience that he had done similar work. Nirenberg said that after the meeting he returned to Washington "feeling very depressed," because he had not realized that Ochoa's lab was working the "important problem of deciphering the genetic code." He "clearly … had to either compete with … Ochoa … or stop working on the problem" (Nirenberg, 2004, p. 49). After a brief 1961 attempt to collaborate rather than compete, Nirenberg concluded that collaboration was out of the question. Later he concluded that, to his horror, he enjoyed the competition, which stimulated him to be more focused, and he "accomplished far more than I would have in its absence" (2004, p. 50).

In approximately two years (1961–1963) the two laboratories published almost twenty full-length papers in the *Proceedings of the National Academy of Sciences of the United States of America* alone, in which they fully defined all aspects of the genetic code. Ochoa noted that the results between the two labs "agreed beautifully." Har Gobind Khorana confirmed and expanded upon much of this work by chemically synthesizing deoxyribonucleotides polymers, of known base composition, and demonstrated that they directed incorporation of specific amino acids into proteins. Thus, what appeared to be a difficult problem was completely resolved in a relatively short period. Furthermore, solving the genetic code arguably opened the way for the disciplinary expansion of molecular biology.

Recognition and Maturity. Ochoa remarked: "Polynucleotide phosphorylase may be considered to have been the Rosetta Stone of the genetic code" (1980, p. 20), a statement recognized, in part, by his receipt, with Kornberg, of the 1959 Nobel Prize in Physiology or Medicine. In his Nobel Prize presentation speech, Theorell commented that their work would have far-reaching impact in fields such as "biochemistry, virus research, genetics, and cancer research." He concluded that Ochoa's work had "helped us to advance quite some distance on the road to understanding the mechanism of life" (Theorell, 1959).

In 1974, after twenty years as chair of biochemistry at NYU, Ochoa retired and accepted an offer to join the Roche Institute of Molecular Biology at Nutley, New

Jersey. The move was apparently rewarding, and Ochoa wrote to Krebs: "I cannot tell you how happy I am here with splendid facilities for work, and with the feeling that I now have time to do what I most like to do" (Krebs, 1976, p. 419). While at Roche, Ochoa maintained an active and productive research program for another decade.

In 1985 he and his wife, Carmen, returned to Spain, where he was already a national hero. Although he spent more than half his life in the United States, and had become a U.S. citizen in 1956, he retained his love of Spain. The love was reciprocal; Grunberg-Manago commented that "Ochoa was indisputably one of the best-known people in his home country" (Grunberg-Manago, 1997, p. 363). Many Spanish streets are named after him, and his portrait is displayed in Madrid restaurants that he visited.

Coda. During his career, Ochoa authored or coauthored more than five hundred papers. Of these, *Science Citation Index* (*SCI*) lists almost three hundred papers from 1945 to 1990; the lab published as many as sixteen papers per year and had a three-year "running average" publication rate of six papers per year. This publication record is impressive; however, publication volume and rate are not the only measures of scientific influence; the scientific community's use of an individual's work is equally important (Hull, 1988). By this indicator as well, Ochoa's career was influential. Almost 20 percent of Ochoa papers listed in the *SCI* database were cited more than a hundred times by other workers. Because a significant majority of papers published are never cited, this citation frequency is remarkable. These data clearly indicate Ochoa's significant scientific impact.

Perhaps the ultimate recognition of a scientist's contribution is in his or her peers' estimation. Ochoa was awarded virtually every public award a scientist can receive; however, perhaps one of the most significant honors was a celebration of his seventieth birthday. In September 1975 Ochoa's former students and colleagues held an international symposium in Barcelona and Madrid and presented papers in six colloquia that covered various fields in which Ochoa had worked: energy metabolism, lipids and saccharides, regulation, nucleic acids and the genetic code, protein biosynthesis, and cell biology. Such celebrations and published Festschrifts for distinguished scientists are not unusual. Few, however, reflect such a tremendous diversity of contributions as the above list indicates or such a distinguished list of speakers. Of the almost fifty papers published, eleven were by Nobel Prize recipients; every author was a member of at least one honorary national scientific academy or society. In addition to the distinguished contributors list, the Festschrift is remarkable in that its dust jacket features a reproduction of a Dalí painting, titled "My Homage to Severo Ochoa." Figures in the painting "symbolize the genetic code messengers, or molecules of polynucleotides, which were synthesized for the first time in Severo Ochoa's laboratory" (Dalí, 1976, p. 445).

Biochemistry's history was written by many great scientists; F. Grande and Carlos Asensio observed, "Severo Ochoa's scientific biography condenses the history of contemporary biochemistry and connects events which have significantly affected the development of the science" (1976, p. 1). Arguably, Ochoa's career reached further than many of his contemporaries. His career began in Germany in what Grande and Asensio call "the golden age of European Biochemistry." As the disciplinary power increasingly swept westward, first to Britain, and then to the United States, life circumstances forced Ochoa to follow that migration. One cannot help but wonder what paths that migration might have followed if a critical friendship or mentor had not provided support. David Hull notes the important role of contingency in both scientific discovery and in individual careers (1988). Severo Ochoa's life and career certainly illustrate the validity of this point.

BIBLIOGRAPHY

The biographical article by Marianne Grunberg-Manago, cited below, includes a complete list of Ochoa's publications.

WORKS BY OCHOA

With José G. Valdecasas. "A Micro Method for the Estimation of Total Creatinine in Muscle." *Journal of Biological Chemistry* 81 (1929): 351–357.

With Carmen G. Ochoa. "Cozymase from Invertebrate Muscle." *Nature* 140 (1937): 1019.

With Rudolph Albert Peters. "Vitamin B_1 and Carboxylase in Animal Tissues." *Biochemical Journal* 32 (1938): 1501–1515.

With Ilona Banga and Rudolph Albert Peters. "Pyruvate Oxidation in Brain. VII. Some Dialysable Components of the Pyruvate Oxidation System." *Biochemical Journal* 33 (1939): 1980–1996.

"Coupling of Phosphorylation with Oxidation of Pyruvic Acid and Brain." *Journal of Biological Chemistry* 138 (1941): 751–773.

With Marianne Grunberg-Manago. "Enzymatic Synthesis and Breakdown of Polynucleotides: Polynucleotide Phosphorylase." *Journal of the American Chemical Society* 77 (1955): 3165–3166.

"Enzymatic Synthesis of Ribonucleic Acid." Nobel Lecture, 11 December 1959. Available from http://nobelprize.org/medicine.

"The Pursuit of a Hobby." *Annual Review of Biochemistry* 49 (1980): 1–30.

OTHER SOURCES

Dale, Henry. NIMR Archives, Box PF15. 30 March 1938. Letter, Henry Dale to Andrew Bennett. National Institute for Medical Research, Mill Hill, London.

Dalí, Salvador. "My Homage to Severo Ochoa." In *Reflections on Biochemistry: In Honour of Severo Ochoa,* edited by A. Kornberg et al., 445. New York: Pergamon Press, 1976.

Ernster, Lars. "P/O Ratios: The First Fifty Years." *FASEB Journal* 7 (1993): 1520–1524.

Garfield, Eugene. "The 1,000 Contemporary Scientists Most-Cited, 1965–1978. Part I. The Basic List and Introduction." *Current Contents,* no. 41 (12 October 1981): 5–14.

Grande, F., and Carlos Asensio. "Biographical Introduction: Severo Ochoa and the Development of Biochemistry." In *Reflections on Biochemistry: In Honour of Severo Ochoa,* edited by Arthur Kornberg et al., 1–14. New York: Pergamon Press, 1976.

Grunberg-Manago, Marianne. "Severo Ochoa: 24 September 1905–1 November 1993." *Biographical Memoirs of Fellows of the Royal Society* 43 (1997): 350–365. The standard Ochoa biography, written by one of his major scientific collaborators. The essay contains a complete list of Ochoa's publications.

Hull, David. *Science as a Process.* Chicago: University of Chicago Press, 1988.

Kornberg, Arthur. "Severo Ochoa (24 September 1905–1 November 1993)." *Proceedings of the American Philosophical Society* 141 (1997): 479–491.

———. "Remembering Our Teachers." *Journal of Biological Chemistry* 276 (2001): 3–11.

———, Bernard L. Horecker, Luis Cornudella, et al., eds. *Reflections on Biochemistry: In Honour of Severo Ochoa.* New York: Pergamon Press, 1976. Festschrift for Ochoa's seventieth birthday, the collection contains many personal reflections on Ochoa.

Kresge, Nicole, Robert D. Simoni, and Robert L. Hill. "Severo Ochoa's Contributions to the Citric Acid Cycle." *Journal of Biological Chemistry* 280 (2005): e8–e10.

Lane, M. Daniel. "The Biotin Connection: Severo Ochoa, Harland Wood, and Feodor Lynen." *Journal of Biological Chemistry* 279 (2004): 39187–39194.

Lipmann, Fritz. "Einar Lundsgaard." *Science* 164 (1969): 246–247.

Nirenberg, Marshall. "Historical Review: Deciphering the Genetic Code—A Personal Account." *Trends in Biochemical Sciences* 29 (2004): 46–54.

Santesmases, María Jesús. "Enzymology at the Core: Primers and Templates in Severo Ochoa's Transition from Biochemistry to Molecular Biology." *History and Philosophy of the Life Sciences* 24 (2002): 193–218.

———. "Severo Ochoa and the Biomedical Sciences in Spain under Franco, 1959–1975." *Isis* 91, no. 4 (December 2000): 706–734.

———, and Emilio Muñoz. "Scientific Organizations in Spain (1950–1970): Social Isolation and International Legitimation of Biochemists and Molecular Biologists on the Periphery." *Social Studies of Science* 27, no. 2 (1997): 187–219.

Singleton, Rivers, Jr. "Harland Goff Wood: An American Biochemist." In *Comprehensive Biochemistry: History of Biochemistry,* Vol. 40, edited by Giorgio Semenza and Rainer Jaenicke. Amsterdam: Elsevier, 1997.

Theorell, Hugo. "The Nobel Prize in Physiology or Medicine 1959, Presentation Speech." Available from http://nobelprize.org/nobel_prizes/medicine/laureates/1959/press.html.

Thieffry, Denis, and Sahotra Sarkar. "Forty Years under the Central Dogma." *Trends in Biochemical Sciences* 23 (1998): 312–316.

Thompson, Robert Henry Stewart, and Alexander G. Ogston. "Rudolph Albert Peters: 13 April 1889–29 January 1982." *Biographical Memoirs of Fellows of the Royal Society* 29 (1983): 494–523.

Rivers Singleton Jr.

OCKHAM, WILLIAM OF

(*b.* Ockham, [later Woking], near London, England, c. 1285; *d.* Munich, Germany, 1347), *logic, philosophy, theology.* For the original article on Ockham see *DSB,* vol. 10.

Ockham's renown is due primarily to his contributions to logic and their impact on ontology, natural philosophy, and theology. He adopted a form of nominalism that is more accurately designated as conceptualism. This postscript focuses on revisions of his biography, contributions to natural philosophy, and influence.

Recent scholarship has revised Ockham's biography on his likely residence at London before and after his period of study at Oxford, scholarly activity at Avignon, date of death and circumstances related to his death, and the location of his burial place in Munich. The completion of the Latin edition of his philosophical and theological works along with translations of several of them has contributed to a better understanding of Ockham's relation to his predecessors and contemporaries, and of his influence on later authors. His conceptualism and account of connotative concepts continue to challenge scholars, and inform our understanding of his contribution to modern empiricism. Likewise, the projected completion of the edition of his political works will likely deepen our understanding of Ockham, making it clearer which ideas were traditional and which link him to modern liberalism.

Life. Ockham entered the Franciscan order around the age of twelve as a novice probably at the London friary, and spent his early years studying the liberal arts and philosophy. In 1306 he was ordained subdeacon at Southwark, London, in the diocese of Winchester. In 1306 or 1307 he began his study of theology at Oxford, and completed the principal requirement of lecturing on the *Sentences* of Peter Lombard by 1319. He probably returned to London to wait for his teaching license. During the next four years he revised his commentary on the first book of the *Sentences,* participated in academic disputations, and wrote some of his major works on logic and natural philosophy.

Ockham's controversial views provoked some to accuse him of heresy. The papacy summoned him to its court at Avignon in 1324. While he awaited the outcome of the investigation, he completed his last treatise on philosophical and theological questions. At the Franciscan friary where he resided, he met other Franciscans who challenged Pope John XXII's views on evangelical poverty, the cornerstone of Franciscan spirituality. When it became clear that the pope was about to condemn even the moderate Franciscan view, Ockham fled with his associates, all of whom were excommunicated. As a result, he never received his doctorate, and eventually ended up in Munich where over the next twenty years he wrote polemical treatises against John XXII and his successors. Contrary to myth, Ockham died impenitent in 1347 probably before the Black Death reached Bavaria. He was buried in the Franciscan cemetery in Munich, which is now the site of the Bavarian National Theater. On the steps to the garage closest to the front entrance of the theater a plaque commemorates Ockham, Orlando di Lasso, and others.

The "Razor." Aside from his extensive works on logic and relevant discussions in the *Sentences* commentary, he wrote several treatises on natural philosophy. Among these are a commentary on Aristotle's *Physics,* a questions-commentary containing 151 questions and two shorter summaries. Although he intended to write commentaries on other organic treatises and on metaphysics, his focus on the *Physics* and his turn to political and moral questions diverted him from that project.

In logic his most important contributions are his so-called razor against superfluous entities and his reactions against philosophers who multiplied the number of existing things by speculating in ways that derive from inconsistencies and a careless use of language. By observing a few simple precautions, Ockham thought, such errors can be avoided. In applying his logical principles, he distinguished between absolute and connotative terms. Absolute terms are substance terms and abstract quality terms that can refer to real things. Connotative terms are concrete quality terms and terms in all of the Aristotelian categories other than substance that can refer to one real thing primarily and to another thing secondarily, but they do not signify things distinct from individual substances and inhering qualities. He applied this distinction extensively, particularly in the analysis of three of the most important topics in Aristotle's *Physics,* motion, time, and place. Ockham did not deny that bodies really move, or that change takes time, or that bodies are in place and move from place to place. He treated all three as connotative terms, the result of which was the elimination of talk about them as individual things that exist independently of the things in motion, in time, and in place.

Natural Philosophy. Ockham's emphasis on eliminating superfluous entities contributed to a more empiricist and less inflationary ontology. Ockham remained an Aristotelian, however, in his acceptance of formal and material causes. He tended, though, to emphasize efficient causes over final causes in nature. Like other scholastics, he made distinctions in the analysis of place and the medium through which bodies move that imply a distinction between a description of motion and a causal analysis of motion. Contrary to Aristotle, Ockham, like Thomas Aquinas, accepted the theoretical possibility of the motion of a body through a vacuum. Because a body cannot exist in two places at the same time, its motion from one side of a postulated vacuum to the other side would require some lapse of time. This led Ockham to distinguish between the conditions of local motion and the causes of greater or lesser speed.

Ockham shared several ideas with other late medieval scholastics, but the clarity of his arguments led later authors to cite him occasionally as an inspiration. For example, several authors concluded that matter and form are not just abstract principles but really existing constituents of things. In Ockham's version really existing physical things are composed of matter and a hierarchy of substantial forms. That doctrine along with his reduction of rarefaction and condensation to a function of the local motions of the parts of a thing inspired later authors to defend atomism. For example, Nicholas of Autrecourt, the German atomist Joachim Jungius, Kenelm Digby, and Thomas Hobbes appealed to Ockhamist doctrines in support of mechanistic analysis and atomism.

Another major consequence of Ockham's doctrine of connotative terms is found in his analysis of mathematics. Where Aristotle prohibited transition from one genus or species to another in proofs to avoid ambiguity and thus fallacious arguments, Ockham tended to relax such prohibitions. Aristotle maintained that we should not compare circular and rectilinear motions, because the difference constitutes a specific difference, meaning that they belong to different species such that any comparison would be fallacious. Ockham's theory of connotation, however, led him to reject Aristotle's prohibition. In Ockham's view *circular* and *rectilinear* do not stand for specifically different entities but express nominal definitions that can be predicated of motions in a way that permits comparison.

More generally, Ockham interpreted Aristotle as allowing for the subordination of a mathematical analysis to physical considerations, the subordination of a physical analysis to mathematical considerations, and even the partial subordination of one science to another. The consequence is that Ockham subdued the logical and ontological restrictions on mathematics, making it a suitable instrument for analyzing any problem that can be quantified or clarified logically by means of mathematics.

Even more startling was Ockham's denial of the traditional doctrine of perceptual and cognitive species, a denial that led him to affirm action at a distance. This argument constitutes an example of Ockham's more empiricist side. Ockham, however, followed the Aristotelian emphasis on efficient causes as deriving from potencies in things, even if his reductionistic tendencies led him to eliminate several speculatively generated entities.

Influence. Ockham's ideas influenced three philosophers at Merton College, Oxford, William Heytesbury, John Dumbleton, and Richard Swineshead, who developed a more mathematical approach that generated some interesting consequences for the mathematical description of change and motion. Among these consequences is the Merton mean-speed theorem, which provides a way of understanding the relation between a uniformly accelerated motion by comparison with a uniform motion over the same time and in the same distance. If a body moves from rest at a uniform rate of acceleration, it will cover the same distance in the same time as the same body moving uniformly at a constant velocity that is half the final velocity of the uniformly accelerated motion. It should be added, however, that medieval philosophers regarded such an analysis as useful for understanding all kinds of changes, including intension and remission of immaterial and incorporeal qualities.

Ockham's influence on Parisian philosophers of the fourteenth century is more complex. Although his conceptualism and critique of inflationary metaphysics influenced Parisian thinkers, they tended to reject his more extreme conclusions by developing moderate interpretations consistent with high medieval scholastic Aristotelianism. For example, the views of John Buridan, Marsilius of Inghen, and Albert of Saxony tend to be more conservative. Nicole Oresme, however, shows how Ockham's influence, even when moderated, contributed to the most original and challenging analysis of nature in the fourteenth century. Like Ockham, Oresme characterized terms such as *motion* as connotative. Oresme's view was not as reductive as Ockham's but he too followed Ockham's critique in applying mathematics to problems of change and variation. He did not deny that motion is a real thing altogether, but affirmed it only as a mode of being. He denied the material or corporeal reality of species and their reality in the sensible world, allowing them only a spatial-temporal reference and thus rendering them intelligible in purely mathematical terms.

The influence of these ideas on later authors is difficult to trace. In general, they inspired more mechanistic thinking or greater emphasis by Aristotelians on mathematical analysis, but most historians consider Galileo Galilei's innovations as surpassing by far the achievements of his predecessors and contemporaries.

SUPPLEMENTARY BIBLIOGRAPHY

WORKS BY OCKHAM

Opera Politica. 3 vols. Manchester, U.K.: Manchester University, 1940–1974.

Opera Philosophica et Theologica. 17 vols. St. Bonaventure, NY: Franciscan Institute, 1967–1988.

"William of Ockham's Commentary on Porphyry." Translated by Eike-Henner W. Kluge. *Franciscan Studies* 33 (1973): 171–254, and 34 (1974): 306–382. Translation of *Expositio in libros artis logicae, prooemium et expositio in librum Porphyrii de Praedicabilibus, Opera Philosophica* 2, 3–131.

Ockham's Theory of Terms. Translated by Michael Loux. Notre Dame, IN: University of Notre Dame, 1974. Translation of *Summa Logicae,* Part 1, *Opera Philosophica* 1, 3–238.

Ockham's Theory of Propositions. Translated by Alfred Freddoso and Henry Schuurman. Notre Dame, IN: University of Notre Dame, 1980. Translation of *Summa Logicae,* Part 2, *Opera Philosophica* 1, 239–356.

Ockham on Aristotle's Physics. Translated by Julian Davies. St. Bonaventure, NY: Franciscan Institute, 1989. Translation of *Brevis summa libri Physicorum, Opera Philosophica* 6, 2–134.

Philosophical Writings: A Selection. Translated by Philotheus Boehner, revised by Stephen Brown. Indianapolis, IN: Hackett, 1990.

Quodlibetal Questions. 2 vols. Translated by Francis Kelley and Alfred Freddoso. New Haven, CT: Yale University, 1991. Translation of *Quodlibeta Septem, Opera Theologica* 9.

Opera Politica. Vol 4. *Auctores Britannici Medii Aevi,* Vol. 14. Oxford: Oxford University, 1997. The political works were edited by Hilary S. Offler, the last volume posthumously by a committee chaired by David Luscombe. John Kilcullen, George Knysh, Volker Leppin, John Scott, and Jan Ballweg are editing Ockham's *Dialogus* for the British Academy. Drafts are available from http://www.britac.ac.uk/pubs/dialogus/ockdial.html.

Demonstration and Scientific Knowledge in William of Ockham. Translated by John Longeway. Notre Dame, IN: University of Notre Dame, 2007. Translation of *Summa Logicae,* Part 3, section 2. *Opera Philosophica* 1, pp. 503–584. The introduction characterizes Ockham as "the founder of European empiricism."

OTHER SOURCES

Adams, Marilyn. *William Ockham.* 2 vols. 2nd ed. Notre Dame, IN: University of Notre Dame, 1989. The most comprehensive study in English.

Beckmann, Jan. *Ockham-Bibliographie 1900–1999.* Hamburg, Germany: Felix Meiner, 1992.

Boehner, Philotheus. *Collected Ariticles on Ockham.* Edited by Eligius Buytaert. St. Bonaventure, NY: Franciscan Institute, 1958. Fundamental articles by Ockham's earliest twentieth-century editor.

Brown, Stephen. "A Modern Prologue to Ockham's Natural Philosophy." *Sprache und Erkenntnis im Mittelalter, Miscellanea Mediaevalia* 13, no. 1 (1981): 107–129. The most authoritative expert on Ockham's physical treatises.

Courtenay, William. "Ockham, Chatton, and the London *Studium:* Observations on Recent Changes in Ockham's Biography." In *Die Gegenwart Ockhams,* edited by Wilhelm Vossenkuhl, Rolf Schönberger, and Otl Aicher, 327–337. Weinheim, Germany: VCH-Verlagsgesellschaft, 1990.

Etzkorn, Girard. "Ockham at Avignon: His Response to Critics." *Franciscan Studies* 59 (2001): 9–19. The latest revision of Ockham's biography.

Franciscan Studies. Commemorative Issues, Vols. 44 and 45, Annual 22–23, 1984–1985. Collection of papers from the celebration at the Franciscan Institute in 1985 of the seventh centenary of Ockham's birth and of the completion of the critical edition. Volume 44 was predated to 1984.

Gál, Gedeon. "William of Ockham Died 'Impenitent' in April 1347." *Franciscan Studies* 42 (1982): 90–95. Gál directed the modern critical edition of Ockham's philosophical and theological works.

Goddu, André. *The Physics of William of Ockham.* Leiden, Netherlands: E.J. Brill, 1984.

———. "William of Ockham's Arguments for Action at a Distance." *Franciscan Studies* 44 (1984): 227–244.

———. "William of Ockham's 'Empiricism' and Constructive Empiricism." In *Die Gegenwart Ockhams,* edited by Wilhelm Vossenkuhl, Rolf Schönberger, and Otl Aicher, 208–231. Weinheim, Germany: VCH-Verlagsgesellschaft, 1990.

———. "Connotative Concepts and Mathematics in Ockham's Natural Philosophy." *Vivarium* 31 (1993): 106–139.

———. "Ockham's Philosophy of Nature." In *The Cambridge Companion to Ockham,* edited by Paul Spade, 143–167. Cambridge, U.K.: Cambridge University Press, 1999.

———. "The Impact of Ockham's Reading of the *Physics* on the Mertonians and Parisian Terminists." *Early Science and Medicine* 6 (2001): 204–237.

Karger, Elizabeth. "Ockham's Misunderstood Theory of Intuitive and Abstractive Cognition." In *The Cambridge Companion to Ockham,* edited by Paul Spade, 204–226. Cambridge, U.K.: Cambridge University Press, 1999. The clearest analysis of Ockham's theory.

Lang, Helen. *Aristotle's Physics and its Medieval Varieties.* Albany: State University of New York, 1992. Indispensable evaluation of medieval interpretations of Aristotle.

Livesey, Steven. "William of Ockham, the Subalternate Sciences, and Aristotle's Prohibition of *metabasis.*" *British Journal for the History of Science* 18 (1985): 127–145. Groundbreaking study.

Maurer, Armand. *The Philosophy of William of Ockham in the Light of Its Principles.* Toronto: Pontifical Institute of Mediaeval Studies, 1999. This is the most accessible book-length study in English.

Miethke, Jürgen. *Ockhams Weg zur Sozialphilosophie.* Berlin: Walter de Gruyter, 1969. The most comprehensive study of Ockham in any language.

Moody, Ernest. *The Logic of William of Ockham.* Reprinted. New York: Russell and Russell, 1965.

———. "Ockham and Aegidius of Rome." In *Studies in Medieval Philosophy, Science, and Logic,* edited by Ernest Moody, 161–188. Berkeley: University of California, 1975. The most influential article on Ockham's account of motion through a void.

Murdoch, John. "*Scientia mediantibus vocibus:* Metalinguistic Analysis in Late Medieval Natural Philosophy." *Sprache und Erkenntnis im Mittelalter, Miscellanea Mediaevalia* 13, no. 1 (1981): 73–106. The best analysis of the logical context of fourteenth-century natural philosophy.

Panaccio, Claude. "Semantics and Mental Language." In *The Cambridge Companion to Ockham,* edited by Paul Spade, 53–75. Cambridge, U.K.: Cambridge University Press, 1999. Best brief study of Ockham's conceptualism and doctrine of connotative terms.

Spade, Paul. "Ockham's Distinctions between Absolute and Connotative Terms." *Vivarium* 13 (1975): 55–76. Reprinted in *Lies, Language and Logic in the Late Middle Ages,* by Paul Spade. London: Variorum Reprints, 1988. Foundational article challenging the coherence and completeness of Ockham's account.

———. *Lies, Language and Logic in the Late Middle Ages.* London: Variorum Reprints, 1988.

———. "Three Versions of Ockham's Reductionist Program." *Franciscan Studies* 56 (1998): 335–346.

———, ed. *The Cambridge Companion to Ockham.* Cambridge, U.K.: Cambridge University Press, 1999. Now standard collection of articles in English.

André Goddu

ODUM, EUGENE PLEASANTS

(*b.* Lake Sunapee, New Hampshire, 17 September 1913; *d.* Athens, Georgia, 10 August 2002), *ecology, ecosystem studies, environmentalism, ornithology, education.*

During the second half of the twentieth century Eugene Odum was the leading proponent of the ecosystem concept in ecology. Taking the concept that had earlier been sketched by the British ecologist Arthur Tansley, Odum made it the central focus of his research. In doing so, he made important changes to Tansley's original ideas. Odum emphasized holism, which Tansley had strongly opposed. He also employed organismal analogies such as

Odum

homeostasis to explain self regulation in ecosystems. This was also foreign to Tansley's original concept. Together with his brother Howard T. Odum, he conducted large-scale experimental studies of energy flow in ecosystems that caught the imagination of a generation of ecologists. Odum's textbook, *Fundamentals of Ecology,* went through five editions and for a time during the 1960s and early 1970s dominated the field. Centered on ecosystems, the textbook effectively promoted ecosystem ecology by persuasively presenting it to generations of students. Odum also effectively used the ecosystem concept to promote conservation and environmental protection. He was recognized by the public as one of the leading environmentalists of the late twentieth century.

Family Influences. Odum was a member of a prominent academic family. He was strongly influenced by his father, the sociologist Howard W. Odum, who was a leading advocate of regionalism. The elder Odum contrasted this sociological approach to the older idea of sectionalism, which emphasized divisiveness and conflict. Regionalism, as opposed to sectionalism, emphasized the growing role of the federal government in fostering cooperation and coordination among the various regions of the nation. From his father, Eugene took the idea of the integration of parts to form a larger social whole. He later claimed that this view encouraged the development of his holistic ecosystem thinking, and in his later writings he routinely referred to his father's work as a basis for understanding the relationship of humans and nature. The New Deal progressivism that his father espoused became the basis for Eugene Odum's optimism about protecting the environment through rational planning based on the application of ecological principles. His father was also a prodigious writer, and he strongly encouraged Eugene to write *Fundamentals of Ecology* when the younger Odum had doubts about his abilities as a textbook author.

Eugene Odum's ideas were also strongly shaped by his younger brother, Howard Thomas, who studied biogeochemistry with G. Evelyn Hutchinson at Yale University and became deeply involved in research on energy transfer and biogeochemical cycling in ecosystems. H. T. Odum wrote the chapters on energy for the first two editions of *Fundamentals of Ecology* and he designed the experimental methods for the pioneering ecosystem studies that the two brothers jointly produced after World War II. Despite some sibling rivalry, the two Odum brothers formed a formidable team. Eugene was particularly skilled at presenting Howard's often esoteric and unorthodox ideas in a way that was readily grasped and widely accepted by professional ecologists and the general public. Unlike his father and his brother, who were sometimes hampered by obscure writing styles and difficulty presenting their broad visions, Eugene Odum wrote in clear prose that proved ideal for writing a successful textbook and the many other books and articles he aimed at general scientific audiences and students. Largely due to the efforts of the Odum brothers, ecosystems became an important part of mainstream ecology during the 1960s. The academic legacy of the Odum family continued to a third generation when Eugene's son William became a professional ecologist.

Eugene Pleasants Odum. UNIVERSITY OF GEORGIA PHOTOGRAPHIC SERVICES.

Education. Odum was a rather indifferent student, although he entered college when he was only fifteen. He later recalled preferring botany to zoology classes because he disliked dissecting animals. However, from early childhood he had a strong interest in birds. As a boy he maintained a journal, the "Briarbridge Bird News," in which he recorded observations of bird life in the area surrounding the family home in Chapel Hill. His father's secretary helped type and mimeograph the articles, and Eugene painted a watercolor portrait of a female catbird feeding her young for the cover for the journal. This writing project expanded when as a college student Odum wrote a regular column titled "Bird Life in Chapel Hill" for the

Odum

local newspaper. By the time that he graduated from the University of North Carolina in 1934 he had published several articles in professional ornithological journals. After completing a master of science degree at the University of North Carolina in 1936, Odum moved to the University of Illinois where he studied under the ornithologist Charles Kendeigh. Apparently because of his lackluster grades, the zoology department moved to reject his application to the PhD program, but Kendeigh intervened on his behalf.

In 1939, Odum completed a dissertation on how the heart rates of passerine birds are affected by environmental factors. Kendeigh suggested the research because a manufacturer of piezoelectric crystals had approached him about using the devices to monitor physiological processes in wild animals. The dissertation research involved placing crystals in birds' nests. The crystal converted the movement of the bird's chest into an electric current which was then transmitted to a pen that recorded the cardiac cycle on a moving strip of paper. Odum's "cardio-vibrometer" provided an innovative method for measuring heart rates under natural conditions and in a noninvasive way. His dissertation was one of the first studies of cardiac physiology in noncaptive animals. The research was later published in *Ecological Monographs.* Despite its physiological focus, this early article already hinted at the holistic philosophy of science that later became closely identified with Odum's thinking. From his perspective, physiology had ecological significance only to the extent that it revealed the functioning of the whole organism in its natural environment. Heart rate, Odum claimed, could be used as an index of the physiological state of the whole animal and its responses to varying environmental conditions. He continued ornithological research during the early years of his career, focusing particularly on the physiological role of fat deposition in migratory birds.

During his studies at the University of Illinois, Odum came under the influence of the ecologist Victor Shelford. At the time Shelford was collaborating with the plant ecologist Frederic Clements on a project to synthesize plant and animal ecology into a more inclusive "bio-ecology." Shelford emphasized biomes (large landscapes characterized by a particular flora and fauna) as the focus of ecological study, and he based this research on a holistic philosophy of science that presented these large-scale ecological entities as superorganisms. Odum later recalled that in his teaching, Shelford was scathing in his denunciation of reductionism in biology which he believed was "anti-ecology," and which he sarcastically identified with the "Woods Hole establishment." Shelford's antireductionistic and organismic views became central parts of Odum's thinking about ecosystems. Odum later recalled that Shelford converted him from being a traditional animal ecologist to a "holistic ecologist." Although a significant intellectual shift, Odum later claimed that it was not a great leap because he simply transferred well-established physiological concepts such as homeostasis from the level of organisms upward to the level of whole ecosystems. Although he usually avoided referring to ecosystems as superorganisms, Odum freely admitted his intellectual debt to Shelford's organismic perspective on ecology. Organismic analogies became a mainstay of Odum's explanations for the stability and self-regulation that he believed were fundamental characteristics of ecosystems.

Early Ecosystem Research. After graduation Odum continued his ornithological research for a short time as naturalist at the Edmund Niles Huyck Preserve in Rensselaerville, New York. In 1940 Odum was hired as an instructor in the zoology department at the University of Georgia. He spent the rest of his career at the university, eventually establishing and directing an institute of ecology. Although he remained an avid bird watcher throughout his life and continued ornithological research, his interests shifted strongly toward studying ecosystems beginning in the early 1950s. This shift probably reflected the influence of Shelford, but it certainly also was stimulated by his brother Howard. After World War II Howard studied with the limnologist G. Evelyn Hutchinson at Yale University. Hutchinson was deeply involved with research on biogeochemical cycles, and together with his postdoctoral fellow, Raymond Lindeman, he pioneered the study of energy flow in aquatic ecosystems. Howard sent his brother copies of Hutchinson's lecture notes, and during the early 1950s Eugene began corresponding directly with Hutchinson. It is significant that Howard wrote the chapters on energy flow for the first two editions of *Fundamentals of Ecology.*

Odum's move to ecosystem ecology was also stimulated by new funding opportunities provided by the Atomic Energy Commission (AEC), which rapidly become a major patron of ecological research. The AEC provided a small grant to the University of Georgia in 1951 to complete a survey of animal populations prior to building a nuclear facility at its Savannah River site near Aiken, South Carolina. Odum convinced the commission to expand this research to include studies of ecological succession and productivity, and he began a long-term study of these processes in the abandoned farmland surrounding the nuclear plant. This small project developed into a laboratory on the site and became an integral part of the fledgling ecological program that Odum was starting at the University of Georgia.

Odum proved a skillful institution builder. Although working at a small, relatively poor state university, he successfully created the Georgia Institute of Ecology, which came to include several branch laboratories as well as the main building at the university. It became one of the premier ecological research and teaching programs in the United States. In a retrospective account of the history of the institute Odum noted the critical role that funding from federal agencies such as the AEC, National Science Foundation, National Institutes of Health, and also private foundations such as the R. J. Reynolds Foundation, which established a marine laboratory for the institute. In compiling this impressive list of successful grants Odum was implicitly acknowledging his skill as an academic entrepreneur.

In 1954 Eugene and Howard Odum were awarded an AEC grant to study productivity on a coral reef at Enewetak Atoll, a major site of nuclear weapons testing during the 1950s. Like other parts of the Marshall Islands, Enewetak became a center for biological, geological, and oceanographic research related to the nuclear testing. The Odum brothers spent six weeks during 1954 studying the ecology of the reef. The product of this research was a thirty-page article published in *Ecological Monographs*. It typified the ecosystem research that would become closely identified with the Odum name.

The Odums found that water flowing over the reef was nutrient poor, and did not contain enough plankton to support the coral polyps. However, the coral animals housed photosynthetic algae inside their bodies. Other biologists had claimed that the algae were parasites that weakened the coral skeleton by burrowing into it. In contrast, the Odums hypothesized that the algae were symbiotic partners with the coral animals forming a mutually beneficial relationship. By measuring dissolved oxygen during the day and night on either side of the reef, the Odums were able to construct an energy budget for the ecosystem. The purpose of the study was to measure the overall "metabolism" of the complete system, balancing the amount of photosynthesis of the symbiotic algae with the respiration of the living community as a whole. This became a theoretical model for ecosystem research, but the Odums claimed that it also served an important practical purpose as a baseline for later studies of the reef as it became increasing affected by nuclear tests. Already the low-level radioactivity in the environment allowed the Odums to produce a radiograph by placing a coral head on a sheet of photographic film.

Finally, the Odum brothers claimed that understanding the stability of coral reefs and the cooperative relationships among the constituent organisms could provide lessons for humans who were increasingly modifying and manipulating natural systems. They described the reef as a highly cooperative system. The coral polyps provided protection for photosynthetic algae that lived inside the small marine animals. In exchange, the algae provided food for the coral. For Eugene Odum, the Japtan reef at Enewetak became a paradigm case of an ancient ecosystem that had developed a high degree of stability through the obligate mutualism of its constituent populations. The Enewetak study won the Mercer Award from the Ecological Society of America in 1956. Completed on a shoestring budget and relying heavily on war-surplus equipment, the Odums' general conclusions were later confirmed and expanded by a much more lavishly funded study of the reef conducted by a team of twenty-five scientists in 1971 during a program called Project Symbios.

Fundamentals of Ecology. During the early 1950s when Odum was pioneering large-scale studies of ecosystem metabolism, he wrote *Fundamentals of Ecology.* The book, originally published in 1953, was meant to be both a comprehensive textbook for students and a reference work for practicing ecologists. Odum later recalled that a major impetus for writing the book came from the condescension that his colleagues in the Zoology Department at the University of Georgia held for ecology. For these traditional zoologists, ecology was little more than descriptive natural history and was not based on truly scientific principles. In response to this criticism, Odum self-consciously began each chapter of the book with a concise statement of an ecological principle, followed by an extended explanation, data, and examples. The book was strongly antireductionistic, a perspective that Odum inherited both from his father's sociology and from Victor Shelford's ecology. Rather than starting with individuals or populations, the early chapters of *Fundamentals of Ecology* were oriented around ecosystem structure and function. Even the chapters on population biology had a strong holistic emphasis that highlighted the importance of group properties such as cooperation and stability. Finally, Odum's textbook had a distinctive environmental perspective. The final section of the book dealt with applied ecology including conservation, wildlife management, pollution, and public health. Odum presented ecologists as professional problem solvers who could use their expert knowledge of ecosystems to solve problems at the interface between science and society. This section of the book was clearly aimed at recruiting biology students to careers in ecology and applied environmental sciences.

In the second edition of the textbook, published in 1959, Odum added a chapter on radiation ecology to the applied ecology section. Despite his well-established relationship with the AEC, Odum had little experience with radiation ecology before 1957, when he was awarded a National Science Foundation grant to study the subject. During the next year he spent time at the Nevada Proving Grounds and the AEC installation at Hanford, Washington. He also conducted research using radioactive tracers to study the population dynamics of ants in Charles Elton's laboratory at Oxford University. Odum's biographer Betty

Odum

Jean Craige claims that sales of *Fundamentals of Ecology* were boosted by the "ban the bomb" movement. If so, it is ironic that Odum embraced environmentalism while relying so heavily on the AEC for financial support. He was not alone in this regard, because during this period many ecologists received financial support from the commission. Odum was conscious of the paradox, and wrote extensively about it both in his textbook and in semipopular articles. Mixing metaphors, Odum described nuclear energy as a two-edged sword, but admitted that it had proven easier to use this sword as a weapon than to fashion it into plowshares. Nonetheless, Odum optimistically believed that the atomic age could provide tools for solving the very environmental problems that it was creating. He pointed to radioactive tracers, which he used for some of his own research, as an example of how nuclear technology could be employed to gain useful insights into ecological processes.

Fundamentals of Ecology eventually went through five editions. It retained its basic outline, although it grew considerably in size and coverage. The third edition, published in 1971, contained a number of new chapters written by other authors on diverse topics including remote sensing, the ecology of space travel, microbial ecology, and mathematical modeling associated with systems ecology. It was now the leading ecology textbook in the United States and was eventually translated into twelve foreign languages. One critic sarcastically commented that the "odum" had become the unit of measurement for textbooks of ecology. However, important changes were occurring in the field and these were reflected in a new generation of textbooks that increasingly challenged *Fundamentals of Ecology* during the 1970s. Most notably, evolutionary ecologists taking a strong Darwinian perspective were redirecting attention from ecosystems to populations. Furthermore, they emphasized the importance of individual fitness and often denied the importance of the group adaptations that Odum believed held populations and communities together. Odum had never been a strong supporter of individual selection which he equated with a "survival of the fittest" mentality, but by the mid-1970s his belief in cooperation based upon group selection began to lose favor with many younger ecologists.

Odum's textbook was unusual in its top-down approach to ecology. Unlike most textbooks both before and since, *Fundamentals of Ecology* moved from ecosystems to the lower levels of biological organization: communities, populations, and individuals. For Odum, the ecosystem was a unifying concept that provided coherence to the discipline. In a short article titled "The New Ecology," Odum claimed that ecologists could rally around the ecosystem much as molecular biologists rallied around the cell. Although this did not happen to the extent that he predicted, Odum's approach did help to significantly reshape modern ecology. His emphasis on ecosystems as fundamental units helped to break down the artificial divide between plant and animal ecology. His emphasis on energy and biochemical cycling also provided a rationale for studying bacteria, fungi, and other groups of organisms that ecologists had previously neglected. The energy flow diagrams from *Fundamentals of Ecology* have become ecological icons that continue to be used in textbooks. Later reactions against some of his ideas notwithstanding, *Fundamentals of Ecology* was the book that graduate students typically studied during one of the most active periods of growth in the discipline of ecology. Odum's colleague Gary Barrett reported that in a survey conducted by the American Institute of Biological Sciences in 2002, *Fundamentals of Ecology* was cited as the textbook that had the greatest impact on the careers of its members.

Holism Defended and Criticized. The holistic, cooperative view of nature that Odum developed in his textbook was also prominently presented in his presidential address to the Ecological Society of America in 1966 and later published as a high-profile article in *Science*. The title, "The Strategy of Ecosystem Development," encapsulated Odum's view of ecosystems as highly organized systems with strong parallels to organisms and human societies. Applying the term *strategy* to ecosystems was controversial both for its anthropomorphism and its implication that group selection was involved in shaping ecosystems. Odum argued that all ecosystems follow a common strategy leading to a steady state equilibrium characteristic of mature systems. He proposed to replace the well-established term *succession* with *development,* highlighting the analogy between the process of orderly changes that he saw in ecosystems and the ontogeny of an organism. The strategy of ecosystem development was summarized in a table of contrasting characteristics of early and mature ecosystems. Odum claimed that during succession maturing ecosystems increasingly developed self-regulation or homeostasis in the same way that organisms did. This ecosystem homeostasis was mediated by such characteristics as high species diversity, niche specialization, complex food webs, high ratios of biomass to production, and increased interdependence among species in the form of obligate mutualism. At the end of the article Odum described how human history had also followed this strategy with "boom-bust" pioneering societies eventually giving way to more stable, mature societies characterized by well-developed systems of civil rights, culture, and law and order.

By his own admission, Odum's article was controversial and the idea that ecosystems are highly organized, self-regulating entities came under considerable criticism. Odum's table of characteristics of young and mature ecosystems continues to appear in some ecology textbooks highlighting its pedagogical usefulness as a capsule summary of important trends in ecological succession. However, Odum's progressive view of nature as stable and cooperative has been rejected by many ecologists who deny progress in nature and view cooperation as competition in disguise. Odum consistently argued that interacting species tend to evolve from primitive parasitism to more advanced forms of mutualism. The coral reef at Enewetak was one such example. Another was the evolution of lichens, which involved a symbiosis of fungus and algae. Odum argued that in primitive lichens the fungus was a parasite that entrapped algae, penetrated their cells, and harvested the products of photosynthesis. In more advanced lichens, Odum believed that the relationship had evolved into mutualism: the algae provided food and the fungus provided nutrients and protection. In these lichens the fungus did not actually penetrate the algal cells, but the two species formed such a tight partnership that neither organism could survive independently. Although not denying that such cases of mutualism may occur, many ecologists today emphasize the instability of such relationships and interpret them as examples of mutual exploitation, rather than true cooperation.

Odum's Environmentalism. Despite his controversial views on the nature of ecosystems, Odum's holistic philosophy of science resonated with many environmentalists. The popular slogan that everything in nature is interconnected, which captured the essence of Odum's position, was a powerful argument for conserving natural habitats, protecting endangered species, and abating pollution. At the height of the environmental movement Odum's picture appeared in popular publications such as *Time* and *Newsweek*. Articles in these news magazines echoed Odum's claim that ecologists were professional problem solvers who had particular expertise in environmental matters.

Increasingly during the 1970s Odum argued that ecology was not simply a biological subdiscipline, but rather an independent and interdisciplinary science that bridged the biological, physical, and social sciences. This bridge-building theme was highlighted in several popular books on ecology, where Odum called for a "bionomics" that would include the value of the work done by natural ecosystems (sometimes referred to as "ecosystem services") in the cost-benefit calculations used by economists. Consciously building on his father's ideas, Odum also argued for a rational "ecosystem management" that would combine perspectives from ecology, sociology, and economics. For example, he approvingly described how choosing sites for nuclear power plants in California now took into account environmental and recreational concerns, as well as profitability. Denying permits for plants near scenic or environmentally sensitive areas might mean higher energy prices, but this "negative feedback" would be beneficial in limiting population growth and urbanization.

Much of Odum's writings on science and society, particularly as related to land use and other environmental issues, evinced the strong concern for social justice that he inherited from his father. At other times, however, he used the more coercive language of control theory which came from his later interest in cybernetics and systems theory. To a large extent this cybernetic way of thinking about both ecosystems and society was derived from his brother, who was one of the founders of a highly theoretical systems ecology. Eugene never moved as far in this direction as Howard, but there was an unresolved tension in his social thought. Some recent critics, notably the writer Alston Chase, condemn Odum and other ecosystem ecologists for providing the intellectual justification for what the critics see as heavy-handed bureaucratic meddling in cases such as the spotted owls in old growth forests in the Pacific Northwest. Odum's view of comprehensive planning based on scientific expertise assumed an activist role for government, and this clashed with the individualism of his critics. In the balance, however, it seems fair to credit Odum with raising public awareness of pressing environmental problems and providing a useful intellectual framework for discussing them.

Odum was a tireless advocate for environmentalism at the state and local level, as well as nationally. He was an award-winning teacher who was comfortable discussing environmental issues to audiences ranging from elementary school classrooms to elite universities. He actively campaigned for environmental protection of natural areas, particularly coastal marshlands. In 1969 he joined a "Save Our Marshes Committee" to prevent phosphate mining along the Georgia coast. His prominence brought national attention to the issue, including quotations in an article in *Life* magazine. He provided testimony before the state legislature and conducted teach-ins at the University of Georgia. In 1970 the state legislature passed a Marshlands Protection Act that was signed into law. For his environmental activism, as well as his writing, Odum was awarded numerous honors by state and national conservation groups. Late in life Odum also became a philanthropist, making substantial contributions to environmental organizations and educational institutions. He had grown wealthy through the sales of his many books and from his various awards and prizes, and before his death he donated over $1.5 million to several universities and environmental organizations. In his will he bequeathed much of his estate to the University of Georgia and its environmental education programs.

Institution Building. Despite his emphasis on cooperation both in nature and society, Eugene Odum was an

Odum

intensely competitive scientist. From the time that he arrived at the University of Georgia he single-mindedly worked to promote ecology and to develop an ecological program that was independent of other university departments, notably zoology and botany. This goal met resistance, particularly during the 1950s when the Zoology Department refused to add ecology to the educational core and rejected Odum's plan to hire another ecologist. Despite this resistance, Odum used funding from the AEC to begin a small ecological research program that eventually became the Savannah River Ecological Laboratory. He also successfully negotiated a gift of land, buildings, and financial support from the tobacco heir Richard J. Reynolds to build a marine laboratory on Sapelo Island. These laboratories later became important parts of the larger ecological program that Odum directed.

During the 1960s and 1970s Odum's national prominence helped to launch a rapid expansion in the ecology program at the University of Georgia. The Georgia Institute of Ecology was officially started in 1967, and a new ecology building was erected in 1974. Odum further supported these developments by endowing ecological research at the institute, using the $150,000 that he received with the Tyler Award for Environmental Achievement in 1977. The gift was eventually matched by the university. Odum directed the Institute of Ecology until his official retirement in 1984, and continued to be active as director emeritus until his death. Odum's dream of having an ecology program fully independent of other academic departments was finally fulfilled in 1993 when the Institute of Ecology began offering its own degree programs.

Family. In 1939 Odum married Martha Ann Huff, a successful watercolor painter. Their son, William Eugene Odum, was a professional ecologist and became the head of the Department of Environmental Sciences at the University of Virginia before his early death from liver cancer. The Odums' second son, Daniel Thomas, was severely retarded and spent his life in a state hospital. After his wife's death Odum continued to write extensively, including a book of short ecological vignettes and a published work of Martha Odum's watercolor paintings. He died of an apparent heart attack while working in his organic garden.

Awards and Honors. Odum was selected to be a delegate to the first "Atoms for Peace" conference held in Geneva, Switzerland, in 1950. He served as president of the Ecological Society of America in 1964. He was elected to the National Academy of Sciences and was an honorary member of the British Ecological Society. In 1974 he received the Eminent Ecologist Award from the Ecological Society of America. Together with his brother Howard T. Odum, he was awarded the Prix de l'Institute de la Vie from the French government in 1975 and the Crafoord Prize from the Royal Swedish Academy of Science in 1987. He received the Distinguished Service Award from the American Institute of Biological Sciences in 1978.

Odum was named Conservationist of the Year in 1976 by the Georgia Wildlife Foundation. In 1977 he received the Tyler Award for Environmental Achievement. He was awarded the Cynthia Pratt Laughlin Medal by the Garden Club of America in 1981. He received the Chevron Conservation Award in 1989 and the Theodore Roosevelt Distinguished Service Award in 1991. He was named Educator of the Year by the National Wildlife Federation in 1983 and received the Environmental Educator Award in 1992 from the Society of Environmental Toxicology and Chemistry.

BIBLIOGRAPHY

WORKS BY ODUM

"Variations in the Heart Rate of Birds: A Study in Physiological Ecology." *Ecological Monographs* 11 (1941): 299–326.

Fundamentals of Ecology. Philadelphia: Saunders, 1953. 2nd ed. 1959. 3rd ed. 1971. 4th ed. 1983. 5th ed. 2005.

With Howard T. Odum. "Trophic Structure and Productivity of a Windward Coral Reef Community on Eniwetok Atoll." *Ecological Monographs* 25 (1955): 291–320.

Ecology: The Link between the Natural and Social Sciences. New York: Holt, Rinehart and Winston, 1963. 2nd ed. 1975.

"The New Ecology." *Bioscience* 14 (July 1964): 14–16.

"The Strategy of Ecosystem Development." *Science* 164 (1969): 262–270.

OTHER SOURCES

Barrett, Gary W. "Eugene Pleasants Odum, 1913–2002," *Biographical Memoirs,* vol. 87. Washington, DC: National Academy of Sciences, 2005.

Barrett, Gary W., and Terry L. Barrett, eds. *Holistic Science: The Evolution of the Georgia Institute of Ecology (1940–2000).* New York: Taylor & Francis, 2001. Odum wrote the foreword and contributed a chapter on the early history of the institute.

Craige, Betty Jean. *Eugene Odum: Ecosystem Ecologist & Environmentalist.* Athens: University of Georgia Press, 2001. This is a useful biography that includes complete lists of Odum's publications and awards to 1999.

Golley, Frank Benjamin. *A History of the Ecosystem Concept in Ecology: More than the Sum of the Parts.* New Haven, CT: Yale University Press, 1993.

Hagen, Joel B. *An Entangled Bank: The Origins of Ecosystem Ecology.* New Brunswick, NJ: Rutgers University Press, 1992.

Joel B. Hagen

ODUM, HOWARD THOMAS (*b.* Durham, North Carolina, 1 September 1924; *d.* Gainesville, Florida, 16 September 2002), *ecology, ecosystem studies, biogeochemistry, thermodynamics, ecological engineering, ecological economics.*

More than any other scientist, Odum shaped the way ecologists think about energy. He pioneered large-scale experimental studies of energy flow in natural ecosystems. His theoretical writings, although often esoteric, strongly influenced the development of the field. Howard wrote the chapters on energy for the early editions of the highly influential textbook, *Fundamentals of Ecology,* authored by his brother Eugene. Howard's early energy-flow diagrams continue to be widely used both in textbooks of ecology and general biology. Together, the Odum brothers helped to established ecosystems as an important focus of ecology during the 1950s and 1960s. Although the concept never quite attained the centrality that they envisioned, ecosystem ecology has become a recognized and well-established field within ecology. During his long career, Howard Odum trained nearly one hundred students. His ideas continue to be developed by these scientists, who are quick to acknowledge his influence and sometimes proudly identify themselves as "Odumites."

Education and Intellectual Influences. Odum's father was the sociologist Howard W. Odum, a leading advocate of regionalism. Regionalism, as opposed to sectionalism, favored active government involvement in fostering cooperation and coordination among the various regions of the nation. The elder Odum encouraged his son to pursue a scientific career, and Odum adopted his father's holistic perspective on human societies. Throughout his career, Odum took a lively interest in topics on the interface between science and society, and he dedicated his most famous book, *Environment, Power, and Society,* to his father.

Odum was also strongly influenced by his brother Eugene, who was eleven years his senior. As a child he learned about biology, particularly bird watching, from Eugene. Following his brother's example, Howard Odum's earliest research was in ornithology, conducted while he was still an undergraduate at the University of North Carolina. This research led to two articles on bird migration and navigation published in the *Auk.* In his later studies of energy flow in ecosystems, organisms and species virtually disappeared from view. Nonetheless, Odum apparently maintained an informal interest in natural history. According to his student John Ewel, Odum was able to identify all of the songbirds of the eastern United States and every North American seashell.

Odum's undergraduate studies were interrupted for three years when he joined the Army Air Corps as a meteorologist during by World War II. His work on predicting hurricanes gained considerable recognition, and he later recalled that it stimulated his interest in studying large, complex systems. After the war, he studied under G. Evelyn Hutchinson at Yale University. During the 1940s Hutchinson was deeply involved with research on biogeochemical cycles. Together with one of his protégés, the postdoctoral fellow Raymond Lindeman, Hutchinson began discussing biogeochemical cycles and energy flow in terms of the new ecosystem concept. He also explored the field of cybernetics to discuss feedback controls in natural systems, including populations and ecosystems.

Arriving in Hutchinson's lab in 1947, five years after Lindeman published a seminal paper on energy flow and biogeochemical cycling in aquatic ecosystems, Odum began a dissertation on the biogeochemistry of strontium. Apparently neither Odum nor Hutchinson anticipated the significance that strontium would later have in the atomic age, but Odum's research was listed in *Life* magazine as one of the fifteen most noteworthy presentations at the 1950 meeting of the American Association for the Advancement of Science. Later published in *Science,* Odum's dissertation research on the strontium content in fossils supported his claim that biogeochemical cycles were maintained in a stable steady state over long periods of geological time. In Odum's view these biogeochemical cycles driven by solar energy could be described as ecosystems.

Large-Scale Experiments. After completing his PhD in 1951, Odum was appointed assistant professor in the Biology Department at the University of Florida. There he began two ambitious experimental studies to measure the overall "metabolism" of ecosystems: one in a freshwater spring in central Florida and the other on a coral reef in the Pacific. For Odum, Silver Springs provided an ideal natural laboratory for studying productivity and the movement of energy through a community of organisms. The flow rate of water from the springs, its temperature, and its chemical content remained relatively constant throughout the year. Therefore, Odum claimed that the system was in a stable state equivalent to what could be artificially produced by a chemostat in a laboratory.

By measuring dissolved oxygen and carbon dioxide upstream and downstream, Odum was able to construct an energy budget comparing photosynthetic productivity of aquatic plants and the respiration of various trophic levels of producers, consumers, and decomposers. He found that most of photosynthetic productivity was consumed by plants themselves, through their own respiration, but that about 12 percent was passed on to herbivores. At each step in the food chain similar respiratory losses were recorded. Odum's diagram of energy flow

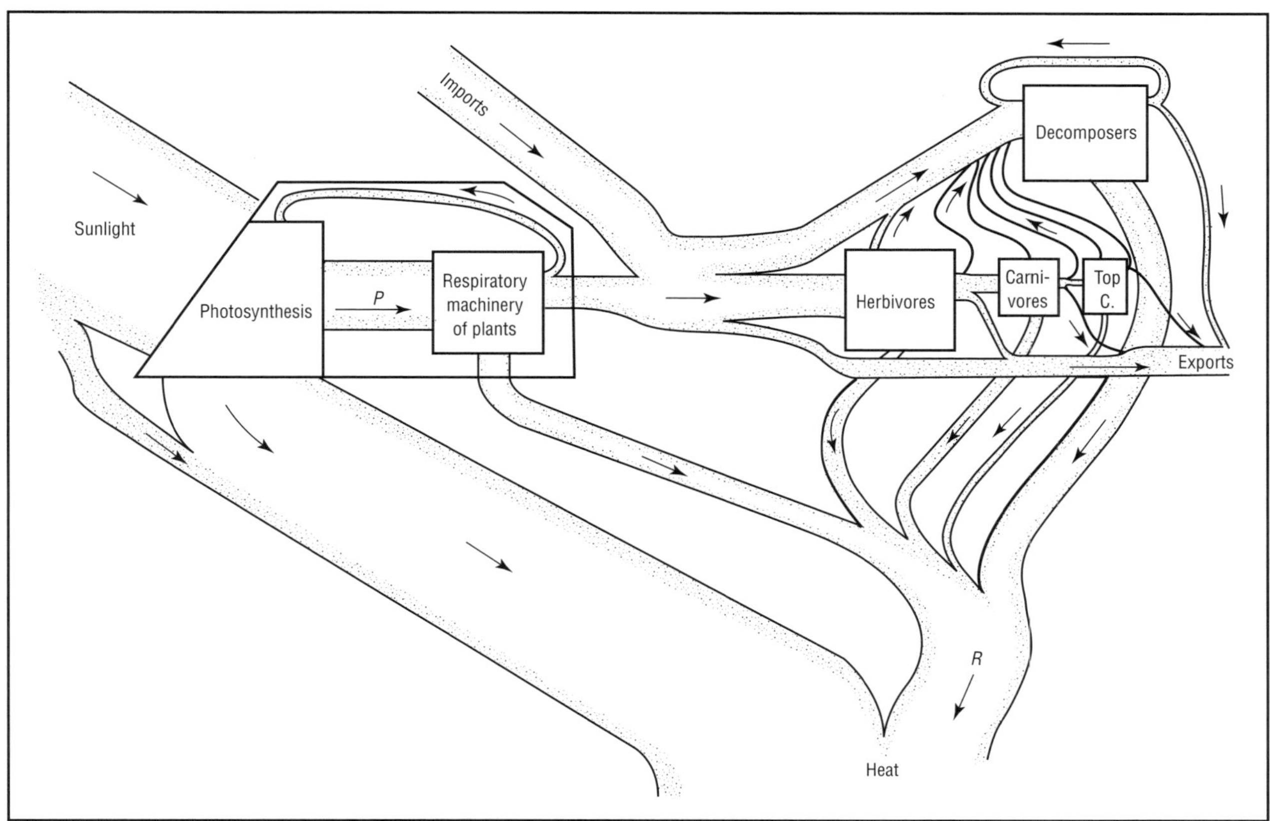

Figure 1. *Howard Odum's energy flow diagram for the Silver Springs ecosytem in Florida.*

through the aquatic system became famous and was widely reproduced in textbooks of ecology and general biology.

While he was completing the study of Silver Springs, Odum joined his brother Eugene in a similar research project supported by the Atomic Energy Commission at Enewetak Atoll. Enewetak was an important site of nuclear weapons testing, and the Odums' ecological study was part of a broader move by the commission to understand the biology, geology, and oceanography of the Marshall Islands and to investigate the effects of radiation on the environment.

During a six-week period in 1954, the Odums applied the techniques that Howard had perfected at Silver Springs to study the metabolism of coral reef community. They discovered that the water passing over the reef was nutrient poor, and did not contain enough plankton to support the coral polyps. However, the coral animals housed photosynthetic algae inside their bodies. Other biologists had claimed that the algae were parasites that weakened the coral skeleton by burrowing into it. In contrast, the Odums concluded that the algae were symbiotic partners with the coral animals forming a mutually beneficial relationship. By measuring dissolved oxygen during the day and night on either side of the reef, the Odums were able to calculate the overall "metabolism" of the complete ecosystem, balancing the photosynthetic productivity of the symbiotic algae with the respiration of the living community as a whole.

They described the reef as a highly cooperative system. The coral polyps provided protection for photosynthetic algae that lived inside the small marine animals. In exchange, the algae provided food for the coral. For the Odums, Enewetak became a paradigm case of an ancient ecosystem that had developed a high degree of stability through the obligate mutualism of its constituent populations. The study, published in *Ecological Monographs,* won the Mercer Award from the Ecological Society of America in 1956.

Throughout his career, Odum pursued daunting experimental studies that would have deterred a less imaginative ecologist. Supported by large grants from the Atomic Energy Commission, he led a team of nearly one hundred scientists in a four-year study (1963–1967) of a tropical rain forest in Puerto Rico. A circular area of the forest approximately 160 meters in diameter was irradiated with radioactive cesium for three months to study the ecological effects of radiation and the ability of the ecosystem to recover from these effects. Odum and his coworkers also constructed a huge plastic cylinder 17 meters tall and about 15 meters in diameter to measure metabolism and transpiration of a section of the forest.

Odum conceived this large-scale study on the model of a military task force, with himself as commander. Individual scientists had to agree not to publish their results before the final report appeared. *A Tropical Rain Forest* was a massive book, some 1,600 pages long and divided into 111 chapters. Although some critics complained about the book's lack of cohesiveness, the study served as the study was a precursor to later "big ecology" projects associated with the International Biological Program and Long Term Ecological Research Program.

Ecological Theory. From the beginning of his career, Odum took a serious interest in ecological theory, particularly the application of thermodynamics to ecosystem processes. As Peter Taylor noted, Odum reduced all of the complexity of ecological systems to energy relationships. Following an idea first proposed by Alfred Lotka during the 1920s, Odum and the chemist Richard Pinkerton formulated their "maximum power principle," which Odum considered to be a new law of thermodynamics. According to this principle, all natural systems sacrifice efficiency to maximize power output. Odum and Pinkerton claimed that this maximum power output occurred when the efficiency of energy production was about half of what was theoretically possible. Turning to another early suggestion by Lotka, Odum argued that natural selection favored the persistence of those biological systems that maximized power output. Thus the maximum power principle provided the basis for understanding the stable state that Odum claimed to find in mature ecosystems including Silver Springs, the coral reef at Enewetak, and the El Verde rain forest in Puerto Rico. Formulated early in his career, this idea unified all of Odum's later work.

One is easily impressed by the mechanistic perspective underlying Odum's theoretical ecology. He and Pinkerton used numerous simple mechanical models such as waterwheels and systems of weights and pulleys to illustrate the maximum power principle. These were more than simple analogies, because Odum viewed the principle as a law of thermodynamics that applied to all open systems.

Even more than mechanical models, Odum was drawn to electrical circuits. During the late 1950s he began to simulate ecosystem dynamics using simple analog computers. Trophic levels and other ecological units were simulated by electronic components such as resistors and capacitors, and energy flow by the current moving through the circuits. Later, he replaced these physical models with a more abstract set of symbols that retained the look of traditional electronic symbols, but which Odum hoped would provide a more general way of representing energy relationships. He explored this new energy circuit language, which he called "energese," in his best-known book, *Environment, Power, and Society.* The 1971 book effectively encapsulated Odum's diverse interests, and concisely presented the ideas that impressed his admirers and alarmed his critics. The circuit diagrams were an important contribution to ecosystem modeling, and some admirers later claimed that they marked the birth of a more general discipline of systems ecology. The diagrams also provided an approach to modeling human interactions with natural systems, laying the conceptual foundation for Odum's forays into ecological engineering and ecological economics.

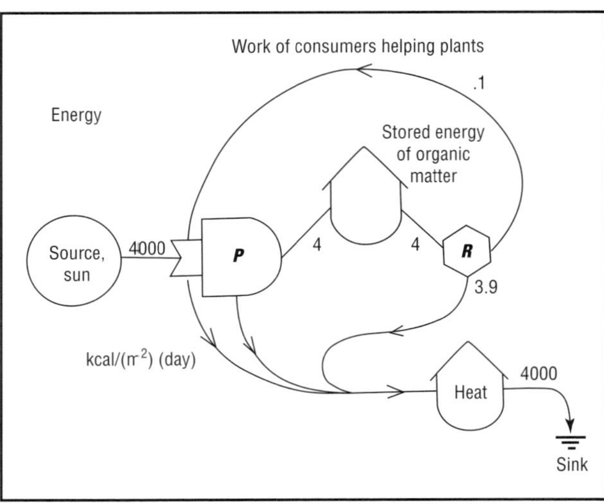

Figure 2. *A circuit diagram of the transformations and storage of energy in an ecosystem using Odum's energy network language.*

Critics decried the circuit diagrams as a misleading analogy that ran counter to well-accepted ecological theories, and perhaps violated common sense. Odum's claim that ecologists should abandon the idea of predators eating their prey and think instead of food being forced through trophic levels by a kind of "ecopotential" struck traditional ecologists as bizarre. Later chapters in Odum's book, which attempted to use energese to explain complex social activities such as politics and religion were idiosyncratic, and were ignored by ecologists.

Ecological Engineering and Ecological Economics. While he was writing *Environment, Power, and Society,* Odum was pioneering the interdisciplinary field of ecological engineering. Together with his graduate students

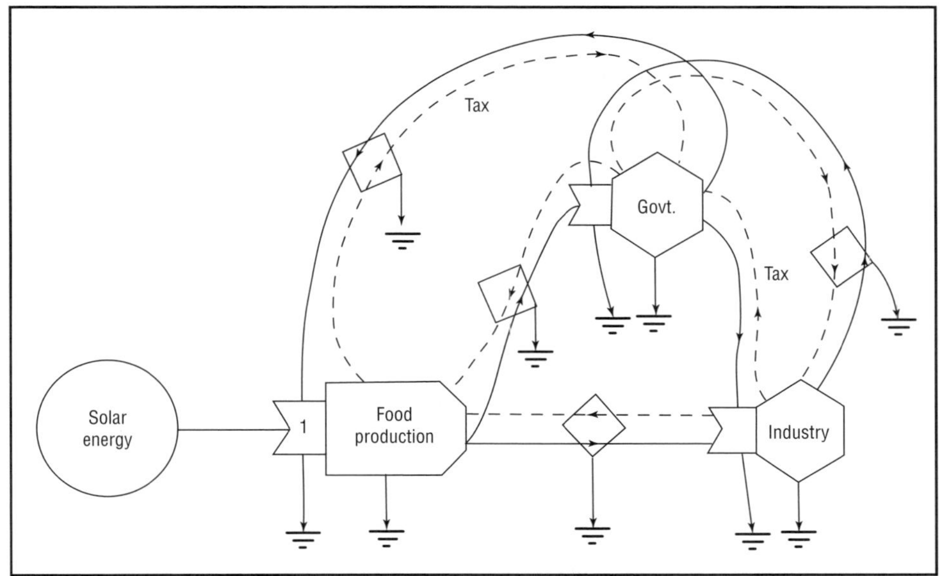

Figure 3. *An energy circuit diagram for an economic system involving three compartments: agriculture, industry, and government.*

he explored the use of wetlands as natural purification systems for human waste. He designed a number of prototypes where partially treated waste was pumped into swamps or other wetlands. These projects, involving over fifty graduate students and numerous faculty members, became a major training ground for ecological engineers. In this context, Odum's idea of a "partnership with nature" appeared to make sense.

During the final thirty years of his career, Odum focused considerable attention on developing an ecological economics. He attempted to derive a set of energy terms that could be used to discuss energy transformations in systems that were both ecological and economic. At a basic level this was a mechanism for bringing ecosystem processes that have no dollar value into economic discourse. He developed the term *emergy* (spelled with an *m*) or "embodied energy" to denote the quantity of energy of one kind required directly or indirectly to produce a service or product. At a more abstract level, his emergy analysis was a continuation of his earlier quest for a universal energy language. Although used by some other ecological economists, it is unclear whether emergy analysis will influence mainstream ecology or economics.

Honors and Awards. Howard and Eugene Odum were jointly awarded the Mercer Prize by the Ecological Society of America (1956), the Prix de l'Institute de la Vie by the French government (1975), and the Crafoord Prize from the Royal Swedish Academy of Science (1987). Howard Odum spent most of his career at the University of Florida (1950–1954, 1970–2002), but at various times also held faculty positions at the University of Texas, University of North Carolina, University of Puerto Rico, and Duke University. He published some fifteen books and three hundred articles.

BIBLIOGRAPHY

WORKS BY ODUM

"The Possible Effect of Cloud Cover on Bird Migration." *Auk* 64 (1947): 316–317.

"The Stability of the World's Strontium Cycle." *Science* 114 (1951): 407–411.

With Eugene P. Odum. "Trophic Structure and Productivity of a Windward Coral Reef at Eniwetok Atoll, Marshall Islands." *Ecological Monographs* 25 (1955): 291–320.

With Richard C. Pinkerton. "Time's Speed Regulator: The Optimum Efficiency for Maximum Power Output in Physical and Biological Systems." *American Scientist* 43 (1955): 331–343.

"Trophic Structure and Productivity of Silver Springs, Florida." *Ecological Monographs* 27 (1957): 55–122.

With Robert F. Pigeon. *A Tropical Rain Forest: A Study of Irradiation and Ecology at El Verde, Puerto Rico.* Oak Ridge, TN: Division of Technical Information, U.S. Atomic Energy Commission, 1970.

Environment, Power, and Society. New York: John Wiley, 1971.

Systems Ecology. New York: John Wiley, 1983.

Environmental Accounting: Emergy and Environmental Decision Making. New York: John Wiley, 1996.

OTHER SOURCES

Ewel, John J. "Resolution of Respect: Howard Thomas Odum (1924–2002)." *Bulletin of the Ecological Society of America* 84 (2003): 13–15.

Golley, Frank Benjamin. *A History of the Ecosystem Concept in Ecology: More than the Sum of the Parts.* New Haven, CT: Yale University Press, 1993.

Hagen, Joel B. *An Entangled Bank: The Origins of Ecosystem Ecology.* New Brunswick, NJ: Rutgers University Press, 1992.

Hall, Charles A. S., ed. *Maximum Power: The Ideas and Applications of H. T. Odum.* Niwot: University of Colorado Press, 1995. Celebrating Odum's sixty-fifth birthday, this Festschrift includes over thirty essays by former students and colleagues.

Mitsch, William J., ed. "Energy-Flow in a Pulsing System: Howard T. Odum." *Ecological Engineering* 3 (1994): 77–105. Mitsch's editorial to this special issue is accompanied by several photographs and twenty-five letters of appreciation dedicated to Odum by former students and colleagues.

Taylor, Peter J. "Technocratic Optimism: H. T. Odum and the Partial Transformation of Ecological Metaphor after World War II." *Journal of the History of Biology* 21 (1988): 213–244.

Joel B. Hagen

OESCHGER, HANS (*b.* Ottenbach, Zürich, Switzerland, 2 April 1927; *d.* Bern, 25 December 1998), *environmental physics, radioactive tracers, climate reconstruction, ice core analysis, carbon cycle modeling, rapid climate change events, earth science, climate change.*

Oeschger was a pioneer in Earth system science based on experimental physics. Working at the Physics Institute of the University of Bern (Switzerland), he developed a counter for low levels of natural radioactivity and thus enabled the use of a number of new environmental tracers. He employed polar ice from Greenland and Antarctica as an archive of information on past changes of the atmosphere's content of greenhouse gases and, with his team, developed various devices measuring their concentrations in small samples. With his colleague Willy Dansgaard, he identified in the Greenland ice cores a series of abrupt climate changes during the last ice age, which have become commonly known as Dansgaard-Oeschger events. Oeschger also developed the first model of the global carbon cycle, which he used to estimate the consequences of anthropogenic (human-produced) emissions of greenhouse gases.

Oeschger grew up in Zürich with a brother and a sister. He married Dori Häuptli in 1955. In 1957 their twin daughters were born.

Oeschger studied physics at the Swiss Federal Institute of Technology (ETH Zürich) where he obtained his diploma in 1951. His primary motivation to study physics was the hope to find "firm ground in the fundamental equations of physics" (Response of Oeschger, 14 May 1998 on the occasion of his departure from the board of ETH) to which complex processes in nature can seemingly be reduced. He then moved to the University of Bern to take up PhD work under the supervision of Friedrich Georg Houtermans, a nuclear physicist trained by James Franck in the legendary physics community at the University of Göttingen (Germany). Houtermans made fundamental contributions to the understanding of energy conversion in stars and the determination of the age of Earth, but he also inspired many young physicists during his professorship at the University of Bern: "Oeschger wanted to become a musician. However, since I [Houtermans] do physics much like an artist, he [Oeschger] now feels quite comfortable in physics" (from obituary speech by daughter Ursula Oeschger, 30 December 1998, Bern).

Experimental Physics: Basis of Environmental Science. While working toward his PhD from 1951 to 1955, Hans Oeschger's task was to set up the first radiocarbon laboratory in Switzerland. Determination of the content of radiocarbon (^{14}C) in organic material was a novel method for dating. As a physicist he was not content to simply implement established technology. Instead he set out to develop a new device with which unprecedented levels of low radioactivity could be measured for the first time. This device, described in his dissertation and now commonly referred to as the Oeschger counter, counted electrons emitted during the decay of the radioactive material. It had a lower background than any other available instrument, owing to a clever anticoincidence technique that dismissed counts that were not caused by the decaying sample. It is still used in the early twenty-first century for conventional radiocarbon dating.

This increased sensitivity was ideally suited for measuring samples with very low concentrations of ^{14}C. For example, water contains dissolved carbon originating from earlier exchange with the atmosphere and therefore also carries the carbon-14 signature of the atmosphere. Separated from contact with the atmosphere, the carbon-14 decays and so offers a means to measure the apparent age of ocean water. In 1959 Oeschger started a collaboration with Roger Revelle and Hans Suess, and spent three months at the Scripps Institution of Oceanography, La Jolla, California. He used his new counter to measure ^{14}C of waters from the deep Pacific Ocean and reported the results at the First International Oceanographic Congress held in New York in 1959. Oeschger's results provided most of the fresh data used to determine for the first time that the apparent age of deep water from the Pacific

Hans Oeschger. AP IMAGES.

Ocean was about 1,500 years. This was reported by George Bien, Norris Rakestraw, and Suess in 1960.

The Oeschger counter enabled the team at the University of Bern to enlarge significantly the palette of natural tracers whose radioisotopes could be measured. In addition to carbon-14, also hydrogen-3, argon-37, argon-39, and krypton-85 were measured with this technique: Measurements were performed in various environments such as the atmosphere, groundwater, ocean water and, eventually, ice from the polar ice sheets. Oeschger reported this important progress in environmental analytics in a series of papers with Houtermans and with his PhD student Hugo Loosli in the 1960s.

In 1963 Oeschger was promoted to associate professor at the University of Bern, and became the head of the Laboratory of Low-Level Counting and Nuclear Geophysics. He embarked on a vigorous program of developing new analytical techniques of measuring weak radioactivity in the environment. Oeschger and "The Bern Team," as he called his group, started to apply these methods to a broad range of fields such as oceanography, hydrology, limnology, and dendrochronology, as well as Quaternary geology. During this time, Oeschger realized that the collaboration of scientists across disciplinary boundaries was crucial if the processes governing the Earth system are to be quantitatively understood. In fact, he was among the first scientists of the "hard-core" physics community to address environmental problems and collaborate with chemists, biologists, geographers, and geologists, while still remaining deeply involved, and internationally respected, in disciplinary research in nuclear geophysics. Oeschger was promoted to full professor at the University of Bern in 1971, and was granted emeritus status in 1992.

Polar Ice as a Climate Archive. The tritium fallout from atmospheric nuclear testing in the early 1960s provided a test bed for the application of the new analytical techniques developed in Bern. With the ice stream of the Great Aletsch Glacier not far from Bern, tritium ($^{3}H^{1}HO$)

was first measured in the surface layers of the firn (granular snow) on Jungfraujoch in 1962. This technique was then applied to ice samples from Greenland as reported in 1963. The next goal was to date Greenland ice using radiocarbon. This marked the start of a long and fruitful collaboration with Chester C. Langway (then at Cold Regions Research and Engineering Laboratory, Hanover, New Hampshire); their report appeared in *Nature* in 1965. In spring 1964, Oeschger visited Greenland for the first time, and in summer 1967 he led a group of scientists during the Expédition Glaciologique Internationale au Groenlande (EGIG). With Danish and American colleagues they melted large quantities of ice for radiocarbon dating. Oeschger also participated in fieldwork at Byrd Station (Antarctica) in 1969.

With access to very old, pristine ice from Greenland and Antarctica, Oeschger and his team at the Physics Institute of the University of Bern continued the effort to build better analytical techniques and equipment suitable for ice samples, in particular gas measurements. The potential of this archive was recognized by P. F. Scholander and colleagues and L. K. Coachman and colleagues in 1956. One of the new analytical techniques was laser absorption spectroscopy, which permitted the determination of concentrations of substances and their isotopes in spite of very small sample sizes. This was described by Bernhard Lehmann, one of Oeschger's PhD students, in 1977. The idea is to use the fundamental physical property of a gas of absorbing photons at specific wavelengths and reemitting them with a delay in a random direction.

This quantum mechanical effect associated with the vibration and rotation of gas molecules has profound implications in Earth system science. For example, water and carbon dioxide (CO_2), and many other gases in the atmosphere, change the radiation balance and are responsible for the greenhouse effect of Earth. In the laboratory, the same effect can be utilized to measure with high precision the concentration of these gases. The absorption of a tuned laser beam shining through the air sample is proportional to the concentration of the absorbing gas. By tuning the wavelength to a value typical for an individual constituent of the gas mixture, concentrations of different gases and even different isotopes can be measured.

A special challenge was the construction of suitable extraction techniques that liberated the air from the enclosing ice matrix in samples from deep ice cores. The successful development was the result of a close collaboration with students as well as skilled technical personnel and long-term associates, and the excellent and dedicated workshop of the Physics Institute of the University of Bern.

This led to arguably the most important contribution of Oeschger and his team in climate research. In 1982 his PhD student Albrecht Neftel published evidence of a substantial reduction of atmospheric concentrations of CO_2 during the last ice age. This study demonstrated for the first time that CO_2 was an important, if not determining, factor for the Earth system to make a transition between ice ages and warm phases. Methane, the third most important greenhouse gas after water vapor and CO_2, showed an even more dramatic increase since preindustrial times and the last ice age. These results were published by Bernhard Stauffer, a former PhD student and later colleague of Hans Oeschger at the University of Bern, in *Science* (1985) and *Nature* (1988).

From Past Changes to Current Concerns. Hans Oeschger was not content with developing experimental devices for environmental measurements, but complemented these achievements with original research into the understanding of various processes in the Earth system. This required quantitative interpretation of the data, and hence models needed to be formulated. In 1975 Oeschger devised the first model of the global carbon cycle with a realistic representation of the relevant ocean processes. The model consisted of a small number of boxes representing different inventories of carbon in the atmosphere, the oceans, and various compartments of the terrestrial biosphere, Although trained as a physicist and familiar with the canonical physical approach of every issue starting from, or reducing to, the fundamental equations of physics, Oeschger realized that the complexity of the Earth system required a radically different yet complementary approach.

With this strategy in mind, he made the necessary simplifications toward one of the first models of the Earth system, which he and his PhD student Uli Siegenthaler then used to estimate the increase of atmospheric CO_2 in response to anthropogenic emissions. They reported their findings in *Science* in 1978. The model became a classic and is used, in variants, in international assessments of climate change by the Intergovernmental Panel on Climate Change. It was also this research that brought Oeschger to the conclusion that scientists, through their insights, have a wider responsibility: "The worst for me." he declared, "would be if there were serious changes in the next five to ten years and we scientists are helpless and did not have the courage to point out these dangerous developments early on" (quote from Global Alliance for Incinerator Alternatives [1995, vol. 4 (1), p. 35]), Oeschger contributed to the first assessment report of the Intergovernmental Panel of Climate Change, which appeared in 1990.

Abrupt Climate Changes: Dansgaard-Oeschger Events. Chester C. Langway (United States), Willy Dansgaard (Denmark), and Hans Oeschger initiated the trinational Greenland Ice Sheet Program (GISP) in 1971 which, after

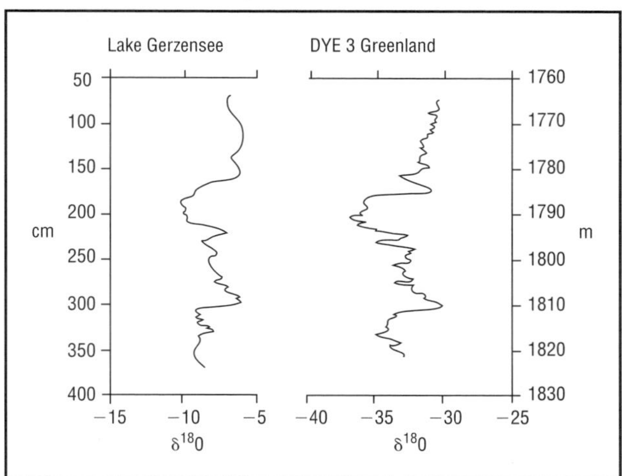

Figure 1. *Image representing the abrupt changes around 12,000 years ago measured in the isotopic composition oxygen of the water molecule in the ice drilled at Dye 3 (Greenland) and in the oxygen molecule of carbonate in lake sediments from Gerzensee (Switzerland) were juxtaposed and thus suggested, for the first time, the large-scale significance of abrupt climate changes identified in Greenland ice cores.*

drilling various shallow cores, culminated in the deep drilling at Dye 3 (65°11'& N, 43°49' W) reaching a depth of 2,037 meters. This deep ice core yielded a wealth of new information about the climate system and its variability during the last 150,000 years. Langway, Oeschger, and Dansgaard, and Oeschger and Langway coedited two books in 1985 and 1989, which strongly influenced ice core science for the coming decades.

One of the surprise findings of the GISP project was reported by Dansgaard and Oeschger in two articles in 1984. They discussed a series of abrupt shifts in the isotope records analyzed in the Greenland ice from Dye 3. Oeschger compared the last of these isotopic shifts around 10,000 BCE to a similar shift found in the carbonate isotope record of Lake Gerzensee, a small proglacial lake near Bern. He concluded correctly that the shifts found in the Greenland ice core therefore represented a much larger-scale climate signal. This early insight has been confirmed in many paleoclimatic archives since then, and these abrupt warming events—twenty-six are recorded in Greenland during the last ice age as reported by the NorthGRIP members in *Nature* in 2004—are commonly referred to as Dansgaard-Oeschger events.

The potential role of changes in ocean circulation for climate jumps was outlined mathematically by oceanographer Henry Stommel as early as 1961. Both Dansgaard and Oeschger were aware of earlier work on marine sediments by William Ruddiman (1981) that showed that the geographical occurrence of cold-loving, surface-dwelling foraminifera in the North Atlantic changed substantially and rapidly in latitude around the same time. While Dansgaard and colleagues in their 1984 article invoked an atmospheric feedback mechanism proposed by Hermann Flohn in 1982, Oeschger and colleagues suggested a complementary hypothesis in 1984, that the ocean circulation might be responsible for these large-scale and rapid climate swings. This was motivated by indications of changes in the atmospheric CO_2 concentrations that were measured on the same ice core and thought to be associated with these rapid climatic changes. They argued that the warm phases are characterized by a rapid turnover rate of the North Atlantic Ocean creating high levels of CO_2, whereas during the ice ages this turnover rate was slow and hence leading to lower concentrations of CO_2.

In a review article that appeared in 1985 Oeschger used the physical analogy of a bistable system to explain abrupt climate change: Triggered by small perturbations, the ocean circulation might switch from one circulation mode to another. Based on these insights, Oeschger was one of the first to point out that the anthropogenic increase of CO_2 could represent such a perturbation. As acknowledged by Wallace Broecker in 1997, this paved the way for more than two decades of intensive research on abrupt climate change (Alley, et al. 2002).

Carrying Global-Change Research Further. Hans Oeschger was an experimental physicist by training and therefore his primary mission was to build devices that could probe the Earth system. His challenging suggestions to students and collaborators would often be disguised in the gentle and informal Swiss-German phrase "Das sötted mir doch chöne mässe" (we ought to be able to measure this), words that on many occasions marked the beginning of a novel method to quantify environmental processes.

His scientific achievements were widely honored. He received the Harold Urey Medal (1987), the Seligman Crystal (1989), the Marcel-Benoist Prize (1991), the Tyler Prize for Environmental Achievement (1996), and the Revelle Medal of the American Geophysical Union (1997). He was a member of the Leopoldina, the Academia Europaea, and a foreign member of the U.S. National Academy of Sciences.

After his formal retirement in 1992, he became active in international research coordination and cofounded PAGES, Past Global Changes, a core project of the International Geosphere-Biosphere Programme with its project office in Bern. Oeschger's vision for this initiative was to bring together all science disciplines concerned with the study of the Earth system and its past changes. Thanks to such efforts, paleoclimatology has transformed from a descriptive field into a mature quantitative science in which changes of environmental conditions can be given

Oeschger

numbers and units. This is the basis of a scientific investigation of the full dynamics of the Earth system and its possible responses to anthropogenic disturbance. These results are of immediate value, but the approach as such may well have broader significance for society: "Real progress in this field will make it possible for society to act based on foresight. The anticipated climate change is only one of the great problems with which society is faced; the thorough way climate change is assessed by the scientific community may serve as an example for addressing other grand challenges" ("Oeschger Receives Revelle Medal," *EOS—Transactions of the American Geophysical Union,* 79 [5], 60–63).

BIBLIOGRAPHY

WORKS BY OESCHGER

"Proportionalzählrohr zur Messung schwacher Aktivitäten weicher β-Strahlung." PhD diss., University of Bern, Switzerland, 1955.

With Norris W. Rakestraw and Hans E. Suess. "Apparent Age of Deep Water in the Pacific Ocean." *International Oceanographic Congress.* New York: American Association for the Advancement of Science, 1959.

With André Renaud and E. Schumacher. "Essai de datation par le tritium des couches de névé du Jungfraufirn et détermination de l'accumulation annuelle." *Bulletin de la Société Vaudoise des Sciences Naturelles* 68 (1962): 49–56.

With André Renaud, E. Schumacher, B. Hughes, and C. Mühlemann. "Tritium Variations in Greenland Ice." *Journal of Geophysical Research* 68 (1963): 3783.

With Friedrich Georg Houtermans, S. Aegerter, and Rama. "Krypton^{81} in der Atmosphäre." *Helvetica Physica Acta* 37 (1964): 177.

With Chester C. Langway, Berhnard Alder, and André Renaud. "Sampling Polar Ice for Radiocarbon Dating." *Nature* 206 (1965): 500–501.

With Hugo H. Loosli. "Detection of ^{39}Ar in Atmospheric Argon." *Earth and Planetary Science Letters* 5 (1968): 191–198.

With Hugo H. Loosli. "^{37}Ar and ^{81}Kr in the Atmosphere." *Earth and Planetary Science Letters* 7 (1969): 67–71.

With Uli Siegenthaler, U. Schotterer, and A. Gugelmann. "A Box Diffusion Model to Study the Carbon Dioxide Exchange in Nature." *Tellus* 27 (1975): 168–192.

With B. Lehmann, M. Wahlen, and R. Zumbrunn. "Isotope Analysis by IR Laser-Absorption Spectroscopy." *Applied Physics* 13 (1977): 153–158.

With Uli Siegenthaler. "Predicting Future Atmospheric Carbon Dioxide Levels." *Science* 199 (1978): 388–395.

With A. Neftel, J. Schwander, B. Stauffer, and R. Zumbrunn. "Ice Core Sample Measurements Give Atmospheric CO_2 Content during the Past 40,000 Yr." *Nature* 295 (1982): 220–223.

With J. Beer, Uli Siegenthaler, B. Stauffer, Willy Dansgaard, and Chester C. Langway. "Late Glacial Climate History from Ice Cores." In *Climate Processes and Climate Sensitivity,* edited by J. E. Hansen and T. Takahashi. Washington, DC: American Geophysical Union, 1984.

With Willy Dansgaard, S. J. Johnsen, H. B. Clausen, D. Dahl-Jensen, N. Gundestrup, and C. U. Hammer. "North Atlantic Climatic Oscillations Revealed by Deep Greenland Ice Cores." In *Climate Processes and Climate Sensitivity,* edited by J. E. Hansen and T. Takahashi. Washington, DC: American Geophysical Union, 1984.

"The Contribution of Ice Core Studies to the Understanding of Environmental Processes." In *Greenland Ice Core: Geophysics, Geochemistry, and Environment,* edited by Chester C. Langway, Hans Oeschger, and Willy Dansgaard. Washington, DC: American Geophysical Union, 1985.

With B. Stauffer, G. Fischer, and A. Neftel. "Increase of Atmospheric Methane Recorded in Antarctic Ice Core." *Science* 229 (1985): 1386–1388.

With B. Stauffer, E. Lochbronner, and J. Schwander. "Methane Concentration in the Glacial Atmosphere Was Only Half That of the Preindustrial Holocene." *Nature* 332 (1988): 812–814.

With Chester C. Langway. *The Environmental Record in Glaciers and Ice Sheets.* Chichester, U.K.: John Wiley & Sons, 1989.

With Intergovernmental Panel on Climate Change (IPCC). *Climate Change: The IPCC Scientific Assessment.* Cambridge, U.K.: Cambridge University Press, 1990.

OTHER SOURCES

Alley, Richard B., Jochem Marotzke, William Nordhaus, et al. *Abrupt Climate Change: Inevitable Surprises.* Washington, DC: National Academy Press, 2002.

Bien, George S., Norris W. Rakestraw, and Hans E. Suess. "Radiocarbon Concentration in Pacific Ocean Water." *Tellus* 12 (1960): 436–443.

Broecker, Wallace S. "Thermohaline Circulation, the Achilles Heel of Our Climate System: Will Man-Made CO_2 Upset the Current Balance?" *Science* 278 (1997): 1582–1588.

Coachman, Lawrence K., Edvard Hemmingsen, and Per F. Scholander. "Gas Enclosures in a Temperate Glacier." *Tellus* 8 (1956): 415–423.

Flohn, Hermann. "Oceanic Upwelling as a Key for Abrupt Climatic Change." *Journal of the Meteorological Society of Japan* 60 (1982): 268–273.

Intergovernmental Panel on Climate Change (IPCC). *Climate Change 2001: The Scientific Basis: Contribution of Working Group I to the Third Assessment Report of the Intergovernmental Panel on Climate Change.* Cambridge, U.K.: Cambridge University Press, 2001.

NorthGRIP Members. "High-Resolution Climate Record of the Northern Hemisphere Back into the Last Interglacial Period." *Nature* 431 (2004): 147–151.

Ruddiman, William F., and Andrew McIntyre. "The Mode and Mechanism of the Last Deglaciation: Oceanic Evidence." *Quaternary Research* 16 (1981): 125–134.

Scholander, Per Fredrik, J. W. Kanwisher, and D. C. Nutt. "Gases in Icebergs." *Science* 123 (1956): 104–105.

Stocker, Thomas. "Hans Oeschger (1927–98)—Pioneer in Environmental Physics." *Nature 397* (1999): 396.

Stommel, Henry Nelson. "Thermohaline Convection with Two Stable Regimes of Flow." *Tellus* 13 (1961): 224–230.

Thomas Stocker

OKEN (OR OKENFUSS), LORENZ

(*b.* Bohlsbach bei Offenburg, Baden, Germany, 1 August 1779; *d.* Zürich, Switzerland, 11 August 1851), *natural science, philosophy, scientific congresses, science journals, science periodicals.* For the original article on Oken see *DSB,* vol. 10.

This postscript gives new insights into Oken's contribution to science during the first half of the nineteenth century. Historical studies since the 1970s show Oken's continued influence upon the professionalization of science through "the Gesellschaft Deutscher Naturforscher und Ärzte" up to contemporary achievements recorded by Heinrich Schipperges and Dietrich von Engelhardt (1987).

Much more research on romanticism, its relationship to naturphilosophie and science illuminates Oken's transitional role in the integration of institutional science: from Isaiah Berlin's (1999) *Roots of Romanticism* to Andrew Cunningham's and Nicholas Jardine's (1990) *Romanticism and the Sciences,* to insights by Dietrich von Engelhardt, from 1990–1999, notably in English translation "Historical Consciousness in the German Romantic Naturforschung" (1990), and Wolfgang Pross's "Lorenz Oken—Naturforschung zwischen Naturphilosophie und Naturwissenschaft" (1991).

Professional and institutional issues are addressed by Wolfgang Schirmacher (1996) and Elinor Shaffer (1990) showing that education for Oken included science, the history of science, and the professionalization of science through textbooks, notably authored by Oken's *Lehrbuch der Naturphilosophie* (1809, 1843) and *Naturgeschichte für Schüler* (1821). The role of popular science was assured by Oken's encyclopedic *Allgemeine Naturgeschichte für alle Stände* (1839–1842) and through the popular journal *Isis* (1818–1848), confirmed by Dietrich von Engelhardt's 1999 encompassing study *Medizinhistoriographie im Zeitalter der Romantic—Eine Wissenschaft Emanzipiert Sich: die Medizinhistoriographie von der Aufklärung bis zur Postmoderne.*

A study at the University of Jena under the directorship of Dr. Olaf Breidbach sheds light on Oken's political persona. The "sonderdruck" (special publication) with Hans-Joachim Fliedner chronicles Oken's political involvement during the 1817 "burschenschaften" demonstrations in *Lorenz Oken (1779–1851) ein Politischer Naturphilosoph.*

Oken and *Naturphilosophie.* Oken embraced romantic science and his worldview was shaped by German romanticism and its philosophy of nature, known as Naturphilosophie (Engelhardt, 1999). Oken studied medicine at Freiburg University and natural history at the Universities of Würzburg and Göttingen. In 1802 he conceptualized the *Abriss der Naturphilosphie* summary and published his *System der Naturphilosophie* the following year. His 1805 *Die Zeugung* (Generation) merited recognition by the followers of Naturphilosophie, and notably by Friedrich Schelling who recommended him for a professorial position at Jena.

Similar to Fichte, Oken erected a total system of nature, encompassing philosophy of nature, science, ethics, and spirit. Fichte's 1806 *Addresses to the German Nation* channeled Oken into employing old-German language in order to revitalize scientific expressions and to avoid French usage in the historical context of the Napoleonic era. Oken embraced Schelling's transcendental philosophy briefly, for example, Schelling's two seminal works: *Ersten Entwurf eines Systems der Naturphilosophie* of 1799, and *Die Weltseele* of 1799–1800, but later, during his Jena years, Oken distanced himself from metaphysical speculations. Johann Fichte's *Wissenschaftslehre* and Schelling's transcendental *Idealphilosophie,* exploring a total system of nature that extended philosophical principles into the physical sciences using mathematical elements of *mathesis* as well as empirical observations, and ordering aspects of nature as stages of a comprehensive metamorphosis. With mathesis as an integral part of Naturphilosophie Oken sought to combine reflection with experiment—through algebraic formulation—aimed at achieving a balanced relationship between knowledge and experience. The schema of Oken's system of naturphilosophie encompassed algebraic + 0—defining the equilibrium he named "metaebene" whereby a synthesis of a new intellectual category of "totalität" (totality) was achieved.

Oken structured a unique classification of animal classes into five major groups according to their sense-organs in *Grundriss der Naturphilosophie,* effectively transforming the Linnaean system. In *Die Zeugung* Oken postulated that life began on the seashore as Urschleim (primal mucous plasm) of "infusoria," cells whose agglomerations and combinations formed into organisms (Engelhardt, 1997). Published in his *Beiträge,* Oken's embryological experiments in 1806, assisted by Dietrich Georg Kieser and Karl Ernst von Baer, foreshadow Mathias Jacob Schleiden's and Theodor Schwann's cell theories.

In Oken's time the level of sophistication with respect to scientific evidence was becoming more professionalized in the context of scientific institutions such as the Gesellschaft Deutscher Naturforscher und Ärzte resulting from the criteria that they set for scientists' membership;

Oken

for example an accredited PhD for presenting their scientific papers at conferences; presenting work in specific domains of science. Oken did hundreds of experiments with chick embryos to gather information on cell theory with Karl Ernst von Baer (1792–l876), comparative embryologist and proponent of epigenetic thinking. Oken pronounced the seminal insight: "ontogeny recapitulates phylogeny." He came under the influence of Schelling at Göttingen and began distancing himself from Schelling's metaphysics of nature in his Jena years

Oken published on the significance of the intermaxillary bone (Zwischenkieferknochen) at his inaugural lecture at Jena in 1807, and in the journal *Isis* in 1817, before Goethe did in 1820. This caused antipathy as a result of priority claims by the latter (Ecker; Pfuhl; Breidbach, Fliedner, and Ries; Schwarz; Schuster).

Oken corresponded on scientific questions with a wide audience that included Louis Napoleon, Anton Mesmer, Richard Owen, and Georges Cuvier. His work was discussed by Britain's renowned morphologist Owen and by anatomists Etienne Geoffroy Saint-Hilaire and Cuvier in France. In 1818 Oken was named a member of the prestigious Deutsche Academie der Naturforscher Leopoldina, legitimating his efforts in science and education. After Oken's death, Ernst Haeckel, founder of monism, cited Oken, as did Alfred Brehm in his popular encyclopedia *Brehm's Tierleben.*

As an esteemed pedagogue, Oken authored textbooks: for example, *Lehrbuch der Naturphilosophie* (Textbook of nature philosophy) and *Naturgeschichte für Schüler* (Natural history for schoolchildren). He became a household name through the encyclopedic *Allgemeine Naturgeschichte für alle Stände* (General natural history for all social classes), focusing education through science. Upon the invitation of Wilhelm von Humboldt, Prussian minister of education, Oken contributed *Über den Wert der Naturgeschichte besonders für die Bildung der Deutschen* (On the value of natural philosophy especially for the education of Germans) on the philosophy of education for the 1810 inaugural of the University of Berlin (Schirmacher). (Oken submitted the paper in 1809 to Wilhelm von Humboldt, upon invitation by Humboldt, the minister of education, intended for the opening of the University of Berlin. Oken did not deliver it in person).

Oken and the Organization of German Science. Oken was a catalyst to the institutionalization and professionalization of German science, acting as agent and mediator in the first half of the nineteenth century. The perpetuation of the Gesellschaft deutscher Naturforscher und Ärzte to this day is testimony of the continued contribution to science that Oken had initiated.

Lorenz Oken. *Lorenz Oken, circa 1815.* HULTON ARCHIVE/GETTY IMAGES.

After the Napoleonic era, the economist Friedrich List signified the unification of fragmented Germany and Europe through a *Zollverein,* a tariff union, while Oken embodied the unification process through science with the "Republic of Intellectuals" (Breidbach, Fliedner, and Ries). As part of the 1817 *Burschenschaften* liberal movement, during the Wartburg festival, Oken led students from Jena University with rallies and speeches. Oken's political activity pitted him against the conservative forces of Goethe and Metternich. Under pressure from Goethe and Saxe-Weimar authorities, Oken chose to continue as publisher and editor of *Isis* when forced to choose between his professorship at Jena and the production of *Isis.* Oken gave up his university career at Jena, dedicating his efforts to the proliferation of science, although the political climate resulted in the 1819 Carlsbad decrees. This decisive event spurred Oken's intensive scientific activities on two different fronts—*Isis* and the Gesellschaft.

A fusion of culture and institution occurred at two levels through Oken's leadership: through *Isis* and through the Gesellschaft. *Isis* was founded in response to the need for a scientific forum to exchange ideas and publish research and discoveries. *Isis* functioned as cultural prism in the context of its time: Advertisements in *Isis* enabled a flourishing trade exchange across international borders.

Oken's aim was to internationalize science through scientific collaboration and exchange.

He contributed to science by increasing the international exchange of information, firstly through *Isis* but foremost through the Gesellschaft's annual conferences as scientists collaborated on scientific projects. *Isis* targeted scientists, students of science, and the general public interested in scientific inventions and new discoveries. The journal included, in addition to scientific information, advertisements; for example, specimens for collection or exchange and announcements concerning special science events, such as the "gesellschaft" conferences. The Gesellschaft Deutscher Naturforscher und Ärzte (GDNÄ) was a scientific society whose originality consisted in staging annual conferences at a different university each year, traveling to German cities as well as to Austria, Chekoslovakia, and Italy. In the 1820s Oken inaugurated the Gesellschaft members' choirs, the "Liedertafel," as a means of socializing at conference banquets; drawing upon the German choral society tradition, such male camaraderie fostered collaboration and unified identity as scientists (Jackson).

As an example of professionalization in science instituted by Oken, for inclusion as member to the GDNÄ certain criteria were stipulated. The member held a doctoral degree from an accredited university, attended annual conferences, presented papers of discoveries, inventions, or "new" science, and became affiliated to specific "sektionen" (a branch of science; e.g., botany, physiology, morphology, embryology, and the like). From 1828 onwards, the GDNÄ had a constitution that was reviewed every five years. Every year it appointed a director of the annual conference and a geschäftsführer (manager of operations) to oversee and manage the conference. Minutes and proceedings of conferences were recorded, read and published. The editorial policy of the journal, as stipulated by Oken, solicited articles of a scientific nature and invited members of the GDNÄ to submit articles for publication. It allowed critiques of articles only if a person who submitted a critique had first submitted an article for publication and had been accepted.

Isis would publish announcements of a professional or science nature but would not advertise venues of a material or frivolous nature; it would not print material of a political nature, nor of a religious nature. *Isis* published the proceedings of the GDNÄ and announced its forthcoming conferences. Oken involved himself with the promotion of the education of science at the high school level, at the technical institutes, and at the universities. His publications of 1809 (3rd ed., 1843) *Lehrbuch der Naturphilosophie*; *Isis* (1817–1848); 1821 (*Naturgeschichte für Schüler*) and 1839–1842 (*Allgemeine Naturgeschichte für alle Stände,* 13 volumes) attest to his life's effort on behalf of science and history education. *Isis* was read by the professional as well as the general public, and his *Lehrbuch* became a reference book for all audiences. Through these efforts Oken promoted understanding and appreciation of science among the broader public while professionalizing science among members of the GDNÄ whose mandate was to promote science at a different university each year.

Oken was a seminal agent in intellectual, scientific, institutional and political endeavors towards the professionalization of science during his lifetime and beyond, contributing to its transformation in Germany and throughout Europe. The Gesellschaft conferences popularized science through members' monthly *Isis* publications of developments, discoveries, and inventions. Similar societies were founded in England, France, Scandinavia, and Italy (Ecker), drawing on the "Okenian" Gesellschaft. The tandem development—*Isis* and the Gesellschaft—professionalized science while at the same time securing its intellectual capital for German and European science in specialized branches (Sektionen der Wissenschaft)—as decreed by the 1828 Gesellschaft conference held in Berlin, under Oken and Alexander von Humboldt, at which hundreds of scientists participated. Notably, the branches of biology, embryology, morphology, physiology, anatomy, and applied medicine were defined by Oken as fields. He taught, researched and published in these areas.

Oken's later professional career, from 1833 until his death in 1851, reestablished his status as a professor of medicine and the rector of the University of Zürich. In 1818 Oken was given the prestigious title "member of the Deutsche Academie der Naturforscher Leopoldina" based on his achievements as editor and publisher of *Isis* and for his numerous scientific publications. He gained considerable status as founder of the Gesellschaft Deutscher Naturforscher und Ärzte in 1822, which became a model for other similar scientific societies. However, the Revolution of 1848 in its sweep across Europe effectively hindered the continuation of *Isis*.

Little is known about Oken's personal life. He married the daughter of Professor John Stark (1753–1811) in 1814 at Jena. They had a son, who died as a result of a duel, and a daughter.

SUPPLEMENTARY BIBLIOGRAPHY

At Göttingen University there is a full archival collection of Isis *(1817–1848). Freiburg University holds an archival collection, being cataloged as of 2007, of Oken's notes, drawings, and sketches, and collected material from his years at Würzburg as well as his period at Freiburg. Under the direction of Olaf Breidbach, Hena University was as of 2007 cataloging material from Oken's Jena University professorship years (1807–1819).*

WORKS BY OKEN

Abriss der Naturphilosphie [Summary of nature philosophy]. Göttingen: Vandenhoek und Ruprecht, 1802.

Die Zeugung. Bamberg, Germany: Göbhardt, 1805.

With Dietrich Georg Kieser. *Beiträge zur vergleichenden Zoologie, Anatomie und Physiologie* [Contributions to comparative zoology, anatomy, and physiology]. 2 vols. Bamberg, Germany: Göbhardt, 1806–1807.

Lehrbuch der Naturphilosophie. 3rd ed. Jena: Frommann, 1809. Zürich: Verlag von Friedrich Schulthess, 1843. Reprinted: Hildesheim, Germany: Georg Olms Verlag, 1991.

Isis von Oken. Periodical. Leipzig: Brockhaus, 1817–1848. Volume 1 includes an account of the Wartburg Festival

Okens Naturgeschichte für Schulen. Leipzig: Brockhaus, 1821.

Allgemeine Naturgeschichte für alle Stände. 13 vols. Stuttgart: Hoffman, 1839–1842.

Isis. Göttingen, 1817–1848.

Über den Wert der Naturgeschichte besonders für die Bildung der Deutschen. Jena: F. Frommann, 1809. Translated as "On the Utility of Natural History" in Schirmacher, 1996.

OTHER SOURCES

Brandt Butscher, Heiderose. "Lorenz Oken and Nineteenth-Century German Romantic Science—Transformation from 'Naturphilosoph' to Professional Scientist through the Institutionalization of Science." PhD diss., York University, Toronto, 2001.

Berlin, Isaiah. *The Roots of Romanticism,* Edited by Henry Hardy. The A. W. Mellon Lectures in the Fine Arts. Princeton, NJ: Princeton University Press, 1999.

Bräuning-Oktavio, Hermann. *Oken und Goethe im Lichte neuer Quellen.* Weimar: Arion, 1959.

Breidbach, Olaf, Hans-Joachim Fliedner, and Klaus Ries, eds. *Lorenz Oken (1779–1851): Ein politischer Naturphilosoph.* Sonderdruck Weimar: Verlag Hermann Böhlaus Nachfolger, 2001

Brehm, Edmund Alfred. *Brehms's Tierleben, Volksausgabe in Einem Band.* [1876] Re-edited in one tome by Wilhelm Bardorff. Berlin: Safari Verlag, 1951.

Cunningham, Andrew, and Nicholas Jardine, eds. *Romanticism and the Sciences.* Cambridge, U.K.: Cambridge University Press, 1990.

Deeg, Karl. "Der letzte Nachfahre des Naturphilosophen Lorenz Oken." *Traunscheiner Wochenblatt,* 10 February 1958. Memorial.

Ecker, Alexander. *Lorenz Oken.* Stuttgart: E. Schweizerbart, 1880. Translated into English by A. Tulk. London: Kegan Paul, Trench & Co., 1883.

Engelhardt, Dietrich von. "Historical Consciousness in the German Romantic 'Naturforschung.'" Translated by Christine Salazar in Cunningham and Jardine, 1990.

———. "Vitalism between Science and Philosophy in Germany around 1800." In *Vitalism from Haller to the Cell Theory,* edited by Guido Cimino and François Duchesneau. Florence: Leo S. Olschki Editore, 1997.

———. "Medizinhistoriographie im Zeitalter der Romantic." In *Eine Wissenschaft emanzipiert sich: Die Medizinhistoriographie von der Aufklärung bis zur Postmoderne,* edited by Ralf Broer. Pfaffenweiler, Germany: Centaurus, 1999.

———. "Die Geschichte der GDNÄ." Available from http://www.gdnae.de/werist/geschi.html.

Fischer, Eugen. "Lorenz Oken, der geniale Naturphilosoph, Streiter für Deutschland." *Mein Heimatland* Sonderdruck 3 (1942).

Fischer, Hans. "Lorenz Oken in Zürich." *Schweizerische Hochschulzeitung* 5 (1956).

Gode-von Aesch, Alexander. *Natural Science in German Romanticism.* New York: AMS Press, 1966.

Heuss, Theodor. Inaugural. Conference Gesellschaft deutscher Naturforscher und Ärzte. University of Freiburg, 1950.

Jackson, Myles W. "Harmonious Investigators of Nature: Music and the Persona of the German Naturforscher in the Nineteenth Century." *Science in Context* (March 2003): 121–145.

Jacyna, L. S. "Romantic Thought and the Origins of Cell Theory." In *Romanticism and the Sciences,* edited by Andrew Cunningham, and Nicholas Jardine. Cambridge, U.K.: Cambridge University Press, 1990.

Kertesz, G. A. "Notes on *Isis* von Oken, 1817–1848." *Isis* 77 (1986): 497–503.

Kuhn-Schnyder, Emil. "Lorenz Oken, 1779–1851—Erster Rektor der Universität Zürich." Zürich: Verlag Hans Rohr, 1980. Lecture celebrating the two-hundredth anniversary of his birth.

Mischer, Sibille. *Der Verschlungene Zug der Seele—Organismus und Entwicklung bei Schelling, Steffens und Oken.* Würzburg: Verlag Königshausen & Neumann, 1997.

Pfannenstiel, Max, and Rudolph Zaunick. *Lorenz Oken und J. W. von Goethe: Dargestellt auf Grund neu erschlossener Quellenzeugnisse.* Leipzig: Johann Ambrosius Barth Verlag, 1941.

Pfannenstiel, Max. "Die Wirbelmetamorphose Okens an Hand Neuer Dokumente." *Berichte der Naturforschenden Gesellschaft Zu Freiburg I. Br.,* 41 (1951): 75–100. Cited by Hermann Bräuning-Oktavio (1959), above.

———. "Oken in Göttingen." *Berichte der Naturforschenden Gesellschaft zu Freiburg i. Br.* (1958).

———. *Kleines Quellenbuch zur Geschichte der Gesellschaft Deutscher Naturforscher und Ärzte: Gedächtnisschrift für die hundertste Tagung der Gesellschaft im Auftrage des Vorstandes der Gesellschaft verfasst.* Berlin: Springer-Verlag, 1958.

Pfuhl, W. "Goethe und die Wirbelstheorie des Schädels." *Medizinische Monatsschrift für allgemeine Medizin und Therapie Wissenschaft* 8: (1949).

Pross, Wolfgang. "Lorenz Oken—Naturforschung zwischen Naturphilosophie und Naturwissenschaft." In Saul, 1991.

Saul, Nicholas, ed. *Die deutsche literarische Romantik und die Wissenschaften.* Publications of the University of London, Institute of Germanic Studies, vol. 47. Munich: Iudicium-Verlag, 1991.

Schipperges, Heinrich, and Dietrich von Engelhardt. *Gesellschaft deutscher Naturforscher und Ärzte—Wissenschaftsgeschichte auf den Versammlungen 1822–1976.* Bibliographie der Vorträge und allgemeine Übersicht. Stuttgart: Wissenschaftliche Verlagsgesellschaft, 1987.

Schirmacher, Wolfgang, ed. *German Essays on Science in the Nineteenth Century.* The German Library, vol. 36. New York: Continuum, 1996.

Schwarz, Walter. "Die Wirbel- und Metamerentheorie des Schädels," Part 2, "Zusammensetzung und Abteilung des Schädels der Wirbeltiere nach den Anschauungen Okens, Goethes und Gegenbaurs." D. Phil. Diss. University of Königsberg, Germany, 1919. Med. Diss. Published Königsberg: Buchdruckerei Otto Kümmel, 1919.

Schuster, Julius. *Oken: Der Mann und sein Werk.* Berlin: W. Junk, 1922. Lecture at the hundredth anniversary meeting of the Gesellschaft Naturforscher und Ärzte in Leipzig.

Shaffer, Elinor S. "Romantic Philosophy and the Organization of the Disciplines: The Founding of the Humboldt University of Berlin." In Cunningham and Jardine, 1990.

Sudhoff, Karl. *Hundert Jahre Deutscher Naturforscher-Versammlungen.* Leipzig, F. C. W. Vogel, 1922. Published by the association for its hundredth annual meeting. Sudhoff was the archivist of the Gesellschaft at that time.

Heiderose Brandt Butscher

OLEINIK, OLGA ARSENIEVNA

(*b.* Kiev, Ukraine, USSR, 2 July 1925; *d.* Moscow, Russia, 13 October 2001), *mathematics, differential equations.*

Oleinik was one of the few outstanding women mathematicians of the twentieth century. The general theory of partial differential equations, which describe the behavior of fluids, gases, elasticity, electromagnetism, and quantum physics, was developed during the last century, and Olga Oleinik was one of the major figures in that process. Her work began principally with elliptic equations (such as the wave equation $u_{xx} + u_{yy} = 0$), but her major contributions were to singular elliptic and parabolic equations and to nonlinear hyperbolic equations (such as $u_{tt} - u_{xx} = 0$).

Life. Oleinik was born in Kiev in Ukraine. Her parents, Arseniev Ivanovic and Anna Petrovna Oleinik, lived in Matusov, a small town near Kiev, where her father was employed in a factory as a bookkeeper. Her life was uneventful until 1941, when Germany invaded the USSR in a lightning campaign. The factory was quickly moved by rail to Perm, Russia, just west of the Urals, and Olga's father was moved with it. The family decided that Olga should accompany him and that the rest of the family would remain in Ukraine (Olga's sister had a small infant). Olga never returned to live in Ukraine.

After completing high school in 1942, Olga attended the local university. Some of the mathematical faculty from the University of Moscow had been evacuated to Perm because of the war, and when they returned to Moscow in 1943 they arranged for Oleinik to become a student at Moscow University. There she studied with and became a lifelong friend of the mathematician Ivan Petrovsky. She attended I. Gelfand's seminar with Olga Ladyzhenskaya and Mark Visik.

In 1947 she obtained her undergraduate degree and in 1954 her doctorate, both under the direction of Petrovsky. Her first thesis was on the topology of real algebraic curves on an algebraic surface; the second thesis was on partial differential equations, a field she stayed with, almost exclusively, for the rest of her life.

She remained at Moscow State University and on Petrovsky's death she succeeded him to become the chair of differential equations, a post she held throughout her life. She was an early visitor to the United States, first in the early 1960s as a delegate to a women's congress. As soon as the Soviet regime softened its restrictions, she worked indefatigably to make Western mathematical literature available to Soviet mathematicians.

Oleinik was married to Lev Alekseevich Chudov during the early 1950s and had a son. Unfortunately the son was mentally disabled, and Oleinik's concern for him and efforts on his behalf took a considerable toll on her professional and emotional life. Oleinik died in Moscow on 13 October 2001, after a long struggle against cancer.

Mathematical Work. In early work, Oleinik considered several types of elliptic equations that had singular coefficients on the boundary, which made them lose their ellipticity. A simple example of such an equation is $(l\text{-}r^2)^{x\ uxx} + u_{yy} = 0$ where $r^2 = x^2 + y^2$ and $a > 0$. Her results, inspired by the work of the Italian mathematician Gaetano Fichera, are still the authority on the subject.

In her 1957 paper "Discontinuous Solutions of Non-Linear Differential Equations," Oleinik introduced a new entropy condition, which is important for deciding which type of shocks could take place in filtration processes. It has become fundamental in the understanding of secondary oil recovery.

In the 1980s she found a greatly simplified proof of Korn's inequality, which is fundamental in studying the equations of elasticity, and applied this result to gain new insight into the so-called St. Venant's principle. Oleinik was one of the founders of homogenization theory for partial differential equations, which shows how to find "average" equations for a highly oscillatory system.

In a series of papers culminating in the text "Matmaticheskie metody v teoil pogranichnogo sloya" (Mathematical methods in boundary-layer theory), Oleinik proved an existence theorem for Ludwig Prandtl's boundary layer equations. This was the basic theory in aero- and hydrodynamics, and the equations were widely used but lacked a strong mathematical framework. There had even been some question about whether there were any valid solutions. Her work also illuminated how the separation of the boundary layer of the fluid from the rigid boundary takes place.

Legacy and Honors. Oleinik published more than three hundred articles and wrote eight books, one of them while recuperating from major knee surgery. She made many mathematical tours in Europe and in the United States. In 1996 she gave the Noether Lecture of the Association for Women in Mathematics at the annual meeting of the American Mathematical Society. She made extensive visits to the University of Rome and to the University of Heidelberg among many other places.

Among the many honors Oleinik received were the Lomonosov Prize in 1964, the medal of the Collège de France, and the first degree medal of Charles University in Prague. In 1995 she was awarded the Order of Honor of the Russian Federation. She was a member of the Soviet Academy of Sciences, a foreign member of the Accademia Nazionale dei Lincei in Rome, and was made doctor honoris causa of the University of Rome in 1984.

Oleinik had a great many students. Among them are N. D. Vvedenskaya, T. D. Wentzel, J. V. Egorov, G. A. Yosifian, S. Kamin, S. N. Kruzhkov, V. Petkov, E. V. Radkevich, G. A. Chechkin, Zhou Yulin, and T. A. Shaposhnikova. Most of them pursued academic and research careers.

BIBLIOGRAPHY

WORKS BY OLEINIK

"On Equations of Elliptic Type Degenerating on the Boundary of a Region" [in Russian]. *Doklady Akademii Nauk SSSR*, n.s., 87 (1952): 885–888.

"Discontinuous Solutions of Non-Linear Differential Equations" [in Russian]. *Uspehi Mat. Nauk*, n.s., 12, no. 3 (1957): 3–73.

With V. A. Kondratiev. "Hardy's and Korn's Type Inequalities and Their Applications." *Rendiconti di Matematica e delle sue Applicazioni*, ser. 7, 10, no. 3 (1990): 641–666.

With V. V. Jikov and S. M. Kozlov. *Homogenization of Differential Operators and Integral Functionals*. Translated by G. A. Yosifian. Berlin: Springer-Verlag, 1994.

With V. N. Samokhin. "Matmaticheskie metody v teoil pogranichnogo sloya" [Mathematical methods in boundary-layer theory]. Moscow: Fizmaslit "Nauka," 1997.

OTHER WORKS

Arnold, V. I., M. I. Vishik, A. S. Kalashnikov, V. P. Maslov, S. M. Nikolskii, and S. P. Novikov. "Olga Arsenievna Oleinik (on her 70th birthday)." *Trudy Seminare imeni I. G. Petrovskogo*, no. 19. Translated in *Journal of Mathematical Sciences* 85, no. 6 (1997): 2249–2259. A short biography of Oleinik and a complete bibliography of her writings from 1986 to 1997.

Jäger, Willi, Peter Lax, and Cathleen Synge Morawetz. "Olga Arsen'evna Oleinik." *Notices of the American Mathematical Society* 50, no. 2 (2002): 220–223.

"Olga Arsenievna Oleinik (On the Occasion of Her Sixtieth Birthday)" [in Russian]. *Trudy Seminare imeni I. G. Petrovskogo* 12 (1987): 3–21. For earlier publications.

Vestnik Moskovskogo Universiteta, Matematika, Mekhanika [Moscow University mathematics and mechanics bulletin] 4 (1975): 122–124 and (1985): 98–102. For earlier publications.

Cathleen Synge Morawetz

OLSON, MANCUR, JR. (*b.* Grand Forks, North Dakota, 22 January 1932; *d.* College Park, Maryland, 19 February 1998), *economics*.

Olson worked across disciplines and was at the center of an interdisciplinary group of scholars who shared many of his views and theoretical stances. In particular they started from the assumption that people are basically rational in their actions, and that this fact allows economists to simplify their explanations of social behavior and to construct broadly applicable theories. Olson was a founding presence in the Public Choice Society, which is one of the most broadly interdisciplinary among such societies.

Raised in North Dakota in an immigrant farming family from Norway, Olson received his B.A. from North Dakota State University in 1954, was a Rhodes Scholar at Oxford from 1954-1956, and earned his PhD from Harvard in 1963. He spent most of his professional life at the University of Maryland, College Park.

In his most influential work, *The Logic of Collective Action* (1965), Olson argued from Paul Samuelson's elegant theory of public goods and their odd pricing problem: The cost of an additional consumer of a public good is zero, therefore the optimal price of it is zero. Samuelson argued that therefore such goods should be provided by the state, although exclusion mechanisms could elicit payment from consumers. In the book, Olson considers public goods that are privately provided through voluntary payments toward their production. His conclusion, of course, is that there will commonly be no provision of such public goods. Everyone will try to freeride and therefore there will be no provision on which to ride. This is the logic of collective action: Anyone's contribution to the provision of a public or collective good will yield vanishingly small benefit to the contributor, typically much smaller than the cost

Olson

of the contribution. No one therefore has any incentive to contribute and the good will not be provided.

Olson's book and its central argument are a striking example of an idea that has often been grasped in specific contexts, but that had not been generalized in a compelling way to make its centrality and importance clear. Many people—going back to Plato and including the philosopher John Stuart Mill, the American labor leader Samuel Gompers, and novelist Joseph Heller—have seen the logic in a specific context, such as theories of social order, union organizing as seen by a theorist and a practitioner, and heroic participation in battle as seen by a novelist. Economists referred to the logic as the "freerider problem," but generally did not go on to elaborate its extremely broad application and importance. Olson's impact in political science was massive. He essentially put an end to traditional group theory, in which it is commonly supposed that the political influence of a group is virtually a linear function of the number of people or voters in the group. In essence, the traditional view is a fallacy of composition: This theory falsely supposed that if people share an interest they will jointly act for it.

This vision of the power of groups reigned from Arthur Bentley to David Bicknell Truman. Many scholars, such as Elmer Eric Schattschneider, argued against the standard view by showing that it did not apply in important cases—the common tack of social scientists who do not have a general theory. Olson provided a general theory and laid the argument of linear power to rest. It remains true that in electoral processes numbers count, but Olson's logic suggests that the organization of voters actually to cast ballots and to vote intelligently remains a problem for the linearity thesis even in elections.

Olson moved fully into political economy in *The Rise and Decline of Nations: Economic Growth, Stagflation, and Social Rigidities* (1982), in which he advanced explanations of political obstacles to economic development, obstacles that can be seen from the perspective of his earlier arguments on collective action. His provocative conclusion is that war, as in World War II, can destroy groups that pose barriers to good economic policies, and can therefore make subsequent development easier and quicker. Olson argued that it can be better to lose a war than to win it, because the winners, such as the United Kingdom, face peace with political barriers to economic development.

Olson's third major project, *Power and Prosperity: Outgrowing Communist and Capitalist Dictatorships* (2000), is the study of the rise of particular kinds of political regimes, and especially of authoritarian regimes that commonly seize power and then attempt to use it to carry out specific programs or merely to enrich the authoritarian leaders. As many traditional political philosophers do, Olson started from an assumption of anarchic organization of a society and then attempted to explain the slow rise of an order that is hierarchical. In both cases he saw potential leaders as bandits. To simplify, he supposed that first there are roving bandits who merely enrich themselves through plunder, killing the golden goose and moving on. Then there are stationary bandits, who are the core of an incipient state. The latter see that there are far greater gains to be made from organizing the society into a productive order that benefits citizens as well as the leaders. There is mutual advantage in stable organization.

This is perhaps strangely similar to the central move of John Rawls's theory of justice (1971). Rawls supposed that a regime of strict equality would suppress incentives to be productive and would therefore not benefit even the worst-off members of the society. The poor could prosper better if many others were unequally rewarded, to induce greater productivity that could be shared with the poorest. Olson recognized that a stable regime that lets producers benefit directly from their own productivity will produce great surpluses that the bandit regime can partially tax away to benefit themselves or their programmatic aims.

Much of the importance of Olson's work is that it crosses disciplinary boundaries. This had a professional cost for Olson because his reputation was split across these disciplines, from economics to political science, sociology, and even history, philosophy, and psychology. In the restrictive academic environment, which encourages division into somewhat narrow disciplines, an Olson seems less central than he actually was. He helped to bring these disciplines together, but, sadly, any great success in meeting this challenge lies still in the future.

Olson was a wonderfully witty person whose presentations at conferences and in the classroom elicited laughter and provided great enjoyment. He was generous to his intellectual challengers and he carefully addressed their arguments, often taking them apart with clever examples and arguments that persuaded. At times, he was the consummate performer, with a great range of physical and facial gestures that enlivened his talk. He died too young of a sudden heart attack after what participants have described as a typical lunch conversation that ranged widely over many issues. His marriage to Alison O. Olson produced a daughter and two sons.

BIBLIOGRAPHY

WORKS BY OLSON

The Logic of Collective Action. Cambridge, MA: Harvard University Press, 1965.

The Rise and Decline of Nations: Economic Growth, Stagflation, and Social Rigidities. New Haven, CT: Yale University Press, 1982.

Power and Prosperity: Outgrowing Communist and Capitalist Dictatorships. Oxford, U.K.: Oxford University Press, 2000.

OTHER SOURCES

Bentley, Arthur F. *The Process of Government.* Chicago: University of Chicago Press, 1908.

Gompers, Samuel. "Discussion at Rochester, N.Y., on the Open Shop—'The Union Shop Is Right'—It Naturally Follows Organization." *American Federationist* 12 (4, 1905): 221–223.

Mill, John Stuart. *Principles of Political Economy.* In *John Stuart Mill: A Selection of His Works,* 7th edition, Vol. 2 and 3, edited by John M. Robson. Toronto: University of Toronto Press, 1966.

Rawls, John. *A Theory of Justice.* Cambridge, MA: Harvard University Press, 1971.

Samuelson, Paul A. "The Pure Theory of Public Expenditure." *Review of Economics and Statistics* 36, no. 4 (1954): 387–389.

Schattschneider, E. E. *The Semi-Sovereign People.* New York: Holt, Rinehart, and Winston, 1960.

Truman, David B. *The Governmental Process: Political Interests and Public Opinion,* 2nd ed. New York: Knopf, 1971.

Russell Hardin

OLYMPIODORUS OF ALEXANDRIA

(*b.* Alexandria, Egypt, *ca.* 495-505; *d.* after 565), *natural philosophy, astrology, alchemy.* For the original article on Olympiodorus of Alexandria see *DSB,* vol. 10.

The conflation of two Olympiodoruses to which the original *DSB* article subscribed stems from a treatise, variously titled "The Alexandrian Philosopher Olympiodorus on the Book *Kat'energeian* (*On the action* or *According to the action)* by Zosimus and on the Sayings of Hermes and the Philosophers" and "The Philosopher Olympiodorus to Petasius, King of Armenia, on the Divine and Sacred Art of the Philosophical Stone." The question of the historical identification of this alchemist named Olympiodorus has been discussed at great length. At first, he was identified with Olympiodorus the historian of Thebes, an opinion shared by a large number of specialists including Marcelin Berthelot. Paul Tannery introduced a series of objections to this identification, and he concluded that the person in question was, on the contrary, Olympiodorus the Neoplatonic commentator of Aristotle.

Life and Works. Neoplatonic philosopher and a student of Ammonius, Olympiodorus taught Platonic and Aristotelian philosophy in Alexandria during the second half of the sixth century. A pagan and a defender of Hellenism, he had as successors Christians such as David (Elias) and Stephanus. Three of his Platonic commentaries are still extant—on the *Alcibiades I,* on the *Gorgias,* and on the *Phaedo*—and two commentaries on Aristotle, the first on the *Categories* (which contains the usual *Prolegomena* to the philosophy of Aristotle) and the other on the *Meteorology* as well as some fragments on the *De interpretatione.* The only one of his works that can be dated with certainty is the commentary to the *Meteorology,* because Olympiodorus mentions in it (52, 31) a comet that supposedly appeared in 565. To Olympiodorus has also been attributed (and probably rightly so) an anonymous commentary on the astrological work (*Eisagôgica*) of Paul of Alexandria, though others have identified the presumed author as Heliodorus.

For a long time, specialists considered Olympiodorus's exegetical activity to lack originality and to be empty of philosophic content. However, he aroused interest from methodological and historical points of view. Indeed, the form of his commentaries, structured according to a certain number of lessons (*praxeis*), with each one containing a general explanation (*theôria*) and the particular explanation of a section of text (generally designated by *lexis*), was considered to be his only truly original contribution to Neoplatonic exegesis. In other respects, Olympiodorus's work is a rich source of information on the cultural conditions and the educational methods of sixth-century Alexandria. It has only been very recently, in the wake of a revival of interest in this author and his commentaries, that he is beginning to be rehabilitated as a thinker or, at least, as an interpreter of Plato and of Aristotle.

In conformity with the tradition of the Alexandrian school, Olympiodorus was interested in Aristotle's logic and in his natural philosophy. His commentary on the *Meteorology* in particular is a work of extreme interest for the history of science. Olympiodorus completed and fixed the Aristotelian classifications of meteorological and chemical phenomena, thus carrying out an immense work of systematizing notions that were sometimes barely sketched out by Aristotle, such as that of the "chemical analysis" (*diagnôsis*) of homogeneous bodies in Book Four. He participated in the debates by commentators on difficult and problematic points in Aristotle's work, as on the theory of vision, on the modality of the heating of air by the sun's rays, and on the origin of the saltiness of the sea. Finally, he conveyed much information on the state of the sciences and techniques of his era, such as mathematics, optics, astronomy, medicine, agriculture, and metallurgy. As for his commentary on Book Four, the first treatise on "chemistry" in Antiquity, Olympiodorus's systematic work is fundamental: He contributed significantly to constituting a new field of inquiry on the properties, the states, and the transformations of sublunary material. His commentary would be the one most frequently consulted not only by Arab and Renaissance authors but also by Greek and medieval alchemists.

Disputed Commentary. Indeed, one of the most interesting texts of the corpus of the Greek alchemists bears the name of Olympiodorus. In the principal manuscript of the corpus, the *Marcianus Graecus* 299 (M), this treatise is titled: "The Alexandrian Philosopher Olympiodorus on the Book *Kat'energeian* (*On the action* or *According to the action)* by Zosimus and on the Sayings of Hermes and the Philosophers." Other manuscripts give it a different title: "The Philosopher Olympiodorus to Petasius, King of Armenia, on the Divine and Sacred Art of the Philosophical Stone." At first identified with Olympiodorus of Thebes, opinions are now divided between the attribution of this treatise to Olympiodorus the Neoplatonist or to a homonymous Olympiodorus or to a pseudepigraph.

The author presented his commentary as a work of both exegesis and doxography. Its originality lies in its explicit claim that Greek philosophy, and especially pre-Socratic philosophy, is the epistemological foundation of transmutation. Indeed, toward the middle of the commentary, Olympiodorus laid out the opinions of nine pre-Socratics (Melissus, Parmenides, Thales, Diogenes, Heracleitus, Hippasus, Xenophanes, Anaximenes, and Anaximander) on the unique principle of things and then sketched a comparison between these positions and those of the principal masters of the art of transmutation (Zosimus, Chymes, Agathodaimon, and Hermes). In other respects, the structure of this treatise remains overall rather discontinuous and incomplete. It has neither preface nor conclusion, it begins and ends *ex abrupto*. The most coherent part is found at the beginning. The author commented on a sentence of Zosimus dealing with the extraction of gold, and he followed the typical pattern of Olympiodorus the commentator: First the *lemma*, the phrase of Zosimus to be commented upon, then a general explanation (*theôria*) and next the detailed exegesis of the terms (*lexis*). As for the rest, the treatise consists of a collection of *excerpta* from ancient authors concerning the principal notions and operations of the art of alchemy, accompanied by commentaries among which can be found other excerpts of Zosimus.

Numerous reasons favor attributing this alchemical work to Olympiodorus the Neoplatonist. First, one can exclude the hypothesis of dealing with a homonym, for the title clearly attributes this treatise to Olympiodorus "philosopher of Alexandria," a philosopher also designated in the alchemical corpus as an "exegete of Plato and Aristotle" and the author of "vast commentaries." Moreover, this author showed that he knew Aristotle well or at least that he came from a milieu in which the Aristotelian system and terminology were thoroughly assimilated. His commentary shows characteristic traits of Neoplatonic exegesis, such as the theme of the apparent obscurity of the language of philosophers, identification of the object of research with a unique principle, the very structure of the doxography dedicated to this principle. Finally, one can spot in it doctrinal and terminological convergences that are evident in both the commentary on Aristotle's *Meteorology* and in other works of Olympiodorus the Neoplatonist.

Nevertheless, because of the discontinuity and the composite character of this alchemical commentary, the identification of Olympiodorus the alchemist with Olympiodorus the Neoplatonic commentator remains a delicate operation that calls for more precision. Indeed, if one compares this text in its present state with the commentaries of Olympiodorus on Plato and Aristotle still extant, as though they were works presenting the same level of completeness, the result could only be unfavorable to the identification of these two figures. In order to support the identification of the two, one must suppose that a lost work written in a more structured form was the source of the alchemical commentary than available. One can then suppose that the present text consists of extracts of a lost alchemical work by Olympiodorus the Neoplatonist (perhaps of a complete commentary on Zosimus's book *On the Action*) arranged by a copyist, or even that the latter copied a work of Olympiodorus up to a certain point, and then added a series of unstructured notes on the principal alchemical operations, accompanied by *excerpta* from other alchemical authors and, probably, from other works by Olympiodorus himself.

SUPPLEMENTARY BIBLIOGRAPHY

WORKS BY OLYMPIODORUS

Commentaries on Plato

Olympiodori In Platonis Gorgiam Commentaria. Edited by Leendert G. Westerink. Leipzig: B.G. Teubner, 1970.

The Greek Commentaries on Plato's Phaedo, vol.I: *Olympiodorus.* Edited by Leendert G. Westerink. Amsterdam: North Holland Publishing, 1976.

Commentary on Plato's Gorgias. Translated with full notes by Robin Jackson, Kimon Lycos, and Harold Tarrant with an introduction by Harold Tarrant. Leiden: Brill, 1998.

Commentaries on Aristotle

Olympiodori in Aristotelis Meteora Commentaria, edited by Wilhelm Stüve. Berlin: G. Remieri, 1900. (= *CAG* 12.2)

Olympiodori Prolegomena et in Categorias Commentarium, edited by Adolf Busse Berlin: G. Remieri,1902. (= *CAG* 12.1)

Heliodori in Paulum Alexandrium commentarium. Edited by Ae. Boer, Otto Neugebauer, and David Pingree. Leipzig: B.G. Teubner, 1962. This includes the anonymous commentary on Paul of Alexandria.

Collection des anciens alchimistes grecs [Collection of Ancient Greek Alchemists], 3 vols. Edited by Marcellin Berthelot and Ch. E. Ruelle. Paris: G. Steinheil, 1887–1888. Reprinted Osnabruck, 1967, II, 69–106; III, 75–115. This includes the alchemical work attributed to Olympiodorus.

De interpretatione. In *Anonymous Commentary on Aristotle's* De interpretatione (*Codex Parisinus Graecus 2064*), edited by Leonardo Taran, pp. 25–41. Meisenheim am Glan: A. Hain, 1978. These are fragments of the commentary on this text.

Commentary on Book IV (French). In *La matière des choses Le livre IV des* Météorologiques *d'Aristote, et son interprétation par Olympiodore* [The Matter of Things. Book IV of Aristotle's *Meteorology* and Its Interpretation by Olympiodorus, with the Revised Greek Text and an Unpublished Translation of His Commentary to Book IV], edited by Cristina Viano. Paris: J. Vrin, 2006.

OTHER SOURCES

Berthelot, Marcellin. *Les Origines de l'alchimie* [The Origins of Alchemy]. Paris, 1885, pp.191–195.

Beutler, Rudolf. "Olympiodoros." In *Encyclopaedie der classischen Altertums-Wissenschaft* [Encyclopedia of Ancient Classical Science] (13), 18, 2, edited by August F. von Pauly, Georg Wissowa, Wilhelm Kroll, et. al, pp. 207-228. Stuttgart: J.B. Metzler, 1949.

Brisson, Luc. "Le corps 'dionysiaque.' L'anthropogonie décrite dans le *Commentaire sur le Phédon de Platon* (1, par. 3–6) attribuée à Olympiodore est-elle Orphique?" ["The 'Dionysiac' Body. The Anthropogenesis Described in the Commentary on Plato's *Phaedo* (1, par. 3–6) attributed to Olympiodorus: Is It Orphic?"]. In *Sophiês Maiêtores. Hommage à Jean Pépin* [Writings In Honor of Jean Pépin], edited by Marie-Odile Goulet-Caze, Goulven Madec, and Denis O'Brien, pp. 481–499. Paris: Institut d'Etudes Augustiniennes, 1992.

Letrouit, Jean. "Datation d'Olympiodore l'Alchimiste" [Dating of Olympiodorus the Alchemist]. *Emerita* 58 (1990): 289–292.

Saffrey, Henri D. "Olympiodoros d'Alexandrie" [Olympiodorus of Alexandria]. In *Dictionnaire des Philosophes antiques* [Dictionary of Ancient Philosophers], IV, directed by Richard Goulet, pp. 769–771. Paris: Éditions du Centre national de la recherche scientifique, 2006.

———. "Olympiodoros d'Alexandrie l'alchimiste" [Olympiodorus of Alexandria the Alchemist]. In *Dictionnaire des Philosophes antiques* [Dictionary of Ancient Philosophers], IV, edited by Richard Goulet, p. 768. Paris: Editions du Centre national de la recherche scientifique, 2006.

Tannery, Paul. "Un fragment d'Anaximène dans Olympiodore le Chimiste" [A Fragment of Anaximenes in Olympiodorus the Chemist], *Archiv für Geschichte der Philosophie,*1 [Archives for the History of Philosophy] (1888), pp. 314–321

Viano, Cristina. "Olympiodore l'alchimiste et les Présocratiques. Une doxographie de l'unité (*De arte Sacra,* § 18–27)" ("Olympiodorus the Alchemist and the Pre-Socratics. A Doxography of Unity, *De arte Sacra,* § 18–27") in *Alchimie: Art, Histoire et Mythes* (Alchemy: Art, History and Myths), edited by Didier Kahn and Sylvain Matton, pp. 95–150. Paris: Société d'étude de l'histoire de l'alchimie., Colloque international,1995.

Warnon, Jean. *Le commentaire attribué à Héliodore sur les* Eisagogika *de Paul d'Alexandrie* (The Commentary Attributed to Heliodorus on the *Eisagogika* of Paul of Alexandria). 192–217. Louvain: Travaux de la Faculté de Philosophie et Lettres de l'Université Catholique, 1967.

Westerink, Leendert G. "Ein astrologisches Kolleg aus dem Jahre 564" [A Lecture on Astrology from the Year 564], *Byzantinische Zeitschrift* (Byzantine Journal) 64 (1971), p. 6–21. Reprinted in *Texts and Studies in Neoplatonismus and Byzantine Literature,* Amsterdam, 1980, pp. 279–294.

Cristina Viano

OLYMPIODORUS OF THEBES (*b.* Thebes, Egypt, ca. 360-385; *d.* after 425), history, geography. For the original article on Olympiodorus see *DSB,* vol. 10.

Photius reported that Olympiodorus defined himself as a "professional poet" (Phot., *Ibid.* 166, 6: *poiêtês…to epitêdeuma*), a term that at the time could designate a writer of either artistic poetry or of prose in the general sense. Certain scholars, attributing to *poiêtês* (Lat. *operator*) the very specific sense of "alchemist" as is found in Greek texts on alchemy, believed him to be the author of a work contained in the Corpus of Greek alchemists, entitled "The Alexandrian Philosopher Olympiodorus on the Book *Kat'energeian* by Zosimus and on the Sayings of Hermes and the Philosophers." This attribution—propagated, among other sources, by the single original *DSB* entry on "Olympiodorus"—is now regarded as false, and the name of the alchemist must be associated instead with that of Olympiodorus of Alexandria, the Neoplatonic commentator of Plato and of Artistotle (see the entry "Olympiodorus of Alexandria").

Life. The earliest known event in the life of Olympiodorus is a mission in 412 for Emperor Honorius to Donatus, leader of the Huns. About 415 he was in Athens and about 423 he went to Egypt, where he visited Nubia, Talmis, Syene (now Aswan), the oasis of Siwa, and the priests of Isis at Philae. He probably lived at times in Byzantium, Ravenna, and Rome; and he knew the latter city well. He was not a Christian. At Athens, Olympiodorus associated with the Sophists and was a friend of the grammarian Philtatius. He was personally acquainted with Valerius, the prefect of Thrace.

Olympiodorus is author of a Greek history, a continuation of the work of Eunapius. The original work, covering the period from 407–425, is preserved only in fragments. The principal source is the *Bibliotheca* of

Photius, the ninth-century patriarch of Constantinople. Another source is the *New History* of Zosimus (*fl.* 490–510). Olympiodorus's history is dedicated to the Emperor Theodosius II and describes in twenty-two books the history of the Western Empire from the seventh consulship of Honorius to the accession of Valentinian III.

More than a history organized around a narrative thread, the work of Olympiodorus presents itself as the objective commentary of an eyewitness to the troubled events that characterized the beginning of the fifth century. Olympiodorus stated that he did not intend to produce a history but that his aim is to furnish "material" for a history (Phot., Bibl. Cod. 80, p. 166, 10). The objectivity and the independence of judgment that he exhibited distinguish his work from that of other historians and made it most interesting for the modern reader. Similarly, the numerous geographic and anthropological digressions that accompany the exposition of what are properly historic facts are of great interest for the history of science. Olympiodorus described the places, the climates, and the peoples that he encountered during his travels. He also related some wondrous phenomena, fantastic stories, and incidents of magic (Phot., *Ibid.* 171= fr. 16 Blockley). In particular, when it is a question of controversial subjects such as the route of Odysseus's voyage (Phot., *Ibid.* 186, 1=fr. 42 Blockley), Olympiodorus stated that he has compared the opinions of other authors, thus showing that he made use of a methodological practice similar to what is known as the *status quaestionis.*

SUPPLEMENTARY BIBLIOGRAPHY

WORKS BY OLYMPIODORUS

Fragmenta Historicorum Graecorum IV. Edited by Karl Muller. 57–68. Paris: 1851.

Historici graeci minores I, edited by Ludwig A. Dindorf, 450–472. Leipzig: B.G. Teubner, 1870. The excerpts from Olympiodorus's historical work, as preserved by Photius, are published here and in Muller.

The Fragmentary Classicising Historian of the Later Roman Empire. Eunapius, Olympiodorus, Priscus and Malchius, 2 vols. Edited by R.C. Blockley, vol. II, 152–220. Liverpool, U.K.: F. Cairns, 1981–1983.

OTHER SOURCES

Haedicke, Walter. "Olympiodoros." In *Encyclopaedie der classischen Altertums-Wissenschaft* [Encyclopedia of Ancient Classical Science] (13), 18, 2, edited by August F. von Pauly, Georg Wissowa, Wilhelm Kroll, et. al, pp. 201-207. Stuttgart: J.B. Metzler, 1949.

Thompson, E. A. "Olympiodoros of Thebes." *Classical Quarterly* 38 (1944): 43–52.

Cristina Viano

OORT, JAN HENDRIK

(*b.* Franeker, Netherlands, 28 April 1900; *d.* Leiden, Netherlands, 5 November 1992), *astronomy, astrophysics, galactic system, radio astronomy.*

Oort is generally regarded as one of the leading astronomers of the twentieth century. He performed very important researches in a number of areas, most notably on the structure and dynamics of the galactic system. Oort also played a crucial part in the development of radio astronomy, in the founding of what became the European Southern Observatory, and in advancing the place of Holland in European and world astronomy.

Early Years. Oort was born in the small town of Franeker in the province of Friesland in the north of the Netherlands. He was one of five children of Abraham Hendrikus Oort and Hannah Faber. Abraham was a psychiatrist and the family left Franeker shortly after Oort's birth when his father became the director of a psychiatric clinic in Oegstgeest near Leiden. Oort went to primary school in Oegstgeest and then to Leiden for secondary school. Encouraged by his parents to follow his interests, Oort decided to study physics at the University of Groningen, which he entered in 1917. After attending lectures by the famous astronomer Jacobus Cornelius Kapteyn, Oort was inspired to switch to astronomy. He later recalled that the most important lessons that Kapteyn taught him as an undergraduate were to link interpretations directly to observations and to be very skeptical about speculations and hypotheses. He put these lessons into effect throughout his career.

Oort took his *doctoral* examination in 1921. This marked the completion of coursework for the degree of doctor of science, but attaining the higher degree would require several more years of study. After the examination Oort became the assistant to Kapteyn's collaborator, Pieter Johannes Van Rhijn, at Groningen. But after a year Oort left to gain experience in the United States. From 1922 to 1924, Oort was an assistant to Frank Schlesinger at the Yale Observatory. Schlesinger was a great authority on fundamental positional astronomy. Oort was trained in astrometry, in particular the use of a zenith telescope to secure very accurate positions of stars. He later judged the experience at Yale as useful, but it did not mesh well with his own aspirations. Hence when Willem de Sitter, director of the observatory at Leiden, offered him a position there, Oort quickly accepted. At first a research assistant, he held various positions until he became a "Professor Extraordinary" and vice director of the Observatory in 1935.

On arriving at Leiden in 1924, Oort tackled a problem he had encountered while at Yale: the properties of the so-called high velocity stars. He found that these stars

Oort

displayed a puzzling and unexplained asymmetry as they were traveling toward one hemisphere of the sky. This asymmetry became apparent when the velocity of the stars was greater than about 65 kilometers per second relative to the Sun; slower moving stars did not display the same behavior. The high velocity stars formed the subject of Oort's doctoral thesis, which he defended at Groningen in May 1926.

In the next year he married Mieke Graadt van Roggen, whom he had first met at a university celebration. The couple had three children between 1928 and 1934, Coenraad, Abraham, and Marijke, and their happy marriage lasted until Oort's death sixty-five years later.

The Galactic System. Kapteyn had died in 1922, but his researches on the structure of the galactic system continued to be extremely influential, particularly among Dutch astronomers. Over the course of his career, Kapteyn had elaborated a model that became known as the Kapteyn universe or Kapteyn system, as well as a set of approaches for working out the structure of our stellar system based on detailed counts of stars. In a paper written at the end of his life, Kapteyn had calculated the limits of the galactic system. Taking the limits of the ellipsoid-shaped system where the density of stars sank to a value of one-hundredth that in the neighborhood of our Sun, then the distance from the center to the edge along the galactic plane was about 25,000 light-years. If measured from the center, it extended for about 5,000 light-years at right angles to that plane. The Sun was roughly 2,000 light-years from the center. Kapteyn had suspected that the high-velocity stars were interlopers that moved through the galactic system, but were not related to it.

The Swedish astronomer Bertil Lindblad treated the high velocity stars in a very different way. By 1926 he had developed a model in which these stars are an integral part of the galactic system, which he divided up into several subsystems. All of the subsystems rotate about a common axis and center. The different subsystems have different degrees of flattening depending on the speeds of rotation of the subsystem. A few years earlier, at the Mount Wilson Observatory in California, Harlow Shapley had advanced the radical idea that the galaxy is much larger than Kapteyn had allowed. In Shapley's scheme, the Sun was far distant from the center of the galactic system, which had a diameter of around 300,000 light-years. For Shapley, the galaxy was framed by the collection of globular star clusters with the center of the system of globular clusters coinciding with the center of the galactic system. But Shapley's vision of the galaxy was controversial and to many astronomers it seemed to rest on dubious assumptions. Lindblad, however, argued that the direction of the center of the galactic system coincided with the direction of the center of system of globular clusters as defined by Shapley.

Oort paid very close attention to Lindblad's researches. Bart Bok, who later became a prominent astronomer in his own right, would later remember that in 1927 Oort was delivering a series of seminars for Bok and three other students at Leiden. Oort, however, skipped two of the seminars after telling the students that he had become bogged down in Lindblad's complex calculations. By the next seminar, Oort had mastered these and had derived his own relatively simple formulas to explain the motions of the stars in terms of a differential galactic rotation. That is, he argued that the galactic system does not rotate as a solid body, but the angular velocity of the stars changes with distance from the center. In his analysis he employed two constants, A and B, which later became known as the Oort constants. Oort now wrote a paper on "Observational Evidence Confirming Lindblad's Hypothesis of a Rotation of the Galactic System." There were, nevertheless, differences to begin with between Lindblad's system and Oort's. In particular, Oort reckoned that the systematic effects he had found in 1927 revealed a large concentration of mass in the central region of the galaxy, whereas Lindblad contended that the greater part of the galactic system is formed by an ellipsoid of constant density.

Other astronomers provided evidence generally interpreted as buttressing Oort's arguments. Indeed, astronomers soon regarded Lindblad and Oort as the codiscoverers of galactic rotation with Oort seen as having furnished its observational proof. There was, however, still a discrepancy between the distances to the center of the galactic system as determined by Shapley's and Oort's estimates from the motions of the stars, 65,000 light-years versus about 20,000 light-years. Shapley had calculated the scale of the galaxy assuming there was negligible interstellar absorption and, except for isolated dark clouds, its effects could effectively be ignored. Kapteyn had worried about the possible effects of absorption. In fact, the possible effects of such absorption were the great unknowns in studies of galactic structure in the first three decades of the century. But in constructing the Kapteyn universe, he came round to the view that it was not significant. In the opinion of many astronomers, however, this assumption was undermined in the early 1930s, with the most compelling evidence being provided by Robert Julius Trumpler at Lick when he measured the distances to open star clusters using two methods. He exploited both the sizes of the clusters and the colors of the stars within them in his distance estimates but found discrepancies in the answers from the two tools. Trumpler calculated that if interstellar absorption was changing the colors of the stars, then the discrepancies were resolved. The amount of interstellar absorption completely undercut the results of Kapteyn's

Oort

attacks on the structure of the galactic system if not the methods he had fashioned. Shapley's model of the galaxy also had to shrink in size, with the result that Oort's and Shapley's estimates of the distance to the galactic center came into line.

Within just a few years of completing his dissertation, Oort had propelled himself into the front rank of younger astronomers. Job offers followed. In 1930 Harvard invited him to become the Willson Professor of Astronomy and in 1932 Columbia University wanted him as the director of its astronomy department. He considered both offers seriously but in the end he chose to stay at Leiden, where he remained for the rest of his career.

Leiden, however, did have its drawbacks. There were no large optical telescopes there (the biggest were a 26-cm visual refractor and a 33-cm astrometric telescope, and both dated from the nineteenth century), and anyway Holland was a poor location from which to pursue optical astronomy. In 1923 an agreement was reached whereby Leiden astronomers had access to the Union Observatory in Johannesburg, South Africa. But the instruments available to Oort there, as at Leiden, were much less powerful than the best of the telescopes in the United States. Hence Oort made a half-year visit in 1932 to the Perkins Observatory in Delaware, Ohio. There he photographed galaxies with a 60-inch reflector in order to measure their luminosity distributions. His goals were to investigate the bulges in spiral galaxies and the forces operating within elliptical galaxies so as to better understand the development and maintenance of spiral structures. But he had very little experience of this sort of observing and overall he was not especially successful.

During the 1930s Oort continued to work principally at problems of galactic structure and dynamics. In 1932, for example, as Kapteyn had a decade earlier, he investigated the forces exerted by the stellar system perpendicular to the galactic plane and the density of stars in this direction. Critical to all aspects of Oort's project was the effort to better determine the effects of interstellar absorption on the brightness and colors of stars, effects that as noted had crippled Kapteyn's investigations. In 1938 Oort wrote on "Absorption and Density Distribution in the Galactic System." This time he performed counts of faint stars at moderate and high galactic latitudes and combined these with data on interstellar absorption drawn from counts of distant galaxies by Edwin Hubble. Among other things, Oort concluded that the obscuring material is confined to a relatively thin layer in the galactic plane.

The style of this 1938 paper was in many respects typical of Oort's scientific writings before the end of World War II and the start of his active involvement in radio astronomy. He was the sole author and it was based on a mastery of the available literature and a very careful compilation and painstaking analysis of a large body of generally available observational evidence. As usual Oort did not employ highly advanced mathematical methods and avoided far-reaching speculations. He closed the paper, for example, by warning that in terms of comparing his results for high and moderate galactic latitudes with data at low latitudes, it might prove advisable to wait for better and more extensive data.

With Oort's growing seniority he assumed extra administrative tasks. In 1934 Willem de Sitter died and Ejnar Hertzsprung became director of the Leiden Observatory. Oort became Hertzsprung's deputy. Like his mentor Kapteyn, Oort was a convinced internationalist when it came to science, and in 1935 his standing in the wider international astronomical community was also underlined when he became general secretary to the International Astronomical Union, the leading international organization of astronomers. Oort did not relinquish this position until 1948, although much of the administrative burden in the war years was carried by Walter Adams at the Mount Wilson Observatory in the United States because of the disruption of communications in war-torn Holland. Oort continued to play a leading part in the running of the union and he would serve as its president from 1958 to 1961.

The War Years and Radio Astronomy. Oort spent part of 1939 in the United States. He arrived back in the Netherlands days before the outbreak of World War II. With the German occupation of the country in 1940, conditions became at best difficult for astronomical research and communications with astronomers outside the Netherlands slowed to a trickle by late 1941.

Oort did continue some research however, including on the Crab Nebula, generally identified as the result of a stellar explosion. During his 1939 U.S. visit, Oort and Nicholas Ulrich Mayall at the Lick Observatory had discussed data on the Crab. These discussions led to papers in 1942, although the final manuscript of one listing Mayall and Oort as coauthors never reached Oort. Oort, however, had authorized Mayall to publish it if this happened. Oort was aided in his research by Jan Julius Lodewijk Duyvendak, a Sinologist at Leiden who had searched Chinese and Japanese records for original observations of the "nova" and produced convincing evidence that the Crab Nebula resulted from a nova viewed from Earth in 1054 CE. In part due to the work of Duyvendak, Mayall, and Oort, Walter Baade confidently identified the Crab Nebula as the result of a Type 1 supernova.

In 1942 Jewish professors were dismissed from the University of Leiden. Oort was a member of a group of professors who met regularly to discuss the problems of

Oort Cloud. *Computer illustration of the Oort cloud.* COURTESY OF DAVID LEVY.

the occupation and the Nazification of the university. After a number of these professors were put into detention camps, Oort, to avoid the same fate, decided to leave for the small village of Hulshorst some 100 kilometers from Leiden (later, in 1944, he moved to Nunspeet). He also resigned from his posts at the university. In effect, he disappeared from view, at least as far as the Germans were concerned.

Oort, nevertheless, stayed in touch with the observatory and was able to continue some astronomical research. On occasion he cycled back to Leiden. He continued to organize work and to deliver unauthorized lectures. Oort also attended scientific meetings of the Nederlandse Astronomenclub.

Despite the isolation of Holland from the outside astronomical world, Oort had come across a paper by an

American engineer, Grote Reber, in a copy of the *Astrophysical Journal* smuggled into the country. Here Reber reported on his investigations of radio emissions from the Milky Way. The great majority of astronomers had paid little heed to Reber's researches, but Oort found this news intriguing. He wondered if radio waves, which would not be impeded by interstellar absorption in the same way as starlight, could be exploited to survey the galaxy. In 1944 Henk C. van de Hulst, a graduate student at Utrecht who had come to work at Leiden, told Oort about a prize that had been offered for an essay on the "Formation of Solid Particles and Condensation in Interstellar Space." Van de Hulst received an honorable mention for his essay, and the interaction between gas and dust was a topic that he and Oort would later pursue further, addressing questions about the heating and evaporation of dust due to nearby stars, for example. But at this time in 1944 Oort gave him another assignment: to review the existing theories on the sources of cosmic radio waves and calculate if spectral lines might exist in the radio spectrum. Oort had grasped that if there were detectable lines in the radio spectrum (as there were absorption and emission lines in the optical section of the electromagnetic spectrum), these could be used, through Doppler shifts of the lines, to investigate the location and rotation of interstellar gas throughout the galactic system, not just the very limited region of several thousand light years to which optical observers were restricted by the effects of interstellar absorption. The lines in the radio spectrum might therefore be extremely powerful probes of galactic structure.

Van de Hulst provided his answers at a meeting of the Nederlandse Astronomenclub at Leiden on 15 April 1944. He had calculated that there should be a spectral line at a wavelength of 21 centimeters due to a switch in the spin of the electron in a hydrogen atom, a so-called hyperfine line. As there was so much hydrogen in the galaxy, van de Hulst reckoned it might even be possible to detect this line, although he was unsure if it would be in emission or absorption. Van de Hulst's results were published in 1945, and, as we shall see shortly, were to prove to be enormously important.

The end of the war meant a rapid end to Hertzsprung's directorship of the Leiden Observatory. Oort succeeded him and also became a full professor. Much of Oort's time was now devoted to improving conditions at the observatory and attending to administrative tasks. But he was also itching to press forward with the radio researches he had started in the war.

Van de Hulst joined the Yerkes Observatory in the United States on a postdoctoral position at the conclusion of the war. He visited Grote Reber and encouraged him to search for the 21-centimeter line, but while Reber later started to build a spectrometer to try to detect the line he did not complete the project. Back at Leiden, Oort stressed the importance of radio observations for studies of the galactic system and interstellar matter. He wanted to build a large dish and radio receiver and sought information from assorted experts on how this might be done. He even wrote to Reber for advice. Oort made his first proposal for a radio telescope to the Dutch Academy of Sciences in late 1945, which then forwarded it to the government. But unlike other nations that had been actively engaged in the development of radar in World War II, the Netherlands was way behind the state of the art, nor were large sums of money available for research expenditures.

Despite the consequent slow start, Oort now showed himself to be an effective political insider with many useful contacts. He was friendly and courteous in his personal dealings although some students found him intimidating as he continually urged them to probe more deeply into a problem. As director at Leiden and the leader of Dutch astronomy, he displayed tenacity in pursuing institutional goals and demonstrated the knack of being able to persuade others of the worth of projects in which he believed. In 1948 Oort helped establish the Stichting voor Radiostraling van Zon en Melkweg (Foundation for radio radiation from the Sun and the Milky Way, also often also known as the Netherlands Foundation for Radio Astronomy). This became the organization that would put radio astronomy onto a secure footing in Holland. Observations got underway in 1948 at Kootwijk (the site of the Dutch Postal and Telephone Company's research station) with the aid of a salvaged antenna originally used in the war by the Germans. But matters moved achingly slowly. The result was that the detection of the 21-centimeter line was made first at Harvard by Harold I. Ewen and Edward M. Purcell in 1951. Shortly after, the line was detected in Holland, and additional confirmation came about a month later from Wilbur Norman Christiansen and J. V. Hindman in Australia. Oort was soon busy searching for an interpretation of the growing number of observations. He reckoned that some of the gas being detected in the plane of the galaxy was at a distance of about 25,000 light-years, far beyond the reach of optical observations to that date.

With the successful detection of the 21-centimeter line, Oort's arguments in favor of a larger instrument to investigate the line grew in force. In 1956 a radio telescope with a dish of diameter 25 meters (it was the biggest in the world for about a year) was built at Dwingeloo. With this instrument in operation, he immediately advocated a still more powerful one. Oort's drive was to be crucial in the establishment in 1970 of the Westerbork Synthesis Radio Telescope, a collection of twelve 25-meter dishes arranged in an east-west line 1.5 kilometers long.

Oort

With his involvement in radio astronomy, Oort became much more of an observational astronomer than he had ever been before. In writing on radio astronomy topics, he now also generally coauthored papers with one or two colleagues. But he maintained his focus on the structure and dynamics of the galactic system. Oort had long suspected that the galaxy is a form of spiral. Proving this, however, was very challenging due to the obstacles thrown up by interstellar absorption and the Sun's position within the galactic system. However, in 1951 the American astronomer William W. Morgan, aided by Donald Osterbrock and Stewart Sharpless, presented what other astronomers regarded as compelling evidence of spiral arms within the galactic system by charting the positions of clouds of ionized hydrogen, HII regions. The solution to the long-standing question of the existence of spiral arms had not come, then, from the sorts of sophisticated star-counting techniques pioneered in large part by Kapteyn and other Dutch astronomers. But the future would lie with radio techniques and Oort, in a joint paper with van de Hulst and C. A. Muller, quickly helped to both confirm and extend Morgan's arguments on spiral arms though radio observations. A few years later Oort coauthored with Frank J. Kerr and Gart Westerhout "The Galactic System as a Spiral Nebula." This paper contained what became a very famous representation of the distribution of neutral hydrogen in the plane of the galaxy, and Oort and his colleagues argued that the Sun is on the inner section of an arm of neutral hydrogen. As Oort had anticipated over a decade earlier, radio observations had indeed made it possible for astronomers to probe the most distant regions of the galactic system.

The European Southern Observatory. In addition to his efforts in establishing the Netherlands at the forefront of radio astronomy by securing powerful radio telescopes, Oort was also eager to secure access to large optical telescopes for Dutch astronomers. The idea for what became the European Southern Observatory was sparked by discussions between Walter Baade, one of the outstanding observational astronomers of his time and very experienced in the use of large telescopes, and Oort. Baade, although based at Mount Wilson in California, very much viewed himself as a European, and he often gave advice to Oort as Oort worked hard and adroitly with various international partners to fashion an observatory to be funded by the governments of a number of European nations. Planning got seriously underway after Oort called a meeting of leading European astronomers in Groningen in 1953. It still took over a decade of demanding diplomacy to reach an agreement between the Netherlands, France, the Federal Republic of Germany, and Sweden (Belgium and Denmark would join a few years later) to establish the European Southern Observatory. The observatory was dedicated on La Silla in Chile in 1969 and went into operation, initially with middle-sized telescopes but larger ones followed.

Comets. In comparison with his studies in galactic and extragalactic astronomy, Oort spent little time on solar system astronomy. However he did perform very important researches on comets. This line of study grew out of the researches of a student at Leiden, A. J. J. van Woerkom, who worked on comets' orbits. His interest piqued by van Woerkom's dissertation, Oort in short order developed his own theory of a cloud of protocomets that surround the solar system. He argued that when the solar system was formed, very many small bodies orbited between Mars and Jupiter. Over time, Jupiter's gravitational force acted to expel many of these objects from the solar system, but some were carried into highly elongated orbits that took them out from the Sun to distances between 50,000 astronomical units and 200,000 astronomical units. Oort further calculated that passing stars could redirect some of these bodies into the inner regions of the solar system, thereby producing a "new" comet. While Oort termed his scheme "speculative" when he advanced it in 1950, it had become widely accepted by the late twentieth century and his proposed cloud of comets has become known as the Oort cloud.

Galaxies and Retirement. In his inaugural lecture as a professor at Leiden in the 1935, Oort had discussed the origin and evolution of the universe and galaxies. He was also deeply interested throughout his career in the clues offered by observations of other galaxies in interpreting our own galaxy. But he began to regularly write scientific papers on other galaxies only in the 1950s. Of particular interest to him were issues of structure that might be significant on a cosmological scale, especially the development of superclusters of galaxies. When he retired in 1970, he chose to speak at his seventieth-birthday symposium on "Galaxies and the Universe."

With retirement he was freed of administrative duties but he continued to be very active in research until well into his eighties, and the last piece he wrote for an astronomical journal was published in the year he died. He won numerous prestigious prizes and awards, as well as honorary doctorates from Brussels, Cambridge, Harvard, Oxford, Turin, and others.

BIBLIOGRAPHY

The collections of the Center for the History of Physics of the American Institute of Physics contain an important oral history with Oort by David DeVorkin taken in 1977.

WORKS BY OORT

"The Stars of High Velocity." Thesis, Groningen University. *Publications of the Kapteyn Astronomical Laboratory at Groningen* 40 (1926): 1–75.

"Observational Evidence Confirming Lindblad's Hypothesis of a Rotation of the Galactic System." *Bulletin of the Astronomical Institute of the Netherlands* 3 (1927): 275–282.

"The Force Exerted by the Stellar System in the Direction Perpendicular to the Galactic Plane and Some Related Problems." *Bulletin of the Astronomical Institute of the Netherlands* 6 (1932): 249–287.

"Absorption and Density Distribution in the Galactic System." *Bulletin of the Astronomical Institute of the Netherlands* 8 (1938): 233–264.

With Nicholas Ulrich Mayall. "Further Data Bearing on the Identification of the Crab Nebula with the Supernova of 1054 A.D.: Part II: The Astronomical Aspects." *Publications of the Astronomical Society of the Pacific* 54 (1942): 95–104.

"Some Phenomena Connected with Interstellar Matter." *Monthly Notices of the Royal Astronomical Society* 106 (1946): 159–179. George Darwin Lecture.

With C. A. Muller. "The Interstellar Hydrogen Line at 1.420 Mc/sec, and an Estimate of Galactic Rotation." *Nature* 168 (1951): 357–358.

"Origin and Development of Comets." *Observatory* 71 (1951): 129–144. Halley Lecture.

With Th. Walraven. "Polarization and Composition of the Crab Nebula." *Bulletin of the Astronomical Institute of the Netherlands* 12 (1956): 285–308.

With Frank J. Kerr and Gart Westerhout. "The Galactic System as a Spiral Nebula." *Monthly Notices of the Royal Astronomical Society* 118 (1958): 379–389.

"Galaxies and the Universe." *Science* 170 (1970): 1363–1370.

"The Development of Our Insight into the Structure of the Galaxy between 1920 and 1940." *Annals of the New York Academy of Sciences* 198 (1972): 255–266.

"The Galactic Center." *Annual Review of Astronomy and Astrophysics* 15 (1977): 295–362.

"Superclusters." *Annual Review of Astronomy and Astrophysics* 21 (1983): 373–428.

"The Origin and Dissolution of Comets," *Observatory* 106 (1986): 186–193. Halley Lecture.

OTHER SOURCES

Blaauw, Adriaan. *ESO's Early History: The European Southern Observatory from Concept to Reality.* Garching, Germany: European Southern Observatory, 1991. Details Oort's role in establishing the European Southern Observatory.

———. *History of the IAU: The Birth and First Half-Century of the International Astronomical Union.* Dordrecht, Netherlands: Kluwer, 1994.

Katgert-Merkelijn, J. K. *The Letters and Papers of Jan Hendrik Oort.* Dordrecht, Netherlands: Kluwer, 1997. Contains a bibliography of Oort's papers.

Kruit, P. C. van der, and Klaass van Berkel. *The Legacy of J. C. Kapteyn: Studies on Kapteyn and the Development of Modern Astronomy.* Dordrecht, Netherlands: Kluwer, 2000. Especially significant for Oort are the chapters by Klaass van Berkel, David H. DeVorkin, and Woodruff T. Sullivan III.

Osterbrock, Donald E. *Walter Baade: A Life in Astrophysics.* Princeton, NJ: Princeton University Press, 2001.

Paul, Erich Robert. "The Death of a Research Programme: Kapteyn and the Dutch Astronomical Community." *Journal for the History of Astronomy* 12 (1981): 77–94.

Smith, Robert W. *The Expanding Universe: Astronomy's Great Debate 1900–1931.* Cambridge, U.K.: Cambridge University Press, 1982.

Woerden, Hugo van, Willem N. Brouw, and Henk C. van de Hulst, eds. *Oort and the Universe: A Sketch of Oort's Research and Person.* Dordrecht, Netherlands: D. Reidel, 1980. Important collection of papers detailing various aspects of Oort's career presented on the occasion of Oort's eightieth birthday.

Robert W. Smith

OPPENHEIMER, J. ROBERT

OPPENHEIMER, J. ROBERT (*b.* New York, New York, 22 April 1904; *d.* Princeton, New Jersey, 18 February 1967), *theoretical physics.* For the original article on Oppenheimer see *DSB,* vol. 10.

The important aspects of Oppenheimer's life were accurately and perceptively highlighted in Rudolf Peierls's 1970 *DSB* entry. Since its writing, many of the details of Oppenheimer's life have come into much sharper focus by virtue of the publication by Alice Kimball Smith and Charles Weiner of many of the letters he wrote before 1945 to his teachers, to his brother, and to his friends; and by virtue of the availability of his extensive *Nachlass* in the archives of the Library of Congress.

The detailed investigations and analyses by historians of the Ethical Culture Society and of its school; of the Sanskrit texts Oppenheimer studied and their canonical meaning; of the organizational structure of Los Alamos and of the technical work carried out there; of Oppenheimer's directorship of Los Alamos, and later of the Institute for Advanced Study; of the details of his governmental advisory activities after World War II, by which time he had become a Cold Warrior; of the illegal behind-the-scene activities of J. Edgar Hoover and his Federal Bureau of Investigation (FBI), and the plotting of Lewis Strauss before the special Atomic Energy Commission (AEC) board was set up to inquire as to Oppenheimer's suitability for a security clearance; of the machinations and illegal actions carried out by the prosecution during the "inquiry" that terminated with the revocation of his clearance in 1954; and of his subsequent activities as a public intellectual and an influential member of the Congress for Cultural Freedom, have resulted in a much more nuanced, context-dependent, and questioning portrait of the man.

Biographical Advances. Since 2000, five biographies have been published that have perceptively described all aspects of his life. All devote some chapters to a depiction of the familial, educational, social, and psychological circumstances that resulted in the precocious, brilliant, arrogant, emotionally immature, privileged Oppenheimer entering adulthood with an almost pathologically "splintered personality," as Isador Rabi had put it.

For their biography of Oppenheimer, Kai Bird and Martin J. Sherwood unraveled the deep crisis Oppenheimer underwent during 1925–1926, the academic year he spent at Cambridge after his graduation from Harvard. Oppenheimer's frustration in his work with Joseph John Thomson at the Cavendish, his general unhappiness with the Cambridge culture, anxieties caused by some sexual encounters, and the cooling of his friendship with some of his Harvard classmates because of their getting married, were catalysts in the breakdown. He became deeply depressed, and jealous of the success of some of the people around him, in particular of Patrick Blackett, a young experimental physicist at the Cavendish some three years his senior who had become his tutor and something of a mentor to him. Sometime in the fall of 1925 he actually left a "poisoned apple" on Blackett's desk, an apple laced with some chemical, possibly cyanide, that might well have caused Blackett great harm. Fortunately, his deed was discovered and Blackett did not eat the apple. But Oppenheimer was hauled before the university authorities and nearly expelled. Only the intervention of his parents, and the promise that he would seek psychiatric help prevented his expulsion. He recovered, immersed himself in the work of Werner Heisenberg, Paul Dirac, and Erwin Schrödinger, and wrote two papers on the application of quantum mechanics to the vibrational and rotational spectra of molecules before leaving Cambridge in late summer 1926 to accept Max Born's invitation to come work with him in Göttingen.

Historians now also have a much better account of all of Oppenheimer's scientific activities during the 1930s, including his astrophysical researches that culminated with his investigations of the formation of what are now known as black holes, the final state of massive stars once they have exhausted their nuclear fuel and implode under gravitational attraction. And they also have a more deeply probing assessment of his involvement with left-wing politics during the 1930s, with such causes as the Spanish Republicans, the California Farm Workers, and the American Federation of Teachers, a branch of which he helped found at Berkeley. Oppenheimer was a member of a group that met regularly to discuss issues of the day. Three out of the four members of that group, which evidently was a secret cell of the Communist Party, were members of the Party. Many of his close friends; his brother and sister-in-law; the woman who had introduced him to left-wing politics and to whom he considered himself engaged for a while, Jean Tatlock; his wife, Katherine "Kitty" Puening Harrison; all had been or were members of the Communist Party. There is no proof that Oppenheimer ever became a card-carrying member of the party or that he accepted party discipline, though he supported many of its activities through Party channels. The possibility that he had been a Communist during the late 1930s, and might even have perjured himself in denying this, has been raised by respected and knowledgeable historians. The issue is not likely to be resolved as it hinges on what various people thought at the time on the basis of his participation of various Communist Party–supported or Party-initiated activities. On the question of perjury, it surely hinges on what Oppenheimer believed. If he thought that signing a card or paying dues——both of which he made it a point never to do——were the key criteria for membership, then his denial that he ever was a member would not be perjury, regardless of what other people thought.

Los Alamos. In his fine "sociological biography" Charles Thorpe makes clear the dynamics involved in the construction of the complex organization of Los Alamos and the simultaneous molding of Oppenheimer's role and authority as its charismatic director. It was a recursive process. The organizational order, the assignment of authority, Oppenheimer's charismatic role and identity were emergent properties of the social and professional interactions of scientists, technicians, military personnel and all the other people that had been brought together to accomplish the military mission of building an atomic bomb and of Oppenheimer's interaction with them. Thorpe also highlights the complementary roles at Los Alamos of Oppenheimer and Gen. Leslie Grove and the nature of their relationship and interactions.

This greater insight into the actions and character of Oppenheimer is the result of recent scholarship that has provided a much better understanding of the context in which his actions took place: scientists as political activists in the United States during the 1930s; the prewar Berkeley milieu; Los Alamos; the post–World War II loyalty-security regime; McCarthyism; the Cold War regime and its impact on intellectuals in the United States and in Europe. Oppenheimer's staunch anticommunism and his deep distrust of the Soviet Union after World War II have been documented by meticulous research. How these views affected his political stand relating to the international control of nuclear energy and nuclear weapons after the rejection of the Acheson-Lilienthal plan by Bernard

J. Robert Oppenheimer. © CORBIS.

Baruch, a close advisor of President Harry S. Truman, and the Soviet's rejection of the Baruch proposal have been clarified by the researches of James Hershberg and others. Similarly, Priscilla McMillan has written a careful and sensitive chronicle and analysis of the deliberate campaign to destroy Oppenheimer that led to the "inquiry" he underwent——a campaign that was responsible for initiating the nuclear arms race between the United States and the Soviet Union that plagued the world for fifty years. Finally, Charles Thorpe's investigation of Oppenheimer's activities in the Congress for Cultural Freedom has revealed an important facet of his life in the aftermath of the revocation of his clearance.

All this recent scholarship corroborates what Cathryn Carson states in the Introduction to *Reappraising Oppenheimer*, the book which she and David Hollinger edited and which is the best entry into recent scholarship on Oppenheimer: "If we can see Oppenheimer in his complexity as something more than a singular individual——as a man mirroring and responding to a panoply of contradictory forces——then we may come closer to capturing his sense that the life he lived had significance beyond its individual confines" (Carson and Hollinger, p. 9).

SUPPLEMENTARY BIBLIOGRAPHY

Oppenheimer's papers are located in the Manuscript Division of the Library of Congress. His papers relating to his directorship of the Institute of Advanced Study (IAS) are located at the IAS. A useful short bibliography compiled on the occasion of a Centennial Conference at Berkeley is available from http://ohst.berkeley.edu/oppenheimer/biblio.html.

WORKS BY OPPENHEIMER

Robert Oppenheimer: Letters and Recollections. Edited by Alice Kimball Smith and Charles Weiner. Cambridge, MA: Harvard University Press. 1980. Many of his pre-1945 letters and a list of his scientific and other published papers.

OTHER SOURCES

Biographical Works

Bernstein, Jeremy. *Oppenheimer: Portrait of an Enigma.* Chicago: Ivan R. Dee, 2004. Provides perspectives on Oppenheimer's strengths as a physicist, written by a member of the contemporary physics community.

Bird, Kai, and Martin J. Sherwin. *American Prometheus: The Triumph and Tragedy of J. Robert Oppenheimer.* New York: Knopf, 2005. Full of detail, the result of almost twenty-five years of scholarship and more than two hundred interviews with Oppenheimer's students, associates, friends, and family.

Carson, Cathryn, and David A. Hollinger, eds. *Reappraising Oppenheimer: Centennial Studies and Reflections.* Berkeley: Office for History of Science and Technology, University of California, Berkeley, 2005. The best entry into the writings *on* J. Robert Oppenheimer. The book also gives a valuable reassessment of Oppenheimer's place in the history of the United States during the twentieth century.

Cassidy, David C. *J. Robert Oppenheimer and the American Century.* New York: Pi Press, 2005. Good description of the changing relationship between science and government.

Herken, Gregg. *Brotherhood of the Bomb: The Tangled Lives and Loyalties of Robert Oppenheimer, Ernest Lawrence, and Edward Teller.* New York: Henry Holt, 2002. Describes rivalries and cooperation among physicists.

Pais, Abraham, with supplemental material by Robert P. Crease. *J. Robert Oppenheimer: A Life.* New York: Oxford University Press, 2006. By a physicist who was also Oppenheimer's neighbor.

Schweber, S. S. *In the Shadow of the Bomb: Bethe, Oppenheimer, and the Moral Responsibility of the Scientist.* Princeton, NJ: Princeton University Press, 2000. Describes the role of Bethe and Oppenheimer in their roles as advisers to the government and emphasizes the moral dilemmas faced by these scientists.

Thorpe, Charles. *Oppenheimer: The Tragic Intellect.* Chicago: University of Chicago Press, 2006. Covers Oppenheimer's activities at Los Alamos and as a public intellectual after World War II.

Directorship of Los Alamos

Rhodes, Richard. *The Making of the Atomic Bomb.* New York: Simon and Schuster, 1986.

Hoddeson, Lillian, P. W. Henriksen, R. A. Meade, et al. *Critical Assembly: A Technical History of Los Alamos during the Oppenheimer Years, 1943–1945.* Cambridge, U.K.: Cambridge University Press, 1993.

Hughes, Jeff. *The Manhattan Project: Big Science and the Atom Bomb.* New York: Columbia University Press, 2003.

Thorpe, Charles, and S. Shapin. "Who Was J. Robert Oppenheimer: Charisma and Complex Organization." *Social Studies of Science* 30 (2000): 545–590.

Development of H-Bombs and Revocation of Clearance

Galison, Peter, and Barton Bernstein. "In Any Light: Scientists and the Decision to Build the Superbomb, 1942–1954." *Historical Studies in the Physical and Biological Sciences* 19, no. 2 (1989): 266–347.

McMillan, Priscilla Johnson. *The Ruin of J. Robert Oppenheimer, and the Birth of the Modern Arms Race.* New York: Viking, 2005.

Rhodes, Richard. *Dark Sun: The Making of the Hydrogen Bomb.* New York: Simon and Schuster, 1995.

York, Herbert F. *The Advisors: Oppenheimer, Teller, and the Superbomb.* San Francisco: W. H. Freeman, 1976. Reprint, Stanford, CA: Stanford University Press, 1989.

AEC Inquiry into Security Clearance

Polenberg, Richard, ed. *In the Matter of J. Robert Oppenheimer: The Security Clearance Hearing.* Ithaca, NY: Cornell University Press, 2002.

U.S. Atomic Energy Commission. *In the Matter of J. Robert Oppenheimer: Transcript of Hearing before Personnel Security Board and Texts of Principal Documents and Letters.* Cambridge, MA: MIT Press. 1971. Covers the 1954 AEC inquiry into Oppenheimer'"s security clearance.

Miscellaneous

Adams, John, and Peter Sellars. *Doctor Atomic.* An opera by the contemporary minimalist American composer John Adams, with libretto by Peter Sellars. It premiered at the San Francisco Opera on 1 October 2005.

Else, Jon, and KTEH-TV (San Jose, California). *The Day after Trinity: J. Robert Oppenheimer and the Atomic Bomb.* A film by Jon Else. Santa Monica, CA: Pyramid Films, 1981.

Kipphardt, Heinar. *In the Matter of J. Robert Oppenheimer: A Play Freely Adapted on the Basis of the Documents by Heinar Kipphardt.* New York: Hill and Wang, 1968.

Silvan Schweber

ORESME, NICOLE

ORESME, NICOLE (*b.* Allemagne [later Fleury sur Orne, near Caen, France], c. 1320; *d.* Lisieux, France, 1382), *mathematics, natural philosophy.* For the original article on Oresme see *DSB,* vol. 10.

Scholarship since the 1970s has enriched the understanding of Oresme's contributions to the history of natural philosophy. There is in the early 2000s a more detailed understanding of the nature of the intellectual environment during his studies at the University of Paris. Analyses of his commentaries on Aristotle's *Physics* and *On the Heavens* reveal Oresme's utilization of the logical and semantical theories of his day. A subsequent critical edition of Oresme's treatise *On Seeing the Stars* shows that he made significant contributions to optics and the study of atmospheric refraction that have previously been overlooked by historians of science.

Early Career. New documentary evidence on Nicole Oresme's earlier academic and ecclesiastical career and a more precise assessment of the University of Paris's institutional setting has contributed to a different overview of Oresme's natural philosophy as well as, more generally, of fourteenth-century philosophy. John Buridan's role in the philosophical training of University of Paris masters such as Nicole Oresme, Albert of Saxony, and Marsilius of Inghen has to be revised, taking into consideration that students only rarely chose their supervising masters; they could attend lectures given by masters as well as disputations outside their Nation, but the notion of "school" must, if one wishes to use it, take into account the peculiar university's institutional habits and procedures. On the basis of University of Paris *rotuli* sent to the papal court with the view of obtaining ecclesiastical benefices for the university masters, the date of Oresme's master's degree has now been determined to be 1341 or 1342, at least six years earlier than previously thought (1348). According to the new chronology, Oresme studied when the diffusion of William of Ockham's doctrines, on logic as well as on natural philosophy, was at its apex; moreover, the spread of the ideas of other English authors such as Thomas Bradwardine and William Heytesbury, whose influence on Oresme's scientific thought is well known, also occurred some years earlier than previously thought. The first years of his academic career in the Faculty of Arts were troubled not only by the diffusion of Ockham's ideas but also by the condemnations of Nicholas of Autrécourt (1346) and Jean de Mirecourt (1347); the work of both masters was of great importance to Oresme's scientific thought.

The Possibility of Scientific Knowledge. According to Nicholas of Autrécourt, scientific knowledge can only be obtained through propositions that can be reduced to the principle of contradiction; this condition drastically reduced the possibility of scientific knowledge in natural philosophy, so much so that masters of arts were urged to discuss in their commentaries on Aristotle's natural works

Oresme

whether a scientific analysis of the problems at issue (usually in the commentaries on the *Physics*) was even possible. Oresme accurately distinguishes two kinds of evident propositions: (1) the perfectly evident ones, whose contrary implies contradiction, typical of mathematics; and (2) the almost perfectly evident ones, whose contrary is not impossible, which are to be found in natural philosophy (*Questions on the Physics*, Book I, Question 3). On this basis he shows that skeptical attitudes are excessive with regard to the possibility of human knowledge about physical events.

The distinction between these two kinds of evidence lets Oresme introduce into natural enquiry the so-called imaginary cases (some of them well known by the historian of science, e.g., the plurality of worlds and the Earth's rotation), which can be proposed because, even though they are not real, they are nonetheless possible. Oresme's belief in the convenience of using mathematics in natural philosophy relies on this ground. So, even if the methods of analysis of the two disciplines must remain different—that is, natural philosophy cannot proceed in a deductive way like mathematics (*Questions on De anima,* Book I, Question1)—some mathematical tools such as points, lines, and surfaces (and the rules of geometry) can be found useful in natural philosophy. Oresme favors the application of geometry to explain not only vision (*perspectiva*), but also physical events, relying explicitly on Robert Grosseteste's writings (and primarily on *De lineis*) and having in mind Aristotle's *scientie mediae* (*Questions on De spera*, Question 1).

Views on Substance and Accident. The change in Oresme's ideas about motion in his commentaries on the *Physics* (*Questions on the Physics,* Book III, where motion is considered a *modus* not different ontologically from the moving body) and *On the soul* (*Questions on De anima,* Book II, Question 15, where it is defined as an accidental property of the moving body) was probably caused by the condemnation of Jean de Mirecourt, who introduced in Paris the ontology of *modi rerum.*

In his only partially edited commentary on the *Physics*, Oresme deals with physical topics such as motion, space, and time systematically relying on the theory of *modi rerum*, according to which accidental properties such as those registered in Aristotle's *Praedicamenta* are to be considered as modifications of the substance, rather than as real beings inhering to real substances. Oresme presents his solution as a third way of dealing with the ontological problems concerning the relationship between substance and accidents, in addition to the "common opinion" defending the reality of accidental properties (at a lower level of substance, in which they inhere), and to the "nominalistic" theory, according to which accidents are not different from substance (with the exception of qualities, in order to avoid dangerous theological implications). In his *Physics* commentary Oresme restates his position (already put forth in the previous books) in book 5, where he discusses the intension and remission of qualitative forms, a basic element in the analysis of natural change and a field in which his contribution toward a geometrical study of qualitative changes and motion is particularly original (see the original *DSB* article). Oresme declares explicitly that his solution is the simplest, and one that can overcome every kind of difficulty (*Questions on the Physics,* Book V, Question 9).

In introducing his theory of *modi rerum* Oresme makes use of semantical tools such as the *complexe significabile* (what can be rendered through a sentence). Only substances can be duly expressed by nouns, while accidents and relations (according to Oresme *modi* or *conditiones rerum*) are to be rendered through sentences in the infinitive form: *aliquod esse album* (that something is white) for the quality "white"; *lapidem aliter se habere quam prius* (that a stone is in a different position as before) for the motion of a stone. This is not the only passage that permits an ascription to him of a deep acquaintance with logic, possibly exceeding the normal university training, even though he never ventured to write a treatise or a commentary on logical topics.

The Limits of Powers. In his commentary *On the Heavens* he deals with the problems of the potential limits of natural substances (*de maximo et minimo*), a topic also discussed by William Heytesbury in his *Regulae solvendi sophismata* and probably introduced in the debates held at the Faculty of Arts in Paris not earlier than the third decade of the fourteenth century. In this commentary Oresme studies the limits of activity of natural powers on the basis of the fourfold distinction typical of the *de maximo et minimo* theory (*maximum quod sic* and *minimum quod non* for the active powers, representing respectively intrinsic and extrinsic limits; *minimum quod sic* and *maximum quod non* for passive powers), and places the limits of active power in an extrinsic limit. The reason for such a choice is to be found in the divisibility of the amount by which the power is greater than resistance (according to the law that in order to have an action the active power must be greater than the resistive one); the limit is to be determined as the least in which the natural power cannot act (*minimum quod non*). In order to reach this solution Oresme relies on the semantical theory of *suppositio* (and specifically on *suppositio confusa tantum,* through which one is not obliged to exhibit a definite limit, in conformity with the infinite divisibility either of the

Oresme

quantity of power or of the space or the temporal duration).

Oresme's systematic use of the *modi rerum* theory in his *Physics* commentary leads to original solutions concerning motion, space, and time, major topics discussed in this book. Viewing motion as a *modus* of the moving body permits him to avoid shortcomings such as the denial of motion (Ockham's solution, reducing motion to the moving body) and the problems that result from considering it as an inherent accident as well (John Buridan's solution); in this case, in fact, it would be very difficult to maintain the basic permanent (*totum simul*) character of accidental forms, motion being essentially continuous.

Oresme maintains the same semi-reductionist attitude toward the other two major physical topics discussed in Aristotle's *Physics*: place and time. These are neither accidental forms nor conceptual devices for describing physical events; they are inner conditions (*conditiones seu modi*) of bodies, properly rendered through adverbs like "here, there, now, yesterday," rather than nouns such as "place" and "time," which would denote them as substances. As for motion, such an ontological commitment gives Oresme the opportunity to elude the problem of the infinite (just because of the insubstantiality of *modi rerum*), making a mathematical analysis easier. Oresme proposes on this basis a definition of place and time different than Aristotle's: Instead of the "innermost motionless boundary of what contains it" (*Aristotle, The Complete Works: Physics*, Book IV, 4, 212a20–21, trans. J. Barnes, 1984)), for Oresme place is the "space filled by the body, which would be empty if the body were removed" (*Questions on the Physics,* Book IV, Question 1); time, rather than the measure of motion (*Physics* IV, 11, 219b1–2) is successive duration (*duratio rerum successiva, Questions on the Physics,* Book IV, Question17), a stronger notion that cannot be reduced exclusively to the measure of duration.

Atmospheric Refraction. A 2006 study of Oresme's treatise *De visione stellarum* reveals yet another example of his major contributions to natural philosophy. Dan Burton (2006) argues that Oresme was the first to make a theoretical study of atmospheric refraction, a phenomenon of great practical import to astronomers as well as of philosophical significance. After all, if the stars are not where they appear to be, how reliable is knowledge gained through the senses? Oresme proposes that light from the stars travels along a curved path in the atmosphere whose density varies uniformly. Thus refraction need not occur only at the interface of two materials, as had been believed by all his predecessors (Grant, 2007). In his mathematical analysis Oresme uses his knowledge of infinite convergent series. Robert Hooke and Isaac Newton later took up this approach to atmospheric refraction and provided a demonstration of Oresme's result.

SUPPLEMENTARY BIBLIOGRAPHY

Albert Douglas Menut's bibliography of Oresme's works ("A Provisional Bibliography of Oresme's Writings," Medieval Studies *28 [1966]: 279–299, and the "Supplementary Note,"* Medieval Studies *31 [1969]: 346–347) has been supplanted by the entry "Nicolaus Oresme" in Olga Weijers,* Le travail intellectuel à la Faculté des Arts de Paris: Textes et maîtres (ca. 1200–1500)*, vol. 6. (Turnhout, Belgium: Brepols, 2005). The great part of Oresme's commentaries on Aristotle's works has been edited, as follows in the "Works" section.*

WORKS BY ORESME

De celo: Claudia Kren, *The Questiones super De celo of Nicole Oresme,* PhD diss., University of Wisconsin, 1965.

Commentary on John of Holiwood's *De spera*: Garrett Droppers, *The Questiones De spera of Nicole Oresme.* PhD diss., University of Wisconsin, 1966.

Metereologics: Stepen C. McCluskey Jr., *Nicole Oresme on Light, Color, and the Rainbow.* PhD diss., University of Wisconsin, 1974. Questions on the third book.

Questio contra divinatores horoscopios: Stefano Caroti, "Nicole Oresme, Quaestio contra divinatores horoscopios," *Archives d'Histoire Doctrinale et Littéraire du Moyen Age* 43 (1976): 201–310.

De sensu et sensato: Jole Agrimi, *Le "Quaestiones de sensu" attribuite a Oresme e Alberto di Sassonia.* Florence: La Nuova Italia, 1983.

Quodlibeta: Bert Hansen, *Nicole Oresme and the Marvels of Nature: A Study of His "De causis mirabilium."* Toronto: Pontifical Institute of Mediaeval Studies, 1985. Parts 1 and 2.

De anima: Benoît Patar, *Nicolai Oresme Expositio et Quaestiones in Aristotelis "De anima."* Edition, étude, critique. Études doctrinales en collaboration avec Claude Gagnon. Louvain-La-Neuve, Louvain, Paris: Éditions de l'Institut Supérieur de Philosophie, Éditions Peeters, 1995.

De generatione et corruptione: Stefano Caroti, ed., *Quaestiones super De generatione et corruptione.* Munich: Bayerische Akademie der Wissenschaften, 1996.

Physica: Stefan Kirschner, ed., *Nicolaus Oresmes Kommentar zur Physik des Aristoteles.* Stuttgart: Franz Steiner Verlag, 1997 (books 3–4; questions 6–9 of book 5). The complete edition edited by Stefano Caroti, Jean Celeyrette, Stefan Kirschner, and Edmond Mazet is forthcoming.

De visione stellarum: Dan Burton, *Nicole Oresme's "De visione stellarum" (On Seeing the Stars): A Critical Edition of Oresme's Treatise on Optics and Atmospheric Refraction, with an Introduction, Commentary, and English Translation.* Leiden: Brill, 2006.

OTHER SOURCES

Bosemberg, Zoe "Nicole Oresme et Robert Grosseteste: La conception dynamique de la matière." In *"Quia inter doctores est magna dissensio": Les débats de philosophie naturelle à Paris au XIVe siècle*, edited by Stefano Caroti and Jean Celeyrette. Florence: Leo S. Olschki, 2004.

Busard, Hubertus L. L. "Die Quellen von Nicole Oresme." *Janus* 58 (1971): 161–193.

Cadden, Joan. "Charles V, Nicole Oresme, and Christine de Pizan: Unities and Uses of Knowledge in Fourteenth-Century France." In *Texts and Contexts in Ancient and Medieval Science: Studies on the Occasion of John E. Murdoch's Seventieth Birthday*, edited by Edith Dudley Sylla and Michael M. McVaugh. Leiden and New York: Brill, 1997.

Caroti, Stefano. "Ordo universalis e impetus nei Quodlibeta di Nicole Oresme." *Archives Internationales d'Histoire des Sciences* 33 (1983): 213–233.

———. "Ein Kapitel der mittelalterlichen Diskussion über reactio: Das novum fundamentum Nicole Oresmes und dessen Widerlegung durch Marsilius von Inghen." In *Historia Philosophiae Medii Aevi. Studien zur Geschichte der Philosophie des Mittelalters: Festschrift für Kurt Flach zu seinem 60. Geburtstag*, edited by Burkhard Mojsisch and Olaf Pluta, vol. 1. Amsterdam and Philadelphia: Grüner, 1991.

———. "Oresme on Motion." *Vivarium* 31 (1993): 8–36.

———. "La position de Nicole Oresme sur la nature du mouvement (*Questiones super Physicam* III, 1–8): Problèmes gnoséologiques, ontologiques et sémantiques." *Archives d'Histoire Doctrinale et Littéraire du Moyen Age* 61 (1994): 303–385.

———. "Nicole Oresme et les *modi rerum*." *Oriens-Occidens* 3 (2000): 115–144.

———. "Time and *Modi Rerum* in Nicole Oresme's *Physics* Commentary." In *The Medieval Concept of Time: Studies on the Scholastic Debate and Its Reception in Early Modern Philosophy*, edited by Pasquale Porro. Leiden and Boston: Brill, 2001.

Celeyrette, Jean. "Le statut des mathématiques dans la *Physique* d'Oresme." *Oriens-Occidens* 3 (2000): 91–113.

———. *Figura/figuratum* par Jean Buridan et Nicole Oresme." In *"Quia inter doctores est magna dissensio": Les débats de philosophie naturelle à Paris au XIVe siècle*, edited by Stefano Caroti and Jean Celeyrette. Florence: Leo S. Olschki , 2004.

———, and Edmond Mazet. "La hierarchie des degrés d'être chez Nicole Oresme." *Arabic Sciences and Philosophy* 8 (1998): 45–65.

Courtenay, William J. "The Early Career of Nicole Oresme." *Isis* 91 (2000): 542–548.

Di Liscia, Daniel A. "Sobre la doctrina de las "Configurationes" de Nicolas de Oresme." *Patristica et Mediaevalia* 11 (1990): 79–105.

———. "Aceleracion y caída de los graves en Oresme: Sobre la inaplicabilidad del teorema de la velocidad media." *Patristica et Mediaevalia* 13 (1992): 61–84; 14 (1993): 41–56.

Grant, Edward. "Scientific Thought in Fourteenth-Century Paris: Jean Buridan and Nicole Oresme." In *Machaut's World: Science and Art in the Fourteenth Century*, edited by Madeleine Pelner Cosman and Bruce Chandler. New York: New York Academy of Sciences, 1978.

———. "Nicole Oresme on Certitude in Science and Pseudo-Science." In *Nicolas Oresme: Tradition et innovation chez un intellectuel du XIVe siècle*, edited by Pierre Souffrin and Alain P. Ségonds. Paris and Padua: Les Belles Lettres–Programma 1+1 Editori, 1988.

———. "Nicole Oresme, Aristotle's 'On the Heavens,' and the Court of Charles V." In *Texts and Contexts in Ancient and Medieval Science: Studies on the Occasion of John E. Murdoch's Seventieth Birthday*, edited by Edith Dudley Sylla and Michael R. McVaugh. Leiden and New York: Brill, 1997.

———. *A History of Natural Philosophy: From the Ancient World to the Nineteenth Century*. Cambridge, U.K.: Cambridge University Press, 2007.

Hugonnard-Roche, Henri. "Logique et philosophie naturelle au XIVe siècle: La critique d'Aristote par Nicole Oresme." In *Actes du 109e Congrès national des Sociétés savantes, Dijon 1984. Section Histoire des sciences et des techniques.* Paris: Comité des Travaux historiques et scientifiques, 1984.

———. "Modalités et argumentation chez Nicole Oresme." In *Nicolas Oresme: Tradition et innovation chez un intellectuel du XIVe siècle*, edited by Pierre Souffrin and Alain P. Ségonds. Paris and Padua: Les Belles Lettres–Programma 1+1 Editori, 1988.

Kirschner, Stefan. "Oresme on Intension and Remission of Qualities in His Commentary on Aristotle's 'Physics.'" *Vivarium* 38 (2000): 255–274.

———. "Oresme's Concepts of Place, Space, and Time in His Commentary on Aristotle's *Physics*." *Oriens-Occidens* 3 (2000): 145–179.

Marshall, Peter. "Nicole Oresme on the Nature, Reflection, and Speed of Light." *Isis* 72 (1981): 357–374.

———. "Parisian Psychology in the Mid-Fourteenth Century." *Archives d'Histoire Doctrinale et Littéraire du Moyen Age* 50 (1983): 101–193.

Lejbowicz, Max. "Argumentation oresmienne et logique divinatoire (quelques remarques sur le *De commensurabilitate*, III)." In *Preuve et raisons à l'Université de Paris: Logique, ontologie et théologie au XIVe siècle*, edited by Zénon Kaluza and Paul Vignaux. Paris: Vrin, 1984.

Mazet, Edmond. "Un aspect de l'ontologie d'Oresme: L'équivocité de l'étant et ses rapports avec la théorie des *complexe significabilia* et avec l'ontologie oresmienne de l'accident." *Oriens-Occident* 3 (2000): 67–89.

———. "Pierre Ceffons et Oresme: Leur relation revisitée." In *"Quia inter doctores est magna dissensio": Les débats de philosophie naturelle à Paris au XIVe siècle*, edited by Stefano Caroti and Jean Celeyrette. Florence: Leo S. Olschki, 2004.

Molland, George A. "Nicole Oresme and Scientific Progress." In *Antiqui und Moderni: Traditionsbewußtsein und Fortschrittsbewußtsein im späten Mittelalter*, edited by Albert Zimmermann. Berlin: De Gruyter, 1974.

———. "The Oresmian Style: Semi-Mathematical, Semi-Holistic." In *Nicolas Oresme: Tradition et innovation chez un intellectuel du XIVe siècle*, edited by Pierre Souffrin and Alain P. Ségonds. Paris and Padua: Les Belles Lettres–Programma 1+1 Editori, 1988.

Quillet, Jeannine, ed. *Autour de Nicole Oresme: Actes du Colloque Oresme organisé à l'Université de Paris XII.* Paris: Vrin, 1990.

———. "Nicole Osreme et la science nouvelle dans le livre du Ciel et du Monde." In *Knowledge and the Sciences in Medieval Philosophy. Proceedings of the Eight International Congress of Medieval Philosophy (SIEPM)*, edited by Simo

Knuuttila, Reijo Työrinoja, and Sten Ebbesen, vol. 2. Helsinki: Societas Philosophica Fennica, 1990.

Rusnock, Paul. "Oresme on Ratios of Lesser Inequality." *Archives Internationales d'Histoire des Sciences* 45 (1995): 263–272.

Sarnowsky, Jürgen. "Nicole Oresme and Albert of Saxony's Commentary on the *Physics*: The Problems of Vacuum and Motion in a Void." In *"Quia inter doctores est magna dissensio": Les débats de philosophie naturelle à Paris au XIVe siècle*, edited by Stefano Caroti and Jean Celeyrette. Florence: Leo S. Olschki, 2004.

Souffrin, Pierre. "La quantification du mouvement chez les scolastiques: La vitesse instantanée chez Nicole Oresme." In *Autour de Nicole Oresme: Actes du Colloque Oresme organisé à l'Université de Paris XII*, edited by Jeannine Quillet. Paris: Vrin, 1990.

Souffrin, Pierre, and Alain P. Ségonds, eds. *Nicolas Oresme: Tradition et innovation chez un intellectuel du XIVe siècle*. Paris and Padua: Les Belles Lettres–Programma 1+1 Editori, 1988.

Taschow, Ulrich. "Die Bedeutung der Musik als Modell für Nicole Oresmes Theorie 'De configurationibus qualitatum et motuum.'" *Early Science and Medicine* 4 (1999): 37–90.

Thijssen, Hans. "Buridan, Albert of Saxony, and Oresme, and a Fourteenth-Century Collection of Quaestiones on the Physics and on De generatione et corruptione." *Vivarium* 24 (1986): 70–82.

Von Plato, Jan. "Nicole Oresme and the Ergodicity of Rotations." *Acta Philosophica Fennica* 32 (1981): 190–197.

Zanin, Fabio. "*Passio corruptiva/passio perfectiva*: A basic Distinction in Oresme's Theory of Knowledge." In *"Quia inter doctores est magna dissensio": Les débats de philosophie naturelle à Paris au XIVe siècle,* edited by Stefano Caroti and Jean Celeyrette. Florence: Leo S. Olschki, 2004.

Stefano Caroti

OSBORN, HENRY FAIRFIELD

(*b.* Fairfield, Connecticut, 8 August 1857; *d.* Garrison, New York, 6 November 1935), *vertebrate paleontology, origins of the mammals, human evolution, museum administrator.*

Although Osborn is best remembered as the outspoken president of the American Museum of Natural History, one of his consuming scientific pursuits was his attempt to show that central Asia was the cradle of the human race. The search was predicated on his belief that spiritual salvation was something that could be proven scientifically or at least had a rational basis. As a result he was tangentially involved in the Piltdown man incident (in which a human fossil skull was hoaxed), was a leading figure in the eugenics movement, and played a small role in the Scopes "monkey trial." Osborn felt, in part, that if he could prove the Asian origin of humans he could show that each human ethnic group had a separate biological origin. If they did then it was justified in treating each ethnic group as either superior or inferior.

Osborn was raised from childhood to believe that salvation was achievable only through the exertion of personal willpower. His mother, Virginia Osborn, was a devout Christian who instilled these values in her son. He took her teachings about the need for personal struggle for salvation and built them into a theory of mammalian evolution in general and human evolution in particular. His system was a quirky and nuanced conglomeration of Lamarkian adaptation, Darwinian selection, spiritual elevation, and the mental gymnastics of metaphysical free will. The question of free will has a long history in Christian theology. It asks if individuals can determine their own destiny or has it been preordained for them. Osborn worked this idea into his evolution theory arguing that humans could determine their own evolution up to a point, but that certain restrictions had been genetically predetermined for them. While his studies of mammalian evolution began in the 1880s, by 1900 he had come to focus on human evolution and central Asia as the source of all mammalian life.

In the intellectual jousting between neo-Lamarckians and neo-Darwinians, Osborn came down, at least initially, on the side of the Lamarckians. Though he was a great admirer of Charles Darwin, Osborn's personal experiences and his belief in straight-line progress in evolution (orthogenesis), as well as his relationship with Edward Drinker Cope (who became something of a mentor to him), drew him away from strict Darwinism and led him to formulate his own explanatory process for evolutionary change. Like Jean-Baptiste Lamarck, Osborn believed an organism could affect its own evolution through the exercise of personal free will. Where Osborn's thinking remained Darwinian was in his belief in the importance of struggle in the equation. In order to blend all this together he tried to reevaluate the fossil record so it would answer both scientific and metaphysical questions. In this way he blended German Romanticism with British empiricism in a pragmatic American fashion.

Following Cope's lead, Osborn centered his studies on fossil teeth. The evolution of teeth, especially horse teeth, was important because in the changes in tooth structure Osborn saw what he believed was the slow, steady, progressive march of evolution. The heart of his evolutionary system was the idea that, as time passed, a species, genera, or phylum went from simple unspecialized forms to more specialized varieties in a series of slow incremental changes. These changes were brought about by the relative exertions of various anatomical parts. These exertions were the result of the organism's attempt to adapt to its environment. Once established, these characters were passed on to the next generation in a linear fashion. Osborn argued that the

Henry Fairfield Osborn. AP IMAGES.

discovery of primitive mammal fossils confirmed the theory that molars had gone through stages beginning with the simple single reptilian, or homodont cone, and proceeding on to the more complex tritubercular (multicone) stage.

Though he was initially unsure just how these characters appeared he rejected the notion that anything happened randomly or was the product of blind chance. Studying variations in fossil teeth convinced him that at least some hereditary characters followed certain predispositions in their development. He saw the tritubercular molars as superior to the nontritubercular forms because they persisted into later ages. As he saw it, the drawback of this process was that as the specialization and complexity of groups increased, so did their inability to adapt to change. Therefore a less specialized, more general type would last longer and so was superior.

Osborn employed the group of mammals known as titanotheres as a model for all mammalian evolutionary schemes. While he accepted natural selection as an important factor in evolution, he was convinced that it was not the central mechanism. He rebuked geneticists that for all their work they had failed to give an explanation for species' origins, feeling only fossils could do so. That organisms adapt to their environment creatively was a process he called aristogenesis. This process operated on a series of rectigradations (a series of inherent genetic advantages and predispositions) that, according to Osborn, were the predestined factors in a genetic pool that give a phyla its special abilities to adapt to changing environmental conditions. Aristogenesis could be called on to overcome obstacles.

Osborn's idea of creative evolution was similar to that of the French philosopher Henri-Louis Bergson (1859–1941), who was not completely satisfied with either Lamarckian or Darwinian evolutionary mechanics. Osborn felt that an élan vital compelled an organism to overcome adversity. Organisms could combine their predestined rectigradations with a fluid willpower to make a unique response to the environment. Osborn said the aristogenes were the characters that evolved into important functional structures. By the 1920s Osborn called on more metaphysical realms—that of the divine—to explain the origins of the aristogenes. He insisted that his study of aristogenesis suggested to him that the modern human line as well as the human soul, were immensely old, had ultimately divine origins, and were not related directly to the primates. Despite being a devout Christian, Osborn opposed the Christian fundamentalists and agreed to appear at Clarence Darrow's request as a defense witness at the Scopes trial in 1925. Confusion over the identity of a fossil tooth, commonly called Nebraska man, contributed to Osborn's last-minute decision not to appear in Tennessee.

He feared his mistake with this misidentified fossil would be used against Scopes in particular and evolution in general as an example of the flawed nature of evolution studies.

As he believed central Asia was the cradle of humans, he sent an expedition to the Gobi Desert in 1921 to search for the earliest human fossils. Led by the museum explorer Roy Chapman Andrews (1884–1960), the Central Asiatic Expeditions lasted until 1930, when local political conditions rendered the situation untenable. Although the expeditions brought back tons of fossil dinosaurs, including the first dinosaur eggs, no human fossil remains were found. Osborn's unique approach to evolution never caught on with the wider scientific community, and his ideas died with him in 1935.

BIBLIOGRAPHY

The Osborn papers at the American Museum of Natural History and the New York Historical Society contain a wealth of information on Osborn, his family, and his work.

OTHER SOURCES

Rainger, Ronald. *An Agenda for Antiquity: Henry Fairfield Osborn and Vertebrate Paleontology at the American Museum of*

Natural History, 1890–1935. Tuscaloosa: University of Alabama Press, 1991.

Regal, Brian. *Henry Fairfield Osborn: Race and the Search for the Origins of Man.* London: Ashgate, 2002.

———. *Human Evolution: A Guide to the Debates.* Santa Barbara, CA: ABC-Clio, 2005.

Brian Regal

OSTWALD, FRIEDRICH WILHELM

(*b.* Riga, Latvia, Russia, 2 September 1853; *d.* Leipzig, Germany, 4 April 1932), *physical chemistry, energetics, color science.* For the original article on Ostwald see *DSB,* vol. 15, Supplement I.

Ostwald was one of the founders, along with Svante Arrhenius and Jacobus Henricus van't Hoff, of the hybrid discipline of physical chemistry and was its most effective organizer and influential spokesman. He was instrumental in winning acceptance for Arrhenius's ionic theory of dissociation. In 1909 Ostwald received the Nobel Prize in Chemistry for his "works on catalysis, as well as for fundamental investigations of chemical equilibrium and reaction velocities" (from the Nobel citation). Ostwald was an imaginative and prolific, although often controversial, apostle of scientific ideas. Beginning in the early 1890s he championed the cause of energetics, first as an energy-based natural science but after around 1900 as a comprehensive worldview. He also championed a variety of other causes, including a novel quantitative theory of colors. Ebullient in personality, Ostwald was a man of great personal charm and an inspiring teacher. Many-sided in his interests—he was a musician and painter as well as a scientist, cultural critic, international organizer, and would-be philosopher—he was actively involved in promoting the broadly humanistic aspirations (e.g., monism, pacifism, and internationalism) shared by many European intellectuals in the first third of the twentieth century.

Biography, Correspondence, *Nachlass.* There is still no authoritative scientific biography of Ostwald, likely because he left an enormous published output consisting of forty-five books, more than five hundred scientific papers, and some five thousand reviews. In addition he edited, at one time or another, six journals, including the *Zeitschrift für physikalische Chemie* (1887–1906) and the *Annalen der Naturphilosophie* (1901–1914) as well as a series of scientific reprints, *Klassiker der exakten Wissenschaften,* to which he appended often revealing introductions and editorial remarks. There is also an enormous *Nachlass,* most of it currently housed in the Berlin-Brandenburgische Akademie der Wissenschaften, only parts of which have been explored. The best account of Ostwald's life and work remains his own *Lebenslinien: Eine Selbstbiographie* in three volumes (1926–1927). A condensed version is "Wilhelm Ostwald" in *Philosophie der Gegenwart in Selbstdarstellungen* (1924). *Wilhelm Ostwald: Mein Vater* (1953), written by Ostwald's daughter Grete, is still useful for its account of his family life. Subsequent works include an uneven miscellanea of twenty-five essays on his life and work collected in the proceedings of an international symposium celebrating the 125th anniversary of Ostwald's birth (1979); Jan-Peter Domschke and Peter Lewandrowski's *Wilhelm Ostwald: Chemiker, Wissenschaftstheoriker, Organisator* (1982); Armin Meisel's "Wilhelm Ostwald: Leben und Werk" (1986); Domschke and Karl Hensel's *Wilhelm Ostwald: Eine Kurzbiographie* (2000), and Mi Gyung Kim's "Wilhelm Ostwald" (2006), a brief but useful essay in English.

More of Ostwald's correspondence with scientific contemporaries has become available to complement the invaluable collections compiled by Hans-Günther Körber in the 1960s. The most important volumes from Berlin are three (1994, 1996, 1997) edited by Regine Zott, probably the foremost German expert on Ostwald's work, and a fourth volume (1998) edited by Joachim Stocklöv.

Additional parts of the *Nachlass* have also been published by the Wilhelm-Ostwald-Gesellschaft zu Grossbothen e.V. in a series of *Sonderhefte* (special issues) of the society. The most important of these are more correspondence editions (1997–2002) with scientific contemporaries, all of them chemists, and various works on Ostwald's color theory (1999–2002). Unfortunately, the society ceased publication in February 2005, when its government funding was not renewed and the bulk of the *Nachlass* was transported to the Berlin Academy. A brief description of the contents of the *Nachlass* is provided by Regine Zott in "Wilhelm Ostwald und sein schriftlicher Nachlass" (1989). A sampling of the contents is given in Uwe Niedersen's "Leben, Wissenschaft, Klassifikation: Aus dem Nachlass Wilhelm Ostwalds" (1992).

Physical Chemistry, Energetics, Color Theory. The work in physical chemistry that made Ostwald's reputation is ably described in Robert Root-Bernstein's "The Ionists: Founding Physical Chemistry, 1872–1890" (1980). The work of Ostwald's many American students is surveyed in John Servos's *Physical Chemistry from Ostwald to Pauling: The Making of a Science in America* (1990). Ostwald's program for energetics is recounted in a series of essays (2007, 2008) by Robert J. Deltete, and a condensed version of Ostwald's energetic theory is contained in "Gibbs and the Energeticists" (1996) by the same author. The application of energetic theory to chemistry was described in 1986 by Arie Leegwater. Ostwald's peculiar understanding of

Friedrich Wilhelm Ostwald. HULTON ARCHIVE/GETTY IMAGES.

irreversibility is examined by Uwe Niedersen in "Die Energetik und der Irreversibilitätsgedanke bei Wilhelm Ostwald" (1983) and "Zu den Problemen von Reversibilität, Irreversibilität und Zeit im Schaffen Wilhelm Ostwalds" (1986). Tensions in his understanding of time are revealed by Hans-Jürgen Krug and Ludwig Pohlmann in "Die Dichotomien der Zeit: Der Zeitbegriff bei Wilhelm Ostwald" (1994). Ostwald's introduction and use of the concepts *mole* and *molar* and their relation to his alleged antiatomism is discussed in two 1982 essays by Yves Noël. The received view that Ostwald was opposed to atomism until his official "conversion" in 1909 is challenged by Britta Görs in *Chemischer Atomismus* (1999). Casper Hakfoort (1992) offers an appraisal of Ostwald's hopes for an energetic worldview, which revives criticism already leveled at Ostwald in his own time by Max Weber in "Energetische Kulturtheorien" (1909). A good overview of Ostwald's color theory is Eugen Ristenpart's *Die Ostwaldsche Farbenlehre und ihre Nutzen* (2000).

Organization, Standardization, Internationalism. Ostwald's pyramidal theory of the structure of science and his ideas about proper scientific organization are contained in two Sonderhefte of the Wilhelm Ostwald Society: *Wissenschaftstheorie und -organization* (2004) and *Das grosse Elixier. Die Wissenschaftslehre* (2004), both of which are critiqued by Friedemann Schmithals in "Abstrakte Wissenschaft oder gute Lehre?" (1999). Ostwald's recommendations for the organization of information and the standardization of documentation are discussed in two useful essays (1991, 1997) by Thomas Hapke. Ostwald's advocacy of an international language is vigorously presented to often skeptical colleagues in another Sonderheft from the Wilhelm-Ostwald-Gesellschaft: *Aus dem Briefwechsel William Ostwalds zur Einführung einer Weltsprache* (1999). His activity on behalf of the German Monist League is ably recounted by Danuta Sobczynska and Ewa Czerwinska (1998), and his attempt to write a "chemical history of culture" is described by Uwe Niedersen in "Chemische Kulturgeschichte: Grundlegung" (1992).

Ostwald's *Grosse Männer* (1910) classified scientists of genius into two broad types, classicists and romanticists, according to mental temperament and "reaction velocity." This classification was described and criticized by Hans Simmer in 1978 and is employed by Robert J. Deltete to illuminate the differences in scientific style between Gibbs and Ostwald in "Josiah Willard Gibbs and Wilhelm Ostwald: A Contrast in Scientific Style" (1996).

The publishers of Ostwald's *Klassiker* celebrated its centenary in 1989 with a special volume describing the history of the project by Lothar Dunsch. By 2005, 297 volumes had appeared. Six essays by Ostwald on the environment were published as volume 257 in 1978, and four essays on the history of science were published as volume 267 in 1985, all from the *Nachlass.*

Updates and Correction. Two additional updates to the original *DSB* entry are an essay by Jindrich Pinkava, "The Relations of W. Ostwald and F. Wald" (1977) and an English translation of Ostwald's *Elektrochemie: Ihre Geschichte und Lehre* as *Electrochemistry. History and Theory,* 2 vols. (1980). A correction concerns Georg Helm, Ostwald's uneasy ally in promoting energetics. Helm was not a physical chemist, although he wrote a textbook on the subject, *Gründzuge der mathematischen Chemie: Energetik der chemischen Erscheinungen* (1894). Instead, he was a mathematician and a mathematical physicist. See the introductory essay by Robert J. Deltete to the English translation of Helm's *Die Energetik nach ihrer geschichtlichen Entwicklung* (*The Historical Development of Energetics;* 2000).

SUPPLEMENTARY BIBLIOGRAPHY

WORKS BY OSTWALD

Autobiography

Lebenslinien. Eine Selbstbiographie. 3 vols. *Lebenslinien: Eine Selbstbiographie. Nach der Ausgabe von 1926/27 überarbeitet*

Ostwald

und kommentiert von Karl Hansel. Stuttgart, Germany: Verlag der Sächsischen Akademie der Wissenschaften zu Leipzig in Kommission bei S. Hirzel, 2003.

Correspondence (Berlin)

Aus dem wissenschaftlichen Briefwechsel Wilhelm Ostwalds. 1. Teil: *Briefwechsel mit Ludwig Boltzmann, Max Planck, Georg Helm und Josiah Willard Gibbs.* 2. Le Teil, France: *Briefwechsel mit Svante Arrhenius und Jacobus Hendricus van't Hoff.* Edited by Hans-Günther Körber. Berlin: Akademie-Verlag, 1961, 1969.

Wilhelm Ostwald und Paul Walden in ihren Briefen. Edited by Regine Zott. Berlin: ERS-Verlag, 1994.

Wilhelm Ostwald und Walther Nernst in ihren Briefen sowie in denen einiger Zeitgenossen. Edited by Regine Zott. Berlin: Engel, 1996.

Fritz Haber in seiner Korrespondenz mit Wilhelm Ostwald sowie in Briefen an Svante Arrhenius. Edited by Regine Zott. Berlin: ERS-Verlag, 1997.

Arthur Rudolf Hantzsch im Briefwechsel mit Wilhelm Ostwald. Edited by Joachim Stocklöv, Berlin: ERS-Verlag, 1998.

Correspondence (Grossbothen)

Sonderhefte der Mitteilungen der Wilhelm-Ostwald-Gesellschaft zu Grossbothen e.V.: *Ernst Beckmann und Wilhelm Ostwald in ihren Briefen* (Sonderheft 1, 1997); *Max Le Blanc und Wilhelm Ostwald in ihren Briefen* (Sonderheft 2, 1998); *Theodor Paul und Wilhelm Ostwald in ihren Briefen* (Sonderheft 3, 1998); *Georg Bredig und Wilhelm Ostwald in ihren Briefen* (Sonderheft 4, 1998); *Robert Luther und Wilhelm Ostwald in ihren Briefen* (Sonderheft 5, 1998); *Carl Schmidt und Wilhelm Ostwald in ihren Briefen* (Sonderheft 9, 2000); *William Ramsay und Wilhelm Ostwald in ihren Briefen* (Sonderheft 11, 2000); *Svante Arrhenius und Wilhelm Ostwald in ihren Briefen* (Sonderheft 15, 2002). Editors of 1-5 are Karl Hansel, Uwe Messow, and Karl Quitzsch; of 9 Roß and Karl Hensel; of 11 David Goodall and Karl Hensel; and of 15 Karl Hensel.

Scientific Work

Gedanken zur Biosphäre: 6 Essays. Eingeleitet und mit Anmerkungen von Hermann Berg. Leipzig, Germany: Geest & Portig, 1978. Ostwald's "Klassiker der exakten wissenschaften," 257.

Electrochemistry: History and Theory. 2 vols. New Delhi: Amerind for the Smithsonian Institution and the National Science Foundation, 1980. English translation of *Elektrochemie: Ihre Geschichte und Lehre.* Leipzig, Germany: Veit & Comp., 1896

Zur Geschichte der Wissenschaft: Vier Manuskripte as dem Nachlass von Wilhelm Ostwald. Mit einer Einführung und Anmerken von Regine Zott. Leipzig, Germany: Geest & Portig, 1985. Ostwald's "Klassiker der exakten wissenschaften, 267.

"Chemische Kulturgeschichte: Grundlegung (1929/30)." Ausgewählt, kommentiert und hrsg. von Uwe Niedersen. *Selbstorganisation* 3 (1992): 287–308. Notes on a hemical account of cultural history

"Kalik oder Schönheitslehre." Ausgewählt, kommentiert und hrsg. von Uwe Niederson. *Selbstorganisation* 4 (1993): 271–295. Ostwald's physical theory of beauty in relation to his color theory.

Aus dem Briefwechsel Wilhelm Ostwalds zur Einführung einer Weltsprache (Sonderheft 6, 1999). Ostwald's advocacy of an international language.

Die Philosophie der Farbe: Briefunterricht zur Farben- und Formenlehre (Sonderheft 13, 2002). Introduction to Ostwald's philosophy of color.

Wissenschaftstheorie und -organization (*Vorträge*) (Sonderheft 19, 2004). Theories about the structure of science.

Das grosse Elixier: Die Wissenschaftslehre (Sonderheft 20, 2004). Ideas about scientific organization.

OTHER SOURCES

Biography

Domschke, Jan-Peter, and Karl Hensel. *Wilhelm Ostwald: Eine Kurzbiographie.* Mitteilungen der Wilhelm-Ostwald-Gesellschaft zu Grossbothen, Sonderheft 10, 2000.

Domschke, Jan-Peter, and Peter Lewandrowski. *Wilhelm Ostwald: Chemiker, Wissenschaftstheoriker, Organisator.* Leipzig, Germany: Urania, 1982.

Internationales Symposium anlässlich des 125: Geburtstages von Wilhelm Ostwald. Berlin: Akademie-Verlag, 1979.

Kim, Mi Gyung. "Wilhelm Ostwald." *HYLE: International Journal for the Philosophy of Chemistry* 12, no. 1 (2006): 141–148.

Meisel, Armin. "Wilhelm Ostwald: Leben und Werk." In *Aufsätze zur Geschichte der Naturwissenschaften und Geographie,* edited by Peter-Günther Hamann, 205–220. Vienna: Österreichische Akademie der Wissenschaften, 1986.

Nachlass

Niedersen, Uwe. "Leben, Wissenschaft, Klassifikation Aus dem *Nachlass* Wilhelm Ostwalds." *Selbstorganisation* 3 (1992): 277–285.

Zott, Regine. "Wilhelm Ostwald und sein schriftlicher *Nachlass.*" *Mitteilungen Gesellschaft Deutscher Chemiker, Fachgruppe Geschichte der Chemie* 2 (1989): 63–66.

Physical Chemistry

Görs, Britta. *Chemischer Atomismus: Anwendung, Veränderung, Alternativen im deutschsprachigen Raum in der zweiten Hälfte des 19. Jahrhunderts.* Berlin: ERS-Verlag, 1999.

Kim, Mi Gyung. "Practice and Representation: Investigative Programs of Chemical Affinity in the Nineteenth Century." PhD diss., University of California, Los Angeles, 1990.

Noel, Yves. "L'adjectif 'molaire,' son introduction, et l'expression de antiatomisme chez Wilhelm Ostwald." *Comptes Rendus du Congrès National des Sociétés Savantes, Section des Sciences* 4 (1982): 361–372.

———. "Les premiers temps de le mole dans l'oeuvre de Wilhelm Ostwald et ses traductions." *Comptes Rendus du Congrès National des Sociétés Savantes, Section des Sciences* 4 (1982): 163–170.

Root-Bernstein, Robert. "The Ionists: Founding Physical Chemistry, 1872–1890." PhD diss, Princeton University, 1980.

Servos, John W. *Physical Chemistry from Ostwald to Pauling: The Making of a Science in America.* Princeton, NJ: Princeton University Press, 1990.

Energetics

Deltete, Robert J. "Gibbs and the Energeticists. " In *No Truth Except in the Details: Essays in Honor of Martin J. Klein,* edited by A. J. Kox and Daniel M. Siegel, 135–169. Dordrecht, Netherlands: Kluwer, 1996.

———. "Wilhelm Ostwald's Energetics 1: Origins and Motivations" and "Wilhem Ostwald's Energetics 2–3: Energetic Theory and Applications." *Foundations of Chemistry* 9, 10 (2007, 2008): 3–56 (first essay).

Hakfoort, Casper. "Science Deified: Wilhelm Ostwald's Energeticist World-view and the History of Scientism." *Annals of Science* 49 (1992): 525–544.

Krug, Hans-Jürgen, and Ludwig Pohlmann. "Die Dichotomien der Zeit: Der Zeitbegriff bei Wilhelm Ostwald." *Selbstorganisation* 5 (1994): 257–278.

Leegwater, Arie. "The Development of Wilhelm Ostwald's Chemical Energetics." *Centaurus* 29 (1986): 314–347.

Niedersen, Uwe. "Die Energetik und der Irreversibilitätsgedanke bei Wilhelm Ostwald." *Wissenschaftliche Zeitschrift der Humboldt Universität, Mathematisch-Naturwissenschaftliche Reihe* 32 (1983): 325–329

———. "Zu den Problemen von Reversibilität, Irreversibilität und Zeit im Schaffen Wilhelm Ostwalds." *Internationale Zeitschrift für Geschichte und Ethik der Naturwissenschaften, Technik und Medizin* 23 (1986): 47–59.

Color Theory

Niedersen, Uwe. "Ästhetik und Zeit: Wilhelm Ostwald über Kunst." *Selbstorganisation* 4 (1993): 251–270. Discusses Ostwald's theory of art and beauty.

Sonderhefte der Mitteilungen der Wilhelm-Ostwald-Gesellschaft zu Grossbothen e.V.: *Wilhelm Ostwald: Bibliographie zur Farbenlehre* (Sonderheft 7, 1999); *Die Farbenlehre Wilhelm Ostwalds: Der Farbenatlas* (Sonderheft 8, 2000); Eugen Ristenpart, *Die Ostwaldsche Farbenlehre und ihre Nutzen* (Sonderheft 12, 2001).

Organization, Standardization, Internationalism

Hapke, Thomas. "Wilhelm Ostwald über Information und Dokumentation." *Mitteilungen Gesellschaft Deutscher Chemiker, Fachgruppe Geschichte der Chemie* 5 (1991): 47–55.

———. "Wilhelm Ostwald und seine Initiativen zur Organisation und Standardisierung naturwissentschaftlicher Publizistik: Enzyklopädismus, Internationalismus und Taylorismus am Beginn des 20. Jahrhunderts." In *Fachschrifttum, Bibliothek und Naturwissenschaft im 19. und 20. Jahrhundert,* edited by Christoph Meinel, 157–174. Wiesbaden, Germany: Harrassowitz, 1997.

Niewöhner, Friedrich. "Zum Begriff 'Monismus' bei Haeckel und Ostwald." *Archiv für Begriffsgeschichte* 24 (1980): 123–126.

Schmithals, Friedemann, "Abstrakte Wissenschaft Oder Gute Lehre? Der Chemiker Wilhelm Ostwald: Lehre Jenseits Einer Fragwudigen Tradition." *Jahrbuch für Universitsitatsgeschichte* 2 (1999): 23–37.

Sobczynska, Danuta, and Ewa Czerwinska. "Szientismus in der Praxis: Das Wirken Wilhelm Ostwalds im deutschen Monistenbund." *Philosophisches Jahrbuch* 105 (1998): 178–194.

Scientific Style

Deltete, Robert J. "Josiah Willard Gibbs and Wilhelm Ostwald: A Contrast in Scientific Style." *Journal of Chemical Education* 73 (1996): 289–294.

Simmer, Hans H. "Ostwalds Lehre vom Romantiker und Klassiker: Eine Typologie des Wissenschaftlers." *Medizinhistorisches Journal* 13 (1978): 277–296.

Klassiker

Dunsch, Lothar. *Ein Fundament zum Gebäude der Wissenschaften: Einhundert Jahre Ostwalds Klassiker der exakten Wissenschaften (1889–1989).* Leipzig, Germany: Geest & Portig, 1989.

Updates and Corrections

Helm, Georg. *The Historical Development of Energetics.* Translated by Robert J. Deltete, with an introductory essay. Dordrecht, Netherlands: Kluwer, 2000. Translation of *Die Energetik nach ihrer geschichtlichen Entwicklung* (1898).

Pinkava, Jindrich. "The Relations of W. Ostwald and F. Wald." *Acta Historiae Rerum Naturalium nec non Technicarum* 9 (1977): 133–148.

Robert J. Deltete

OVCHINNIKOV, YURY ANATOLYEVICH (*b.* Moscow, U.S.S.R., 2 August 1934; *d.* Moscow, 17 February 1988), *bioorganic chemistry, physicochemical biology.*

Ovchinnikov is associated with an important period in the history of advancement of physicochemical biology in the Soviet Union. A talented disciple of the outstanding representatives of the classical school of bioorganic chemists and biochemists, he carved out a brilliant career as an academic scientist. His success largely depended on his ability to formulate problems and to organize well-coordinated and integrated large research teams. His personal qualities as a researcher and his talent as a science administrator allowed him to implement major research projects based on original approaches and to obtain pioneering results both in the field of the classical studies of protein and nucleic acids structure and in the new areas of physicochemical biology, genetic engineering, and other biotechnologies.

In contrast to many academic scientists tending to avoid political activities, Ovchinnikov joined the Communist Party in 1962 when he was only beginning his scientific career, which facilitated his future promotions. At the age of thirty-six he became a director of a major research institute and a full member of the U.S.S.R. Academy of Sciences, later to become the chair of the academy's section that consolidated all chemical engineering and biological institutions under the Academy of Sciences. This opened up enormous possibilities for him to set up new research centers, conduct large-scale research, and establish important international contacts, and allowed him to influence formation of scientific policy concerning a wide scope of issues and to implement his own research plans. In spite of the fact that in the Cold War the policies of the U.S.S.R. government to which Ovchinnikov was quite close were strongly criticized by the West, being a member of Supreme Soviet of the Russian Federation (the R. F. parliament) and sitting on numerous advisory boards and committees, he became an authority in the international scientific community as evidenced by his longstanding membership in international scientific organizations, editorial boards of international scientific journals, academies, and European universities, as well as by the comments of prominent scientists who had met with him personally.

Biography and Career. Yury Ovchinnikov's father, Anatoly Ivanovich, who was one of the prominent design engineers working in the aircraft industry in 1937, was subjected to Stalin's repressions and died in 1946. His wife, with three children, were deported to Siberia where they spent the difficult war (1941–1945) and postwar years. Having graduated from the secondary school in Krasnoyarsk with a gold medal (1952), Yury gained entrance to the Chemical Faculty of Moscow State University. He majored in the study of organic syntheses and proved to be a bright student. Being a gregarious person, he joined the students' theater as an actor and even received an invitation to become a professional actor which he, however, declined and continued his studies as a postgraduate student under the guidance of Yury A. Arbouzov.

In the course of postgraduate studies (1957–1959) Ovchinnikov became acquainted with Mikhail M. Shemyakin, who at that time was a corresponding member of the U.S.S.R. Academy of Sciences and director of research program dedicated to chemical synthesis of antibiotics. These were times of rapid advancement of antibiotic chemistry. Scientists focused not only on the studies of natural antibiotics but also on the possibilities for obtaining their synthetic analogs. As part of this program, young Ovchinnikov performed the synthesis of several model compounds and, as part of the development of the complete synthesis scheme, elucidated their transformations. Working side by side with such accomplished professionals as Arbouzov, Shemyakin, and Mikhail Kolosov helped Ovchinnikov in his scientific career.

After finishing his postgraduate studies in 1960, he joined the Institute of Natural Compounds Chemistry (INCCh) newly established by Shemyakin under the U.S.S.R. Academy of Sciences (after 1965, the Institute of Bioorganic Chemistry, or IBCh). Having defended his thesis in 1961, he received an invitation to study the chemistry of depsipeptides—atypical peptides containing, besides amino acids, hydroxy acid residues and possessing antibiotic activity. This study marked the beginning of working his way into "Big Science." Mikhail Shemyakin noticed Yury standing out among other young researchers with his efficiency, orderliness, and tenacity. He realized that Ovchinnikov had all the makings of a leader and soon made him deputy director in 1963. In 1964, Ovchinnikov went to Zürich for training under Vladimir Prelog (Eidgenössische Technische Hochschule Zürich, Switzerland). During the period from 1964 till 1970, Ovchinnikov together with his coworkers performed the synthesis of a number of natural depsipeptides and their analogs. In 1966, he defended his postdoctoral thesis. In contrast to the doctoral thesis (which in the U.S.S.R. was called the *kandidat* dissertation), under the procedure established in the state system for training scientific researchers, this work did not require participation of a more senior scientific advisor and was supposed to demonstrate the excellent professional skills of the scientist.

In 1967, Ovchinnikov was appointed head of the Laboratory of Peptide Chemistry at the IBCh and in 1968, supported by Shemyakin, who chaired the respective branch of the academy, he was elected a corresponding member of the U.S.S.R. Academy of Sciences. Due to Yury Ovchinnikov's unflagging energy as well as his administrative abilities and position, the Laboratory of Peptide Chemistry soon became a major research center consolidating the best specialists in the field of peptide chemistry and protein structure and function. The results obtained during this period were presented in a comprehensive report to the plenary session of twenty-third International Union of Pure and Applied Chemistry Congress, which was the first IUPAC Congress to be conducted in the U.S.S.R. (Riga, 1970).

On the last day of the congress, its president and IBCh director Mikhail Shemyakin died suddenly. By the resolution of presidium of the academy, Yury Ovchinnikov was appointed director of the institute, and in 1970, he was elected a full member of the academy. His administrative career received a new impetus: In 1970 and 1971, he was chief academic secretary for the presidium of the U.S.S.R. Academy of Sciences; from 1973 to 1978, he chaired the Section of Chemical Engineering Sciences and was a member of the presidium of the U.S.S.R. Academy of Sciences, and in 1974, he became vice president of the Academy of Sciences.

The U.S.S.R. Academy of Sciences was traditionally regarded by the government as a think tank of Soviet science that defined the strategy for the development of science across the Soviet Union. Academician Ovchinnikov, besides being an important member of the academy administration, was also a high-ranking member of the Communist Party, having been a delegate to the three so-called epochal congresses of the Communist Party (CPSU) in 1976, 1981, and 1986. From 1976 to 1980, he served as a member of the CPSU Central Inspection Commission; from 1980 to 1988, he was an alternate member of the CPSU Central Committee.

These circumstances allowed him to act as a mediator between the scientific community and the government, creating necessary conditions for the realization of the high potential of the Russian scientists and helping Soviet biological sciences out of stagnation. Because of the then-current practices of long-term and rigid planning of scientific research activities and the lack of alternative sources of funding other than state financing, the organizers of the new research programs were forced to apply directly to the U.S.S.R. authorities with any proposals in order to change the established system of priorities.

Discoveries made within the new disciplines such as physicochemical-molecular biology, which led to an understanding of molecular mechanisms of key processes at the cellular level, offered great potential for applying more scientific discoveries to such vitally important spheres as medicine, agricultural production, and environmental protection. This could be achieved through the technical re-equipment of research institutions and reformation of biological education in the country where science for had many decades suffered under ideological dictates that hindered the development of several scientific disciplines, genetics above all.

Consolidated activities of authoritative members of the scientific community—physicists, chemists, and biologists—resulted in the removal of a ban on studies in the field of classical genetics and the establishment of the new radiobiological research units: the Institute of Radiation and Physicochemical Biology (IRPChB) under the U.S.S.R. Academy of Sciences and the Department of Radiobiology at the Institute of Atomic Energy under the military department "Minsredmash" (the predecessor of the Ministry of Atomic Power), as well as the Institute of Biophysics (IBPh), Institute of Protein Research (IPR), and Institute of Natural Compounds Chemistry (INCCh, now IBCh). It took years to obtain all the necessary approvals and to coordinate all the actions necessary to implement the decisions passed by presidium of the U.S.S.R. Academy of Sciences in 1957. The IRPChB and the INCCh opened in 1959, while the IBPh and the IPR could finally deploy extensive research work only after the new research center was built in the suburbs of Moscow (Pushchino-Na-Oke, 1966). Early in the 1970s Ovchinnikov established a new department at the IPR to perform research in the field of structural chemistry of peptides.

His laboratory and some others in the U.S.S.R. Academy of Sciences successfully approached the government for funding, using military interest in developing the means of protection against biological weapons and creating new kinds of weapons. This became a reality thanks to Ovchinnikov's activities as the vice-president of the Academy and as the indisputable leader of physico-chemical biology in the U.S.S.R at that time. The evaluation of research work conducted at specialized institutions that were inspired by Academician Ovchinnikov and carried out by the Committee of Academic Scientists (a committee of the Academy of Sciences and the Academy of Medical Sciences), revealed the inadequacy of the theoretical and experimental foundations of existing institutions. These findings led the government to promote fundamental disciplines that could provide the foundations for biotechnologies allowing the design of microorganisms and biological materials with predetermined properties intended for a vast scope of practical tasks. Three consecutive governmental decrees in 1974, 1981 and 1985 enabled technical re-equipment of research institutions, creation of the new research and educational centers, and the implementation of major research projects.

Some Russian and Western scientists have come to believe that Ovchinnikov was a leader in the Soviet Union's biological weapons program, including work banned by the 1972 Biological and Toxin Weapons Convention. But the books and articles charging Ovchinnikov do not include references to written documentation that could definitely prove his involvement.

In spite of always being preoccupied, Yury Ovchinnikov was devoted to his family and paid much attention to his children. He was married twice, having three children (a daughter and two sons) born in the first marriage, with Tatiana Kirenskaya (divorced in 1982), and two daughters from the second marriage, with Tatiana Marchenko. He drew his strength and found comfort in his family both when he was actively working and, especially, during the last two difficult years of his life. He died from an incurable malignant disease at the age of fifty-four.

Organization of International Cooperation. Under the guidance of Yury Ovchinnikov, the IBCh under the U.S.S.R. Academy of Sciences in the 1970s and 1980s flourished until it became equal to advanced research centers of the West in bioorganic chemistry and several areas of physicochemical biology. In the institute's activities much attention was given to international cooperation. The development of original approaches to research and the achievement of important results attracted many specialists. Ovchinnikov, who often made trips to Europe and the United States, facilitated participation of large groups of the Soviet scientists in the conferences held in the West, while the institute hosted highly specialized symposia with the participation of foreign colleagues. As an official representative of the U.S.S.R. and the Academy of Sciences, he introduced the practice of regular bipartite meetings between Soviet and foreign (American, German, French, Italian, Swedish) scientists sharing the latest information concerning various issues. Major international conferences were conducted in Moscow by the IBCh. The institute was charged with the organization of the FEBS (Federation of European Biochemical Societies) Conference in 1984.

In the eyes of the international scientific community Ovchinnikov presented a picture of a perfect scientist and a statesman who looked more North American than Soviet: extremely competent, influential, efficient, responsible, nimble, and charming. He was an ardent adherent to concentrating efforts on a limited scope of work that led to tangible results, as well as centralization of scientific research management. His last attempt to consolidate institutions conducting research in the sphere of molecular biology and bioengineering into a large conglomerate managed by a single administrative center (similar to the already existing All-Union Oncological and Cardiological Centers) proved to be unsuccessful. The scientific community, represented by a meeting convened by the vice president of the U.S.S.R. Academy of Sciences, did not support his idea. Knowing Ovchinnikov's tenacity, it might be safely assumed that only his illness and death that soon followed prevented him from realizing his idea in one form or another.

Ovchinnikov chaired the Federation of European Biochemical Societies, was a member of the Committee on Peptide Chemistry, the international Institute for Energy Resources and Ecology (Sweden), the European Academy of Arts, Sciences, and Humanities, and the American Philosophical Society. For many years Ovchinnikov served as editor in chief and member of the editorial board of a great number of Soviet and international journals. He was elected foreign or honorary member of more than fifteen academies and universities in Europe and South America. He received an impressive numbers of awards and prizes: the Gold Medal of the CIBA Foundation (1979), the Gold Medal "For Services to Science and Mankind," given by the Academy of Science of Czechoslovak Socialist Republic (1974), and three Orders of Lenin (1975, 1981, 1984). He was a hero of Socialist Labor (1981).

Research: Depsipeptides. The problem of developing methods for the synthesis of natural compounds with exotic structure, such as atypical peptides that contain, in addition to D- and L amino acids, hydroxy acid residues, and rings containing a great number of links (macrocycles), was chosen by M. Shemyakin in the early 1960s. Ovchinnikov joined this work, which was modest in the beginning but developed in a very interesting manner. The chemists successfully synthesized the antibiotics *enniatins* A and B, compounds whose structures had been proposed back in the 1940s. However, the first products of the achieved synthesis were significantly different in their physicochemical properties from the natural substances and particularly devoid of any antibacterial activity. There was no doubt that the methods used for establishing these compounds' structures were correct and, besides, another cyclic depsipeptide, *sporidesmolide I* (a neutral fungal metabolite), had been synthesized employing the same technique. The only possible conclusion was that the earlier proposed structure of *enniatin* A and B was incorrect. In the following, the analysis of physicochemical parameters of several newly synthesized compounds differing in the number of links in the macrocycle established the correct structures.

Ovchinnikov obtained a whole series of macrocyclic depsipeptides applying a generic method for their synthesis. Their systematic study yielded extensive data concerning the influence on ring formation of the three-dimensional dynamic structure (the so-called conformation) of amino acids and hydroxy acids. Conformational studies, in the 1960s, where an exciting and promising area of chemical research.

In 1964, Ovchinnikov (together with H. Gerlach and V. Prelog) realized that the relationship between structure and biological function could not be established without profound conformational studies. In 1967, Ovchinnikov's laboratory began systematic investigations of the conformational states of peptides, using nuclear magnetic resonance spectroscopy (NMR, Vladimir Bystrov). A number of new regularities were established including the interchangeability of the ester and amide bonds in many natural peptides with their biological activity retained.

The topochemical principle of transformation of biologically active peptides was established, according to which the creation of new bioactive molecules could be achieved through profound modifications of the molecules provided that the *spatial locations of specific groups,* defining their biological activity, were retained. The ideas first proposed in this pioneering work were further developed both in the U.S.S.R. and abroad, setting the foundations for creating new biologically active peptides—hormones, antibiotics, neuropeptides, enzyme substrates, and inhibitors. In the course of these studies it was demonstrated that not only x-ray structural analysis could be used in structural studies of large molecules, but also NMR, and other spectroscopic techniques x-ray analysis required the compound under analysis to be in a crystalline state. Other spectroscopic methods, in contrast, provided information

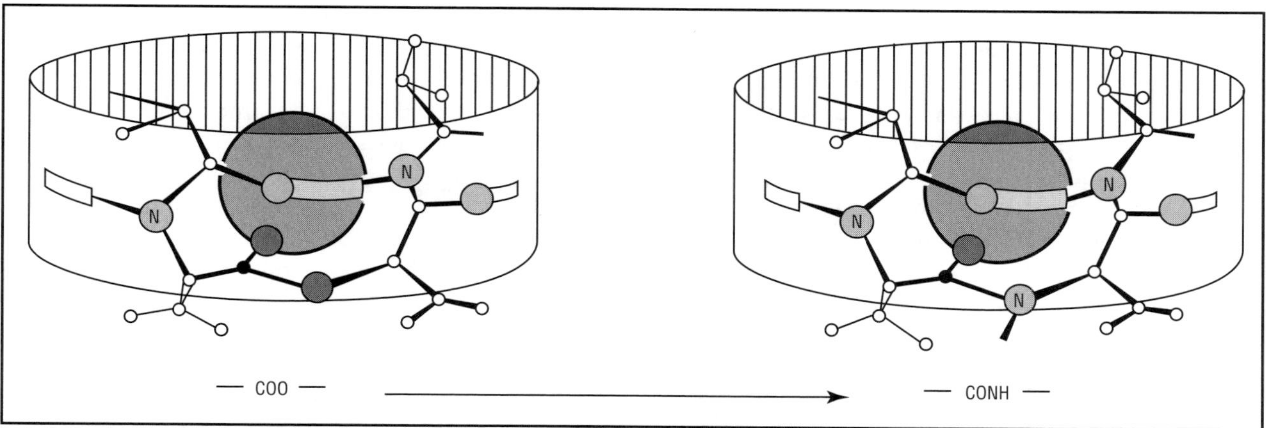

Figure 1. *Two valinomycin bracelet-like structures: A_1 (left) and A_2 (right).*

on the structures of compounds in solution and thus allowed one to follow their dynamics, for instance the formation of depsipeptide complexes with metal ions.

By that time reports had already appeared in the literature concerning the ability of valinomycin and the enniatins to increase the permeability of lipid membranes (such as the cell membrane) to alkaline metal ions. It was believed that their antibacterial properties depended on this effect. *Valinomycin* selectively binds potassium (K^+) ions in solution, forming stable complexes (with a macrocycle-to-cation ration of 1:1), and demonstrates unique, unsurpassable Na^+, K^+-selectivity in complex formation. The enniatins bind practically every alkaline and alkaline-earth cation with considerably less selectivity, with 1, 2 or even 3 cations per macrocycle in the complex. Such complexes are responsible for ion transport, and selectivity of transmembrane transport depends on selectivity of complexation. The bound ion is always positioned in the center of the cavity of the depsipeptide molecule. The size of the valinomycin cavity is rigidly limited by the bracelet-like system of six intramolecular bonds, which explains valinomycin's inability to bind sodium (Na^+) ions. Enniatin molecules are more labile, which allows them to adjust the size of the cavity to the size of the bound ion. Peripheral parts of both valinomycin and enniatin complexes are hydrophobic, which allows them to freely migrate across the lipid zones of the membranes (see Figure 1). Thus this work resulted in the identification of the molecular origin of such fundamental biological phenomena as *selective transport of metal ions across membranes* (presentation at the IUPAC Congress in Riga, 1970).

Research: Primary Structure of Soluble Proteins. Having become the head of the first major laboratory in the U.S.S.R. engaged in studies of protein structure, Ovchinnikov directed his researchers towards the investigation of the primary structure (amino acid sequence) of proteins and peptides whose functions had been already established. The determination of the amino acid sequence of aspartate aminotransferase (a key enzyme of nitrogen metabolism) from the heart muscle of pigs was the first major success of Ovchinnikov's laboratory. He and his coworkers became the partners of the team of biochemists led by Alexander E. Braunstein (Institute of Molecular Biology in the U.S.S.R. Academy of Sciences), the author of the fundamental discovery of enzymatic transamination.

Knowledge of the primary structure of an enzyme was necessary for elucidation of its reaction mechanism. The joint work took several years to complete and resulted in the determination of the complete amino acid sequence of a protein consisting of 412 amino acid residues. In addition to the laboratory at the IBCh, Ovchinnikov was department head at the IPR (Pushchino), where the primary structures of several physiologically important proteins (cobra, bee and scorpion *venom toxins* and plant protein *leghaemoglobin)*, several *bacterial proteins* (proteins from ribosomal subparticles, elongation factor G from *Escherichia coli,* etc.) were established (1971–1979).

These studies proved to be extremely efficient due to the excellent organization of work based on the combination of classical approaches (enzymatic and chemical methods of sequencing) with an original mass-spectrometric technique for the determination of amino acid sequence that Boris Rozynov, Anatoly Kiryushkin, and Yury Ovchinnikov developed in the Moscow laboratory for the analysis of short peptide sequences.

The best-known work of Ovchinnikov's team was the determination of the primary structure of the most important enzyme in the transcription process, *DNA-dependent RNA polymerase.* This was a protein comprising several subunits, two of which were formed by a giant polypeptide chain consisting of 1,300 amino acid residues. In this work chemical methods and the genetic engineering approach were combined. Genes of the large subunits of RNA polymerase were isolated, inserted into plasmids, and sequenced. At the same time determination of the structure of peptides from the same subunits proceeded in parallel with and independently from gene sequencing, which ensured correctness of the results. It was particularly important because the structures already published by other laboratories were found to contain mistakes. Determination of the structure of RNA polymerase set the foundation for extensive studies on the mechanism of action of this enzyme as well as genetic and biochemical studies. This work was awarded the 1984 U.S.S.R. State Prize.

Research: Membrane Proteins. Studies of ion-transporting protein systems present in biological membranes continued Ovchinnikov's earlier works on *depsipeptide ion carriers,* becoming the next step in the investigation of the mechanism of ion transport across membranes, on the one hand, and a move to a higher level of the studies of protein structure and functions, on the other.

It is well known that the function of transporting ions and molecules across the membranes that separate the cells and the organelles is performed by specialized membrane complexes in a strictly controlled manner. The systems of active transport of ions across the membranes (i.e., energy-dependent transport against a concentration gradient), the so-called *ion pumps,* play the key role in the processes of ion transport. The function of Na^+, K^+-adenosine triphosphatase (Na^+, K^+-ATPase), the most common transport enzyme in the animal world, is to maintain a nonequilibrium distribution of cations between the cell and its environment (inside the cell, the concentration of K^+ is thirty times higher and the concentration of Na^+ is ten times lower than in the intercellular space). The gradient of ion concentration created by Na^+, K^+-ATPase acts as a driving force for the active transport of other substances (sugars, amino acids) into the cell.

Research on membrane proteins required the development of high-technology physical methods for their isolation and analysis. These were fundamentally different from those used for globular soluble proteins. This work laid the grounds for further molecular and genetic studies of the systems for active transport of ions in human cells, important for revealing the causes of some pathological conditions. Thus, in the course of studies, members of Ovchinnikov's laboratory and Eugene Sverdlov and his coauthors (in Edward Budovsky's laboratory at the INCCh , later in Sverdlov's laboratory in IBCh) for the first time established the existence in the human genome of a family of five genes differing in nucleotide sequences specific for the different tissues (kidney, brain, thyroid, and liver cells). Their expression in all cases results in the synthesis of catalytically active protein Na^+, K^+-ATPase differing in nucleotide sequences specific for the different tissues. The tissue-specific expression of genes was shown to be subjected to a tissue-specific control and also depended on the developmental stage. This finding perhaps may be attributed to various functions of proteins belonging to this family.

Chronologically, Na^+, K^+-ATPase structure was established after the determination of amino acid sequence of *bacteriorhodopsin* (1978). The investigation of the molecular mechanisms of photoreception was not only the first success of Ovchinnikov's laboratory in the field of membrane proteins but also pioneering work, because the IBC staff pushed by their director won the competition with Har Gobind Khorana's laboratory (USA), thus becoming the authors of the primary structure of the first integral membrane protein to be sequenced by chemical, enzymic and physical methods. Visual processes in animals depend on 11-*cis* retinal, a light-sensitive component of *rhodopsin.* Because the numerous attempts of biochemists to isolate pure and biologically active rhodopsin from animal sources had failed, an easier object was chosen as a model—*bacteriorhodopsin,* which contained a stereoisomer of *retinal.* In 1981, the same authors in Ovchinnikov's laboratory managed to master the difficulties and determined the structure of rhodopsin from the bovine retina.

Research: Genetic Engineering and Microbial Synthesis. In the late 1970s, Ovchinnikov directed the work at the IBCh and its affiliates toward the improvement of chemical synthesis methods, the directed mutagenesis of DNA, and the creation of microorganisms producing peptides and proteins that were alien to them. *Leuenkephalin* (opioid neuropeptide, 1979), human *interferon* α_2 (antiviral and antitumor protein, 1981), and *proinsulin* (human insulin precursor).

To implement plans for production of compounds to be used in medicine and agriculture based on the above mentioned and similar biotechnologies, in 1985 he succeeded in obtaining approval for the organization of the research and engineering complex "biogen," which consolidated twenty-six research, engineering, and producing organizations. Two products, interferon and proinsulin, were brought to actual production and introduced into medical practice. Development of the new technologies boosted by Ovchinnikov undoubtedly led to better quality of research in the fields of molecular and cellular biology in the U.S.S.R.

BIBLIOGRAPHY

WORKS BY OVCHINNIKOV

With Vadim T. Ivanov, Anatoly A. Kiryushkin, and Mikhail M. Shemyakin. "Synthesis of Cyclic Depsipeptides." In *Peptides: Proceedings of the Fifth European Symposium, September 1962,* edited by Geoffrey Tyndale Young. New York: Macmillian and Oxford: Pergamon, 1963.

With Mikhail M. Shemyakin, Anatoly A. Kiryushkin, E. I. Vinogradova, et al. "Mass-Spectrometric Determination of the Amino Acid Sequence in Peptides." *Nature* 5047 (1966): 361–366.

With V. K. Antonov, L. D. Bergelson, Vadim T. Ivanov, et al. "Depsipeptides and Peptides as Chemical Tools for Studying Ion Transport through Biological Membranes." *Abstracts of Communications Presented at the Meeting of the Federation of European Biochemical Societies, Madrid, 7-11th April 1969.* Madrid, 1969.

With Vadim T. Ivanov, I. A. Line, N. D. Abdullayev, et al. "Physicochemical Basis of Functioning of Biological Membranes: The Conformation of Valinomycin and Its K^{+-} Complex in Solution." *Biochemical and Biophysical Research Communications* 34, no. 6 (1969): 803–811.

With Vadim T. Ivanov and Alexander M. Shkrob. *Membrane-Active Complexones.* B. B. A. Library, vol. 12. Amsterdam: Elsevier, 1974.

With Vadim T. Ivanov. "Recent Developments in the Structure-Functional Studies of Peptide Ionophores." *Biochemistry of Membrane Transport,* edited by G. Semenza and Ernesto Carafoli. FEBS Symposium, no. 42. Berlin: Springer-Verlag, 1977.

With V. M. Lipkin, N. N. Modyanov, O. Yu. Chertov, et al. "Primary Structure of α-subunits of DNA-dependent RNA-polymerase from *Escherichia coli.*" *FEBS Letters* 1 (1977): 108–111.

With N. G. Abdulayev, M. Yu. Feigina, and N. A. Lobanov. "The Structural Basis of the Functioning of Bacteriorhodopsin: An Overview." *FEBS Letters* 2 (1979): 219–224.

With Yuri B. Alakhov, Yuri P. Bundulis, M. A. Dovgas, et al. "Rhodopsin and Bacteriorhodopsin: Structure-Function Relationships." *FEBS Letters* 2 (1982): 179–191.

With E. D. Sverdlov, G. S. Monastirskaya, R. L. Allikmets, et al. " Semeistvo Genov Na+, K+-atfasy cheloveka ne meneye pyati genov i (ili) psevdogenov, gomologichnikh (-subyedinitse" [The Family of Human Na+- K+- ATPase's Geens]. *Doklady of Academy of Sciences of the U.S.S.R.* 291, no. 3 (1987): 731–738.

OTHER SOURCES

Alibek, Ken, and Stephen Handelman. *Biohazard: The Chilling True Story of the Largest Covert Biological Weapons Program in the World—Told from the Inside by the Man Who Ran It.* London: Hutchinson, 1999.

Ivanov, Vadim T., ed. *Yuri Anatolyevich Ovchinnikov. Zhizn i nauchnaya deyatelnost* [Yuri A. Ovchinnikov: Life and Scientific Activity]. Moscow: Nauka, 1991. Collection of articles-memoirs (Vladimir Prelog, Dorothy Crowfoot-Hodgkin, Alexandr A. Bayev, Mikhael A. Ostrovsky, and other Russian and foreign scientists).

Levina, Elena S., and Alexander E. Sedov. "Molecular Biology in the Soviet Russia (An Essay)." *Molecular Biology* (Moscow) 34, no. 3 (2000): 420–447. Stages of the evolvement and development of the major directions of physicochemical biology in the U.S.S.R. from the 1950s to the 1980s, including a short outlines of the lives and activities of the leading scientists in the context of the history of science and the history of the state.

Shoham, Dany, and Ze'ev Wolfson. "The Russian Biological Weapons Program: Vanished or Disappeared?" *Critical Reviews in Microbiology* 30 (2004): 241–261.

"Yuri Anatolyevich Ovchinnikov." In *Materialy k bio-bibliographii uchenikh SSSR.* [Yury A. Ovchinnikov. In Materials for a Biobibliography of Scientists of the U.S.S.R., Chemical Sciences Series]. Moscow: Nauka, 1991. Review, main dates of Ovchinnikov's life and activity (in Russian), the list of publications (500).

Elena S. Levina

OWEN, RICHARD (*b.* Lancaster, England, 20 July 1804; *d.* London, England, 18 December 1892), *comparative anatomy, vertebrate paleontology, evolutionary biology.* For the original article on Owen see *DSB*, vol. 10.

Since the early 1980s, a major repositioning of Owen has taken place, as historians of evolutionary biology began tracing the roots of Darwinism to scientific traditions that previously had been considered inimical to the theory of evolution, such as natural theology and idealist morphology. Owen, who conventionally was marginalized and cast in the role of Charles Darwin's main creationist opponent, has been reappraised as a major representative of those traditions and, beyond that, as a proponent of evolution theory himself, albeit evolution of a non-Darwinian kind.

Moreover, the emergence within historical scholarship of attempts to understand the growth of science in terms of its institutions and the recognition that museums of natural history were significant sites of scientific practice has led to a more fundamental reevaluation of Owen yet. Rather than being seen in the first instance as a participant in the nineteenth-century debate about the origin of species, he has been appraised as a leader of the Victorian museum movement. Placed in the context of his museum career ambitions and attainments, Owen has received a more differentiated understanding of his contributions to comparative anatomy and vertebrate paleontology.

Owen

Museum Curator at Hub of Empire. Owen made his living as a museum curator, being employed during the 1827–1856 period at the Hunterian Museum and during 1856–1883 at the British Museum. From early on in his professional career he pursued the ideal of a separate national museum of natural history, one that would exhibit nature according to his museological rules. He later addressed the issue in a rare treatise of its kind, *On the Extent and Aims of a National Museum of Natural History* (1862). Initially, he transformed the Royal College of Surgeons' Hunterian Museum into a major center for the study of comparative anatomy and vertebrate paleontology, in a conscious effort to keep up with Georges Cuvier's Parisian Muséum d'Anatomie Comparée.

To this end, Owen led the Hunterian Museum away from the narrow purpose of surgical training. When he was blocked in carrying this through to the full, Owen left the employment of the Royal College of Surgeons to accept an appointment at the British Museum (BM), where he became the first superintendent of the natural history collections. However, his marginal position at the BM, especially in relation to its librarian Anthony Panizzi (1797–1879), and the inadequacy of the accommodation for the collections in his care were among further reasons for Owen to seek the establishment of a separate museum of natural history. In this he succeeded by securing the creation of the British Museum (National History), or BM(NH), in South Kensington, which was inaugurated in 1881. It was Owen who created the Natural History Museum as it is known in the early twenty-first century, one of the greatest "cathedrals of science" to be built anywhere and the crowning achievement of his career.

Like Georges Cuvier (1769–1832), Owen was not a field naturalist but a museum man who never undertook a major journey of exploration but who, at the vantage point of his institutional position, orchestrated the collecting of natural history specimens, obtaining many rare and precious ones, early on from London's Zoological Gardens, but increasingly also from around the British Isles and indeed from around the world. He succeeded in turning the Hunterian Museum and the BM(NH) into centers for the cataloging, exhibiting, and storing of trophy treasures from Britain's colonial empire. The enormous range as well as the novelty of his numerous research papers reflect Owen's position at this metropolitan hub of empire.

Functionalist Studies. For the purchase of specimens, the expansion of exhibition and storage space, and his museum plans in general, Owen needed the approval and cooperation of his employers and patrons, and to a significant extent his science took on the qualities of the factions from which he sought support. Among Owen's early and most effective patrons was the Oxford geologist William Buckland (1784–1856), who gave Owen access to the liberal Tory prime minister Robert Peel (1788–1850). Following Peel's death by accident, his political mantle fell on William Ewart Gladstone (1809–1898), the founder of the Liberal Party and thrice prime minister. Owen's museum endeavors were by and large a Peelite-Gladstonian enterprise, and much of what Owen attained in terms of institutional and career advancement, including various national honors, such as a civil list pension (1842) and a knighthood (Knight Commander; 1884), came to him from a circle of mainly Oxonian liberal Anglicans.

These men regarded natural history as a form of natural theology, and the Paleyan proclivities of the network of Owen's museum patrons were ably and, at times sensationally, accommodated by him. From his early monograph on the pearly nautilus to his reconstruction of the leonine marsupial *Thylacoleo carnifex*, Owen interpreted organic diversity in terms of Cuvierian functionalism, explaining organic form in terms of its function and providing instances of perfect adaptation.

Idealist Morphology and Vertebrate Archetype. A majority of Owen's metropolitan colleagues were not Oxbridge educated but, like Owen himself, had received their education outside England, in Edinburgh or additionally on the Continent. From there they brought with them a different epistemology than Cuvierian-Paleyan functionalism, namely the idealism of Romantic nature philosophy, which explained physical reality—especially organic diversity—in terms of the transcendental logic of form rather than functional adaptation.

In London, German idealism was articulated by Samuel Taylor Coleridge and Thomas Carlyle as well as by Coleridge's disciple, the surgeon Joseph Henry Green, to whose influence Owen was exposed at the Royal College of Surgeons, where Green delivered Hunterian Lectures on a rotating scheme before Owen himself in 1837 began delivering the lectures as the sole Hunterian professor. Moreover, Owen was intellectually indebted to William Whewell, one of the rare Oxbridge thinkers to communicate idealist thought. In this largely metropolitan subculture, Owen developed a research program of transcendental morphology, bringing the prior accomplishments of Lorenz Oken, Carl Gustav Carus, and other Continental anatomists to an internationally admired level of perfection. It was Owen's declared ambition to unify the functionalist and transcendentalist approaches, but in this he did not succeed.

Owen began working systematically on problems of transcendental anatomy in 1841, as part of his curatorial task of cataloging the extensive osteological collections of

Owen

the Hunterian Museum. From this work he extracted the materials for his comprehensive account of transcendental osteology, which he presented to the British Association for the Advancement of Science (BAAS) in 1846 in the form of a major report, subsequently published under the title *On the Archetype and Homologies of the Vertebrate Skeleton* (1849). In this and earlier reports to the BAAS (1839, 1841, 1842, 1843), he made major improvements in classification and terminology, adding several significant taxonomic categories, most famously the *Dinosauria* (1841), from which Owen, ever since dinosaurs first entered the wider sphere of public interest at the Great Exhibition of 1851, has derived considerable vicarious renown.

To demonstrate the inadequacy of the functionalist method, Owen cited the development of the skull, because it had been the skull with which transcendental morphology in Germany had been most notably associated. Functional adaptation could not explain that in all classes of vertebrates, as a rule, the foetal skull is composed of the same number of uncoalesced pieces, arranged in the same general way. In marsupials or birds, for example, it does not play the role it has in placental mammals of making birth safer. A more comprehensive view had to be taken, which Owen did by adopting the vertebrate theory of the skull, that is, the notion that the skull is to be understood as a series of metamorphosed vertebrae, just as, at the other end of the vertebral column, the sacrum represents several fused vertebrae. The basic building block of the skeleton was the vertebra, and the uncoalesced skull bones in backboned foetuses can be explained as parts of separate cephalic vertebrae.

Thus the skeleton could be seen as a series of ideal vertebrae, most closely represented in real life by the bony framework of fishes. Owen called the fish-like concatenation of virtually undifferentiated vertebrae the vertebrate archetype. It represented the skeleton in its most elementary form, with only a hint of the modifications that are to be found in real vertebrates, and to which all skeletal forms, including those of humans, could be traced back by a careful study of their homological relationships.

Owen gave a precise definition to the concepts—at that time fuzzily defined—of *analogy* and *homology*: he defined an analogue as "A part or organ in one animal which has the same function as another part or organ in a different animal"; he defined a homologue, by contrast, as "The same organ in different animals under every variety of form and function" (1848, p. 7).

Origin of Species by Natural Means. With his notion of an archetype—which Owen soon after its initial enunciation in terms of an expression of an immanent force redefined as a Platonic blueprint of design in the mind of the Creator—he shifted the evidence for the existence of a supreme designer from concrete adaptations to an abstract plan—from special to general teleology. Divine contrivance was to be recognized not so much in the characteristics of individual species but in their common ground-plan. In other words, species could have originated by natural means, not by miraculous creation. To this belief Owen gave cautious, some would say cryptic, expression in a variety of publications, for example in his *On the Nature of Limbs* (1849). Strong criticism from his Paleyite patrons turned Owen privately into a evolutionist, but he enormously resented it when later he was portrayed by Darwin as a creationist. And indeed, over a period of some four decades, from the mid-1840s to the mid-1880s, he explicitly and repeatedly expressed—in articles, monographs, a textbook, and letters—his belief in a natural origin of species. He belatedly formulated his mature theory of saltatory descent in the concluding chapter of his *On the Anatomy of Vertebrates* (3 volumes, 1866–1868), separately published as the *Derivative Hypothesis of Life and Species* (1868).

Richard Owen. HULTON ARCHIVE/GETTY IMAGES.

The question remained, however, what the "natural means" were. With respect to this issue Owen and Darwin parted company. To Owen, natural selection could only explain the extinction of species, not their diverging

Owen

origins. Moreover, like many of his German colleagues, Owen conflated the questions of the origin of species with that of the origin of life, and natural selection seemed ineffectual at the primordial level of abiogenesis. Owen was a pivotal figure in the emergence of the evolutionary view of life forms as indicated by fossils. He was a strong advocate of the notion that the paleontological record is progressive, arguing in an anonymous *Quarterly Review* (1851) critique of Charles Lyell's steady-state view of the geological past that the succession of fossils through time shows a distinct development from lower to higher. For Owen, this progressive change was a process guided by divine purpose. He believed in an orthogenetic-saltational process of organic unfolding, driven by an inherent tendency to change, not by contingent, gradualist, and external forces such as natural selection.

The phenomenon of metagenesis provided Owen with a visualizing aid for his notion of evolution. In the booklet *On Parthenogenesis, or the Successive Production of Procreating Individuals from a Single Ovum* (1849), he described the phenomenon of alternating generations in the reproductive cycles of, for example, aphids, jellyfish, or flukeworms. Characteristic of such metagenetic cycles is that the individual generations can differ in form from each other as much as different species or even genera, families, and orders do. One could imagine that under particular circumstances the cycle might be broken, and the separate stages go on reproducing. In this way wholly new species might originate.

The Hippocampus Controversy. Owen applied his saltational theory of the origin of species also to humans and, in the Christian antislavery tradition of Johann Friedrich Blumenbach and James Cowles Prichard, stressed the unity of mankind and the gap that exists between humans and the higher apes. Based on a series of comparative studies of the anthropoid apes, he placed humans in a subclass of their own, the *Archencephala*, pointing to a number of specific cerebral features, in particular the *hippocampus minor*. This led to a prolonged controversy with Thomas Henry Huxley who, in an effort to prove a Darwinian origin of *Homo sapiens*, argued that apes also possess a *hippocampus minor* and that the lowest races of mankind are closer to these apes than to Englishmen. The controversy was fought out highly publicly at successive annual meetings of the BAAS, at Oxford (1860), Manchester (1861), and Cambridge (1862). Huxley outclassed Owen as a controversialist and tactician, and has been regarded as both the victor and the person who got it right. Detailed reexamination has disclosed the complexity of the case, however, and shows that on both sides issues of personality and politics structured the scientific debate.

SUPPLEMENTARY BIBLIOGRAPHY

WORKS BY OWEN

On the Archetype and Homologies of the Vertebrate Skeleton. London: J. van Voorst, 1848.

On the Nature of Limbs. London: J. van Voorst, 1849.

On Parthenogenesis, or the Successive Production of Procreating Individuals from a Single Ovum. London: J. van Voorst, 1849.

"Lyell: On Life and Successive Development." *Quarterly Review* 89 (1851): 412–451.

On the Extent and Aims of a National Museum of Natural History. London: Saunders, Otley, 1862.

On the Anatomy of Vertebrates. 3 vols. London: Longmans, Green, 1866–1868.

Derivative Hypothesis of Life and Species. London: Longmans, Green, 1868.

The Hunterian Lectures in Comparative Anatomy May–June, 1837. Edited by Phillip R. Sloan. Chicago: University of Chicago Press, 1992.

OTHER SOURCES

Amundson, Ron. "Typology Reconsidered: Two Doctrines on the History of Evolutionary Biology." *Biology and Philosophy* 13 (1998): 153–177.

Branagan, David. "Richard Owen in the Antipodean Context." *Journal and Proceedings of the Royal Society of New South Wales* 125 (1992): 95–102.

Camardi, Giovanni. "Richard Owen, Morphology, and Evolution." *Journal of the History of Biology* 34 (2001): 481–515.

Cosans, Christopher. "Anatomy, Metaphysics, and Values: The Ape Brain Debate Reconsidered." *Biology and Philosophy* 9 (1994): 129–165.

Desmond, Adrian. *Archetypes and Ancestors: Palaeontology in Victorian London, 1850–1875.* London: Blond & Briggs, 1982.

———. *The Politics of Evolution: Morphology, Medicine, and Reform in Radical London.* Chicago: University of Chicago Press, 1989.

Gross, Charles G. "Hippocampus Minor and Man's Place in Nature: A Case Study in the Social Construction of Neuroanatomy." *Hippocampus* 3 (1993): 403–415.

Gruber, Jacob W. "Owen, Richard." In *Oxford Dictionary of National Biography*, edited by H. C. G. Matthew and Brian Harrison. Oxford: Oxford University Press, 2004.

———, and John C. Thackray. *Richard Owen Commemoration: Three Studies.* London: Natural History Museum, 1992.

Ospovat, Dov. *The Development of Darwin's Theory: Natural History, Natural Theology, and Natural Selection, 1838–1859.* Cambridge, U.K.: Cambridge University Press, 1981.

Padian, Kevin. "A Missing Hunterian Lecture on Vertebrae by Richard Owen, 1837." *Journal of the History of Biology* 28 (1995): 333–368.

———. "The Rehabilitation of Sir Richard Owen." *BioScience* 47 (1997): 446–453.

Panchen, Alec L. "Richard Owen and the Concept of Homology." In *Homology: The Hierarchical Basis of*

Owen

Comparative Biology, edited by Brian K. Hall. San Diego: Academic, 1994.

Richards, Evelleen. "A Question of Property Rights: Richard Owen's Evolutionism Reassessed." *British Journal for the History of Science* 20 (1987): 129–171.

———. "A Political Anatomy of Monsters, Hopeful and Otherwise: Teratogeny, Transcendentalism, and Evolutionary Theorizing." *Isis* 85 (1994): 377–411.

Richards, Robert J. *The Meaning of Evolution: The Morphological Construction and Ideological Reconstruction of Darwin's Theory.* Chicago: University of Chicago Press, 1992.

Rupke, Nicolaas A. "Richard Owen's Hunterian Lectures on Comparative Anatomy and Physiology, 1837–55." *Medical History* 29 (1985): 237–258.

———. "Richard Owen's Vertebrate Archetype." *Isis* 84 (1993), 231–251.

———. *Richard Owen: Victorian Naturalist.* New Haven, CT: Yale University Press, 1994.

Sloan, Phillip R. "Whewell's Philosophy of Discovery and the Archetype of the Vertebrate Skeleton: The Role of German Philosophy of Science in Richard Owen's Biology." *Annals of Science* 60 (2003): 39–61.

Smith, C. U. M. "Worlds in Collision: Owen and Huxley on the Brain." *Science in Context* 10 (1997): 343–365.

Wilson, Leonard G. "The Gorilla and the Question of Human Origins: The Brain Controversy." *Journal of the History of Medicine and Allied Sciences* 51 (1996): 184–207.

Nicolaas A. Rupke